Lecture Notes in Computer Science 12674

More information about this subseries at http://www.springer.com/series/7410

Nikita Borisov · Claudia Diaz (Eds.)

Financial Cryptography and Data Security

25th International Conference, FC 2021
Virtual Event, March 1–5, 2021
Revised Selected Papers, Part I

 Springer

Editors
Nikita Borisov
University of Illinois at Urbana-Champaign
Urbana, IL, USA

Claudia Diaz
KU Leuven
Leuven, Belgium

ISSN 0302-9743 ISSN 1611-3349 (electronic)
Lecture Notes in Computer Science
ISBN 978-3-662-64321-1 ISBN 978-3-662-64322-8 (eBook)
https://doi.org/10.1007/978-3-662-64322-8

LNCS Sublibrary: SL4 – Security and Cryptology

This Springer imprint is published by the registered company Springer-Verlag GmbH, DE part of Springer Nature
The registered company address is: Heidelberger Platz 3, 14197 Berlin, Germany

Preface

FC 2021, the 25th International Conference on Financial Cryptography and Data Security, was held online during March 1–5, 2021.

We received an all-time record of 223 submissions, of which 6 were desk rejected due to non-compliance with page limits and 217 were considered for review. Of these, 54 were included in the program, 47 as regular papers, four as short papers, and three as Systematization of Knowledge (SoK) papers; a 25% acceptance rate. Revised papers appear in these proceedings.

The review process was double-blind and carried out entirely online via the HotCRP review platform. The review period lasted about 10 weeks, taking place between the end of September and the beginning of December 2020. Papers received four reviews on average. The review period was followed by an online discussion, which was at times extensive—two papers received 27 comments and the median discussion had five comments. After discussion, papers were either accepted, rejected, or conditionally accepted, with a Program Committee (PC) member assigned in the latter case to shepherd the paper and ensure that specific improvements were made. One of the conditionally accepted papers could not be included in the program due to a technical flaw discovered during the shepherding process.

We are grateful to the 127 Program Committee members and 94 external reviewers who reviewed all the submissions and provided thoughtful and constructive feedback, which considerably strengthened the quality of the final program. Two reviewers stood out in terms of the quality of their reviews and were named "Distinguished Reviewers": Zeta Avarikioti and Dionysis Zindros. Additionally, we would like to recognize reviewers whose contributions went above and beyond the expectations of a regular PC member: Joseph Bonneau, Christian Cachin, Jeremy Clark, Juan Garay, Arthur Gervais, Katharina Kohls, Johannes Krupp, Wouter Lueks, Sarah Meiklejohn, Pedro Moreno-Sanchez, Bart Preneel, Marko Vukolić, Riad Wahby, and Ren Zhang. Finally, we would like to recognize three external reviewers for their outstanding service: Christian Badertscher, Ankit Gangwal, and Henning Seidler.

FC 2021 no longer distinguished between two "tracks", one on traditional financial cryptography and another on blockchain research, and instead had a single track with a wide variety of topics including blockchain-related papers. When classifying papers into these two broad categories, we found that 72% of submitted papers were on topics related to blockchain research, while only 55% of accepted papers fell in that category. The accepted papers were organized according to their topic into 12 sessions: Smart Contracts, Anonymity and Privacy in Cryptocurrencies, Secure Multi-party Computation, System and Application Security, Zero-knowledge Proofs, Blockchain Protocols, Payment Channels, Mining, Scaling Blockchains, Authentication and Usability, Measurement, and Cryptography.

Due to the COVID-19 global pandemic, a physical meeting was impossible; instead FC 2021 was held as a four-day online event. Papers were presented in 12 sessions, with a short live presentation followed by a question-and-answer session with the audience.

Authors also recorded a longer paper presentation of 20–30 minutes that is available online, linked from the conference website. In addition to the 12 regular paper sessions, the program included a Rump session, a keynote talk on "Signature and Commitment" by Whitfield Diffie, a keynote Fireside Chat with SEC Commissioner Hester Peirce, a General Assembly, and a social hour at the end of each day. We are grateful to all the session chairs for their service. And we would like to offer special thanks to Kay McKelly and Kevin McCurley for providing and managing the online conference platform. We would also like to thank Sergi Delgado Segura and Rafael Hirschfeld for their service as conference general chairs, and the IFCA directors and Steering Committee for their help organizing the conference during this particularly challenging year.

Finally, we would like to thank the sponsors of the conference for their generous support: our Platinum sponsor Novi; our Gold sponsors Chainalysis and IBM; and our Silver sponsors NTT Research and Protocol Labs.

August 2021   Nikita Borisov
                                                               Claudia Diaz

Organization

General Chairs

Sergi Delgado Segura Talaia Labs, UK
Rafael Hirshfeld   Unipay Technologies, The Netherlands

Program Committee Chairs

Nikita Borisov   University of Illinois at Urbana-Champaign, USA
Claudia Diaz   KU Leuven, Belgium

Steering Committee

Joseph Bonneau   New York University, USA
Rafael Hirshfeld   Unipay Technologies, The Netherlands
Andrew Miller   University of Illinois at Urbana-Champaign, USA
Monica Quaintance Kadena, USA
Burton Rosenberg University of Miami, USA

Program Committee

Ittai Abraham   VMware Research, Israel
Gunes Acar   KU Leuven, Belgium
Shashank Agrawal Western Digital Research, USA
Ross Anderson   University of Cambridge, UK
Elli Androulaki   IBM Research—Zurich, Switzerland
Diego F. Aranha   Aarhus University, Denmark
Man Ho Au   The University of Hong Kong, China
Zeta Avarikioti   ETH Zurich, Switzerland
Erman Ayday   Case Western Reserve University, USA,
        and Bilkent University, Turkey
Foteini Baldimtsi   George Mason University, USA
Shehar Bano   Novi and Facebook, UK
Iddo Bentov   Cornell Tech, USA
Bobby Bhattacharjee University of Maryland, USA
Alex Biryukov   University of Luxembourg, Luxembourg
Dan Boneh   Stanford University, USA
Joseph Bonneau   New York University, USA
Karima Boudaoud Université Côte d'Azur, France
Ioana Boureanu   University of Surrey, UK

Xavier Boyen	Queensland University of Technology, Australia
Rainer Böhme	University of Innsbruck, Austria
Jeffrey Burdges	Web 3 Foundation, Switzerland
Benedikt Bünz	Stanford University, USA
Christian Cachin	University of Bern, Switzerland
L. Jean Camp	Indiana University, USA
Srdjan Capkun	ETH Zurich, Switzerland
Pern Hui Chia	Google, USA
Tom Chothia	University of Birmingham, UK
Jeremy Clark	Concordia University, Canada
Shaanan Cohney	University of Pennsylvania, USA, and University of Melbourne, Australia
George Danezis	University College London and Novi, UK
Sanchari Das	University of Denver, USA
Vensa Daza	Pompeu Fabra University, Spain
Jean Paul Degabriele	TU Darmstadt, Germany
Matteo Dell'Amico	EURECOM, France
Sven Dietrich	City University of New York, USA
Benjamin Edwards	Cyentia Institute, USA
Tariq Elahi	University of Edinburgh, UK
Kaoutar Elkhiyaoui	IBM Research, Switzerland
William Enck	North Carolina State University, USA
Zekeriya Erkin	Delft University of Technology, The Netherlands
Ittay Eyal	Technion, Israel
Antonio Faonio	EURECOM, France
Dario Fiore	IMDEA Software Institute, Spain
Ben Fisch	Stanford University, USA
Simone Fischer-Hübner	Karlstad University, Sweden
Juan Garay	Texas A&M University, USA
Christina Garman	Purdue University, USA
Arthur Gervais	Imperial College London, UK
Esha Ghosh	Microsoft Research, USA
Thomas Gross	Newcastle University, UK
Jens Grossklags	Technical University of Munich, Germany
Feng Hao	University of Warwick, UK
Ethan Heilman	Boston University, USA
Urs Hengartner	University of Waterloo, Canada
Ryan Henry	University of Calgary, Canada
Jori Herrera-Joancomartí	Universitat Autònoma de Barcelona, Spain
Jaap-Henk Hoepman	Radboud University and University of Groeningen, The Netherlands
Nicholas Hopper	University of Minnesota, USA
Kévin Huguenin	University of Lausanne, Switzerland
Stephanie Hurder	Prysm Group, USA
Alice Hutchings	University of Cambridge, UK
Marc Juarez	University of Southern California, USA

Sreeram Kannan	University of Washington, USA
Gabriel Kaptchuk	Boston University, USA
Ghassan Karame	NEC Laboratories Europe, Germany
Aniket Kate	Purdue University, USA
Stefan Katzenbeisser	University of Passau, Germany
Aggelos Kiayias	University of Edinburgh and IOHK, UK
Katharina Kohls	Ruhr University Bochum, Germany
Markulf Kohlweiss	University of Edinburgh and IOHK, UK
Johannes Krupp	CISPA Helmholtz Center for Information Security, Germany
Albert Kwon	Badge Biometrics, USA
Aron Laszka	University of Houston, USA
Kirill Levchenko	University of Illinois at Urbana-Champaign, USA
Jiasun Li	George Mason University, USA
Benjamit Livshits	Brave Software and Imperial College London, USA
Wouter Lueks	EPFL, Switzerland
Xiapu Luo	The Hong Kong Polytechnic University, China
Loi Luu	Kyber Network, Singapore
Travis Mayberry	US Naval Academy, USA
Patrick McCorry	anydot, UK
Catherine Meadows	US Naval Research Laboratory, USA
Sarah Meiklejohn	University College London, UK
Andrew Miller	University of Illinois at Urbana-Champaign, USA
Pedro Moreno-Sanchez	IMDEA Software Institute, Spain
Steven Murdoch	University College London, UK
Neha Narula	MIT Media Lab, USA
Kartik Nayak	Duke University, USA
Russell O'Connor	Blockstream, Canada
Satoshi Obana	Hosei University, Japan
Simon Oya	University of Waterloo, Canada
Giorgos Panagiotakos	University of Athens, Greece
Olivier Preira	UC Louvain, Belgium
Andrew Poelstra	Blockstream, USA
Bart Preneel	KU Leuven, Belgium
Cristina Pérez-Solà	Universitat Oberta de Catalunya, Spain
Elizabeth A. Quaglia	Royal Holloway, University of London, UK
Joel Reardon	University of Calgary, Canada
Ling Ren	University of Illinois at Urbana-Champaign, USA
Alfredo Rial	University of Luxembourg, Luxembourg
Stefanie Roos	TU Delft, The Netherlands
Burton Rosenberg	University of Miami, USA
Ahmad-Reza Sadeghi	TU Darmstadt, Germany
Reihaneh Safavi-Naini	University of Calgary, Canada
Alessandra Scafuro	North Carolina State University, USA
Nolen Scaife	University of Colorado Boulder, USA
Jean-Pierre Seifert	TU Berlin, Germany

Abhi Shelat	Northeastern University, USA
Jared M. Smith	Oak Ridge National Laboratory, USA
Yonatan Sompolinsky	The Hebrew University of Jerusalem, Israel
Kyle Soska	Carnegie Mellon University, USA
Douglas Stebila	University of Waterloo, Canada
Vanessa Teague	University of Melbourne, Australia
Alin Tomescu	VMware Research, USA
Luke Valenta	Cloudflare Research, USA
Aad van Moorsel	Newcastle University, UK
Marie Vasek	University College London, UK
Pramod Viswanath	University of Illinois at Urbana-Champaign, USA
Artemij Voskobojnikov	University of British Columbia, Canada
Marko Vukolić	IBM Research, Switzerland
Riad S. Wahby	Stanford University, USA
Nick Weaver	International Computer Science Institute, USA
Edgar Wieppl	University of Vienna and SBA Research, Austria
Phillipp Winter	The Tor Project, USA
Jiangshan Yu	Monash University, Australia
Fan Zhang	Chainlink and Duke University, USA
Ren Zhang	Nervos, China
Dionysis Zindros	University of Athens, Greece
Aviv Zohar	The Hebrew University of Jerusalem, Israel

Additional Reviewers

Abramova, Svetlana	Farhang, Sadegh
Akand, Mamun	Feher, Daniel
Alupotha, Jayamine	Fietkau, Julian
Avizheh, Sepideh	Fischer, Felix
Badertscher, Christian	Fletcher, Christopher
Bag, Samiran	Fröwis, Michael
Bagaria, Vivek	Gangwal, Ankit
Beck, Gabrielle	Govinden, Jérôme
Bentov, Iddo	Guimarães, Antônio Carlos
Bissias, George	Gupta, Abhinav
Buhren, Robert	Haffey, Preston
Cascudo, Ignacio	Haque, Abida
Chatzigiannis, Panagiotis	Harishankar, Madhumitha
Choi, Kevin	Humbert, Mathias
Das, Sourav	Islami, Lejla
Daveas, Stelios	Jao, David
Diamond, Parker	Ji, Yan
Elichai, Turkel	Karadzic, Vukasin
Ersoy, Oguzhan	Karakostas, Dimitris
Escudero, Daniel	Karantaidou, Ioanna

Kasper, Daniel
Keller, Patrik
Knapp, Jodie
Kolonelos, Dimitris
Lagorio, Giovanni
Leonardos, Nikos
Li, Tianyu
Linvill, Kirby
Litos, Orfeas
Lorenzo, Martinico
Madhusudan, Akash
Maier, Dominik
Marmolejo Cossío, Francisco
Martinico, Lorenzo
Mazorra, Bruno
McMenamin, Conor
Medley, Liam
Nabi, Mahmudun
Nadahalli, Tejaswi
Navarro-Arribas, Guillermo
Polydouri, Andrianna
Posa, Tibor
Prabhu Kumble, Satwik
Raghuraman, Srinivasan
Ribaudo, Marina
Rovira, Sergi
Sarenche, Roozbeh

Seidler, Henning
Sharifian, Setareh
Shrestha, Nibesh
Silde, Tjerand
Simkin, Mark
Sliwinski, Jakub
Sutton, Michael
Syrmoudis, Emmanuel
Tairi, Erkan
Takahasi, Akira
Terner, Benjamin
Tikhomirov, Sergei
Vadaraj, Srikar
Vitto, Giuseppe
Volkhov, Mikhail
Weber, Brian
Wilsiol, Nils
Wyborski, Shai
Xiang, Zhuolun
Xue, Haiyang
Yang, Rupeng
Zacharakis, Alexandros
Zacharias, Thomas
Zamyatin, Alexei
Zapico, Arantxa
Zhang, Xinyuan

Contents – Part I

Secure Multi-party Computation

System and Application Security

Zero-Knowledge Proofs

Contents – Part II

Blockchain Protocols

Payment Channels

Measurement

Cryptography

Smart Contracts

Attacking the DeFi Ecosystem with Flash Loans for Fun and Profit

Kaihua Qin[(✉)], Liyi Zhou, Benjamin Livshits, and Arthur Gervais

Imperial College London, London, UK
{kaihua.qin,liyi.zhou,b.livshits,a.gervais}@imperial.ac.uk

Abstract. Credit allows a lender to loan out surplus capital to a borrower. In the traditional economy, credit bears the risk that the borrower may default on its debt, the lender hence requires upfront collateral from the borrower, plus interest fee payments. Due to the atomicity of blockchain transactions, lenders can offer *flash loans*, i.e., loans that are only valid within one transaction and must be repaid by the end of that transaction. This concept has lead to a number of interesting attack possibilities, some of which were exploited in February 2020.

This paper is the first to explore the implication of transaction atomicity and flash loans for the nascent decentralized finance (DeFi) ecosystem. We show quantitatively how transaction atomicity increases the arbitrage revenue. We moreover analyze two existing attacks with ROIs beyond 500k%. We formulate finding the attack parameters as an *optimization problem* over the state of the underlying Ethereum blockchain and the state of the DeFi ecosystem. We show how malicious adversaries can efficiently maximize an attack profit and hence damage the DeFi ecosystem further. Specifically, we present how two previously executed attacks can be "boosted" to result in a profit of 829.5k USD and 1.1M USD, respectively, which is a boost of $2.37\times$ and $1.73\times$, respectively.

1 Introduction

A central component of our economy is *credit*: to foster economic growth, market participants can borrow and lend assets to each other. If credit creates new and sustainable value, it can be perceived as a positive force. Abuse of credit, however, necessarily entails negative future consequences. Excessive debt can lead to a debt default—i.e., a borrower is no longer capable to repay the loan plus interest payment. This leads us to the following intriguing question: What if it were possible to offer credit without bearing the risk that the borrower does not pay back the debt? Such a concept appears impractical in the traditional financial world. No matter how small the borrowed amount, and how short the loan term, the risk of the borrower defaulting remains. If one were absolutely certain that a debt would be repaid, one could offer loans of massive volume – or lend to individuals independently of demographics and geographic location, effectively providing capital to rich and poor alike.

ⓒ International Financial Cryptography Association 2021
N. Borisov and C. Diaz (Eds.): FC 2021, LNCS 12674, pp. 3–32, 2021.
https://doi.org/10.1007/978-3-662-64322-8_1

Given the peculiarities of blockchain-based smart contracts, *flash loans* emerged. Blockchain-based smart contracts allow to programmatically enforce the atomic execution of a transaction. A flash loan is a loan that is only valid within one atomic blockchain transaction. Flash loans fail if the borrower does not repay its debt before the end of the transaction borrowing the loan. That is because a blockchain transaction can be reverted during its execution if the condition of repayment is not satisfied. Flash loans yield three novel properties, absent in traditional finance:

- **No debt default risk:** A lender offering a flash loan bears no risk that the borrower defaults on its debt[1]. Because a transaction and its instructions must be executed atomically, a flash loan is not granted if the transaction fails due to a debt default.
- **No need for collateral:** Because the lender is guaranteed to be paid back, the lender can issue credit without upfront collateral from the borrower: a flash loan is non-collateralized.
- **Loan size:** Flash loans can be taken from public smart contract-governed liquidity pools. Any borrower can borrow the entire pool at any point in time. As of September 2020, the largest flash loan pool Aave [13] offers in excess of 1B USD [1].

To the best of our knowledge, this is the first paper that investigates flash loans. **This paper makes the following contributions:**

- **Flash loan usage analysis.** We provide a comprehensive overview of how and where the technique of flash loans can and is utilized. At the time of writing, flash loan pool sizes have reached more than 1B USD.
- **Post mortem of existing attacks.** We meticulously dissect two events where talented traders realized a profit of each about 350k USD and 600k USD with two independent flash loans: a *pump and arbitrage* from the 15th of February 2020 and an *oracle manipulation* from the 18th of February 2020.
- **Attack parameter optimization framework.** Given the interplay of six DeFi systems, covering exchanges, credit/lending, and margin trading, we provide a framework to quantify the parameters that yield the maximum revenue an adversary can achieve, given a specific trading attack strategy. We show that an adversary can maximize the attack profit efficiently (in less than 13ms) due to the atomic transaction property.
- **Quantifying opportunity loss.** We show how the presented flash loan attackers have forgone the opportunity to realize a profit exceeding 829.5k USD and 1.1M USD, respectively. We realize this by finding the optimal adversarial parameters the trader should have employed, using a parametrized optimizer. We experimentally validate the opportunity loss on a locally deployed blockchain mirroring the attacks' respective blockchain state.
- **Impact of transaction atomicity on arbitrage.** We show quantitatively how atomicity reduces the risk of revenue from arbitrage. Specifically, by analyzing 6.4M transactions, we find that the expected arbitrage reward

---

[1] Besides the risk of smart contract vulnerabilities.

decreases by 123.49 ± 1375.32 USD and 1.77 ± 10.59 USD for the DAI/ETH and MKR/ETH markets respectively when the number of intermediary transactions reaches $5,000$.

Paper Organization: The remainder of the paper is organized as follows. Section 2 elaborates on the DeFi background. Section 3 dissects two known flash loan attacks. Section 4 proposes a framework to optimize the attack revenues and Sect. 5 evaluates the framework on the two analyzed attacks. Section 6 analyses the implications of the atomic transaction property. Section 7 provides a discussion. We conclude the paper in Sect. 8.

2   Background

Decentralized ledgers, such as Bitcoin [44], enable the performance of transactions among a peer-to-peer network. At its core, a blockchain is a chain of blocks [17,44], extended by miners crafting new blocks that contain transactions. Smart contracts [49] allow the execution of complicated transactions, which forms the foundation of decentralized finance, a conglomerate of financial cryptocurrency-related protocols. These protocols for instance allow to lend and borrow assets [4,39], exchange [11,24], margin trade [3,24], short and long [3], and allow to create derivative assets [4]. At the time of writing, the DeFi space accounts for over 8B USD in smart contract locked capital among different providers. The majority of the DeFi platforms operate on the Ethereum blockchain, governed by the Ethereum Virtual Machine (EVM), where the trading rules are governed by the underlying smart contracts. A decentralized exchange is typically referred to as DEX. We refer to the on-chain DeFi actors as traders and distinguish among the two types of traders:

Liquidity Provider: a trader with surplus capital may choose to offer this capital to other traders, e.g., as collateral within a DEX or lending platform.

Liquidity Taker: a trader which is servicing liquidity provider with fees in exchange for accessing the available capital.

2.1   DeFi Platforms

We briefly summarize relevant DeFi platforms for this work.

Automated Market Maker (AMM) DEX: While many exchanges follow the limit order book design [34,35,40], an alternative exchange design is to collect funds within a liquidity pool, e.g., two pools for an AMM asset pair X/Y [11,34]. The state (or depth) of an AMM market X/Y is defined as (x, y), where x represents the amount of asset X and y the amount of asset Y in the liquidity pool. Liquidity providers can deposit/withdraw in both assets X and Y to in/decrease liquidity. The simplest AMM mechanism is a constant product market maker, which for an arbitrary asset pair X/Y, keeps the product $x \times y$ constant during trades. When trading on an AMM exchange, there can be a difference between the expected price and the executed price, termed *slippage* [10]. Insufficient liquidity and other front-running trades can cause slippage on an AMM [52]. We assume that a constant product AMM ETH/WBTC market is supplied with 10 ETH and 10 WBTC (i.e., the exchange rate is 1 ETH/WBTC). A trader can purchase 5 WBTC with 10 ETH (cf. $10 \times 10 = (10 + 10) \times (10 - 5)$) at an effective price of 2 ETH/WBTC. Hence, the slippage is $\frac{2-1}{1} = 100\%$.

Margin Trading: Trading on margin allows a trader to take under-collateralized loans from the trading platform and trade with these borrowed assets to amplify the profit (i.e., leverage). On-chain margin trading platforms remain in control of the loaned asset (or the exchanged asset) and hence is able to liquidate when the value of the trader's collateral drops too low.

Credit and Lending: With over 3B USD total locked value, credit represents one of the most significant recent use-cases for blockchain based DeFi systems. Due to the lack of legal enforcement when borrowers default, they are required to provide between 125% [24] to 150% [39] collateral of an asset x to borrow 100% of another asset y (i.e., over-collateralization).

2.2   Reverting EVM State Transitions

The Ethereum blockchain is in essence a replicated state machine. To achieve a state transition, one applies as input transactions that modify the EVM state following rules encoded within deployed smart contracts. A smart contract can be programmed with the logic of reverting a transaction if a particular condition is not met during execution. The EVM state is *only* altered if a transaction executes successfully, otherwise, the EVM state is reverted to the previous, non-modified state.

Flash Loans. Flash loans are possible because the EVM allows the reversion of state changes. A flash loan is only valid within a single transaction and relies on the atomicity of blockchain (and, specifically, EVM) transactions within a single block. Flash loans entail two important new financial properties: First, a borrower does not need to provide upfront collateral to request a loan of any size, up to the flash loan liquidity pool amount. Any borrower, willing to pay the required transaction fees (which typically amounts to a few USD) is an eligible borrower. Second, risk-free lending: If a borrower cannot pay back the loan, the flash loan transaction fails. Ignoring smart contract and blockchain vulnerabilities, the lender is hence not exposed to the risks of a debt default.

2.3   Flash Loan Usage in the Wild

To our knowledge, the Marble Protocol introduced the concept of flash loans [8]. Aave [13] is one of the first DeFi platforms to widely advertise flash loan capabilities (although others, such as dYdX also allow the non-documented possibility to borrow flash loans) since January 2020. At the time of writing, Aave charges a constant 0.09% interest fee for flash loans and amassed a total liquidity beyond 1B USD [1]. In comparison, the total volume of U.S. corporation debt reached 10.5T USD in August, 2020 [12].

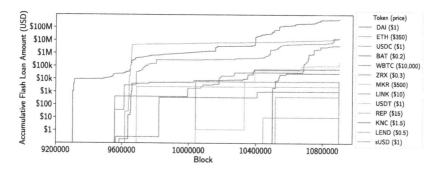

Fig. 1. Accumulative flash loan amounts of 13 cryptocurrencies on Aave. Note that the y-axis is a logarithmic scale.

By gathering all blockchain event logs from Aave with a full archive Ethereum node, we find 5,616 flash loans issued from the Aave smart contract (cf. 0x398eC7346DcD622eDc5ae82352F02bE94C62d119) between the 8th of January, 2020 and the 20th of September, 2020. In Fig. 1, we show the accumulative flash loan amounts of 13 different loan currencies. Among them, DAI is the most popular with the accumulative amount of 447.2M USD. We inspect and classify the Aave flash loan transactions depending on which platforms the flash loans interact with (cf. Fig. 11 in Appendix A). We notice that most flash loans interact with lending/exchange DeFi systems and that the flash loan's transaction costs (i.e., gas) appear significant (at times beyond 4M gas, compared to 21k gas for regular Ether transfer). The dominating use cases are arbitrage and liquidation. Further details are presented in Appendix A.

Flash Loan Arbitrage Example: The value of an asset is typically determined by the demand and supply of the market, across different exchanges. Due to a lack of instantaneous synchronization among exchanges, the same asset can

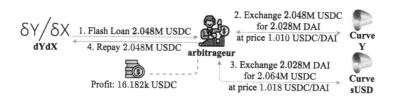

Fig. 2. High-level executions of a flash loan based arbitrage transaction 0xf7498a2546c3d70f49d83a2a5476fd9dcb6518100b2a731294d0d7b9f79f754a: *(1)* flash loan; *(2)* exchange USDC for DAI in Curve Y pool; *(3)* exchange DAI for USDC in Curve sUSDC pool; *(4)* repay. Note that Curve provides several on-chain cryptocurrency markets, also known as pools.

be traded at slightly different prices on different exchanges. *Arbitrage* is the process of exploiting price differences among exchanges for a financial gain [46]. In Fig. 2, we present, as an example, the execution details of a flash loan based arbitrage transaction on the 31st of July, 2020. The arbitrageur borrowed a flash loan of 2.048M USDC, performed two exchanges, and realized a profit of 16.182k USDC (16.182k USD). This example highlights how given atomic transactions, a trader can perform arbitrage on different on-chain markets, without the risk that the prices in the DEX would intermediately change. Flash loans moreover remove the currency volatility risk for arbitrageurs. In Sect. 6, we quantify the implications of transaction atomicity on arbitrage risks.

Besides arbitrage, we noticed another two use cases for flash loans: *(i)* wash trading (fraudulent inflation of trading volume), *(ii)* loan collateral swapping (instant swapping from one collateral to another), and also a variation of flash loan, *(iii)* flash minting (the momentarily token in- and decrease of an asset). We elaborate further on these in Appendix B and provide real-world examples.

2.4   Related Work

There is a growing body of work focusing on various forms of manipulation and financially-driven attacks in cryptocurrency markets.

Crypto Manipulation: Front-running in cryptocurrencies has been extensively studied [5,18,22,25,32,52]. Remarkably, Daian *et al.* [22] introduce the concept of miner extractable value (MEV) and analyze comprehensively the exploitability of ordering blockchain transactions. Our work focuses on flash loans, which qualify as a potential MEV that miners could exploit. Gandal *et al.* [26] demonstrate that the unprecedented spike in the USD-BTC exchange rate in late 2013 was possibly caused by price manipulation. Recent papers focus on the phenomenon of pump-and-dump for manipulating crypto coin prices [28,33,51].

Smart Contract Vulnerabilities: Several exploits have taken advantage of smart contract vulnerabilities (e.g., the DAO exploit [9]). The most commonly known smart contract vulnerabilities are re-entrance, unhandled exceptions, locked ether, transaction order dependency and integer overflow [37]. Many tools and techniques, based on fuzzing [31,36,50], static analysis [19,47,48], symbolic execution [37,43,45], and formal verification [14,16,27,29,30], emerged to detect and prevent these vulnerabilities. In this work, we focus on DeFi economic security, which might not result from a single contract vulnerability and could involve multiple DeFi platforms.

3   Flash Loan Post-Mortem

Flash loans enable anyone to have instantaneous access to massive capital. This section outlines how that can have negative effects, as we explain two attacks facilitated by flash loans yielding an ROI beyond 500k%. We evaluate the proposed DeFi attack optimization framework (cf. Sect. 4) on these two analyzed attacks (cf. Sect. 5).

3.1   Pump Attack and Arbitrage (PA&A)

On the 15th of February, 2020, a flash loan transaction (cf. 0xb5c8bd9430b 6cc87a0e2fe110ece6bf527fa4f170a4bc8cd032f768fc5219838 at an ETH price of 264.71 USD/ETH), followed by 74 transactions, yielded a profit of $1,193.69$ ETH (350k USD) given a transaction fee of 132.36 USD (cumulative $50,237,867$ gas, 0.5 ETH). We show in Sect. 5.1 that the adversarial parameters were not optimal, and that the adversary could have earned a profit exceeding 829.5k USD.

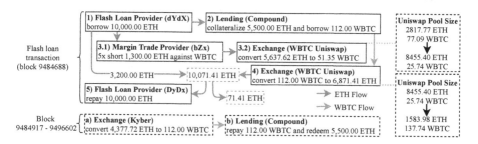

Fig. 3. The pump attack and arbitrage. The attack consists of two parts, a flash loan and several loan redemption transactions.

Attack Intuition: The core of PA&A is that the adversary pumps the price of ETH/WBTC on a constant product AMM DEX (Uniswap) with the leveraged funds of ETH in a margin trade. The adversary then purchases ETH at a "cheaper" price on the distorted DEX market (Uniswap) with the borrowed WBTC from a lending platform (Compound). As shown in Fig. 3, this attack mainly consists of two parts. For simplicity, we omit the conversion between ETH and WETH (the 1:1 convertible ERC20 version of ETH).

Flash Loan (Single Transaction): The first part of the attack (cf. Fig. 3) consists of 5 steps within a single transaction. In step ①, the adversary borrows a flash loan of $10,000.00$ ETH from a flash loan provider (dYdX). In step ②, the adversarial trader collateralizes $5,500.00$ ETH into a lending platform (Compound) to borrow 112.00 WBTC. Note that the adversarial trader does not return the 112.00 WBTC within the flash loan. This means the adversarial trader takes the risk of a forced liquidation against the $5,500.00$ ETH collateral if the price fluctuates. In steps ③, the trader provides $1,300$ ETH to open a short position for ETH against WBTC (on bZx) with a $5\times$ leverage. Upon receiving this request, bZx transacts $5,637.62$ ETH on an exchange (Uniswap) for only 51.35 WBTC (at 109.79 ETH/WBTC). Note that at the start of block 9484688, Uniswap has a total supply of $2,817.77$ ETH and 77.09 WBTC (at 36.55 ETH/WBTC). The slippage of this transaction is significant with $\frac{109.79-36.55}{36.55} = 200.38\%$. In step ④, the trader converts 112.00 WBTC borrowed from lending platform (Compound) to $6,871.41$ ETH on the DEX

(Uniswap) (at 61.35 ETH/WBTC). We remark that the equity of the adversarial margin account is negative after the margin trading because of the significant price movement. The pump attack could have been avoided if bZx checked the negative equity and reverted the transaction. At the time of the attack, this logic existed in the bZx contracts but was not invoked properly. In step ⑤, the trader pays back the flash loan plus an interest of 10^{-7} ETH. After the flash loan transaction (i.e., the first part of PA&A), the trader gains 71.41 ETH, and has a debt of 112 WBTC over-collateralized by 5,500 ETH (49.10 ETH/WBTC). If the ETH/WBTC market price is below this loan exchange rate, the adversary can redeem the loan's collateral as follows.

Loan Redemption: The second part of the trade consists of two recurring steps, (step ⓐ - ⓑ), between Ethereum block 9484917 and 9496602. Those transactions aim to redeem ETH by repaying the WBTC borrowed earlier (on Compound). To avoid slippage when purchasing WBTC, the trader executes the second part in small amounts over a period of two days on the DEX (Kyber, Uniswap). In total, the adversarial trader exchanged 4,377.72 ETH for 112 WBTC (at 39.08 ETH/WBTC) to redeem 5,500.00 ETH.

Identifying the Victim: We investigate who of the participating entities is losing money. Note that in step ③ of Fig. 3, the short position (on bZx) borrows $5,637.62 - 1,300 = 4,337.62$ ETH from the lending provider (bZx), with 1,300 ETH collateral. Step ③ requires to purchase WBTC at a price of 109.79 ETH/WBTC, with both, the adversary's collateral and the pool funds of the liquidity provider. 109.79 ETH/WBTC does not correspond to the market price of 36.55 ETH/WBTC prior to the attack, hence the liquidity provider overpays by nearly 3× of the WBTC price.

How Much are the Victims Losing: We now quantify the losses of the liquidity providers. The loan provider lose 4,337.62 (ETH from loan providers) - 51.35 (WBTC left in short position) × 39.08 (market exchange rate ETH/WBTC) = 2,330.86 ETH. The adversary gains 5,500.00 (ETH loan collateral in Compound) - 4,377.72 (ETH spent to purchase WBTC) + 71.41 (part 1) = 1,193.69 ETH.

More Money is Left on the Table: Due to the attack, Uniswap's price of ETH was reduced from 36.55 to 11.50 ETH/WBTC. This creates an arbitrage opportunity, where a trader can sell ETH against WBTC on Uniswap to synchronize the price. 1,233.79 ETH would yield 60.65 WBTC, instead of 33.76 WBTC, realizing an arbitrage profit of 26.89 WBTC (286,035.04 USD).

3.2   Oracle Manipulation Attack

We proceed to detail a second flash loan attack, which yields a profit of 2,381.41 ETH (c. 634.9k USD) within a single transaction (cf. 0x762881b07feb63c436 dee38edd4ff1f7a74c33091e534af56c9f7d49b5ecac15, on the 18th of February, 2020, at an ETH price of 282.91 USD/ETH) given a transaction fee of 118.79 USD. Before diving into the details, we cover additional background knowledge.

We again show how the chosen attack parameters were sub-optimal and optimal parameters would yield a profit of 1.1M USD instead (cf. Sect. 5.2).

Price Oracle: One of the goals of the DeFi ecosystem is to not rely on trusted third parties. This premise holds both for asset custody as well as additional information, such as asset pricing. One common method to determine an asset price is hence to rely on the pricing information of an on-chain DEX (e.g., Uniswap). DEX prices, however, can be manipulated with flash loans.

Attack Intuition: The core of this attack is an oracle manipulation using a flash loan, which lowers the price of sUSD/ETH. In a second step, the adversary benefits from this decreased sUSD/ETH price by borrowing ETH with sUSD as collateral.

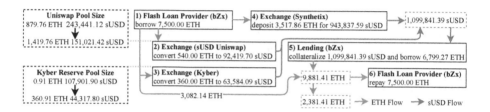

Fig. 4. The oracle manipulation attack.

Adversarial Oracle Manipulation: We identify a total of 6 steps within this transaction (cf. Fig. 4). In step ①, the adversary borrows a flash loan of 7,500.00 ETH (on bZx). In the next three steps (②,③,④), the adversary converts a total of 4,417.86 ETH to 1,099,841.39 sUSD (at an average of 248.95 sUSD/ETH). The exchange rates in step ② and ③ are 171.15 and 176.62 sUSD/ETH respectively. These two steps decrease the sUSD/ETH price to 106.05 sUSD/ETH on Uniswap and 108.44 sUSD/ETH on Kyber Reserve, which are collectively used as a price oracle of the lending platform (bZx). Note that Uniswap is a constant product AMM, while Kyber Reserve is an AMM following a different formula (cf. Appendix C). The trade on the third market (Synthetix) in step ④ is yet unaffected by the previous trades. The adversarial trader then collateralizes all the purchased sUSD (1,099,841.39) to borrow 6,799.27 ETH (at $\frac{\text{exchange rate}}{\text{collateral factor}} = \max(106.05, 108.44) \times 1.5 = 162.66$ sUSD/ETH on bZx). Now the adversary possesses 6,799.27+3,082.14 ETH and in the last step repays the flash loan amounting to 7,500.00 ETH. The adversary, therefore, generates a revenue of 2,381.41 ETH while only paying 0.42 ETH (118.79 USD) transaction fees.

Identifying the Victim: The adversary distorted the price oracle (Uniswap and Kyber) from 268.30 sUSD/ETH to 108.44 sUSD/ETH, while other DeFi platforms remain unaffected at 268.30 sUSD/ETH. Similar to the pump attack and arbitrage, the lenders on bZx are the victims losing assets as a result of the distorted price oracle. The lender lost 6,799.27 ETH - 1,099,841 sUSD, which is estimated to be 2,699.97 ETH (at 268.30 sUSD/ETH). The adversary gains 6,799.27 (ETH from borrowing) - 3,517.86 (ETH to purchase sUSD) - 360 (ETH to purchase sUSD) - 540 (ETH to purchase sUSD) = 2,381.41 ETH.

4 Optimizing DeFi Attacks

The atomicity of blockchain transactions guarantees the continuity of the action executions. When the initial state is deterministically known, this trait allows an adversary to predict the intermediate results precisely after each action execution and then to optimize the attacking outcome by adjusting action parameters. In light of the complexity of optimizing DeFi attacks manually, we propose a *constrained optimization framework* that is capable of optimizing the action parameters. We show, given a blockchain state and an attack vector composed of a series of DeFi actions, how an adversary can efficiently discover the optimal action parameters that maximize the resulting expected revenue.

4.1 System and Threat Model

The system considered is limited to one decentralized ledger which supports pseudo-Turing complete smart contracts (e.g., similar to the Ethereum Virtual Machine; state transitions can be reversed given certain conditions).

We assume the presence of one computationally bounded and economically rational adversary $\mathbb{A}$. $\mathbb{A}$ attempts to exploit the availability of flash loans for financial gain. While $\mathbb{A}$ is not required to provide its own collateral to perform the presented attacks, the adversary must be financially capable to pay transaction fees. The adversary may amass more capital which possibly could increase its impact and ROI.

4.2 Parametrized Optimization Framework

We start by modeling different components that may engage in a DeFi attack. To facilitate optimal parameter solving, we quantitatively formalize every endpoint provided by DeFi platforms as a state transition function $S' = \mathcal{T}(S; p)$ with the constraints $\mathcal{C}(S; p)$, where S is the given state, p are the parameters chosen by the adversary and S' is the output state. The state can represent, for example, the adversarial balance or any internal status of the DeFi platform, while the constraints are set by the execution requirements of the EVM (e.g., the Ether balance of an entity should never be a negative number) or the rules defined by the respective DeFi platform (e.g., a flash loan must be repaid before the transaction termination plus loan fees). When quantifying profits, we ignore the loan interest/fee payments and transaction fees, which are negligible in the present DeFi attacks. The constraints are enforced on the input parameters and output states to ensure that the optimizer yields valid parameters.

We define the balance state function $\mathcal{B}(\mathbb{E}; X; S)$ to denote the balance of currency X held by entity $\mathbb{E}$ at a given state S and require Eq. 1 to hold.

$$\forall(\mathbb{E}, X, S), \ \mathcal{B}(\mathbb{E}; X; S) \geq 0 \tag{1}$$

The mathematical DeFi models applied in this work are detailed in Appendix C.

Our parametrized optimizer is designed to solve the optimal parameters that maximizes the revenue given an on-chain state, DeFi models and attack vector. An attack vector specifies the execution order of different endpoints across various DeFi platforms, depending on which we formalize a unidirectional chain of transition functions (cf. Eq. 2).

$$S_i = \mathcal{T}_i(S_{i-1}; p_i) \tag{2}$$

By nesting transition functions, we can obtain the cumulative state transition functions $\mathcal{ACC}_i(S_0; p^{1:i})$ that satisfies Eq. 3, where $p^{1:i} = (p_1, ..., p_i)$.

$$
\begin{aligned}
S_i &= \mathcal{T}_i(S_{i-1}; p_i) = \mathcal{T}_i(\mathcal{T}_{i-1}(S_{i-2}; p_{i-1}); p_i) \\
&= \mathcal{T}_i(\mathcal{T}_{i-1}(...\mathcal{T}_1(S_0, p_1)...; p_{i-1}); p_i) = \mathcal{ACC}_i(S_0; p^{1:i})
\end{aligned}
\tag{3}
$$

Therefore the constraints generated in each step can be expressed as Eq. 4.

$$\mathcal{C}_i(S_i; p_i) \Longleftrightarrow \mathcal{C}_i(\mathcal{ACC}_i(S_0; p^{1:i}); p_i) \tag{4}$$

We assume an attack vector composed of N transition functions. The objective function can be calculated from the initial state S_0 and the final state S_N (e.g., the increase of the adversarial balance).

$$\mathcal{O}(S_0; S_N) \Longleftrightarrow \mathcal{O}(S_0; \mathcal{ACC}(S_0; p^{1:N})) \tag{5}$$

Given the initial state S_0, we formulate an attack vector into a constrained optimization problem with respect to all the parameters $p^{1:N}$ (cf. Eq. 6).

$$
\begin{aligned}
\text{maximize} \quad & \mathcal{O}(S_0; \mathcal{ACC}(S_0; p^{1:N})) \\
\text{s.t.} \quad & \mathcal{C}_i(\mathcal{ACC}_i(S_0; p^{1:i}); p_i) \quad \forall i \in [1, N]
\end{aligned}
\tag{6}
$$

5   Evaluation

In the following, we evaluate our parametrized optimization framework on the existing attacks described in Sect. 3. We adopt the Sequential Least Squares Programming (SLSQP) algorithm from SciPy[2] to solve the constructed optimization problems. Our framework is evaluated on a Ubuntu 18.04.2 machine with 16 CPU cores and 32 GB RAM.

---

[2] https://www.scipy.org/. We use the `minimize` function in the `optimize` package.

5.1 Optimizing the Pump Attack and Arbitrage

We first optimize the pump attack and arbitrage. Figure 5 summarizes the notations and the on-chain state when the attack was executed (i.e., S_0). We use these blockchain records as the initial state in our evaluation. X and Y denote ETH and WBTC respectively. In the PA&A attack vector, we intend to tune the following two parameters, (i) p_1: the amount of X collateralized to borrow Y (cf. step ② and ③ in Fig. 3) and (ii) p_2: the amount of X collateralized to short Y (cf. step ④ in Fig. 3). Following the methodology specified in Sect. 4.2, we derive the optimization problem and the corresponding constraints, which are presented in Fig. 6. We detail the deriving procedure in Appendix D. We remark that there are five linear constraints and only one nonlinear constraint, which implies that the optimization can be solved efficiently.

We repeated our experiment for 1,000 times, the optimizer spent 6.1ms on average converging to the optimum. The optimizer provides a maximum revenue of 2,778.94 ETH when setting the parameters $(p_1; p_2)$ to (2,470.08; 1,456.23), while in the original attack the parameters (5,500; 1,300) only yield 1,171.70 ETH. Due to the ignorance of trading fees and precision differences, there is a minor discrepancy between the original attack revenue calculated with our model and the real revenue which is 1,193.69 ETH (cf. Sect. 3). This is a 829.5k USD gain over the attack that took place, using the price of ETH at that time. We experimentally validate the optimal PA&A parameters by forking the Ethereum blockchain with Ganache [6] at block 9484687 (one block prior to the original attack transaction). We then implement the pump attack and arbitrage in solidity v0.6.3. The revenue of the attack is divided into two parts: part one from the flash loan transaction, and part two which is a follow-up operation in later blocks (cf. Sect. 3) to repay the loan. For simplicity, we chose to only validate the first part, abiding by the following methodology: (i) We apply the parameter output of the parametrized optimizer, i.e., $(p_1; p_2) = (2,470.08; 1,456.23)$ to the adversarial validation smart contract. (ii) Note that our model is an approximation of the real blockchain transition functions. Hence, due to the inaccuracy of our model, we cannot directly use the precise model output, but instead use the model output as a guide for a manual, trial, and error search. We find 1,344

Description	Variable	Value
Maximum Amount of ETH to flash loan	v_X	10,000
Collateral Factor	cf	0.75
Collateralized Borrowing Exchange Rate	er	36.48
Maximum Amount of WBTC to Borrow	z_Y	155.70
Uniswap Reserved ETH	$u_X(S_0)$	2,817.77
Uniswap Reserved WBTC	$u_Y(S_0)$	77.08
Over Collateral Ratio	ocr	1.153
Leverage	ℓ	5
Maximum Amount of ETH to leverage	w_X	4,858.74
Market Price of WBTC	p_m	39.08

Objective function	$u_X(S_0) + \frac{p_2 \times \ell}{ocr} - u_X(S_4) - p_2 - \frac{p_1 \times cf \times p_m}{er}$
Constraints	$p_1 \geq 0, \, p_2 \geq 0$
	$v_X - p_0 - p_1 \geq 0$
	$z_Y - \frac{p_1 \times cf}{er} \geq 0$
	$w_X + p_2 - \frac{p_2 \times \ell}{ocr} \geq 0$
	$B_0 + u_X(S_0) + \frac{p_2 \times \ell}{ocr} - u_X(S_4) - p_1 - p_2 \geq 0$

Fig. 5. Initial on-chain states of the PA&A.

Fig. 6. Generated PA&A constraints. $u_X(S_4)$ is nonlinear with respect to p_1 and p_2.

is the maximum value of p_2 that allows the successful adversarial trade. *(iii)* Given the new p_2 constraint, our optimizer outputs the new optimal parameters $(2, 404; 1, 344)$. *(iv)* Our optimal adversarial trade yields a profit of $1, 958.01$ ETH on part one (as opposed to 71.41 ETH) and consumes a total of 3.3M gas.

5.2   Optimizing the Oracle Manipulation Attack

In the oracle manipulation attack, we denote X as ETH and Y as sUSD, while the initial state variables are presented in Fig. 7. We assume that $\mathbb{A}$ owns zero balance of X or Y. There are three parameters to optimize in this attack, *(i)* p_1: the amount of X used to swap for Y in step 2); *(ii)* p_2: the amount of X used to swap for Y in step 3); *(iii)* p_3: the amount of X used to exchange for Y in step 4). We summarize the produced optimization problem and its constraints in Fig. 8, of which five constraints are linear and the other two are nonlinear. We present the details in Appendix E.

We execute our optimizer $1, 000$ times, resulting in an average convergence time of 12.9 ms. The optimizer discovers that setting $(p_1; p_2; p_3)$ to $(898.58; 546.80; 3, 517.86)$ results in $6, 323.93$ ETH in profit for the adversary. This results in a gain of 1.1M USD instead of 634.9k USD. We fork the Ethereum blockchain with Ganache at block 9504626 (one block prior to the original adversarial transaction) and again implement the attack in solidity v0.6.3. We validate that executing the adversarial smart contract with parameters $(p_1; p_2; p_3) = (898.58; 546.8; 3, 517.86)$ renders a profit of $6, 262.28$ ETH, while the original attack parameters yield $2, 381.41$ ETH. The attack consumes 11.3M gas (which fits within the current block gas limit of 12.5M gas, but wouldn't have fit in the block gas limit of February 2020). By analyzing the adversarial validation contract, we find that 460 is the maximum value of p_2 which reduces the gas consumption below 10M gas. Similar to Sect. 5.1, we add the new constraint to the optimizer, which then gives the optimal parameters $(714.3; 460; 3, 517.86)$. The augmented validation contract renders a profit of $4, 167.01$ ETH and consumes 9.6M gas.

Description	Variable	Value
Maximum ETH to flash loan	v_X	$7, 500$
Uniswap Reserved ETH	$u_X(S_0)$	879.757
Uniswap Reserved sUSD	$u_Y(S_0)$	$243, 441.12$
Liquidity Rate	lr	0.00252
Min. sUSD Price of Kyber Reserve	minP	0.0037
Max. sUSD Price of Kyber Reserve	maxP	0.0148
Inventory of ETH in Kyber Reserve	$k_X(S_0)$	0.90658
Market Price of sUSD	p_m	0.00372719
Max. sUSD to Buy	maxY	$943, 837.59$
Collateral Factor	cf	0.667
Max. ETH to Borrow	z_Y	$11, 086.29$

Objective function	$\mathcal{B}(\mathbb{A}; Y; S_4) \times cf \times P_Y(M; S_2) - p_1 - p_2 - p_3$
Constraints	$p_1 \geq 0, \; p_2 \geq 0, \; p_3 \geq 0$
	$v_X - p_1 - p_2 - p_3 \geq 0$
	$maxP - minP \times e^{lr \times (k_X(S_0) + p_2)} \geq 0$
	$maxY - \frac{p_3}{p_m} \geq 0$
	$z_Y - \mathcal{B}(\mathbb{A}; Y; S_4) \times cf \times P_Y(M; S_2) \geq 0$

Fig. 7. Initial on-chain states of the oracle manipulation attack.

Fig. 8. Constraints generated for the oracle manipulation attack. $\mathcal{B}(\mathbb{A}; Y; S_4)$, $P_Y(M; S_2)$ are nonlinear components with respect to p_1, p_2, p_3.

6   Implications of Transaction Atomicity

In an atomic blockchain transaction, actions can be executed collectively in sequence, or fail collectively. Technically, operating DeFi actions in an atomic transaction is equivalent to acquiring a lock on all involved financial markets to ensure no other market agent can modify market states intermediately, and releasing the lock after executing all actions in their sequence.

To quantify objectively the impact of transaction atomicity (specifically, how the transaction atomicity impacts arbitrage profit), we proceed with the following methodology. We consider the arbitrages that involve two trades T_A and T_B to empirically compare the atomic and non-atomic arbitrages (cf. Fig. 9). We define the atomic and non-atomic arbitrage profit as follows.

Atomic Arbitrage Profit ($aarb$): is defined as the gain of two atomically executed arbitrage trades T_A and T_B on exchange A and B.

Non-atomic Arbitrage Profit ($naarb$): is defined as the arbitrage gain, if T_A executes first, and T_B's execution follows after i intermediary transactions.

Conceptually, a non-atomic arbitrage requires the arbitrageur to lock assets for a short time (order of seconds/minutes). Those assets are exposed to price volatility. The arbitrageur can at times realize a gain, if the asset increases in value, but equally has the risk of losing value. A trader engaging in atomic arbitrage is not exposed to this volatility risk, which we denote as *holding value*.

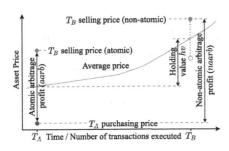

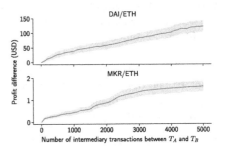

Fig. 9. On the impact of transaction atomicity on arbitrage. The arbitrageur submits the first trade T_A, which aims to purchase an asset at a "cheaper" prices (●) and sell the asset on another exchange at a "higher" price (◉). In a non-atomic environment, T_B is not immediately executed after T_A. The holding value is the in/decrease in price when holding the asset between T_A and T_B.

Fig. 10. Simulated impact of intermediary transactions on arbitrage revenue. The average reward decreases by 123.49 ± 1375.32 USD and 1.77±10.59 USD for the DAI/ETH and MKR/ETH markets respectively, at 350 USD/ETH, for 5,000 intermediary transactions. Note that we present the 95% bootstrap confidence interval of mean [23] for readability.

Holding Value (hv)**:** is defined as the change in the averaged price of the given asset pair on the two exchanges, which represents the asset value change during the non-atomic execution period.

We introduce holding value to neutralize the price volatility and can hence objectively quantify the financial advantage of atomic arbitrage. Given these variables, we define the *profit difference* in Eq. 7.

$$\text{profit difference} = aarb \text{ - } (naarb \text{ - } hv) \tag{7}$$

We simulate atomic and non-atomic based on $6,398,992$ transactions we collect from the Ethereum mainnet (from block 10276783 onwards). We insert 0 - $5,000$ blockchain transactions following the trade transaction T_A. Note that 0 intermediary transaction is equivalent to the atomic arbitrage. The insertion order follows the original execution order of these transactions, some of which may be irrelevant to the arbitrage. We present the simulated profit difference in Fig. 10. We observe that the average profit difference reaches 123.49 ± 1375.32 USD and 1.77 ± 10.59 USD for the DAI/ETH and MKR/ETH markets respectively when the number of intermediary transactions increases to $5,000$.

7   Discussion

The current generation of DeFi had developed organically, without much scrutiny when it comes to financial security; it, therefore, presents an interesting security challenge to confront. DeFi, on the one hand, welcomes innovation and the advent of new protocols, such as MakerDAO, Compound, and Uniswap. On the other hand, despite a great deal of effort spent on trying to secure smart contacts [21,31,38,48,50], and to avoid various forms of market manipulation, etc. [15,41,42], there has been little-to-no effort to secure entire *protocols*.

As such, DeFi protocols join the ecosystem, which leads to both exploits against protocols themselves as well as multi-step attacks that utilize several protocols such as the two attacks in Sect. 3. In a certain poignant way, this highlights the fact the DeFi, lacking a central authority that would enforce a strong security posture, is ultimately vulnerable to a multitude of attacks by design. Flash loans are merely a mechanism that *accelerates* these attacks. It does so by requiring no collateral (except for the minor gas costs), which is impossible in the traditional fiance due to regulations. In a certain way, flash loans democratize the attack, opening this strategy to the masses. As we anticipate in the earlier version of this paper, following the two analyzed attacks, economic attacks facilitated by flash loans become increasingly frequent, which have incurred a total loss of over 100M USD [7].

Determining What is Malicious: An interesting question remains whether we can qualify the use of flash loans, as clearly malicious (or clearly benign). We believe this is a difficult question to answer and prefer to withhold the value judgment. The two attacks in Sect. 3 are clearly malicious: the PA&A involves manipulating the WBTC/ETH price on Uniswap; the oracle manipulation attack involves price oracle by manipulatively lowering the price of ETH against sUSD on Kyber. However, the arbitrage mechanism, in general, is not malicious — it is merely a consequence of the decentralized nature of the DeFi ecosystem, where many exchanges and DEXs are allowed to exist without much coordination with each other. As such, arbitrage will continue to exist as a phenomenon, with good and bad consequences. Despite the lack of absolute distinction between flash loan attacks and legitimate applications of flash loans, we attempt to summarize two characteristics that appear to apply to malicious flash loan attacks: *(i)* the attacker benefits from a distorted state created artificially in the flash loan transaction (e.g., the pumped market in the PA&A and the manipulated oracle price); *(ii)* the attacker's profit causes the loss of other market participants (e.g., the liquidity providers in the two analyzed attacks in Sect. 3).

We extend our discussion in Appendix F.

8   Conclusion

This paper presents an exploration of the impact of transaction atomicity and the flash loan mechanism on the Ethereum network. While proposed as a clever mechanism within DeFi, flash loans are starting to be used as financial attack vectors to effectively pull money in the form of cryptocurrency out of DeFi. In this paper, we analyze existing flash loan-based attacks in detail and then proceed to propose optimizations that significantly improve the ROI of these attacks. Specifically, we are able to show how two previously executed attacks can be "boosted" to result in a revenue of 829.5k USD and 1.1M USD, respectively, which is a boost of $2.37\times$ and $1.73\times$, respectively.

Acknowledgments. We thank the anonymous reviewers and Johannes Krupp for providing valuable comments and helpful feedback that significantly strengthened the paper. We are moreover grateful to the Lucerne University of Applied Sciences and Arts for generously supporting Kaihua Qin's Ph.D.

A   Classifying Flash Loan Use Cases

In Fig. 11, we present the DeFi platforms that use a total of $5,615$ Aave flash loan transactions[3] between the 8th of January, 2020 and the 20th of September, 2020. We find that more than 30% of the flash loans are interacting with Kyber, MakerDAO, and Uniswap. Compound and MakerDAO accumulate 433.81M USD flash loans which occupy 90% of the total flash loan amount. On average, a flash transaction uses 1.43M gas, while the most complex one consumes 6.3M gas.

---

[3] We collect in total $5,616$ flash loans with one transaction performing two flash loans.

B   Flash Loan Use Cases

B.1   Wash Trading

The trading volume of an asset is a metric indicating its popularity. The most popular assets therefore are supposed to be traded the most—e.g., Bitcoin to

DeFi Platforms	Transactions	Amount (USD)	Mean gas
Kyber, MakerDAO, Uniswap	1826	6.91M	1.64M±465.69k
Kyber, MakerDAO, OasisDEX, Uniswap	817	6.75M	1.38M±324.09k
Compound, MakerDAO	320	433.81M	1.49M±333.16k
0x, Kyber, MakerDAO, Uniswap	231	888.17k	1.76M±595.93k
Compound	228	5.98M	1.22M±501.97k
0x, Compound, Curve, MakerDAO	168	115.82k	1.31M±603.77k
0x, Kyber, MakerDAO, OasisDEX, Uniswap	153	2.12M	1.80M±432.11k
Compound, Curve	143	1.75M	2.06M±281.84k
MakerDAO	122	8.86M	934.39k±230.73k
0x, Compound, Curve	103	103.00k	1.27M±249.15k
Compound, MakerDAO, Uniswap	93	120.18k	1.31M±314.83k
Kyber, Uniswap	92	80.54k	985.68k±711.43k
0x, MakerDAO	87	1.70M	1.18M±120.70k
Bancor, Compound, Kyber, MakerDAO, Uniswap	77	8.45k	2.14M±705.27k
0x, Uniswap	68	32.97k	694.76k±129.58k
MakerDAO, Uniswap	68	40.83k	1.01M±254.51k
0x, OasisDEX	57	23.79k	716.40k±132.51k
Kyber, MakerDAO	53	437.65k	2.06M±641.44k
0x, Kyber, MakerDAO	42	639.36k	1.78M±352.44k
Compound, Kyber, MakerDAO, Uniswap	37	185.30k	2.72M±740.48k
0x, Kyber, Uniswap	30	23.81k	1.30M±285.27k
Bancor, Compound, Kyber, MakerDAO, OasisDEX, Uniswap	30	13.46k	2.05M±666.87k
Compound, Uniswap	29	45.58k	1.14M±293.59k
MakerDAO, OasisDEX	27	114.31k	823.62k±139.90k
Uniswap	25	56.34k	672.12k±404.84k
0x, Compound, MakerDAO	22	88.57k	1.81M±274.23k
Kyber	21	41.73k	803.54k±207.92k
Compound, Curve, MakerDAO	20	3.10M	1.93M±665.87k
Compound, Kyber, Uniswap	13	18.04k	1.82M±430.46k
0x, Kyber, OasisDEX, Uniswap	13	11.99k	1.42M±291.46k
0x, OasisDEX, Uniswap	12	15.68k	789.94k±193.06k
Compound, Kyber, MakerDAO, OasisDEX, Uniswap	11	63.12k	3.20M±893.03k
0x	9	8.48k	590.03k±111.78k
Kyber, OasisDEX, Uniswap	8	42.55k	858.12k±255.44k
0x, Compound, Curve, Kyber, MakerDAO, Uniswap	7	6.98k	1.87M±301.64k
Kyber, MakerDAO, OasisDEX	6	130.31k	1.84M±512.57k
0x, Compound, MakerDAO, Uniswap	5	2.64k	2.02M±149.59k
Bancor, Compound, Kyber, Uniswap	5	564.52	3.83M±1.50M
Others	537	6.87M	670.22k± 568.05k
Total	5,615	481.20M	1.43M± 605.97k

Fig. 11. Classifying the usage of flash loans in the wild, based on an analysis of transactions between the 8th of January, 2020 and the 20th of September, 2020 on Aave [13]. *Others* include the platform combinations that appear less than five times and the ones of which the owner platforms are unknown to us. The total amount is calculated at the price – DAI ($1); ETH ($350); USDC ($1); BAT ($0.2); WBTC ($10,000); ZRX ($0.3); MKR ($500); LINK ($10); USDT ($1); REP ($15), KNC ($1.5), LEND ($0.5), sUSD ($1).

date enjoys the highest trading volume (reported up to 50T USD per day) of all cryptocurrencies.

Malicious exchanges or traders can mislead other traders by artificially inflating the trading volume of an asset. In September 2019, 73 out of the top 100 exchanges on Coinmarketcap [20] were wash trading over 90% of their volumes [2]. In centralized exchanges, operators can easily and freely create fake trades in the backend, while decentralized exchanges settle trades on-chain. Wash trading on DEX thus requires wash traders to hold and use real assets. Flash loans can remove this "obstacle" and wash trading costs are then reduced to the flash loan interest, trading fees, and (blockchain) transaction fees, e.g., gas. A wash trading endeavor to increase the 24-h volume by 50% on the ETH/DAI market of Uniswap would for instance cost about 1,298 USD (cf. Fig. 12). We visualize in Fig. 12 the required cost to create fake volumes in two Uniswap markets. At the time of writing, the transaction fee amounts to 0.01 USD, the flash loan interests range from a constant 1 Wei (on dYdX) to 0.09% (on Aave), and exchange fees are about 0.3% (on Uniswap).

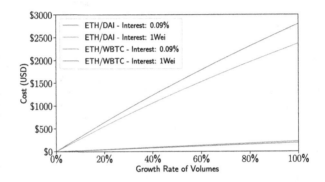

Fig. 12. Wash trading cost on two Uniswap markets with flash loans costing 0.09% (Aave) and a constant of 1 Wei (dYdX) respectively. The 24-h volumes of ETH/DAI and ETH/WBTC market were 963,786 USD and 67,690 USD respectively (1st of March, 2020).

Wash Trading Example: On March 2nd, 2020, a flash loan of 0.01 ETH borrowed from dYdX performed two back-and-forth trades (first converted 0.01 ETH to 122.1898 LOOM and then converted 122.1898 LOOM back to 0.0099 ETH) on Uniswap ETH/LOOM market (cf. 0xf65b384 ebe2b7bf1e7bd06adf0daac0413defeed42fd2cc72a75385a200e1544). The 24-h trading volume of the ETH/LOOM market increased by 25.8% (from 17.71 USD to 22.28 USD) as a result of the two trades.

B.2   Collateral Swapping

We classify DeFi platforms that rely on users providing cryptocurrencies [13, 24, 39] as follows: (i) a DeFi system where a new asset is minted and backed-

```
contract FlashMintableCoin is ERC20 { [...]
    function flashMint(uint256 amount) {
        // mint coins and transfer them
        mint(msg.sender, amount);
        // borrower uses the loan
        Borrower(msg.sender).execute(amount);
        // reverts if not have enough to burn
        burn(msg.sender, amount);
}}
```

Fig. 13. Flash mint example.

up with user-provided collateral (e.g., MakerDAO's DAI or SAI [39]) and (ii) a DeFi system where long-term loans are offered and assets are aggregated within liquidity pools (e.g., margin trading [3] or long term loans [13]). Once a collateral position is opened, DeFi platforms store the collateral assets in a vault until the new/borrowed asset are destroyed/returned. Because cryptocurrency prices fluctuate, this asset lock-in bears a currency risk. With flash loans, it is possible to replace the collateral asset with another asset, even if a user does not possess sufficient funds to destroy/return the new/borrowed asset. A user can close an existing collateral position with borrowed funds, and then immediately open a new collateral position using a different asset.

Collateral Swapping Example: On February 20th, 2020, a flash loan borrowed 20.00 DAI (from Aave) to perform a collateral swap (on MakerDAO), cf. 0x5d5bbfe0b666631916adb8a56821b204d97e75e2a852945ac7396a82e207e0ca. Before this transaction, the transaction sender used 0.18 WETH as collateral for instantiating 20.00 DAI (on MakerDAO). The transaction sender first withdraws all WETH using the 20.00 DAI flash loan, then converts 0.18 WETH for 178.08 BAT (using Uniswap). Finally the user creates 20.03 DAI using BAT as collateral, and pays back 20.02 DAI (with a fee to Aave). This transaction converts the collateral from WETH to BAT and the user gained 0.01 DAI, with an estimated gas fee of 0.86 USD.

B.3   Flash Minting

Cryptocurrency assets are commonly known as either inflationary (further units of an asset can be mined) or deflationary (the total number of units of an asset are finite). Flash minting is an idea to allow an instantaneous minting of an arbitrary amount of an asset—the newly-mined units exist only during one transaction. It is yet unclear where this idea might be applicable to, the minted assets could momentarily increase liquidity.

Flash Minting Example: A flash mint function (cf. Fig. 13) can be integrated into an ERC20 token, to mint an arbitrary number of coins within a transaction only. Before the transaction terminates, the minted coins will be burned. If the available amount of coins to be burned by the end of the transaction is less than those that were minted, the transaction is reverted (i.e., not executed). An example ERC20 flash minting code could take the following form (cf. 0x09b4c8200f0cb51e6d44a1974a1bc07336b9f47f):

C   DeFi Models

In the following, we detail the quantitative DeFi models applied in this work. Note that we do not include all the states involved in the DeFi attacks but only those relevant to the constrained optimization.

Flash Loan: We assume a flash loan platform $\mathbb{F}$ with z_X amount of asset X, which the adversary $\mathbb{A}$ can borrow. The required interest to borrow b of X is represented by $\mathrm{interest}(b)$.

State: In a flash loan, the state is represented by the balance of $\mathbb{A}$, i.e., $\mathcal{B}(\mathbb{A}; X; S)$. Transitions: We define the transition functions of **Loan** in Eq. 8 and **Repay** in Eq. 9, where the parameter b_X denotes the loaned amount.

$$\mathcal{B}(\mathbb{A}; X; S') = \mathcal{B}(\mathbb{A}; X; S) + b_X$$
$$\text{s.t.} \quad z_X - b_X \geq 0 \tag{8}$$

$$\mathcal{B}(\mathbb{A}; X; S') = \mathcal{B}(\mathbb{A}; X; S) - b_X - \mathrm{interest}(b_X)$$
$$\text{s.t.} \quad \mathcal{B}(\mathbb{A}; X; S) - b_X - \mathrm{interest}(b_X) \geq 0 \tag{9}$$

Fixed Price Trading: We define the endpoint `SellXforY` that allows the adversary $\mathbb{A}$ to trade q_X amount of X for Y at a fixed price p_m. `maxY` is the maximum amount of Y available for trading.

State: We consider the following state variables:

- Balance of asset X held by $\mathbb{A}$: $\mathcal{B}(\mathbb{A}; X; S)$
- Balance of asset Y held by $\mathbb{A}$: $\mathcal{B}(\mathbb{A}; Y; S)$

Transitions: Transition functions of `SellXforY` are defined in Eq. 10.

$$\mathcal{B}(\mathbb{A}; X; S') = \mathcal{B}(\mathbb{A}; X; S) - q_X$$
$$\mathcal{B}(\mathbb{A}; Y; S') = \mathcal{B}(\mathbb{A}; Y; S) + \frac{q_X}{\mathsf{p}_m}$$
$$\text{s.t.} \quad \mathcal{B}(\mathbb{A}; X; S) - q_X \geq 0$$
$$\mathrm{maxY} - \frac{q_X}{\mathsf{p}_m} \geq 0 \tag{10}$$

Constant Product Automated Market Maker: The constant product AMM is with a market share of 77% among the AMM DEX, the most common AMM model in the current DeFi ecosystem [11]. We denote by $\mathbb{M}$ an AMM instance with trading pair X/Y and exchange fee rate f.

State: We consider the following states variables that can be modified in an AMM state transition.

- Amount of X in AMM liquidity pool: $u_X(S)$, which equals to $\mathcal{B}(\mathbb{M}; X; S)$
- Amount of Y in AMM liquidity pool: $u_Y(S)$, which equals to $\mathcal{B}(\mathbb{M}; Y; S)$
- Balance of X held by $\mathbb{A}$: $\mathcal{B}(\mathbb{A}; X; S)$
- Balance of Y held by $\mathbb{A}$: $\mathcal{B}(\mathbb{A}; Y; S)$

Transitions: Among the endpoints of $\mathbb{M}$, we focus on SwapXforY and SwapYforX, which are the relevant endpoints for the DeFi attacks discussed within this work. p_X is a parameter that represents the amount of X the adversary intends to trade. $\mathbb{A}$ inputs p_X amount of X in AMM liquidity pool and receives o_Y amount of Y as output. The constant product rule [11] requires that Eq. 11 holds.

$$u_X(S) \times u_Y(S) = (u_X(S) + (1-f)p_X) \times (u_Y(S) - o_Y) \tag{11}$$

We define the transition functions and constraints of SwapXforY in Eq. 12 (analogously for SwapYforX).

$$\mathcal{B}(\mathbb{A}; X; S') = \mathcal{B}(\mathbb{A}; X; S) - p_X$$
$$\mathcal{B}(\mathbb{A}; Y; S') = \mathcal{B}(\mathbb{A}; Y; S) + o_Y$$
$$u_X(S') = u_X(S) + p_X$$
$$u_Y(S') = u_Y(S) - o_Y$$
$$\text{where} \quad o_Y = \frac{p_X \times (1-f) \times u_Y(S)}{u_X(S) + p_X \times (1-f)}$$
$$\text{s.t.} \quad \mathcal{B}(\mathbb{M}; X; S) - p_X \geq 0 \tag{12}$$

Because an AMM DEX $\mathbb{M}$ transparently exposes all price transitions on-chain, it can be used as a price oracle by the other DeFi platforms. The price of Y with respect to X given by $\mathbb{M}$ at state S is defined in Eq. 13.

$$p_Y(\mathbb{M}; S) = \frac{u_X(S)}{u_Y(S)} \tag{13}$$

Automated Price Reserve: The automated price reserve is another type of AMM that automatically calculates the exchange price depending on the assets held in inventory. We denote a reserve holding the asset pair X/Y with $\mathbb{R}$. A minimum price minP and a maximum price maxP is set when initiating $\mathbb{R}$. $\mathbb{R}$ relies on a liquidity ratio parameter lr to calculate the asset price. We assume that $\mathbb{R}$ holds $k_X(S)$ amount of X at state S. We define the price of Y in Eq. 14.

$$P_Y(\mathbb{R}; S) = \text{minP} \times e^{lr \times k_X(S)} \tag{14}$$

The endpoint ConvertXtoY provided by $\mathbb{R}$ allows the adversary $\mathbb{A}$ to exchange X for Y.

State: We consider the following state variables:

- The inventory of X in the reserve: $k_X(S)$, which equals to $\mathcal{B}(\mathbb{R}; X; S)$
- Balance of X held by $\mathbb{A}$: $\mathcal{B}(\mathbb{A}; X; S)$

– Balance of Y held by $\mathbb{A}$: $\mathcal{B}(\mathbb{A}; Y; S)$

Transitions: We denote as h_X the amount of X that $\mathbb{A}$ inputs in the exchange to trade against Y. The exchange output amount of Y is calculated by the following formulation.

$$j_Y = \frac{e^{-lr \times h_X} - 1}{lr \times P_Y(\mathbb{R}; S)}$$

We define the transition functions within Eq. 15.

$$k_X(S') = k_X(S) + h_X$$
$$\mathcal{B}(\mathbb{A}; X; S') = \mathcal{B}(\mathbb{A}; X; S) - h_X$$
$$\mathcal{B}(\mathbb{A}; Y; S') = \mathcal{B}(\mathbb{A}; Y; S) + j_Y$$
$$\text{where} \quad j_Y = \frac{e^{-lr \times h_X} - 1}{lr \times P_Y(\mathbb{R}; S)}$$
$$\text{s.t.} \quad \mathcal{B}(\mathbb{A}; X; S) - h_X \geq 0$$
$$P_Y(\mathbb{R}; S') - minP \geq 0$$
$$maxP - P_Y(\mathbb{R}; S') \geq 0 \qquad (15)$$

Collateralized Lending and Borrowing: We consider a collateralized lending platform $\mathbb{L}$, which provides the `CollateralizedBorrow` endpoint that requires the user to collateralize an asset X with a collateral factor cf (s.t. $0 < cf < 1$) and borrows another asset Y at an exchange rate er. The collateral factor determines the upper limit that a user can borrow. For example, if the collateral factor is 0.75, a user is allowed to borrow up to 75% of the value of the collateral. The exchange rate is for example determined by an outsourced price oracle. z_Y denotes the maximum amount of Y available for borrowing.

State: We hence consider the following state variables and ignore the balance changes of $\mathbb{L}$ for simplicity.

– Balance of asset X held by $\mathbb{A}$: $\mathcal{B}(\mathbb{A}; X; S)$
– Balance of asset Y held by $\mathbb{A}$: $\mathcal{B}(\mathbb{A}; Y; S)$

Transitions: The parameter c_X represents the amount of asset X that $\mathbb{A}$ aims to collateralize. Although $\mathbb{A}$ is allowed to borrow less than his collateral would allow for, we assume that $\mathbb{A}$ makes use of the entirety of his collateral. Equation 16 shows the transition functions of `CollateralizedBorrow`.

$$\mathcal{B}(\mathbb{A}; X; S') = \mathcal{B}(\mathbb{A}; X; S) - c_X$$
$$\mathcal{B}(\mathbb{A}; Y; S') = \mathcal{B}(\mathbb{A}; Y; S) + b_Y$$
$$\text{where} \quad b_Y = \frac{c_X \times cf}{er}$$
$$\text{s.t.} \quad \mathcal{B}(\mathbb{A}; X; S') - c_X \geq 0; z_Y - b_Y \geq 0 \qquad (16)$$

A can retrieve its collateral by repaying the borrowed asset through the endpoint `CollateralizedRepay`. We show the transition functions in Eq. 17 and for simplicity ignore the loan interest fee.

$$\mathcal{B}(\mathbb{A}; \mathsf{X}; \mathsf{S}') = \mathcal{B}(\mathbb{A}; \mathsf{X}; \mathsf{S}) + c_{\mathsf{X}}$$
$$\mathcal{B}(\mathbb{A}; \mathsf{Y}; \mathsf{S}') = \mathcal{B}(\mathbb{A}; \mathsf{Y}; \mathsf{S}) - b_{\mathsf{Y}}$$
$$\text{s.t.} \quad \mathcal{B}(\mathbb{A}; \mathsf{Y}; \mathsf{S}) - b_{\mathsf{Y}} \geq 0 \tag{17}$$

Margin Trading: A margin trading platform $\mathbb{T}$ allows the adversary $\mathbb{A}$ to short/long an asset Y by collateralizing asset X at a leverage ℓ, where $\ell \geq 1$.

We focus on the `MarginShort` endpoint which is relevant to the discussed DeFi attack in this work. We assume $\mathbb{A}$ shorts Y with respect to X on $\mathbb{F}$. The parameter d_{X} denotes the amount of X that $\mathbb{A}$ collateralizes upfront to open the margin. w_{X} represents the amount of X held by $\mathbb{F}$ that is available for the short margin. $\mathbb{A}$ is required to over-collateralize at a rate of ocr in a margin trade. In our model, when a short margin (short Y with respect to X) is opened, $\mathbb{F}$ performs a trade on external X/Y markets (e.g., Uniswap) to convert the leveraged X to Y. The traded Y is locked until the margin is closed or liquidated.

State: In a short margin trading, we consider the following state variables:

- Balance of X held by $\mathbb{A}$: $\mathcal{B}(\mathbb{A}; \mathsf{X}; \mathsf{S})$
- The locked amount of Y: $\mathcal{L}(\mathbb{A}; \mathsf{Y}; \mathsf{S})$

Transitions: We assume $\mathbb{F}$ transacts from an external market at a price of emp. The transition functions and constraints are specified in Eq. 18.

$$\mathcal{B}(\mathbb{A}; \mathsf{X}; \mathsf{S}') = \mathcal{B}(\mathbb{A}; \mathsf{X}; \mathsf{S}) - c_{\mathsf{X}}$$
$$\mathcal{L}(\mathbb{A}; \mathsf{Y}; \mathsf{S}') = \mathcal{L}(\mathbb{A}; \mathsf{Y}; \mathsf{S}) + l_{\mathsf{Y}}$$
$$\text{where} \quad l_{\mathsf{Y}} = \frac{d_{\mathsf{X}} \times \ell}{\text{ocr} \times \text{emp}}$$
$$\text{s.t.} \quad \mathcal{B}(\mathbb{A}; \mathsf{X}; \mathsf{S}) - c_{\mathsf{X}} \geq 0; w_{\mathsf{X}} + d_{\mathsf{X}} - \frac{d_{\mathsf{X}} \times \ell}{\text{ocr}} \geq 0 \tag{18}$$

D   Optimizing the Pump Attack and Arbitrage

In the following, we detail the procedure of deriving the pump attack and arbitrage optimization problem. Figure 5 summarizes the on-chain state when the attack was executed (i.e., S_0). X and Y denote ETH and WBTC respectively. For simplicity, we ignore the trading fees in the constant product AMM (i.e., $f = 0$ for $\mathbb{M}$). The endpoints executed in the pump attack and arbitrage are listed in the execution order as follows.

1. `Loan` (dYdX)
2. `CollateralizedBorrow` (Compound)
3. `MarginShort` (bZx) & `SwapXforY` (Uniswap)

4. `SwapYforX` (Uniswap)
5. `Repay` (dYdX)
6. `SellXforY` & `CollateralizedRepay` (Compound)

In the pump attack and arbitrage vector, we intend to tune the following two parameters, *(i)* p_1: the amount of X collateralized to borrow Y in the endpoint 2) and *(ii)* p_2: the amount of X collateralized to short Y in the endpoint 3). Following the procedure of Sect. 4.2, we proceed with detailing the construction of the constraint system.

0): We assume the initial balance of X owned by A is B_0 (cf. Eq. 19), and we refer the reader to Fig. 5 for the remaining initial state values.

$$\mathcal{B}(A; X; S_0) = B_0 \tag{19}$$

1) Loan. A gets a flash loan of X amounts $p_1 + p_2$ in total

$$\mathcal{B}(A; X; S_1) = B_0 + p_1 + p_2$$

with the constraints

$$p_1 \geq 0, p_2 \geq 0, v_X - p_1 - p_2 \geq 0$$

2) `CollateralizedBorrow`: A collateralizes p_1 amount of X to borrow Y from the lending platform L

$$\mathcal{B}(A; X; S_2) = \mathcal{B}(A; X; S_1) - p_1 = B_0 + p_2$$

$$\mathcal{B}(A; Y; S_2) = \frac{p_1 \times cf}{er}$$

with the constraint $z_Y - \dfrac{p_1 \times cf}{er} \geq 0$

3) `MarginShort` & `SwapXforY`. A opens a short margin with p_2 amount of X at a leverage of ℓ on the margin trading platform T; T swaps the leveraged X for Y at the constant product AMM M

$$\mathcal{B}(A; X; S_3) = \mathcal{B}(A; X; S_2) - p_2 = B_0$$

$$u_X(S_3) = u_X(S_0) + \frac{p_2 \times \ell}{ocr}$$

$$u_Y(S_3) = \frac{u_X(S_0) \times u_Y(S_0)}{u_X(S_3)}$$

$$\mathcal{L}(A; Y; S_3) = u_Y(S_0) - u_Y(S_3)$$

with the constraint $w_X + p_2 - \dfrac{p_2 \times \ell}{ocr} \geq 0$

4) `SwapYforX`. A dumps all the borrowed Y at M

$$\mathcal{B}(A; Y; S_4) = 0$$

$$u_Y(S_4) = u_Y(S_3) + \mathcal{B}(A; Y; S_2)$$

$$u_X(S_4) = \frac{u_X(S_3) \times u_Y(S_3)}{u_Y(S_4)}$$

$$\mathcal{B}(A; X; S_4) = B_0 + u_X(S_3) - u_X(S_4)$$

5) Repay. $\mathbb{A}$ repays the flash loan

$$\mathcal{B}(\mathbb{A}; X; S_5) = \mathcal{B}(\mathbb{A}; X; S_4) - p_1 - p_2$$

with the constraint $\mathcal{B}(\mathbb{A}; X; S_4) - p_1 - p_2 \geq 0$

6) SellXforY & CollateralizedRepay. $\mathbb{A}$ buys Y from the market with the market price p_m and retrieves the collateral from $\mathbb{L}$

$$\mathcal{B}(\mathbb{A}; X; S_6) = \mathcal{B}(\mathbb{A}; X; S_5) + p_1 - \mathcal{B}(\mathbb{A}; Y; S_2) \times p_m$$

The objective function is the adversarial ETH revenue (cf. Eq. 20).

$$\mathcal{O}(S_0; p_1; p_2) = \mathcal{B}(\mathbb{A}; X; S_6) - B_0$$

$$= u_X(S_0) + \frac{p_2 \times \ell}{\mathsf{ocr}} - u_X(S_4) - p_2 \qquad (20)$$

$$- \frac{p_1 \times \mathsf{cf} \times p_m}{\mathsf{er}}$$

E   Optimizing the Oracle Manipulation Attack

In the oracle manipulation attack, X denotes ETH and Y denotes sUSD. Again, we ignore the trading fees in the constant product AMM (i.e., $f = 0$ for $\mathbb{M}$). The initial state variables are presented in Fig. 7. We assume that $\mathbb{A}$ owns zero balance of X or Y. We list the endpoints involved in the oracle manipulation attack vector as follows.

1. **Loan** (bZx)
2. **SwapXforY** (Uniswap)
3. **ConvertXtoY** (Kyber reserve)
4. **SellXforY** (Synthetix)
5. **CollateralizedBorrow** (bZx)
6. **Repay** (bZx)

We construct the constrained optimization problem as follows.

1) Loan: $\mathbb{A}$ gets a flash loan of X amounts $p_1 + p_2 + p_3$

$$\mathcal{B}(\mathbb{A}; X; S_1) = p_1 + p_2 + p_3$$

with the constraints

$$p_1 \geq 0, p_2 \geq 0, p_3 \geq 0, v_X - p_1 - p_2 - p_3 \geq 0$$

2) SwapXforY: $\mathbb{A}$ swaps p_1 amount of X for Y from the constant product AMM $\mathbb{M}$

$$\mathcal{B}(\mathbb{A}; X; S_2) = \mathcal{B}(\mathbb{A}; X; S_1) - p_1 = p_2 + p_3$$

$$u_X(S_2) = u_X(S_0) + p_1$$

$$u_Y(S_2) = \frac{u_X(S_0) \times u_Y(S_0)}{u_X(S_2)}$$

$$\mathcal{B}(\mathbb{A}; Y; S_2) = u_Y(S_0) - u_Y(S_2)$$

3) ConvertXtoY: $\mathbb{A}$ converts p_2 amount of X to Y from the automated price reserve $\mathbb{R}$

$$\mathcal{B}(\mathbb{A}; X; S_3) = \mathcal{B}(\mathbb{A}; X; S_2) - p_2 = p_1$$
$$k_X(S_3) = k_X(S_0) + p_2$$
$$P_Y(\mathbb{R}; S_3) = \mathsf{minP} \times e^{\mathsf{lr} \times k_X(S_3)}$$
$$\mathcal{B}(\mathbb{A}; Y; S_3) = \mathcal{B}(\mathbb{A}; Y; S_2) + \frac{e^{-\mathsf{lr} \times p_2} - 1}{\mathsf{lr} \times P_Y(\mathbb{R}; S_0)}$$
$$\text{s.t.} \quad \mathsf{maxP} - P_Y(\mathbb{R}; S_3) \geq 0$$

4) SellXforY: $\mathbb{A}$ sells p_3 amount of X for Y at the price of p_m

$$\mathcal{B}(\mathbb{A}; X; S_4) = \mathcal{B}(\mathbb{A}; X; S_3) - p_3 = 0$$
$$\mathcal{B}(\mathbb{A}; Y; S_4) = \mathcal{B}(\mathbb{A}; Y; S_3) + \frac{p_3}{\mathsf{p}_m}$$

with the constraint $\mathsf{maxY} - \dfrac{p_3}{\mathsf{p}_m} \geq 0$

5) CollateralizedBorrow: $\mathbb{A}$ collateralizes all owned Y to borrow X according to the price given by the constant product AMM $\mathbb{M}$ (i.e., the exchange rate $\mathsf{er} = \frac{1}{P_Y(\mathbb{M}; S_2)}$)

$$\mathcal{B}(\mathbb{A}; Y; S_5) = 0$$
$$\mathcal{B}(\mathbb{A}; X; S_5) = \mathcal{B}(\mathbb{A}; Y; S_4) \times \mathsf{cf} \times P_Y(\mathbb{M}; S_2)$$

with the constraint

$$z_Y - \mathcal{B}(\mathbb{A}; Y; S_4) \times \mathsf{cf} \times P_Y(\mathbb{M}; S_2) \geq 0$$

6) Repay: $\mathbb{A}$ repays the flash loan

$$\mathcal{B}(\mathbb{A}; X; S_6) = \mathcal{B}(\mathbb{A}; X; S_5) - p_1 - p_2 - p_3$$

with the constraint $\mathcal{B}(\mathbb{A}; X; S_5) - p_1 - p_2 - p_3 \geq 0$

The objective function is the remaining balance of X after repaying the flash loan (cf. Eq. 21).

$$\begin{aligned} \mathcal{O}(S_0; p_1; p_2; p_3) &= \mathcal{B}(\mathbb{A}; X; S_6) \\ &= \mathcal{B}(\mathbb{A}; X; S_5) - p_1 - p_2 - p_3 \\ &= \mathcal{B}(\mathbb{A}; Y; S_4) \times \mathsf{cf} \times P_Y(\mathbb{M}; S_2) \\ &\quad - p_1 - p_2 - p_3 \end{aligned} \tag{21}$$

F   Extended Discussion

In the following, we extend our discussion in Sect. 7.

Responsible Disclosure: It is somewhat unclear how to perform responsible disclosure within DeFi, given that the underlying vulnerability and victim are not always perfectly clear and that there is a lack of security standards to apply. We plan to reach out to Aave, Kyber, and Uniswap to disclose the contents of this paper.

Does Extra Capital Help: The main attraction of flash loans stems from them not requiring collateral that needs to be raised. One can, however, wonder whether extra capital would make the attacks we focus on more potent and the ROI greater. Based on our results, extra collateral for the two attacks of Sect. 3 would not increase the ROI, as the liquidity constraints of the intermediate protocols do not allow for a higher impact.

Potential Defenses: Here we discuss several potential defenses. However, we would be the first to admit that these are not foolproof and come with potential downsides that would significantly hamper normal interactions.

- Should DEX accept trades coming from flash loans?
- Should DEX accept coins from an address if the previous block did not show those funds in the address?
- Would introducing a delay make sense, e.g., in governance voting, or price oracles?
- When designing a DeFi protocol, a single transaction should be limited in its abilities: a DEX should not allow a single transaction triggering a slippage beyond 100%.

Looking into the Future: In the future, we anticipate DeFi protocols eventually starting to comply with a higher standard of security testing, both within the protocol itself, as well as part of integration testing into the DeFi ecosystem. We believe that eventually, this may lead to some form of DeFi standards where it comes to financial security, similar to what is imposed on banks and other financial institutions in traditional centralized (government-controlled) finance. We anticipate that either whole-system penetration testing or an analytical approach to modeling the space of possibilities like in this paper are two ways to improve future DeFi protocols.

Generality of the Optimization Framework: We show in Sect. 5 that our optimization framework performs efficiently on a given attack vector. To discover new attacks on a blockchain state with the framework, we may need to iterate over all the combinations of DeFi actions. The search space thus explodes as the number of DeFi actions increases. Our optimization framework requires to model every DeFi action manually. This, however, makes the framework less handy for users who are unfamiliar with the mathematical formulas of the DeFi actions. To make the framework more accurate, we can build gas consumption and block gas limit into the models, which requires to comprehend every DeFi action explicitly. We leave the automation of modeling for future work.

References

1. Aavewatch - live protocol stats! https://aavewatch.now.sh/
2. Bti market surveillance report - september 2019 - bti. https://www.bti.live/bti-september-2019-wash-trade-report/, Accessed 24 Feb 2020
3. bzx - a protocol for tokenized margin trading and lending. https://bzx.network/
4. Compound. https://compound.finance/
5. Consensys/0x-review: Security review of 0x smart contracts. https://github.com/ConsenSys/0x-review
6. Ganache — truffle suite. https://www.trufflesuite.com/ganache
7. Home — prevent flash loan attacks. https://preventflashloanattacks.com/
8. marbleprotocol/flash-lending: Flash lending smart contracts. https://github.com/marbleprotocol/flash-lending
9. Report of investigation pursuant to section 21(a) of the securities exchange act of 1934: The dao. https://www.sec.gov/litigation/investreport/34-81207.pdf
10. Slippage definition & example. https://www.investopedia.com/terms/s/slippage.asp
11. Uniswap. https://uniswap.org/
12. U.s. corporate debt soars to record $10.5 trillion - marketwatch. www.marketwatch.com/story/u-s-corporate-debt-soars-to-record-10-5-trillion-11598921886#:~:text=U.S.%20corporations%20now%20owe%20a,new%20BofA%20Global%20Research%20report
13. Aave: Aave Protocol (2020). https://github.com/aave/aave-protocol
14. Amani, S., Bégel, M., Bortin, M., Staples, M.: Towards verifying ethereum smart contract bytecode in isabelle/hol. In: Proceedings of the 7th ACM SIGPLAN International Conference on Certified Programs and Proofs, pp. 66–77 (2018)
15. Bentov, I., et al.: Tesseract: real-time cryptocurrency exchange using trusted hardware. In: Conference on Computer and Communications Security (2019)
16. Bhargavan, K., et al.: Formal verification of smart contracts: short paper. In: Proceedings of the 2016 ACM Workshop on Programming Languages and Analysis for Security, pp. 91–96 (2016)
17. Bonneau, J., Miller, A., Clark, J., Narayanan, A., Kroll, J.A., Felten, E.W.: Sok: research perspectives and challenges for bitcoin and cryptocurrencies. In: 2015 IEEE Symposium on Security and Privacy (SP), pp. 104–121. IEEE (2015)
18. Breidenbach, L., Daian, P., Tramèr, F., Juels, A.: Enter the hydra: towards principled bug bounties and exploit-resistant smart contracts. In: 27th {USENIX} Security Symposium ({USENIX} Security 18), pp. 1335–1352 (2018)
19. Brent, L., et al.: Vandal: a scalable security analysis framework for smart contracts (2018). arXiv preprint arXiv:1809.03981
20. CoinMarketCap: Bitcoin market capitalization (2019)
21. Crytic: Echidna: Ethereum fuzz testing framework. https://github.com/crytic/echidna
22. Daian, P., et al.: Flash Boys 2.0: frontrunning, transaction reordering, and consensus instability in decentralized exchanges. In: IEEE Security and Privacy 2020 (2020)
23. DiCiccio, T.J., Efron, B.: Bootstrap confidence intervals. In: Statistical Science, pp. 189–212 (1996)
24. dYdX: dYdX (2020). https://dydx.exchange/

25. Eskandari, S., Moosavi, S., Clark, J.: SoK: transparent dishonesty: front-running attacks on blockchain. In: Bracciali, A., Clark, J., Pintore, F., Rønne, P.B., Sala, M. (eds.) FC 2019. LNCS, vol. 11599, pp. 170–189. Springer, Cham (2020). https://doi.org/10.1007/978-3-030-43725-1_13

26. Gandal, N., Hamrick, J., Moore, T., Oberman, T.: Price manipulation in the Bitcoin ecosystem. J. Monet. Econ. **95**(4), 86–96 (2018)

27. Grishchenko, I., Maffei, M., Schneidewind, C.: A semantic framework for the security analysis of ethereum smart contracts. In: Bauer, L., Küsters, R. (eds.) POST 2018. LNCS, vol. 10804, pp. 243–269. Springer, Cham (2018). https://doi.org/10.1007/978-3-319-89722-6_10

28. Hamrick, J., et al.: The economics of cryptocurrency pump and dump schemes (2018)

29. Hildenbrandt, E., et al.: Kevm: a complete semantics of the ethereum virtual machine. Technical report (2017)

30. Hirai, Y.: Defining the ethereum virtual machine for interactive theorem provers. In: Brenner, M., Rohloff, K., Bonneau, J., Miller, A., Ryan, P.Y.A., Teague, V., Bracciali, A., Sala, M., Pintore, F., Jakobsson, M. (eds.) FC 2017. LNCS, vol. 10323, pp. 520–535. Springer, Cham (2017). https://doi.org/10.1007/978-3-319-70278-0_33

31. Jiang, B., Liu, Y., Chan, W.: Contractfuzzer: fuzzing smart contracts for vulnerability detection. In: Proceedings of the 33rd ACM/IEEE International Conference on Automated Software Engineering, pp. 259–269. ACM (2018)

32. Kalodner, H.A., Carlsten, M., Ellenbogen, P., Bonneau, J., Narayanan, A.: An empirical study of namecoin and lessons for decentralized namespace design. In: WEIS. Citeseer (2015)

33. Kamps, J., Kleinberg, B.: To the moon: defining and detecting cryptocurrency pump-and-dumps. Crime Sci. **7**(1), 1–18 (2018). https://doi.org/10.1186/s40163-018-0093-5

34. Kyber: Kyber (2020). https://kyber.network/

35. Labs, A.: Idex: a real-time and high-throughput ethereum smart contract exchange. Technical report (2019)

36. Liu, C., Liu, H., Cao, Z., Chen, Z., Chen, B., Roscoe, B.: Reguard: finding reentrancy bugs in smart contracts. In: 2018 IEEE/ACM 40th International Conference on Software Engineering: Companion (ICSE-Companion), pp. 65–68. IEEE (2018)

37. Luu, L., Chu, D.H., Olickel, H., Saxena, P., Hobor, A.: Making smart contracts smarter. In: Proceedings of the ACM SIGSAC Conference on Computer and Communications Security, pp. 254–269 (2016). https://doi.org/10.1145/2976749.2978309, http://dl.acm.org/citation.cfm?doid=2976749.2978309

38. Luu, L., Chu, D.H., Olickel, H., Saxena, P., Hobor, A.: Making smart contracts smarter. In: Proceedings of the 2016 ACM SIGSAC Conference on Computer and Communications Security, pp. 254–269 (2016)

39. Maker: Makerdao (2019). https://makerdao.com/en/

40. MakerDao: Intro to the oasisdex protocol (2019). Accessed 12 Nov 2019, https://github.com/makerdao/developerguides/blob/master/Oasis/intro-to-oasis/intro-to-oasis-maker-otc.md

41. Mavroudis, V.: Market manipulation as a security problem (2019). arXiv preprint arXiv:1903.12458

42. Mavroudis, V., Melton, H.: Libra: fair order-matching for electronic financial exchanges (2019). arXiv preprint arXiv:1910.00321

43. Mueller, B.: Mythril-reversing and bug hunting framework for the ethereum blockchain (2017)

44. Nakamoto, S.: Bitcoin: a peer-to-peer electronic cash system (2008)
45. Nikolić, I., Kolluri, A., Sergey, I., Saxena, P., Hobor, A.: Finding the greedy, prodigal, and suicidal contracts at scale. In: Proceedings of the 34th Annual Computer Security Applications Conference, pp. 653–663 (2018)
46. Shleifer, A., Vishny, R.W.: The limits of arbitrage. J. Finan. **52**(1), 35–55 (1997)
47. Tikhomirov, S., Voskresenskaya, E., Ivanitskiy, I., Takhaviev, R., Marchenko, E., Alexandrov, Y.: Smartcheck: static analysis of ethereum smart contracts. In: Proceedings of the 1st International Workshop on Emerging Trends in Software Engineering for Blockchain, pp. 9–16 (2018)
48. Tsankov, P., Dan, A., Drachsler-Cohen, D., Gervais, A., Buenzli, F., Vechev, M.: Securify: practical security analysis of smart contracts. In: Proceedings of the 2018 ACM SIGSAC Conference on Computer and Communications Security, pp. 67–82. ACM (2018)
49. Wood, G.: Ethereum: a secure decentralised generalised transaction ledger. Ethereum Project Yellow Paper (2014)
50. Wüstholz, V., Christakis, M.: Harvey: a greybox fuzzer for smart contracts (2019). arXiv:1905.06944
51. Xu, J., Livshits, B.: The anatomy of a cryptocurrency pump-and-dump scheme. In: Proceedings of the Usenix Security Symposium (2019)
52. Zhou, L., Qin, K., Torres, C.F., Le, D.V., Gervais, A.: High-frequency trading on decentralized on-chain exchanges (2020). arXiv preprint arXiv:2009.14021

The Eye of Horus: Spotting and Analyzing Attacks on Ethereum Smart Contracts

Christof Ferreira Torres[1]([⊠]) [iD], Antonio Ken Iannillo[1] [iD], Arthur Gervais[2] [iD], and Radu State[1] [iD]

[1] SnT, University of Luxembourg, Avenue J. F. Kennedy 29, 1855 Luxembourg, Luxembourg
{christof.torres,antonioken.iannillo,radu.state}@uni.lu
[2] Imperial College London, Exhibition Rd., South Kensington, London, UK
a.gervais@imperial.ac.uk

Abstract. In recent years, Ethereum gained tremendously in popularity, growing from a daily transaction average of 10K in January 2016 to an average of 500K in January 2020. Similarly, smart contracts began to carry more value, making them appealing targets for attackers. As a result, they started to become victims of attacks, costing millions of dollars. In response to these attacks, both academia and industry proposed a plethora of tools to scan smart contracts for vulnerabilities before deploying them on the blockchain. However, most of these tools solely focus on detecting vulnerabilities and not attacks, let alone quantifying or tracing the number of stolen assets. In this paper, we present HORUS, a framework that empowers the automated detection and investigation of smart contract attacks based on logic-driven and graph-driven analysis of transactions. HORUS provides quick means to quantify and trace the flow of stolen assets across the Ethereum blockchain. We perform a large-scale analysis of all the smart contracts deployed on Ethereum until May 2020. We identified 1,888 attacked smart contracts and 8,095 adversarial transactions in the wild. Our investigation shows that the number of attacks did not necessarily decrease over the past few years, but for some vulnerabilities remained constant. Finally, we also demonstrate the practicality of our framework via an in-depth analysis on the recent Uniswap and Lendf.me attacks.

Keywords: Ethereum · Smart contracts · Attack detection · Forensics

1 Introduction

As of today, Ethereum [47] revolutionized the way digital assets are traded by being the first to introduce the concept of Turing-complete smart contracts on the blockchain. These are programs that are executed and stored across the blockchain. However, due to the tamper-resistant nature of blockchains, smart

© International Financial Cryptography Association 2021
N. Borisov and C. Diaz (Eds.): FC 2021, LNCS 12674, pp. 33–52, 2021.
https://doi.org/10.1007/978-3-662-64322-8_2

contracts can no longer be modified once deployed. At the time of writing, Ethereum has a market capitalization of over 42 billion USD, making it the second most valuable cryptocurrency on the market [4]. As of writing, WETH, the most valuable Ethereum smart contract holds more than 2 billion USD worth of ether (Ethereum's own cryptocurrency) [13]. Moreover, Ethereum grew in the past 4 years from a daily transaction average of 10K in January 2016 to an average of 500K in January 2020 [12]. Such an increase in value and popularity attracts abuse and the lack of a governing authority has led to a "Wild West"-like situation, where several attackers began to exploit vulnerable smart contracts to steal their funds. In the past, several smart contracts hosting tens of millions of USD were victims to attacks (e.g., [24,35,50]). Hence, over the past few years a rich corpus of research works and tools have surfaced to identify smart contract vulnerabilities (e.g., [2,15,18,21,23,26,29,43,44]). However, most of these tools only focus on analyzing the bytecode of smart contracts and not their transactions or activities. Only a small number leverages transactions to detect attacks (e.g., [3,36,48]), whereas the majority either requires the Ethereum client to be modified or large and complex attack detection scripts to be written. Moreover, none of these tools allow to directly trace stolen assets after their detection.

In this work, we introduce HORUS, a framework capable of automatically detecting and analyzing smart contract attacks from historical blockchain data. Besides detecting attacks, the framework also provides means to quantify and trace the flow of stolen assets across Ethereum accounts. The framework replays transactions without modifying the Ethereum client and encodes their execution as logical facts. Attacks are then detected using Datalog queries, making the framework easily extendable to detect new attacks. Stolen funds are traced by loading detected transactions into a graph database and performing transaction graph analysis. Using our framework, we conduct a longitudinal study that spans the entire past Ethereum blockchain history, from August 2015 to May 2020, consisting of over 3 million smart contracts. One of the fundamental research questions we are investigating is whether these years of efforts have yielded visibly fewer attacks in the wild. If the tools proposed herein are effective, one could argue that attacks should have declined over time. To quantify the answer to this question, we start by investigating whether attacks occur continuously, or if they appear sporadically. While most well-known attacks carry significant monetary value, we wonder whether smaller, but ongoing attacks may occur more often and remain rather occluded.

Contributions. We present the design and implementation of HORUS, a framework that helps identifying smart contract attacks based on a sequence of blockchain transactions using Datalog queries. In addition, the framework extracts the quantity of stolen funds, including ether as well as tokens, and traces them across accounts to support behavioral studies of attackers. We provide a longitudinal study on the security of Ethereum smart contracts of the past 4.5 years, and find 8,095 attacks in the wild, targeting a total of 1,888 vulnerable contracts. Finally, we perform a forensic analysis of the recent Uniswap and Lendf.me hacks.

The remainder of the paper is organized as follows. Section 2 introduces background on smart contracts and the Ethereum virtual machine. Section 3 presents our framework. Our evaluation is discussed in Sect. 4. Section 5 analyzes our results and presents our forensic analysis on the Uniswap and Lendf.me incidents. Finally, Sect. 6 and Sect. 7 discuss related work and conclude our paper, respectively.

2 Background

Smart Contracts. Although, the notion of smart contracts is not new [41], the concept only became wide-spread with the release of Ethereum in 2015. Ethereum smart contracts are fully-fledged programs that are different from traditional programs in several ways. They are deterministic as they must be executed across a network of mutually distrusting nodes. Once deployed, smart contracts cannot be removed or updated, unless they have been explicitly designed to do so. Furthermore, every smart contract has a balance that keeps track of the amount of ether owned by the contract, and a value storage that allows to keep state across executions. They are usually developed using a high-level programming language, such as Solidity [46], that compiles into low-level bytecode. This bytecode is interpreted by the Ethereum Virtual Machine (EVM).

Transactions. The deployment and execution of smart contracts occurs via transactions. Smart contracts are identifiable via a unique 160-bit address that is generated during deployment. Transactions may only be initiated by externally owned accounts (EOA)[1]. Smart contract functions are triggered by encoding the function signature and arguments in the data field of a transaction. A fallback function is executed whenever the provided function name is not implemented. Transactions may also contain a given amount of ether that shall be transferred from one account to another. Smart contracts may call other smart contracts during execution, thus, a single transaction may trigger further transactions, so-called internal transactions.

Ethereum Virtual Machine. The EVM is a stack-based virtual machine that supports a Turing-complete set of instructions allowing smart contracts to store data and interact with the blockchain. The EVM uses a gas mechanism to associate costs to the execution of instructions. This guarantees termination and prevents denial-of-service attacks. The EVM holds a machine state $\mu = (g, pc, m, i, s)$ during execution, where g is the gas available, pc is the program counter, m represents the memory contents, i is the active number of words in memory, and s is the content of the stack.

3 The Horus Framework

In this section, we provide details on the design and implementation of the HORUS framework. HORUS automates the process of conducting longitudinal

---

[1] EOAs are accounts controlled via private keys that have no associated code.

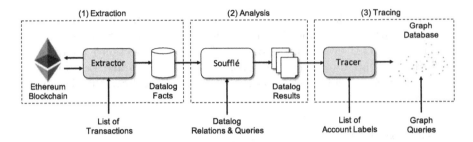

Fig. 1. Architecture of HORUS. Shaded boxes represent custom components, whereas boxes highlighted in white represent off-the-shelf components.

studies of attacks on Ethereum smart contracts. The framework has the capability to detect and analyze smart contract attacks from historical data. Moreover, the framework also provides means to trace the flow of stolen assets across Ethereum accounts. The latter is particularly useful for studying the behavior of attackers. Figure 1 provides an overview on the architecture of HORUS. The framework is organized as an EAT (extract, analyse, and trace) pipeline consisting of three different stages:

(1) **Extraction:** The extraction stage takes as input a list of transactions from which execution related information is extracted and stored as Datalog facts.

(2) **Analysis:** The analysis stage takes as input a set of Datalog relations and queries, which together identify attacks on the extracted Datalog facts.

(3) **Tracing:** The tracing stage retrieves a list of attacker accounts obtained via the analysis and fetches all transactions related to these accounts (including normal transactions, internal transactions and token transfers). Afterwards, a graph database is created, which captures the flow of funds (both ether and tokens) from and to these accounts. Further, the database can be augmented with a list of labeled accounts to enhance the tracing of stolen assets.

In the following, we describe each of the three pipeline stages in more detail. The entire framework was written in Python using roughly 2,000 lines of code[2].

3.1   Extraction

The role of the extractor is to request from the Ethereum client the execution trace for a list of transactions and to convert them into logic relations that reflect the semantics of their execution. An execution trace consists of an ordered list of executed EVM instructions. Each record in that list contains information such as the executed opcode, program counter, call stack depth, and current stack values. Unfortunately, execution traces cannot be obtained directly from historical blockchain data, they can only be recorded during contract execution. Fortunately, the Go based Ethereum client (Geth) provides a debug functionality via the `debug_traceTransaction` and `debug_traceBlockByNumber` functions, which gives us the ability to replay the execution of any given past transaction or

---

[2] Code and data are publicly available at https://github.com/christoftorres/Horus.

block and retrieve its execution trace. Execution traces are requested via Remote Procedure Call (RPC). Previous works [3, 34, 36, 48, 49], did not rely on RPC as it is too slow. Instead, they modified Geth to speed up the process of retrieving execution traces. However, this has the limitation that users cannot use Geth's default version, but are required to use a modified version, and changes will need to be carried over every time a new version of Geth is released. Moreover, at the time of writing, none of these works publicly disclosed their modified version of Geth, which not only makes it difficult to reproduce their results, but also to conduct future studies. Therefore, rather than modifying Geth, we decided to improve the speed on the retrieval of execution traces via RPC. We noticed that execution traces contain a number of information that is irrelevant for our analysis. Fortunately, Geth allows us to inject our own execution tracer written in JavaScript [42]. Through this mechanism, we are able to reduce the size of the execution traces and improve execution speed, without actually modifying Geth. For example, our JavaScript code removes the current program counter, the remaining gas and the instruction's gas cost from the execution trace. Moreover, instead of returning a complete snapshot of the entire stack and memory for every executed instruction, our code only returns stack elements and memory slices that are relevant to the executed instruction.

```
.decl opcode(step:number, op:Opcode, tx_hash:symbol)
.decl data_flow(step1:number, step2:number, tx_hash:symbol)
.decl arithmetic(step:number, op:Opcode, operand1:Value, operand2:Value,
    arithmetic_result:Value, evm_result:Value)
.decl storage(step:number, op:Opcode, tx_hash:symbol, caller:Address,
    contract:Address, index:Value, value:Value, depth:number)
.decl condition(step:number, tx_hash:symbol)
.decl erc20_transfer(step:number, tx_hash:symbol, contract:Address, from:
    Address, to:Address, value:Value)
.decl call(step:number, tx_hash:symbol, op:Opcode, caller:Address, callee:
    Address, input:symbol, value:Value, depth:number, call_id:number,
    call_branch:number, result:number)
.decl selfdestruct(step:number, tx_hash:symbol, caller:Address, contract:
    Address, destination:Address, value:Value)
.decl block(block_number:number, gas_used:number, gas_limit:number,
    timestamp:number)
.decl transaction(tx_hash:symbol, tx_index:number, block_number:number, from
    .Address, to:Address, input:symbol, gas_used:number, gas_limit:number,
    status:number)
```

Listing 1. List of Datalog facts extracted by HORUS.

Listing 1 shows the list of Datalog facts that our extractor produces by iterating through each of the records of the execution traces and encoding relevant information. While most facts are related to low level EVM operations (e.g., `call`), others are related to high level operations. For example, the `erc20_transfer` fact refers to the ERC-20 token event "Transfer" that is emitted whenever tokens are transferred, where `contract` denotes the address of the token contract, and `from` and `to`, denote the sender and receiver of the tokens, respectively. It is important to note that this list can easily be modified or extended to support different studies from the one proposed in this paper

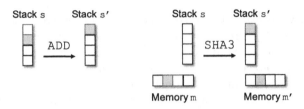

Fig. 2. The example on the left depicts the propagation of taint via the ADD instruction, where the result pushed onto stack s' becomes tainted because the second operand on stack s was tainted. The example on the right depicts the propagation of taint via the SHA3 instruction, where the result pushed onto stack s' becomes tainted because the memory m was tainted.

by modifying the extractor, analyzer and tracer. Besides using the default types number and symbol, we also define our own three new types: Address for 160-bit values, Opcode for the set of EVM opcodes, and Value for 256-bit stack values.

Dynamic Taint Analysis. The extractor leverages dynamic taint analysis to track the flow of data across instructions. Security experts can then use the data_flow fact to check if data flows from one instruction to another. Taint is introduced via sources, then propagated across the execution and finally checked if it flows into sinks. Sources represent instructions that might introduce untrusted data (e.g., CALLDATALOAD or CALLDATACOPY), whereas sinks represent instructions that are sensitive locations (e.g., CALL or SSTORE). We implemented our own dynamic taint analysis engine. The engine loops through every executed instruction and checks whether the executed instruction is a source, for which the engine then introduces taint by tagging the affected stack value, memory region or storage location according to the semantics defined in [47]. We implemented the stack using an array structure following LIFO logic. Memory and storage are implemented using a Python dictionary that maps memory and storage addresses to values. Taint propagation is performed at the byte level (see examples in Fig. 2).

Execution Order. Attacks such as the Parity wallets hacks were composed of two transactions being executed in a specific order. To detect such multi-transactional attacks, our framework encodes a total order across multiple transactions via the triplet $o = (b, t, s)$, where b is the block number, t is the transaction index, and s is the execution step. The execution step is a simple counter that is reset at the beginning of the execution of a transaction and its value is incremented after each executed instruction. An execution step is bound to a transaction index, which is on the other hand bound to a block number. As such, our framework is able to precisely identify the execution order of any instruction across multiple transactions and the entire blockchain history.

3.2 Analysis

The second stage of our pipeline uses a Datalog engine to analyze whether a given list of Datalog relations and queries match any of the previously extracted Datalog facts. These Datalog queries identify adversarial transactions, i.e., malicious transactions that successfully carried out a concrete attack against a smart contract by exploiting a given vulnerability. Our framework uses Soufflé as its Datalog engine. Soufflé compiles Datalog relations and queries into a highly optimized C++ executable [22]. In the following, we provide Datalog queries for detecting reentrancy, Parity wallet hacks, integer overflows, unhandled exceptions and short address attacks. Although, a number of smart contract vulnerabilities exist [1], in this work we focus on those that are ranked by the NCC Group as the top 10 smart contract vulnerabilities [30] and for which we can extract the amount of ether or tokens that were either stolen or locked.

Reentrancy. Reentrancy occurs whenever a contract calls another contract, and the called contract calls back the original contract (i.e., a re-entrant call) before the state in the original contract has been updated appropriately. We detect reentrancy by identifying cyclic calls originating from the same caller and calling the same callee (see Listing 2). We check if two successful **calls** (i.e., result is 1), share the same transaction **hash**, **caller**, **callee**, **id** and **branch**, where the second call has a higher call **depth** than the first call. Afterwards, we check if there are two **storage** operations with the same call depth as the first call, where the first operation is an **SLOAD** and occurs before the first call, and the second operation is an **SSTORE** and occurs after the second call.

```
Reentrancy(hash, caller, callee, depth2, amount) :-
    storage(step1, "SLOAD", hash, _, caller, index, _, depth1),
    call(step2, hash, _, caller, callee, _,        _, depth1, id, branch, 1),
    call(step3, hash, _, caller, callee, _, amount, depth2, id, branch, 1),
    storage(step4, "SSTORE", hash, _, caller, index, _, depth1),
    depth1 < depth2, step1 < step2, step3 < step4, !match("0", amount).
```

Listing 2. Datalog query for detecting reentrancy attacks.

Parity Wallet Hacks. In this paper, we focus on detecting the two Parity wallet hacks [35,50]. Both hacks were due faulty access control implementations that allowed attackers to set themselves as owners, which allowed them to perform critical actions such as the transfer of funds or the destruction of contracts. We detect the first Parity wallet hack by checking if there exist two **transactions** t_1 and t_2, both containing the same sender and receiver, where the first 4 bytes of t_1's input match the function signature of the **initWallet** function (i.e., e46dcfeb), and if the first 4 bytes of t_2's input match the function signature of the **execute** function (i.e., b61d27f6) (see Listing 3). Afterwards, we check whether there is a **call**, which is part of t_2 and where t_2 is executed after t_1 (i.e., block1 < block2; block1 = block2, index1 < index2).

```
ParityWalletHack1(hash1, hash2, caller, callee, amount) :-
    transaction(hash1, index1, block1, from, to, input1, _, _, 1),
    substr(input1, 0, 8) = "e46dcfeb",
    transaction(hash2, index2, block2, from, to, input2, _, _, 1),
    substr(input2, 0, 8) = "b61d27f6",
    call(_, hash2, "CALL", caller, callee, _, amount, _, 1),
    (block1 < block2; block1 = block2, index1 < index2).
```

Listing 3. Datalog query for detecting the first Parity wallet hack.

We detect the second Parity wallet hack in a very similar way to the first one, except that in this case we check if t_2's input matches the function signature of the kill function (i.e., cbf0b0c0) and t_2 contains a selfdestruct (see Listing 4).

```
ParityWalletHack2(hash1, hash2, contract, destination, amount) :-
    transaction(hash1, index1, block1, from, to, input1, _, _, 1),
    substr(input1, 0, 8) = "e46dcfeb",
    transaction(hash2, index2, block2, from, to, input2, _, _, 1),
    substr(input2, 0, 8) = "cbf0b0c0",
    selfdestruct(_, hash2, _, contract, destination, amount),
    (block1 < block2; block1 = block2, index1 < index2).
```

Listing 4. Datalog query for detecting the second Parity wallet hack.

Integer Overflows. We detect integer overflows by checking if data from CALLDATALOAD or CALLDATACOPY opcodes flows into an arithmetic operation, where the arithmetic result does not match the result returned by the EVM. Afterwards, we check whether the result of the arithmetic operation flows into an SSTORE storage operation and an erc20_transfer occurs, where the amount is one of the two operands used in the arithmetic computation (see Listing 5). Please note that in this work, we only focus on detecting integer overflows related to ERC-20 tokens, since token smart contracts have been identified in the past to be frequent victims of integer overflows [32,33].

```
IntegerOverflow(hash, from, to, amount) :-
    (opcode(step1, "CALLDATALOAD", hash);
     opcode(step1, "CALLDATACOPY", hash)),
    arithmetic(step2, _, operand1, operand2, arithmetic_res, evm_res),
    arithmetic_res != evm_res, (operand1 = amount; operand2 = amount),
    storage(step3, "SSTORE", hash, _, _, _, _, 1),
    data_flow(step1, step2, hash), data_flow(step2, step3, hash),
    erc20_transfer(_, hash, _, from, to, amount), !match("0", amount).
```

Listing 5. Datalog query for detecting integer overflow attacks.

Unhandled Exception. Inner calls executed by smart contracts may fail and by default only the state changes caused by those failed calls are rolled back. It is the responsibility of the developer to check the result of every call and perform proper exception handling. However, many developers forget or decide to ignore the handling of such exceptions, resulting in funds not being transferred to their rightful owners. We detect an unhandled exception by checking whether a call with opcode "CALL" failed (i.e., result is 0) with an amount larger than zero and where the result was not used in a condition (see Listing 6).

```
UnhandledException(hash, caller, callee, amount) :-
    call(step, hash, "CALL", caller, callee, _, amount, _, 0),
    !match("0", amount), !used_in_condition(step, hash).
```

Listing 6. Datalog query for detecting unhandled exceptions.

Short Address. The ERC-20 functions transfer and transferFrom take as input a destination address and a given amount of tokens. During execution the

EVM will add trailing zeros to the end of the transaction input if the transaction arguments are not correctly encoded as chunks of 32 bytes, thereby shifting the input bytes to the left by a few zeros, and therefore unwillingly increase the number of tokens to be transferred. However, attackers can exploit this fact by generating addresses that end with trailing zeros and omit these zeros, to then trick another party (e.g., web service) into making a call to `transfer/transferFrom` containing the attacker's malformed address. We detect a short address attack by first checking if the first 4 bytes of a `transaction`'s input match either the function signature of `transfer` (i.e., a9059cbb) or `transferFrom` (i.e., 23b872dd). Then, for the function `transfer` we check whether the length of the input is smaller than 68 (i.e., 4 bytes function signature, 32 bytes destination address, and 32 bytes amount), and for the function `transferFrom` we check whether the length of the input is smaller than 100 (i.e., 4 bytes function signature, 32 bytes from address, 32 bytes destination address, and 32 bytes amount), and finally we check if an `erc20_transfer` occurred (see Listing 7).

```
ShortAddress(hash, from, to, amount) :-
  transaction(hash, _, _, input, _, _, 1, _),
  (substr(input, 0, 8) = "a9059cbb", strlen(input) / 2 < 68;
   substr(input, 0, 8) = "23b872dd", strlen(input) / 2 < 100),
  erc20_transfer(_, hash, _, from, to, amount), !match("0", amount).
```

Listing 7. Datalog query for detecting short address attacks.

3.3   Tracing

The final stage of our pipeline is the tracing of stolen assets, such as ether and tokens, from attacker accounts to labeled accounts (e.g., exchanges). The tracer starts by extracting sender addresses and timestamps from malicious transactions that have been identified via the Datalog analysis. Sender addresses are assumed to be accounts belonging to attackers. Afterwards, the tracer uses Etherscan's API to retrieve for each sender address all its normal transactions, internal transactions and token transfers, and loads them into a Neo4j graph database. We rely on a third-party service such as Etherscan to retrieve normal transactions, internal transactions and token transfers, because a default Ethereum node does not provide this functionality out-of-the-box. Accounts are encoded as vertices and transactions as directed edges between those vertices. We differentiate between three types of accounts: attacker accounts, unlabeled accounts, and labeled accounts. Every account type contains an address. Labeled accounts contain a category (e.g., exchange) and a label (e.g., Kraken 1). We obtain categories and labels from Etherscan's large collection of labeled accounts[3]. We downloaded a total of 5,437 labels belonging to 204 categories. We differentiate between three different types of transactions: normal transactions, internal transactions, and token transactions. Each transaction type contains a transaction value, transaction hash, and transaction date. Token transactions contain a

---

[3] https://etherscan.io/labelcloud.

token name, token symbol and number of decimals. Transactions can be loaded either backwards or forwards. Loading transactions forwards allows us to track where attackers sent their stolen funds to, whereas loading transactions backwards allows us to track where attackers received their funds from. We start with the attacker's account when loading transactions and recursively load transactions for neighboring accounts that are part of the same transaction for up to a given number of hops. We do not load transactions for accounts with more than 1,000 transactions. This is to avoid bloating the graph database with transactions from mixing services, exchanges or gambling smart contracts. Moreover, when loading transactions backwards, we only load transactions that occurred before the timestamp of the attack, whereas when loading transactions forwards, we only load transactions that occurred after the timestamp of the attack. Finally, when all transactions are loaded, security experts can query the graph database using Neo4j's own graph query language called Cypher, to trace the flow of stolen funds. Evidently, our tracing is only effective up to a certain point, since mixing services and exchanges prevent further tracing. Nonetheless, our tracing is still useful to study whether attackers send their funds to mixers or exchanges and to identify which services are being used and to what extend.

4 Evaluation

In this section, we demonstrate the scalability and effectiveness of our framework by performing a large-scale analysis of the Ethereum blockchain and comparing our results to those presented in previous works.

Dataset. We used the Ethereum ETL framework [28] to retrieve a list of transactions for every smart contract deployed up to block 10 M. We collected a total of 697,373,206 transactions and 3,362,876 contracts. The deployment timestamps of the collected contracts range from August 7, 2015, to May 4, 2020. We filtered out contracts without transactions and removed transactions that have a gas limit of 21,000 (i.e., do not execute code). Moreover, similar to [36], we skipped all the transactions that were part of the 2016 denial-of-service attacks, as these incur high execution times [40]. After applying these filters, we ended up with a final dataset of 1,234,197 smart contracts consisting of 371,419,070 transactions. During the extraction phase, HORUS generated roughly 700 GB of Datalog facts on the final dataset.

Experimental Setup. All experiments were conducted using a machine with 64 GB of memory and an Intel(R) Core(TM) i7-8700 CPU with 12 cores clocked at 3.2 GHz, running 64-bit Ubuntu 18.04.5 LTS. Moreover, we used Geth version 1.9.9, Soufflé version 1.7.1, and Neo4j version 4.0.3.

4.1   Results

Table 1. Summary of detected vulnerable contracts and adversarial transactions.

	Results		Validation		
Vulnerability	Contracts	Transactions	TP	FP	p
Reentrancy	46	2,508	45	1	0.97
Parity Wallet Hacks	600	1,852	600	0	1.00
Parity Wallet Hack 1	596	1,632	596	0	1.00
Parity Wallet Hack 2	238	238	238	0	1.00
Integer Overflow	125	443	65	0	1.00
Overflow (*Addition*)	37	139	25	0	1.00
Overflow (*Multiplication*)	23	120	20	0	1.00
Underflow (*Subtraction*)	104	352	68	0	1.00
Unhandled exception	1,068	3,100	100	0	1.00
Short address	55	275	5	0	1.00
Total unique	1,888	8,095			

Table 1 summarizes our results: we found 1,888 attacked contracts and 8,095 adversarial transactions. From these contracts, 46 were attacked using reentrancy, 600 were attacked during the Parity wallet hacks, 125 were attacked via integer overflows, 1,068 suffered from unhandled exceptions, and 55 were victims of short address attacks. For the Parity wallet hacks, we find that the majority was attacked during the first hack. We also observe that most contracts that are vulnerable to integer overflows, were attacked via an integer underflow.

4.2   Validation

We confirm our framework's correctness, by comparing our findings to those reported by previous works for which results were publicly available. Also, we solely compare our finding to works that similarly to HORUS, focus on detecting attacks rather than vulnerable contracts. In cases where the results were not publicly available, we manually inspected the source code and transactions of flagged contracts using Etherscan. Table 1 summarizes the results of our validation in terms of true positives (TP), false positives (FP) and precision (p). Overall our framework achieves a high precision of 99.54%.

Reentrancy. First, we compare our results to those of SEREUM [36]. The authors reported a total of 16 vulnerable contracts, where 14 are false positives. The true positives include the DAO [6] and the DSEthToken [8] contract, which HORUS has also identified. HORUS has flagged none of the 14 false positives. Next, we compare our results to ÆGIS [14,16]. HORUS successfully detected the 7 contracts that were reported by ÆGIS. Then, we compare our results to SODA [3]. HORUS identified 25 of the 26 contracts that were flagged as true positives by SODA. We analyzed the remaining contract (0x59abb8006b30d7357869760d21b4965475198d9d) and found that it is not vulnerable to reentrancy, which is in line with what other previous works discovered [48]. For the 5 false positives reported by SODA, we detected 3 of them, where two (0xd4cd7c881f5ceece4917d856ce73f510d7d0769e and 0x72f60eca0 db681127421569412966115f1f97982e) are actual true positives and have been misclassified by SODA. The other one (known as HODLWallet [9]) is indeed a false positive. Afterwards, we compare our results with those of ETHSCOPE [48]. HORUS detected 45 out of the 46 true positives reported by ETHSCOPE. The non-reported contract is the DarkDAO [7], which did not suffer from a reentrancy attack and is, therefore, a false positive. In terms of false positives, HORUS only has one in common with ETHSCOPE, namely the aforementioned HODLWallet contract. The other two false positives that ETHSCOPE reported were correctly identified as true negatives by HORUS. Finally, we compare our results with those of Zhou et al. [51]. HORUS found 22 of the 26 contracts that have been reported as true positives by Zhou et al. We inspected the remaining 4 contracts and found that they are false positives.

Parity Wallet Hacks. For the first Parity wallet hack, we compared our results to those reported by ÆGIS and Zhou et al. ÆGIS reported 3 contracts, which have also been found by HORUS. Next, Zhou et al. reported 622 contracts, of which HORUS found 596. We analyzed the remaining 26 contracts and found that these are false positives. After analyzing their list of transactions, we could not find evidence of the two exploiting transactions, namely `initWallet` and `execute`. For the second Parity wallet hack, we compared our results to those of ÆGIS. HORUS found 238 contracts, of which 236 were also reported by ÆGIS. The remaining two are true positives and have not been identified by ÆGIS.

Integer Overflow. We compared our findings to those of Zhou et al. The authors found 50 contracts, whereas we found 125 contracts. HORUS detected 49 of the 50 contracts reported by Zhou et al. We analyzed the undetected contract (0xa9a8ec071ed0ed5be571396438a046a423a0c206) and found no evidence of an integer overflow. Besides our comparison with Zhou et al., we also tried to analyze manually the source code of the reported contracts. We were able to obtain the source code for 65 of the 125 reported contracts. Our manual inspection identified that all of the contracts are true positives. They either contained a faulty arithmetic check or no arithmetic check at all.

Unhandled Exception. Since none of the previous works analyzed unhandled exceptions, we manually analyzed the source code of the contracts reported by HORUS. However, we limited our validation to a random sample of 100 contracts since manually analyzing 1,068 contracts is infeasible. We find that all of the 100 contracts contained in their source code either a direct call or a function call that did not check the return value. Therefore, we conclude that HORUS reports no false positives on the detection of unhandled exceptions.

Short Address. We compared our results to those reported by SODA. SODA detected 726 contracts and 6,599 transactions, whereas HORUS detected 55 contracts and 275 transactions. After further investigation, we found that the contracts and transactions detected by HORUS were also detected by SODA. We also found that SODA reported transactions that failed or where the transferred amount was zero, while HORUS only reported transactions that were successful and where an ERC-20 transfer event was successfully triggered with an amount larger than zero. Moreover, we were able to obtain the source code for 5 of the reported contracts and confirm that the `transfer` or `transferFrom` functions contained inside those contracts do not validate the input length of parameters.

5   Analysis

In this section, we demonstrate the practicality of HORUS in detecting and analyzing real-world smart contract attacks via an analysis of our evaluated results and a case study on the recent Uniswap and Lendf.me incidents.

5.1   Volume and Frequency of Attacks

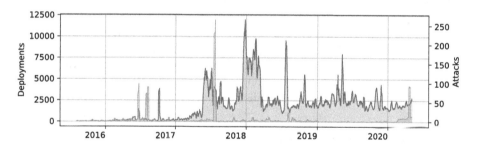

Fig. 3. Weekly average of daily contract deployments and attacks over time.

Figure 3 depicts the weekly average of daily attacks in comparison to the weekly average of daily deployments. We state that the peak of weekly deployed contracts was at the end of 2017, and that the largest volume of weekly attacks occurred before this peak. Moreover, most attacks seem to occur in clusters of the same day. We suspect that attackers scan the blockchain for similar vulnerable contracts and exploit them at the same time. The first three spikes in the attacks correspond to the DAO and Parity wallet hacks, whereas the last spike corresponds to the recent Uniswap/Lendf.me hacks.

Figure 4 depicts the occurrences of adversarial transactions per vulnerability type that we measured during our evaluation. While reentrancy attacks seem

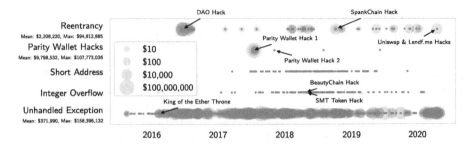

Fig. 4. Volume and frequency of smart contract attacks over time.

to occur more sporadically, other types of vulnerabilities such as unhandled exceptions are triggered rather continuously. Overall, we see that over time less contracts became victims to short address attacks and integer overflows, suggesting that smart contracts have become more secure over the past few years. However, we also see that smart contracts still remain vulnerable to well-known vulnerabilities such as reentrancy and unhandled exceptions, despite automated security tools being available. Figure 4 also illustrates for each adversarial transaction the amount of USD that was either stolen (reentrancy and Parity wallet hack 1) or locked (unhandled exception and Parity wallet hack 2). The USD amounts were calculated by multiplying the price of one ether at the time of the attack times the ether extracted via our Datalog query. We do not provide USD amounts for short address attacks and integer overflows, because these attacks involve stolen ERC-20 tokens and we were not able to obtain the historical prices of these tokens. We can see that the DAO hack and the first Parity wallet hack remain the two most devastating attacks in terms of ether stolen, with ether worth 94,812,885 USD and 107,773,036 USD, respectively. We marked well-known incidents such as the DAO hack, or the two Parity wallet hacks for the reader's convenience and to demonstrate that HORUS is able to detect them.

5.2   Forensic Analysis on Uniswap and Lendf.me Incidents

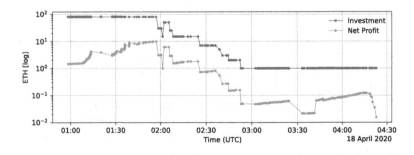

Fig. 5. Invested ETH and net profit made by Uniswap attackers over time.

Uniswap. On April 18, 2020, attackers were able to drain a large amount of ether from Uniswap's liquidity pool of ETH-imBTC [11]. They purposely chose the imBTC token as it implements the ERC777 standard, which would allow them to register a callback function and therefore perform a reentrancy attack on Uniswap. The attackers would start by purchasing imBTC tokens for ETH. Afterward, they would exchange half of the purchased imBTC tokens within the same transaction back to ETH. However, the latter would trigger a callback function that the attackers registered before the attack, allowing them to take control and call back the Uniswap contract to exchange the remaining half of imBTC tokens to ETH before the conversion rate was updated. Thus, the attackers could trade the second batch of imBTC tokens at a more profitable conversion rate. Interestingly, this vulnerability was known to Uniswap and was publicly disclosed precisely a year before the attack [5].

We used HORUS to extract and analyze all the transactions mined on that day, and identified a total of 525 transactions performing reentrancy attacks against Uniswap with an accumulated profit of 1,278 ETH (232,239.46 USD). The attack began at 00:58:19 UTC and ended roughly 3.5 h later at 04:22:58 UTC. Figure 5 depicts a timeline of the attack, showing the amount of ether that the attackers invested and the net profit they made per transaction. We see that the net profit goes down over time. The highest profit made for a single transaction was roughly 9.79 ETH (1,778.72 USD), while the lowest profit was 0.01 ETH (2.73 USD). The attackers began their attack by purchasing tokens for roughly 80 ETH and went over time down to 1 ETH. Moreover, we see that the profit was mostly tied to the amount of ether that the attackers were investing (i.e., using to purchase imBTC tokens). However, we also see that sometimes there were some fluctuations, where the attackers were making more profit while they would invest the same amount of ether. This is probably due to other participants trading imBTC on Uniswap during the attack and therefore influencing the exchange rates. In the last step, we traced the entire ether flow from the attackers account for up to 5 hops using HORUS's tracing capabilities. Our transaction graph analysis reveals that the attackers exchanged roughly 702 ETH (55% of the stolen funds) for tokens on different exchanges: 589 ETH on Uniswap for WETH, DAI, USDC, BAT, and MKR, 31 ETH on Compound, and 82 ETH on 1inch.exchange. The latter is of particular interest for law enforcement agencies as 1inch.exchange keeps track

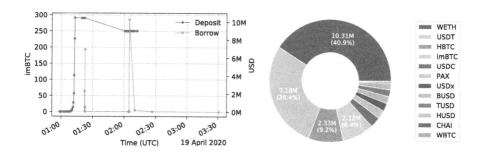

Fig. 6. Deposited and borrowed tokens by Lendf.me attackers over time.

of IP addresses of transactions performed over their platform [37], which can be useful in deanonymizing the attackers.

Lendf.me. On April 19, 2020, attackers were able to drain all of Lendf.me's liquidity pools [10]. Similar to the Uniswap hack, the attackers exploited the fact that Lendf.me was trading imBTC and could register a callback function to perform a reentrancy attack. The attackers would start by depositing x amount of imBTC tokens into Lendf.me's liquidity pool. Next, still within the same transaction, they would deposit another amount y, however, this time triggering the callback function registered by the attackers, which would withdraw the previously deposited x tokens from Lendf.me. By the end of the transaction, the imBTC balance of the attackers on the imBTC token contract would be $x - y$, but the imBTC balance on the Lendf.me contract would be $x + y$, thereby increasing their imBTC balance on Lendf.me by x without actually depositing it. Similar to Uniswap, the issue here is that the user's balance is only updated after the transfer of tokens, thus the update is based on data before the transfer and therefore ignoring any updates made in between.

Using HORUS, we extracted and analyzed all the transactions mined on that day. We identified a total of 46 transactions performing reentrancy attacks against Lendf.me, and 19 transactions using the stolen imBTC tokens to borrow other tokens. Figure 6 shows on the left the amount of imBTC tokens that the attackers deposited during the attack and the amount of USD that the attackers made by borrowing other tokens. The right-hand side of Fig. 6 depicts the number of tokens in USD that the attackers borrowed from Lendf.me. The attackers borrowed from 12 different tokens, worth together 25,244,120.74 USD, where 10.31M USD are only from borrowing WETH. The attackers launched their attack at 00:58:43 UTC and stopped 2 h later at 02:12:11 UTC. They started depositing low amounts of imBTC and increased their amounts over time up to 291.35 imBTC. The borrowing started at 01:22:27 UTC and ended at 03:30:42 UTC. Finally, we used HORUS to trace the flow of tokens from the attackers account for up to 3 hops. We found that the attackers initially traded some parts of the stolen tokens for other tokens on ParaSwap, Compound, Aave, and 1inch.exchange. However, at 14:16:52 UTC, thus about 10 h later, the attackers started sending all the stolen tokens back to Lendf.me's admin account (0xa6a6783828ab3e4a9db54302bc01c4ca73f17efb). Lendf.me then moved all the tokens into a recovery account (0xc88fcc12f400a0a2cebe87110dcde0dafd2 9f148) where users could then reclaim their tokens.

6   Related Work

Static Analysis. Researchers proposed a number of tools to detect smart contract vulnerabilities via static analysis. Luu et al. [26] proposed OYENTE, the first symbolic execution tool for smart contracts. Other tools such as OSIRIS [15], combine symbolic execution and taint analysis to detect integer bugs. MYTHRIL [29] uses a mix of symbolic execution and control-flow checking. MAIAN [31] employs inter-procedural symbolic execution. TEETHER [25] automatically generates exploits for smart contracts. HONEYBADGER [17] performs symbolic execution to detect honeypots. However, symbolic execution is often unable to explore all program states, making it generally unsound. Formal verification tools were proposed [27,45], together with a formal definition of the EVM [20]. ETHBMC [18] uses bounded model checking to detect vulnerabilities, whereas ETHOR [38] uses reachability analysis. ZEUS [23] verifies the correctness of smart contracts using abstract interpretation and model checking. SMARTCHECK [43] checks Solidity source code against XPath patterns. VERIS-MART [39] leverages counter example-based inductive synthesis to detect arithmetic bugs. SECURIFY [44] extracts semantic information from the dependency graph to check for compliance and violation patterns using Datalog. VANDAL [2] converts EVM bytecode to semantic logic relations and checks them against Datalog queries. The main difference between these works and ours, is that they analyze the bytecode of smart contracts, whereas we analyze the execution of transactions.

Dynamic Analysis. Although less apparent, a number of dynamic approaches have also been proposed. ECFCHECKER [19] enables the runtime detection of reentrancy attacks via a modified EVM. SEREUM [36] proposes a modified EVM to protect deployed smart contracts against reentrancy attacks. ÆGIS [14,16] presents a smart contract and a DSL to protect against all kinds of runtime attacks. SODA [3] uses a modified Ethereum client to inject custom modules for the online detection of malicious transactions. Perez et al. [34] use Datalog to study the transactions of vulnerable smart contracts that have been detected by previous works. ETHSCOPE [48] loads historical data into an Elasticsearch database and adds dynamic taint analysis to the client to analyze transactions. Zhou et al. [51] study attacks and defenses by encoding transactional information as action trees and result graphs. TXSPECTOR [49] is a concurrent work to ours and adopts the Datalog facts proposed by VANDAL. However, these facts were designed to analyze bytecode and do not allow to detect multi-transactional attacks. In contrast to these works, our work does not modify the Ethereum client. Instead, we dynamically inject our custom tracer into the client. We also provide a new set of Datalog facts that allow to check for multi-transactional attacks and describe data flows between instructions via dynamic taint analysis. Finally, none of the aforementioned tools provide means to trace stolen assets across the Ethereum blockchain.

7   Conclusion

A wealth of automated vulnerability detection tools for Ethereum smart contracts were proposed over the past years. This raises the question whether the security of smart contracts has improved. In this paper, we presented the design and implementation of an extensible framework for carrying out longitudinal studies on detecting, analyzing, and tracing of smart contract attacks. We analyzed transactions from August 2015 to May 2020 and identified 8,095 attacks as well as 1,888 vulnerable contracts. Our analysis revealed that while the number of attacks seems to have decreased for attacks such as integer overflows, unhandled exceptions and reentrancy attacks still seem to remain present despite an abundance of new smart contract security tools. Finally, we also presented an in-depth analysis on the recent Uniswap and Lendf.me incidents.

Acknowledgments. We would like to thank the anonymous reviewers and Johannes Krupp for their valuable comments and feedback. This work was partly supported by the Luxembourg National Research Fund (FNR) under grant 13192291.

References

1. Atzei, N., Bartoletti, M., Cimoli, T.: A survey of attacks on ethereum smart contracts (SoK). In: Maffei, M., Ryan, M. (eds.) POST 2017. LNCS, vol. 10204, pp. 164–186. Springer, Heidelberg (2017). https://doi.org/10.1007/978-3-662-54455-6_8
2. Brent, L., et al.: Vandal: a scalable security analysis framework for smart contracts (2018). arXiv preprint arXiv:1809.03981
3. Chen, T., et al.: Soda: a generic online detection framework for smart contracts. In: Proceedings of the Network and Distributed System Security Symposium (NDSS'20) (2020)
4. CoinMarketCap: Top 100 Cryptocurrencies by Market Capitalization (2020). https://coinmarketcap.com
5. ConsenSys Diligence: Uniswap Audit (2019). https://github.com/ConsenSys/Uniswap-audit-report-2018-12
6. Etherscan: The DAO (2016). https://etherscan.io/address/0xbb9bc244d798123fde783fcc1c72d3bb8c189413
7. Etherscan: The Dark DAO (2016). https://etherscan.io/address/0x304a554a310c7e546dfe434669c62820b7d83490
8. Etherscan: DSEthToken (2017). https://etherscan.io/address/0xd654bdd32fc99471455e86c2e7f7d7b6437e9179
9. Etherscan: HODLWallet (2018). https://etherscan.io/address/0x4a8d3a662e0fd6a8bd39ed0f91e4c1b729c81a38
10. Etherscan: Lendf.Me - MoneyMarket (2019). https://etherscan.io/address/0x0eee3e3828a45f7601d5f54bf49bb01d1a9df5ea
11. Etherscan: Uniswap: imBTC (2019). https://etherscan.io/address/0xffcf45b540e6c9f094ae656d2e34ad11cdfdb187
12. Etherscan: Ethereum Daily Transactions Chart (2020). https://etherscan.io/chart/tx
13. Etherscan: Wrapped Ether (2020). https://etherscan.io/address/0xc02aaa39b223fe8d0a0e5c4f27ead9083c756cc2
14. Ferreira Torres, C., Baden, M., Norvill, R., Jonker, H.: ÆGIS: smart shielding of smart contracts. In: Proceedings of the 2019 ACM SIGSAC Conference on Computer and Communications Security, pp. 2589–2591 (2019)
15. Ferreira Torres, C., Schütte, J., State, R.: Osiris: hunting for integer bugs in ethereum smart contracts. In: Proceedings of the 34th Annual Computer Security Applications Conference, ACSAC '18, pp. 664–676. ACM, New York (2018). https://doi.org/10.1145/3274694.3274737
16. Ferreira Torres, C., Steichen, M., Norvill, R., Fiz Pontiveros, B., Jonker, H.: ÆGIS: shielding vulnerable smart contracts against attacks. In: Proceedings of the 15th ACM Asia Conference on Computer and Communications Security (ASIA CCS'20), Taipei, Taiwan, 5–9 October 2020 (2020)

17. Ferreira Torres, C., Steichen, M., State, R.: The art of the scam: demystifying honeypots in ethereum smart contracts. In: 28th USENIX Security Symposium (USENIX Security 19), pp. 1591–1607. USENIX Association, Santa Clara (2019)
18. Frank, J., Aschermann, C., Holz, T.: ETHBMC: a bounded model checker for smart contracts. In: 29th USENIX Security Symposium (USENIX Security 20). USENIX Association, Boston (2020)
19. Grossman, S., et al.: Online detection of effectively callback free objects with applications to smart contracts. In: Proceedings of the ACM on Programming Languages, vol. 2, no. POPL, p. 48 (2017)
20. Hildenbrandt, E., et al.: Kevm: a complete formal semantics of the ethereum virtual machine. In: 2018 IEEE 31st Computer Security Foundations Symposium (CSF), pp. 204–217 (2018)
21. Jiang, B., Liu, Y., Chan, W.: Contractfuzzer: fuzzing smart contracts for vulnerability detection. In: Proceedings of the 33rd ACM/IEEE International Conference on Automated Software Engineering, pp. 259–269. ACM (2018)
22. Jordan, H., Scholz, B., Subotić, P.: SOUFFLÉ: on synthesis of program analyzers. In: Chaudhuri, S., Farzan, A. (eds.) CAV 2016. LNCS, vol. 9780, pp. 422–430. Springer, Cham (2016). https://doi.org/10.1007/978-3-319-41540-6_23
23. Kalra, S., Goel, S., Dhawan, M., Sharma, S.: Zeus: analyzing safety of smart contracts. In: NDSS, pp. 1–12 (2018)
24. Finley, K.: A $50 million hack just showed that the DAO was all too human (2016). https://www.wired.com/2016/06/50-million-hack-just-showed-dao-human/
25. Krupp, J., Rossow, C.: teether: Gnawing at ethereum to automatically exploit smart contracts. In: 27th USENIX Security Symposium (USENIX Security 18), pp. 1317–1333 (2018)
26. Luu, L., Chu, D.H., Olickel, H., Saxena, P., Hobor, A.: Making smart contracts smarter. In: Proceedings of the 2016 ACM SIGSAC Conference on Computer and Communications Security - CCS'16, pp. 254–269. ACM Press, New York (2016). https://doi.org/10.1145/2976749.2978309
27. Mavridou, A., Laszka, A.: Tool demonstration: FSolidM for designing secure ethereum smart contracts. In: Bauer, L., Küsters, R. (eds.) POST 2018. LNCS, vol. 10804, pp. 270–277. Springer, Cham (2018). https://doi.org/10.1007/978-3-319-89722-6_11
28. Evgeny, M.: Ethereum ETL v1.3.0 (2019). https://github.com/blockchain-etl/ethereum-etl
29. Mueller, B.: Smashing ethereum smart contracts for fun and real profit. In: The 9th annual HITB Security Conference (2018)
30. NCC Group: Decentralized Application Security Project (or DASP) Top 10 of 2018 (2018). https://dasp.co
31. Nikolić, I., Kolluri, A., Sergey, I., Saxena, P., Hobor, A.: Finding the greedy, prodigal, and suicidal contracts at scale. In: Proceedings of the 34th Annual Computer Security Applications Conference, pp. 653–663. ACM (2018)
32. PeckShield - batchOverflow Bug: ALERT: New batchOverflow Bug in Multiple ERC20 Smart Contracts (CVE-2018-10299) (2018). https://blog.peckshield.com/2018/04/22/batchOverflow/
33. PeckShield - proxyOverflow Bug : New proxyOverflow Bug in Multiple ERC20 Smart Contracts (CVE-2018-10376) (2018). https://blog.peckshield.com/2018/04/25/proxyOverflow/
34. Perez, D., Livshits, B.: Smart contract vulnerabilities: vulnerable does not imply exploited. In: 30th USENIX Security Symposium (USENIX Security 21). USENIX Association, Vancouver (2021)

35. Petrov, S.: Another parity wallet hack explained (2017). https://medium.com/@Pr0Ger/another-parity-wallet-hack-explained-847ca46a2e1c
36. Rodler, M., Li, W., Karame, G., Davi, L.: Sereum: protecting existing smart contracts against re-entrancy attacks. In: Proceedings of the Network and Distributed System Security Symposium (NDSS'19) (2019)
37. Ryan   Sean   Adams   (2020).   https://twitter.com/RyanSAdams/status/1252574107159408640
38. Schneidewind, C., Grishchenko, I., Scherer, M., Maffei, M.: ethor: practical and provably sound static analysis of ethereum smart contracts (2020). arXiv preprint arXiv:2005.06227
39. So, S., Lee, M., Park, J., Lee, H., Oh, H.: Verismart: a highly precise safety verifier for ethereum smart contracts. In: 2020 IEEE Symposium on Security and Privacy (SP), pp. 1678–1694. IEEE (2020)
40. StackExchange: Why is my node synchronization stuck/extremely slow at block 2,306,843? (2016). https://ethereum.stackexchange.com/questions/9883/why-is-my-node-synchronization-stuck-extremely-slow-at-block-2-306-843
41. Szabo, N.: Formalizing and securing relationships on public networks. First Monday **2**(9) (1997)
42. Szilágyi, P.: Go-Ethereum Management APIs - JavaScript-based tracing (2020). https://github.com/ethereum/go-ethereum/wiki/Management-APIs#javascript-based-tracing
43. Tikhomirov, S., Voskresenskaya, E., Ivanitskiy, I., Takhaviev, R., Marchenko, E., Alexandrov, Y.: Smartcheck: static analysis of ethereum smart contracts. In: 2018 IEEE/ACM 1st International Workshop on Emerging Trends in Software Engineering for Blockchain (WETSEB), pp. 9–16. IEEE (2018)
44. Tsankov, P., Dan, A., Drachsler-Cohen, D., Gervais, A., Buenzli, F., Vechev, M.: Securify: practical security analysis of smart contracts. In: Proceedings of the 2018 ACM SIGSAC Conference on Computer and Communications Security, pp. 67–82. ACM (2018)
45. Wang, Y., et al.: Formal specification and verification of smart contracts for azure blockchain (2019). https://www.microsoft.com/en-us/research/publication/formal-specification-and-verification-of-smart-contracts-for-azure-blockchain
46. Wood, G.: Solidity 0.6.8 documentation (2020). https://solidity.readthedocs.io/en/v0.6.8/
47. Wood, G., et al.: Ethereum: a secure decentralised generalised transaction ledger. Ethereum Proj. Yellow Paper **151**(2014), 1–32 (2014)
48. Wu, L., et al.: Ethscope: a transaction-centric security analytics framework to detect malicious smart contracts on ethereum (2020). arXiv preprint arXiv:2005.08278
49. Zhang, M., Zhang, X., Zhang, Y., Lin, Z.: TXSPECTOR: uncovering attacks in ethereum from transactions. In: 29th USENIX Security Symposium (USENIX Security 20), pp. 2775–2792. USENIX Association (2020)
50. Zhao, W.: $30 Million: Ether Reported Stolen Due to Parity Wallet Breach (2017). https://www.coindesk.com/30-million-ether-reported-stolen-parity-wallet-breach
51. Zhou, S., Yang, Z., Xiang, J., Cao, Y., Yang, Z., Zhang, Y.: An ever-evolving game: evaluation of real-world attacks and defenses in ethereum ecosystem. In: 29th USENIX Security Symposium (USENIX Security 20), pp. 2793–2810. USENIX Association (2020)

Timelocked Bribing

Tejaswi Nadahalli[1]([✉]), Majid Khabbazian[2], and Roger Wattenhofer[1]

[1] ETH Zürich, Zürich, Switzerland
tejaswin@ethz.ch
[2] University of Alberta, Edmonton, Canada

Abstract. A Hashed Time Lock Contract (HTLC) is a central concept in cryptocurrencies where some value can be spent either with the
preimage of a public hash by one party (Bob) or after a timelock expires
by another party (Alice). We present a bribery attack on HTLC's where
Bob's hash-protected transaction is censored by Alice's timelocked transaction. Alice incentivizes miners to censor Bob's transaction by leaving
almost all her value to miners in general. Miners follow (or refuse) this
bribe if their expected payoff is better (or worse). We explore conditions
under which this attack is possible, and how HTLC participants can protect themselves against the attack. Applications like Lightning Network
payment channels and Cross-Chain Atomic Swaps use HTLC's as building blocks and are vulnerable to this attack. Our proposed solution uses
the hashpower share of the weakest known miner to derive parameters
that make these applications robust against this bribing attack.

Keywords: Bitcoin · HTLC · Bribe · Miner extractable value

1 Introduction

Bitcoin started the modern cryptocurrency revolution by removing trusted intermediaries and replacing them with a dynamic set of miners. These miners validate transactions and are paid by the system in the form of block rewards and
also by transaction participants in the form of fees. Rational miners will always
choose higher fee transactions than lower-fee ones, and this behavior will get
reinforced over time as block rewards decrease to zero [1]. This setup has often
raised ([2–4]) the possibility of miners being bribed by transaction participants
to favor one participant over the other. Typical bribing attacks envision the paying party (Alice) cheating the paid party (Bob) by Alice double-spending the
same value in a separate transaction paying back to Alice. Miners are bribed by
Alice to include the double-spending transaction in the blockchain by forking it
and orphaning the block with the first transaction, thereby cheating Bob of the
payment from the first transaction. These bribery attacks, however, operate at
a block level because, to be cheated, Bob needs to be convinced that the first
transaction is buried in the blockchain by k blocks (in Bitcoin, $k = 6$). Before
this happens, Bob should ideally not honor the first transaction, but monitor

© International Financial Cryptography Association 2021
N. Borisov and C. Diaz (Eds.): FC 2021, LNCS 12674, pp. 53–72, 2021.
https://doi.org/10.1007/978-3-662-64322-8_3

the public Bitcoin blockchain. If a transaction where Alice double-spends the same bitcoins back to herself is seen, and Bob's transaction is abandoned in an orphaned block, Bob should not honor Alice's first transaction by not giving Alice the goods and services that were promised.

A more sophisticated concept of transactions exists where Bob *does* want Alice to pay the transaction value back to herself, but only after some time has elapsed. During this time, Bob reserves the option of getting paid himself from the same payment source. This complex transaction structure is the building block for financial contracts like escrows, payment channels, atomic swaps, etc. The required time delay is implemented using a blockchain artefact called *timelocks*. A rudimentary version of timelocks (nLocktime) was in the first Bitcoin implementation by Satoshi Nakamoto in 2009 [5]. More sophisticated timelocks that lock transactions, specific bitcoins, or specific script execution paths were added later [6–8]. Bitcoin script allows for timelocks to be combined with hashlocks in an OR condition to create a new kind of transaction called Hash Timelocked Transactions (HTLC). As we will see later, HTLC's open the possibility of transaction level bribing of miners where miners do not have to orphan mined blocks, but just have to ignore a *currently valid* transaction and wait for the timelocked bribe to become valid. Additionally, in this attack, the bribe is endogenous to the transactions and does not have to be implemented externally through public bulletin boards or other third party smart contracts. Bribery attacks that operate at a transaction level are far more insidious compared to block orphaning bribery attacks. Block orphaning attacks undermine the native cryptocurrency's trust with the larger community and could be detrimental to the briber's financial position in general. Transaction level bribery, on the other hand, targets specific contracts on the blockchain and could go unnoticed as the larger cryptocurrency system hums along. This sort of an attack, where a miner has visibility into the pool of transactions that are waiting for confirmation (mempool) and can include or not include a transaction in their mined block is discussed in a more general setting in [9] under the umbrella term "Miner Extractable Value".

1.1   HTLC

HTLC's are a type of smart contract that use preimage resistance of cryptographic hash functions, along with timelocks, to enable an escrow service. Say we have a buyer who has some bitcoin and wants to buy some goods/services from a seller. The buyer commits their bitcoin into a contract which is locked by an OR condition of:

– Preimage to a cryptographic hash. This is the payment path. The buyer creates a random secret preimage and cryptographically hashes it to get a digest. This digest is used to lock the payment path. The buyer will reveal the preimage to the seller once the buyer has possession of the goods/services. The seller can use this preimage and their own signature to send the funds to an address they control. The exchange of the preimage for the goods/services can be implemented in a variety of ways, leading to different applications.

– A timelock. This is the refund path. The buyer sets a timelock after which the funds are refunded back. This path is to ensure that the funds do not get locked in the contract if the seller aborts.

This transaction (HTLC_TXN) is broadcast and is confirmed on the Bitcoin blockchain to a sufficient depth to be considered finalized. The seller then exchanges their goods and services for the preimage of the hash from the buyer. This exchange process is independent of the transaction itself. Each application that uses HTLC's has its own way of doing this exchange. For example, Atomic Swaps rely on another public blockchain to reveal the secret preimage. After the exchange is done, the seller will attempt to move the UTXO created in HTLC_TXN's payment path to an address that the seller controls with a simpler unencumbered transaction (SELLER_TXN) that uses the seller's signature and the preimage received from the buyer. If the exchange is not done, the buyer waits for the timelock to expire, and uses the REFUND_TXN to send the funds back to themselves.

1.2 Bribing Attack

The attack can begin after the HTLC_TXN is confirmed and the buyer already has the goods/services for which the buyer committed the funds for. If the buyer acts in good faith and does nothing, there is no attack. If the buyer acts in bad faith, the buyer will try to censor SELLER_TXN from being included in any future block. The buyer broadcasts the REFUND_TXN (which sends the funds back to the buyer) and chains it with a BRIBE_TXN, which sends the funds from the buyer to any miner who mines it by leaving the output field empty. Note that in the BRIBE_TXN, the buyer can send an ϵ amount to themselves. This makes the bribe not just a griefing attack (where the attacker does not profit), but marginally profitable. Also note that SELLER_TXN and the pair [REFUND_TXN, BRIBE_TXN] spend the same UTXO and are inherently incompatible. If one of them is confirmed on the blockchain, the other becomes invalid. In the rest of this paper, we will use BRIBE_TXN and the pair [REFUND_TXN, BRIBE_TXN] interchangeably. Pseudo-code for these transactions are in Appendix Λ.

Bitcoin's consensus rules govern what transactions can be included in a block by miners, but does not say anything about what transactions miners can or cannot ignore. It gives the benefit of the doubt to miners, allowing the possibility that miners have not seen a specific transaction because of network delays/failures. Miners could be (or not be) interested in a transaction because its fees are high (or low). In our attack scenario, miners see SELLER_TXN and BRIBE_TXN at the same time. But as per the consensus rules, miners cannot include BRIBE_TXN immediately because it is timelocked. But crucially, there is no obligation to include the SELLER_TXN immediately either. As blocks go by, BRIBE_TXN becomes valid and can be included in the blockchain and SELLER_TXN is censored, with the sale proceeds going to the miners and the buyer, but not to the seller. The seller could increase their fees to compete with the timelocked bribe, but that would come out of their own pocket, as they have already handed out the goods and services to the buyer.

In the following sections, we show how the two main applications of HTLC's: Lightning Payment Channels and Atomic Swaps, are both vulnerable to this bribing attack.

1.3 Payment Channels

Payment channels [10,11] are a promising solution to the scalability problem in cryptocurrencies like Bitcoin and Ethereum, which have low transaction throughputs. Lightning Network's [11] payment channels rely on HTLC's to enforce the revocation of older commitment transactions. In our attack scenario, Alice and Bob have a payment channel that they have updated over time using many commitment transactions. Both Alice and Bob keep their own copy of the commitment transaction, where their copy can be broadcast by them, and will lock their side of the channel balance with an HTLC and the counterparty's side with a regular payment. This means that in the case of a channel closure, the broadcaster has to wait for his payment, but the counterparty can withdraw funds immediately. Without loss of generality, we can assume that in one such update (u_1), the entire channel balance was in Bob's favor, and Alice has zero balance in her favor. In a subsequent update (u_2), Alice delivers some goods/services to Bob, and after u_2, the entire channel balance is in Alice's favor and Bob has zero balance on his side of the channel. As a part of the Lightning Protocol, during u_2's negotiation, Bob gives Alice the preimage (p_1) of a hash that lets her punish him if u_1 ever makes it to the blockchain.

The briber (in our case, Bob) broadcasts an outdated commitment transaction u_1 (called Revoked Commitment Transaction in Lightning). This has one output which is an HTLC. He then follows it up by broadcasting the bribing transaction: BRIBE_TXN. Note that the BRIBE_TXN is timelocked and should be invalid till the timelock expires. The victim (Alice in our case), sees u_1 on the blockchain, and using her knowledge of the revocation preimage, sends the corresponding SELLER_TXN (called Breach Remedy Transaction in Lightning) to the pool of transactions to be included in the blockchain, Note that SELLER_TXN should be valid immediately as it has no timelock on it. But if all miners wait for the BRIBE_TXN's timelock to expire, and during that time ignore the SELLER_TXN, the bribing attack is successful. The amount that goes from the BRIBE_TXN to the miner does not matter to Bob because he already has the equivalent goods/services from Alice for that value. Therefore, he is bribing with what he has already spent.

Lightning Network uses HTLC's to also implement payment hops from, say, Alice to Bob through Carol - where Alice and Bob do not have a direct payment channel between each other, but both have a channel to Carol. HTLC's are used here to ensure that Carol can use her channels to send funds from Alice to Bob without Carol's own funds being put at risk. Either the entire payment goes through from Alice to Bob through Carol (who gets the routing fees), or the entire payment is aborted, and all parties retain their own pre-payment balances. Using a series of messages [12], Alice, Bob, and Carol communicate using an off-chain protocol and negotiate a series of commitment transactions that each have an additional HTLC that sends the new payment from Alice to Bob through Carol. These HTLC's have a different payment specific secret preimage and its associated hash that locks the hashlock arm of the HTLC. They also have a lower timeout value (compared to the channel's timeout value) that refunds this particular payment back to the source in case any other node along the payment route aborts the payment. These hops do not affect the bribing attack model: an outdated commitment transaction can still be broadcast by the briber and the victim has to respond.

1.4 Atomic Swaps

Atomic Swaps are a way to exchange cryptocurrencies between two separate public blockchain systems (say, between Bitcoin and Litecoin) without involving a trusted third party [13,14]. TierNolan's classic Atomic Swap construction [15] relies on two HTLC_TXN's to get around the trusted third party. Alice and Bob have their own HTLC_TXN's in the blockchains whose assets they have. These HTLC_TXN's will enable corresponding SELLER_TXN's to the other party and REFUND_TXN's to themselves. Alice initiates her side of the swap by publishing an HTLC on her blockchain which has a timelock of $2 \cdot t$ and hash of a secret preimage that only she knows. Bob accepts the swap by publishing his own HTLC on his blockchain with a timelock of $1 \cdot t$ and the same hash whose preimage he *does not* know. Alice then redeems Bob's HTLC by revealing her secret through a SELLER_TXN on Bob's blockchain. Bob's knowledge of this secret (by monitoring Bob's public blockchain) enables Bob to publish his own SELLER_TXN on Alice's blockchain, thereby completing the swap.

In the atomic swap described above, Alice can try to censor Bob's SELLER_TXN with her own BRIBE_TXN on her blockchain that lets her keep assets on Bob's blockchain, and leave most of her bribing profits on her own blockchain to miners. This way, Alice only profits if her attack succeeds, and has no possibility of a loss. Ideally, this should not be possible because Bob's SELLER_TXN is valid from the moment he gets to know of Alice's secret preimage, and Alice's BRIBE_TXN is invalid at that time. But if all miners are made aware of Alice's BRIBE_TXN, the bribing attack might succeed.

2 Analysis

In this section, we analyze the parameters under which this bribing attack is successful. As Alice and Bob both have to agree on the HTLC for it to be valid, they can control these parameters to avoid the attack. The HTLC parameters are:

- T: denotes the number of blocks needed until the BRIBE_TXN becomes valid. This is the HTLC's timelock expressed in terms of number of blocks.
- f: fee offered by Alice to miners to confirm her SELLER_TXN.

– b: bribe offered by Bob to miners to confirm his BRIBE_TXN. Note that b is
  not explicitly called out in the transaction because all unclaimed outputs of
  a transaction go to the miner who confirms it. Typically, $b > f$.

There are parameters of the network that Alice and Bob do not control. These are
the percentages of the total hashpower that identifiable miners control. Uniden-
tifiable miners are grouped in a catch-all group. Miners are identified based on
their coinbase transaction indicators (see Sect. 3.1 for more details). Let there
be n miners M_j, $1 \le j \le n$, each with a fraction p_j of the total hashpower.

2.1 Assumptions

– Miners are rational and choose the most profitable strategy on what transactions to include in their blocks while conforming to the consensus rules of
  Bitcoin. Their goal is to maximize expected payoff, and not mine altruistically.
– Miners are also rational in the sense that they will not choose a dominated
  strategy when they can choose one that is not. A strategy s is dominated
  by strategy s' if the payoff for playing strategy s is strictly greater than the
  payoff for playing s', independent of other players' strategies.
– Miners do not create forks. If a transaction is included in a valid block, miners
  build the blockchain on top of that block.
– Relative hashpowers of miners is common knowledge. Currently, almost all
  Bitcoin blocks are mined by mining pools, and almost all of these blocks
  have an identifiable signature in the coinbase transaction that allows them to
  identify this relative share of hashpowers.
– Relative hashpowers of miners stay constant over the duration of the bribing
  attack.
– The attacker and the victim of the bribery attack have no hashpower of their
  own.
– Timelocks are expressed in number of blocks, and we are thus operating in a
  setting where block generation is equivalent to clock ticks.
– Block rewards and fees generated by transactions external to our setting are
  constant and have no bearing on the attack itself.
– All miners can see timelocked transactions that are valid in the future. Currently, the most popular Bitcoin implementation, Bitcoin Core, does not allow
  timelocked transactions that are "valid in the future" to enter its pool. Consequently, it does not forward such transactions through the peer to peer
  network. This is not a consensus rule, but rather an efficiency gain whereby
  allowing only valid transactions to enter the pool and propagate across the
  peer to peer network reduces network and memory load. We assume that
  SELLER_TXN and BRIBE_TXN are visible to all miners immediately after they
  are broadcast by their respective parties. Also, some mining pools run "transaction accelerator" services where they cooperate with other mining pools to
  get visibility to transactions that pay an extra fee (on top of the blockchain
  fee). We assume that malicious buyers have access to such services.

2.2 Setting

We analyze this attack by modeling the sequence of blocks being mined as a (Markov) game, called the *bribing game*. A bribing game has n miners, and runs in $T+1$ sequential stages. Stages represent periods between two mined blocks. In each stage, every miner has two possible actions: *follow* or *refuse* (corresponding to a miner excluding the SELLER_TXN from the miner's block template or not). After all miners play their action, a single miner is randomly selected as the leader of the stage. In other words, after all the miners have decided on their block template, a single miner wins the proof of work lottery and this miner's block extends the blockchain.

Let $B_1, B_2, \ldots, B_T$ be all the blocks that can include SELLER_TXN. Let B_{T+1} be the block that includes BRIBE_TXN. Note that BRIBE_TXN cannot be included in $B_1, B_2, \ldots, B_T$ as it's not valid then. Let $\mathcal{E}_{i,j}$ denote the event that miner j is selected as the leader of stage i. The events $\mathcal{E}_{i,j}$ are independent of each other and the actions taken by miners. $\mathcal{E}_{i,j}$ represents block B_i being mined by miner M_j. In addition, the *selection probability* of miner j for block i is given by:

$$\forall i, j \quad Pr(\mathcal{E}_{i,j}) = p_j,$$

which corresponds to the hashpower of miner M_j. Each stage is in either of two states: *active* or *inactive*. The game starts in an active stage (i.e., the first stage is active). Stage i, $i > 1$, becomes inactive if the leader of stage $i-1$ plays the action *refuse* (corresponds to including SELLER_TXN), or if stage $i-1$ is already inactive. Therefore, if one stage becomes inactive, all the following stages become inactive. This intuitively makes sense because once SELLER_TXN is confirmed, it stays confirmed in subsequent blocks and more importantly, BRIBE_TXN is invalid after that. The payoffs for each stage i are determined by whether $1 \le i \le T$ or if $i = T + 1$.

- $1 \le i \le T$: If the leader plays *refuse*, the payoff is $f > 0$. If the leader plays *follow*, the payoff is 0. Non-leaders' payoff is always 0.
- $i = T + 1$: Leader's payoff is $b > 0$. Non-Leaders' payoff is 0.

Let us call a miner M_j *strong* if $p_j \ge \frac{f}{b}$; otherwise we call M_j *weak*. Note that the bribing attack is successful if all miners follow the bribe (i.e., they always ignore SELLER_TXN). This corresponds to the strategy profile in which all miners play the action *follow* in all stages. Without loss of generality, there are two possible distributions of hashpowers among miners:

- All miners are strong; i.e., $p_j \ge \frac{f}{b}$ for $1 \le j \le n$.
- At least one miner is weak; i.e., $\exists p_j$ s.t. $p_j < \frac{f}{b}$ for $1 \le j \le n$.

In the next sections, we analyze both of these distributions.

2.3 All Miners Are Strong

Lemma 1. *If all miners are strong (i.e., $p_j \ge \frac{f}{b}$ for $1 \le j \le n$), then the strategy profile in which every miner plays* follow *in all stages is an equilibrium.*

Proof. Consider Miner j (M_j), and assume that all other miners follow the bribe in all stages. We show that following the bribe in all stages is the best response for M_j as well. If M_j follows the bribe in all stages, they will earn $p_j \cdot b$ in expectation. This is because, when all miners play *follow* in all stages, stage $T + 1$ will be active, and its leader, which is M_j with probability p_j, earns b.

If M_j plays *refuse* with non-zero probability in at least one stage. Let $x > 0$ be the probability that stage $T+1$ becomes inactive as the result of M_j's actions. In other words, x is the probability that M_j plays *refuse* in a Stage $1 \leq i \leq T$ in which they are selected as the leader. Note that other miners cannot make stage $T+1$ inactive as they always play *follow* and only M_j is including SELLER_TXN in their block template. The expected payoff of M_j is, therefore, $x \cdot f + (1-x) \cdot p_j \cdot b$, which is not more than $p_j \cdot b$, because $p_j \geq \frac{f}{b}$ and $x > 0$.

Note that when all miners are strong, the equilibrium shown in Lemma 1 (which favours bribery) exists no matter how large T is. As of this writing, the average fees for Bitcoin transactions since the beginning of 2019 is around 0.00003 BTC (author's own analysis of the Bitcoin blockchain). The average balance held by a lightning channel is 0.026 BTC [16]. If we use these values, we get the equilibrium stated in Lemma 1 exists if each miner has over 0.115% of the total hash power of the entire Bitcoin network. Due to the permissionless and anonymous nature of Bitcoin, however, we can never be sure that the weakest miner has a hash power above 0.115% of the total hash power. However, we can inspect the Bitcoin blockchain to guesstimate the distribution of hashpowers among known mining pools, and recommend channel parameters based on that. We treat this in more detail in Sect. 3. Next, we consider the case where at least one miner is weak. We show that, in this case, the value of T matters.

2.4   One Miner is Weak

Recall that when a stage becomes inactive, all its followup stages become inactive as well. Moreover, all miners receive zero payoff in an inactive stage, irrespective of what they play. Note that, for every miner (weak or strong), playing *follow* at state $T + 1$ is the strictly dominant strategy if stage $T + 1$ is active. This is because the expected payoff of a miner in an active stage $T + 1$ is $p_j b$ if they play *follow*, and $p_j f$ (which is smaller than $p_j b$) if they play *refuse*. In the next lemma, we show that in active stages other than stage $T + 1$, playing *refuse* is the strictly dominant strategy for weak miners.

Lemma 2. *In any active stage i, $1 \leq i \leq T$, playing* refuse *is the strictly dominant strategy for any weak miner.*

Proof. A miner earns b if stage $T + 1$ is active and this miner is selected as the leader of stage $T + 1$. Therefore, the probability that a Miner j (M_j) earns b is at most p_j. From the definition of weakness, for M_j, we have $p_j \cdot b < f$. So, if stage $T + 1$ is active, the weak miner gets an expected payoff less than f. Additionally, in stages $< T$, the probability that a miner earns f is strictly less than one, because, no matter how large T is, there is always a non-zero chance that the miner never gets selected as a leader. Therefore, across all stages up to and including stage $T+1$, the expected payoff of a weak miner is always strictly less than f.

Assume M_j is weak (i.e., $p_j < \frac{f}{b}$), and plays *follow* in an active stage i, $1 \leq i \leq T$. We now show that playing *refuse* in stage i will improve her payoff. Suppose M_j plays *refuse* instead of *follow* in the active stage i. If M_j is not selected as the leader of stage i, then the game remains the same as the case where M_j played *follow*. If M_j is selected as the leader, however, they will earn f. This is an improvement over the *expected payoff* of M_j from the previous paragraph, which is strictly less than f.

2.5   The Elimination of Dominated Strategies

By Lemma 2, playing *refuse* is the strictly dominant strategy for every weak miner; any other strategy is strictly dominated. Hence, we can simplify the analysis of the bribing game by eliminating strictly dominated strategies. Let us call a bribing game *safe* if after eliminating strictly dominated strategies, the only action left for each miner (strong or weak) in stage one is to play *refuse*. If every miner plays *refuse* in stage one, the game is effectively over as other stages become inactive immediately after, with SELLER_TXN confirmed and BRIBE_TXN becoming invalid.

Recollect that, if all the miners are strong, the bribing game is not safe no matter how large T is (Lemma 1). By the next theorem, however, the game is safe if there is at least one weak miner, and T is large enough.

Theorem 1. *Suppose there is at least one weak miner, and*

$$T > \frac{\log \frac{f}{b}}{\log(1 - p_w)} \tag{1}$$

where p_w is the sum of the selection probabilities of weak miners. Then, the bribing game is safe.

Proof. By Lemma 2, playing *refuse* is the strictly dominant strategy for every weak miner in each stage i, $1 \leq i \leq T$. By eliminating the dominated strategies of weak miners, we get a smaller game in which weak miners play *refuse* in every stage i, $1 \leq i \leq T$.

Consider a strong miner M, who plays *follow* in stage 1. Their reward for playing *follow* is only possible at stage $T+1$. Let α be the probability that stage $T+1$ will be active. Since weak miners only play *refuse* in the first T stages, we get

$$\alpha \leq (1 - p_w)^T$$

$$\leq (1 - p_w)^{\frac{\log \frac{f}{b}}{\log(1 - p_w)}}$$

$$\leq \frac{f}{b(1 - p_w)}$$

where $(1 - p_w)^T$ is the probability that no weak miner is selected as a leader in the first T stages. Thus, the expected payoff of M at stage $T + 1$ is less than

$$\frac{f}{b(1 - p_w)} \cdot (1 - p_w).b = f$$

where $\frac{f}{b(1-p_w)}$ is an upper bound on the probability that stage $T + 1$ is active, and $(1-p_w)$ is an upper bound on the probability that M is selected as the leader of stage $T + 1$. Note that the probability that M earns f prior to stage $T + 1$ is strictly less than one. Therefore, at the beginning of stage 1, the expected payoff of M is strictly less than f. Now, if M plays *refuse* (instead of *follow*) in the first stage, we will have two possibilities. First possibility is that M is selected as the leader of stage 1, in which case M earns f, which is strictly more than its expected payoff. In the second possibility where M is not selected as the leader of stage 1, the game remains identical to the original case where M plays *follow*. This implies that M is better off playing *refuse* in the first stage, which concludes the proof. We remark that this result does not imply that M is better off playing *refuse* in every stage. In fact, as the game proceeds to new stages, the expected payoff of M can change, and M may choose to play *follow*.

2.6   The Elimination of Dominated Strategies of Strong Miners

A bribing game with parameters f and b may be safe for a significantly smaller T than what is given in Theorem 1. In its proof, we eliminated only strictly dominated strategies of weak miners. In principle, we can continue the process by eliminating strictly dominated strategies of strong miners as well. To do so, we can first sort the strong miners according to their selection probabilities. Starting with the strong miner with the smallest selection probability, and an upper bound of T from Theorem 1, we can calculate the minimum number of initial stages in which the miner is strictly better off playing *refuse*. We then eliminate the strictly dominated strategies of that miner, and move to the next strong miner. At the end of this iterated elimination process, if all miners play *refuse* in the first stage, then the game is proven to be safe. As we iterate from time period 0 to time period T, the value of t where all miners play refuse for the *last* time shows us that if we had begun the game at this point, the game would have been safe in the first stage itself. This new starting point of the game results in the new ending point being at $T_{new} = T_{old} - t$. In this new setting, the game is safe in the first stage. The actual algorithm to find t and an accompanying worked example are presented in Appendix B. T_{new} is lower than T, and now, with just one weak miner, and elimination of dominated strategies of all miners, the game is safe for lower values of T. This lower value of T makes the usage of HTLC's more practical and convenient.

3   Solutions

In the introduction, we pointed out that the two main applications of HTLC's: Lightning Channels and Atomic Swaps, are both vulnerable to this bribing attack. In this section, we first analyze the Bitcoin blockchain to get an estimate of the hashpower share of known mining pools. This lets us find parameters that can harden the HTLC constructions in each of these applications such that they are not vulnerable to the bribing attack. In the case of Atomic Swaps, to use these parameters, we propose a modification to the classic atomic swap protocol.

3.1 Mining Pools and Their Hashpower Shares

We try to find the weakest known miners in the Bitcoin ecosystem by analyzing the miners of the 16000 blocks from Block #625000. We know the coinbase transaction indicators of larger mining pools. Using these, we can attribute mined blocks to known mining pools. Looking at these blocks, we can estimate each of these mining pools' share of the total hashpower based on how many blocks they have mined. Mining pools and their hashpower shares are shown in Table 1. We see that the weakest known pools are under 1% of the total hashpower, and this leads to our proposed fixes for both Lightning Channels and Atomic Swaps.

Table 1. Hashpower of 16000 blocks from block #625000

Mining pool	Hashpower	Mining pool	Hashpower
F2Pool	15.7937%	BTCTOP	2.6313%
PoolIn	15.5563%	NovaBlock	0.9500%
BTC.com	12.2688%	SpiderPool	0.6125%
AntPool	12.1625%	Bitcoin.com	0.1938%
Huobi	6.5875%	UkrPool	0.0938%
58COIN	6.3000%	SigmaPool	0.0750%
ViaBTC	5.7875%	OkKong	0.0688%
OKEX	5.6437%	NCKPool	0.0625%
Unknown	4.0687%	MiningCity	0.0500%
SlushPool	3.8188%	KanoPool	0.0250%
Lubian.com	3.6938%	MiningDutch	0.0187%
Binance	3.5375%		

3.2 Lightning

In the Lightning Network specifications (specifically, from Bolt 2 [17]), we have the following parameters:

- *channel_reserve_satoshis*: Each side of a channel maintains this reserve so it always has something to lose if it were to try to broadcast an old, revoked commitment transaction. Currently, this is recommended to be 1% of the total value of the channel. This is the amount that the cheated party can utilize as extra fees without dipping into their own side of the channel.

- *to_self_delay*: This is the number of blocks that the counterparty's self outputs must be delayed in case a channel closes unilaterally from the counterparty's side. In one popular Lightning client: c-lightning [18], this is set by default to 144 blocks (approximately 1 day). In another popular Lightning client: LND [19], it is scaled in a range from 1 day to 14 day based on the channel value.

We do not find any documented reasons on why these important parameters are set the way they are. Based on the analysis from Sects. 2.4 and 2.5, and the distribution of hashpowers, we can formulate what these values ought to be. First, we note that *channel_reserve_satoshis* on the victim's side of this bribing attack can be used by the victim to increase their fees to thwart the attack. We posit that *channel_reserve_satoshis* being at 1% is reasonable, given that there are many known miners whose hashpower is less than 1% of the total hashpower of all miners. If it were lower than, say, 0.03%, as per Sect. 2.3, the channel would be always vulnerable to this bribing attack.

We then set $\frac{f}{b}$ to be 0.01, and calculate the total *weak* hashpower to be 0.0215 (from Table 1). Based on Theorem 1, we get $T > 212$ blocks. This is larger than the suggested default of *to_self_delay* at 144 blocks. So, if the channel operator is paranoid, they can set *to_self_delay* to this higher value of 212. We can plug in the hashpowers from Table 1 into Algorithm 1, with $f = 1$ and $b = 100$ and we get a value of $T = 54$ blocks. If the channel operator is *#reckless* and believes that miners eliminate strictly dominated strategies of other miners (a stronger assumption than just assuming that weak miners exist), they can open channels with this much lower timelock value. Note that these values do not actually impact the usage of the Lightning Network, but are merely security parameters that ensure that both parties are adequately protected in case the other party decides to bribe miners.

3.3   Atomic Swaps

Atomic Swaps that have Bitcoin on one side need to take Bitcoin's block time of 10 min into account. Even if the other blockchain in question (say Litecoin) has faster block generation, till Bitcoin's transactions are not confirmed, the atomic swap in question cannot be considered executed. Commercial platforms like Komodo [20] use 15,600 s (26 blocks) as the HTLC's timelock value when they setup swaps between Bitcoin-like currencies or ERC-20 style tokens. Other works [14,21,22] have suggested that a timelock period of 1 day (144 blocks) is a good default.

Based on Theorem 1, we get $\frac{f}{b} = 0.68$ at $T = 26$ blocks and $\frac{f}{b} = 0.122$ at $T = 144$ blocks. A fee to bribe ratio of 0.68 (for $T = 26$ blocks) is quite high. This suggests that $T = 26$ blocks does not provide enough security for reasonable values of fee to bribe ratios. At 144 blocks, we have a reasonable fee to bribe ratio of 0.122.

Unlike Lightning channel's *channel_reserve_satoshis*, due to its inherently asymmetric nature, there is no simple way to encode this extra fee in the atomic swap itself. Alice has to convince Bob upfront that she will not attempt the bribing attack when it is Bob's turn to redeem his side of the swap. One way of achieving this is for Bob to offer a lower value than what Alice wants. This way, if Alice attempts the bribery attack, Bob can increase his SELLER_TXN fees to the amount dictated by Theorem 1 or Algorithm 1. But if Alice does not attempt to bribe, this atomic swap setup is unfair to her as she is getting a lower value from Bob than what she is offering to Bob.

To solve this, we present an extension to the classic Atomic Swap protocol that allows a way for Alice to include extra fees in the swap for Bob to use to "counter-bribe" *only* if Alice attempts to bribe.

Risk Free Atomic Swap: Here, as with the classic protocol, Alice creates a (random) secret preimage and hashes it to get her "locking string". Alice creates a transaction that commits her swap amount such that Bob can claim this amount only if he knows the preimage. The "refund" part of this transaction, instead of sending the amount back to Alice after a timelock, sends it to a multisig controlled by both Alice and Bob. Alice also creates a second transaction that uses this multisig controlled output as its first input, and another unrelated input from Alice which adds the extra fees required to make the swap risk-free. The total output of this second transaction is sent to Bob *only* if he has the secret preimage, or to Alice after a timelock. This pair of transactions is created by Alice; the second transaction is pre-signed by Bob and needs to be held by Alice before she broadcasts the first transaction. These transactions, and the accompanying flowchart are listed in detail in Appendix C. Based on whether Alice or Bob abort the swap, or Alice bribes miners, or Alice and Bob complete a normal swap, a combination of these transactions will be broadcast on the both blockchains by Alice and/or Bob as depicted by the flow chart.

4 Related Work

There are two major strands of censorship attacks in blockchains. Ignore attacks (that incentivize miners to ignore certain transactions) and fork attacks (that incentivize miners to orphan blocks with certain transactions by forking the blockchain).

4.1 Ignore Attacks

Ignore Attacks are presented in [23,24], and [25]. In [23], smart contracts in a "funding blockchain" are used to censor transactions in a "target blockchain". Funding blockchains need to support powerful smart contract primitives to be able to program these attacks – typically Ethereum is used. Two such attack smart contracts presented in [23] are Pay-per-Miner and Pay-per-Block. In Pay-per-Miner, every miner gets a bribe at the end of the bribing period if the bribing attack succeeds, even if the miner followed the bribe or not. A weak miner could refuse the bribe, and attempt to mine with the SELLER_TXN, but not succeed in mining a block. This miner would still be eligible for the bribe at the end. This contract does not consider a weak miner's lower probability of mining the final block with the bribe and hence, overpays. In Pay-Per-Block, every miner is paid incrementally per block during the bribing period. This attack also bribes weak miners who go against the bribe, and thus have a higher expected reward at the end of the bribing period. Both these attacks would get better if miners could cryptographically prove to the smart contract that they are following the bribe.

Concurrent to our work, a similar timelocked bribing attack is presented in [25]. They consider the situation where all miners are strong (i.e., $p_j \geq \frac{f}{b}$ for all miners $1 \leq j \leq n$), and like us, they conclude that the bribing attack will be successful and is independent of the bribing period T. To alleviate this situation where all miners are strong and bribing attacks could happen, they propose a modified construction of the HTLC called MAD-HTLC (Mutually Assured Destruction HTLC). MAD-HTLC adds a second transaction chained to the HTLC with a collateral from the bribing counterparty to ensure that they have something to lose if they attempt to bribe. However, [25] does not consider weak miners, or elimination of dominated strategies - which we show lead to HTLC parameters that can be adjusted to safeguard against this bribing attack with any distribution of miner hashpowers and values of f and b. Our approach also doesn't need a modification to the HTLC construction and the associated collateral and extra transaction costs.

Transaction Pinning [26] tries to make a transaction inherently unprofitable to mine, independent of any future bribe. The attacker, who can validly spend one of the target transaction's outputs broadcasts multiple low fee-rate transactions that spends their path of the target transaction. This makes the entire transaction package unprofitable to mine, thereby censoring the first transaction, which the victim can spend through another path. To remedy this, the victim can use CPFP carve-outs [27] to bump up the fee-rate of the censored transaction and still get it confirmed by a miner. To enable this, Lightning Channels will allow "anchor outputs" [28] to let either party bump up their fees without being blocked by the counterparty.

These types of Ignore Attacks rely on being able to setup and communicate incentives (in the present, or in the future) to miners such that the most profitable strategy for each miner is to wait for the incentive. Whether these incentives succeed or not, depends on the current value available to miners, the future value promised to miners, and the ability of miners to be able to extract these values. Unlike previous research, our work takes into account *all* these parameters.

4.2   Fork Attacks

Fork Attacks go back a long way, with the earliest one discussed on bitcointalk.org being *feather forking* [2]. In this attack, a miner wants to censor a specific transaction and announces on some public bulletin board that they will not add blocks on top of any block that contains this specific transaction. If this miner has a reasonable chance of getting a block, other rational miners will follow them instead of mining "normally" and hence forgo the fees of the censored transaction. Feather forking is also analyzed under the Pay-per-Commit contract in [23]. Feather forking relies on a miner committing to the attack, and this being common knowledge among all miners. This attack relies on both a funding cryptocurrency blockchain to set up the attack and a way to communicate with all miners that the attack is going to happen.

Miners can be also incentivized to fork the Bitcoin blockchain with "Whale Transactions" [3]. Here, the attacker waits for a target transaction to be confirmed to a sufficient depth to get the corresponding goods and services from their victim. After that, the attacker tries to fork the blockchain by successively broadcasting transactions that have high fees (whale transactions) and also reverse the target transaction. These whale transactions are then included in blocks of the blockchain fork that rational miners might follow. The authors evaluate the relationship between confirmation depth, the attacker's secret mining lead, the attacker's hashpower, the whale transaction fees and whether these attacks are profitable. External smart contracts on platforms like Ethereum can be used [4,24] to incentivize Bitcoin miners to abandon the honest blockchain suffix and mine on top of a briber's fork. In [24], the attacker chooses the set of transactions to be mined for each block, and hands it out to miners through the smart contract. This is similar to how mining pools operate. Miners get rewarded in the "funding cryptocurrency" (Ether, in this case). Incentivizing every Bitcoin miner with Ether given the relative size of the two systems seems far fetched to us.

Fork Attacks rely on attackers being able to incentivize rational miners to orphan a reasonable length suffix of the blockchain. The attack succeeds if it is conducted after the primary transaction has been thought confirmed by the victim. Given that most proof-of-work cryptocurrencies have a probabilistic notion of finality, these attacks are feasible. On the other hand, Bitcoin has seen fewer and fewer orphan blocks over time [29], and the possibility of this kind of attack is considerably lower now than they were in, say, 2015.

5   Conclusion

In this work, we observe that HTLC's are vulnerable to an "in-band" bribing attack where the HTLC initiator (buyer, in our case) can receive goods and services offline and then prevent the seller from getting their due share by bribing miners. This bribe can only work if the "time value" of waiting for the bribe is worthwhile for all miners. A rather self-evident observation is that when the timelock on the bribe expires and the bribe transaction is still valid, it will be claimed in the immediate next block as the fee on it is considerably higher than normal transaction fees. Additionally, stronger miners are likely to mine any specific block - and therefore more likely to mine the block in which the bribe is valid and available. Therefore, we posit that weaker miners will ignore the bribe altogether and will attempt to mine the seller's transaction while the timelock holds and the fee on the seller's transaction is good enough. This leads us to the relationship between the fee to bribe ratio and the distribution of miners' hashpowers. Based on this analysis, we propose Lightning Channel parameters that make them resistant to this kind of bribing attack. In Atomic Swaps, our analysis also proposes a fee for the victim to safeguard themselves. To enable that, we propose a modification to the classic Atomic Swap protocol that can bring in this fee into the swap and still keep it fair for both parties.

Appendix A   Transactions in Pseudo Bitcoin Script

HTLC Transaction:

```
HTLC_TXN: { txid: HTLC_TXN_TXID
  vin: [{ txid: SOURCE_TXN_ID that pays the buyer.
    scriptSig: <buyer's sig for SOURCE_TXN_ID> }]
  vout: [{ value: <value>
    scriptPubKey: IF
                    OP_HASH160 <digest> OP_EQUALVERIFY
                    <seller_pubkey_1>
                  OP_ELSE
                    <delay> OP_CSV OP_DROP <buyer_pubkey_1>
                  OP_ENDIF OP_CHECKSIG }]
}
```

Seller Transaction, spending from the hashlocked path:

```
SELLER_TXN: { txid: SELLER_TXN_TXID
  vin: [{ txid: HTLC_TXN_TXID
    scriptSig: <seller_sig_1> <preimage> OP_TRUE }]
  vout: [{ value: <value>
    scriptPubKey: <seller_pubkey_2> OP_CHECKSIG }]
}
```

Refund Transaction, spending from the timelocked path: REFUND_TXN:

```
REFUND_TXN: { txid: REFUND_TXN_TXID
  vin: [{ txid: HTLC_TXN_TXID
    scriptSig: <buyer_sig_1> OP_FALSE
    sequence: <delay> }]
  vout: [{ scriptPubKey: <buyer_pubkey_2> OP_CHECKSIG }]
}
```

Bribe Transaction, which leaves the output values to miners: BRIBE_TXN:

```
BRIBE_TXN: { txid: BRIBE_TXN_TXID
  vin: [{ txid: REFUND_TXN_TXID
    scriptSig: <buyer_sig_2> }]
  vout: [{ // Empty output. Entire amount goes to the miner }]
}
```

Appendix B   Iterated Removal of Dominated Strategies

The FIND_T procedure receives as input a list of mining hashpowers (leader selection probabilities), and the values of parameters f and b. As output, it returns the lowest value of T such that all miners refuse the bribe in the first stage of the game. It uses the inner procedure CALCULATE_BRIBERY_MATRIX to determine the behavior of more strong miners at each block when less strong miners' strategies get dominated (Fig. 1).

Example (Table 2): Let's take the case of 4 miners with hashpower shares $\mathbb{P} = [0.1, 0.2, 0.3, 0.4]$, $f = 11, b = 100$. Applying Theorem 1, we get an upper bound of T to be 21. Running the procedure CALCULATE_BRIBERY_MATRIX returns the matrix shown in Table 2, with "1" standing for *refuse* and "0" standing for

---

```
 1: procedure CALCULATE_BRIBERY_MATRIX(P, f, b, T)
 2:     B ← [][]   ▷ Bribery Matrix where B[j][i] represents whether miner_j follows the
        bribe at block_i
 3:     for j ← 0 to length(P) do
 4:         if P[j] < f/b then
 5:             B[j] ← [1, 1, ...1]
                        ⎵⎵⎵⎵⎵
                          T
 6:         else
 7:             B[j] ← [0, 0, ...0]
                        ⎵⎵⎵⎵⎵
                          T
 8:             for t_x ← 1 to T do
 9:                 P_h ← 1
10:                 for t_y ← 1 to t_x do
11:                     sum ← 0
12:                     for k ← 0 to j do
13:                         sum ← sum + B[k][t_y] · P[k]
14:                     P_h ← P_h * (1 − sum)
15:                 expected_bribe = P_h * P[j] * b
16:                 if f > expected_bribe then
17:                     B[j][t_x] = 1
18:     return B

19: procedure FIND_T(P, f, b)                          ▷ P is the array of miners' hashpowers
20:     assert(at least 1 value in P > f/b)
21:     P = sorted(P)                                                       ▷ Ascending
22:     T = ⌈ log f/b / log(1−p_w) ⌉                                   ▷ From Theorem 1
23:     B = CALCULATE_BRIBERY_MATRIX(P, f, b, T)
24:     for i ← 1 to T do
25:         for j ← 0 to length(P) do
26:             if B[j][i] == 0 then
27:                 return T − (i − 1)
28:     return T
```

Fig. 1. Iterated removal of dominated strategies

follow. Note that this matrix shows the conservative scenario of T = 21 blocks (as given by Theorem 1. The aim of this algorithm is to find a more aggressive (lower) value of T which we get if we eliminate dominated strategies of strong miners. We now go through the actions of each miner.

Table 2. Bribery matrix, worked example

Blocks	0.1	0.2	0.3	0.4
Block #1	1	1	1	1
Block #2	1	1	1	1
Block #3	1	1	1	1
Block #4	1	1	1	1
Block #5	1	1	1	1
Block #6	1	1	1	1
Block #7	1	1	1	1
Block #8	1	1	1	1
Block #9	1	1	1	1
Block #10	1	1	1	1
Block #11	1	1	1	1
Block #12	1	1	1	1
Block #13	1	1	1	1
Block #14	1	1	1	1
Block #15	1	1	1	1
Block #16	1	1	0	0
Block #17	1	0	0	0
Block #18	1	0	0	0
Block #19	1	0	0	0
Block #20	1	0	0	0
Block #21	1	0	0	0

The miner with hashpower 0.1 (p_0) will play *refuse* at every block because we have $T > \frac{\log \frac{f}{b}}{\log(1-p_w)}$. The miner with hashpower 0.2 (p_1) will play *refuse* as long as the expected bribe (payable at $T+1$) calculated at a particular block is lower than the fees that they would earn if they mine that block. In this case, $(1-p_w)^t \cdot p_1 \cdot b < f$ till $t = 6$ for values of $f = 11, b = 100, p_w = 0.1$. This means that p_1 will start playing *follow* as we get closer to $t = T$ (specifically when we are 5 blocks away from T). The miner with hashpower 0.3 (p_3) will play *refuse* along similar lines, by looking at the actions of miners p_0 and p_1 over the different blocks. One thing to notice is that at block #16, p_2 will act assuming that p_0 and p_1 will both play *refuse*. At block #17, p_2 will act assuming that

p_0 will play *refuse* and p_1 will play *follow*. This is implemented in the algorithm by using the 0's and 1's in the bribery matrix and using them as factors in line #13 of the CALCULATE_BRIBERY_MATRIX procedure. This way, on line #13, we only use miners who play *refuse* at each block to calculate the expected bribe.

In the main procedure FIND_T, we then find the last block in which all miners play *refuse* and return that as the result. In the real world, we can give a 5–6 block cushion on top of this, and it will still be significantly lower than the upper bound of T.

Appendix C   Risk Free Atomic Swaps

Please check the IACR Eprint version of this paper for pseudo-code transactions and flow chart of the risk free atomic swap.

References

1. Bonneau, J., Miller, A., Clark, J., Narayanan, A., Kroll, J.A., Felten, E.W.: SOK: research perspectives and challenges for bitcoin and cryptocurrencies. In: 2015 IEEE Symposium on Security and Privacy, pp. 104–121. IEEE (2015)
2. Miller, A.: Feather-forks: enforcing a blacklist with sub-50% hash power. https://bitcointalk.org/index.php?topic=312668.0. Accessed 7 May 2020
3. Liao, K., Katz, J.: Incentivizing Blockchain Forks via Whale Transactions. In: Brenner, M., Rohloff, K., Bonneau, J., Miller, A., Ryan, P.Y.A., Teague, V., Bracciali, A., Sala, M., Pintore, F., Jakobsson, M. (eds.) FC 2017. LNCS, vol. 10323, pp. 264–279. Springer, Cham (2017). https://doi.org/10.1007/978-3-319-70278-0_17
4. McCorry, P., Hicks, A., Meiklejohn, S.: Smart Contracts for Bribing Miners. Cryptology ePrint Archive, Report 2018/581. https://eprint.iacr.org/2018/581
5. Nakamoto, S.: bitcoin core source code, version 0.1.0. https://bitcointalk.org/index.php?topic=68121.0. Accessed 7 May 2020
6. Friedenbach, M., BtcDrak, Dorier, N., kinoshitajona: BIP68: Relative lock-time using consensus-enforced sequence numbers. https://github.com/bitcoin/bips/blob/master/bip-0068.mediawiki. Accessed 7 May 2020
7. Todd, P.: BIP68: CHECKLOCKTIMEVERIFY. https://github.com/bitcoin/bips/blob/master/bip-0065.mediawiki. Accessed 7 May 2020
8. BtcDrak, Friedenbach, M., Lombrozo, E.: BIP112. Checksequenceverify. https://github.com/bitcoin/bips/blob/master/bip-0112.mediawiki. Accessed 7 May 2020
9. Daian, P., et al.: Flash boys 2.0: frontrunning in decentralized exchanges, miner extractable value, and consensus instability. In: 2020 IEEE Symposium on Security and Privacy (SP), pp. 910–927. IEEE (2020)
10. Decker, C., Wattenhofer, R.: A Fast and Scalable Payment Network with Bitcoin Duplex Micropayment Channels. In: Pelc, A., Schwarzmann, A.A. (eds.) SSS 2015. LNCS, vol. 9212, pp. 3–18. Springer, Cham (2015). https://doi.org/10.1007/978-3-319-21741-3_1
11. Poon, J., Dryja, T.: The Bitcoin Lightning Network: Scalable Off-Chain Instant Payments (2016)
12. BOLT Authors: Lightning Network Specifications, Bolt 3. https://github.com/lightningnetwork/lightning-rfc/blob/master/03-transactions.md. Accessed 7 May 2020

13. Herlihy, M.: Atomic cross-chain swaps. In: Proceedings of the 2018 ACM Symposium on Principles of Distributed Computing, pp. 245–254. ACM (2018)

14. Han, R., Lin, H., Yu, J.: On the optionality and fairness of atomic swaps. In: Proceedings of the 1st ACM Conference on Advances in Financial Technologies, pp. 62–75. AFT 2019, Association for Computing Machinery (2019). doi: 10.1145/3318041.3355460

15. Atomic Swaps: https://bitcointalk.org/index.php?topic=193281.msg2224949 Accessed 7 May 2020

16. 1ML: https://1ml.com/. Accessed 7 May 2020

17. BOLT Authors: Lightning Network Specifications, Bolt 2. https://github.com/lightningnetwork/lightning-rfc/blob/master/02-peer-protocol.md. Accessed 7 May 2020

18. C-Lightning Authors: c-lightning - a Lightning Network implementation in C. https://github.com/ElementsProject/lightning. Accessed 7 May 2020

19. LND Authors: LND: The Lightning Network Daemon. https://github.com/lightningnetwork/lnd. Accessed 7 May 2020

20. Atomic Swaps Explained: The Ultimate Beginner's Guide. https://komodoplatform.com/atomic-swaps/. Accessed 7 May 2020

21. BitMEX Research: Atomic Swaps and Distributed Exchanges: The Inadvertent Call Option. https://blog.bitmex.com/atomic-swaps-and-distributed-exchanges-the-inadvertent-call-option/. Accessed 7 May 2020

22. Robinson, D.: HTLCs Considered Harmful. https://cyber.stanford.edu/sites/g/files/sbiybj9936/f/htlcs_considered_harmful.pdf. Accessed 7 May 2020

23. Winzer, F., Herd, B., Faust, S.: Temporary censorship attacks in the presence of rational miners. In: IEEE Security & Privacy on the Blockchain (IEEE S & B) (2019). https://eprint.iacr.org/2019/748

24. Judmayer, A., et al.: Pay-To-Win: Incentive Attacks on Proof-of-Work Cryptocurrencies. Cryptology ePrint Archive, Report 2019/775. https://eprint.iacr.org/2019/775

25. Tsabary, I., Yechieli, M., Eyal, I.: MAD-HTLC: Because HTLC is Crazy-Cheap to Attack (2020)

26. Transaction Pinning. https://bitcoinops.org/en/topics/transaction-pinning/. Accessed 7 May 2020

27. CPFP Carve-out. https://bitcoinops.org/en/topics/cpfp-carve-out/. Accessed 7 May 2020

28. Anchor Outputs. https://github.com/lightningnetwork/lightning-rfc/pull/688. Accessed 7 May 2020

29. An orphan block on the bitcoin (btc) blockchain. https://en.cryptonomist.ch/2019/05/28/orphan-block-bitcoin-btc-blockchain/. Accessed 7 May 2020

Shielded Computations in Smart Contracts Overcoming Forks

Vincenzo Botta[1], Daniele Friolo[1]([⊠]), Daniele Venturi[2], and Ivan Visconti[1]

[1] DIEM, University of Salerno, Fisciano, Italy
friolo@di.uniroma1.it
[2] Department of Computer Science, Sapienza University of Rome, Rome, Italy

Abstract. In this work, we consider executions of smart contracts for implementing secure multi-party computation (MPC) protocols on forking blockchains (e.g., Ethereum), and we study security and delay issues due to forks. In this setting, the classical double-spending problem tells us that messages of the MPC protocol should be confirmed on-chain before playing the next ones, thus slowing down the entire execution.

Our contributions are twofold:
- For the concrete case of fairly tossing multiple coins with penalties, we notice that the lottery protocol of Andrychowicz et al. (S&P '14) becomes insecure if players do not wait for the confirmations of several transactions. In addition, we present a smart contract that instead retains security even when all honest players immediately answer to transactions appearing on-chain. We analyze the performance using Ethereum as testbed.
- We design a compiler that takes any "digital and universally composable" MPC protocol (with or without honest majority), and transforms it into another one (for the same task and same setup) which maintains security even if all messages are played on-chain without delays. The special requirements on the starting protocol mean that messages consist only of bits (e.g., no hardware token is sent) and security holds also in the presence of other protocols. We further show that our compiler satisfies fairness with penalties as long as honest players only wait for confirmations once.

By reducing the number of confirmations, our protocols can be significantly faster than natural constructions.

Keywords: MPC · Blockchain · Finality · Forks · Smart contracts

1 Introduction

The rise of blockchains[1] is progressively changing the way transactions are executed over the Internet. Indeed, the traditional client-server paradigm turns out

---

[1] We use the terms "blockchain" and "distributed ledger" interchangeably.

D. Friolo—Part of the work done during his PhD at Department of Computer Science, Sapienza University of Rome, Italy.

N. Borisov and C. Diaz (Eds.): FC 2021, LNCS 12674, pp. 73–92, 2021.
https://doi.org/10.1007/978-3-662-64322-8_4

to be insufficient when many parties want to perform a distributed computation, especially in cases where features like public verifiability and automatic punishment are desired. Blockchains through the execution of smart contracts naturally allow many players to perform a joint computation, even when they are not simultaneously online; moreover, they allow to publicly check the actions of all players[2] and enforce a proper behavior through financial punishments.

Forks, Finality and Double Spending. Typical blockchains experience some delays before a transaction can be considered confirmed. Indeed, a large part of the most used blockchains consists of a list of blocks that can temporary fork. In such cases, fork-resolution mechanisms decide which branch is eventually part of the list of blocks and which one is discarded, at the price of cutting off some transactions that for some time have appeared on the blockchain. These finality limitations generate delays and uncertainty, and a significant effort has been made recently to design blockchains with better finality [8,9,12,15,26,27].

It is well known that the existence of transactions that appear and then disappear from a blockchain is the source of the (in)famous double-spending attack. The solution to the double spending problem is pretty harsh: the receiver of a payment will have to wait long time (i.e., until the transaction is confirmed and becomes irreversible) before taking future actions. Obviously, this can be problematic when an entire process consists of many sequential transactions and the confirmation time is long.

The double spending problem does not seem to extend to the case where another on-chain transaction is connected to the payment transaction. Indeed, in this case, if as a consequence of a fork the payment transaction disappears, then the connected transaction disappears too. This chaining of transactions related to the same process can be easily implemented through smart contracts.

Insecurity of Smart Contracts with hasty Players. Since transactions are not immediately confirmed in a forking blockchain, the full execution of a smart contract with multiple sequential transactions might take too long. It would thus be natural to speed up the execution of smart contracts by playing messages immediately. Indeed, as mentioned above, by appropriately chaining the transactions of a smart contract, attacks exploiting the cancellation of a transaction like in the double-spending attack are not effective,[3] and therefore playing immediately without waiting confirmations could be a valid option.

However, we notice that forks can help an adversary to mount more subtle attacks. For example, let us consider a smart contract executed by two players, Alice and Bob, willing to establish jointly a random string: 1) Alice starts the protocol by sending to the smart contract a commitment to a random string r_1; 2) Bob sends a random string r_2 to the smart contract; 3) Alice then opens the commitment, and if the opening is valid the common string is defined to be

---

[2] We will often use the two terms "party" and "player" as synonyms.

[3] Since we are considering protocols running entirely on-chain, double spending attacks can not be exploited to avoid the payment of some off-chain service.

$r = r_1 \oplus r_2$. For concreteness, say that Alice is honest and Bob is corrupted, and assume that a fork happens after Alice already sent the commitment. If Bob runs the protocol honestly on the first branch, he gets to see Alice's opening, and thus he can completely bias the output on the other branch by just sending $r'_2 = r' \oplus r_1$ to the smart contract, for any value r' of his choice. The above scenario can be a serious threat for integrity of data and even confidentiality in other protocols. This motivating example clearly shows that, unless one has proven some kind of resilience to forks, it is certainly preferable to always wait that transactions are confirmed, at the price of having very slow executions of a smart contract. Such slowness could be unacceptable in some applications.

Why MPC on Blockchains? Blockchains offer public verifiability of distributed computations, in the sense that in case of dispute everyone can verify what happened and when. Moreover, smart contracts can automatically punish whoever violates some a-priori established rules. Clearly, the above advantages are useful also when players are running a privacy-preserving computation, in the form of a multi-party computation (MPC) protocol.

A popular example of MPC that can benefit from a blockchain is e-voting, since public verifiability is an important property of remote elections and several systems rely on a bulletin board that can be instantiated with a blockchain. Another well known example is the one illustrated by Andrychowicz et al. [1,2] who, despite the very limited expressive power of Bitcoin transactions, have shown how to use blockchains to obtain fairness through penalties to MPC protocols with dishonest majority, somehow circumventing the impossibility result of Cleve [11] (that holds without assuming setup).

Note that executing an MPC protocol on-chain allows players not to be online all at the same time. Moreover, differently from protocols running on a TCP/IP WAN where players must know each other's IP address beforehand[4], with the aid of a ledger any player can join a protocol execution by just reading[5] a transaction containing the required information (e.g., the functionality, minimum number of parties, or any other identifying information).

The above features, and the dilemma about playing immediately risking security or waiting for confirmation making the entire process very slow, motivate our work aiming at obtaining smart contracts for fast/fair/secure/publicly-verifiable MPC protocols on forking blockchains.

We remark that at least some of the aforementioned advantages provided by our constructions do not come already from the use of payment channels. Consider for instance payment channels allowing to run a computation in large part off-chain. The use of similar channels for MPC would require players to be simultaneously online with point-to-point connections, therefore suffering of the issues discussed above.

---

[4] We remark that executing a protocol on a payment channel does not offer any advantage in terms of anonymity with respect to an off-chain execution.

[5] Blockchain identifiers are usually public pseudonyms not necessarily correlated with the real user identities. This feature offers some privacy compared to IP addresses.

1.1 Our Contributions

Fair Lottery with Penalties and Fully Hasty Players. In Andrychowicz et al. [1,2] and in Kumaresan et al. [6,20] it was shown how to obtain fairness (i.e., the adversary should be discouraged from avoiding that honest players learn the output after he gets it) through penalties. The idea is that a player should deposit some coins of the underlying cryptocurrency and the smart contract should return the coins back only in case the player completes correctly the execution of the protocol defined by the smart contract.

In light of the negative result by Cleve [11] on achieving fairness without honest majority, we will also consider fairness with penalties. Recall that we are planning to do so still admitting that the blockchain could fork and trying to obtain fast executions avoiding as much as possible to wait for confirmations of transactions.

We analyze a variant of the attack described earlier that can be applied to a smart contract based on Andrychowicz *et al.* [1,2] protocol for securely realizing multi-party lotteries[6] The main difference with the toy example from above is that in their work each player commits to a random value r_i between 1 and n (where n is the total number of participants to the lottery), and then, after all the commitments have been opened, the winner of the lottery is defined to be the player $w = r_1 + \ldots + r_n \pmod{n} + 1$. An appealing feature of this protocol is that it achieves fairness with penalties: if a malicious player aborts the protocol (e.g., it does not open the commitment before a certain time bound), then a previously deposited amount of coins is automatically transferred to the honest players (i.e., to those that correctly opened the commitment on time).

We note that in the protocol of Andrychowicz et al. it is vital that players are non-hasty and therefore post new transactions only after the previous ones are already confirmed on the blockchain. Indeed, in the presence of hasty players, a malicious party can commit to a value r_i such that $\sum_i r_i \pmod{n} + 1 = i$, assuming that all players already opened the commitments on a minor branch of a fork. As our main contribution, in Sect. 3, we circumvent the limitations of [1,2], and present a smart contract that implements the lottery functionality[7] remaining secure even in the presence of hasty players. Fairness with penalties can be added without affecting the efficiency of the protocol. In fact, the smart contract we design is more general, in that it allows the players to establish a common, uniformly random, string (which in turn allows to run a lottery). When referring to our protocol depending on the context we will sometimes say lottery protocol and sometimes parallel coin-tossing protocol.

The main idea in our construction consists of combining unique signatures [24] and random oracles (similarly to constructions of verifiable random

---

[6] Protocols of [1,2] is based on Bitcoin, but this makes no difference for our attack.

[7] We specify that our smart contract implements a parallel coin-tossing protocol. In some cases, we say that our smart contract implements a lottery protocol since we are interested in comparing our protocol with the lottery protocol of Andrychowicz et al. We remark that the output of a coin-tossing protocol can be used to compute a lottery winner.

functions) as follows: first of all, players compute unique signatures on input the concatenation of the ordered sequence of their public keys. Notice that as long as at least one player is honest, we have a long string that no PPT player could predict when selecting his public key. Then this long string is given in input to a random oracle, returning a uniformly distributed string as an output. The simulator will program the random oracle to force in the simulation the same random string obtained in the ideal-world execution.

There is still an attack that can be mounted. Assume that in the presence of a fork the entire protocol is executed in a branch. The adversary could take advantage of the output in one branch to decide to play the same first round or a different first round in the other branch biasing successfully the distribution of the output. To circumvent this problem, we make executions in different branches completely independent by also passing a branch id as input to the unique signature evaluation procedure. As branch id we take the hash of the block containing the last deposit. Therefore, when a protocol is entirely run in a branch, we have that the two branch ids are different and thus there is no point in adaptively choosing the same or a different message in another branch. Indeed, in any case, the outputs in different branches will be completely independent. In order to deal with multiple executions of the real-world protocol in different branches, we will also have a simulator that will play multiple times in the ideal world. Since the output of the protocol is a random string, it can be then used in many applications, not only to run a multi-party lottery. Note that our protocol is around 50% more efficient than the lottery of Andrychowicz et al. Let's say that t is the number of blocks needed for transaction confirmation, then our lottery protocol can be run by using only $t + 1$ blocks, whereas Andrychowicz et al. requires $2 \cdot t$ blocks to be completed.

Notice that this result makes no use of finality of transactions on a blockchain except from the one needed for calculating the output. The protocol can be run in the presence of fully hasty players, and is therefore very efficient.

We stress that we consider the adversary as a player that tries to exploit the existence of forks in order to bias the output of the smart contract. We are not modelling the adversary of the smart contract as a player that has control over forks, deciding which branch will eventually be discarded and which one will become permanently part of the blockchain. Obviously, a powerful adversary that has control over the forks can always play the protocol with a different input on each branch to then select the one that produced the output that she likes the most. This is unavoidable when there is little use of finality of transactions. Nevertheless, notice that in many cases this is not a problem. Indeed think of the need of establishing a random string to then use it as first round of a statistically hiding commitment scheme or as common reference string for a non-interactive zero-knowledge proof. In such scenarios the adversary can freely select a random string from any polynomially large set of randomly sampled strings without compromising any security. In other cases like playing bingo, the fact that the adversary can decide the string out of several candidates can be an issue.

Defining On-Chain MPC with Hasty Players. We model the execution of a smart contract through transactions sent by different players is a computation involving multiple parties, and therefore when considering "security" of such computations we naturally refer to secure MPC. We formalize how to execute an MPC protocol in the presence of a blockchain. Our definition builds on the model of blockchain protocols, introduced in [16,25]. A blockchain protocol allows players to keep a consistent record of transactions satisfying: (i) *consistency* (i.e., the view of the blockchain obtained by different players is identical up to pruning k blocks from the chain); and (ii) *liveness* (i.e., if all honest parties attempt to broadcast a message, then after w rounds, an honest party will see that message at depth k in the ledger).

Hence, running an MPC protocol π with the aid of a blockchain protocol simply means that the players exchange messages using the blockchain. Intuitively, a player is called *non-hasty* if she always waits that the previous messages are confirmed on the blockchain before sending the next one. On the other hand, a *hasty player* sends her next message by just looking at her current view of the blockchain (without pruning blocks). Apart from these changes, security is defined similarly as in the standard real-ideal world paradigm. Intuitively, in a protocol running with hasty players, block confirmation is not needed. However, if parties wants to keep a natural blockchain feature like public verifiability, the last message exchanged in the protocol must be necessary confirmed. Throughout the paper, when we talk about no confirmation we implicitly assume the last message is confirmed for public verifiability guarantees.

The definition of security in the presence of hasty players has importance in forking blockchains, in which miners can discard non-confirmed blocks, achieving consensus on other blocks. Our definition applies to forking sidechains too.

General-Purpose MPC with Hasty Players and Fairness with Penalties. Having motivated the problem of running MPC protocols on forking blockchains, we show a general compiler to obtain smart contracts that implements ideal multi-party functionalities retaining security in the presence of forks and allowing players to be hasty.[8]

In order to preserve security in the presence of forks, our compiler makes sure that, whenever an execution of the MPC protocol is repeated in multiple branches, each honest player protects herself from attacks exploiting forks by refusing to play again a message of the same execution of the protocol in case the blockchain shows a different prefix in the transcript of the execution. Specifically, if on one branch $\mathcal{B}_2$ there is a player that changes the message already played in a different branch $\mathcal{B}_1$, then each honest player that played already in $\mathcal{B}_1$ and is asked to play again on input a different prefix in $\mathcal{B}_2$ will abort the execution in

---

[8] In this work all our positive results consist of on-chain protocols for secure computation that are stand-alone secure, with security preserved under sequential composition. The reason why we do not try to obtain universal composability is that existing notions of universal composability with a ledger [10] rely on non-forking ledger functionalities and therefore on non-hasty players.

$\mathcal{B}_2$. Clearly, this strategy forces a unique execution regardless of forks, and thus security holds even in the presence of fully hasty players. For more details about our compiler and its extension adding fairness with penalties see Sect. 4.

1.2 Related Work

Following [1,2], other works focus on achieving fairness with penalties for different applications of interest, including lotteries [6], decentralized poker [7,22], and general-purpose computation [4,6,19,21,23]. In the more recent work of [4] the authors proposed a fair with penalties MPC protocol with increased efficiency of the off-chain phase. In particular, the line of works by Kumaresan et al. relies on an elegant paradigm working in two phases: 1) during the first phase, players run an MPC protocol to obtain the output in hidden form (e.g., a secret sharing of the output); since the output is hidden, such a protocol can be executed off chain, as malicious aborts do not violate fairness; 2) during the second phase, the output is reconstructed in a fair manner on chain. Unfortunately, the security of this paradigm in the presence of hasty players is difficult to assess, as protocols relying on intermediate ideal functionalities (such as the "claim-or-refund" and "multi-lock" functionality [6,20], or a smart contract functionality [4]), although implementable using Bitcoin or Ethereum, may be insecure when executed with hasty players. Moreover, known results about designing protocols in a hybrid model allowing to make calls to a functionality are applicable only to the classical setting where multiple executions of the same instance of the protocol due to forks are not possible. Also note that performing a large part of the computation off chain hinders one of the main advantages of blockchain-aided MPC (i.e., public verifiability of the entire process). Our results, in contrast, consider MPC protocols executed completely on-chain through smart contracts.

A different line of works, shows how to perform MPC in the presence of an abstract transaction ledger [3,10,16,18,28], of which Bitcoin and Ethereum are possible implementations. However, such an idealized ledger does not account for the possibility of forks, thus (implicitly) meaning that the players using it are modeled as non-hasty.

Our main contribution is a protocol to jointly generate a random beacon. It is known that there exist protocols suited for blockchains generating random values. A well known implementation is RANDAO [30]. The smart contract introduced in RANDAO is similar to a smart contract implementation of the Andrychowicz et al. lottery protocol [2].

As we show in Sect. 3 even this smart contract is subject to attacks in case some party does not wait for the confirmation of the first phase of the protocol. On the contrary, our lottery protocol described in Sect. 3.1 is secure even if parties do not wait for block confirmations.

2 Threat Model

Our n-party parallel coin-tossing (PCT) protocol in the presence of hasty players is secure w.r.t. dishonest majority, meaning that it can tolerate up to $n-1$

corrupted players. We assume that the blockchain adversary is computationally bounded, and when there is a fork in the blockchain, we pragmatically assume that the adversary has negligible impact on deciding which branch will be confirmed. Our generic compiler can be secure in the presence of hasty players w.r.t. dishonest majority when the protocol to be compiled is secure w.r.t. dishonest majority. We point out that if one would like to consider a very strong adversary with even 49% of the computational power of the network, then clearly our assumption does not hold. However, we stress that with such an adversary even the 6-block rule in Bitcoin does not make much sense. To guarantee that a delicate transaction (i.e., the coinbase transaction) is confirmed with a strong enough adversary, up to 144 blocks are necessary in Bitcoin [31], meaning 1 day to communicate even a single protocol message. Therefore if one would like to consider such strong adversaries even a protocol requiring one confirmation might be impractical.

We will also consider adversaries mounting DoS attacks through aborts. In our context the adversary can mount this attack by causing an abort to the protocol by e.g. not playing anymore and, in our generic compiler, also by sending different messages on different branches, making honest players abort the execution. Such adversaries have the only purpose of penalizing honest players that will therefore waste time and transaction fees and perhaps restarting the protocol from scratch.

3   Parallel Coin Tossing

A coin-tossing protocol allows a set of players to agree on a uniformly random string, and has many important applications (e.g., it allows to easily implement a decentralized lottery). Our protocol leverages standard techniques to achieve fairness with penalties, but does not require finality (thus allowing players to be fully hasty). We start summarizing the protocol of [2] below and we show that their protocol becomes completely insecure in the presence of hasty players. This naturally leads to our new protocol, which we describe and analyze in Sect. 3.1.

The Protocol of Andrychowicz et al. Recall that in the Bitcoin ledger, each account is associated to a pair of keys (pk, sk), where pk is the verification key of a signature scheme—representing the address of an account—while sk is the corresponding secret key used to sign (the body of) the transactions. Each block on the ledger contains a list of transactions, and new blocks are issued by an entity called *miner*. The blockchain is maintained via a consensus mechanism based on proof of work; users willing to add a transaction to the ledger forward it to the miners, which will try to include it in the next minted block.

In the description below, we say that a transaction is *valid* if it is computed correctly (i.e., the signature is valid, the coins have not been spent already, and so on), and that it is *confirmed* if it appears in the common-prefix of all the miners (i.e., it is at least k-blocks deep in the ledger). Each transaction Tx includes:

- A set of input transactions $Tx_1, Tx_2, \cdots$ from which the coins needed for the actual transaction Tx are taken;
- A set of input scripts containing the input for the output scripts of $Tx_1, Tx_2, \cdots$;
- An output script defining in which condition Tx can be claimed;
- The number of coins taken from the redeemed transactions;
- A time lock t specifying when Tx becomes valid (i.e., a time-locked transaction won't be accepted by the miners before time t has passed).

The construction by [1,2] relies on a primitive called *time-locked commitment*. Let n denote the number of parties. Each party P_j creates $n - 1$ $Commit_{i \neq j}^j$ transactions containing a commitment to its lottery value. In particular, the output script of such a transaction ensures that it can be claimed either by P_j via an $Open_i^j$ transaction exhibiting a valid opening for the commitment, or by another transaction that is signed by both P_j and P_i. Before posting these transactions on the ledger, P_j creates a time-locked transaction $PayDeposit_i^j$ redeeming $Commit_i^j$, sends it off-chain to each $P_{i \neq j}$, and finally posts all the $Commit_i^j$ transactions on the ledger. In case P_j does not open the commitment before time τ, then each recipient of a $PayDeposit_i^j$ transaction can sign it and post it on the ledger; since time τ has passed, the miners will now accept the transaction as a valid transaction redeeming $Commit_i^j$. More in details:

Deposit phase: Each player P_j computes a commitment $y_j = Hash(x_j \| \delta_j)$, where δ_j is some randomness, sends off-chain the $PayDeposit_i^j$ transactions (with time-lock τ) to each $P_{i \neq j}$, and posts the $Commit_i^j$ transactions.

Betting phase: P_j bets one coin in the form of a transaction $PutMoney_j$ (redeeming a previous transaction held by P_j, and with P_j's signature as output script). All the players agree and sign off-chain a $Compute$ transaction taking as input all the $(PutMoney_j)_{j \in [n]}$ transactions, and then the last player that receives the $Compute$ transaction posts it on the ledger. In order to claim this transaction, a player $P_{w'}$ must exhibit the openings of the commitments of all participants: The script checks that the openings are valid, computes the index of the winner w (as a function of the values $x_1, \ldots, x_n$), and checks that $w' = w$ (i.e., the only participant that can claim the $Compute$ transaction is the winner of the lottery).

Compensation phase: After time τ, in case some player P_j did not send all of its $\{Open_i^j\}_{i \in [n], i \neq j}$ transactions, all the other players $P_{i \neq j}$ can post the $PayDeposit_i^j$ transaction, thus obtaining a compensation.

A Simple Attack in the Presence of Hasty Players. The main idea behind our attack is that, in the presence of hasty players, the protocol's messages can end-up answering messages appeared on (still) unconfirmed blocks. By looking at different branches of a fork, an attacker can try to change an old (in the sense that even an answer to it has already been published on-chain) unconfirmed transaction by re-posting it, with the hope that it will end-up on a different branch and become part of the common prefix. This essentially corresponds to a reset attack on the protocol.

The construction described above relies on the (implicit) assumption that the players are non-hasty. In particular, each player P_j should wait to post its $\mathsf{PutMoney}_i^j$ transaction only after all the Commit_i^j transactions are confirmed on the ledger, in such a way that all players are aligned on the same branch (and so the miners have the $\{\mathsf{Commit}_i^j\}_{i \in [n], j \neq i}$ transactions in their common prefix). In the case of hasty players, when a fork occurs, an attacker can take advantage of the openings of the other parties played in a faster branch in order to bias the result of the lottery on a slower branch. If eventually the slower branch remains permanently in the blockchain, then clearly the attack is successful.

For concreteness, let us focus on Blum's coin tossing, in which the winner is defined to be $w = x_1 + \ldots + x_n \bmod n + 1$. Consider the following scenario:

- The (hasty) players $P_1, \ldots, P_n$ run a full instance of the protocol; note that this requires at least 3 blocks.
- The attacker P_n hopes to see a fork containing all the $\{\mathsf{Commit}_j^i\}$ transactions of the other $n - 1$ players.
- Since the attacker P_n now knows the openings $x_1, \ldots, x_{n-1}$, it can post a new set of $\{\mathsf{Commit}'^i_n\}_{i \in [n], i \neq n}$ transactions containing a commitment to a value x'_n such that $x_1 + \ldots + x_{n-1} + x'_n \bmod n + 1 = n$.

In case the new set of transactions ends up on a different branch which is finally included in the common prefix, P_n wins the lottery. In the next section, we propose a new protocol that does not suffer from this problem.

3.1   Our PCT Protocol

We now present a parallel coin-tossing (PCT) protocol on blockchain that is secure in the presence of hasty players. The main challenge that we face is that the protocol must prevent an adversary from choosing adaptively her contribution to the coin tossing in a branch of a fork, after possibly seeing the contributions of the other players in different branches.

We tackle this problem by requiring that each honest party computes his contribution by evaluating a unique signature (see the full version for the formal definition) upon input the public keys of all players. Notice that if the adversary A sees some signatures in a branch, and changes her public key in another branch, then A cannot predict the signatures of the honest players on this other branch by the unforgeability property of the signature scheme, and thus A will not manage to bias the final output. Hence, we hash the concatenation of all the signatures in order to determine the final output. Assuming that the hash function is modelled as a random oracle, we would like to argue that the output of the protocol looks uniform.

However, the following subtlety arises. Assume without loss of generality that only P_n is corrupt and that the protocol proceeds until the end on a given branch of the blockchain. Denote by pk_n the public key chosen by the attacker. Further, assume that A notices another branch where all honest players have already sent their public keys. Now, the adversary can either: (i) publish a different public key pk'_n, or (ii) publish the same public key pk_n as in the other branch. In case A "likes" the outcome of the protocol on the first branch, she will choose option (ii) and thus can bias the protocol output.

To avoid the above attack, we identify each branch with a string bid that is uniquely associated to it, and include bid as part of the message to sign. Intuitively, this solves the previous problem as, even if all the public keys stay the same on two different branches, the value bid will change thus ensuring that the protocol output will also be different (and uniformly random). We proceed with a more detailed description of our protocol (see also Fig. 1).[9]

- One of the players chooses a random value sid that represents the identifier of the current protocol execution, and publishes sid on the blockchain.
- Each player P_i willing to participate generates the public and private keys for the unique signature $(pk_i, sk_i) \leftarrow_{\$} \mathsf{Gen}(1^\lambda)$, and publishes pk_i on the blockchain.
- Each player P_i lets $y_i = \mathsf{Sign}(sk_i, pk_1||\cdots||pk_n||sid||bid)$, where bid is the hash of the blockchain[10] up to the block that contains the last public key, and publishes y_i on the blockchain.
- Each player P_i checks that $\mathsf{Verify}(pk_j, x, y_j) = 1$ for all $j \neq i$, where $x = pk_1||\cdots||pk_n||sid||bid$, and outputs $\mathsf{Hash}(y_1||\cdots||y_n)$.

We stress that thanks to the value bid, the protocol execution becomes branch dependent. In particular, the chances of success of a corrupted P_j to bias the output are not affected by the potential use of different public keys in branches of a fork corresponding to a protocol run with a given sid.

Security Analysis. Let f^{pct} be the n-party functionality that picks a uniformly random string ω and sends it to all the n parties. The theorem below establishes the security of our coin-tossing protocol in the (programmable) random oracle (RO) model. We note that the security of the original protocol by Andrychowicz et al. [1,2] also relies on the RO heuristic, as do all currently known analysis of blockchain protocols [14,25].

Proofs can be found in the full version.

Theorem 1. *If* (Gen, Sign, Verify) *is a unique signature scheme, the protocol of Fig. 1 securely implements the functionality* f^{pct} *in the presence of hasty players and malicious adversaries with aborts, in the programmable RO model.*

---

[9] Note that our protocol can be run on generic blockchains. In the full version, we provide an implementation using Ethereum smart contracts, but the protocol can also be implemented in Bitcoin using the opcode OP_RETURN in case players do not need to get fairness with penalties.

[10] For efficiency the hash can be more simply applied to the block containing pk_n. Nevertheless, for the sake of simplicity of the protocol description and of the security analysis we will stick with hashing the entire blockchain.

Parallel Coin Tossing Protocol π^*_{pct}

Let (Gen, Sign, Verify) be a signature scheme with message space $\mathcal{M} = \{0,1\}^*$, and Hash : $\{0,1\}^* \to \{0,1\}^\lambda$ be a hash function.

- P_1 picks $sid \leftarrow^\$ \{0,1\}^\lambda$, and runs Broadcast($sid$).
- For each $i \in [n]$, P_i generates $(pk_i, sk_i) \leftarrow^\$ \text{Gen}(1^\lambda)$ and runs Broadcast(pk_i).
- For each $i \in [n]$, P_i executes $\mathcal{B}_i \leftarrow^\$ \text{GetRecords}(1^\lambda, \text{UpdateState}(1^\lambda))$ until all public keys $pk_1, \ldots, pk_n$ are contained in $\mathcal{B}_i$, and then defines $bid := \text{Hash}(\mathcal{B}_i)$.
- For each $i \in [n]$, P_i computes $y_i = \text{Sign}(sk_i, x)$, where $x = pk_1 || \ldots || pk_n || sid || bid$ and runs Broadcast(y_i).
- For each $i, j \in [n]$, with $i \neq j$, P_i checks that Verify(pk_i, x, y_i) = 1, and, if so, it outputs Hash($y_1 || \cdots || y_n$) and else it aborts.

Fig. 1. Our new protocol for parallel coin tossing.

Fairness with Penalties. We now discuss how to augment the protocol π^*_{pct} in order to achieve fairness with penalties. First of all, each party should publish also a deposit along with her public key on the blockchain. The deposit can be redeemed by showing a valid signature on the value $x = pk_1 || \cdots || pk_n || sid || bid$.

Assume that P_n is corrupted. The adversary can wait that the honest parties publish their value $y_1, \ldots, y_{n-1}$ on a given branch, and thus locally compute the output Hash($y_1 || \cdots || y_n$), where y_n is P_n's signatures on x corresponding to public key pk_n. Now, if P_n does not like the output it can either: (i) publish y_n in any case , or (ii) decide not to publish y_n. In case (i), P_n plays honestly, takes back his deposit and every player obtains the output. In case (ii), P_n aborts the protocol, but loses her deposit.

Note that the penalty mechanism for our protocol is too sophisticated for the scripting language used in Bitcoin. Instead in Ethereum we can design a smart contract to define the PCT protocol, having fairness with penalties and without penalizing the efficiency.

In the full version we give details about how the smart contract works.

We call $\tilde{\pi}^*_{pct}$ the fair (with penalties) version of protocol π^*_{pct}. The informal description of the smart contract used in $\tilde{\pi}^*_{pct}$ is given in Fig. 2 and the protocol is described below:

(i) *Setup phase:* At the beginning, one of the players creates the smart contract. When the contract is posted on the blockchain, the constructor automatically generates a unique session identifier sid.

(ii) *Deposit phase:* For each $i \in [n]$, P_i can decide to participate to the PCT protocol by triggering the function deposit to send a safety deposit and his public key pk_i of an unique signature scheme. After time1 blocks have passed, if $(pk_1, \ldots, pk_n)$ are collected by the smart contract, it computes bid as Hash($\mathcal{B}$), where $\mathcal{B}$ is the blockchain that contains $(pk_1, \ldots, pk_n)$. The deposit phase ends and parties can start to redeem their deposit.

(iii) *Claim phase:* For each $i \in [n]$, P_i can claim his deposit back by triggering the function `claim` of the smart contract and sending a value y_i such that $\mathsf{Verify}(pk_i, x, y_i) = 1$, where $x = pk_1 || \cdots || pk_n || sid || bid$, and pk_i is the public key of P_i. After `time2` blocks have passed, the claim phase ends and the smart contract computes and publishes the output as $\mathsf{Hash}(y_1 || \cdots || y_n)$.

The **Parallel Coin Tossing Smart Contract** runs with players $\mathsf{P}_1, \ldots, \mathsf{P}_n$ and consists of two main functions **deposit** and **claim** and two fixed timestamps **time1,time2** and a session id sid.

Deposit Phase: In round t_1, when **deposit**(pk_i) together with d coins is triggered from a party P_i, store (i, pk_i). Then, if $(pk_1, \ldots, pk_n)$ are stored, compute and store $bid := \mathsf{Hash}(\mathcal{B})$ and proceed to the Claim Phase. Otherwise, for all i, if the message (i, pk_i) has been stored, send back d coins to P_i and terminate.

Claim Phase: In round t_2, when **claim**(i, y_i) is triggered from P_i, check if $\mathsf{Verify}(pk_i, x, y_i) = 1$, where $x = pk_1 || \cdots || pk_n || sid || bid$. If the check is correct send d coins back to P_i.

Compute Phase: If, after **time2**, all the y_i are correctly claimed, compute and publish $\mathsf{Hash}(y_1, \ldots, y_n)$.

Fig. 2. Smart contract for parallel coin tossing.

Theorem 2. *If* $(\mathsf{Gen}, \mathsf{Sign}, \mathsf{Verify})$ *is a unique signature scheme,* $\tilde{\pi}^*_{\mathsf{pct}}$ *described in Fig. 2 securely realizes* f^{pct} *and satisfies fairness with penalties in the presence of hasty players and malicious adversaries, in the programmable RO model.*

A Remark on DoS Attacks. Note that in $\tilde{\pi}^*_{\mathsf{pct}}$ there is no need to fix the identity of the participants "before" the execution of the protocol. We can consider the case in which a party P_i participates to a protocol execution only after she triggers the `deposit` function giving as an input her public key. Our PCT protocol can be executed even if only two parties decide to participate and thus n does not need to be fixed beforehand. Moreover, `time1` is independent of n and of the number of blocks to wait for considering a transaction confirmed. Registered parties are not incentivized to abort the protocol (i.e., by not triggering the `claim` function) due to financial compensation (parties must send a collateral deposit together with the first message). This makes DoS attacks in which the attacker aborts the protocol multiple times (making honest parties waste time and money) financially inconvenient.

3.2   Experimental Evaluation

We also provide some experiments to show noticeable improvements in our PCT protocol with respect to the lottery protocol of Andrychowicz et al. in terms of the number of blocks needed for completion of the protocol. Since the confirmation time has a considerable impact on the overall communication with respect to the number of rounds, we measure the efficiency of on-chain protocols in terms of the number of blocks[11].

We evaluate the efficiency of π^*_{pct} compared with the protocol from [1,2]. To evaluate the efficiency in the best case we consider the following assumptions:

- Transactions in the last k blocks are considered not confirmed yet.
- All parties send the message at round i of the protocol as soon as they read all messages from round $i-1$ on $\mathcal{B}_i^{\lceil k}$, where k is 0 in case of hasty executions.
- Whenever a player broadcasts a transaction, it appears in the next block.
- All messages in a round of the MPC protocol fit in a single block.

In case of non-hasty executions if we have a ρ-round MPC protocol π running on the blockchain, the number of blocks needed to complete the execution with the previous assumption is $\rho \cdot k$.

Analysis. We now give a comparison between our coin-tossing protocol and the one of Andrychowicz et al. To allow for a fair comparison between our coin-tossing protocol and the one presented in [1,2], we implemented both protocols in Solidity using Ethereum smart contracts.[12] See the full version for the code of the smart contracts.

For both protocols, in the deposit phase, a timeout $\bar{t}$ must be provided by the contract creator, so that players have enough time to send their deposits together with the corresponding additional information required by the protocol. In the ideal conditions described above, the timeout can be of just one block. The same argument applies to the opening phase of [1,2]. A comparison is described below:

- *Lottery:* Due to the expressiveness of smart contracts, our implementation of [1,2] requires one step less than the original implementation using in bitcoin. Specifically, we can embed the betting phase in the commit/deposit phase, by just requiring that the players deposit 1 more coin. Since in their setting block confirmation is required at each step, the overall execution takes exactly $3 \cdot k$ blocks (including one round for posting the smart contract).
- *Our PCT:* As proven in Sect. 3.1, our PCT protocol can be executed in fully-hasty mode. The entire execution consists of $2 + k$ blocks (including 1 block for posting the contract and confirmation of the output). In the worst case, where all messages will appear to the state of the honest player after k blocks for each step, the overall execution takes $3 \cdot k$, as much as [2].

GAS Consumption. As it can be seen in Fig. 3, PCT is more expensive in terms of GAS consumption than Lottery. It is well motivated by the fact that Lottery uses only hash function to compute the commitments and no other expensive

---

[11] Notice that whenever players are all online and ready to play, the execution should be fast and waiting for confirmations of all messages would be painful.

[12] Notice that the average time for a new block to appear is around 15 s [13].

computations. Our PCT protocol needs also unique signatures. Our GAS calculation for unique signature is based on the BLS signatures implementation provided for testing in [29], but improved implementations could potentially lower the GAS consumption. It can be seen anyway as an affordable cost to pay to achieve efficiency still maintaining the same security guarantees.

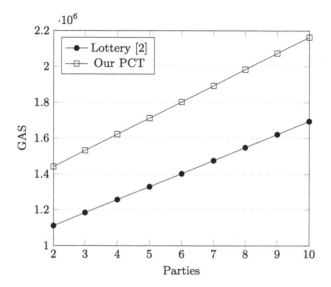

Fig. 3. GAS consumption comparison between our smart contract implementation of PCT (Sect. 3.1) protocol and the Lottery of Andrychowicz et al. [2] (Sect. 3).

4   Our Generic Compiler

Our compiler starts from the observation that a stand-alone MPC protocol could be insecure when executed on a blockchain. To be concrete, a rewinding simulator of the MPC protocol can not be used to prove the security of the on-chain MPC protocol, since rewinding would have the unclear meaning of rewinding the blockchain. Moreover, we do not want to give control of the blockchain to the simulator (i.e., no control of the majority of the stake, of the computational power, and so on) since our result aims at being generic w.r.t. the type of blockchain used. Essentially, the simulator is going to incarnate just the honest players of the MPC protocol during the simulation. In order perform a simulation in the presence of a concurrently played blockchain protocol, (i.e., rewinding is not possible and the blockchain is generic and therefore not controlled by the simulator), we therefore require the initial protocol π received in input by the compiler to be universally composable secure. This guarantees the existence of a straight-line simulator and allows us to avoid simulators that "control" the blockchain[13],

---

[13] Typically a simulator that controls the blockchain requires some specific assumptions on the blockchain like in [16] where only some restricted proof-of-stake blockchains were compatible with the simulation.

therefore allowing the applicability of our results to generic blockchains. Additionally, we require π to have only "digital" communication since players when running the protocol on-chain must produce messages that consists of bits only. Therefore an exchange of hardware (e.g., PUFs) in π can not be accepted.

Notice that the original protocol might require private and authenticated channels. Since the entire traffic of our protocol will be redirected to the blockchain, we will use public-key encryption and digital signatures. The first message of each player in the compiled protocol will consist of a pair of public keys, one to receive encrypted messages and one to allow others to verify signatures of messages.

Compiler Description. Intuitively our transformation proceeds as follows. Our starting point is any MPC protocol π UC-securely computing an n-party functionality $f : (\{0,1\}^*)^n \rightarrow (\{0,1\}^*)^n$ in the presence of malicious players (with aborts). Hence, the honest players fix the random tape for running π and simply execute protocol π by broadcasting their messages on the blockchain. Furthermore, each honest player P_i keeps track of the longest protocol transcript α_i generated so far and, in the presence of a fork, aborts the execution in case the view on a given branch is not consistent with α_i. This intuitively ensures that the underlying protocol π is run only once, even in the presence of forks.

Since the initial protocol π may require private channels between the players, we need to augment the above transformation in such a way that subsets of honest parties can exchange messages in a confidential and authenticated manner. Let $m_{i,j}^{(r)}$ be the message that P_i sends to P_j at the generic round r. The latter is achieved by having P_i encrypting $m_{i,j}^{(r)}$ using the public encryption key ek_j of P_j, and then signing the resulting ciphertext $c_{i,j}^{(r)}$ with its own private signing key sk_i, which is the standard way of building a secure channel. We refer the reader to the full version for a formal description.

On Fairness Through Penalties. To obtain a fair with penalties protocol π_{fair}, we use the following technique, borrowed from [6,20]. Let's consider a protocol π' running with parties $P_1, \ldots, P_n$ for a functionality f' that, given the output $y \leftarrow f(x_1, \ldots, x_n)$, where x_i is the input of player P_i, secret shares y into $(\sigma_1, \ldots, \sigma_n)$ (for a full threshold sharing scheme), generates a set of commitments $C = (\gamma_1, \ldots, \gamma_n)$ such that γ_i is the commitment of σ_i. Each player P_i obtains as an output the pair (C, σ_i)[14]. The fair protocol with penalties in the presence of hasty players can be obtained as follows: (i) We compile π' with our generic compiler, obtaining π'_{bc}. (ii) In our protocol π_{fair}, parties $P_1, \ldots, P_n$ first engage in π'_{bc}. After π'_{bc} ends, each P_i obtains the output (C, σ_i). Now, each P_i has a limited time t_1 to send his tuple C to a smart contract together with a payment of some deposit. (iii) If everyone sent the same tuple C, each player P_i has another time shift t_2 to send their share σ_i of γ_i to receive back their deposit. Else, if after t_2, $(\sigma_1, \ldots, \sigma_n)$ are posted to the smart contract, each P_i

---

[14] P_i implicitly receives also a decommitment information of γ_i.

can reconstruct the output by using all collected shares. Else, players that have not opened their shares within t_2, will be penalized since their coins will remain frozen forever into the smart contract.

We prove that fairness can be achieved if honest parties playing π_{fair} wait for confirmation only of step (ii). The reason for requiring the confirmation of phase (ii) is that otherwise the adversary can try to generate an abort during the execution of π'_{bc} after learning the output of the entire protocol π_{fair} on a different branch. Now, let's say that t is the time needed for transaction confirmation in the blockchain, and r the number of rounds of π'_{bc}, π_{fair} requires around $r + 2t$ blocks to complete the on-chain execution (including output confirmation). To maintain security of Kumaresan et al. protocols by blindly posting messages on-chain, the overall execution requires around $r \cdot t$ blocks to be successfully terminated. More details are provided in the full version.

Remark on DoS Attacks. Note that in our construction deposits can be made at the end of step (ii) since adversaries trying to violate fairness can be spotted only during step (iii). Therefore an adversary can freely abort the execution before step (iii). Intuitively, by taking as input a protocol achieving identifiable abort [17] that is publicly verifiable[15], a player cheating in any point of the protocol execution can be successfully spotted and punished. This can be done by making a player posting a smart contract that will act as an external judge that exploits public verifiability of the underlying protocol. Unfortunately, protocols compiled with our construction would lose the identifiable abort property. This is due to the fact that the adversary can make honest players aborting by running two correct executions of the underlying protocol on two branches but using different messages. In such case, the two executions would be both considered valid in both branches by the smart contract mentioned above.

5 Conclusions

We have focused on MPC protocols implemented on forking blockchains using smart contracts, and have shown how to design such protocols allowing players to be hasty (i.e., without being delayed by finality limitations).

Our work shows that, beyond the double-spending attack, there are other issues that can affect both security and privacy of MPC protocols implemented by a smart contract. On the negative side, we showed that a well-known MPC protocol implemented via smart contracts becomes insecure in the presence of forks and hasty players (because the adversary can play adaptively on a branch of a fork depending on the information observed on the other branch). On the positive side, we have shown smart contracts within on-chain MPC protocols that remain secure even when there are forks and players are hasty.

Moreover we have also discussed how to get fairness with penalties. This allows us to get smart contracts that are simultaneously safe, fair and fast. We

---

[15] An efficient construction can be found at [5].

have also provided in Sect. 3.2 some experiments to show noticeable improvements of our PCT protocol with respect to the lottery protocol of Andrychowicz et al. in terms of number of blocks needed for completion of the protocol and gas consumption of the smart contracts.

Acknowledgments. We thank Michele Ciampi, Fabio Massacci, Mark Simkin and Roberto Zunino for remarkable comments on this work. We also thank Andrew Miller for useful feedback on a previous version of our paper. Research supported by the European Union's Horizon 2020 research and innovation programme under grant agreement No 780477 (project PRIViLEDGE), and in part by GNCS–INdAM, Region Campania (Italy), and the research project SPECTRA funded by Sapienza University of Rome.

References

1. Andrychowicz, M., Dziembowski, S., Malinowski, D., Mazurek, L.: Secure multiparty computations on bitcoin. In: 2014 IEEE Symposium on Security and Privacy, SP 2014, Berkeley, CA, USA, May 18–21, 2014, pp. 443–458. IEEE Computer Society (2014)
2. Andrychowicz, M., Dziembowski, S., Malinowski, D., Mazurek, L.: Secure multiparty computations on bitcoin. Commun. ACM **59**(4), 76–84 (2016)
3. Badertscher, C., Maurer, U., Tschudi, D., Zikas, V.: Bitcoin as a transaction ledger: a composable treatment. In: Katz, J., Shacham, H. (eds.) CRYPTO 2017. LNCS, vol. 10401, pp. 324–356. Springer, Cham (2017). https://doi.org/10.1007/978-3-319-63688-7_11
4. Baum, C., David, B., Dowsley, R.: Insured MPC: efficient secure computation with financial penalties. In: Bonneau, J., Heninger, N. (eds.) FC 2020. LNCS, vol. 12059, pp. 404–420. Springer, Cham (2020). https://doi.org/10.1007/978-3-030-51280-4_22
5. Baum, C., Orsini, E., Scholl, P., Soria-Vazquez, E.: Efficient constant-round MPC with identifiable abort and public verifiability. In: Advances in Cryptology - CRYPTO 2020 - 40th Annual International Cryptology Conference, CRYPTO 2020, Santa Barbara, CA, USA, August 17-21, 2020, Proceedings, Part II. pp. 562–592
6. Bentov, I., Kumaresan, R.: How to use bitcoin to design fair protocols. In: Garay, J.A., Gennaro, R. (eds.) CRYPTO 2014. LNCS, vol. 8617, pp. 421–439. Springer, Heidelberg (2014). https://doi.org/10.1007/978-3-662-44381-1_24
7. Bentov, I., Kumaresan, R., Miller, A.: Instantaneous decentralized poker. In: Takagi, T., Peyrin, T. (eds.) ASIACRYPT 2017. LNCS, vol. 10625, pp. 410–440. Springer, Cham (2017). https://doi.org/10.1007/978-3-319-70697-9_15
8. Buterin, V., Griffith, V.: Casper the friendly finality gadget. CoRR abs/1710.09437 (2017)
9. Chan, T.H.H., Pass, R., Shi, E.: Pala: a simple partially synchronous blockchain. Cryptology ePrint Archive, Report 2018/981 (2018). https://eprint.iacr.org/2018/981
10. Choudhuri, A.R., Goyal, V., Jain, A.: Founding secure computation on blockchains. In: Ishai, Y., Rijmen, V. (eds.) EUROCRYPT 2019. LNCS, vol. 11477, pp. 351–380. Springer, Cham (2019). https://doi.org/10.1007/978-3-030-17656-3_13

11. Cleve, R.: Limits on the security of coin flips when half the processors are faulty (extended abstract). In: Proceedings of the 18th Annual ACM Symposium on Theory of Computing, 28–30 May, 1986, Berkeley, California, USA, pp. 364–369. ACM (1986)

12. Dinsdale-Young, T., Magri, B., Matt, C., Nielsen, J.B., Tschudi, D.: Afgjort: a partially synchronous finality layer for blockchains. In: Galdi, C., Kolesnikov, V. (eds.) SCN 2020. LNCS, vol. 12238, pp. 24–44. Springer, Cham (2020). https://doi.org/10.1007/978-3-030-57990-6_2

13. Ethereum team: The ethereum average block time chart. https://etherscan.io/chart/blocktime. Accessed 11 June 2020

14. Garay, J., Kiayias, A., Leonardos, N.: The bitcoin backbone protocol: analysis and applications. In: Oswald, E., Fischlin, M. (eds.) EUROCRYPT 2015. LNCS, vol. 9057, pp. 281–310. Springer, Heidelberg (2015). https://doi.org/10.1007/978-3-662-46803-6_10

15. Gilad, Y., Hemo, R., Micali, S., Vlachos, G., Zeldovich, N.: Algorand: scaling byzantine agreements for cryptocurrencies. In: Proceedings of the 26th Symposium on Operating Systems Principles, Shanghai, China, 28–31 October, 2017, pp. 51–68. ACM (2017)

16. Goyal, R., Goyal, V.: Overcoming cryptographic impossibility results using blockchains. In: Kalai, Y., Reyzin, L. (eds.) TCC 2017. LNCS, vol. 10677, pp. 529–561. Springer, Cham (2017). https://doi.org/10.1007/978-3-319-70500-2_18

17. Ishai, Y., Ostrovsky, R., Zikas, V.: Secure multi-party computation with identifiable abort. In: Garay, J.A., Gennaro, R. (eds.) CRYPTO 2014. LNCS, vol. 8617, pp. 369–386. Springer, Heidelberg (2014). https://doi.org/10.1007/978-3-662-44381-1_21

18. Kiayias, A., Zhou, H.-S., Zikas, V.: Fair and robust multi-party computation using a global transaction ledger. In: Fischlin, M., Coron, J.-S. (eds.) EUROCRYPT 2016. LNCS, vol. 9666, pp. 705–734. Springer, Heidelberg (2016). https://doi.org/10.1007/978-3-662-49896-5_25

19. Kosba, A.E., Miller, A., Shi, E., Wen, Z., Papamanthou, C.: Hawk: the blockchain model of cryptography and privacy-preserving smart contracts. In: IEEE Symposium on Security and Privacy, SP 2016, San Jose, CA, USA, 22–26 May, 2016, pp. 839–858. IEEE Computer Society (2016)

20. Kumaresan, R., Bentov, I.: How to use bitcoin to incentivize correct computations. In: Proceedings of the 2014 ACM SIGSAC Conference on Computer and Communications Security, Scottsdale, AZ, USA, 3–7 November, 2014, pp. 30–41. ACM (2014)

21. Kumaresan, R., Bentov, I.: Amortizing secure computation with penalties. In: Proceedings of the 2016 ACM SIGSAC Conference on Computer and Communications Security, Vienna, Austria, 24–28 October, 2016, pp. 418–429. ACM (2016)

22. Kumaresan, R., Moran, T., Bentov, I.: How to use bitcoin to play decentralized poker. In: Proceedings of the 22nd ACM SIGSAC Conference on Computer and Communications Security, Denver, CO, USA, October 12–16, 2015, pp. 195–206. ACM (2015)

23. Kumaresan, R., Vaikuntanathan, V., Vasudevan, P.N.: Improvements to secure computation with penalties. In: Proceedings of the 2016 ACM SIGSAC Conference on Computer and Communications Security, Vienna, Austria, 24–28 October, 2016, pp. 406–417. ACM (2016)

24. Lysyanskaya, A.: Unique signatures and verifiable random functions from the DH-DDH separation. In: Yung, M. (ed.) CRYPTO 2002. LNCS, vol. 2442, pp. 597–612. Springer, Heidelberg (2002). https://doi.org/10.1007/3-540-45708-9_38

25. Pass, R., Seeman, L., Shelat, A.: Analysis of the blockchain protocol in asynchronous networks. In: Coron, J.-S., Nielsen, J.B. (eds.) EUROCRYPT 2017. LNCS, vol. 10211, pp. 643–673. Springer, Cham (2017). https://doi.org/10.1007/978-3-319-56614-6_22

26. Pass, R., Shi, E.: Hybrid consensus: Efficient consensus in the permissionless model. In: 31st International Symposium on Distributed Computing, DISC 2017, 16–20 October 2017, Vienna, Austria. LIPIcs, vol. 91, pp. 39:1–39:16 (2017)

27. Pass, R., Shi, E.: Thunderella: Blockchains with Optimistic Instant Confirmation. In: Nielsen, J.B., Rijmen, V. (eds.) EUROCRYPT 2018. LNCS, vol. 10821, pp. 3–33. Springer, Cham (2018). https://doi.org/10.1007/978-3-319-78375-8_1

28. Scafuro, A., Siniscalchi, L., Visconti, I.: Publicly verifiable proofs from blockchains. In: Lin, D., Sako, K. (eds.) PKC 2019. LNCS, vol. 11442, pp. 374–401. Springer, Cham (2019). https://doi.org/10.1007/978-3-030-17253-4_13

29. Solidity team: Solidity bls signatures. https://github.com/kfichter/solidity-bls, smart contract implementation of BLS Signatures

30. Randao's Team: Randao: A dao working as rng of ethereum. https://github.com/randao/randao

31. Bitcoin Wiki: Confirmation in bitcoin. https://en.bitcoin.it/wiki/Confirmation

A Formal Model of Algorand Smart Contracts

Massimo Bartoletti[1(✉)], Andrea Bracciali[2], Cristian Lepore[2], Alceste Scalas[3], and Roberto Zunino[4]

[1] Università degli Studi di Cagliari, Cagliari, Italy
bart@unica.it
[2] Stirling University, Stirling, UK
[3] Technical University of Denmark, Lyngby, Denmark
[4] Università degli Studi di Trento, Trento, Italy

Abstract. We develop a formal model of Algorand stateless smart contracts (stateless ASC1). We exploit our model to prove fundamental properties of the Algorand blockchain, and to establish the security of some archetypal smart contracts. While doing this, we highlight various design patterns supported by Algorand. We perform experiments to validate the coherence of our formal model w.r.t. the actual implementation.

1 Introduction

Smart contracts are agreements between two or more parties that are automatically enforced without trusted intermediaries. Blockchain technologies reinvented the idea of smart contracts, providing trustless environments where they are incarnated as computer programs. However, writing secure smart contracts is difficult, as witnessed by the multitude of attacks on smart contracts platforms (notably, Ethereum)—and since smart contracts control assets, their bugs may directly lead to financial losses.

Algorand [20] is a late-generation blockchain that features a set of interesting features, including high-scalability and a no-forking consensus protocol based on Proof-of-Stake [7]. Its smart contract layer (ASC1) aims to mitigate smart contract risks, and adopts a non-Turing-complete programming model, natively supporting atomic sets of transactions and user-defined assets. These features make it an intriguing smart contract platform to study.

The official specification and documentation of ASC1 consists of English prose and a set of templates to assist programmers in designing their contracts [1,3]. This conforms to standard industry practices, but there are two drawbacks:

1. Algorand lacks a mathematical model of contracts and transactions suitable for formal reasoning on their behaviour, and for the verification of their properties. Such a model is needed to develop techniques and tools to ensure that contracts are correct and secure;

© International Financial Cryptography Association 2021
N. Borisov and C. Diaz (Eds.): FC 2021, LNCS 12674, pp. 93–114, 2021.
https://doi.org/10.1007/978-3-662-64322-8_5

2. furthermore, even preliminary informal reasoning on non-trivial smart contracts can be challenging, as it may require, in some corner cases, to resort to experiments, or direct inspection of the platform source code.

Given these drawbacks, we aim at developing a formal model that:

o1. is high-level enough to simplify the design of Algorand smart contracts and enable formal reasoning about their security properties;
o2. expresses Algorand contracts in a simple declarative language, similar to PyTeal (the official Python binding for Algorand smart contracts) [5];
o3. provides a basis for the automatic verification of Algorand smart contracts.

Contributions. This paper presents:

- a *formal model of stateless ASC1* providing a solid theoretical foundation to Algorand smart contracts (Sect. 2). Such a model formalises both Algorand accounts and transactions (Sects. 2.1–Sect. 2.4, Sect. 2.6), and smart contracts (Sect. 2.5);
- a validation of our model through experiments [4] on the Algorand platform;
- the formalisation and proof of some *fundamental properties of the Algorand state machine*: no double spending, determinism, value preservation (Sect. 2.7);
- an *analysis of Algorand contract design patterns* (Sect. 3.2), based on several non-trivial contracts (covering both standard use cases, and novel ones). Quite surprisingly, we show that stateless contracts are expressive enough to encode arbitrary finite state machines;
- the proof of relevant *security properties of smart contracts* in our model;
- a *prototype tool* that compiles smart contracts (written in our formal declarative language) into executable TEAL code (Sect. 4).

Our formal model is faithful to the actual ASC1 implementation; by objectives o.1–o.3, it strives at being high-level and simple to understand, while covering the most commonly used primitives and mechanisms of Algorand, and supporting the specification and verification of non-trivial smart contracts (Sect. 3.2, Sect. 4). To achieve these objectives, we introduce minor high-level abstractions over low-level details: e.g., since TEAL code has the purpose of accepting or rejecting transactions, we model it using expressions that evaluate to *true* or *false* (similarly to PyTEAL); we also formalise different transaction types by focusing on their function, rather than their implementation. Our objectives imply that we do *not* aim at covering all the possible TEAL contracts with bytecode-level accuracy, and our Algorand model is *not* designed as a full low-level formalisation of the behavior of the Algorand blockchain. We discuss the differences between our model and the actual Algorand platform in Sect. 5. Due to space constraints, we provide the proofs of our statements in a separate technical report [14].

2   The Algorand State Machine

We present our formal model of the Algorand blockchain, including its smart contracts (stateless ASC1), incrementally. We first define the basic transactions that generate and transfer assets (Sect. 2.1–Sect. 2.3), and then add atomic groups of transactions (Sect. 2.4), smart contracts (Sect. 2.5), and authorizations (Sect. 2.6). We discuss the main differences between our model and Algorand in Sect. 5.

Table 1. Summary of notation.

$a, b, \ldots$	Users (key pairs)	$\mathbb{T}_{lv} \subseteq \mathbb{T}$	Transactions in last Δ_{max} rounds
$x, y, \ldots \in \mathbb{X}$	Addresses	$f_{asst} \in \mathbb{A} \to \mathbb{X}$	Asset manager
$\tau, \tau', \ldots \in \mathbb{A}$	Assets	$f_{lx} \in (\mathbb{X} \times \mathbb{N}) \to \mathbb{N}$	Lease map
$v, w, \ldots \in 0..2^{64} - 1$	Values	$f_{frz} \in \mathbb{X} \to 2^{\mathbb{A}}$	Freeze map
$\sigma, \sigma' \in \mathbb{A} \to \mathbb{N}$	Balances	$\Gamma, \Gamma', \ldots$	Blockchain states
$x[\sigma]$	Accounts	$\models \sigma$	Valid balance
$t, t', \ldots \in \mathbb{T}$	Transactions	$f_{lx}, r \models t$	Valid time constraint
$e, e', \ldots$	Scripts	$\mathcal{W} \models \mathcal{T}, i$	Authorized transaction in group
$r, r' \ldots \in \mathbb{N}$	Rounds	$[\![e]\!]_{\mathcal{T},i}^{\mathcal{W}}$	Script evaluation

2.1   Accounts and Transactions

We use $a, b, \ldots$ to denote public/private key pairs (k_a^p, k_a^s). Users interact with Algorand through pseudonymous identities, obtained as a function of their public keys. Hereafter, we freely use a to refer to the public or the private key of a, or to the user associated with them, relying on the context to resolve the ambiguity. The purpose of Algorand is to allow users to exchange **assets** $\tau, \tau', \ldots$ Besides the Algorand native cryptocurrency Algo, users can create custom assets.

   We adopt the following notational convention:

- lowercase letters for single entities (e.g., a user a);
- uppercase letters for *sets* of entities (e.g., a set of users A);
- calligraphic uppercase letters for *sequences* of entities (e.g., list of users $\mathcal{A}$).

Given a sequence $\mathcal{L}$, we write $|\mathcal{L}|$ for its length, $set(\mathcal{L})$ for the set of its elements, and $\mathcal{L}.i$ for its ith element ($i \in 1..|\mathcal{L}|$); ε denotes the empty sequence. We write:

- $\{x \mapsto v\}$ for the function mapping x to v, and having domain equal to $\{x\}$;
- $f\{x \mapsto v\}$ for the function mapping x to v, and y to $f(y)$ if $y \neq x$;
- $f\{x \mapsto \bot\}$ for the function undefined at x, and mapping y to $f(y)$ if $y \neq x$.

Accounts. An **account** is a deposit of one or more crypto-assets. We model accounts as terms $x[\sigma]$, where x is an **address** uniquely identifying the account, and σ is a **balance**, i.e., a finite map from assets to non-negative 64-bit integers. In the concrete Algorand, an address is a 58-characters word; for mathematical elegance, in our model we represent an address as either:

– a **single user** a. Performing transactions on a[σ] requires a's authorization;
– a pair $(\mathcal{A}, n)$, where $\mathcal{A}$ is a sequence of users, and $1 \leq n \leq |\mathcal{A}|$, are **multisig (multi-signature)** addresses. Performing transactions on $(\mathcal{A}, n)[\sigma]$ requires that at least n users out of those in $\mathcal{A}$ grant their authorization;[1]
– a **script**[2] e. Performing transactions on e[σ] requires e to evaluate to *true*.

pay	snd, rcv, val, asst	snd transfers val units of asst to rcv (possibly creating rcv)
close	snd, rcv, asst	snd gives asst to rcv and removes it (if Algo, closes snd)
gen	snd, rcv, val	snd mints val units of a new asset, managed by rcv
optin	snd, asst	snd opts in to receive units of asset asst
burn	asst	asst is removed from the creator (if sole owner)
rvk	snd, rcv, val, asst	asst's manager transfers val units of asset from snd to rcv
frz	snd, asst	asst's manager freezes snd's use of asset asst
unfrz	snd, asst	asst's manager unfreezes snd's use of asset asst
delegate	snd, asst, rcv	asst's manager delegates asst to new manager rcv

Fig. 1. Transaction types. Fields type, fv, lv, lx are common to all types.

Each balance is required to own Algos, have at least 100000 micro-Algos for each owned asset, and cannot control more than 1000 assets. Formally, we say that σ is a **valid balance** (in symbols, $\models \sigma$) when:[3]

$$\mathsf{Algo} \in \mathrm{dom}\,(\sigma) \;\wedge\; \sigma(\mathsf{Algo}) \geq 100000 \cdot |\,\mathrm{dom}\,(\sigma)| \;\wedge\; |\,\mathrm{dom}\,(\sigma)| \leq 1001$$

Transactions. Accounts can append various kinds of **transactions** to the blockchain, in order to, e.g., alter their balance or set their usage policies. We model transactions as records with the structure in Fig. 1. Each transaction has a type, which determines which of the other fields are relevant.[4] The field snd usually refers to the subject of the transaction (e.g., the *sender* in an assets transfer), while rcv refers to the *receiver* in an assets transfer. The fields asst and val refer, respectively, to the affected asset, and to its amount. The fields fv ("first valid"), lv ("last valid") and lx ("lease") are used to impose time constraints.

Algorand groups transactions into **rounds** $r = 1, 2, \ldots$ To establish *when* a transaction t is valid, we must consider both the current round r, and a **lease map** f_{lx} binding pairs (address, lease identifier) to rounds: this is used to enforce mutual exclusion between two or more transactions (see e.g. the *periodic payment*

---

[1] W.l.o.g., we consider a single-user address a equivalent to $(\mathcal{A}, n)$ with $\mathcal{A} = \langle a \rangle$, $n = 1$.
[2] We formalize scripts (i.e., smart contracts) later on, in Sect. 2.5.
[3] Since the codomain of σ is $\mathbb{N}$, the balance entry $\sigma(\mathsf{Algo})$ represents micro-Algos.
[4] In Algorand, the actual behaviour of a transaction may depend on both its type and other conditions, e.g., which optional fields are set. For instance, *pay* transactions may also close accounts if the CloseRemainderTo field is set. For the sake of clarity, in our model we prefer to use a richer set of types; see Sect. 5 for other differences.

contract in Sect. 3). Formally, we define the ***temporal validity of a transaction*** t by the predicate $f_{lx}, r \models t$, which holds whenever:

$$t.\text{fv} \le r \le t.\text{lv} \quad \text{and} \quad t.\text{lv} - t.\text{fv} \le \Delta_{max} \quad \text{and}$$
$$\left(t.\text{lx} = 0 \quad \text{or} \quad (t.\text{snd}, t.\text{lx}) \notin \text{dom}\,(f_{lx}) \quad \text{or} \quad r > f_{lx}(t.\text{snd}, t.\text{lx})\right)$$

First, the current round must lie between $t.\text{fv}$ and $t.\text{lv}$, whose distance cannot exceed Δ_{max} rounds[5]. Second, t must have a null lease identifier, or the identifier has not been seen before (i.e., $f_{lx}(t.\text{snd}, t.\text{lx})$ is undefined), or the lease has expired (i.e., $r > f_{lx}(t.\text{snd}, t.\text{lx})$). When performed, a transaction with non-null lease identifier acquires the lease on $(t.\text{snd}, t.\text{lx})$, which is set to $t.\text{lv}$.

2.2 Blockchain States

We model the evolution of the Algorand blockchain as a labelled transition system. A ***blockchain state*** Γ has the form:

$$\text{x}_1[\sigma_1] \mid \cdots \mid \text{x}_n[\sigma_n] \mid r \mid T_{lv} \mid f_{asst} \mid f_{lx} \mid f_{frz} \qquad (1)$$

where all addresses x_i are distinct, $\mid$ is commutative and associative, and:

- r is the current round;
- T_{lv} is the set of performed transactions whose "last valid" time lv has not expired. This set is used to avoid double spending (see Theorem 1);
- f_{asst} maps each asset to the addresses of its ***manager*** and ***creator***;
- f_{lx} is the ***lease map*** (from pairs (address, integer) to integers), used to ensure mutual exclusion between transactions;
- f_{frz} is a map from addresses to sets of assets, used to ***freeze assets***.

We define the ***initial state*** Γ_0 as $\text{a}_0[\{\text{Algo} \mapsto v_0\}] \mid 0 \mid \emptyset \mid f_{asst} \mid f_{lx} \mid f_{frz}$, where $\text{dom}\,(f_{asst}) = \text{dom}\,(f_{lx}) = \text{dom}\,(f_{frz}) = \emptyset$, a_0 is the initial user address, and $v_0 = 10^{16}$ (which is the total supply of 10 billions Algos).

  We now formalize the ASC1 state machine, by defining how it evolves by single transactions (Sect. 2.3), and then including atomic groups of transactions (Sect. 2.4), smart contracts (Sect. 2.5), and the authorization of transactions (Sect. 2.6).

2.3 Executing Single Transactions

We write $\Gamma \xrightarrow{t}_1 \Gamma'$ to mean: ***if*** the transaction t is performed in blockchain state Γ, then the blockchain evolves to state Γ'.[6] We specify the transition relation $\rightarrow_1$ through a set of inference rules (see [14, Fig. 5 in Appendix] for the full definition): each rule describes the effect of a transaction t in the state Γ of Eq. (1). We now illustrate all cases, depending on the transaction type ($t.\text{type}$).

---

[5] Δ_{max} is a global consensus parameter, set to 1000 at time of writing.

[6] Note that $\Gamma \xrightarrow{t}_1 \Gamma'$ does not imply that transaction t ***can*** be performed in Γ: in fact, t might require an authorization. We specify the required conditions in Sect. 2.6.

When $\tau \in \text{dom}(\sigma)$, we use the shorthand $\sigma + v{:}\tau$ to update balance σ by adding v units to token τ; similarly, we write $\sigma - v{:}\tau$ to decrease τ by v units:

$$\sigma + v{:}\tau \ \equiv \ \sigma\{\tau \mapsto \sigma(\tau) + v\} \qquad\qquad \sigma - v{:}\tau \ \equiv \ \sigma\{\tau \mapsto \sigma(\tau) - v\}$$

Pay to a New Account. Let $t.\text{snd} = x_i$ for some $i \in 1..n$, let $t.\text{rcv} = y \notin \{x_1, \dots, x_n\}$ (i.e., the sender account x is already in the state, while the receiver y is not), and let $t.\text{val} = v$. The rule has the following preconditions:

c1. t does not cause double-spending ($t \notin T_{\text{lv}}$);
c2. the time interval of the transaction, and its lease, are respected ($f_{\text{lx}}, r \models t$);
c3. the updated balance of x_i is valid ($\models \sigma_i - v : \text{Algo}$);
c4. the balance of the new account at address y is valid ($\models \{\text{Algo} \mapsto v\}$).

If these conditions are satisfied, the new state Γ' is the following:

$$x_i[\sigma_i - v{:}\text{Algo}] \mid y\,[\{\text{Algo} \mapsto v\}] \mid \cdots \mid r \mid T_{\text{lv}} \cup \{t\} \mid f_{asst} \mid upd(f_{\text{lx}}, t) \mid f_{frz}$$

In the new state, the Algo balance of x_i is decreased by v units, and a new account at y is created, containing exactly the v units taken from x_i. The balances of the other accounts are unchanged. The updated lease mapping is:

$$upd(f_{\text{lx}}, t) = \begin{cases} f_{\text{lx}}\{(t.\text{snd}, t.\text{lx}) \mapsto t.\text{lv}\} & \text{if } t.\text{lx} \neq 0 \\ f_{\text{lx}} & \text{otherwise} \end{cases}$$

Note that all transaction types check conditions c1. and c2. above; further, all transactions check that updated account balances are valid (as in c3. and c4.).

Pay to an Existing Account. Let $t.\text{snd} = x_i$, $t.\text{rcv} = x_j$, $t.\text{val} = v$, and $t.\text{asst} = \tau$. Besides the common checks, performing t requires that x_j has "opted in" τ (formally, $\tau \in \text{dom}(\sigma_j)$), and τ must not be frozen in accounts x_i and x_j (formally, $\tau \notin f_{frz}(x_i) \cup f_{frz}(x_j)$). If $x_i \neq x_j$, then in the new state the balance of τ in x_i is decreased by v units, and that of τ in x_j is increased by v units:

$$x_i[\sigma_i - v{:}\tau] \mid x_j[\sigma_j + v{:}\tau] \mid \cdots \mid r \mid T_{\text{lv}} \cup \{t\} \mid f_{asst} \mid upd(f_{\text{lx}}, t) \mid f_{frz}$$

where all accounts but x_i and x_j are unchanged. Otherwise, if $x_i = x_j$, then the balance of x_i is unchanged, and the other parts of the state are as above.

Close. Let $t.\text{snd} = x_i$, $t.\text{rcv} = x_j \neq x_i$, and $t.\text{asst} = \tau$. Performing t has two possible outcomes, depending on whether τ is Algo or a user-defined asset. If $\tau = \text{Algo}$, we must check that σ_i contains *only* Algos. If so, the new state is:

$$x_j[\sigma_j + \sigma_i(\text{Algo}){:}\text{Algo}] \mid \cdots \mid r \mid T_{\text{lv}} \cup \{t\} \mid f_{asst} \mid upd(f_{\text{lx}}, t) \mid f_{frz}$$

where the new state no longer contains the account x_i, and all the Algos in x_i are transferred to x_j. Instead, if $\tau \neq$ Algo, performing t requires to check only that x_i actually contains τ, and that x_j has "opted in" τ. Further, τ must not be frozen for addresses x_i and x_j, i.e. $\tau \notin f_{frz}(x_i) \cup f_{frz}(x_j)$. The new state is:

$$x_i[\sigma_i\{\tau \mapsto \bot\}] \mid x_j[\sigma_j + \sigma_i(\tau):\tau] \mid \cdots \mid r \mid T_{lv} \cup \{t\} \mid f_{asst} \mid upd(f_{lx}, t) \mid f_{frz}$$

where τ is removed from x_i, and all the units of τ in x_i are transferred to x_j.

Gen. Let $t.\mathsf{snd} = x_i$, $t.\mathsf{rcv} = x_j$, and $t.\mathsf{val} = v$. Performing t requires that x_i has enough Algos to own another asset, i.e. $\models \sigma_i\{\tau \mapsto v\}$, where τ is the (fresh) identifier of the new asset. In the new state, the balance of x_i is extended with $\{\tau \mapsto v\}$, and f_{asst} is updated, making x_j the manager of τ. The new state is:

$$x_i[\sigma_i\{\tau \mapsto v\}] \mid \cdots \mid r \mid T_{lv} \cup \{t\} \mid f_{asst}\{\tau \mapsto (x_j, x_i)\} \mid upd(f_{lx}, t) \mid f_{frz}$$

Opt in. Let $t.\mathsf{snd} = x_i$ and $t.\mathsf{asst} = \tau$. Performing t requires that τ already occurs in Γ, and that x_i has enough Algos to store it. If the balance σ_i does not have an entry for τ, in the new state σ_i is extended with a new entry for τ:

$$x_i[\sigma_i\{\tau \mapsto 0\}] \mid \cdots \mid r \mid T_{lv} \cup \{t\} \mid f_{asst} \mid upd(f_{lx}, t) \mid f_{frz}$$

Otherwise, if x_i's balance has already an entry for τ, then σ_i is unchanged.

Burn. Let $t.\mathsf{snd} = x_i$ and $t.\mathsf{asst} = \tau$. Performing t requires that x_i is the creator of τ, and that x_i stores *all* the units of τ (i.e., there are no units of τ in other accounts). In the resulting state, the token τ no longer exists:

$$x_i[\sigma_i\{\tau \mapsto \bot\}] \mid \cdots \mid r \mid T_{lv} \cup \{t\} \mid f_{asst}\{\tau \mapsto \bot\} \mid upd(f_{lx}, t) \mid f_{frz}$$

Note that this transaction requires an authorization by the asset manager of τ, which is recorded in f_{asst}. (We address this topic in Sect. 2.6.)

Revoke. Let $t.\mathsf{snd} = x_i$ and $t.\mathsf{rcv} = x_j$. Performing t requires that both x_i and x_j are already storing the asset τ, and that τ is not frozen for x_i and x_j. In the new state, the balance of x_i is decreased by $v = t.\mathsf{val}$ units of the asset $\tau = t.\mathsf{asst}$, and the balance of x_j is increased by the same amount:

$$x_i[\sigma_i - v:\tau] \mid x_j[\sigma_j + v:\tau] \mid \cdots \mid r \mid T_{lv} \cup \{t\} \mid f_{asst} \mid upd(f_{lx}, t) \mid f_{frz}$$

The effect of a *rvk* transaction is essentially the same as *pay*. The difference is that *rvk* must be authorized by the manager of the asset τ, while *pay* must be authorized by the sender x_i (see Sect. 2.6).

Freeze and Unfreeze. A *frz* transaction t with $t.\mathsf{snd} = x_i$ and $t.\mathsf{asst} = \tau$ updates the mapping f_{frz} into f'_{frz}, such that $f'_{frz}(x_i) = f_{frz}(x_i) \cup \{\tau\}$, whenever the asset τ is owned by x_i. This effectively prevents any transfers of the asset τ to/from the account x_i. The dual transaction *unfrz* updates the mapping f_{frz} into f'_{frz} such that $f'_{frz}(x_i) = f_{frz}(x_i) \setminus \{\tau\}$.

Delegate. A *delegate* transaction t with $t.\mathsf{snd} = x_i$, $t.\mathsf{rcv} = x_j$ and $t.\mathsf{asst} = \tau$ updates the manager of τ, provided that $f_{asst}(\tau) = (x_i, x_i)$, for some x_k. In the updated mapping $f_{asst}\{\tau \mapsto (x_j, x_k)\}$, the manager of τ is x_j.

Initiating a New Round. We model the advancement to the next round of the blockchain as a state transition $\Gamma \xrightarrow{\checkmark}_1 \Gamma'$. In the new state Γ', the round is increased, and the set T_{lv} is updated as $T'_{lv} = \{t \in T_{lv} \mid t.\mathsf{lv} > r\}$. The other components of the state are unchanged.

2.4   Executing Atomic Groups of Transactions

Atomic transfers allow state transitions to atomically perform *sequences* of transactions. To atomically perform a sequence $\mathcal{T} = t_1 \cdots t_n$ from a state Γ, we must check that all the transactions t_i can be performed *in sequence*, i.e. the following precondition must hold (for some $\Gamma_1, \ldots, \Gamma_n$):

$$\Gamma \xrightarrow{t_1}_1 \Gamma_1 \quad \cdots \quad \Gamma_{n-1} \xrightarrow{t_n}_1 \Gamma_n$$

If so, the state Γ can take a *single*-step transition labelled $\mathcal{T}$. Denoting the new transition relation with $\rightarrow$, we write the atomic execution of $\mathcal{T}$ in Γ as follows:

$$\Gamma \xrightarrow{\mathcal{T}} \Gamma_n$$

$e ::= v$	constant
$\mid e \circ e$	arithmetic ($\circ \in \{+, -, <, \leq, =, \geq, >, *, /, \%, \text{ and}, \text{ or }\}$)
$\mid \mathsf{not}\ e$	negation
$\mid \mathsf{txlen}$	number of transactions in the atomic group
$\mid \mathsf{txpos}$	index of current transaction in the atomic group
$\mid \mathsf{txid}(n)$	identifier of n-th transaction in the atomic group
$\mid \mathsf{tx}(n).\mathsf{f}$	value of field f of n-th transaction in the atomic group
$\mid \mathsf{arg}(n)$	n-th argument of the current transaction
$\mid \mathsf{H}(e)$	hash
$\mid \mathsf{versig}(e, e, e)$	signature verification

Syntactic sugar: $false ::= 1 = 0$ $true ::= 1 = 1$ $\mathsf{tx.f} ::= \mathsf{tx}(\mathsf{txpos}).\mathsf{f}$ $\mathsf{txid} ::= \mathsf{txid}(\mathsf{txpos})$
$\mathsf{if}\ e_0\ \mathsf{then}\ e_1\ \mathsf{else}\ e_2 ::= (e_0\ \mathsf{and}\ e_1)\ \mathsf{or}\ ((\mathsf{not}\ e_0)\ \mathsf{and}\ e_2)$

Fig. 2. Smart contract scripts (inspired by PyTeal [5]).

2.5   Executing Smart Contracts

In Algorand, custom authorization policies can be defined with a smart contract language called TEAL [6]. TEAL is a bytecode-based stack language, with an official programming interface for Python (called PyTeal): in our formal model, we take inspiration from the latter to abstract TEAL bytecode scripts as terms, with the syntax in Fig. 2. Besides standard arithmetic-logical operators, TEAL includes operators to count and index all transactions in the current atomic group, and to access their id and fields. When firing transaction involving scripts, users can specify a sequence of **arguments**; accordingly, the script language includes operators to know the number of arguments, and access them. Further, scripts include cryptographic operators to compute hashes and verify signatures.

The **script evaluation function** $[\![e]\!]_{\mathcal{T},i}^{\mathcal{W}}$ (Fig. 3) evaluates e using 3 parameters: a sequence of arguments $\mathcal{W}$, a sequence of transactions $\mathcal{T}$ forming an atomic group, and the index $i < |\mathcal{T}|$ of the transaction containing e. The script $\mathsf{tx}(n).\mathsf{f}$ evaluates to the field f of the nth transaction in group $\mathcal{T}$. The size of $\mathcal{T}$ is given by txlen, while txpos returns the index i of the transaction containing the script being evaluated. The script $\mathsf{arg}(n)$ returns the nth argument in $\mathcal{W}$. The script $\mathsf{H}(e)$ applies a public hash function H to the evaluation of e. The script $\mathsf{versig}(e_1, e_2, e_3)$ verifies a signature e_2 on the message obtained by concatenating the enclosing script and e_1, using public key e_3. All operators in Fig. 3 are *strict*: they fail if the evaluation of any operand fails.

2.6   Authorizing Transactions, and User-Blockchain Interaction

As noted before, the mere existence of a step $\Gamma \xrightarrow{t}_1 \Gamma'$ does not imply that t can actually be issued. For this to be possible, users must provide a sequence $\mathcal{W}$ of **witnesses**, satisfying the **authorization predicate** associated with t; such a predicate is uniquely determined by the **authorizer address** of t, written $auth(t, f_{asst})$. For transaction types *close*, *pay*, *gen*, *optin* the authorizer address is t.snd; for *burn*, *rvk*, *frz* and *unfrz* on an asset τ it is the asset manager $f_{asst}(\tau)$. Intuitively, if $auth(t, f_{asst}) = \mathsf{x}$, then $\mathcal{W}$ authorizes t iff:

1. if x is a multisig address $(\mathcal{A}, n)$, then $\mathcal{W}$ contains at least n signatures of t, made by users in $\mathcal{A}$; (if x is a single-user address a: see footnote 1)
2. if x is a script e, then e evaluates to *true* under the arguments $\mathcal{W}$.

$$[\![v]\!]_{\mathcal{T},i}^{\mathcal{W}} = v \qquad [\![e \circ e']\!]_{\mathcal{T},i}^{\mathcal{W}} = [\![e]\!]_{\mathcal{T},i}^{\mathcal{W}} \circ_{\perp} [\![e']\!]_{\mathcal{T},i}^{\mathcal{W}} \qquad [\![\text{not } e]\!]_{\mathcal{T},i}^{\mathcal{W}} = \neg_{\perp}[\![e]\!]_{\mathcal{T},i}^{\mathcal{W}}$$

$$[\![\mathsf{tx}(n).\mathsf{f}]\!]_{\mathcal{T},i}^{\mathcal{W}} = (\mathcal{T}.n).\mathsf{f} \ (0 \leq n < |\mathcal{T}|) \qquad [\![\mathsf{txid}(n)]\!]_{\mathcal{T},i}^{\mathcal{W}} = \mathcal{T}.n \ (0 \leq n < |\mathcal{T}|)$$

$$[\![\mathsf{txlen}]\!]_{\mathcal{T},i}^{\mathcal{W}} = |\mathcal{T}| \qquad [\![\mathsf{txpos}]\!]_{\mathcal{T},i}^{\mathcal{W}} = i \qquad [\![\mathsf{arg}(n)]\!]_{\mathcal{T},i}^{\mathcal{W}} = \mathcal{W}.n \ (0 \leq n < |\mathcal{W}|)$$

$$[\![\mathsf{H}(e)]\!]_{\mathcal{T},i}^{\mathcal{W}} = H([\![e]\!]_{\mathcal{T},i}^{\mathcal{W}}) \quad [\![\mathsf{versig}(e_1, e_2, e_3)]\!]_{\mathcal{T},i}^{\mathcal{W}} = ver_k(m, s) \ \begin{pmatrix} m = (\mathcal{T}.i.\mathsf{snd}, [\![e_1]\!]_{\mathcal{T},i}^{\mathcal{W}}) \\ s = [\![e_2]\!]_{\mathcal{T},i}^{\mathcal{W}} \ \ k = [\![e_3]\!]_{\mathcal{T},i}^{\mathcal{W}} \end{pmatrix}$$

Fig. 3. Evaluation of scripts in Fig. 2.

We now formalize the intuition above. Since the evaluation of scripts depends on a whole group of transactions $\mathcal{T}$, and on the index i of the current transaction within $\mathcal{T}$, we define the authorization predicate as $\mathcal{W} \models \mathcal{T}, i$ (read: "$\mathcal{W}$ authorizes the ith transaction in $\mathcal{T}$"). Let $sig_A(m)$ stand for the set of signatures containing $sig_a(m)$ for all $a \in A$; then, $\mathcal{W} \models \mathcal{T}, i$ holds whenever:

1. if $auth(\mathcal{T}.i, f_{asst}) = (\mathcal{A}, n)$, then $|set(\mathcal{W}) \cap sig_{set(\mathcal{A})}(\mathcal{T}, i)| \geq n$
2. if $auth(\mathcal{T}.i, f_{asst}) = e$, then $[\![e]\!]_{\mathcal{T},i}^{\mathcal{W}} = true$

Note that, in general, the sequence of witnesses $\mathcal{W}$ is not unique, i.e., it may happen that $\mathcal{W} \models \mathcal{T}, i$ and $\mathcal{W}' \models \mathcal{T}, i$ for $\mathcal{W} \neq \mathcal{W}'$. For instance, the *Oracle* contract in Sect. 3 accepts transactions with witnesses of the form $0\,s$ or $1\,s'$, where the first element of the sequence represents the oracle's choice, and the second element is the oracle's signature.

Given a *sequence of sequences* of witnesses $\mathbf{W} = \mathcal{W}_0 \cdots \mathcal{W}_{n-1}$ with $n = |\mathcal{T}|$, the **group authorization predicate** $\mathbf{W} \models \mathcal{T}$ holds iff $\mathcal{W}_i \models \mathcal{T}, i$ for all $i \in 0..n-1$.

User-Blockchain Interaction. We model the interaction of users with the blockchain as a transition system. Its states are pairs (Γ, K), where Γ is a blockchain state, while K is the set of authorization bitstrings currently known by users. The transition relation $\xrightarrow{\ell}$ (with $\ell \in \{w, \checkmark, \mathbf{W}:\mathcal{T}\}$) is given by the rules:

$$\frac{}{(\Gamma, K) \xrightarrow{w} (\Gamma, K \cup \{w\})} \qquad \frac{\Gamma \xrightarrow{\checkmark} \Gamma'}{(\Gamma, K) \xrightarrow{\checkmark} (\Gamma', K)} \qquad \frac{\Gamma \xrightarrow{\mathcal{T}} \Gamma' \quad set(\mathbf{W}) \subseteq K \quad \mathbf{W} \models \mathcal{T}}{(\Gamma, K) \xrightarrow{\mathbf{W}:\mathcal{T}} (\Gamma', K)}$$

With the first two rules, users can broadcast a witness w, or advance to the next round. The last rule gathers from K a sequence of witnesses $\mathbf{W}$, and lets the blockchain perform an atomic group of transactions $\mathcal{T}$ if authorized by $\mathbf{W}$.

2.7   Fundamental Properties of ASC1

We now exploit our formal model to establish some fundamental properties of ASC1. Theorem 1 states that the same transaction t cannot be issued more than once, i.e., there is no *double-spending*. In the statement, we use $\rightarrow^* \xrightarrow{\mathcal{T}} \rightarrow^*$ to denote an arbitrarily long series of steps including a group of transactions $\mathcal{T}$.

Theorem 1 (No double-spending). *Let* $\Gamma_0 \rightarrow^* \xrightarrow{\mathcal{T}} \rightarrow^* \Gamma \xrightarrow{\mathcal{T}'} \Gamma'$. *Then, no transaction occurs more than once in* $\mathcal{T}\mathcal{T}'$.

Define the *value* of an asset τ in a state $\Gamma = x_1[\sigma_1] \mid \cdots \mid x_n[\sigma_n] \mid r \mid \cdots$ as the sum of the balances of τ in all accounts in Γ:

$$val_\tau(\Gamma) = \sum_{i=1}^{n} val_\tau(\sigma_i) \qquad \text{where } val_\tau(\sigma) = \begin{cases} \sigma(\tau) & \text{if } \tau \in dom(\sigma) \\ 0 & \text{otherwise} \end{cases}$$

Theorem 2 states that, once an asset is minted, its value remains constant, until the asset is eventually burnt. In particular, since Algos cannot be burnt (nor minted, unlike in Bitcoin and Ethereum), their amount remains constant.

Theorem 2 (Value preservation). *Let $\Gamma_0 \to^* \Gamma \to^* \Gamma'$. Then:*

$$val_\tau(\Gamma') = \begin{cases} val_\tau(\Gamma) & \text{if } \tau \text{ occurs in } \Gamma \text{ and it is not burnt in } \Gamma \to^* \Gamma' \\ 0 & \text{otherwise} \end{cases}$$

Theorem 3 establishes that the transition systems $\to$ and $\Rightarrow$ are deterministic: crucially, this allows reconstructing the blockchain state from the transition log. Notably, by item 3 of Theorem 3, witnesses only determine whether a state transition happens or not, but they do not affect the new state. This is unlike Ethereum, where arguments of function calls in transactions may affect the state.

Theorem 3 (Determinism). *For all $\lambda \in \{\checkmark, \mathtt{J}\}$ and $\ell \in \{\checkmark, w\}$:*

1. *if $\Gamma \xrightarrow{\lambda} \Gamma'$ and $\Gamma \xrightarrow{\lambda} \Gamma''$, then $\Gamma' = \Gamma''$;*
2. *if $(\Gamma, K) \xrightarrow{\ell} (\Gamma', K')$ and $(\Gamma, K) \xrightarrow{\ell} (\Gamma'', K'')$, then $(\Gamma', K') = (\Gamma'', K'')$;*
3. *if $(\Gamma, K) \xrightarrow{\mathbf{W}:\mathtt{J}} (\Gamma', K')$ and $(\Gamma, K) \xrightarrow{\mathbf{W}':\mathtt{J}} (\Gamma'', K'')$, then $\Gamma' = \Gamma''$ and $K' = K'' = K$.*

3 Designing Secure Smart Contracts in Algorand

We now exploit our formal model to design some archetypal smart contracts, and establish their security (Sect. 3.2). First, we introduce an attacker model.

3.1 Attacker Model

We assume that cryptographic primitives are secure, i.e., hashes are collision resistant and signatures cannot be forged (except with negligible probability). A *run* $\mathcal{R}$ is a (possibly infinite) sequence of labels $\ell_1 \ell_2 \cdots$ such that $(\Gamma_0, K_0) \xrightarrow{\ell_1} (\Gamma_1, K_1) \xrightarrow{\ell_2} \cdots$, where Γ_0 is the initial state, and $K_0 = \emptyset$ is the initial (empty) knowledge; hence, as illustrated in Sect. 2.6, each label ℓ_i in a run $\mathcal{R}$ can be either w (broadcast of a witness bitstring w), $\mathbf{W}:\mathtt{J}$ (atomic group of transactions $\mathtt{J}$ authorized by $\mathbf{W}$), or $\checkmark$ (advance to next round). We consider a setting where:

- each user a has a *strategy* Σ, i.e. a PPTIME algorithm to select which label to perform among those permitted by the ASC1 transition system. A strategy takes as input a finite run $\mathcal{R}$ (the past history) and outputs a single enabled label ℓ. Strategies are *stateful*: users can read and write a private unbounded tape to maintain their own state throughout the run. The initial state of a's tape contains a's private key, and the public keys of all users;[7]

---

[7] Notice that new public/private key pairs can be generated during the run, and their public parts can be communicated as labels w.

– an **adversary** Adv who controls the scheduling with her stateful **adversarial strategy** Σ_{Adv}: a PPTIME algorithm taking as input the current run $\mathcal{R}$ and the labels output by the strategies of users (i.e., the steps that users are trying to make). The output of Σ_{Adv} is a single label ℓ, that is appended to the current run. We assume the adversarial strategy Σ_{Adv} can delay users' transactions by at most δ_{Adv} rounds, where δ_{Adv} is a given natural number.[8]

A set Σ of strategies of users and Adv induces a distribution of runs; we say that run $\mathcal{R}$ is **conformant** to Σ if $\mathcal{R}$ is sampled from such a distribution. We assume that infinite runs contain infinitely many ✓: this *non-Zeno condition* ensures that neither users nor Adv can perform infinitely many transactions in a round.

3.2   Smart Contracts

We now exploit our model to specify some archetypal ASC1 contracts, and reason about their security. To simplify the presentation, we assume $\delta_{Adv} = 0$, i.e., the adversary Adv can start a new round (performing ✓) only if all users agree.[9] The table below summarises our selection of smart contracts, highlighting the design patterns they implement.

Use case/Pattern	Signed witness	Timeouts	Commit/ reveal	State machine	Atomic transfer	Time windows
Oracle	✓	✓				
HTLC		✓	✓			
Mutual HTLC [14, §B.1]		✓	✓		✓	
$O(n^2)$-collateral lottery		✓	✓		✓	
0-collateral lottery [14, §B.2]		✓	✓	✓	✓	
Periodic payment						✓
Escrow [14, §B.3]	✓			✓		
Two-phase authorization		✓		✓		✓
Limit order [14, §B.4]		✓			✓	
Split [14, §B.5]		✓			✓	

Oracle. We start by designing a contract which allows either a or b to withdraw all the Algos in the contract, depending on the outcome of a certain boolean event. Let o be an oracle who certifies such an outcome, by signing the value 1 or 0. We model the contract as the following script:

$$\textit{Oracle} \triangleq \text{tx.type} = \textit{close} \text{ and tx.asst} = \text{Algo and } ((\text{tx.fv} > r_{max} \text{ and tx.rcv} = \text{a})$$
$$\text{or } (\text{arg}(0) = 0 \text{ and versig}(\text{arg}(0), \text{arg}(1), \text{o}) \text{ and tx.rcv} = \text{a})$$
$$\text{or } (\text{arg}(0) = 1 \text{ and versig}(\text{arg}(0), \text{arg}(1), \text{o}) \text{ and tx.rcv} = \text{b}))$$

---

[8] Without this assumption, Adv could arbitrarily disrupt deadlines: e.g., Σ_{Adv} could make a *always* lose lottery games (like the ones below) by delaying a's transactions.

[9] All results can be easily adjusted for $\delta_{Adv} > 0$, but this would require more verbose statements to account for possible delays introduced by Adv.

Once created, the contract accepts only *close* transactions, using two arguments as witnesses. The argument $\mathsf{arg}(0)$ contains the outcome, while $\mathsf{arg}(1)$ is o's signature on $(Oracle, \mathsf{arg}(0))$, i.e., the concatenation between the script and the first argument. The user b can collect the funds in *Oracle* if o certifies the outcome 1, while a can collect the funds if the outcome is 0, or after round r_{max}.

Theorem 4 below proves that *Oracle* works as intended. To state it, we define T_p as the set of transactions allowing a user p to withdraw the contract funds:

$$T_p = \{t \mid t.\mathsf{type} = close, \ t.\mathsf{snd} = Oracle, \ t.\mathsf{rcv} = p, \ t.\mathsf{asst} = \mathsf{Algo}\}$$

The theorem considers the following strategies for a, b, and o:

- Σ_a: wait for $s = sig_o(Oracle, 0)$; if s arrives at round $r \leq r_{max}$, then immediately send a transaction $t \in T_a$ with $t.\mathsf{fv} = r$ and witness $0\ s$; otherwise, at round $r_{max} + 1$, send a transaction $t \in T_a$ with $t.\mathsf{fv} = r_{max} + 1$;
- Σ_b: wait for $s' = sig_o(Oracle, 1)$; if s' arrives at round r, immediately send a transaction $t \in T_b$ with $t.\mathsf{fv} = r$ and witness $1\ s'$;
- Σ_o: do one of the following: *(a)* send o's signature on $(Oracle, 0)$ at any time, or *(b)* send o's signature on $(Oracle, 1)$ at any time, or *(c)* do nothing.

Theorem 4. *Let* $\mathcal{R}$ *be a run conforming to some set of strategies* Σ, *such that: (i)* $\Sigma_o \in \Sigma$; *(ii)* $\mathcal{R}$ *reaches, at some round before* r_{max}, *a state* $Oracle[\sigma] \mid \cdots$; *(iii)* $\mathcal{R}$ *reaches the round* $r_{max} + 2$. *Then, with overwhelming probability:*

(1) if $\Sigma_a \in \Sigma$ *and* o *has not sent a signature on* $(Oracle, 1)$, *then* $\mathcal{R}$ *contains a transaction in* T_a, *transferring at least* $\sigma(\mathsf{Algo})$ *to* a*;*
(2) if $\Sigma_b \in \Sigma$ *and* o *has sent a signature on* $(Oracle, 1)$ *at round* $r \leq r_{max}$, *then* $\mathcal{R}$ *contains a transaction in* T_b, *transferring at least* $\sigma(\mathsf{Algo})$ *to* b*.*

Notice that in item (1) we are only assuming that a and o use the strategies Σ_a and Σ_o, while b and Adv can use *any* strategy (and possibly collude). Similarly, in item (2) we are only assuming b's and o's strategies.

Hash Time Lock Contract (HTLC). A user a promises that she will either reveal a secret s_a by round r_{max}, or pay a penalty to b. More sophisticated contracts, e.g. gambling games, use this mechanism to let players generate random numbers in a fair way. We define the HTLC as the following contract, parameterised on the two users a, b and the hash $h_a = H(s_a)$ of the secret:

$$HTLC(a, b, h_a) \triangleq \mathsf{tx.type} = close \text{ and } \mathsf{tx.asst} = \mathsf{Algo} \text{ and }$$
$$((\mathsf{tx.rcv} = a \text{ and } \mathsf{H}(\mathsf{arg}(0)) = h_a) \text{ or } (\mathsf{tx.rcv} = b \text{ and } \mathsf{tx.fv} \geq r_{max}))$$

The contract accepts only *close* transactions with receiver a or b. User a can collect the funds in the contract only by providing the secret s_a in $\mathsf{arg}(0)$, effectively making s_a public.[10] Instead, if a does not reveal s_a, then b can collect the

---

[10] If s_a is a sufficiently long bitstring generated uniformly at random, collision resistance of the hash function ensures that only a (who knows s_a) can provide such an $\mathsf{arg}(0)$.

funds after round r_{max}. We state the correctness of $HTLC$ in Theorem 5; first, let T_p be the set of transactions allowing user p to withdraw the contract funds:

$$T_p \; = \; \{t \mid t.\text{type} = close, \; t.\text{snd} = HTLC(a, b, h_a), \; t.\text{rcv} = p, \; t.\text{asst} = \text{Algo}\}$$

We consider the following strategies for a and b:

- Σ_a: at a round $r < r_{max}$, send a $t \in T_a$ with $t.\text{fv} = r$ and witness s_a;
- Σ_b: at round r_{max}, check whether any transaction in T_a occurs in $\mathcal{R}$. If not, then immediately send a transaction $t \in T_b$ with $t.\text{fv} = r_{max}$.

Theorem 5. *Let $\mathcal{R}$ be a run conforming to some set of strategies Σ, such that: (i) $\mathcal{R}$ reaches, at some round before r_{max}, a state $HTLC(a, b, h_a)[\sigma] \mid \cdots$; (ii) $\mathcal{R}$ reaches the round $r_{max} + 1$. Then, with overwhelming probability:*

(1) if $\Sigma_a \in \Sigma$, then $\mathcal{R}$ contains a transaction in T_a, transferring at least $\sigma(\text{Algo})$ to a;

(2) if $\Sigma_b \in \Sigma$ and $\mathcal{R}$ does not contain the secret s_a before round $r_{max} + 1$, then $\mathcal{R}$ contains a transaction in T_b, transferring at least $\sigma(\text{Algo})$ to b.

Lotteries. Consider a gambling game where n players bet 1 Algo each, and the winner, chosen uniformly at random among them, can redeem n Algos. A simple implementation, inspired by [9–11] for Bitcoin, requires each player to deposit $n(n-1)$ Algos as collateral in an HTLC contract.[11] For $n = 2$ players a and b, such deposits are transferred by the following transactions:

$$t_{Ha} \; = \; \{\text{type} : pay, \text{snd} : a, \text{rcv} : HTLC(a, b, h_a), \text{val} : 2, \text{asst} : \text{Algo}, \dots\}$$
$$t_{Hb} \; = \; \{\text{type} : pay, \text{snd} : b, \text{rcv} : HTLC(b, a, h_b), \text{val} : 2, \text{asst} : \text{Algo}, \dots\}$$

The bets are stored in the following contract, which determines the winner as a function of the secrets, and allows her to withdraw the whole pot:

$$Lottery \triangleq \text{tx.type} = close \text{ and tx.asst} = \text{Algo and } H(\arg(0)) = h_a \text{ and } H(\arg(1)) = h_b$$
$$\text{and if } (\arg(0) + \arg(1)) \, 2 = 0 \text{ then tx.rcv} = a \text{ else tx.rcv} = b$$

with $h_a \neq h_b$.[12] Players a and b start the game with the atomic transactions:

$$\mathcal{T}_{a,b} \; = \; t_{Ha} \, t_{Hb} \, t_{La} \, t_{Lb} \quad \text{where:}$$
$$t_{La} \; = \; \{\text{type} : pay, \text{snd} : a, \text{rcv} : Lottery, \text{val} : 1, \text{asst} : \text{Algo}, \dots\}$$
$$t_{Lb} \; = \; \{\text{type} : pay, \text{snd} : a, \text{rcv} : Lottery, \text{val} : 1, \text{asst} : \text{Algo}, \dots\}$$

The transaction t_{La} creates the contract with a's bet, and t_{Lb} completes it with b's bet. At this point, there are two possible outcomes:

(a) both players reveal their secret. Then, the winner can withdraw the pot, by performing a *close* action on the *Lottery* contract, providing as arguments the two secrets, and setting her identity in the rcv field;

---

[11] A zero-collateral lottery is presented in [14, §B.2].
[12] This check prevents a replay attack: if a chooses $h_a = h_b$, then b cannot win.

(b) one of the players does not reveal the secret. Then, the other player can withdraw the collateral in the other player's HTLC (and redeem her own).

To formalise the correctness of the lottery, consider the sets of transactions:

$$
\begin{aligned}
T_{\mathsf{p,q}}^{secr} &= \{t \mid t.\mathsf{type} = close, t.\mathsf{snd} = HTLC(\mathsf{p,q},h_\mathsf{p}), t.\mathsf{rcv} = \mathsf{p}, t.\mathsf{asst} = \mathsf{Algo}\} \\
T_{\mathsf{p,q}}^{tout} &= \{t \mid t.\mathsf{type} = close, t.\mathsf{snd} = HTLC(\mathsf{p,q},h_\mathsf{p}), t.\mathsf{rcv} = \mathsf{q}, t.\mathsf{asst} = \mathsf{Algo}\} \\
T_{\mathsf{p}}^{lott} &= \{t \mid t.\mathsf{type} = close, t.\mathsf{snd} = Lottery, t.\mathsf{rcv} = \mathsf{p}, t.\mathsf{asst} = \mathsf{Algo}\}
\end{aligned}
$$

and consider the following strategy Σ_a for a (the one for b is analogous):

1. at some $r < r_{max}$, send a transaction $t \in T_{\mathsf{a,b}}^{secr}$ with $t.\mathsf{fv} = r$ and witness s_a;
2. if some transaction in $T_{\mathsf{b,a}}^{secr}$ occurs in $\mathcal{R}$ at round $r' < r_{max}$, then extract its witness s_b and compute the winner; if a is the winner, immediately send a transaction $t \in T_\mathsf{a}^{lott}$ with $t.\mathsf{fv} = r'$ and witness $s_\mathsf{a}s_\mathsf{b}$;
3. if at round r_{max} no transaction in $T_{\mathsf{b,a}}$ occurs in $\mathcal{R}$, immediately send a transaction $t \in T_{\mathsf{b,a}}^{tout}$ with $t.\mathsf{fv} = r_{max}$.

Theorem 6 below establishes that the lottery is fair, implying that the expected payoff of player a following strategy Σ_a is at least negligible; instead, if a does not follow Σ_a (e.g., by not revealing her secret), the expected payoff may be negative; analogous results hold for player b. This result can be generalised for $n > 2$ players, with a collateral of $n(n-1)$ Algos. As in the HTLC, we assume that s_a and s_b are sufficiently long bitstrings generated uniformly at random.

Theorem 6. *Let $\mathcal{R}$ be a run conforming to a set of strategies Σ, such that: (i) $\mathcal{R}$ contains, before r_{max}, the label $\mathcal{T}_{\mathsf{a,b}}$; (ii) $\mathcal{R}$ reaches round $r_{max} + 1$. For $\mathsf{p} \neq \mathsf{q} \in \{\mathsf{a,b}\}$, if $\Sigma_\mathsf{p} \in \Sigma$, then: (1) $\mathcal{R}$ contains a transaction in $T_{\mathsf{p,q}}^{secr}$, transferring at least 2 Algo to p; (2) the probability that $\mathcal{R}$ contains $T_{\mathsf{q,p}}^{tout}$ or T_p^{lott}, which transfer at least 1 Algo to p, is $\geq \frac{1}{2}$ (up-to a negligible quantity).*

Periodic Payment. We want to ensure that a can withdraw a fixed amount of v Algos at fixed time windows of p rounds. We can implement this behaviour through the following contract, which can be refilled when needed:

$$
PP(p,d,n) \triangleq \mathsf{tx.type} = pay \text{ and } \mathsf{tx.val} = v \text{ and } \mathsf{tx.asst} = \mathsf{Algo} \text{ and}
$$
$$
\mathsf{tx.rcv} = \mathsf{a} \text{ and } \mathsf{tx.fv} \% p = 0 \text{ and } \mathsf{tx.lv} = \mathsf{tx.fv} + d \text{ and } \mathsf{tx.lx} = n
$$

The contract accepts only *pay* transactions of v Algos to receiver a. The conditions $\mathsf{tx.fv} \% p = 0$ and $\mathsf{tx.lv} = \mathsf{tx.fv} + d$ ensure that the contract only accepts transactions with validity interval $[k\,p, k\,p+d]$, for $k \in \mathbb{N}$. The condition $\mathsf{tx.lx} = n$ ensures that *at most* one such transactions is accepted for each time window.

Finite-State Machines. Consider a set of users A who want to stipulate a contract whose behaviour is given by a finite-state machine with states $q_0, \ldots, q_n$. We can implement such a contract by representing each state q_i as a script e_i; the current state/script holds the assets, and each state transition $q_i \to q_j$ is a clause in e_i which enables a *close* transaction to transfer the assets to e_j. This clause requires tx.rcv $= e_j$—except in case of loops, which cannot be encoded directly:[13] in this case, we identify the next state as tx.rcv $= \mathsf{arg}(0)$, also requiring all users in A to sign $\mathsf{arg}(0)$ to confirm its correctness. To ensure that any user in A can trigger a state transition (by firing the corresponding transaction), their signatures must be exchanged before the contract starts. We show an instance of this pattern as the two-phase authorization contract below.

An alternative technique is based on quines. As before, a state transition $q_i \to q_j$ is rendered as a transaction which closes e_i and transfers the balance to e_j. Here, all such scripts e_k have the same code, except for a single state constant k which occurs at a specific offset, and which represents the current state. To verify that tx.rcv represents a legit next state, e_i requires a witness w such that: (i) tx.rcv is equal to the hash of w, and the state constant j within w is indeed a next state for i; (ii) tx.snd is equal to the hash of w', where w' is obtained from w by replacing the state constant j with the current state i. Performing these checks could be possible by using concatenation and substring operators.[14]

Two-Phase Authorization. We want a contract to allow user c to withdraw some funds, but only if authorized by a and b. We want a to give her authorization first; if b's authorization is not given within $p \geq \Delta_{max}$ rounds, then anyone can fire a transaction to reset the contract to its initial state. We model this contract with two scripts: *P1* represents the state where no authorization has been given yet, while *P2* represents the state where a's authorization has been given. Conceptually, the contract implements a finite-state machine, looping between two states until the contract funds are withdrawn by c.

$P1 \triangleq$ tx.type $= close$ and tx.asset $=$ Algo and versig(txid, arg(0), a) and
  tx.rcv $= P2$ and tx.fv % $(4*p) = 0$ and tx.lv $=$ tx.fv $+ \Delta_{max}$

$P2 \triangleq$ tx.type $= close$ and tx.asset $=$ Algo and
  ((versig(txid, arg(0), b) and tx.rcv $=$ c) or
  (versig(arg(0), arg(1), a_1) and versig(arg(0), arg(2), b_1) and
  tx.rcv $= \mathsf{arg}(0)$ and tx.fv % $(4*p) = 2*p$ and tx.lv $=$ tx.fv $+ \Delta_{max}$))

The scripts *P1* and *P2* use a time window with 4 frames, each lasting p rounds. Script *P1* only accepts *close* transactions which transfer the balance to *P2*; the time constraint ensures that such transactions are sent in the first time frame. The script *P2* accepts two kinds of transactions: *(a)* transfer the balance to c, using an authorization by b; *(b)* transfer the balance to *P1*, in the 4th time frame.

---

[13] This is because Algorand contracts cannot have circular references: contract accounts are referenced by script hashes, and no script can depend on its own hash.

[14] In Algorand, these operators are available only for **LogicSigVersion** ≥ 2.

```
{                                      {
      "type": "pay",                        "type": "axfer",
      "snd": x,                             "snd": x,
      "rcv": 0,                             "asnd": x,
      "close": y,                           "arcv": 0,
      "amt": 0                              "aclose": y,
}                                           "xaid": tau,
                                            "aamt": 0
                                       }
```

Fig. 4. Translation of a *close* transaction (left: τ = Algo, right: $\tau \neq$ Algo).

Note that in *P2* we cannot use the (intuitively correct) condition tx.rcv = *P1*, as it would introduce a circularity. Instead, we apply the state machines technique described above: we require tx.rcv = arg(0), with arg(0) signed by both a and b,[15] and assume that these signatures are exchanged before the contract starts.

4   From the Formal Model to Concrete Algorand

We now discuss how to translate transactions and scripts in our model to concrete Algorand. We first sketch how to compile our scripts into TEAL. The compilation of most constructs is straightforward. For instance, a script $e + e'$ is compiled by using the opcode +, and similarly for the other arithmetic and comparison operators, and for the cryptographic primitives. The logic operators and, or are compiled via the opcode bnz, to obtain the short-circuit semantics. The not operator is compiled via the opcode !. The operator txid(*n*) is compiled as gtxn n TxID, txlen is compiled as global GroupSize, txpos is compiled as txn GroupIndex, and arg(*n*) as arg n.

Finally, compiling the script tx(*n*).f depends on the field f. If f is fv, lv, or lx, then the compilation is gtxn n i, where i is, respectively, FirstValid, LastValid, or Lease. For the other cases of f, the compilation of tx(*n*).f generates a TEAL script which computes f by decoding the concrete Algorand transaction fields, and making them available in the scratch space. This decoding is detailed in Table 2 in [14]. From the same table we can also infer how to translate transactions in the model to concrete Algorand transactions. For instance, translating a transaction of the form:

$$\{\text{type} : \textit{close}, \text{ snd} : x, \text{ rcv} : y, \text{ asst} : \tau\}$$

results in the concrete transaction in Fig. 4 (where we omit the irrelevant fields).

Our modelling approach is supported by a prototype tool, called **secteal** (*secure TEAL*), and accessible via a web interface at:

http://secteal.cs.stir.ac.uk/

The core of the tool is a compiler that translates smart contracts written as expressions, based on the script language (Sect. 2.5), into executable TEAL byte-code. In its current form, **secteal** supports experimentation with our model, and

---

[15] We use other key pairs a_l and b_l to avoid confusion with the signatures on txid.

is provided with a series of examples from Sect. 3.2. Users can also compile their own `secteal` contracts, paving the way to a declarative approach to contract design and development. `secteal` is a first building block toward a comprehensive IDE for the design, verification, and deployment of contracts on Algorand.

5   Conclusions

This work is part of a wider research line on formal modelling of blockchain-based contracts, ranging from Bitcoin [12,28,32] to Ethereum [18,23–26,31], Cardano [19], Tezos [17], and Zilliqa [33]. These formal models are a necessary prerequisite to rigorously reason on the security of smart contracts, and they are the basis for automatic verification. Besides modelling the behaviour of transactions, in Sect. 3.1 we have proposed a model of attackers: this enables us to prove properties of smart contracts in the presence of adversaries, in the spirit of long-standing research in the cryptography area [8,9,13,16,22,29,30].

Differences Between Our Model and Algorand. Besides not modelling the consensus protocol, to keep the formalization simple, we chose to abstract from some aspects of ASC1, which do not appear to be relevant to the development of (the majority of) smart contracts. First, we are not modelling some transaction fields: among them, we have omitted the **fee** field, used to specify an amount of Algos to be paid to nodes, and the **note** field, used to embed arbitrary bitstrings into transactions. We associate a single manager to assets, while Algorand uses different managers for different operations (e.g., the freeze manager for $frz/unfrz$ and the clawback manager for rvk). We use two different transactions types, pay and $close$, to perform asset transfers and account closures: in Algorand, a single pay transaction can perform both. Note that we can achieve the same effect by performing the pay and $close$ transactions within the same atomic group. Although Algorand relies on 7 transaction types, the behaviour of some transactions needs to be further qualified by the combination of other fields (e.g., freeze and unfreeze are obtained by transactions with the same type **afrz**, but with a different value of the **AssetFrozen** field). While this is useful as an implementation detail, our model simplifies reasoning about different behaviours by explicitly exposing them in the transaction type. In the same spirit, while Algorand uses different transaction types to represent actions with similar functionality (e.g., transferring Algos and user-defined assets are rendered with different transaction types, **pay** and **axfer**), we use the same transaction type (e.g., pay) for such actions. Our model does not encompass some advanced features of Algorand, e.g.: rekeying accounts, key registration transactions (**keyreg**), some kinds of asset configuration transaction (e.g., decimals, default frozen, different managers), and application call transactions.[16] Our script language substantially covers TEAL opcodes with **LogicSigVersion=1**, but for a few exceptions, e.g. bitwise operations, different hash functions, jumps.

---

[16] Application call transactions are used to implement *stateful* contracts, and therefore are outside the scope of this paper.

Related Work. Besides featuring an original consensus protocol based on proof-of-stake [20], Algorand has also introduced a novel paradigm of (stateless) smart contracts, which differs from the paradigms of other mainstream blockchains. On the one hand, Algorand follows the *account-based* model, similarly to Ethereum (and differently from Bitcoin and Cardano, which follow the UTXO model). On the other hand, Algorand's paradigm of stateless contracts diverges from Ethereum's stateful contracts: rather, it resembles Bitcoin's, where contracts are based upon custom transaction redeem conditions. Besides these differences, Algorand natively features user-defined assets, while other platforms render them as smart contracts (e.g., by implementing ERC20 and ERC721 interfaces in Ethereum). Overall, these differences demand for a formal model that is substantially different from the models devised for the other blockchain platforms.

Our formalization of the Algorand's script language is close, with respect to the level of abstraction, to the model of Bitcoin script developed in [12]. Indeed, both works formalise scripts in an expression language, abstracting from the bytecode. A main difference between Algorand and Ethereum is that Ethereum contracts are stateful: their state can be updated by specific bytecode instructions; instead, (stateless) TEAL scripts merely authorize transactions. Consequently, a difference between our model and formal models of Ethereum contracts is that the semantics of our scripts has no side effects. In this way, our work departs from most literature on the formalization of Ethereum contracts, where the target of the formalization is either the bytecode language EVM [24,25,31], or the high-level language Solidity [15,21,27].

Future Work. Our formal model of Algorand smart contracts can be expanded depending on the evolution of the Algorand framework. In mid August 2020, Algorand has introduced *stateful* ASC1 contracts [2], enriching contract accounts with a persistent key-value store, accessible and modifiable through a new kind of transaction (which can use an extended set of TEAL opcodes). To accommodate stateful contracts in our model, we would need to embed the key-value store in contract accounts, and extend the script language with key-value store updates. The rest of our model (in particular, the semantics of transactions and the attacker model) is mostly unaffected by this extension. Future work could also investigate declarative languages for stateful Algorand smart contracts, and associated verification techniques. Another research direction is the mechanization of our formal model, using a proof assistant: this would allow machine-checking the proofs developed by pencil-and-paper in [14, §D]. Similar work has been done e.g. for Bitcoin [32] and for Tezos [17].

Acknowledgements. The authors are partially supported by: Conv. Fondazione di Sardegna & Atenei Sardi project F74I19000900007 *ADAM* (Massimo Bartoletti); The Data Lab, Innovation Center (Cristian Lepore); EU Horizon 2020 project 830929 *CyberSec4Europe*, and Industriens Fonds Cyberprogram 2020-0489 *Security-by-Design in Digital Denmark (Sb3D)* (Alceste Scalas), and MIUR PON *Distributed Ledgers for Secure Open Communities* (Roberto Zunino).

References

1. Algorand developer docs (2020). https://developer.algorand.org/docs/
2. Algorand developer docs: stateful smart contracts (2020). https://developer.algorand.org/docs/features/asc1/stateful/
3. Algorand developer docs: Transaction Execution Approval Language (TEAL) (2020). https://developer.algorand.org/docs/reference/teal
4. ASC1 coherence-checking experiments (2020). https://github.com/blockchain-unica/asc1-experiments
5. PyTeal: Algorand smart contracts in Python (2020). https://github.com/algorand/pyteal
6. Transaction execution approval language (TEAL) specification (2020) https://developer.algorand.org/docs/reference/teal/specification/
7. Alturki, M.A., et al.: Towards a verified model of the algorand consensus protocol in coq. In: Sekerinski, E., et al. (eds.) FM 2019. LNCS, vol. 12232, pp. 362–367. Springer, Cham (2020). https://doi.org/10.1007/978-3-030-54994-7_27
8. Andrychowicz, M., Dziembowski, S., Malinowski, D., Mazurek, Ł: Fair two-party computations via bitcoin deposits. In: Böhme, R., Brenner, M., Moore, T., Smith, M. (eds.) FC 2014. LNCS, vol. 8438, pp. 105–121. Springer, Heidelberg (2014). https://doi.org/10.1007/978-3-662-44774-1_8
9. Andrychowicz, M., Dziembowski, S., Malinowski, D., Mazurek, L.: Secure multiparty computations on Bitcoin. In: IEEE S & P, pp. 443–458 (2014). https://doi.org/10.1109/SP.2014.35, first appeared on Cryptology ePrint Archive http://eprint.iacr.org/2013/784
10. Andrychowicz, M., Dziembowski, S., Malinowski, D., Mazurek, L.: Secure multiparty computations on Bitcoin. Commun. ACM **59**(4), 76–84 (2016). https://doi.org/10.1145/2896386
11. Atzei, N., Bartoletti, M., Cimoli, T., Lande, S., Zunino, R.: SoK: unraveling bitcoin smart contracts. In: Bauer, L., Küsters, R. (eds.) POST 2018. LNCS, vol. 10804, pp. 217–242. Springer, Cham (2018). https://doi.org/10.1007/978-3-319-89722-6_9
12. Atzei, Nicola, Bartoletti, Massimo, Lande, Stefano, Zunino, Roberto: A formal model of bitcoin transactions. In: Meiklejohn, Sarah, Sako, Kazue (eds.) FC 2018. LNCS, vol. 10957, pp. 541–560. Springer, Heidelberg (2018). https://doi.org/10.1007/978-3-662-58387-6_29
13. Banasik, W., Dziembowski, S., Malinowski, D.: Efficient zero-knowledge contingent payments in cryptocurrencies without scripts. In: Askoxylakis, I., Ioannidis, S., Katsikas, S., Meadows, C. (eds.) ESORICS 2016. LNCS, vol. 9879, pp. 261–280. Springer, Cham (2016). https://doi.org/10.1007/978-3-319-45741-3_14
14. Bartoletti, M., Bracciali, A., Lepore, C., Scalas, A., Zunino, R.: A formal model of Algorand smart contracts. CoRR abs/2009.12140v3 (2020). https://arxiv.org/abs/2009.12140v3
15. Bartoletti, M., Galletta, L., Murgia, M.: A minimal core calculus for solidity contracts. In: Pérez-Solà, C., Navarro-Arribas, G., Biryukov, A., Garcia-Alfaro, J. (eds.) DPM/CBT -2019. LNCS, vol. 11737, pp. 233–243. Springer, Cham (2019). https://doi.org/10.1007/978-3-030-31500-9_15
16. Bentov, I., Kumaresan, R.: How to use bitcoin to design fair protocols. In: Garay, J.A., Gennaro, R. (eds.) CRYPTO 2014. LNCS, vol. 8617, pp. 421–439. Springer, Heidelberg (2014). https://doi.org/10.1007/978-3-662-44381-1_24
17. Bernardo, B., Cauderlier, R., Hu, Z., Pesin, B., Tesson, J.: Mi-Cho-Coq, a framework for certifying tezos smart contracts. In: FM 2019. LNCS, vol. 12232, pp. 368–379. Springer, Cham (2020). https://doi.org/10.1007/978-3-030-54994-7_28

18. Bhargavan, K., et al.: Formal verification of smart contracts. In: PLAS (2016). https://doi.org/10.1145/2993600.2993611

19. Chakravarty, M.M.T., Chapman, J., MacKenzie, K., Melkonian, O., Peyton Jones, M., Wadler, P.: The extended UTXO model. In: Bernhard, M., et al. (eds.) FC 2020. LNCS, vol. 12063, pp. 525–539. Springer, Cham (2020). https://doi.org/10.1007/978-3-030-54455-3_37

20. Chen, J., Micali, S.: Algorand: a secure and efficient distributed ledger. Theor. Comput. Sci. **777**, 155–183 (2019). https://doi.org/10.1016/j.tcs.2019.02.001

21. Crafa, S., Di Pirro, M., Zucca, E.: Is solidity solid enough? In: Bracciali, A., Clark, J., Pintore, F., Rønne, P.B., Sala, M. (eds.) FC 2019. LNCS, vol. 11599, pp. 138–153. Springer, Cham (2020). https://doi.org/10.1007/978-3-030-43725-1_11

22. Delgado-Segura, S., Pérez-Solà, C., Navarro-Arribas, G., Herrera-Joancomartí, J.: A fair protocol for data trading based on bitcoin transactions. Fut. Gener. Comput. Syst. (2017). https://doi.org/10.1016/j.future.2017.08.021

23. Grishchenko, I., Maffei, M., Schneidewind, C.: Foundations and tools for the static analysis of ethereum smart contracts. In: Chockler, H., Weissenbacher, G. (eds.) CAV 2018. LNCS, vol. 10981, pp. 51–78. Springer, Cham (2018). https://doi.org/10.1007/978-3-319-96145-3_4

24. Grishchenko, I., Maffei, M., Schneidewind, C.: A semantic framework for the security analysis of ethereum smart contracts. In: Bauer, L., Küsters, R. (eds.) POST 2018. LNCS, vol. 10804, pp. 243–269. Springer, Cham (2018). https://doi.org/10.1007/978-3-319-89722-6_10

25. Hildenbrandt, E., et al.: KEVM: a complete formal semantics of the Ethereum Virtual Machine. In: IEEE Computer Security Foundations Symposium (CSF), pp. 204–217. IEEE Computer Society (2018). https://doi.org/10.1109/CSF.2018.00022

26. Hirai, Y.: Defining the ethereum virtual machine for interactive theorem provers. In: Brenner, M., et al. (eds.) FC 2017. LNCS, vol. 10323, pp. 520–535. Springer, Cham (2017). https://doi.org/10.1007/978-3-319-70278-0_33

27. Jiao, J., Kan, S., Lin, S., Sanán, D., Liu, Y., Sun, J.: Semantic understanding of smart contracts: Executable operational semantics of Solidity. In: IEEE Symposium on Security and Privacy, pp. 1695–1712. IEEE (2020). https://doi.org/10.1109/SP40000.2020.00066

28. Klomp, R., Bracciali, A.: On symbolic verification of bitcoin's SCRIPT language. In: Garcia-Alfaro, J., Herrera Joancomartí, J., Livraga, G., Rios, R. (eds.) DPM/CBT-2018. LNCS, vol. 11025, pp. 38–56. Springer, Cham (2018). https://doi.org/10.1007/978-3-030-00305-0_3

29. Kumaresan, R., Bentov, I.: How to use Bitcoin to incentivize correct computations. In: ACM CCS, pp. 30–41 (2014). https://doi.org/10.1145/2660267.2660380

30. Kumaresan, R., Moran, T., Bentov, I.: How to use Bitcoin to play decentralized poker. In: ACM CCS, pp. 195–206 (2015). https://doi.org/10.1145/2810103.2813712

31. Luu, L., Chu, D.H., Olickel, H., Saxena, P., Hobor, A.: Making smart contracts smarter. In: ACM CCS, pp. 254–269 (2016). https://doi.org/10.1145/2976749.2978309

32. Rupić, K., Rozic, L., Derek, A.: Mechanized formal model of Bitcoin's blockchain validation procedures. In: Workshop on Formal Methods for Blockchains (FMBC@CAV). OASIcs, vol. 84, pp. 7:1–7:14. Schloss Dagstuhl - Leibniz-Zentrum für Informatik (2020). https://doi.org/10.4230/OASIcs.FMBC.2020.7
33. Sergey, I., Nagaraj, V., Johannsen, J., Kumar, A., Trunov, A., Hao, K.C.G.: Safer smart contract programming with Scilla. Proc. ACM Program. Lang. 3(OOPSLA), 185:1–185:30 (2019). https://doi.org/10.1145/3360611

Anonymity and Privacy
in Cryptocurrencies

Everything You Ever Wanted to Know About Bitcoin Mixers (But Were Afraid to Ask)

Jaswant Pakki[✉], Yan Shoshitaishvili, Ruoyu Wang, Tiffany Bao, and Adam Doupé

Arizona State University, Tempe, USA
{jpakki1,yans,fishw,tbao,doupe}@asu.edu

Abstract. The lack of fungibility in Bitcoin has forced its userbase to seek out tools that can heighten their anonymity. Third-party Bitcoin mixers use obfuscation techniques to protect participants from blockchain transaction analysis. In recent years, various centralized and decentralized Bitcoin mixing methods were proposed in academic literature (e.g., CoinJoin, CoinShuffle). Although these methods strive to create a threat-free environment for users to preserve their anonymity, public Bitcoin mixers continue to be associated with theft and poor implementation. This paper explores the public Bitcoin mixer ecosystem to identify if today's mixing services have adopted academia's proposed solutions. We perform real-world interactions with publicly available mixers to analyze both implementation and resistance to common threats in the mixing landscape. We present data from 21 publicly available mixing services on the deep web and clearnet.

Our results highlight a clear gap between public and proposed Bitcoin mixers in both implementation and security. We find that the majority of key security features proposed by academia are not deployed in any public Bitcoin mixers that are trusted most by Bitcoin users. Today's mixing services focus on presenting users with a *false sense of control* to gain their trust rather than employing secure mixing techniques.

1 Introduction

In May of 2019, European Union authorities seized Bestmixer, a mixing service that advertised to eradicate any criminal history associated with a user's Bitcoin. After an investigation, authorities asserted that the majority of the $200 million that traveled through the service had "a criminal origin or destination" [6].

Bitcoin mixing services are not illegal by nature: Their guarantee to obfuscate a trail of funds appeals to benign users who seek anonymity, and various centralized mixing services are available to the public today. The techniques implemented by these services have a direct impact on user privacy and security. For example, Bestmixer claimed to eradicate all "order history completely and automatically in 24 h" [5]. This claim was proven false when authorities seized

© International Financial Cryptography Association 2021
N. Borisov and C. Diaz (Eds.): FC 2021, LNCS 12674, pp. 117–146, 2021.
https://doi.org/10.1007/978-3-662-64322-8_6

IP-addresses, transactions logs, wallet addresses, and chat messages that were stored on multiple Bestmixer servers.

The dual use of mixing services, by both privacy-wary users and cyber-criminals, provides two motivations for their study. Aiding the former, security researchers in academia have proposed plethora designs and implementations for secure mixing [11,12,15,16,22–25]. Hunting the latter, researchers developed techniques that are capable of tracking Bitcoins through deployed mixers [10,19,21]. However, a gap remains: Despite active research in Bitcoin mixing and *un-mixing*, it is unclear on what techniques current, actually deployed dual-use Bitcoin mixers base their operation and, thus, it is unclear what security properties their users can expect. The effect of this is clear: Although protocols for ideal mixing exist, the majority of publicly available services are still associated with distrust and scam accusations [7].

In this paper, we provide the first *active* and systematic measurement of the current public Bitcoin mixing ecosystem to identify if academically proposed solutions are adopted. The key challenge of this measurement is to scalably analyze public mixers and correlate our observations with academically proposed solutions. Another challenge is the majority of public mixers are black-box services, which do not have their code available to the public. To tackle these challenges, we perform real-world mixer interactions with five public mixers to identify *actual behaviors* that are indicative of their implementation and their resistance to common threats. We leverage our direct interactions, the public nature of Bitcoin's blockchain, and mixer-specific features to identify these behaviors.

Our results highlight a gap of implementation and security between academically proposed mixing solutions and actual public mixers. For example, our security analysis identifies a lack of coin theft prevention in *all five public mixers studied*, even though solutions exist, such as Obscuro [23]. Our results also include mixer-specific characteristics that would benefit from longitudinal research.

Overall, this paper makes the following contributions:

- We provide an overview of the current Bitcoin mixing service landscape, both regarding published academic literature and through information that is collected from actual public mixers.
- We conduct active experiments with five popular public mixing services to collect data and transaction IDs of real-world mixer interactions.
- We perform an implementation and security analysis on our mixing dataset. Among other insights, we determined that none of the studied public mixers implement cutting-edge security properties as proposed by academia.

2   Background

Bitcoin mixing services provide their users with improved anonymity by leveraging inherent characteristics of both Bitcoin and blockchain technology. Before diving into the details of mixers, here we present background knowledge on Bitcoin itself and discuss prior research work that is related to Bitcoin mixers.

Bitcoin and Blockchain. Bitcoin (BTC) is a decentralized digital currency that relies on a peer-to-peer (P2P) distributed network to store and check the validity of transaction data [20]. This data is stored on a public ledger where users are identified by pseudonymous addresses (we will discuss the security implications of these addresses further in Sect. 2). The blockchain is the underlying architecture of the public ledger. Each block holds the hash of its predecessor and a Merkle tree of transactions. Any change in transaction information would lead to a different Merkle root hash and hash of the block itself.

Another integral part of Bitcoin's implementation is its use of the Elliptic Curve Digital Signature Algorithm (ECDSA). The pseudonymous addresses users create are each derived from corresponding public/private key pairs stored in user's wallets. To prevent forgery of transactions, Bitcoin users sign created transactions with their private key. When transaction information is sent out to nodes in the P2P network, they use the sender's public key to validate that the transaction was signed by the corresponding private key.

Anonymity in Bitcoin. Bitcoin uses pseudonymous addressing to identify its users. While these users are capable of creating as many addresses as they would like, they are not required to do so. In turn, researchers have used clustering, transaction analysis, taint analysis, and behavior analysis to track patterns and build relationships between public keys [9,13,14,17,18]. The official Bitcoin website highlights potential threats to user anonymity and clearly states that the currency is not anonymous [1].

Bitcoin Transactions. Bitcoin makes use of a transaction-based public ledger. Inputs and outputs of transactions are referred to as Unspent Transaction Outputs (UTXOs). Transactions consume UTXOs as inputs and create new ones as outputs. UTXOs can only be used in full or not at all. It is quite unlikely that a UTXO will match the exact requested spent amount. Thus, the majority of Bitcoin transactions have two outputs. While the recipient receives one output, the left over (change output) amount is sent back to the sender at a new address.

Transaction metadata includes public keys, input and output UTXOs, size of the transaction, and hash of the transaction as a unique identifier. Transaction inputs also include signatures using the sender's private key; this allows anyone to use the sender's public key to verify the validity of the signed transaction.

Related Work. In 2013, Moser *et al.* [19] explored Bitcoin Fog, BitLaundry, and the Send Shared functionality of Blockchain.info to attempt tracing their outputs back to their input accounts in a series of experiments. They identified that two of the services, Bitcoin Fog and Blockchain.info, successfully obfuscated their funds. They were successfully able to trace their BitLaundry outputs back to their original inputs using Blockchain.info's transaction graph functionality which has since been deprecated. In 2015, Novetta [21] conducted experiments with BitMixer, BitLaunder, Shared Coin, and Bitcoin Blender to identify provable links in mixing schemes, identify fingerprints of individual mixers, and

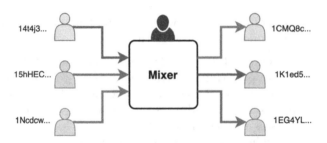

Fig. 1. High-Level diagram of a Bitcoin mixer with three participants and a centralized mixer run by an operator. The participants send their Bitcoin to the mixer. From its pool of collected Bitcoin, the mixer returns funds to participants' specified output addresses such that they are not returned their initial deposit.

identify if mixing can be detected on the blockchain. The study found fingerprinting patterns in the services based on recurring addresses, fees, and branching patterns. Balthasar and Hernandez-Castro [10] interacted with DarkLaunder, Bitlaunder, CoinMixer, Helix, and Alphabay and identified security and privacy limitations in the services. Their work highlights the need for secure and privacy-aware protocols to improve the Bitcoin mixing ecosystem.

3   Bitcoin Mixers

Bitcoin mixers are services that offer the ability to obfuscate users' funds. Figure 1 depicts the general functionality of a mixer with three users. Each user sends their Bitcoins into the service and is returned another user's input to a different address. This output is associated with a completely different transaction history. The mixer operator runs the service and is aware of all connections (permutations) between inputs and outputs. Although this high-level view may seem easily traceable, mixers use obfuscation techniques that make it difficult to trace transactions and identify mixing service use on the blockchain.

Obfuscation Techniques. Since their inception, mixing services have adapted to threats stemming from transactional analysis. Traceable characteristics of transactions include the mixer's input address, the user's address, the amount sent to and from the service, and the timestamps of input and output transactions. The mixer input address is presented to the user to send their funds to the service. If the same input address was used for all users, it would be simple to identify mixing participants and the Bitcoin the mixer has in its pool. To avoid this, mixers generate new input addresses for each user. Additionally, the user's address could be traceable if kept consistent throughout the mixing interaction. Therefore, mixers allow their participants to specify multiple output addresses.

Patterns in amounts and timestamps of transactions could also indicate mixer use. Because network fees are public information, mixers add private, randomized mixing fees to each transaction. Additionally, mixing delays are used to make blockchain analysis more difficult. There are more than 300,000 Bitcoin transactions every 24 h [8]. Thus, it is in mixing participants' best interest that delays are maximized. While the majority of services randomize fees and delays, some allow users to customize these features.

Threats. Trust is incredibly important for the success of a Bitcoin mixer. As third-party services, they must convince users that funds will be properly mixed and returned. Thus, mixers often offer features for users to check the status of their mix or proudly promote positive reviews from forum posts. Still, Bitcoin mixers are continuously accused of scams and poor implementation [7].

While mixers may pose threats to their participants' funds and anonymity, users and external attackers also contribute to the threat landscape. Some of the threats posed by users and external attackers, such as tracing transactions, are mitigated with obfuscation features. Others, such as coin theft, can be mitigated by the proposed mixer implementations that will be discussed in Sect. 4. The majority of current mixing implementations involve a centralized third party that is run by an all-powerful operator. The threats that are posed by this mixer operator are much more difficult to detect. In this paper, we focus our security analysis on the following threats presented by Tran *et al.* [23]:

Permutation Leak: An adversary is able to access mixing logs or a database pertaining to the permutation between input and output addresses.

Coin Theft: An adversary steals the input coins by providing users with an alternative address or by compromising the mixer's address. The mixer operator can also steal users' funds.

Dropping of Participants: A malicious mixer operator can deny participation to selected benign users to reduce the anonymity set.

Small Mixing Set Size: The mixing set size during each round is directly indicative of the quality of the mix. A large mixing set ensures anonymity and protection against blockchain analysis.

Join-then-abort: An adversarial participant disrupts the mix by aborting the mixing protocol before its execution.

4   Academic Mixing Techniques

In response to the threats facing Bitcoin mixers, the Bitcoin community and academic literature have proposed alternative methods to improve trust and eliminate threats. In this section, we discuss the general architecture of four decentralized and four centralized proposed mixing protocols.

4.1   Decentralized Mixing Protocols

The intrinsic anonymity in the Bitcoin ecosystem makes trusting a third party that runs a mixing service highly risky. Therefore, decentralized mixing protocols strive to avoid the use of a third party. Most of the following protocols assume a decentralized method for users to find other participants, which is called *boot-strapping*. Generally, decentralized protocols suffer from limited scalability and long wait times to find mixing peers.

CoinJoin. CoinJoin is a method for multiple transactions from multiple senders to be combined into one transaction [15]. Without any modification to the current Bitcoin protocol, this technique makes it difficult for outside entities to identify the corresponding recipient for each input. Users may collaborate to identify a uniform output amount and combine their transactions into one. In turn, senders face lower transaction fees and lessen the transactions on the Bitcoin network. Additionally, participants of CoinJoin transactions do not face risk of theft: each participant must sign the transaction before it is considered valid.

CoinShuffle. Ruffing *et al.* [22] presented CoinShuffle in 2014. The mixing protocol requires no third party, is compatible with the existing Bitcoin network, and uses CoinJoin to execute transactions. The protocol assumes that users have a secure, decentralized method to express their interest in participation. Output address shuffling and a final CoinJoin transaction eliminate the risk of permutation leak and coin theft attacks.

CoinParty. Ziegeldorf *et al.* [25] proposed CoinParty, a mixing protocol with multiple one-to-one transactions to and from escrow addresses. While compatible with the existing Bitcoin network, CoinParty uses secure multi-party computation for users to collaborate. Temporary threshold ECDSA escrow addresses eliminate the risk of coin theft if $2/3$ of the participants are benign users. Similar to CoinShuffle, output addresses are shuffled to avoid permutation leaks.

Xim. Bissias *et al.* [11] explored the threats presented by Sybil-based denial-of-service attacks to Bitcoin mixing services. They present Xim, a two-party mixing implementation. Unlike the previously described methods, Xim provides a decentralized method for finding mixing participants. Joining a mix interaction requires both participants to spend funds. The requirement to pay to advertise and respond to desired mixing partners make Sybil attacks difficult.

4.2   Centralized Mixing Protocols

Centralized mixing protocols aim to secure a scheme where an untrusted third party exists, and participants send their funds through these centralized services.

OBSCURO. Tran *et al.* [23] presented a centralized Bitcoin mixer using Trusted Execution Environments (TEEs). OBSCURO addresses the threats posed by mixing operators to lessen the control they have on the functionality and day-to-day activity of the service. To do so, the mixer codebase is isolated from the rest of the system. Users are given the ability to verify the isolated functionalities using remote attestation and are guaranteed a large mixing set size. OBSCURO's implementation requires no changes to the existing Bitcoin network and is generic such that it can be implemented with any TEE technique.

Mixcoin. Bonneau *et al.* [12] propose Mixcoin, a Bitcoin mixing protocol that provides accountability to expose malicious centralized mixers. To do so, signed warranties are implemented between the participants and the service. If any wrongdoing occurs on the mixer's part, users have proof of an agreement between both parties to post on public forums. Warranties can be verified by publicly available information such as transactions or public keys. Thus, Mixcoin provides an incentive for mixers to operate in a trustworthy manner. The protocol assumes there are various mixers M_i, and each mixer has a warranty signing key K_{M_i} which is consistently used to sign warranties with each participant. Thus, the mixer's reputation relies heavily on the use of their key. Although accountability is achieved, the mixer can steal funds from its users and potentially leak permutations between inputs and outputs.

Blindcoin. Valenta and Rowan [24] address Mixcoin's susceptibility to permutation leak attacks with Blindcoin. Without any changes to the existing Bitcoin protocol, a blind signature scheme and an append-only public log are added onto the Mixcoin protocol. The user includes a blinded token consisting of their output address and a nonce in their initial offer to the mixing service. The use of this token eliminates the threat of a permutation leak attack by the mixer operator. In addition, the mixing service is required to post this blinded token to an append only public log. As a result, Blindcoin ensures accountability while keeping the mapping of input to output addresses secret. However, Blindcoin does not prevent coin theft since the mixer can still steal funds from its users.

TumbleBit. Heilman *et al.* [16] present TumbleBit, a unidirectional and unlinkable payment hub protocol. TumbleBit is completely compatible with the current Bitcoin protocol and relies on an untrusted centralized intermediary $\mathcal{M}$ to transfer funds between users. TumbleBit's transactions are sent off-blockchain and are not affected by the latency issues in Bitcoin. These payments are essentially off-blockchain puzzles generated through interactions with $\mathcal{M}$.

5   Public Mixing Services

Today's most popular Bitcoin mixing services are centralized to avoid scalability and participant bootstrapping issues inherent in decentralized methods. To begin our analysis of the current mixing service landscape, we first gathered a list of centralized mixers. The majority of these mixers were posted as service announcements on Bitcointalk, a key forum for Bitcoin-related discussions. Appendix A.1 outlines the characteristics we collected for each mixing service. Our findings are displayed in Table 1 with some of these characteristics omitted for simplicity. A ✓ signifies that the service offers the feature while a ✗ indicates lack of the feature. Any field marked with a dash was not found or not applicable to the service. Note that the information presented is solely based on the data that is available on each mixer's website or Bitcointalk forum posts as of May 1st, 2020 and does not involve any actual transactions.

Popularity Analysis. Our next step was to identify a metric to rank mixing services based on popularity for in-depth analysis. As seen in Table 1, every mixing service has a Tor mirror that is highly recommended. These sites have a .onion extension and cannot be indexed by standard search engines. As a result, identifying the amount of traffic for each service is quite difficult.

To address this obstacle, we first categorized mixers into two categories: Trusted and Untrusted. We based this categorization on service support and user activity on the Bitcointalk forum. Trusted mixers displayed consistent communication with an active user base on the forum and had zero scam accusations at the time of the study. Untrusted mixers displayed a lack of communication with their users and had one or more scam accusations. Any mixer without a service announcement on Bitcointalk or an inactive open-source community was also

Table 1. The inclusion of various Bitcoin mixer features on current Bitcoin mixing services. This data is based solely on publicly available information on the mixer's website or Bitcointalk forum posts as of May 1st, 2020 and does not involve any transactions. Furthermore, the mixers are categorized as Trusted or Untrusted based on their standing and activity on the Bitcointalk forum.

	Mixer	Year	Account	Mixing Fees	Distribution Control	Delay	Multiple Output Addr	Multiple Input Addr	Tor	Clearnet	Bitcointalk	Open Source	Min. Blocks	Forum Posts	Scam Accusation(s)
Trusted	Samourai Whirlpool	2015	✗	✓	✓	✗	✓	✗	✓	✓	✗	✓	–	–	–
	CryptoMixer	2016	✗	✓	✓	✓	✓	✓	✓	✓	✓	✗	1	356	✗
	Mixer.money	2016	✗	✓	✗	✓	✓	✗	✓	✓	✓	✗	–	151	✗
	BitCloak	2016	✗	✓	✗	✓	✓	✗	✓	✓	✓	✗	1	174	✗
	ChipMixer	2017	✗	✗	✓	✓	✓	✗	✓	✓	✓	✗	1	1887	✗
	BitMix.biz	2017	✗	✓	✗	✓	✓	✗	✓	✓	✓	✗	1	147	✗
	FoxMixer	2017	✗	✓	✓	✓	✓	✗	✓	✓	✓	✗	6	39	✗
	Wasabi Wallet	2018	✗	✓	✗	✗	✓	✗	✓	✓	✗	✓	–	–	–
	MixTum	2018	✗	✓	✗	✓	✓	✗	✓	✓	✓	✗	1	99	✗
	Bitcoin Mixer	2019	✗	✓	✓	✓	✓	✗	✓	✓	✓	✗	1	108	✗
	Sudoku Wallet	2019	✗	✓	✗	✓	✓	✗	✓	✓	✓	✗	3	68	✗
Untrusted	Bitcoin Fog	2011	✓	✓	✓	✓	✓	✓	✓	✗	✓	✗	6	647	✓
	PenguinMixer	2017	✗	✓	✗	✓	✓	✗	✓	✗	✗	✓	2	–	–
	Blender.io	2017	✗	✓	✗	✓	✓	✗	✓	✓	✓	✗	3	103	✓
	BMC Mixer	2017	✗	✓	✗	✓	✓	✓	✓	✗	✓	✗	2	2	✗
	SmartMix	2019	✗	✓	✓	✓	✓	✗	✓	✓	✓	✗	3	170	✓
	Mixer Tumbler	2019	✗	✓	✗	✓	✗	✗	✓	✓	✓	✗	3	17	✗
	AtoB Mixer	2019	✗	✓	✗	–	✓	✗	✓	✓	✓	✗	–	102	✓
	Anonymix	2020	✗	✓	✓	✓	✓	✗	✓	✓	✗	✗	1	–	–
	BlockMixer	2020	✗	✓	–	–	✗	✗	✓	✓	✓	✗	3	1	✗
	DarkWeb Mixer	–	✗	✓	✗	–	✓	✗	✓	✗	✗	✗	–	–	–

marked as Untrusted due to a lack of information from its user base. The only exceptions to this categorization were Samourai Wallet's Whirlpool and Wasabi Wallet. Although these services do not have Bitcointalk service announcements, they were categorized as Trusted due to their active community and open-source implementation.

After analysis of forum posts, 11 mixers were Trusted and 10 were Untrusted. We chose five web-based Trusted services for in-depth analysis: ChipMixer, Mix-Tum, Bitcoin Mixer, CryptoMixer, and Sudoku Wallet. These services were chosen based on their popularity and unique features. We did not select any Untrusted mixing services for this in-depth analysis due to ethical concerns.

ChipMixer. was established in 2017. With over 95 pages of Bitcointalk forum posts and no scam allegations, the service is the most popular mixer. ChipMixer is a unique implementation with the introduction of *chips*. It generates addresses and funds them with increments of 0.001 BTC up to 8.192 BTC. These addresses are provided to ChipMixer's participants along with their corresponding private keys as outputs. Rather than executing on-blockchain transactions, users are expected to import the given private keys to their wallets off-blockchain. Thus, there is no link between funds deposited to ChipMixer and the chips given to participants. Users may split, merge, even *bet or donate* the given chips before withdrawal using the corresponding private keys. These features can be used multiple times, in any order, and on individual chips.

While ChipMixer does not require an account, users are given a session token and an input address that lasts for seven days. The service also gives users the option to destroy their sessions prematurely within this seven-day period, and service logs are kept for the same length. Mixing fees are purely donation-based and users may choose to donate any amount of their given chips. On withdrawal, users are given a cryptographically signed receipt proving that the funds are coming from ChipMixer. Additionally, users are given the option to receive a voucher code and use the non-withdrawn chips in other ChipMixer interactions.

MixTum. was established in 2018. The service claims to have a separate pool of Bitcoin from cryptocurrency stock exchanges such as Binance, OKEex, and DigiFinex. MixTum guarantees that participant funds are not mixed within a pool of other user's Bitcoin and instead outputs are from exchanges.

MixTum is a traditional Bitcoin mixer that sends on-block-chain transactions to return participant funds. Mixing fees are up to 5% (randomized) plus 0.00015 BTC for the output network fee. Users can specify up to two output addresses which receive multiple payments when funds are returned. The number of payments and distribution of funds between these addresses is randomized by the service. In addition, randomized delays of up to six hours are implemented on output transactions. MixTum provides users with a PGP signed letter of guarantee with information regarding the mixing interaction.

MixTum offers a free trial with the minimum required amount of 0.001 BTC, one output address, and no mixing fees. Although MixTum claims logs are not kept, they do keep data regarding participant interactions until the completion of the output transaction or until the session expires in seven days.

Bitcoin Mixer. was established in 2019. The service provides its users with a Mix ID to check the status of their mix. The minimum input amount accepted is 0.0002 BTC. When multiple output addresses are specified (up to seven), users can control the distribution and delays for each. Delays for each output address range from less than one hour (rapid) to 12 h. The service keeps logs for up to seven days but gives users the option to manually delete their session details. The mixing fees for Bitcoin Mixer are 0.25% plus 0.000001 BTC per output.

CryptoMixer. was established in 2016. The service's initial announcement on Bitcointalk stated that it has over 2,000 BTC in reserve. CryptoMixer leveraged the trust of reputable Bitcointalk users to verify the services pool of funds [2–4].

CryptoMixer allows a minimum input of 0.001 BTC. The maximum input changes based off of the amount of Bitcoin in its reserve. Accounts are not required, and instead users are given a CryptoMixer code to identify their sessions. This code can be used in future sessions to receive discounts and ensure previous inputs are not returned. CryptoMixer's site claims it has a 100% zero-logs policy but also states that transaction details are routinely deleted. Based on the fees, delays, distribution, and number of output addresses set, participants are given a security level for their mix. The Standard, Silver, and Gold security levels offer higher thresholds for obfuscation. For example, the Standard level offers up to 24-hour delays while Gold offers up to 96 h.

Unlike the other services, CryptoMixer allows users to generate an unlimited number of input addresses to send their funds. Each input address also comes with a verifiable, digitally signed letter of guarantee, proving that it was generated by the service. Each given address is valid for 24 h.

Sudoku Wallet was established in 2019. The service is a single-use wallet which outputs private keys rather than on-blockchain transactions. These outputs are of two to four addresses funded from previously executed CoinJoin transactions. The distribution between these addresses is not configurable by the user. There is no minimum or maximum input enforced. Sudoku Wallet does not require accounts but provides users with a wallet key to access their session before it is automatically deleted in seven days. The service claims to have a strict "no logs" policy. To send funds to Sudoku Wallet, one input address is provided along with its corresponding private key. The mixing fee is randomized from 0.5% to 1% plus the CoinJoin fee which is described as the number of output addresses involved in the CoinJoin times the transaction fee.

6 Evaluation

In this section, we describe the methodology of our in-depth experiments on five chosen mixers to understand more about the implementation of these mixer services. In addition, we outline our results of the experiments conducted with each mixer. Detailed results are included in Appendix B with transaction IDs.

6.1 Methodology

The experiments are real-world interactions with five public mixing services: ChipMixer, MixTum, Bitcoin Mixer, CryptoMixer, and Sudoku Wallet. Our goal is to identify if these mixers have adopted implementation and security solutions provided by the academic literature discussed in Sect. 4. Overall, we use data from Table 1 and our experiments to compare implementation and security of the five services with the proposed mixing protocols from Sect. 4.

We conducted three trials of experiments: each consisted of one transaction with each of five mixing services. We ensured that all five interactions during a trial were finished before moving onto the next. To estimate the necessary amount of funds to execute all 15 mixer interactions, we set a constant network fee of 0.50 USD (0.000053 BTC) and calculated the worst-case mixing fees for each service. The total fees were estimated to be 57.25 USD (0.00635 BTC). To account for changing network fees, unexpected mixer fees, or coin theft, we determined 100 USD (0.011 BTC) would be sufficient to execute all three trials.

During the first trial, input amounts were set to the minimum required by each service. Inputs were gradually raised in the second and third trials. We increased the obfuscation parameters from trial to trial when customizable. This included longer delays, a higher number of output addresses, and higher fees. The public nature of the blockchain allowed for comparison between interactions with a single service to identify unexpected behavior. We specify the exact parameters, input, and output values for each trial in the results for each service in Appendix B. To calculate the mixing fees for on-blockchain transactions the total BTC sent to and from the mixing service (excluding network fees) were subtracted.

Table 2. Data collected during our experiments with each studied mixer along with their description.

Data field	Description
Obfuscation parameters	Obfuscation features set (number of output addresses, delays, distribution, etc.)
Input amount	Amount sent to mixer (before network fees)
Input network fee	Network fee on transaction to mixer (BTC)
Input address	Address given to user by mixer to send initial funds
Time in	Date and time of input transaction
Input transaction ID	Transaction ID of input transaction
Output amount	Amount sent back to user's deposit address(es)
Output network Fee	Amount of network fees on transaction(s) to deposit address(es)
Time out	Date and time output transactions are sent from mixer
Output transaction ID	Transaction ID of output transaction
Mixer fee	Service fee collected
Additional information	Information unique to service: Letter of Guarantee, Special Mixing Code, Receipt, etc.

All five mixers offer a Tor mirror, so we used the Tor Browser. To store, receive, and send Bitcoin, we used the desktop wallet Electrum. We maintained two separate wallets for legacy and SegWit functionality. All transactions were labeled according to their corresponding mixer and trial number. In addition to collecting screenshots of every mixing interaction, the data described in Table 2 was recorded. This includes transaction information such as the input and output transaction IDs, the obfuscation parameters, and unique information for each service including letters of guarantee. Next, we will discuss the general steps taken and any special data collected for each service.

Setup. Before beginning the first trial, we purchased 100 USD worth of Bitcoin from the exchange Coinbase. At the time, this equated to 0.01788742 BTC. Then, we created two separate Electrum wallets: Legacy and SegWit.

ChipMixer. There are five general steps in interactions with ChipMixer. During Step 1, users are given their session token and told to save it permanently to access their session for the next seven days. Step 2 is the Deposit step: send at least 0.001 BTC in one transaction to a given input address, wait for one network confirmation on this transaction, and then refresh the page. During this step, users are also able to enter voucher codes from previous interactions to use funds that have not been withdrawn. At Step 3, users have a full view of their current chips grouped by value and have the ability to split, merge, commonize, bet, and donate. On this page, they are also given the option to withdraw or receive a voucher for chips. These two options directly lead to Step 4, the withdrawal. Users are given the private key to their withdrawn chips and steps on how to import this key to Electrum, Bitcoin Core, or to a JSON file. As another option, they can sweep the chips to a desired output address. Before the final step, a signed receipt is offered for download. In Step 5, sessions can be destroyed.

We created a new session for each trial with ChipMixer. The session token was recorded to test its validity after the seven-day period or after sessions were manually deleted. The given input address and the input transaction ID was noted to identify patterns in the movement of funds. Chipmixer's method of returning funds does not involve output addresses, so we used the SegWit wallet for all three trials. We considered the obfuscation parameters for ChipMixer to be the set of features used (split, merge, and donate) as well as the method of withdrawal. Commonize and betting were not used in all three trials. We attempted both sweep and private key transfer withdrawals to identify effects on traceability. Before destroying each session, we attempted to access each session's signed receipt to verify the signature.

Results. The results from each ChipMixer trial are displayed in Appendix B.1 Table 6. In our trials with ChipMixer, we did not encounter any unexpected mixing fees. In Trial 1, we swept the private keys to our Electrum wallet with an on-blockchain transaction (requiring network fees). In Trial 2, we transferred the private keys to our Electrum wallet off-blockchain (no network fees). In all three trials, we could not access the signed receipt offered by ChipMixer due to an internal server error.

MixTum. In MixTum for Step 1, users enter up to two output addresses. In Step 2, users are given an input address along with its corresponding QR code. In addition, a signed letter of guarantee is provided for download.

Trials for MixTum were attempted with both legacy and SegWit addresses. The only customizable obfuscation parameter was the number of output addresses. On Step 2, all letters of guarantee were downloaded and signatures were verified using GnuPG. Transactions from MixTum were analyzed for their distribution and randomized delay. Mixing fees were also checked to see if they were accurately calculated. Input and Output transaction IDs were used to gain insight about the movement of funds.

Results. Table 7 in Appendix B.2 displays the obfuscation parameters, total input, total output, output network fees, and mixing fees pertaining to each trial with MixTum. For all three trials, signed letters of guarantee were successfully downloaded and verified. MixTum's calculator output displayed a smaller value than received on all three trials. In Trials 2 and 3, mixing fees were up to 5% plus 0.00015 BTC as advertised. However, Trial 1 charged a mixing fee of 0 BTC.

Bitcoin Mixer. In Step 1, users specify up to seven output addresses each with distribution (%) and delay (rapid to 12 h). In Step 2, the service provides a Mix ID and an input address. After delays, the output transactions are executed. In Step 3, users review their mix information and can delete their mix.

In Step 1, we attempted specifying both legacy and SegWit addresses to Bitcoin Mixer. The main obfuscation parameters for this service were the number of output addresses, percentage distribution, and delay. We heightened the intensity of these parameters from trial to trial and verified the accuracy of distributions and delays. Mix IDs for each session were noted to check their validity after deletion of the mix. After receiving outputs, we calculated the mixing fees to identify unexpected behavior. In all three trials, we deleted our mix information.

Results. Table 8 in Appendix B.3 outlines the obfuscation parameters, input, output, and mixer fees associated with each Bitcoin Mixer trial. The distributions, mixing fees, and outputs were accurately calculated. Outputs were generally received 20 to 30 min early, indicating randomization of delays. The deletion of Mix IDs was successful in all three trials.

CryptoMixer. In Step 1, users specify up to 10 output addresses and set the delay and distribution for each. Users can then specify their preferred service fee. The combination of these three obfuscation parameters determines the security level of the mix. On the same page, CryptoMixer's calculator displays the expected amount that each output address will receive. Before continuing to Step 2, the CryptoMixer code can be entered. In Step 2, a letter of guarantee is presented along with an input address. As input transactions are made the service displays the received amounts and their confirmations. If the amount is not sufficient, the service specifies the expected output as a negative value. Finally, users are also provided with a CryptoMixer code to use with future transactions.

Trials with CryptoMixer were conducted with both legacy and SegWit addresses. The customizable obfuscation parameters for this service include the number of input and output addresses, delay, distribution, and service fee. While Trial 1 was customized to fall under the Standard security level, Trial 2 and 3 were both set to the Silver security level. We recorded the output values displayed from the service's calculator to check for accuracy. The CryptoMixer code from Trial 1 was used in Trial 2 to test its effectiveness against receiving previous inputs. Finally, the letter of guarantee was downloaded for each input address in all three trials and both the signature and contents were verified.

Results. Appendix B.4 Table 9 displays the obfuscation parameters, input, output, and mixer fees associated with each CryptoMixer trial. The service's calculator displayed accurate outputs based on the set mixing fee for each trial. We did not receive any output from CryptoMixer on Trials 2 and 3. We were successfully able to download and verify the letters of guarantee provided by the service. Additionally, we received five-digit CryptoMixer codes in each trial but could not evaluate the effectiveness of their use.

Sudoku Wallet. In Step 1, users are presented with a wallet key. In Step 2, an input address is presented along with its corresponding private key. After three confirmations on the input transaction(s), the user can proceed. In Step 3, two to four addresses with balances adding up to the user's input amount minus mixing fees are presented along with their private keys. The user then has the option to sweep these funds or import the private keys to their wallet. In Step 4, users are urged to delete their wallet and generate a new one to mix more funds.

We created a new wallet for each transaction and recorded the wallet key to check its validity after deletion. In Step 2, we noted the input address and its private key. The obfuscation parameter for Sudoku Wallet is limited to the method of withdrawing the funds. In Step 3, we recorded the given output addresses and calculated the mixing fee to identify unexpected behavior. We studied the history of these output addresses to ensure they used CoinJoin transactions.

Results. Appendix B.5 Table 10 displays the obfuscation parameters, input, output, output network fees, and mixer fees associated with each Sudoku Wallet trial. Mixing fees for each trial were inconsistent and unverifiable with any previously executed CoinJoin transactions. Trial 1 had a mixer fee of 0 BTC while Trial 3 had a fee of 0.0027 BTC (90% of the input).

7 Analysis

In this section, we provide an implementation and security analysis of the five public mixing services.

7.1 Implementation Analysis

We use the data gathered in Sect. 5 regarding current public mixers and our experiments (discussed in Sect. 6) to identify the adoption of academically proposed solutions in ChipMixer, MixTum, Bitcoin Mixer, CryptoMixer, and Sudoku Wallet.

Table 3 outlines which mixing services include key characteristics of proposed solutions in their implementation. The characteristics selected include CoinJoin, shuffling of output addresses in one transaction, multisignature escrows, TEXT field use to share data, signed warranties, blinding, and off-blockchain transactions. Each of these characteristics are used in at least one of the academically proposed solutions.

ChipMixer. Through tracing our input transactions and outputs received by ChipMixer, we identified that funds sent to the service are routinely involved in the creation of chips ranging from 0.001 BTC to 8.192 BTC. For example, our Trial 1 input of 0.001 BTC was involved in the creation of five chips of 8.192 BTC. The creation of these chips involves a transaction resembling CoinJoin. The transaction includes UTXOs sent to ChipMixer by users as its input set. The output is a set of chips of a uniform size. Unlike CoinShuffle, this CoinJoin is solely created with funds available in ChipMixer's wallet. Thus, the need for multiple signatures and shuffling of output addresses is eliminated.

Table 3. The inclusion of academically proposed techniques in the five studied public mixers. The five mixers exhibit a lack of adoption of proposed techniques. Output address shuffling, multisignature escrows, the use of TEXT fields in transactions, remote attestation, and blinding are not implemented by any of the services studied.

	CoinJoin [15, 22]	Output Address Shuffling [22, 25]	Multisig Escrow [16, 25]	TEXT Field Use [11, 23]	Remote Attestation [23]	Signed Warranty [12, 24]	Blinding [16, 24]	Off-Blockchain Txns [11, 16]
ChipMixer	✓	✗	✗	✗	✗	✗	✗	✓
MixTum	✗	✗	✗	✗	✗	✓	✗	✗
Bitcoin Mixer	✗	✗	✗	✗	✗	✗	✗	✗
CryptoMixer	✗	✗	✗	✗	✗	✓	✗	✗
Sudoku Wallet	✗	✗	✗	✗	✗	✗	✗	✓

ChipMixer incorporates off-blockchain transactions by giving users the option to split, merge, bet, commonize, and donate their given chips. These options have an impact on the amount and distribution of the mix without executing multiple on-blockchain transactions. The withdrawal of funds via importing private keys is also done off-blockchain. Thus, a complete ChipMixer mixing interaction can be done with only one on-blockchain input transaction. This is comparable to TumbleBit and its incorporation of off-blockchain puzzles to send Bitcoin between two users.

ChipMixer claims to provide a signed receipt on withdrawal of chips. Although the service was unable to provide this receipt in all three trials, we do not believe it is comparable to the signed warranties produced in Mixcoin and Blindcoin. While ChipMixer's signed receipt aims to prove the origin of output funds, Mixcoin and Blindcoin's signed warranty outlines the terms of the mix before any input or output.

Overall, our analysis did not provide any evidence that ChipMixer implements signed warranties, blinding, remote attestation, output address shuffling, or multisignature escrow addresses.

MixTum. MixTum offers a PGP signed letter of guarantee before any inputs to the service. The letters for all three trials included the generated input address, the output address(es), the maximum mixing time, the deadline for users to send their input by, and the maximum service fee. This guarantee can be compared to the signed warranty provided in Mixcoin which includes the value to be mixed, the deadline for the input to be sent, the deadline for the service to return funds, the output address, the mixing fee rate, a nonce, and the number of confirmations required on the input. Mixcoin's protocol requires that users create the terms of the mix and provide them to the service. In the case of MixTum, the service creates the majority of the terms including the fee and deadline to return funds. Overall, the PGP signed letter of guarantee from MixTum provides enough information to identify a breach in protocol and holds the service accountable.

We did not identify any evidence that MixTum incorporates CoinJoin, output address shuffling, multisignature escrow addresses, TEXT field use, remote attestation, blinding, or off-blockchain transactions.

Bitcoin Mixer. Through our analysis and experiments with Bitcoin Mixer, we identified that the service does not implement any of the proposed mixing solutions found in CoinShuffle, CoinParty, Xim, OBSCURO, Mixcoin, Blindcoin, or TumbleBit. The service does not implement CoinJoin transactions or shuffle output addresses of multiple users in one transaction. In addition, Bitcoin Mixer does not implement multisignature escrow addresses, TEXT fields in transactions, remote attestation, a signed warranty, blinding, or off-blockchain transactions.

CryptoMixer. CryptoMixer provides a signed letter of guarantee along with each input address. Unlike MixTum, CryptoMixer's letter of guarantee is signed using its Bitcoin private key. This letter provides confirmation of the origin of the input address, distribution of funds to each output address, delay for each output address, deadline for inputs, minimum and maximum input allowed, and mixing fee. This guarantee can be compared to the signed warranty provided in Mixcoin. In this case, the user specifies output addresses, delays, distributions, and the fees. Thus, CryptoMixer's letter of guarantee ensures accountability and can be used against the service in case of a breach of protocol.

Overall, the signed warranty was the only academically proposed solution adopted by CryptoMixer. We did not identify any evidence of CoinJoin, output address shuffling, multisignature escrow addresses, TEXT field use, remote attestation, blinding, or off-blockchain transactions.

Sudoku Wallet. Sudoku Wallet claims to provide funds from pre-mixed Coin-Join transactions. Blockchain analysis in all three trials revealed that inputs were not involved in uniform output CoinJoin transactions after being sent to the service. Additionally, outputs had not been involved in uniform output CoinJoin interactions in recent history. Thus, we do not believe the service uses CoinJoin transactions. However, Sudoku Wallet does make use of off-blockchain transactions on withdrawal. Like ChipMixer, the use of private keys as outputs ensures that outputs are not detectable on the blockchain.

Overall, we did not identify any evidence of CoinJoin transactions, output address shuffling, multisignature escrow addresses, TEXT field use, remote attestation, signed warranties, or blinding.

7.2 Security Analysis

We build our security analysis upon OBSCURO's security analysis performed on CoinJoin, CoinShuffle, CoinParty, Xim, Mixcoin, Blindcoin, and TumbleBit [23]. We expand on their academically proposed Bitcoin mixer comparison by performing similar analysis on the five mixing services included in this study. Table 4

Table 4. A security comparison of the five public mixing services against the threats presented in Sect. 3. All five services lack prevention against coin theft, relationship anonymity attacks, and do not guarantee participation. A similar table conducting a security comparison of academically proposed mixers is provided in OBSCURO [23].

	Coin Theft Prevention	Relationship Anonymity	Participation Guarantee	Large Mixing Set Guarantee	Join-then-abort Resistance	Minimum On-Chain Txns
ChipMixer	✗	✗	✗	✗	✓	1
MixTum	✗	✗	✗	✗	✓	2
Bitcoin Mixer	✗	✗	✗	✗	✓	2
CryptoMixer	✗	✗	✗	✓	✓	2
Sudoku Wallet	✗	✗	✗	✗	✓	1

displays the results of this analysis. We compare the mixers based on their resistance to the threats outlined in Sect. 3.

Coin Theft. The five mixers in the study do not have protections in place against coin theft. ChipMixer, Bitcoin Mixer, and Sudoku Wallet provide no proof of origin for the provided input address, making it possible for adversaries or malicious mixer operators to steal funds. MixTum and CryptoMixer provide signed letters of guarantee, making it difficult for an attacker to inject their own address. However, the letter of guarantee is ineffective against malicious mixer operators. Although it sets accountability, users can still have their funds stolen. Mixcoin and Blindcoin suffer from the same protections against a malicious operator. Thus, six out of eight mixing services in OBSCURO's analysis implement protections against coin theft. For example, CoinJoin, CoinShuffle, and TumbleBit use multisig addresses to ensure all parties are involved in the movement of funds.

ChipMixer and Sudoku Wallet provide private keys as outputs. Importing these keys to a wallet may be appealing because of its off-blockchain nature, however it leaves users susceptible to coin theft. The mixing service could still access the private key and sweep the funds to a separate address without user permission.

Relationship Anonymity. Relationship anonymity is not guaranteed in any of five mixing services. Malicious mixing operators can directly learn the permutation between inputs and outputs. Additionally, all five services store or log session data for at least a limited amount of time, providing a tempting target for adversaries. In comparison, five out of eight proposed mixing services from Obscuro's analysis provide a method to ensure relationship anonymity. For example, CoinParty and CoinShuffle use output address shuffling while Blindcoin and TumbleBit use blinding.

Participation Guarantee. All five public mixers lack resistance against dropping participants. This is common in protocols that involve a mixer operator who can control the mixer's worldview. In comparison, five out of eight protocols studied in OBSCURO's analysis guarantee participation for all users. The only centralized protocol included in these five is OBSCURO. In its implementation, selective dropping of participants results in a DoS attack because of the protocols dependence on public bulletin boards.

Large Mixing Set Guarantee. Of all five services, CryptoMixer was the only to guarantee a large mixing set size. For public mixing services, we view the mixing set to be the pool of UTXOs that the mixing service controls. To guarantee a large mixing set, CryptoMixer provided reputable Bitcointalk users with access to a list of their owned addresses along with signatures for each. The users confirmed that the service had nearly 2,000 BTC in their pool. In comparison, two out of eight proposed services provide a guarantee of a large mixing set. For example, OBSCURO refunds user inputs when a minimum number of participants is not reached. Mixcoin, Blindcoin, and TumbleBit do not include an agreement of a minimum mixing set size in their centralized protocols. In decentralized protocols such as CoinJoin, CoinShuffle, and CoinParty, users are guaranteed a small set due to the communication overhead and long wait times with larger anonymity sets.

Join-then-abort Resistance. All five public mixing services provide resistance against join-then-abort attacks. Users are unable to abort the mixing protocol after funds have been sent to the given input address. In comparison, five out of eight proposed protocols also provide resistance against this attack. In CoinJoin implementations, like CoinShuffle, users are able to disrupt the mix by disapproving of the final transaction.

Minimum On-Chain Transactions. The number of on-block-chain transactions for the five mixers in this study is similar to the proposed protocols in OBSCURO's analysis. Aside from Xim, which requires three ads on-blockchain before the four transactions in Barber's Fair Exchange, and TumbleBit, which uses two escrow channels, the proposed protocols require one to two transactions.

7.3   Additional Interesting Behavior

Our experiments on ChipMixer, MixTum, CryptoMixer, and Sudoku Wallet revealed additional, interesting behavior associated with each service. We believe these behaviors represent an opportunity for a long-term study to learn more about the underlying service implementation.

ChipMixer. ChipMixer generates new chips by creating transactions which resemble traditional CoinJoin with uniform output chip values ranging from 0.001 BTC to 8.192 BTC. The set of inputs for these chip generation transactions is comprised of UTXOs adding up to the exact amount necessary to create the specified number of chips. In turn, chip generation does not include change transactions in its output. We identified this pattern in all four of our input transactions with ChipMixer. Additionally, we were able to trace these created chips to identify outputs to other users. It is possible that a large number of inputs could be sent to ChipMixer to gain a better understanding of their pool of chips. Appendix C.1 provides some example chip generation transactions.

Although ChipMixer claims logs and session information is deleted in seven days, we found that our session tokens for all three trials were still valid after 16 days. This could indicate that deletion of logs and session tokens is manually done by the mixer operator.

ChipMixer incorporates various features that focus on providing users with an illusion of control over their funds. However, off-blockchain transactions such as split and merge essentially have no impact on the chips available in ChipMixer's pool. In addition, voucher codes carry no value outside of the service.

MixTum. MixTum is built upon Jambler.io, a mixing platform that provides the source code to start a mixer. The letter of guarantee and the input address are generated from Jambler.io, and the platform pays MixTum a commission on completion of each mixing interaction. Jambler.io claims to obtain funds from cryptocurrency exchanges and use a scoring algorithm to only mix with "pure" funds.

MixTum's typical mixing fees are up to 5% + 0.00015 BTC. However, in Trial 1 we sent the minimum 0.001 BTC, we received an output of 0.001 BTC. The transaction fee on this output was 0.00024227 BTC. Thus, the service did not charge a mixing fee and lost money. This was tested twice with the same result.

CryptoMixer. CryptoMixer returned an output in Trial 1 even though the service stated that the input amount was less than required. In Trial 2, we identified that the service does not accept transactions less than the minimum 0.001 BTC. However, CryptoMixer's calculator still recognizes inputs less than the minimum and calculates accordingly. We believe CryptoMixer treats all inputs to a session as donations if an input less than the minimum is detected before an output transaction is scheduled. The first three inputs for Trial 2 were 0.001 BTC, 0.001 BTC, and 0.0005 BTC. All three received their first confirmation at the same time. We believe CryptoMixer recognized that one of these inputs was less than 0.001 BTC and treated all inputs as donations as a result. In Trial 3, we learned that input addresses do not accept more than one transaction. Our second transactions were not recognized and CryptoMixer did not send an output. Overall, CryptoMixer has poor implementation and lacks proper documentation.

Sudoku Wallet. On the presentation of the input address, Sudoku Wallet also provides a corresponding private key. We believe this is done to give users the illusion that they still have access to their funds. However, in all three of our trials, Sudoku Wallet moved the funds associated with the input address before we obtained our output. For example, in Trial 1, we swept our outputs at 12:51 AM, however the input address funds had been moved to a separate address at 12:33 AM. This shows how simple coin theft is when mixers output private keys.

Sudoku Wallet's mixing fees are described as 0.5% to 1% (randomized) plus the CoinJoin fee. However, mixing fees were inconsistent in all three trials. We were not able to identify any CoinJoin transactions to calculate the fees in each output's blockchain history. Thus, more transactions will need to be executed to understand the mixing fees.

During Trial 3, the provided wallet key was entered onto the Sudoku Wallet website. We received an error stating that the Bitcoin Client function `loadwallet()` verification failed. This error reveals that Sudoku Wallet creates a new wallet for each user to keep track of balances. This is the only implementation of separate wallet creation. Although Sudoku Wallet states that logs are not maintained, this is similar to logging transaction data for each participant.

8   Discussion and Limitations

Our analysis shows a clear disconnect between the five publicly available mixers studied and academically proposed solutions. Key characteristics of these solutions have not been widely adopted by today's most trusted Bitcoin mixing services. We found that none of the five public mixing services we tested use the proposed features of output address shuffling, multisignature escrow addresses,

TEXT fields in transactions, remote attestation, or blinding. The only three characteristics adopted include CoinJoin, signed warranties, and off-blockchain transactions.

All five mixers performed poorly in security analysis. The lack of prevention against coin theft, permutation leaks, and dropping of participants in public services shows that these services are not built to prioritize security and anonymity concerns addressed in academic literature. Rather, most services appear to be focused on providing their users with the illusion of control over their mix. On a positive note, centralized mixers displayed complete resistance against join-and-abort attacks, unlike proposed decentralized solutions. CryptoMixer also leverages Bitcointalk to guarantee a minimum mixing set size.

To gain credibility and trust from their users, today's mixers must employ a combination of key characteristics provided by proposed academic solutions. Public mixing services should advertise the use of proven solutions from academic literature, use trusted third-party remote attestation services, provide signed letters of guarantee, and adopt open-source practices. Mixers should also aim to leverage the solidified trust users have with reputable members of Bitcointalk and actively engage with their participants. Output addresses can be encrypted with the mixer's public key and included in the TEXT field of input transactions to lessen the threat of selective dropping of participants. Although it would result in higher network fees, mixers should identify a minimum mixing set size and ensure outputs include multiple users rather than one-to-one transactions. The use of private keys as outputs must be eliminated from services to ensure safety against coin theft.

Ultimately, our trials were quite lightweight. A higher number of trials with larger transactions could lead to a more in-depth understanding of the reasoning behind certain mixer behavior. Our understanding of mixer features relies heavily on information collected from each service's website as well as posts from Bitcointalk. A long-term analysis of both trusted and untrusted services could paint a better picture of the ever-changing features being implemented into the public mixing atmosphere. Additionally, this study could be expanded to include open-source wallets that provide their own mixing implementations such as Wasabi Wallet and Samourai Wallet.

9   Conclusion

The Bitcoin mixing ecosystem attracts a wide range of users, many of whom simply wish to remain anonymous. The association of scams and poor implementation by these services has led to the proposal of secure protocols in academic literature. These proposed solutions provide methods to ensure accountability for mixing services and secure communication between participants without the leakage of input and output permutations. Through real world mixer interactions, we identified that there exists a disconnect in both implementation and resistance to common mixing threats between today's public mixing services and academically proposed solutions. We strongly believe that the disparities identified in this work represent an overall lack of regard for secure implementation. Although mixing services are often associated with criminal activity, the adoption of secure mixing methods could better their reputation and provide a foundation for future Bitcoin mixer research.

Acknowledgement. We would like to express our gratitude to the anonymous reviewers for their valuable feedback. This work was supported in part by the National Science Foundation (NSF) in grants 2000792, 1651661, and 1703644.

A   Appendix 1

A.1   Public Mixer Characteristics

(See Table 5).

Table 5. Mixer characteristics collected for our initial analysis of the public Bitcoin mixer landscape.

Characteristic	Description
Min	Minimum mixing amount allowed
Max	Maximum mixing amount allowed
Account	Is registration required to participate?
Fees	Mixing fees
Time	Time to finish mixing
Delay	Amount of delay on mixing output
Logs	Amount of time service keeps logs
Input addresses	Number of input addresses given to user
Output addresses	Number of output addresses user may specify
Distribution control	Does the user have control of the distribution of funds across their specified output addresses?
Minimum blocks	Number of network confirmations needed before mixing begins
Additional features	Additional unique features (letter of guarantee, receipt, check mix function, etc.)
Tor	Hidden service URL
Clearnet	Clearnet URL
Established	Year established
Bitcointalk	Bitcointalk service announcement URL
Forum posts	Number of forum posts as of May 1st, 2020
Scam accusation(s)	Does the mixer have any unresolved scam accusations?

B   Appendix 2

B.1   ChipMixer Results

Table 6. Results for ChipMixer trials.

Trial	Obfuscation parameters	Input (BTC)	Output (BTC)	Output network fees (BTC)	Mixer fees (BTC)	Txn IDs
1	sweep	0.001	0.000921	0.000079	0	[1]
2	split, donate, merge, withdraw	0.003	0.002	0	0.001	[2]
3	voucher, sweep	0.004	0.00381195	0.00018805	0	[3]

[1] I_1: 467e3de55595849259650ef0dfdcad22b945bf98cc99cb0cc5d2f4ad6c4a9c9b
O_1: 5e2673cb8e845aa41ba7c04b1aa6b1da415bffa87d01806f4e762133964694e1
[2] I_1: a0e9c07185369c217f740ee06a8b3499dd15d365647c78f34e6d3195132eb99b
I_2: 3a8f4b06c8d30dcb333376b7168df3c1a93812086f5c31cf7c104715d2dc0d3b
O_1: 6647ea4eaf7b6968101e2618a21608d4111f836aec7cf1589972f678a5a06ad4
[3] I_1: 7675b43440cd2ac9c95134085262c1df8a8284ac4daeb9223402084363f53405
I_2: 2fac417838683750b879e743811cea0c263efc0bf8c24a72b5f80cb393b78578
O_1: 47a373922147c11b3a7b3d0675a62bf94c6d1e1d8252e915ca8bef83e37a0cd2
O_2: 0755d63c3e989810bb8b0f65e852845d8c9538446278f438f0ca3a5f99310e00

Trial 1. In Trial 1, 0.001 BTC was sent in one transaction, I_1, from the SegWit wallet. Within 30 s of the first confirmation on this input, we received one chip of 0.001 BTC. In Step 3, we were given the option to donate, withdraw, or receive a voucher. Options to split or merge were unavailable. We chose to withdraw our chips and proceeded to Step 4. We attempted to download the signed receipt but received an internal server error. Next, we chose to sweep the chip to the SegWit wallet with a network fee of 0.000079 BTC. The interaction resulted in 0 BTC mixing fees and our final output, O_1, was 0.000921 BTC.

Trial 2. In Trial 2, 0.003 BTC was sent to ChipMixer in two separate transactions from the SegWit wallet, I_1 and I_2. These transactions were 0.002 BTC and 0.001 BTC. The service provided one chip of 0.002 BTC (chip 1) and one of 0.001 BTC (chip 2). We split chip 1 into two chips of 0.001 BTC. Then, we donated one of these chips to ChipMixer and did not identify any movement of funds from the input address. Next, we merged the two remaining 0.001 BTC chips into one 0.002 BTC chip. On Step 4, we attempted to access the signed receipt but received an internal server error. We chose to withdraw our final chip by importing the private key into a new wallet. Importing resulted in 0 BTC network fees and 0 BTC mixer fees. The output to our wallet, O_1, was 0.002 BTC.

Trial 3. In Trial 3, two separate sessions were created. In the first session, transaction I_1 of 0.001 BTC was sent to ChipMixer and withdrawn for a voucher. The service provided a 53 character alphanumeric code. In the second session, transaction I_2 of 0.003 BTC was sent to the given input address. The voucher code from the first session was also redeemed. In total, the service provided two 0.001 BTC and one 0.002 BTC chips. On withdrawal, the chips were swept into the SegWit wallet. This resulted in two on-blockchain transactions with outputs of 0.00190361 BTC and 0.00190834 BTC, O_1 and O_2. The network fees associated with these transactions were 0.00009639 BTC and 0.00009166 BTC respectively. The total mixer fee was 0 BTC.

B.2   MixTum Results

Table 7. Results for MixTum trials.

Trial	Obfuscation parameters	Input (BTC)	Output (BTC)	Output network fees (BTC)	Mixer fees (BTC)	Txn IDs
1	1 Output	0.001	0.001	0.00024227	0	4
2	2 Outputs	0.002	0.001762	0.0004707	0.000238	5
3	2 Outputs	0.003	0.00276	0.00049838	0.00024	6

4 I_1: 0cf2b5ae532f7efb78133b0cf63b8a11af658dba5cab810a6125cb8c81433896
O_1: 41102ce0aab86f143bd836cecae1495c1c4dbb3cf4b2b4ee19e2f7e9c8dd264b
5 I_1: 3acc63ef655aed1a47323aeace7d3107ce8e26dc046a3a05998b284aa9221d91
O_1: 24b0e68ee157eef4567ce853198f1af5196fc0ffbfa875e20a84044bf6b82de0
O_2: 9f60da6b97b39c6de65f7b7e59def229fe990a70c66ab1263a71f7d262aac9ca
6 I_1: 32328f8ea37163f06894e3ddd8620e4bfb93c1b968b70a1c7973d5fa4e81ffb3
I_2: 3863aab6e6f84f4da584975b9719511954ebc10a0ceca918b26f250d3553b211
O_1: da0f4c46f528f4df7d7383eee5064e69759403410f63049f4fe59341f1ee9991
O_2: 8ac7f54fb2fa52811d07ff3fa5f7031f8499e0d63ba37691e8979612e3107181
O_3: d9cf6777e294f2936f9219cbd10a4926f93986fa9d79829e72e6f422eae1e59f

Trial 1. In Trial 1, one legacy output address was specified. A SegWit output address was attempted but was not accepted by the service. One input transaction, I_1, of 0.001 BTC was sent to a compatibility format input address provided by MixTum. Within five minutes, an output transaction, O_1 of 0.001 BTC was received. The network fee on the output was 0.00024227 BTC and mixing fees were 0 BTC.

Trial 2. In Trial 2, two legacy output addresses were specified. One input transaction, I_1, of 0.002 BTC was sent to a compatibility format input address provided by MixTum. The first output, O_1, of 0.001 BTC was received in one hour and 14 min. The network fee on this transaction was 0.00024227 BTC. A second output, O_2, of 0.000762 BTC was received in four hours and 55 min with a network fee of 0.00022843. The overall mixing fee for this interaction was equal to 4.4% of the input plus 0.00015 BTC.

Trial 3. In Trial 3, two legacy output addresses were specified. Two input transactions, I_1 and I_2, were sent to a compatibility format input address provided by MixTum. I_1 was 0.002 BTC and I_2 was 0.001 BTC. The first output address received two output transactions, O_1 and O_2, of 0.0004 BTC and 0.001 BTC 47 min after the input. The second output address received an output, O_3, of 0.00136 BTC in 52 min. The network fees for these output transactions were 0.00017997 BTC, 0.00017305 BTC, and 0.00014536 BTC respectively. The overall mixing fee for this trial was 3% of the input amount plus 0.00015 BTC.

B.3   Bitcoin Mixer Results

Table 8. Results for Bitcoin Mixer trials.

Trial	Obfuscation parameters	Input (BTC)	Output (BTC)	Mixer fees (BTC)	Txn IDs
1	1 Output rapid delay	0.0002	0.0001985	0.0000015	7
2	3 Outputs distribution (%): 35, 35, 30 delay (hr): 1, 2, 2	0.0004	0.000396	0.000004	8
3	5 Outputs distribution (%): 13.3, 5.36, 21.98, 30.72, 28.64 delay (hr): 1, 2, 5, 10, 12	0.0006	0.0005935	0.0000065	9

[7] I_1: 1e986fcb917e3b6702f7c0855ef97bb63852f3a7b4b732c979c24a650d83d60a
O_1: 1752cc1c59e086a41e5eff494a3e949220585174df969524ba0315ff43baacc1
[8] I_1: f3ea2711301deda2a6e1721a6cb535c8d989a9536089c72b1df693ec72d3a979
O_1: a445e5f62e7a7aaccbb5f0094dead98ff340f00fa461bb02bcebb5c39209ce39
O_2: b29103754707b9553948efe16e0f0f2ed24afd9344851ae6aba53d48d6295188
O_3: a38b52879b069709aa7baa3928b71f3c2ebb8dcfbce23b481fc0f5b00f00afe1
[9] I_1: 101a29a16be3357b5b9733e9cb5576d735ba4526f0937071a1bc43158e4cf4ab
O_1: 1423cc8eadc7be5b71c25286244ca9815479691a816c545eb46ce9d40ae6d3c8
O_2: fa5bb1ade1c6e99ffa964ad5b76f005c4e6c4b740b1697fd664e43f0f8522e2a
O_3: a1d08152d1e5e9d75996591e69b663f0eefb96fa31f06fd6ca907084d2e04f26
O_4: 61ef79f1ff7ae348a453f4e1d073ce5cf7a732d6c0e50d9fe04d0005eec142f4
O_5: 32ad310b25f2f4f11288e8115fce4126526643f49afc5c5e80f081bab3d853b1

Trial 1. In Trial 1, one output SegWit address was specified with rapid delay. The service provided a compatibility format input address and a mix ID. One transaction, I_1, of 0.0002 BTC was sent to this address. Within 30 s of the first network confirmation, an output transaction, O_1, of 0.0001985 BTC was received. Overall, the interaction had a mixing fee of 0.0000015 BTC.

Trial 2. In Trial 2, three legacy output addresses were specified. Delay and distribution among these addresses was set to be 1 h with 35%, 2 h with 35%, and 2 h with 30% respectively. The service provided one compatibility format input address. One transaction, I_1, of 0.0004 BTC was sent to this address. The first output address received output O_1 of 0.0001386 BTC in 43 min. The second received output O_2 of 0.0001386 BTC in 1 h and 44 min. The third received output O_3 of 0.0001188 BTC in 1 h and 44 min. The overall mixing fee for this trial was 0.000004 BTC.

Trial 3. In Trial 3, five SegWit output addresses were specified. Delay and distribution was set to be 1 h with 13.3%, 2 h with 5.36%, 5 h with 21.98%, 10 h with 30.72%, and 12 h with 28.64% respectively. The service provided one compatibility format input address. One transaction, I_1, of 0.0006 BTC was sent to this address. Output O_1 of 0.00007894 BTC was received by the first output address in 31 min. Output O_2 of 0.00003181 BTC was received by the second output address in 1 h and 26 min. Output O_3 of 0.00013045 BTC was received by the third output address in 4 h and 26 min. Output O_4 of 0.00018232 BTC was received by the fourth output address in 9 h and 26 min. Finally, output O_5 of 0.00016998 BTC was received by the fifth output address in 11 h and 26 min. The overall mixing fee for this trial was 0.0000065 BTC.

B.4   CryptoMixer Results

Table 9. Results for CryptoMixer trials.

Trial	Obfuscation parameters	Input (BTC)	Output (BTC)	Mixer fees (BTC)	Txn IDs
1	1 Output 2 Input 0.5060% fee 1 h 15 min delay	0.001	0.00049494	0.00050506	10
2	CryptoMixer Code 3 Outputs 4 Inputs distribution (%): 20.05, 19.96, 59.99 delays: 3hr 7m, 9hr 1min, 15hr 2min	0.002	0	0	11
3	3 Outputs 2 Inputs distribution (%): 20.43, 19.85, 59.72 delays: 3hr 3min, 9hr 8min, 15hr 4min	0.002	0	0	12

[10] I_1: a02d447aae65ce5d671b2cf1ba183cf08399655f17ed26269c0124e0cf4f5e3d
I_2: 73e8f1f233c9ca966f7ab34a4074a558269b37cfb65c4f1a3482f66b8d6e3c6f
O_1: f60a746dd452f1c687f0ff92849ede81ecbe7787440f2906c47385f0d9279fcd
[11] I_1: 1268643164dddfee0fce627295fb6c26d62dadb418630c3601e812feb612d0fe
I_2: 02667f20e8355136aec0295409c5d689bf8a7a9ec1302e8a2941154ec565062e
I_3: 1c2bfe577e9bb80cbbd2d56108145d640112128b4518348676b468032f947b62
I_4: 9b5e7617ee123c10e697c838d9d061118c3749bf0b89c12107c6daf0df2f798d
[12] I_1: fb930e8d5c9ffe10edc40f880671da7bc8370eee101bc46a20e9fafc0ceb4ddb
I_2: 5d010989689bae4d4ec4bd4e9c3984a4632548fa15aeac9ea90d94f15fc2928d

Trial 1. In Trial 1, one SegWit output address was specified. Additionally, the mixing service fee and delay were set to 0.5060% and 1 h and 15 min respectively. This qualified for a Standard security level. The service provided a five character alphanumeric CryptoMixer code and one legacy format input address with its corresponding letter of guarantee. One transaction, I_1, of 0.001 BTC was sent to this address. The service's calculator stated that the output would be 0.00049494 BTC. However, after one confirmation the service displayed an error stating that the "amount is less than required." The error did not disappear and the number of confirmations on our original input did not update after the first detected confirmation. Assuming the service expected an additional payment of 0.00049494 BTC, we generated a second input address and executed another input transaction, I_2. However, this was ignored by the service. After 1 h and 21 min of the first input, we received output O_1 of 0.00049494 BTC with a network fee 0.00007749 BTC. The overall mixing fee for this interaction was 0.00050506 BTC.

Trial 2. In Trial 2, the CryptoMixer code from Trial 1 was used and three legacy output addresses were specified. Delay and distribution for these output addresses was 3 h and 7 min with 20.05%, 9 h and 1 min with 19.96%, and 15 h and 2 min with 59.99% respectively. The mixing fee was set to 1.0176%. These parameters qualified the interaction for a Silver security level. The service provided the same CryptoMixer code from Trial 1 and we manually generated four legacy format input addresses. The letter of guarantee for each of these addresses was successfully downloaded. Input transactions I_1, I_2, I_3, and I_4 were executed with 0.001 BTC, 0.001 BTC, 0.0005 BTC, and 0.001 BTC respectively. The service's calculator stated that 0.00039386 BTC, 0.00039209 BTC, and 0.001178 BTC would be deposited to out output addresses. However, no outputs were received.

Trial 3. In Trial 3, no CryptoMixer code was used and three legacy output addresses were specified. Delay and distribution for these output addresses was 3 h and 3 min with 20.43%, 9 h and 8 min with 19.85%, and 15 h and 4 min with 59.72% respectively. The mixing service fee was set to 1.0820%. These parameters qualified this trial for Silver security level. We received a new five character CryptoMixer code and manually generated two legacy format input addresses. The letter of guarantee for each of these addresses was successfully downloaded. Input transactions I_1 and I_2 were executed with 0.001 BTC each. However, we received the same error from Trial 1 stating "amount is less than required." For both inputs the service stated 0.00051082 BTC was pending. Thus, two transactions of 0.0005 BTC and 0.00001082 BTC were sent to each input address. However, the service did not identify these transactions and no outputs were received.

B.5   Sudoku Wallet Results

Table 10. Results for Sudoku Wallet trials.

Trial	Obfuscation parameters	Input (BTC)	Output (BTC)	Output network fees (BTC)	Mixer fees (BTC)	Txn IDs
1	sweep	0.001	0.00087261	0.00012739	0	[13]
2	sweep	0.002	0.00171162	0.00024839	0.00003999	[14]
3	sweep	0.003	0.0000769	0.00022310	0.0027	[15]

[13] I_1: 1f5996ac5b80fcc2df3cc44894ecbdd4e26a35ae20f076ff242d112900bc4898
O_1: d37438550d5418c26b3b9a0cadc20007d80d12177b096ef286c53ef10cad11c9
[14] I_1: 778e990edf67d546bd8eeae911107Re3R1a7ac7d0eff9sebbdda8b13bb0d275d2
O_1: a03076b11384abf4cd1e3df92b327c324af910e14914c6038b60e037814935c9
[15] I_1: 3c18b011a01f243d2cace66c07cf6016385ffa20f55e0cbdfccf34fa96f18088
O_1): 310ec6f888c9db47c1d24410f5a38b3b40461b378a355f0363faaed8f5166443

Trial 1. Sudoku Wallet provided a 25 character alphanumeric wallet key. The service then presented an input address with its corresponding private key. We sent one transaction, I_1, of 0.001 BTC to this input address. After the service detected three confirmations on this input, we were able to view two output addresses funded with 0.00059025 BTC and 0.00040975 BTC along with their private keys. These funds were then swept to our SegWit wallet through an on-blockchain transaction, O_1. The network fee for this transaction was 0.00012739

BTC and 0.00087261 BTC was the final output. The overall mixing fee for this interaction was 0 BTC.

Trial 2. Sudoku Wallet provided a new 25 character alphanumeric wallet key. The service presented an input address with its corresponding private key. We sent one transaction, I_1, of 0.002 BTC to this address. After three confirmations, we were presented three output addresses with 0.00066667 BTC, 0.00064667 BTC, and 0.00064667 BTC. These funds were then swept to our legacy wallet through an on-blockchain transaction, O_1. The network fee for this transaction was 0.00024839 BTC and 0.00171162 BTC was the final output. The overall mixing fee for this interaction was 0.00003999 BTC.

Trial 3. We received a new 25 character alphanumeric wallet key. We sent one transaction, I_1, of 0.003 BTC to the given input address. After three confirmations, we were presented three output addresses of 0.0001 BTC each with corresponding private keys. These funds were swept to our SegWit wallet through an on-blockchain transaction. O_1. The network fee for this transaction was 0.00022310 BTC and 0.0000769 BTC was the final output. The overall mixing fee for this interaction was 0.0027 BTC.

C   Appendix 3

C.1   Chip Generation Transactions

(See Table 11).

Table 11. Example chip generation transactions.

Chip size (BTC)	Transaction ID
8.192	a3098c6d8961c6674ad4590a3b50c2ca213d833b49a2c774ce5248cabed135a2
0.256	5b7bfd2f60d6058344cdb59fe64d3c1402378c3489210de2a6d18a34e1c0bd5b
4.096	66c3429e06f5e8732717bbeba30d7df28f81a785c4018ad0a269959bbd37bce6

References

1. Protect your privacy (2013). http://bitcoin.org/en/protect-your-privacy
2. Cryptomixer.io fast, secure and reliable bitcoin mixer (since 2016) (2016). https://bitcointalk.org/index.php?topic=1484009.msg15350012#msg15350012
3. Cryptomixer.io fast, secure and reliable bitcoin mixer (since 2016) (2016). https://bitcointalk.org/index.php?topic=1484009.msg15256505#msg15256505
4. Cryptomixer.io fast, secure and reliable bitcoin mixer (since 2016) (2016). https://bitcointalk.org/index.php?topic=1484009.msg15428183#msg15428183
5. Bestmixer.io the future of bitcoin mixing! technology is here (2018). https://bitcointalk.org/index.php?topic=3140140.0

6. Multi-million euro cryptocurrency laundering service bestmixer.io taken down (2019). https://www.europol.europa.eu/newsroom/news
7. list bitcoin mixers bitcoin tumblers websites (2020). https://bitcointalk.org/index. php?topic=2827109.msg29058223#msg29058223
8. Bitcoin charts & graphs - blockchain (2020). https://www.blockchain.com/en/ charts
9. Alsalami, N., Zhang, B.: Sok: a systematic study of anonymity in cryptocurrencies. In: 2019 IEEE Conference on Dependable and Secure Computing (DSC), pp. 1–9 (2019). https://doi.org/10.1109/DSC47296.2019.8937681
10. de Balthasar, T., Hernandez-Castro, J.: An analysis of bitcoin laundry services. In: NordSec (2017)
11. Bissias, G., Ozisik, A.P., Levine, B.N., Liberatore, M.: Sybil-resistant mixing for Bitcoin. In: Proceedings of the ACM Conference on Computer and Communications Security, WPES '14, pp. 149–158. ACM (2014). https://doi.org/10.1145/ 2665943.2665955
12. Bonneau, J., Narayanan, A., Miller, A., Clark, J., Kroll, J.A., Felten, E.W.: Mixcoin: anonymity for bitcoin with accountable mixes. In: Christin, N., Safavi-Naini, R. (eds.) FC 2014. LNCS, vol. 8437, pp. 486–504. Springer, Heidelberg (2014). https://doi.org/10.1007/978-3-662-45472-5_31
13. Delgado-Segura, S., et al.: Txprobe: discovering bitcoin's network topology using orphan transactions. In: Financial Cryptography (2018)
14. DuPont, J., Squicciarini, A.C.: Toward de-anonymizing bitcoin by mapping users location. In: Proceedings of the 5th ACM Conference on Data and Application Security and Privacy, CODASPY '15, pp. 139–141. Association for Computing Machinery, New York (2015). https://doi.org/10.1145/2699026.2699128
15. . Maxwell, G: CoinJoin: bitcoin privacy for the real world (2013). https:// bitcointalk.org/index.php?topic=279249
16. Heilman, E., AlShenibr, L., Baldimtsi, F., Scafuro, A., Goldberg, S.: TumbleBit: an untrusted bitcoin-compatible anonymous payment hub. In: NDSS. Internet Society (2017). https://doi.org/10.14722/ndss.2017.23086
17. Koshy, P., Koshy, D., McDaniel, P.: An analysis of anonymity in bitcoin using P2P network traffic. In: Christin, N., Safavi-Naini, R. (eds.) FC 2014. LNCS, vol. 8437, pp. 469–485. Springer, Heidelberg (2014). https://doi.org/10.1007/978-3-662-45472-5_30
18. Meiklejohn, S., et al.: A fistful of bitcoins: characterizing payments among men with no names. In: Proceedings of the 2013 Conference on Internet Measurement Conference, IMC '13, pp. 127–140. Association for Computing Machinery, New York (2013). https://doi.org/10.1145/2504730.2504747
19. Möser, M., Böhme, R., Breuker, D.: An inquiry into money laundering tools in the bitcoin ecosystem. In: 2013 APWG eCrime Researchers Summit, pp. 1–14 (2013)
20. Nakamoto, S.: Bitcoin: a peer-to-peer electronic cash system (2009). http://www. bitcoin.org/bitcoin.pdf
21. Novetta, L.: Survey of bitcoin mixing services: Tracing anonymous bitcoins. Technical repory, McLean, VA (2015). https://www.novetta.com/wp-content/uploads/ 2015/10/NovettaBiometrics_BitcoinCryptocurrency_WP-W_9182015.pdf
22. Ruffing, T., Moreno-Sanchez, P., Kate, A.: CoinShuffle: practical decentralized coin mixing for bitcoin. Technical report (2014)
23. Tran, M., Luu, L., Suk Kang, M., Bentov, I., Saxena, P.: Obscuro: a bitcoin mixer using trusted execution environments. In: ACSAC '18 (Annual Computer Security Applications Conference), ACSAC '18, vol. 18, pp. 692–701. ACM, New York (2018). https://doi.org/10.1145/3274694.3274750

24. Valenta, L., Rowan, B.: Blindcoin: blinded, accountable mixes for bitcoin. In: Brenner, M., Christin, N., Johnson, B., Rohloff, K. (eds.) FC 2015. LNCS, vol. 8976, pp. 112–126. Springer, Heidelberg (2015). https://doi.org/10.1007/978-3-662-48051-9_9

25. Ziegeldorf, J.H., Grossmann, F., Henze, M., Inden, N., Wehrle, K.: CoinParty: secure multi-party mixing of bitcoins. In: CODASPY 2015 - Proceedings of the 5th ACM Conference on Data and Application Security and Privacy, pp. 75–86. ACM (2015). https://doi.org/10.1145/2699026.2699100

PERIMETER: A Network-Layer Attack on the Anonymity of Cryptocurrencies

Maria Apostolaki$^{(\boxtimes)}$, Cedric Maire, and Laurent Vanbever

ETH Zürich, Zürich, Switzerland
apmaria@ethz.ch

Abstract. Cryptocurrencies are widely used today for anonymous transactions. Such currencies rely on a peer-to-peer network where users can broadcast transactions containing their pseudonyms and ask for approval. Previous research has shown that application-level eavesdroppers, meaning nodes connected to a large portion of the Bitcoin peer-to-peer network, are able to deanonymize multiple users by tracing back the source of transactions. Yet, such attacks are highly visible as the attacker needs to maintain thousands of outbound connections. Moreover, they can be mitigated by purely application-layer countermeasures.

This paper presents a stealthier and harder-to-mitigate attack exploiting the interactions between the networking and application layers. Particularly, the adversary combines her access over Internet infrastructure with application-layer information to deanonymize transactions. We show that this attack, namely PERIMETER, is practical in today's Internet, achieves high accuracy in Bitcoin, and generalizes to encrypted cryptocurrencies *e.g.,* Ethereum.

Keywords: Deanonymization · Bitcoin · Ethereum · Blockchain · BGP · Routing attack · Network-layer attack

1 Introduction

Anonymity is among the essential properties of any cryptocurrency [38]. The most successful cryptocurrencies today *i.e.,* Bitcoin and Ethereum, are pseudonymous [27]: clients are able to securely transact while using pseudonyms that cannot be trivially mapped to their real-world identities. Cryptocurrencies operate using a peer-to-peer (P2P) network of nodes. When a node performs a transaction, it sends the transaction to its peers, which propagate it further. Consequently, an adversary that listens to *all* exchanged messages can map each transaction to the IP address of the node that created it, effectively deanonymizing that node.

Multiple attacks have exploited this transaction broadcasting mechanism to map Bitcoin pseudonyms to their originating IP address [20,22,34,40]. To do so, they use a "supernode": a seemingly regular node that connects to all active

© International Financial Cryptography Association 2021
N. Borisov and C. Diaz (Eds.): FC 2021, LNCS 12674, pp. 147–166, 2021.
https://doi.org/10.1007/978-3-662-64322-8_7

Bitcoin nodes and listens to the transactions they relay. [1] Yet, such attacks are highly noticeable [33], as the "supernode" establishes 50–117 new connections to *every* reachable Bitcoin client. Moreover, such attacks can be mitigated by purely application-level countermeasures. For instance, the diffusion broadcast mechanism mitigates the attacks presented in [20,34], while Dandelion [23] and its improvements [28] reduce the effectiveness of the attack presented in [22].

In this work, we introduce PERIMETER: a stealthier, harder-to-mitigate, network-level attack. PERIMETER relies on an attack vector that has been overlooked: leveraging access to the Internet infrastructure. Connections of any cryptocurrency are inevitably routed over the Internet, thus accessible to multiple Autonomous Systems (ASes) and Internet Exchange Points (IXPs). As a result, a malicious AS or IXP that combines her access to the Internet infrastructure with application-level knowledge can perform a cross-layer deanonymization attack. Our routing analysis of the Bitcoin network reveals that such attacks are practical in today's Internet. Indeed, we found that at least 6 distinct network adversaries can deanonymize more than 35% of the Bitcoin clients (see Sect. 5). The PERIMETER attack is stealthier than previous attacks, as it is completely passive (no need for new connections); and harder to mitigate, as the attacker's power is dependent on the Internet routing protocol (BGP) *i.e.,* not on the application protocol.

PERIMETER is composed of two phases. In the first phase, the attacker eavesdrops on the victim's connections at the *packet-level* to collect information about the transactions the victim propagates to its peers. In the second phase, the attacker analyzes this information to distinguish the victim's transactions.

The attacker eavesdrops on the victim's connections by directly reading each packet's payload *i.e.,* not by establishing connections. In effect, the attack is undetectable and equally effective against nodes, which do not accept connections *e.g.,* NATed notes. Notably, unlike previous work on network-level attacks [17,48], which require the attacker to control *all* connections of a victim, PERIMETER works with just a fraction. We experimentally show that an adversary intercepting only 25% of the victim's connections can deanonymize it with 70% accuracy (see Sect. 6).

The adversary distinguishes the victim's transactions using anomaly detection (Isolation Forest [35]). The victim's transactions appear as anomalies as they have a distinct propagation pattern. For example, in Bitcoin, the victim will send a transaction that it generated to an unusually high portion of its peers compared to other transactions. Unlike previous work on deanonymizing Bitcoin clients that rely solely on the time difference between announcements of the same transaction across nodes [20,22,33,34], PERIMETER is agnostic to it. As a result, PERIMETER is not sensitive to broadcast protocol changes *e.g.,* diffusion, trickle, etc. Instead, PERIMETER leverages the victim's interactions with its peers to infer whether the victim knew a transaction before its peers.

PERIMETER generalizes to encrypted cryptocurrencies. Taking the popular Ethereum as an example, we observe that an AS or IXP-level adversary is a

---

[1] Similar techniques could be applied to Ethereum.

practical threat for two main reasons. First, similarly to the Bitcoin network, the Ethereum network is affected by the centralization of the Internet traffic. Indeed, we observe that for the majority of clients there are 4 distinct adversaries intercepting 30% of their connections (see Sect. 5). Second, a network adversary can infer the victim's peers by eavesdropping on the IP packets, as their header is inevitably unencrypted. This combined with the lack of randomness in broadcasting transactions (*e.g.*, diffusion), makes traditional attacks (solved in Bitcoin) such as Koshy et al. [34] effective.

To summarize, we make the following key contributions:

- A novel attack vector against anonymity that is effective against Bitcoin (Sects. 3, 4) and generalizes to encrypted cryptocurrencies.
- A thorough analysis of the Bitcoin and Ethereum networks from the routing perspective using real-world control-plane data. Our analysis demonstrates the feasibility of such an attack in today's Internet (Sect. 5).
- An evaluation of PERIMETER's practicality using both realistic simulations and "in-the-wild" experiments against Bitcoin clients (Sect. 6).
- A comprehensive set of deployable countermeasures (Sect. 7).

2   Background

In this section, we briefly describe Bitcoin, Ethereum, and Internet routing.

2.1   Bitcoin Workings

Bitcoin is a currency that does not rely on any central authority or trusted party. Instead, Bitcoin relies on a peer-to-peer (P2P) network in which nodes use a consensus mechanism to jointly agree on an append-only log of all the transactions that ever happened, the *blockchain*. Bitcoin users are associated with one or multiple cryptographic pseudonyms, which cannot be trivially mapped to the user's real-world identities. Thus, we say that Bitcoin is pseudonymous. Attempts to map pseudonyms to real-world identities constitute deanonymization attacks.

To transfer funds among each other, Bitcoin clients issue transactions in which they declare the transfer of a certain amount of Bitcoin from their Bitcoin pseudonym to one (or multiple) others. Transactions need to be propagated in the network, verified by all nodes, and eventually added to the blockchain. Upon receiving a new transaction, a Bitcoin client advertises it to its peers using an "inv" message that includes the hash of the transaction. The peers which are unaware of an advertised transaction request it by replying to the advertisement with a "getdata" message that includes the hash of the transaction. Finally, a Bitcoin client sends the transaction to those peers that request it with a "tx" message.

The Bitcoin Core has included two modifications that affect the way transactions are propagated.[2] First, a client advertises transactions with independent,

---

[2] We mention the modifications that are relevant to our work.

exponential delays to its peers. This broadcast mechanism is called *diffusion* and was introduced as a countermeasure against deanonymization attacks. Second, the diffusion delay that a client adds before an advertisement to a given peer differs depending on which initiated the connection between them. Particularly, a Bitcoin node halves the delay for peers to which it initialized the connection as these are less of a privacy concern [3].

2.2   Ethereum Workings

Ethereum supports decentralized applications that are backed by smart contracts: protocols or small pieces of software running on top of the Ethereum network and performing irreversible transactions with no third-party intervention. In the context of Ethereum, a transaction is a data structure describing the exchange of Ether signed with the private key corresponding to a users' pseudonym. Similar to Bitcoin, Ethereum relies on a P2P network of nodes and is pseudonymous. In contrast to Bitcoin, though, all Ethereum communications are encrypted [11]. Thus, an on-path eavesdropper cannot read the exchanged messages.

The Ethereum protocol also differs from the Bitcoin protocol in the way transactions are broadcasted. Ethereum broadcasts newly learned transactions without delay across transmissions. It also makes use of an advertisement system, but only for a subset of its neighbor peers. In particular, consider an Ethereum (Geth [6]) node with n peers, each time it learns a new transaction, the node broadcasts it to $\lfloor \sqrt{n} \rfloor$ of its peers and then it advertises it to the remaining $n - \lfloor \sqrt{n} \rfloor$ peers, excluding those which is already aware of it.

2.3   Internet Routing

The Internet is composed of smaller networks called Autonomous Systems (AS). Each AS contains multiple hosts that are addressed with a unique IP. ASes build physical connections to each other to exchange traffic under certain economic agreements. Oftentimes, ASes also participate in Internet eXchange Points (IXPs). In this case, multiple ASes connect to a single physical location and exchange traffic. BGP [9] is the routing protocol that regulates how IP packets are forwarded in the Internet. Particularly, BGP computes the unidirectional AS-paths along which traffic from each host will reach its destination. ASes and IXPs in this AS-path forward traffic, and thus they can eavesdrop, drop, or delay it.

3   Overview

In this section, we give an overview of the PERIMETER attack before we elaborate on its workings in Sect. 4. In particular, we first describe the attacker's goal, profile, and procedure (Sect. 3.1). Next, we illustrate the PERIMETER attack against a Bitcoin client with an example (Sect. 3.2). Finally, we describe how the attack generalizes to Ethereum (Sect. 3.3).

3.1   PERIMETER at a High-Level

Attacker's Goal. The attacker's goal is to deanonymize a specific node, meaning to map the IP of a victim node to the transaction(s) it created.[3] Concretely, the attacker's goal is to compute a set of transactions that contains (most of) the victim's transaction(s) (*i.e.,* maximize true positives) and as few as possible transactions created by other nodes (*i.e.,* minimize false positives). We refer to this set of transactions as the victim's *anonymity set.*

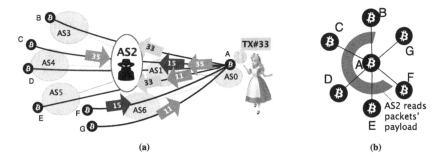

(a)   (b)

Fig. 1. (a) From the networking viewpoint, the attacker (AS2) naturally *i.e.,* according to BGP, intercepts some of the victim's connections. (b) From the application viewpoint, the attacker (partially) surrounds the victim without establishing any new connection. Surrounding the victim allows the attacker (AS2) to read the unencrypted Bitcoin messages the victim node A sends and receives.

Attacker's Profile. The attacker is an Autonomous System (AS) or Internet eXchange Point (IXP) that naturally (*i.e.,* according to BGP's calculations) intercepts any direction of X% of the victim's connections and knows the victim's IP.[4] Due to the centralization of the Internet traffic, multiple ASes and IXPs intercept a large portion of a host's connections even if they are not their direct provider, as we show in Sect. 5.

Attack Procedure. The attack consists of eavesdropping on the victim's connections and analyzing collected data to distinguish the victim's transaction(s). Concretely, the adversary first leverages her position in the Internet to gain visibility over the transactions that the victim propagates. We refer to this process as *surrounding* since the adversary creates a logical circle around the victim across which she can observe the incoming and outgoing information. Notably, the adversary surrounds the victim in a purely passive and undetectable manner, as she only observes traffic that she anyway forwards. Next, the adversary

---

[3] Such an attack is very harmful to the victim because an attacker can often link all other transactions the victim made to the deanonymized one [39].

[4] Finding the IP of a person is practical as it is revealed every time this person visits a website or an application *e.g.,* skype call.

computes statistics on the transactions the victim advertises and uses anomaly detection to find the victim's transactions. Useful statistics include the number of times the victim or its peers sent or received a transaction.

3.2 PERIMETER in Action

An Example Scenario. Figure 1a illustrates how an attacker running PERIME-TER can deanonymize Bitcoin transactions. This network is composed of seven ASes (AS0 - AS6), some of which host Bitcoin clients (nodes A-G). Traffic between each pair of nodes is forwarded following the AS-path that BGP calculates. As a result, AS2 intercepts the connections between node A and nodes B, C, D and E. Assume that AS2 is malicious and aims at deanonymizing Alice's transactions. AS2 knows the IP of the node on which Alice runs her Bitcoin wallet, namely the IP of node A. Thus, AS2 aims at mapping node A to the transaction(s) it generates, TX#33 in this example.

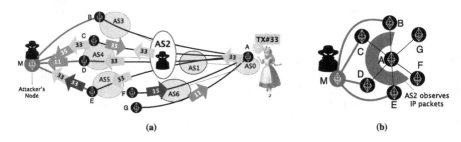

(a)   (b)

Fig. 2. To deanonymize Alice's transaction in Ethereum, the attacker (AS2) connects to some of the victim's peers. AS2 infers some of the victim's peers' IPs by eavesdropping on the victim's connections. (b) In effect, the attacker indirectly surrounds the victim from the application viewpoint.

PERIMETER Attack on Bitcoin. AS2 eavesdrops on the victim's connections that she naturally intercepts and creates the initial anonymity set from the transactions that node A propagates *i.e.,* TX #15, TX #11, TX #35, and TX #33. From the application viewpoint, AS2 has passively formed a (partial) logical circle around the victim, as illustrated in Fig. 1b. Next, AS2 tries to reduce the size of the anonymity set by removing transactions that are most likely not generated by the victim. AS2 knows that a Bitcoin node only receives transactions it requests and only requests transactions it does not know already. Thus, AS2 excludes TX #35 from the anonymity set as AS2 has observed node A receiving TX #35 from node C. AS2 cannot use the same technique for TX #15 and TX #11 because AS2 does not intercept the victim's connections to the nodes from which it received these transactions, *i.e.,* nodes F and G. Instead, AS2 uses anomaly detection to find the victim's transaction, which appears as an anomaly with respect to its propagation pattern. For instance, the number of peers that requested TX #33 from node A is higher for TX #33 than for any other transaction. We elaborate on the anomaly detection procedure and the features used in Sect. 4.

3.3   Generalizing PERIMETER to Ethereum

Figure 2a illustrates the same attack scenario as before but with nodes A-G belonging to the Ethereum network. We now explain how AS2 could use PERIMETER to deanonymize node A in this case. Unlike Bitcoin, Ethereum connections are encrypted, meaning that AS2 cannot directly read the content of the messages the victim exchanges with its peers. To deanonymize an Ethereum client, AS2 uses the observation made by Biryukov et al. [20] according to which a node can be uniquely identified in a single session by its directly connected neighboring nodes. Unlike in the attack presented by Biryukov et al. [20] that used a Bitcoin-specific flaw to infer connections, in PERIMETER, the attacker can infer the IP addresses of the victim's peers by reading the unencrypted headers of the packets the victim node A inevitably sends and receives. After connecting to some of the victim's peers,[5] distinguishing the victim's transactions (across those its peers propagate) is strictly more straightforward than for Bitcoin. That is the case as most Ethereum nodes (geth version [6]) advertise the new transactions immediately to their peers. From the application viewpoint, the adversary has again partially surrounded the victim, as seen in Fig. 2b.

4   PERIMETER Workings

Having described the PERIMETER attack at the high-level in Sect. 3, we now elaborate on PERIMETER's technical details. Concretely, we describe how the attacker (i) distinguishes Bitcoin traffic (Sect. 4.1); (ii) retrieves propagated transactions (Sect. 4.2); and (iii) uses anomaly detection (Isolation Forest) to find the victim's transaction(s) (Sect. 4.3). Finally, we discuss the features the attacker uses (Sect. 4.4).

4.1   Recognizing Bitcoin Traffic

The adversary surrounds the victim node and reads the data exchanged in the Bitcoin connections to create the initial anonymity set. To do so, the adversary first needs to distinguish Bitcoin traffic across all the connections she intercepts. The adversary can easily distinguish Bitcoin traffic since most clients use a particular TCP port, i.e., 8333. Notably, the adversary can recognize the Bitcoin connections, even between clients using another TCP port. To do so, the adversary can search on the packet payload to find known Bitcoin message types,

---

[5] Ethereum facilitates connecting to a client using its IP (i.e., discovery v4 UDP packet).

e.g., "inv" or "getdata". Indeed, the adversary can perform string searching at line-rate even in commodity hardware [32]. Importantly, the adversary performs string search on a single packet per connection. Once she finds a Bitcoin message in a packet of a connection, she can use a filter that matches on the 4-tuple of the TCP connection (*i.e.,* IP addresses and TCP ports) to distinguish it.

4.2   Creating the Initial Anonymity Set

To create the initial anonymity set, the attacker needs to distinguish all transactions that the victim itself or its peers have advertised. This is challenging as Bitcoin messages can be split among multiple packets, and those packets can be re-ordered, lost, and re-transmitted while being transferred in the Internet. As a result, concatenating each Bitcoin connection's payloads (packet stream) would not result in the complete list of messages that the corresponding clients exchanged (message stream). To reconstruct the message stream, the adversary can use tools such as GoPacket [7] that leverage the sequence number contained in the TCP header.

Next, the adversary includes in the anonymity set the hashes of the transactions that are included in three types of messages, namely "inv", "getdata", and "tx". Finally, the adversary calculates statistics per transaction hash. Particularly, she calculates the number of "inv", "getdata", and "tx" that are sent and received per transaction.

4.3   Analyzing Data

Having collected the initial anonymity set, the adversary needs to reduce it to the transactions that the victim created. Doing so is challenging for two reasons. First, the number of transactions the victim propagates is orders of magnitude higher than those that it creates. Second, the adversary does not have ground truth to train on (*e.g.,* transactions that the victim created).

To address these challenges, the adversary formulates the problem to an unsupervised anomaly detection problem, meaning a problem that requires identifying data points that differ from the norm (i.e., anomalies) in an unlabeled dataset. Doing so allows the attacker to train directly on the traffic she observes, leveraging the fact that the victim's transactions are a tiny minority compared to all transactions the victim propagates. As a result, the attacker can learn the most common propagation pattern and distinguish the victim's transactions as anomalies. Indeed, the victim's transactions will exhibit different propagation patterns, *e.g.,* the victim will propagate the transaction it generates to more peers compared to other transactions.

The attacker uses an Isolation Forest (IF) [35,36] to solve this unsupervised anomaly detection problem since IF is more efficient, expressive, and interpretable than clustering-based approaches or neural networks. Concretely, IF is more efficient, especially with high-dimensional data, than distance-based methods, including classical nearest-neighbor and clustering-based approaches. This is because IF is a tree-based machine learning algorithm that directly identifies anomalies by isolating outliers in the data rather than first defining the normal behavior and calculating point-based distances. Finally, in contrast to neural network methods, such as autoencoders, IF is easy to interpret, and it is not too sensitive to parameter tuning. IF achieves this by building an ensemble of decision trees to partition the data points. To create these trees, IF recursively generates partitions by randomly selecting a feature and then selecting a random split value between the minimum and the maximum value of the selected feature. The number of required random splits to isolate a sample averaged over a forest of such random trees determines the normality of a sample. IF leverages the observation that anomalies are more natural to isolate, and thus they need fewer splits on average than normal data points.

4.4   Feature Selection

We started our feature investigation with a pool of features, including some timing-related and some interaction-related (*i.e.,* related to the interaction between the victim and its peers). Using cross-validation in our simulation runs (see Sect. 6.1), we selected three interaction-related features: *(i)* number of "getdata" messages; *(ii)* number of "tx" messages; and *(iii)* the portion of clients which requested a transaction. Next, we describe the features in detail and explain why they allow the victim's transaction(s) to stand out as anomalies.

The number of "getdata" messages that the victim received per transaction: This is equivalent to the number of times the victim sent a transaction. Thus, the adversary can capture this feature independently of the direction of the victim's connections she intercepts. A Bitcoin client will only send a "getdata" for an advertised transaction if it has not received this transaction before. Thus, the victim is expected to receive more "getdata" for a transaction it created, as its peers are unlikely to have received it from others.

The number of "tx" messages the victim received per transaction: If the victim received a transaction from one of its peers, then the victim could not have created it. That is because, in order for the victim to receive a transaction, it should have requested this transaction from its peer, and thus, it should not have known this transaction beforehand. The number of "tx" the victim received for a transaction is equivalent to the number of "getdata" the victim sent. In effect, an AS-level (or IXP-level) adversary would be able to calculate this feature independently of the direction of traffic she intercepts, namely *to* or *from* the victim node.

The portion of clients that requested a transaction from the victim across those the victim advertised this transaction to: This feature is similar to the number of "getdata" with one critical difference. It considers that because of diffusion, the victim might delay advertising its transaction to some of the peers so much that they learn it from elsewhere. The victim's transaction will have a high request/advertisement ratio because the victim knows about the transaction much earlier than its peers.

5   PERIMETER's Practicality

As we described in Sect. 3, an effective PERIMETER attacker needs to naturally intercept some of the victim's connections. In this section, we show that this attacker model is practical, taking into consideration both real-world Internet routing and the two biggest cryptocurrency peer-to-peer networks, namely the Bitcoin and the Ethereum networks. To that end, we first investigate how likely it is for a given cryptocurrency client to be vulnerable to PERIMETER. We found that for 50% of the Bitcoin (60% of the Ethereum) clients, there are at least four distinct network adversaries that can intercept 30% of their connection. Second, we investigate how likely it is for a random transaction to be deanonymized. We found that only five network adversaries (if they were colluding) would be able to deanonymize the majority of transactions created in Bitcoin. We describe our methodology in Sect. 5.1 before we summarize our results in Sect. 5.2.

5.1   Methodology

To realistically evaluate the practicality of the PERIMETER attack, we simulated BGP [9], the default routing protocol in the Internet. Particularly, for each pair of ASes in the Internet, we compute the BGP AS-path: the sequences of ASes and IXPs that can intercept packets sent by clients hosted in this AS pair. We then calculated the ability of various ASes and IXPs to perform various-powered PERIMETER attacks against the Bitcoin and Ethereum clients. Notably, we augment the routing analysis of the Bitcoin network presented in [17] by adding IXP links and by analyzing the Ethereum network.

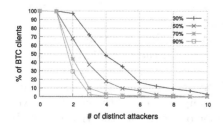 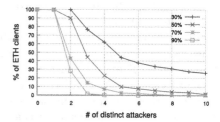

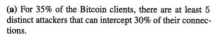

(a) For 35% of the Bitcoin clients, there are at least 5 distinct attackers that can intercept 30% of their connections.

(b) For 37% of the Ethereum clients, there are at least 6 distinct attackers that can intercept 30% of their connections.

Fig. 3. Both Bitcoin and Ethereum are vulnerable to PERIMETER's attacker model.

We used three datasets for our evaluation: *(i)* the IPs of the Ethereum and Bitcoin clients; *(ii)* the BGP advertised routes; and *(iii)* the publicly-available economic relationship among ASes and IXPs.

Ethereum & Bitcoin IPs to ASes. We fetched the IPs of the Bitcoin and Ethereum from publicly available data [12,13]. We removed onion addresses as we could not assign them to actual IPs. Next, we inferred the most-specific prefix and the AS hosting each Bitcoin and Ethereum client. To that end, we processed almost a million BGP routes (covering all Internet prefixes) advertised on BGP sessions maintained by 6 RIPE BGP collectors [10] (rrc00- rrc05). We do the mapping by associating each prefix to the origin AS advertising it.

AS-Level Topology and Forwarding Paths. To infer an AS-level topology, we used the economic relationships between ASes provided by CAIDA [25]. An AS-level topology is a directed graph in which each node corresponds to an AS, and each link represents an inter-domain connection between two neighboring ASes. Each link is also labeled with the business relationship between the two ASes (customer, peer, or provider). We augmented our AS-level topology with IXP links provided by CAIDA [26] following the methodology in [15,37].

Our augmented AS-level topology is composed of ∼67 K ASes, more than ∼700 IXPs, and ∼4M links. Our datasets were collected in September 2019. We computed the actual forwarding paths on our AS-level topology following the routing tree algorithm described in [30].

5.2   Findings

Using the Internet topology described in Sect. 5.1, we calculated how vulnerable individual clients are to PERIMETER and how likely it is for a transaction to be deanonymized.

The Majority of Bitcoin Clients are Vulnerable to PERIMETER by Multiple Potential Attackers. We calculated the number of distinct attackers able to intercept a fraction of the potential victims' connections. We summarize our results in Fig. 3a. The x-axis corresponds to the number of distinct attackers that can perform a PERIMETER attack against the portion of the Bitcoin clients shown in the y-axis. We consider four attack types depending on the fraction of the victim's traffic that the attacker intercepts. Specifically, we consider attackers intercepting 30%, 50%, 70%, and 90%, which correspond to different lines in the plots. As expected, all Bitcoin clients are vulnerable to PERIMETER by their own provider, which intercepts >90% of their connections. Interestingly though, >90% of all Bitcoin clients are also vulnerable to PERIMETER by at least one more network adversary. Moreover, we observe that for 50% of the Bitcoin clients, there are at least 4 attackers able to intercept 30% of their connections. This is worrying as such adversaries can deanonymize Bitcoin clients with at least 70% accuracy, as we observe from our experiments in the Bitcoin Mainnet (see Sect. 6). Worse yet, for 20% of the Bitcoin clients, there are at least 4 potential attackers that can perform the PERIMETER attack leveraging their access to 50% of the victims' connections.

PERIMETER's Attacker Model is Practical in the Ethereum Network. We plot the same results for Ethereum in Fig. 3b. We observe that Ethereum is slightly more vulnerable than Bitcoin to a passive AS-level (or IXP-level) adversary. Particularly, we observe that for most clients, there are four distinct network adversaries intercepting 30% of their connections. Observe that these adversaries can almost effortlessly infer 30% of the clients' peers. This is worrying considering that geth [6], the most used Ethereum version [12], does not implement diffusion or any other randomized broadcast mechanism.

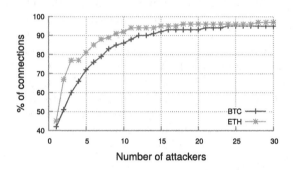

Fig. 4. 5 network adversaries intercept 72% (80%) of all possible Bitcoin (Ethereum) connections.

Few Well-Established Attackers Can Perform a Network-Wide Deanonymization Attack. Figure 4 illustrates the cumulative percentage of connections that can be intercepted by an increasing number of ASes or IXPs (*e.g.*, by colluding with each other). We observe that only ten ASes/IXPs together intercept 90% of the Ethereum clients and 85% of the Bitcoin clients. If those ten network providers decided to collude, they would be able to deanonymize 85% of all transactions in Bitcoin and able to infer at least 90% of the Ethereum peer-to-peer graph. This is especially alarming considering that the attack is entirely passive; thus, there is no reputation risk involved in performing it. As an intuition, the list of the most powerful attackers include ASes such as Amazon, Alibaba, DigitalOcean, and OVHcloud but also large IXPs such as DataIX Novosibirsk, the Amsterdam Internet Exchange, the Hong Kong Internet Exchange, and London Internet Exchange.

6   PERIMETER's Effectiveness

We evaluate the effectiveness of PERIMETER in simulation (Sect. 6.1) and in the wild (Sect. 6.2). We found that an attacker intercepting 25% of the victim's connections can deanonymize a client with 70% accuracy in the Bitcoin Mainnet. Unsurprisingly, the PERIMETER attack appears even more effective in simulation.

6.1 PERIMETER in Simulation

We evaluated PERIMETER using a realistic simulation whose delays we have tuned based on Internet-wide measurements. We elaborate on our methodology before we describe our results.

Simulator. We modeled the entire Bitcoin networks by extending the realistic event-driven simulator used in [17]. We used the 0.19.1 version of the Bitcoin Core as a reference for the behavior of the Bitcoin clients. Among other implementation details, we simulated diffusion: the poisson delay that a node waits before advertising a new transaction to each peer and the preference to outgoing connections in advertising and in requesting transactions [3]. We simulated all nodes whose IPs were reachable, and we could locate in the Internet as described in Sect. 5.

Simulating Internet Delays. To realistically model Internet delays among clients in our simulation, we leveraged the RIPE Atlas platform. RIPE Atlas [1] is a data collection system composed of a global network of devices, called probes, that can actively perform Internet measurements. In particular, to estimate the delay between each pair of Bitcoin nodes, we measure the delay between probes in the ASes hosting these Bitcoin nodes. Indeed, Internet delay between two particular hosts located in any AS-pair is representative of the delay between any pair of hosts in the same AS-pair. That is because the Internet path between any pair of hosts in the same AS-pair is common. We performed ping measurements for each pair of ASes say (ASA, ASB) in which there are at least two Bitcoin clients (*e.g.,* one Bitcoin client in ASA and one in ASB) and at least one RIPE probe available (*i.e.,* either in ASA or in ASB). If multiple probes existed in the same AS, we used one for each prefix in which at least one client is hosted. We perform each measurement at least three times and use the median delay. Our measurement campaign lasted 7 h and included ~50 K pings. We leveraged delay measurements available from RIPE atlas [2] to add the delays of AS-pairs, which we could not measure ourselves. Together these delay measurements cover 72% of the Bitcoin connections.

We configure the delay of each node pair in the simulation with a randomly-selected value across the delays measured in the corresponding AS-pairs. We validated our augmented simulator by ensuring that the median transaction propagation delay aligns with the value reported in [14].

Procedure. We simulated a total of 10000 transactions, among which 100 were created by the victim client. We use 70% of all transactions for training and 30% for testing. For feature selection, we use 5-fold cross-validation on the training set. We run the attack assuming the adversary intercepts a fraction of the victim's connection *i.e.,* 25%, 50%, 75%, 100%.

Results. We summarize our results in Table 1. We observe that an attacker can always (*i.e.,* almost independently of the percentage of connections she intercepts) deanonymize the victim with 100% true positive and low false-positive rate. This is expected because the simulated environment is idealized. In particular, *all* clients run the same code, are benign and are in the same condition

Table 1. In simulation, an adversary deanonymizes the victim with 100% accuracy even when intercepting 25% of its connections.

Simulation	25%	50%	75%	100%
True positives	1	1	1	1
False positives	0.002%	0.002%	0.001%	0%

Table 2. In the wild, an adversary deanonymizes the victim with 90% accuracy when intercepting 50% of its connections.

Mainnet	25%	50%	75%	100%
True positives	0.7	0.9	0.9	1
False positives	0.002%	0.003%	0.003%	0.0%

concerning load. Such an environment creates a straightforward case for anomaly detection.

6.2 PERIMETER in the Wild

We evaluated PERIMETER on the actual Bitcoin network. We describe our methodology before we describe our results.

Methodology. For our in-the-wild experiment, we used as victim a Bitcoin node version 0.19.1 of the Bitcoin Core running. Since we only attack our own node, our experiment is ethical: we did not disturb the normal operation of the Bitcoin network in any way. We configured our victim to not listen for incoming connections but instead only connect to a predefined set of peers randomly selected across those in [13].[6] We capture a total of ~30 K of transactions, among which 10 transactions were created by our victim. As the attack is completely passive, we use the same transactions to measure the effectiveness of various powered adversaries. In particular, we run the attack assuming the adversary intercepts a fraction of the victim's connection i.e., 25%, 50%, 75%, 100%.

We split the resulting dataset into the training and testing sets. We used all the victim's transactions and 30% of the transactions from other clients as the testing set. We included all of the victim's transactions in the testing to have a more accurate estimate of true positives. In any case, the victim's transactions are too few to affect the training of the model. We used the remaining 70% of transactions from other clients as the training set. Finally, we used the features we selected in the simulation, and we describe them in Sect. 4.4.

Results. Table 2 summarizes our results. We observe that an adversary intercepting only 25% of the victim's connections can deanonymize it with 70% true positives and only 0.002% false positives. Moreover, an adversary intercepting 50% of a client's connections (or more) can deanonymize the victim with 90% accuracy (or above). As a baseline, consider that previous attacks using "supernodes" report accuracies of 11%–60% [20] and 75% [22], thus lower than PERIMETER. This demonstrates the effectiveness of a network-layer attacker exploiting her access over the Internet infrastructure.

---

[6] We do not allow incoming connections to prevent attacks from light clients during the experiment.

7   Countermeasures

The PERIMETER attack poses a serious and practical threat to the anonymity properties of Bitcoin, as shown in Sect. 5 and Sect. 6. We argue that such a threat should and can be avoided for current and future cryptocurrencies by employing the following countermeasures.

Encrypting Traffic. One of the most critical enablers of the PERIMETER attack is that traffic is routed over the Internet unencrypted. Undoubtedly, encrypting Bitcoin's traffic would make the currency more anonymous, from the PERIMETER's perspective. Still, encryption alone cannot adequately mitigate the threat of passive AS-level adversaries. Observe that the PERIMETER attack generalizes to Ethereum, whose traffic is encrypted, even though, in this case, the attacker also needs to establish new connections.

Using Fake Peers. PERIMETER generalizes to encrypted cryptocurrencies (*e.g.,* Ethereum) because of the networking footprint of its clients. Particularly, a PERIMETER attacker can infer a client's peers by eavesdropping on this client's connections. Inferring a client's peers is critical for its deanonymization [34]. To shield against this attack, a client could establish connections to 'fake" peers with which it does not interact in practice, effectively deceiving a potential attacker into connecting to irrelevant clients. In doing so, the client should not request or store any transaction from fake peers; neither should it not advertise new transactions to them. In effect, the client obfuscates its footprint from a networking attacker.

Obfuscating the Client's State. One of the key features used to deanonymize Bitcoin clients in the PERIMETER attack is whether the victim requested (or received) a particular transaction from any of its observed peers. By requesting a transaction, the client reveals to a networking attacker (or potentially malicious client) that they do not know about a transaction and thus that they have not created it. As a result, the adversary can safely exclude some transactions, effectively decreasing the initial anonymity set. This is also true for the Ethereum geth client [6]. To avoid this, a client should also request the transactions it creates from peers that advertise them. While by doing so, the client increases its load without learning anything new, it also deprives potential attackers of an extremely effective feature. Notably, obfuscating the transactions a client knows by requesting them is aligned with obfuscating the transactions a light client is interested in by requesting more transactions (*i.e.,* using Bloom Filters in Bitcoin's BIP37 [31]).

Routing-Aware Transactions' Requests. Instead of requesting more transactions to obfuscate its state, a client can achieve a similar effect by carefully selecting the peer from which it requests an unknown transaction. Particularly, a client should request transactions in a routing-aware manner, meaning avoid requesting multiple transactions from clients whose connections are intercepted by the same AS or IXP. In effect, an adversary is unlikely to have an accurate view of which transactions the victim knew.

Routing-Aware Transactions' Advertisement. While PERIMETER does not directly use timing information, previous works [20,22,34] have shown the need for obfuscating the first-ever propagation of a transaction from each node. In fact, this need has motivated countermeasures, such as the adoption of diffusion in the Bitcoin Core and the creation of Dandelion [28]. We argue that such improvements need to also account for AS-level adversaries. Particularly in diffusion, one could increase the delay for clients whose path contains a very common AS or IXP. Similarly, the first node to advertise a transaction in the Dandelion protocol could be selected (in addition to the current criteria) such that the created traffic does not often traverse the same AS or IXP.

Using Tor or VPN Services. The goal of the PERIMETER attacker is to link transactions to IP addresses. Thus, if a client manages to obfuscate its IP address by using Tor or a VPN service, it should be protected against some of the potential attackers. Unfortunately, this statement is only partially true. Tor is anonymous by design but has performance and security limitations, while a VPN is less anonymous but more robust. Regarding Tor, a network adversary can easily prevent the client from using Tor either by exploiting the Dos mechanism [21] or by merely dropping the corresponding traffic. Observe that the latter is possible as the IPs of all Tor relays are publicly known, and the adversary might intercept the corresponding connections. Even if the client manages to use Tor, it would still be vulnerable to deanonymization by a network attacker that leverage timing analysis [47]. On the contrary, using a VPN service would be an effective countermeasure if the VPN provider is used by other Bitcoin users and/or the victim is not using the same VPN provider for additional communication. Indeed, an attacker would still be able to map the victim's transactions to the VPN provider's IP. Thus, it is critical that the attacker cannot also trivially map the victim's identity to the VPN provider's IP.

8   Related Work

Deanonymizing Cryptocurrency Transactions. Researchers have studied Bitcoin's anonymity properties from two angles: the blockchain analysis and the traffic analysis of the P2P network. From the blockchain-analysis angle, several papers have shown that linking transactions made by the same user relying on publicly available blockchain data is possible [16,39,41–43] even across sessions. These works are orthogonal to ours. From the traffic-analysis angle, several papers have shown that linking transactions to IPs is possible by analyzing data collected from one or multiple "supernodes" [20,22,34,40], which establish connections to all reachable clients. Unlike, PERIMETER such attacks are visible as the attacker needs to maintain thousands of outbound connections. Moreover, these attacks can be mitigated by existing techniques such as diffusion, increasing delay to inbound connections [3], and Dandelion [23,28].

AS-Level Adversaries. AS-level attacks can be active or passive [46]. In an active attack, the adversary performs BGP hijacks. Active adversaries can partition the Bitcoin network [17], deanonymize Tor [47], and compromise certificate authorities' infrastructure [19]. While effective, active AS-level adversaries are highly visible. In a passive attack, the adversary operates on traffic that she naturally intercepts. Passive adversaries can eclipse clients [48] and delay blocks [17]. PERIMETER is orthogonal to the above works as it acts against anonymity while being completely invisible (passive attacker).

Measuring Cryptocurrency Networks. Apostolaki et al. [17] presented the first analysis of the Bitcoin network from the routing perspective. Our analysis augments this by including IXPs in the AS-level topology and by analyzing the Ethereum network. Gencer et al. [29] analyzed both Ethereum and Bitcoin from the bandwidth, availability, and geographic distribution perspective but not from the routing perspective. Finally, Saad et al. [45] presented a measurement analysis on the AS distribution, location, and performance of Bitcoin clients, also not considering Internet routing.

Countermeasures. To the best of our knowledge, none of the existing countermeasures against previous attacks protects against PERIMETER. Countermeasures against deanonymization attacks such as Dandelion [23,28] do not prevent AS-level attacks as the selection of the first peer who receives a new transaction is independent of the AS-level topology. Relay networks such as Falcon [4], SABRE [18], and FIBRE [5] are irrelevant to PERIMETER as they focus on block propagation. Mixing protocols [24,44] allow users to obscure transaction history but cannot prevent a PERIMETER attacker from mapping the IP of a node with a transaction that this node created. Finally, a recent modification in Bitcoin Core [8] reduces the chances of a client to select peers from the same AS by improving IP bucketing. While this might be effective against [48], it cannot prevent PERIMETER. That is because this selection only affects outgoing connections, and most importantly, it does not consider the AS-path.

9   Conclusion

This paper presented PERIMETER, the first passive network-level deanonymization attack that is practical and effective against Bitcoin. We showed that PERIMETER is stealthier than previous deanonymization attacks while achieving higher accuracy. We revealed that Bitcoin and Ethereum are vulnerable to the PERIMETER's attacker model based on real-world data. While PERIMETER poses a severe threat to Bitcoin and similar cryptocurrencies, we also explained a comprehensive list of deployable countermeasures.

References

1. About: What is RIPE Atlas? https://atlas.ripe.net/landing/about/
2. Announcing Daily RIPE Atlas data archives. https://labs.ripe.net/Members/petros_gigis/announcing-daily-ripe-atlas-data-archives
3. Bitcoin Core diffusion delay. https://github.com/bitcoin/bitcoin/blob/da4cbb7927497ca3261c1504c3b85dd3f5800673/src/net_processing.cpp#L3813

4. Fast Internet Bitcoin Relay Engine. https://www.falcon-net.org
5. FIBRE. https://bitcoinfibre.org/
6. Go Ethereum: Official Go implementation of the Ethereum protocol. https://github.com/ethereum/go-ethereum
7. GoPacket. https://github.com/google/gopacket
8. p2p: supplying and using asmap to improve IP bucketing in addrman. https://github.com/bitcoin/bitcoin/pull/16702
9. RFC 1267 - Border Gateway Protocol 3 (BGP-3). https://tools.ietf.org/html/rfc1267
10. RIPE RIS Raw Data. https://www.ripe.net/data-tools/stats/ris/ris-raw-data
11. The RLPx Transport Protocol. https://github.com/ethereum/devp2p/blob/master/rlpx.md
12. Ethereum Mainnet Statistics (2020). https://www.ethernodes.org
13. GLOBAL BITCOIN NODES DISTRIBUTION (2020). https://bitnodes.io/
14. Propagation of Transactions and Blocks (2020). https://dsn.tm.kit.edu/bitcoin/#propagation
15. Ager, B., Chatzis, N., Feldmann, A., Sarrar, N., Uhlig, S., Willinger, W.: Anatomy of a large european ixp. In: Proceedings of the ACM SIGCOMM 2012 Conference on Applications, Technologies, Architectures, and Protocols for Computer Communication, SIGCOMM 2012, pp. 163–174. ACM (2012). https://doi.org/10.1145/2342356.2342393. https://doi.org/10.1145/2342356.2342393
16. Androulaki, E., Karame, G.O., Roeschlin, M., Scherer, T., Capkun, S.: Evaluating user privacy in bitcoin. In: Sadeghi, A.-R. (ed.) FC 2013. LNCS, vol. 7859, pp. 34–51. Springer, Heidelberg (2013). https://doi.org/10.1007/978-3-642-39884-1_4
17. Apostolaki, M., Zohar, A., Vanbever, L.: Hijacking bitcoin: Routing attacks on cryptocurrencies. In: S&P '17 (May). https://doi.org/10.1109/SP.2017.29
18. Apostolaki, M., Marti, G., Müller, J., Vanbever, L.: Sabre: protecting bitcoin against routing attacks. In: Proceedings of the 26th Annual Network and Distributed System Security Symposium, pp. 02A1. Internet Society (2019)
19. Birge-Lee, H., Sun, Y., Edmundson, A., Rexford, J., Mittal, P.: Bamboozling certificate authorities with {BGP}. In: 27th USENIX Security Symposium (USENIX Security 18), pp. 833–849 (2018)
20. Biryukov, A., Khovratovich, D., Pustogarov, I.: Deanonymisation of clients in bitcoin p2p network. In: CCS 2014
21. Biryukov, A., Pustogarov, I.: Bitcoin over tor isn't a good idea. In: 2015 IEEE Symposium on Security and Privacy, pp. 122–134. IEEE (2015)
22. Biryukov, A., Tikhomirov, S.: Deanonymization and linkability of cryptocurrency transactions based on network analysis. In: EuroS&P 2019 (2019)
23. Bojja Venkatakrishnan, S., Fanti, G., Viswanath, P.: Dandelion: Redesigning the bitcoin network for anonymity. POMACS (2017)
24. Bonneau, J., Narayanan, A., Miller, A., Clark, J., Kroll, J.A., Felten, E.W.: Mixcoin: anonymity for bitcoin with accountable mixes. In: Christin, N., Safavi-Naini, R. (eds.) FC 2014. LNCS, vol. 8437, pp. 486–504. Springer, Heidelberg (2014). https://doi.org/10.1007/978-3-662-45472-5_31
25. The CAIDA AS relationship dataset - 20191001. http://data.caida.org/datasets/as-relationships/serial-1/
26. The caida ixps dataset - 201910. http://data.caida.org/datasets/ixps/ix-asns_201910.jsonl. Accessed 12 Mar 2020
27. Extance, A.: The future of cryptocurrencies: bitcoin and beyond. Nature News 526(7571), 21 (2015)

28. Fanti, G., Venkatakrishnan, S.B., Bakshi, S., Denby, B., Bhargava, S., Miller, A., Viswanath, P.: Dandelion++: lightweight cryptocurrency networking with formal anonymity guarantees. POMACS (2018)
29. Gencer, A.E., Basu, S., Eyal, I., van Renesse, R., Sirer, E.G.: Decentralization in bitcoin and ethereum networks. In: Meiklejohn, S., Sako, K. (eds.) FC 2018. LNCS, vol. 10957, pp. 439–457. Springer, Heidelberg (2018). https://doi.org/10.1007/978-3-662-58387-6_24
30. Goldberg, S., Schapira, M., Hummon, P., Rexford, J.: How secure are secure inter-domain routing protocols. ACM SIGCOMM Comput. Commun. Rev. **40**(4), 87–98 (2010)
31. Hearn, M., Corallo, M.: Connection bloom filtering. bitcoin improvement proposal 37 (2012)
32. Jepsen, T., Alvarez, D., Foster, N., Kim, C., Lee, J., Moshref, M., Soulé, R.: Fast string searching on pisa. In: Proceedings of the 2019 ACM Symposium on SDN Research, pp. 21–28 (2019)
33. Khalilov, M.C.K., Levi, A.: A survey on anonymity and privacy in bitcoin-like digital cash systems. IEEE Commun. Surv. Tutorials **20**(3), 2543–2585 (2018)
34. Koshy, P., Koshy, D., McDaniel, P.: An analysis of anonymity in bitcoin using P2P network traffic. In: Christin, N., Safavi-Naini, R. (eds.) FC 2014. LNCS, vol. 8437, pp. 469–485. Springer, Heidelberg (2014). https://doi.org/10.1007/978-3-662-45472-5_30
35. Liu, F.T., Ting, K.M., Zhou, Z.H.: Isolation forest. In: 2008 Eighth IEEE International Conference on Data Mining, pp. 413–422. IEEE (2008)
36. Liu, F.T., Ting, K.M., Zhou, Z.H.: Isolation-based anomaly detection. ACM Trans. Knowl. Discovery Data (TKDD) **6**(1), 1–39 (2012)
37. Luckie, M., Huffaker, B., Dhamdhere, A., Giotsas, V., Claffy, K.: As relationships, customer cones, and validation. In: Proceedings of the 2013 Conference on Internet Measurement Conference, pp. 243–256 (2013)
38. Matetic, S., Wüst, K., Schneider, M., Kostiainen, K., Karame, G., Capkun, S.: BITE: Bitcoin lightweight client privacy using trusted execution
39. Meiklejohn, S., Pomarole, M., Jordan, G., Levchenko, K., McCoy, D., Voelker, G.M., Savage, S.: A fistful of bitcoins: characterizing payments among men with no names. In: Proceedings of the 2013 Conference on Internet Measurement Conference, pp. 127–140 (2013)
40. Neudecker, T., Hartenstein, H.: Could network information facilitate address clustering in bitcoin? In: Brenner, M., Rohloff, K., Bonneau, J., Miller, A., Ryan, P.Y.A., Teague, V., Bracciali, A., Sala, M., Pintore, F., Jakobsson, M (eds.) FC 2017. LNCS, vol. 10323, pp. 155–169. Springer, Cham (2017). https://doi.org/10.1007/978-3-319-70278-0_9
41. Ober, M., Katzenbeisser, S., Hamacher, K.: Structure and anonymity of the bitcoin transaction graph. Future Internet **5**(2), 237–250 (2013)
42. Reid, F., Harrigan, M.: An analysis of anonymity in the bitcoin system. In: Security and Privacy in Social Networks, pp. 197–223. Springer (2013)
43. Ron, D., Shamir, A.: Quantitative analysis of the full bitcoin transaction graph. In: Sadeghi, A.-R. (ed.) FC 2013. LNCS, vol. 7859, pp. 6–24. Springer, Heidelberg (2013). https://doi.org/10.1007/978-3-642-39884-1_2
44. Ruffing, T., Moreno-Sanchez, P., Kate, A.: Coinshuffle: practical decentralized coin mixing for bitcoin. In: European Symposium on Research in Computer Security, pp. 345–364. Springer (2014)
45. Saad, M., Cook, V., Nguyen, L., Thai, M.T., Mohaisen, A.: Partitioning attacks on bitcoin: Colliding space, time and logic. Technical report (2019)

46. Sun, Y., Apostolaki, M., Birge-Lee, H., Vanbever, L., Rexford, J., Chiang, M., Mittal, P.: Securing internet applications from routing attacks. arXiv preprint arXiv:2004.09063 (2020)
47. Sun, Y., Edmundson, A., Vanbever, L., Li, O., Rexford, J., Chiang, M., Mittal, P.: RAPTOR: routing attacks on privacy in tor. In: 24th USENIX Security Symposium (USENIX Security 2015), pp. 271–286 (2015)
48. Tran, M., Choi, I., Moon, G.J., Vu, A.V., Kang, M.S.: A stealthier partitioning attack against bitcoin peer-to-peer network. In: S&P 2020

An Empirical Analysis of Privacy in the Lightning Network

George Kappos[1($\boxtimes$)], Haaroon Yousaf[1], Ania Piotrowska[1,2], Sanket Kanjalkar[3], Sergi Delgado-Segura[4], Andrew Miller[3,5], and Sarah Meiklejohn[1]

[1] University College London, London, UK
h.yousaf@ucl.ac.uk
[2] Nym Technologies, Neuchatel, Switzerland
[3] University of Illinois Urbana-Champaign, Urbana, USA
[4] PISA Research, Paris, France
[5] IC3, New York, USA

Abstract. Payment channel networks, and the Lightning Network in particular, seem to offer a solution to the lack of scalability and privacy offered by Bitcoin and other blockchain-based cryptocurrencies. Previous research has focused on the scalability, availability, and crypto-economics of the Lightning Network, but relatively little attention has been paid to exploring the level of privacy it achieves in practice. This paper presents a thorough analysis of the privacy offered by the Lightning Network, by presenting several attacks that exploit publicly available information about the network in order to learn information that is designed to be kept secret, such as how many coins a node has available or who the sender and recipient are in a payment routed through the network.

1 Introduction

Since its introduction in 2008, Bitcoin [29] has become the most widely adopted cryptocurrency. The decentralized and permissionless nature of Bitcoin allows all users to join the network and avoids the need for intermediaries and authorities who control the flow of money between them. Instead, the validity of each transaction is verified by a consensus decision made by the network participants themselves; valid transactions are then recorded in the public blockchain. The blockchain thus acts as a ledger of all transactions that have ever taken place.

The need to broadcast transactions to all peers in the network and store them in a permanent ledger, however, presents two problems for the longevity of blockchain-based cryptocurrencies. First, it imposes severe scalability limitations: the Bitcoin blockchain today is over 300 GB, and Bitcoin can achieve a throughput of only ten transactions per second. Other cryptocurrencies achieve somewhat higher throughputs, but there is an inherent tradeoff in these broadcast-based systems between throughput and security [11,14]. Second, the

---

G. Kappos and H. Yousaf—Contributed equally. Full version of paper available at https://arxiv.org/abs/2003.12470.

N. Borisov and C. Diaz (Eds.): FC 2021, LNCS 12674, pp. 167–186, 2021.
https://doi.org/10.1007/978-3-662-64322-8_8

transparent nature of the ledger means anyone can observe the flow of coins, identify the counterparties to a transaction, and link different transactions. This has been shown most decisively for Bitcoin [4,27,35,39,41], but this type of analysis extends even to cryptocurrencies that were explicitly designed with privacy in mind [6,17,19,23,28,34,48].

The most promising solutions that have been deployed today to address the issue of scalability are so-called "layer-two" protocols [15], with the Lightning Network (LN) [33] emerging as the most popular one since its launch in March 2018. In Lightning, pairs of participants use the Bitcoin blockchain to open and close *payment channels* between themselves. Within a channel, these two users can make arbitrarily many *off-chain* payments between themselves, without having to use the blockchain. Beyond a single channel, Lightning supports multi-hop payment routing, meaning even participants who are not connected directly can still route payments through a broader *payment channel network* (PCN). Nodes in the network are incentivized to route payments by a fee they can charge for payments they forward.

In addition to the promise it shows in improving scalability, Lightning also seems to address the issue of privacy. As we elaborate on in Sect. 2, the nodes in the network and most of the channels in the network are publicly known in order to build up the PCN (although some channels may be kept private), as is the *capacity* of a given channel, meaning the maximum payment value that can be routed through it. The individual *balances* associated with the channel, however, are kept secret. Furthermore, payments are not broadcast to all peers and are not stored in a public ledger. Even if a payment passes through multiple channels, onion routing is used to ensure that each node on the path can identify only its immediate predecessor and successor.

As is the case with ledger-based cryptocurrencies, however, the gap in Lightning between the potential for privacy and the reality is significant, as we show in this work. In particular, we consider four main privacy properties promised by LN [2,24]:

Private channels should allow two nodes to share a channel but keep its existence, along with all of its information (capacity, participants, etc.), hidden from the rest of the network. We explore this property in Sect. 3.2 by presenting a heuristic that identifies on-chain funding of private channels and one or even both of the participants.

Third-party balance secrecy says that although the capacity of the channel is public, the respective balances of the participants should remain secret. We explore this property in Sect. 4 by presenting and evaluating a generic method by which an active attacker (i.e., one opening channels with nodes in the network) can discover channel balances.

On-path relationship anonymity says that intermediate nodes routing the payment should not learn which other nodes, besides their immediate predecessor or successor, are part of the payment's route. We explore this property in Sect. 5, where we leverage an LN simulator we developed (described in

Sect. 5.1) to evaluate the ability of an intermediate node to infer the sender and recipient in payments that it routes.

Off-path payment privacy says that any node not involved in routing a payment should not infer any information regarding the routing nodes or the payment value. We explore this property in Sect. 6 by presenting and evaluating a method by which an active attacker can use the ability to discover balances to form *network snapshots*. By comparing consecutive network snapshots, the attacker can infer payments by identifying where and by how much the balances of channels changed.

1.1 Ethical Considerations

The attacks presented in Sects. 5 and 6 are evaluated on a simulated network rather than the live one, but our attack in Sect. 4 is evaluated on the live test network. As in related active attacks on Bitcoin [7,8,22], we made every effort to ensure that our attacks did not interfere with the normal functioning of the network: the messages sent during the attack have no abnormal effect and do not cost any money to process, and their volume is relatively modest (we sent at most 24 messages per node we attacked). We thus believe that they did not have any long- or short-term destructive effect on the nodes that processed them. We disclosed the results of this paper to the developers of the three main LN clients and the liquidity provider Bitrefill in February 2020, and have discussed the paper with the Lightning developers since then.

1.2 Related Work

We consider as related all research that focuses on the Lightning Network, particularly as it relates to privacy. Most of the previous research has focused on the scalability, utility and crypto-economic aspects of LN [9,20,21,24,45], or on its graph properties [26,40]. Rohrer et al. [37] study the susceptibility of LN to topology-based attacks, and Tochner et al. [44] present a DoS attack that exploits how multi-hop payments are routed. Among other findings, they show that the ten most central nodes can disrupt roughly 80% of all paths using their attack. Pérez-Solà et al. [32] present an attack that diminishes the capacity of a node's channels, preventing it from participating in the network. Tikhomirov et al. [42] show how a wormhole attack prevents honest intermediaries from participating in routing payments.

In terms of privacy, Malavolta et al. [25] identify a new attack exploiting the locking mechanism, which allows dishonest users to steal payment fees from honest intermediaries along the path. They propose anonymous multi-hop locks as a more secure option. Nowatowski and Tøn [31] study various heuristics in order to identify Lightning transactions on the Bitcoin blockchain. Concurrently to our work, Romiti et al. [38] developed several heuristics to link Bitcoin wallets to Lightning entities. One of their heuristics is similar to the *tracing heuristic* we develop in Sect. 3.2, but their goal is to create augmented Bitcoin clustering methods rather than identify private channels. As we describe further in Sect. 4, others have performed balance discovery attacks [16,30,43]. The main limitation of these attacks is that they rely on specifics of the error messages the attacker receives, so may easily become irrelevant as the network evolves. We overcome this limitation by presenting a *generic* attack (in Sect. 4), as well as investigating the implications of such an attack more broadly (in Sect. 6).

Béres et al. [5] look briefly at the question of finding the sender and recipient of a payment. Similarly to our work, they develop an LN traffic simulator based on publicly available network snapshots and information published by certain node owners. Their work considers only single-hop payments, however, and does not look at other privacy properties. There are a number of other Lightning network studies that use a network simulator [9,10,13,49]. Several of these simulators were used to perform economic analysis of the Lightning network [9,13,49], while the CLoTH simulator [10] provides only performance statistics (e.g., time to complete a payment, probability of payment failure, etc.). However, all of those simulators make several simplifying assumptions about the topology, path selection algorithm, and distribution of payments. As such, they are not suitable for an analysis of its privacy properties.

2 Background

In order to open a Lightning *channel*, two parties deposit bitcoins into a 2-of-2 *multi-signature* address, meaning any transaction spending these coins would need to be signed by both of them. These funds represent the channel *capacity*; i.e., the maximum amount of coins that can be transferred via this channel. Once a channel is established, its participants can use it to exchange arbitrarily many payments, as long as either has a positive balance. They can also close the channel using a Bitcoin transaction that sends them their respective balances from the 2-of-2 multi-signature address.

Most users, however, are not connected directly, so instead need to *route* their payments through the global Lightning Network. Here, nodes are identified by public keys, and edges represent channels, which are publicly associated with a *channel identifier* cid, the channel capacity C, and a *fee* fee that is charged for routing payments via this channel. Privately, edges are also implicitly associated with the *inward* and *outward balances* of the channel. Except for *private* channels, which are revealed only at the time of routing, the topology of this network and its public labels are known to every peer.

When routing a payment, the sender (Alice) uses *onion routing* to hide her relationship with the recipient (Bob). Alice selects the entire path to Bob (*source routing*), based on the capacities and fees of the channels between them. The eventual goal is that each intermediate node on this path forwards the payment to its successor, expecting that its predecessor will do the same so its balance will not change. The nodes cannot send the money right away, however, because it may be the case that the payment fails. To thus create an intermediate state, LN uses *hashed time-lock contracts* (*HTLCs*), which allow for time-bound conditional payments. In summary, the protocol follow five basic steps to have Alice pay Bob:

1. **Invoicing** Bob generates a secret x and computes the hash h of it. He issues an *invoice* containing h and some payment amount amt, and sends it to Alice.
2. **Onion routing** Alice picks a path $A \rightarrow U_1 \rightarrow \cdots \rightarrow U_n \rightarrow B$. Alice then forms a Sphinx [12] packet destined for Bob and routed via the U_i nodes. Alice then sends the outermost onion packet $onion_1$ to U_1.
3. **Channel preparation** Upon receiving $onion_i$ from U_{i-1}, U_i decodes it to reveal: cid, which identifies the next node U_{i+1}, the amount amt_i to send them, a timeout t_i, and the packet $onion_{i+1}$ to forward to U_{i+1}. Before sending $onion_{i+1}$ to U_{i+1}, U_i and U_{i-1} *prepare* their channel by updating their intermediate state using an HTLC, which ensures that if U_{i-1} does not provide U_i with the pre-image of h before the timeout t_i, U_i can claim a refund of their payment. After this is done, U_i can send $onion_{i+1}$ to U_{i+1}.
4. **Invoice settlement** Eventually, Bob receives $onion_{n+1}$ from U_n and decodes it to find (amt, t, h). If amt and h match what he put in his invoice, he sends the invoice pre-image x to U_{n-1} in order to redeem his payment of amt. This value is in turn sent backwards along the path.
5. **Channel settlement** At every step on the path, U_i and U_{i+1} use x to *settle* their channel; i.e., to confirm the updated state reflecting the fact that amt_i was sent from U_i to U_{i+1} and thus that amt was sent from Alice to Bob.

3 Blockchain Analysis

3.1 Data and Measurements

The Lightning network can be captured over time by periodic snapshots of the public network graph, which provide ground-truth data about nodes (identifiers, network addresses, status, etc.) and their channels (identifiers, capacity, endpoints, etc.). To obtain a comprehensive set of snapshots, we used data provided to us by (1) our own lnd client, (2) one of the main c-lightning developers, and (3) scraped user-submitted (and validated) data from 1ML[1] and LN Bigsun.[2] To analyze on-chain transactions, we also ran a full Bitcoin node, using the BlockSci tool [18] to parse and analyze the raw blockchain data.

Our LN dataset included the hash of the Bitcoin transaction used to open each channel. By combining this with our blockchain data, we were thus able to identify when channels closed and how their funds were distributed. In total, we identified 174,378 channels, of which 135,850 had closed with a total capacity of 3315.18 BTC. Of the channels that closed, 69.22% were claimed by a single output address (i.e., the channel was completely unbalanced at the time of closure), 29.01% by two output addresses, and 1.76% by more than two outputs.

3.2 Private Channels

Private channels provide a way for two Lightning nodes to create a channel but not announce it to the rest of the network. In this section, we seek to understand

---

[1] https://1ml.com/.
[2] https://ln.bigsun.xyz/.

the extent to which private channels can nevertheless be identified, to understand their privacy limitations as well as the scope of our remaining attacks on the public network.

We first provide an upper bound on the number of private channels using a *property heuristic*, which identifies Bitcoin transactions that seem to represent the opening and closing of channels but for which we have no public channel identifier.

Property Heuristic. To align with our LN dataset, we first looked for all Bitcoin transactions that (1) occurred after January 12, 2018 and (2) before September 7, 2020, and (3) where one of the outputs was a P2WSH address (which LN channels have to be, according to the specification). We identified 3,500,312 transactions meeting these criteria, as compared with the 174,378 public channels opened during this period. We then identified several common features of the known opening transactions identified from our dataset: (i) 99.91% had at most two outputs, which likely represents the funder creating the channel and sending themselves change; (ii) 99.91% had a single P2WSH output address; (iii) 99.85% had a P2WSH output address that received at most 16,777,215 satoshis, which at the time of our analysis is the maximum capacity of an LN channel; (iv) 99.99% had a P2WSH output that appeared at most once as both an input and output, which reflects its "one-time" usage as a payment channel and not as a reusable script; and (v) 99.99% were funded with either a WitnessPubHeyHash address or ScriptHash address.

By requiring our collected transactions to also have these features and excluding any transactions involved in opening or closing public channels, we were left with 267,674 potential transactions representing the opening of private channels. If the outputs in these transactions had spent their contents (i.e., the channel had been closed), then we were further able to see how they did so, which would provide better evidence of whether or not they were associated with the Lightning Network. Again, we identified the following features based on known closing transactions we had from our network data: (i) 100% had a non-zero sequence number, as required by the Lightning specification [2]; (ii) 100% had a single input that was a 2-of-2 multisig address, again as required by the Lightning design; and (iii) 98.24% had at most two outputs, which reflects the two participants in the channel.

By requiring our collected opening transactions to also have a closing transaction with these three features, we were left with 77,245 pairs of transactions that were potentially involved in opening and closing private channels. Again, this is just an upper bound, since there are other reasons to use 2-of-2 multisigs in this way that have nothing to do with Lightning.

We identified 77,245 pairs of transactions that were potentially involved in opening and closing private channels, but likely has a high false positive rate. We thus developed a *tracing heuristic*, which follows the "peeling chain" [27] initiated at the opening and closing of public channels to identify any associated private channels.

Tracing Heuristic. We next look not just at the properties of individual transactions, but also at the flow of bitcoins between transactions. In particular, we observed that it was common for users opening channels to do so in a "peeling chain" pattern [27]. This meant they would (1) use the change in a channel opening transaction to continue to create channels and (2) use the outputs in a channel closing transaction to open new channels. Furthermore, they would often (3) co-spend change with closing outputs; i.e., create a channel opening transaction in which the input addresses were the change from a previous opening transaction and the output from a previous closing one.

By systematically identifying these operations, we were able to link together channels that were opened or closed by the same Lightning node by following the peeling chain both forwards and backwards. Going backwards, we followed each input until we hit a transaction that did not seem to represent a channel opening or closure, according to our property heuristic. Going forwards, we identified the change address in a transaction, again using the property heuristic to identify the channel creation address and thus isolate the change address as the other output, and continued until we hit one of the following: (1) a transaction with no change output or one that was unspent, meaning we could not move forwards, or (2) a transaction that did not satisfy the property heuristic. We also did this for all of the outputs in a known channel closing transaction, to reflect the second pattern identified above.

We started with the 174,378 public channels identified in our LN dataset. By applying our tracing heuristic, we ended up with 27,386 additional channel opening transactions. Of these, there were 27,183 that fell within the same range of blocks as the transactions identified by our property heuristic.

Using the tracing heuristic, however, not only identified private channels but also allowed us to cluster together different channels (both public and private), according to the shared ownership of transactions within a peeling chain [27]. To this end, we first clustered together different channels according to their presence in the same peeling chain, and then looked at the public channels within each cluster and calculated the common participant, if any, across their endpoints. If there was a single common participant, then we could confidently tag them as the node responsible for opening all of these channels.

In order to find the other endpoint of each private channel, we followed the closing outputs of the channel's closing transaction, whenever applicable, leveraging the second and third observed patterns in the tracing heuristic. In particular, when a closing output was spent in order to open a new channel, we performed the same clustering operation as earlier. We failed to identify the second participant in each channel only when the channel was still open, the channel was closed but the closing output was still unspent, or the closing output was used for something other than Lightning.

Out of the 27,183 transactions we identified as representing the opening of private channels, we were able to identify both participants in 2,035 (7.5%), one participant in 21,557 (79.3%), and no participants in 3,591 (13.2%). Our identification method applies equally well, however, to public channels. We were able to identify the opening participant for 155,202 (89.0%) public channels. Similarly, for the public channels that were already closed, which represent 185,860 closing outputs, we were able to associate 143,577 (77.25%) closing outputs with a specific participant.

4 Balance Discovery

Previous attacks designed to discover the balances associated with individual channels (as opposed to just their capacity) [16,30,43] exploited debug information as an *oracle*. In these attacks, an attacker opens a channel with a node and routes a fake payment hash, with some associated amount amt, through its other channels. Based on the error messages received and performing a binary search on amt (i.e., increasing amt if the payment went through and decreasing it if it failed), the attacker efficiently determines the exact balance of one side of the channel. In this section we perform a new *generic* attack on the LN testnet. As compared to previous attacks, our attacker must run two nodes rather than one. If error messages are removed or made generic in the future, however, our attack would continue to work whereas previous attacks would not.

The Attack. In our attack, an attacker running nodes A and D needs to form a path $A \rightarrow B \rightarrow C \rightarrow D$, with the goal of finding the balance of the channel $B \rightarrow C$. This means our attacker needs to run two nodes, one with a channel with outgoing balance (A), and one with a channel with incoming balance (D). Creating the channel $A \rightarrow B$ is easy, as the attacker can just open a channel with B and fund it themselves. Opening the channel $C \rightarrow D$ is harder though, given that the attacker must create incoming balance.

Today, there are two main options for doing this. First, the attacker can open the channel $C \rightarrow D$ and fund it themselves, but assign the balance to C rather than to D (this is called funding the "remote balance"). This presents the risk, however, that C will immediately close the channel and take all of its funds. We call this approach unassisted channel opening. The second option is to use a *liquidity provider* (e.g., Bitrefill[3] or LNBIG[4]), which is a service that sells channels with incoming balance.[5] We call this assisted channel opening.

Once the attacker has created the channels $A \rightarrow B$ and $C \rightarrow D$, they route a random payment hash H to D, via B and C, with some associated amount amt. If D receives H, this means the channel from B to C had sufficient balance to route a payment of amount amt. If D did not receive H after some timeout, the attacker can assume the payment failed, meaning amt exceeded the balance from B to C. Either way, the attacker can (as in previous attacks) repeat the process using a binary search on amt. Eventually, the attacker discovers the balance of the channel as the maximum value for which D successfully receives H.

---

[3] https://www.bitrefill.com/.

[4] http://lnbig.com/.

[5] Bitrefill, for example, sells a channel with an incoming balance of 5000000 satoshis (the equivalent at the time of writing of 493.50 USD) for 8.48 USD.

To a certain extent, this attack generalizes even to the case in which there is more than one intermediate channel between the two attacker nodes. In this more general case, however, the above method identifies the bottleneck balance in the entire path, rather than the balance of an individual channel. In the event of a payment failure though, the current C-lightning and LND clients return an *error index*, which is the position of the node at which the payment failed. This means that an attacker would know exactly where a payment failed along a longer path. We chose not to use this index when implementing our attack, in order to keep it fully generic and to test just the basic version, but leave an attack that does use this index as interesting future research.

Attack Results. We performed this attack on testnet on September 3 2020. We ran two LN nodes and funded all our channels (unassisted), both locally and remotely, which required a slight modification of the client (as fully funding a remote channel is restricted by default). We opened channels with every accessible node in the network. At the time of the attack there were 3,159 nodes and 9,136 channels, of which we were able to connect to 103 nodes and attack 1,017 channels. We were not able to connect to a majority of the overall nodes, which happened for a variety of reasons: some nodes did not publish an IPv4 address, some were not online, some had their advertised LN ports closed, and some refused to open a channel.

Of these 1,017 channels, we determined the balance of 568. Many (65%) of the channels were fairly one-sided, meaning the balance of the attacked party was 70% or more of the total capacity. We received a variety of errors for the channels where we were unsuccessful, such as *TemporaryChannelFailure*, or we timed out as the client took more than 30 s to return a response.

We did not carry out the attack on mainnet due to cost and ethical considerations, but believe it likely that the attack would perform better there. This is because there is no cost for forgetting to close open channels on testnet or maintain a node, whereas on mainnet a user is incentivized by an opportunity cost (from fees) to ensure a node is maintained and its channels are active.

Attacker Cost. In our experiment we used testnet coins, which are of essentially no value, so the monetary cost for us to perform this attack was negligible. To understand the practical limitations of this attack, however, we estimate the minimum cost on mainnet. When creating the outgoing channel $A \rightarrow B$, the attacker must pay for the opening and closing transaction fees on the Bitcoin blockchain. At the time of our attack, this was 0.00043 BTC per transaction. They must also remotely fund the recipient node with enough *reserve satoshis* to allow the forwarding of high payments, which at present are 1% of the channel capacity. To create the incoming channel $C \rightarrow D$, the attacker can use liquidity providers like Bitrefill, who at the time of writing allow users to buy channels with 0.16 BTC incoming capacity for 0.002604 BTC.

Purchasing the cheapest incoming liquidity available today would cost the attacker 0.00086 BTC and 0.005 BTC on hold, enabling routes to 4,811 channels (with a total capacity of 45 BTC). This would require opening 2,191 channels with a maximum channel capacity of 0.04998769 BTC. In total, this would require the attacker to spend 1.097 BTC and put 109.53 BTC on hold.

5 Path Discovery

We now describe how an *honest-but-curious* intermediate node involved in routing the payment can infer information regarding its path, and in particular can identify the sender and recipient of the payment. Our strategy is similar to a passive variant of a predecessor attack [46] proposed against the Crowds [36] anonymous communication network. Our strategy can be further extended by analyzing the sparse network connectivity and limited number of potential paths due to channel capacity.

In contrast to previous work [5], we consider not only single-hop routes but also routes with multiple intermediate nodes. The only assumption we make about the adversary's intermediate node is that it keeps its channel balanced, which can be easily done in practice.

We define $\Pr_S$ and $\Pr_R$ as the probability that the adversary successfully discovers, respectively, the sender and recipient in a payment. Following our notation, Béres et al. claim, based on their own simulated results, that $\Pr_S = \Pr_R$ ranges from 0.17 to 0.37 depending on parameters used in their simulation. We show that this probability is actually a lower bound, as it does not take into account multiple possible path lengths or the chance that a payment fails (their simulation assumes that all payments succeed on the first try).

The strategy of our honest-but-curious adversary is simple: they always guess that their immediate predecessor is the sender. In other words, if we define H as the adversary's position along the path, they always assume that $H = 1$. Similarly, they always guess that their immediate successor is the recipient. We focus on the probability of successfully guessing the sender; the probability of successfully guessing the recipient can be computed in an analogous way.

Successful Payments. We start by analyzing the success probability of this adversary in the case of a successful payment, which we denote as $\Pr_S^{\mathsf{succ}}$. We define as $\Pr[L = \ell]$ the probability of a path being of length ℓ, and as $\Pr[H = h \mid L = \ell]$ the probability that the adversary's node is at position h given that the path length is ℓ. According to the Lightning specification [2], the maximum path length is 20. By following the strategy defined above, we have that

$$\Pr_S^{\mathsf{succ}} = \sum_{n=3}^{20} \Pr[L = \ell \mid \mathsf{succ}] \cdot \Pr[H = 1 \mid L = \ell, \mathsf{succ}]$$

$$= \Pr[L = 3 \mid \mathsf{succ}]$$

$$+ \sum_{n=4}^{20} \Pr[L = \ell \mid \mathsf{succ}] \cdot \Pr[H = 1 \mid L = \ell, \mathsf{succ}]$$

since $\Pr[H = 1 \mid L = 3, \mathsf{succ}] = 1$ given that the adversary is the only intermediate node in this case. Hence, $\Pr[L = 3 \mid \mathsf{succ}]$ is a lower bound on $\Pr_S$.

To consider the overall probability, we focus on the conditional probabilities $\Pr[H = 1 \mid L = \ell, \mathsf{succ}]$. If all nodes form a clique,[6] then it would be almost equally probable for any node to be in any hop position $H = h$. (The only reason the distribution is not entirely uniform is that some channels may be chosen more often than others, depending on the relative fees they charge, but an adversary could choose fees to match its neighbors as closely as possible.) In this case then, the probability that $H = 1$ is just $1/(\ell - 2)$.

Failed Payments. Similarly, in case the payment fails, we define the probability $\Pr_S^{\mathsf{fail}}$ as

$$\Pr_S^{\mathsf{fail}} = \sum_{\ell=3}^{20} \Pr[L = \ell \mid \mathsf{fail}] \cdot \Pr[H = 1 \mid L = \ell, \mathsf{fail}].$$

This is the same formula as for $\Pr_S^{\mathsf{succ}}$ so far, but we know that $\Pr[L = 3 \mid \mathsf{fail}] = 0$, since if the adversary is the only intermediate node the payment cannot fail. Furthermore, the conditional probability $\Pr[H = 1 \mid L = \ell, \mathsf{fail}]$ is different from the probability $\Pr[H = 1 \mid L = \ell, \mathsf{succ}]$, as the fact that a payment failed reveals information to the adversary about their role as an intermediate node. In particular, if an intermediate node successfully forwards the payment to their successor but the payment eventually fails, the node learns that their immediate successor was not the recipient and thus that the failed path was of length $L \geq 4$ and their position is not $L - 1$. This means that $\Pr[L = \ell \mid \mathsf{fail}]$ becomes $\Pr[L = \ell \mid \mathsf{fail}, \ell \geq 4]$. We thus get

$$\Pr_S^{\mathsf{fail}} = \Pr[L = 4 \mid \mathsf{fail}, \ell \geq 4]$$
$$+ \sum_{\ell=5}^{20} \Pr[L = \ell \mid \mathsf{fail}] \cdot \Pr[H = 1 \mid L = \ell, \mathsf{fail}].$$

This gives $\Pr[L = 4 \mid \mathsf{fail}, \ell \geq 4]$ as a lower bound in the case of a failed payment. As we did in the case of successful payments, we assume a clique topology as the best case for this adversary's strategy, in which their chance of guessing their position is $1/(\ell - 3)$ (since they know they are not the last position). We thus obtain

$$\Pr_S^{\mathsf{fail}} = \Pr[L = 4 \mid \mathsf{fail}, \ell \geq 4] + \sum_{\ell=5}^{20} \Pr[L = \ell \mid \mathsf{fail}] \cdot \frac{1}{\ell - 3}.$$

5.1   Lightning Network Simulator

In order to investigate the success of this on-path adversary, we need measurements that it would require significant resources to obtain from the live network, such as the average path length for a payment. Given the financial and

---

[6] This would rather be a clique excluding a link between the sender and recipient, since otherwise they would presumably use their channel directly.

ethical concerns this would raise, we make the same decision as in previous work [5,9,10,13,49] to develop a Lightning network simulator to perform our analysis. We implemented our simulator in 2,624 lines of Python 3 and will release it as open-source software.

Network Topology. As mentioned in Sect. 2, we represent the network as a graph $G = (V, E)$. We obtain the information regarding V and E from the snapshots we collected, as described in Sect. 3.1, which also include additional information such as capacities and fees. The network topology view of our simulator is thus an exact representation of the actual public network.

Geolocation. Nodes may publish an IPv4, IPv6 or .onion address, or some combination of these. If a node advertised an IPv4 or IPv6 address then we used it to assign this node a corresponding geolocation. This enabled us to accurately simulate TCP delays on the packets routed between nodes, based on their distance and following previous studies [14] in using the global IP latency from Verizon.[7] For nodes that published only a .onion, we assign delays according to the statistics published by Tor metrics, given the higher latency associated with the Tor network.[8]

Path Selection. As discussed in Sect. 2, the route to the destination in LN is constructed solely by the payment sender. All clients generally aim to find the shortest path in the network, meaning the path with the lowest amount of fees. As shown by Tochner et al. [44], however, both the routing algorithm and the fee calculation differ across the three main choices of client software: lnd, c-lightning, and eclair. We could not easily extract or isolate the routing algorithms from these different implementations, so chose to implement all three versions of the path finding algorithm ourselves. We did this using Yen's k-shortest path algorithm [47] and the networkx Dijkstra's SPF algorithm.[9]

Software Versions. Our collected snapshots did not include information about software versions, so we scraped the Owner Info field for each node listed on the 1ML website. Although in 91% of the cases this field is empty, the results allow us to at least estimate the distribution of the client software. We obtained information about 370 nodes and found that 292 were lnd, 54 were c-lightning, and 24 were eclair. We randomly assign software versions to the remaining nodes in the network according to this distribution, and then modify the weight function in the path finding algorithm according to the software version.

Payment Parameters. Our first parameter, t_{pay}, represents the total daily number of payments happening in LN. For this, we use an estimate from LNBIG [3], the largest node that holds more than 40% of the network's total

---

[7] https://enterprise.verizon.com/terms/latency/.

[8] https://metrics.torproject.org/onionperf-latencies.html.

[9] https://networkx.github.io/documentation/stable/reference/algorithms/shortest_paths.html.

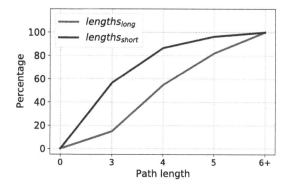

Fig. 1. Average path length.

capacity at the time of writing. According to LNBIG, the total number of routed transactions going through the network is 1000–1500 per day, but this does not take into account the payments performed via direct channels. Given this estimation, we use two values for t_{pay}: 1000, representing a slight underestimate of today's volume, and 10,000, representing a potential estimate for the future of LN.

We also define as endpoints the parameter that determines the sender and the recipient of a payment. We define two values for this parameter: *uniform*, which means that the payment participants are chosen uniformly at random, and *weighted*, which means the participants are chosen randomly according to a weighted distribution that takes into account their number of direct channels (i.e., their degree). Similarly, we use values to determine the values of payments. When values is *cheap*, the payment value is the smallest value the sender can perform, given its current balances. When values is *expensive*, the payment value is the biggest value the sender can send.

5.2   Simulation Results

Given the parameters t_{pay}, endpoints, and values, we ran two simulation instances, with the goal of finding the worst-case and best-case scenarios for the on-path adversary. Based on the respective probabilities for $\Pr_S^{succ}$ and $\Pr_S^{fail}$, we can see that the worst case is when the path is long and the payment is likely to succeed, while the best case is when the path is short and the payment is likely to fail. Since the total volume t_{pay} does not affect the path length, we use $t_{pay} = 1000$ for both instances. Each simulation instance was run using the network and node parameters scraped on September 1, 2020.

In our first simulation, $lengths_{long}$, our goal was to capture the adversary's worst case. This meant we chose endpoints $=$ *uniform*, so that the choice of sender and receiver was not biased by connectivity, and thus paths were not short due to their potentially high connectivity. Similarly, we chose values $=$ *cheap* to minimize the probability of having a payment fail. For our second

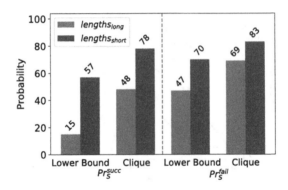

Fig. 2. Probability of correctly identifying the sender given successful and failed payment. For detailed simulation settings of lengths$_{\text{long}}$ and lengths$_{\text{short}}$ see Sect. 5.2

simulation, lengths$_{\text{short}}$, our goal was to capture the adversary's best case, so we chose endpoints = *weighted* to ensure highly connected nodes were picked more often and thus paths were shorter. We also chose values = *expensive*, leading to many balance failures.

As shown in Fig. 1, even when we attempted to maximize the path length in lengths$_{\text{long}}$, 14.98% of paths still consist of only one hop. In lengths$_{\text{short}}$, 56.65% of paths consisted of a single hop. This interval agrees with recent research, which argues that 17–37% of paths have only one intermediate node [5]. The main reason the paths are short even in lengths$_{\text{long}}$ is that the network topology and the client path finding algorithm have a much larger effect on the path length than endpoints or values.

Beyond the results in Fig. 1, running our simulator enabled us to estimate the probabilities $\Pr[L = \ell]$ for $3 \leq \ell \leq 20$ for both the best- and worst-case scenario for the adversary. We now use those results to compute the probabilities $\Pr_S^{\text{succ}}$ and $\Pr_S^{\text{fail}}$ for the case where our adversary is successful only when it is impossible to be wrong (LowerBound) as well as in the case of a clique topology (clique), as shown in Fig. 2. Here the clique topology is the worst possible topology for the adversary, since a less complete topology would allow the adversary to rule out nodes that cannot be involved in the payment and thus increase their confidence.

$\Pr_S^{\text{succ}}$ is bounded from below when $L = 3$, since in that case the adversary can never be wrong. Similarly, $\Pr_S^{\text{fail}}$ is bounded from below when $L = 4$. In the case of a successful payment, the lower bound on $\Pr_S^{\text{succ}}$ ranges from 15% (lengths$_{\text{long}}$) to 57% (lengths$_{\text{short}}$). On the other hand, the lower bound of $\Pr_S^{\text{fail}}$ increases with the percentage of unsuccessful attempts, up to 83% (lengths$_{\text{short}}$), which is significantly higher than any previously recorded experiment. This is also not just a theoretical result: according to recent measurements, 34% of payments fail on the first try [1].

Our measurements show that even an adversary following an extremely simple strategy can have a high probability of inferring the sender of a payment routed through their node, especially in the case in which the payment fails.

This is likely due to LN's highly centralized topology, which means paths are short and often involve the same intermediate nodes, as well as the fact that clients are designed to find the cheapest—and thus shortest—paths. Without changes in the client or the network topology, it is thus likely that intermediate nodes will continue to be able to violate on-path relationship anonymity.

6   Payment Discovery

In this section, we analyze the off-path payment privacy in Lightning, in terms of the ability of an attacker to learn information about payments it did not participate in routing.

Informally, our attack works as follows: using the balance discovery attack described in Sect. 4, the attacker constructs a *network snapshot* at time t consisting of all channels and their associated balances. It then runs the attack again at some later time $t + \tau$ and uses the differences between the two snapshots to infer information about payments that took place by looking at any paths that changed. In the simplest case that only a single payment took place between t and $t + \tau$ (and assuming all fees are zero), the attacker can see a single path in which the balances changed by some amount amt and thus learn everything about this payment: the sender, the recipient, and the amount amt. More generally, two payments might overlap in the paths they use, so an attacker would need to heuristically identify such overlap and separate the payments accordingly.

6.1   Payment Discovery Algorithm

We define τ to be the interval in which an attacker is able to capture two snapshots, S_t and $S_{t+\tau}$, and let $G_{\text{diff}} = S_{t+\tau} - S_t$ be the difference in balance for each channel. Our goal is then to decompose G_{diff} into paths representing distinct payments. More specifically, we construct paths such that (1) each edge on the path has the same amount (plus fees), (2) the union of all paths results in the entire graph G_{diff}, and (3) the total number of paths is minimal. This last requirement is to avoid splitting up multi-hop payments: if there is a payment from A to C along the path $A \to B \to C$, we do not want to count it as two (equal-sized) payments of the form A to B and B to C.

We give a simple algorithm that solves the above problem under the assumption the paths are disjoint. This assumption may not always hold, but we will see in Sect. 6.3 that it often holds when the interval between snapshots is relatively short. Our algorithm proceeds iteratively by "merging" payment paths. We initially consider each non-zero edge in G_{diff} as a distinct payment. We then select an arbitrary edge with difference amt, and merge it with any adjacent edges with the same amount (plus the publicly known fee f) until no edge of weight amt can be merged.

$$A \xrightarrow{\text{amt}+f_{A,B}+f_{B,C}} B, \; B \xrightarrow{\text{amt}+f_{B,C}} C \; \Rightarrow \; \text{infer payment A to C}$$

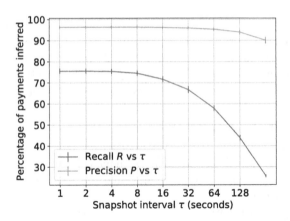

Fig. 3. The precision and recall of our payment discovery attack, based on the snapshot interval τ (in log scale). The error bars show 95% confidence intervals over five simulation runs.

We then remove this path from G_{diff} and continue with another edge. Asymptotically the running time of this algorithm is $O(|E|^2)$ for E edges; given the size and sparsity of Lightning Network today this means it runs in under a second.

There are several ways this algorithm can make incorrect inferences. First, it would incorrectly merge two same-valued payments A to B and B to C occurring end-to-end. Second, our algorithm does not attempt to resolve the case that a single channel is used for multiple payments in an interval. Looking ahead to Sect. 6.3, our experiments show this happens infrequently when the snapshot intervals are short enough. Finally, as we saw in Sect. 4, balance discovery may fail for some (or many) channels in the network. Our algorithm takes a conservative approach designed to minimize the false positive rate: as a final filtering step, it suppresses any pairs of inferred payments with approximately the same amount (within a small threshold of two satoshis).

6.2   Attack Simulation

We denote the attacker's precision by P (the number of correctly detected payments divided by the total number of detected payments) and recall by R (the number of correctly detected payments divided by the number of actual payments). We are primarily interested in understanding how these performance metrics depend on the interval at which an attacker takes snapshots (τ).

To answer these questions we leverage the simulator we developed in Sect. 5.1, and extend it to include the balance discovery attack from Sect. 4. Due to the fact that 98% of the errors in this attack were because a node was not online or did not participate in any payments, we set a 0.05 probability of it failing on a functional channel in which both nodes are online. In keeping with the discussion in Sect. 5.1, we use $t_{\text{pay}} = 2000$ as the total number of payments per day and sample the senders and recipients randomly from all nodes in the network. In terms of payment value, our simulation is a pessimistic scenario where the payment amounts are very small (1000 satoshis on average) but fluctuate uniformly within a small range around this average (±10 satoshis). This is pessimistic because it is close to the worst-case scenario, in which all payments have identical amounts, but two factors make it likely that real-world payments would have much greater variation: (1) payments are denominated in fine-grained units (1 satoshi = 10^{-8} BTC), and (2) wallets typically support generating payment invoices in units of fiat currency by applying the real-time Bitcoin exchange rate, which is volatile.

6.3   Simulated Attack Results

In order to figure out the effect of the snapshot interval τ on P and R, we take balance inference snapshots of the entire network for varying time intervals, ranging from $\tau = 1$ second to $\tau = 2^8$ seconds. Each time, we run the simulator for a period of 30 days, amounting to 60,000 payments in total. Figure 3 shows the relationship between τ and the number of payments inferred and confirms the intuition that the attack is less effective the longer the attacker waits between snapshots, as this causes overlap between multiple payments. At some point, however, sampling faster and faster offers diminishing returns; e.g., for $\tau = 32$ seconds, the attacker has a recall R of 66%, which increases slowly to 74.1% for $\tau = 1$ second. With a realistic minimum of $\tau = 30$ seconds, which is the time it took us and others to run the balance discovery attack on a single channel [16]), the attacker has a recall of more than 67%. Because of our final filtering step in our discovery algorithm, we have a precision P very close to 95% for smaller values of τ.

7   Conclusions

In this paper, we systematically explored the main privacy properties of the Lightning Network and showed that, at least in its existing state, each property is susceptible to attack. Unlike previous work that demonstrated similar gaps between theoretical and achievable privacy in cryptocurrencies, our research does not rely on patterns of usage or user behavior. Instead, the same interfaces that allow users to perform the basic functions of the network, such as connecting to peers and routing payments, can also be exploited to learn information that was meant to be kept secret. This suggests that these limitations may be somewhat inherent, or at least that avoiding them would require changes at the design level rather than at the level of individual users.

Acknowledgements. George Kappos, Haaroon Yousaf and Sarah Meiklejohn are supported in part by EPSRC Grant EP/N028104/1, and in part by the EU H2020 TITANIUM project under grant agreement number 740558. Sanket Kanjalkar and Andrew Miller are supported by the NSF under agreement numbers 1801369 and 1943499. Sergi Delgado-Segura was partially funded by EPSRC Grant EP/N028104/1.

References

1. The lightning conference: of channels, flows and icebergs talk by Christian Decker. https://www.youtube.com/watch?v=zk7hcJDQH-I
2. Lightning network specifications. https://github.com/lightningnetwork/lightning-rfc
3. Person behind 40% of LN's capacity: "I have no doubt in Bitcoin and the Lightning Network". https://www.theblockcrypto.com/post/41083/person-behind-40-of-lns-capacity-i-have-no-doubt-in-bitcoin-and-the-lightning-network
4. Androulaki, E., Karame, G.O., Roeschlin, M., Scherer, T., Capkun, S.: Evaluating user privacy in bitcoin. In: Sadeghi, A.-R. (ed.) FC 2013. LNCS, vol. 7859, pp. 34–51. Springer, Heidelberg (2013). https://doi.org/10.1007/978-3-642-39884-1_4
5. Béres, F., Seres, I.A., Benczúr, A.A.: A cryptoeconomic traffic analysis of Bitcoins lightning network. arXiv:1911.09432 (2019)
6. Biryukov, A., Feher, D., Vitto, G.: Privacy aspects and subliminal channels in Zcash. In: Proceedings of the 2019 ACM SIGSAC Conference on Computer and Communications Security (2019)
7. Biryukov, A., Khovratovich, D., Pustogarov, I.: Deanonymisation of clients in Bitcoin P2P network. In: Proceedings of ACM CCS (2014)
8. Bogatyy, I.: Linking 96% of Grin transactions. https://github.com/bogatyy/grin-linkability
9. Brânzei, S., Segal-Halevi, E., Zohar, A.: How to charge lightning. arXiv:1712.10222 (2017)
10. Conoscenti, M., Vetrò, A., De Martin, J.C., Spini, F.: The cloth simulator for HTLC payment networks with introductory lightning network performance results. Information **9**, 223 (2018)
11. Croman, K., et al.: On scaling decentralized blockchains. In: Clark, J., Meiklejohn, S., Ryan, P.Y.A., Wallach, D., Brenner, M., Rohloff, K. (eds.) FC 2016. LNCS, vol. 9604, pp. 106–125. Springer, Heidelberg (2016). https://doi.org/10.1007/978-3-662-53357-4_8
12. Danezis, G., Goldberg, I.: Sphinx: a compact and provably secure mix format. In: 30th IEEE Symposium on Security and Privacy (2009)
13. Engelmann, F., Kopp, H., Kargl, F., Glaser, F., Weinhardt, C.: Towards an economic analysis of routing in payment channel networks. In: Proceedings of the 1st Workshop on Scalable and Resilient Infrastructures for Distributed Ledgers (2017)
14. Gervais, A., Karame, G.O., Wüst, K.., Glykantzis, V., Ritzdorf, H., Capkun, S.: On the security and performance of proof of work blockchains. In: Proceedings of the 2016 ACM SIGSAC Conference on Computer and Communications Security (2016)
15. Gudgeon, L., Moreno-Sanchez, P., Roos, S., McCorry, P., Gervais, A.: Off the chain transactions. IACR Cryptology ePrint Archive, Sok (2019)
16. Herrera-Joancomartí, J., Navarro-Arribas, G., Ranchal-Pedrosa, A., Pérez-Solà, C., Garcia-Alfaro, J.: On the difficulty of hiding the balance of lightning network channels. In: Proceedings of the 2019 ACM Asia Conference on Computer and Communications Security (CCS) (2019)
17. Hinteregger, A., Haslhofer, B.: An empirical analysis of Monero cross-chain traceability. In: Proceedings of the 23rd International Conference on Financial Cryptography and Data Security (FC) (Short paper) (2019)
18. Kalodner, H.A., Goldfeder, S., Chator, A., Möser, M., Narayanan, A.: BlockSci: design and applications of a blockchain analysis platform. arXiv:1709.02489 (2017)

19. Kappos, G., Yousaf, H., Maller, M., Meiklejohn, S.: An empirical analysis of anonymity in Zcash. In: 27th *USENIX* Security Symposium 2018 (2018)
20. Khalil, R., Gervais, A.: Revive: rebalancing off-blockchain payment networks. In: Proceedings of the 2017 ACM SIGSAC Conference on Computer and Communications Security, pp. 439–453 (2017)
21. Khan, N., State, R.: Lightning network: a comparative review of transaction fees and data analysis. In: Prieto, J., Das, A.K., Ferretti, S., Pinto, A., Corchado, J.M. (eds.) BLOCKCHAIN 2019. AISC, vol. 1010, pp. 11–18. Springer, Cham (2020). https://doi.org/10.1007/978-3-030-23813-1_2
22. Koshy, P., Koshy, D., McDaniel, P.: An analysis of anoymity in Bitcoin using P2P network traffic. In: International Conference on Financial Cryptography and Data Security (FC) (2014)
23. Kumar, A., Fischer, C., Tople, S., Saxena, P.: A traceability analysis of Monero's blockchain. In: Foley, S.N., Gollmann, D., Snekkenes, E. (eds.) ESORICS 2017. LNCS, vol. 10493, pp. 153–173. Springer, Cham (2017). https://doi.org/10.1007/978-3-319-66399-9_9
24. Malavolta, G., Moreno-Sanchez, P., Kate, A., Maffei, M., Ravi, S.: Concurrency and privacy with payment-channel networks. In: Proceedings of the 2017 ACM SIGSAC Conference on Computer and Communications Security (2017)
25. Malavolta, G., Moreno-Sanchez, P., Schneidewind, C., Kate, A., Maffei, M.: Anonymous Multi-Hop Locks for blockchain scalability and interoperability. In: Proceedings of NDSS (2018)
26. Martinazzi, S.: The evolution of lightning network's topology during its first year and the influence over its core values. arXiv preprint arXiv:1902.07307 (2019)
27. Meiklejohn, S., et al.: A fistful of Bitcoins: characterizing payments among men with no names. In: Proceedings of the 2013 Conference on Internet Measurement Conference. ACM (2013)
28. Möser, M., et al.: An empirical analysis of traceability in the Monero blockchain. In: Proceedings on Privacy Enhancing Technologies (2018)
29. Nakamoto, S.: Bitcoin: a peer-to-peer electronic cash system. Technical report, Manubot (2019)
30. Nisslmueller, U., Foerster, K.-T., Schmid, S., Decker, C.: Toward active and passive confidentiality attacks on cryptocurrency off-chain networks (2020)
31. Nowostawski, M., Tøn, J.: Evaluating methods for the identification of off-chain transactions in the Lightning Network. Appl. Sci. **9**(12), 2519 (2019)
32. Pérez-Solà, C., Ranchal-Pedrosa, A., Herrera-Joancomartí, J., Navarro-Arribas, G., García-Alfaro, J.: LockDown: balance availability attack against lightning network channels. In: Bonneau, J., Heninger, N. (eds.) FC 2020. LNCS, vol. 12059, pp. 245–263. Springer, Cham (2020). https://doi.org/10.1007/978-3-030-51280-4_14
33. Poon, J., Dryja, T.: The bitcoin lightning network: scalable off-chain instant payments (2016)
34. Quesnelle, J.: On the linkability of Zcash transactions (2017)
35. Reid, F., Harrigan, M.: An analysis of anonymity in the bitcoin system. In: Altshuler Y., Elovici Y., Cremers A., Aharony N., Pentland A. (eds.) Security and Privacy in Social Networks. Springer, New York (2013). https://doi.org/10.1007/978-1-4614-4139-7_10
36. Reiter, M.K., Rubin, A.D.: Crowds: anonymity for web transactions. ACM Trans. Inf. Syst. Secur. **1**(1), 66–92 (1998)

37. Rohrer, E., Malliaris, J., Tschorsch, F.: Discharged payment channels: quantifying the lightning network's resilience to topology-based attacks. In: 2019 IEEE European Symposium on Security and Privacy Workshops (EuroS&PW), pp. 347–356. IEEE (2019)

38. Romiti, M., Victor, F., Moreno-Sanchez, P., Haslhofer, B., Maffei, M.: Cross-layer deanonymization methods in the lightning protocol (2020)

39. Ron, D., Shamir, A.: Quantitative analysis of the full bitcoin transaction graph. In: Sadeghi, A.-R. (ed.) FC 2013. LNCS, vol. 7859, pp. 6–24. Springer, Heidelberg (2013). https://doi.org/10.1007/978-3-642-39884-1_2

40. Seres, I.A., Gulyás, L., Nagy, D.A., Burcsi, P.: Topological analysis of Bitcoin's lightning network. arXiv:1901.04972 (2019)

41. Spagnuolo, M., Maggi, F., Zanero, S.: BitIodine: extracting intelligence from the bitcoin network. In: Christin, N., Safavi-Naini, R. (eds.) FC 2014. LNCS, vol. 8437, pp. 457–468. Springer, Heidelberg (2014). https://doi.org/10.1007/978-3-662-45472-5_29

42. Tikhomirov, S., Moreno-Sanchez, P., Maffei, M.: A quantitative analysis of security, anonymity and scalability for the lightning network. Cryptology ePrint Archive, Report 2020/303 (2020). https://eprint.iacr.org/2020/303

43. Tikhomirov, S., Pickhardt, R., Biryukov, A., Nowostawski, M.: Probing channel balances in the lightning network (2020)

44. Tochner, S., Schmid, S., Zohar, A.: Hijacking routes in payment channel networks: a predictability tradeoff. arXiv:1909.06890 (2019)

45. Werman, S., Zohar, A.: Avoiding deadlocks in payment channel networks. In: Garcia-Alfaro, J., Herrera-Joancomartí, J., Livraga, G., Rios, R. (eds.) DPM/CBT -2018. LNCS, vol. 11025, pp. 175–187. Springer, Cham (2018). https://doi.org/10.1007/978-3-030-00305-0_13

46. Wright, M.K., Adler, M., Levine, B.N., Shields, C.: The predecessor attack: an analysis of a threat to anonymous communications systems. ACM Trans. Inf. Syst. Secur. 7(4), 489–522 (2004)

47. Yen, J.Y.: An algorithm for finding shortest routes from all source nodes to a given destination in general networks. Q. Appl. Math. 27, 526–530 (1970)

48. Yu, Z., Au, M.H., Yu, J., Yang, R., Xu, Q., Lau, W.F.: New empirical traceability analysis of CryptoNote-style blockchains. In: Proceedings of the 23rd International Conference on Financial Cryptography and Data Security (FC) (2019)

49. Zhang, Y., Yang, D., Xue, G., CheaPay: an optimal algorithm for fee minimization in blockchain-based payment channel networks. In: IEEE International Conference on Communications (ICC) (2019)

Cross-Layer Deanonymization Methods in the Lightning Protocol

Matteo Romiti[1]([⊠]) [iD], Friedhelm Victor[2] [iD], Pedro Moreno-Sanchez[3] [iD],
Peter Sebastian Nordholt[5], Bernhard Haslhofer[1] [iD], and Matteo Maffei[4]

[1] AIT - Austrian Institute of Technology, Vienna, Austria
{matteo.romiti,bernhard.haslhofer}@ait.ac.at
[2] Technische Universität Berlin, Berlin, Germany
friedhelm.victor@tu-berlin.de
[3] IMDEA Software Institute, Madrid, Spain
pedro.moreno@imdea.org
[4] Technische Universität Wien, Vienna, Austria
matteo.maffei@tuwien.ac.at
[5] Chainalysis, New York City, USA
psn@chainalysis.com

Abstract. Bitcoin (BTC) pseudonyms (layer 1) can effectively be de-anonymized using heuristic clustering techniques. However, while performing transactions off-chain (layer 2) in the Lightning Network (LN) seems to enhance privacy, a systematic analysis of the anonymity and privacy leakages due to the interaction between the two layers is missing. We present (Please, find the full version of this paper with appendix at https://arxiv.org/abs/2007.00764.) clustering heuristics that group BTC addresses, based on their interaction with the LN, as well as LN nodes, based on shared naming and hosting information. We also present linking heuristics that link 45.97% of all LN nodes to 29.61% BTC addresses interacting with the LN. These links allow us to attribute information (e.g., aliases, IP addresses) to 21.19% of the BTC addresses contributing to their deanonymization. Further, these deanonymization results suggest that the security and privacy of LN payments are weaker than commonly believed, with LN users being at the mercy of as few as five actors that control 36 nodes and over 33% of the total capacity. Overall, this is the first paper to present a method for linking LN nodes with BTC addresses across layers and to discuss privacy and security implications.

1 Introduction

Payment channel-networks (PCNs) have emerged as a promising alternative to mitigate the scalability issues with current cryptocurrencies. These layer-2 protocols, built on-top of layer-1 blockchains, allow users to perform transactions without storing them on the Bitcoin (BTC) blockchain. The idea is that two users create a funding transaction that locks coins, thereby creating a payment channel between them [6]. Further payments no longer require on-chain transactions but rather peer-to-peer mutual agreements on how to distribute the coins

© International Financial Cryptography Association 2021
N. Borisov and C. Diaz (Eds.): FC 2021, LNCS 12674, pp. 187–204, 2021.
https://doi.org/10.1007/978-3-662-64322-8_9

locked in the channel. At any point, both users can decide to close the channel by creating a settlement transaction that unlocks the coins and distributes them according to the last agreed balance.

While there are different payment channel designs, the BTC Lightning Network (LN) [16] is the most widespread PCN implementation to date. At the time of writing (September 2020), according to 1ml.com, the LN features a network of 13, 902 public active nodes, 37, 003 channels and a total capacity of more than 1, 108.70 BTC, worth 11, 569, 618 USD.

Apart from scalability, PCNs are considered beneficial to improve the well-known lack of privacy of cryptocurrencies [4], where the anonymity claim stemming from the usage of pseudonyms in on-chain transactions has been largely refuted from both academia and industry [12]. The key to an effective deanonymization of BTC pseudonyms lies in heuristic methods, which cluster addresses that are likely controlled by the same entity [14]. In practice, entities correspond to user wallets or software services (e.g., hosted wallet, exchange) that control private keys on behalf of their users.

In this work, we challenge the widespread belief that the LN greatly improves privacy by showing for the first time how LN nodes can be linked to BTC addresses, which results in a bi-directional privacy leakage affecting LN and BTC itself. Related research [8,13,15,17,18] already focused on security and privacy aspects on the PCN layer, but, so far, none of them focused on linking off-chain LN nodes to on-chain BTC addresses. This is a challenging task because such links are not provided explicitly in the LN protocol as they would severely affect the privacy of node operators (e.g., revealing their business to competitors).

Our Contributions. Our methodology is structured in two main strategies: (i) heuristics on layer 1, to create clusters of BTC addresses controlled by the same actor, and on layer 2, clusters of LN nodes; and (ii) heuristics to link these clusters across layers. In Sect. 4, we present four novel on-chain clustering heuristics (star, snake, collector, proxy), which group BTC addresses based on their interaction patterns with the LN. With these heuristics, we can cluster 19.39% of all BTC entities funding an LN channel, and 13.40% of all entities closing a channel. We also present an LN node clustering heuristic leveraging public announcements of aliases and IP addresses, which allows us to group 1, 251 nodes into 301 clusters. In Sect. 5, we present two novel cross-layer linking algorithms. One exploits that the same BTC address can be used to close one channel and then re-use the coins to open a new channel, which allows us to link 26.48% of the LN nodes to 20.96% BTC addresses in our dataset, when combined with the previous on- and off-chain clustering heuristics. The other algorithm exploits the reuse of a single BTC entity for opening several channels to different LN nodes and it allows us to link 29.61% of the addresses to 45.97% of nodes.

Given these results, we finally discuss the impact of our deanonymization techniques on the privacy of BTC entities as well as the security and privacy of the LN. In a nutshell, we are able to (i) attribute 21.19% of the BTC addresses with information from the LN (e.g., IP addresses); (ii) measure the centralized

control of the capacity in the LN and observe that as few as five actors consisting
of 36 nodes control over 33% of the total capacity; (iii) show that as few as five
users can threaten the security of the LN by means of (possibly targeted) DoS
attacks and violate the privacy of over 60% of the cheapest payment paths
because they are routed through them.

For the reproducibility of the results, we make our dataset and our implementation available at https://github.com/MatteoRomiti/lightning_study[1].

2   Background and Problem Statement

We now define the simplified model and terminology used throughout this paper,
elaborating then on the cross-layer linkage problem, as well as on related work
in this area. For further details on PCNs, we refer to recent surveys [6,9].

2.1   BTC Blockchain (Layer 1)

A BTC **address** a is a tuple containing (i) a number of coins (in Satoshis)
associated to this address; and (ii) an excerpt of the BTC script language that
denotes the (cryptographic) conditions under which a can be used in a transaction. Although in principle it is possible that a can be spent under any condition that can be expressed in the BTC script language, in practice most of the
addresses share a few conditions: (i) requiring a signature σ on the transaction
verifiable under a given public key pk; and (ii) requiring two signatures $\{\sigma_1, \sigma_2\}$
verifiable with two given public keys pk_1 and pk_2 (i.e., multisig address). We say
that an address a is owned by a user if she can produce the required signature/s.

A BTC **transaction** tx is identified by txid computed as the hash of the *body*
of tx, i.e., $H(\mathsf{Input}, \mathsf{Output})$. Input denotes the set of addresses set as input and
being spent in tx; and Output is the set of addresses set as output. A transaction
can have also a change output, where coins and address are owned by the same
user controlling the inputs.

We define a BTC **entity** e as a set $e := \{a_i\}$ of addresses controlled by
the same user as clustered with the well-known and effective [7] co-spending
heuristic [14]. This heuristic assumes that if two addresses (i.e. a_1 and a_2) are
used as inputs in the same transaction while one of these addresses along with
another address (i.e. a_2 and a_3) are used as inputs in another transaction, then
the three addresses (a_1, a_2, a_3) are likely controlled by the same actor.

A **BTC wallet** is the software used by a BTC user to handle BTC addresses
owned by her. A wallet may correspond to a BTC entity, if addresses are reused.

2.2   Nodes and Payment Channels in the LN (Layer 2)

A **node** n in the Lightning Network (LN) is a tuple $n := (\mathsf{nid}, \mathsf{IP}, \mathsf{Alias})$, where
nid is the identifier of the node; IP denotes the IP address associated with the
node, and Alias the associated lexical label.

---

[1] The proprietary attribution data from Chainalysis is not included in the published
dataset. The reader can contact the company for further inquiry.

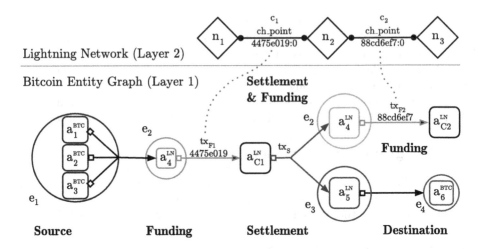

Fig. 1. Life cycle of an LN channel. At layer 1, a source entity e_1 tops up entity e_2 that is then used in tx_{F1} as funding entity of the channel c_1 represented by multisig address a_{C1}^{LN}. The channel c_1 is established at layer 2 between the nodes n_1 and n_2. The channel c_1 is then closed with the settlement transaction tx_S sending the funds back to two settlement entities, e_2 and e_3. The former, e_2, reuses these coins in tx_{F2} to fund another channel (c_2) between n_2 and n_3 represented at layer 1 by the multisig address a_{C2}^{LN}. The coins in the other settlement entity, e_3, are instead collected into a destination entity e_4, not directly involved in the LN.

A **payment channel** c is then created between two nodes and denoted by the tuple $c := (\mathsf{chpoint}, n_1, n_2)$, where $\mathsf{chpoint}$ denotes the channel's endpoint that is set to the identifier $tx.\mathsf{txid}$ of the funding transaction tx that created the channel. As the transaction may have several outputs, $\mathsf{chpoint}$ also contains the output index of the multisig address that locks the funds in the channel (e.g., $\mathsf{chpoint:choutindex}$); while n_1 and n_2 are the nodes of the channel.

An **LN wallet** is the software used by an LN user to manage her node, as well as the channels of this node. In practice, an LN wallet comes with an integrated BTC wallet to open and close channels in the LN. Recent releases of two LN wallet implementations (*lnd* and *c-lightning*) [5,19] enable opening/closing a channel using an external BTC wallet.

2.3   Cross-Layer Interaction

In this section, we describe the interaction between BTC and the LN by means of the example illustrated in Fig. 1. Assume Alice wants to open a payment channel with Bob. Further, assume that Alice has a BTC wallet with coins in address a_1^{BTC} and she wants to open a payment channel with Bob. Additionally assume that Alice has never interacted with the LN before and only has an LN wallet, whose integrated BTC wallet handles a_4^{LN}. In this setting, the lifetime of the payment channel between Alice and Bob is divided into the following phases:

Replenishment. Alice first transfers coins from her BTC wallet (represented by entity $e_1 := \{a_1^{BTC}, a_2^{BTC}, a_3^{BTC}\}$) to her LN wallet (entity $e_2 := \{a_4^{LN}\}$), to top up the LN wallet from the BTC wallet. We call e_1 the **source** entity as it is used as the source of funds to be later used in the LN.

Funding. Alice can now open a channel with Bob by first computing a *deposit* address a_{C1}^{LN} shared between Alice and Bob. In the next step, Alice creates a **funding transaction** tx_{F1} where $tx_{F1}.\mathsf{Input} := a_4^{BTC}$, $tx_{F1}.\mathsf{Output} := a_{C1}^{LN}$, and $tx_{F1}.\mathsf{txid} := H(tx_{F1}.\mathsf{Input}, tx_{F1}.\mathsf{Output})$.[2] After tx_{F1} appears on the BTC blockchain, the payment channel c_1 between Alice and Bob is effectively open. The channel c_1 is then represented in the payment channel network as the tuple $(c_1.\mathsf{chpoint}, n_1, n_2)$, where n_1 and n_2 are nodes belonging to Alice and Bob.

Payment. After the channel c_1 is open, during the *payment* phase, both Alice and Bob can pay each other by exchanging authenticated transactions in a peer-to-peer manner authorizing the updates of the balance in the channel. Following our example, Alice and Bob create a **settlement transaction** tx_S where $tx_S.\mathsf{Input} := a_{C1}^{LN}$, $tx_S.\mathsf{Output} := \{a_4^{LN}, a_5^{LN}\}$ so that a_4^{LN} belongs to Alice, and a_5^{LN} belongs to Bob. The cornerstone of payment channels is that Alice and Bob do not publish tx_S in the BTC blockchain. Instead, they keep it in their memory (i.e., off-chain) and locally update the balances in their channel c_1. Both Alice and Bob can repeat this process several times to pay each other.

Settlement. When the channel is no longer needed, Alice and Bob can close the channel by submitting the last agreed settlement transaction into the BTC blockchain, thereby unlocking the coins from a_{C1}^{LN} into two BTC addresses, each belonging to one of them with a number of coins equal to the last balance they agreed off-chain. In practice, the settlement transaction may have more than two outputs: Alice can pay Bob to a third address where Bob needs to provide data other than a signature to redeem the coins (e.g., the valid preimage of a hash value before a certain timeout as defined in the Hash Time Lock Contract [1]).

Collection. After the settlement transaction appears in the BTC blockchain, Bob gets the coins in his LN wallet. As a final step, Bob might want to get his coins into a different BTC wallet of his own. For that, Bob transfers funds from a_5^{LN} to a_6^{BTC}, which we call **destination** address.

We note several points here. First, the addresses involved in the lifetime of payment channels could have been clustered into entities. In such a case, we refer to the source/funding/settlement/destination entity involved in the steps instead of the particular address itself. In our example, Alice owns entity e_1 that controls (among others) a_1^{BTC} and we thus say that entity e_1 is the *source* entity in the replenishment step. Second, the same entity can be used at the same time for settlement and funding. Finally, Alice gets the coins from the channel with Bob in entity e_2 that is then reused later to open a new payment channel.

---

[2] Although theoretically a payment channel can be dual-funded (i.e., Bob also contributes x_1 to the funding transaction), this feature is under discussion in the community [3] and currently only single-funded channels are implemented in practice.

2.4 The Cross-Layer Linking Problem

A starting point, as shown in Fig. 1, is to identify the funding transaction tx_{F1} corresponding to the payment channel $c_1 := (\mathsf{chpoint}, n_1, n_2)$, by finding the transaction (and the output index) that fulfills the condition $tx_{F1}.\mathsf{txid} = c_1.\mathsf{chpoint}$. While this is trivial, we cannot assert that the entity e_2 in $tx_{F1}.\mathsf{Input}$ also controls n_1, as it could also be that e_2 controls n_2. Similarly, while we can deterministically get the settlement transaction tx_S used to close the channel c_1, we cannot unambiguously link each settlement entity to the corresponding node.

The goal of this work is to cluster BTC entities based on their interactions with the LN and then unambiguously link these clusters to LN nodes that are under their control. Technically, this corresponds to finding a function that takes a set of LN channels as input and returns tuples of the form (entity, node) for which it can be asserted that the LN node is controlled by the linked BTC entity.

2.5 Related Work

Single-layer security attacks on the LN topology were the focus of many recent studies: Rohrer et al. [17] measured the LN topology and found that the LN is highly centralized and vulnerable to targeted (e.g., DoS) attacks. Similarly, Seres et al. [18] found that the LN provides topological stability under random failures, but is structurally weak against rational adversaries targeting network hubs. Also, Martinazzi and Flori [13] have shown that the LN is resilient against random attacks, but very exposed to targeted attacks, e.g., against central players. Lin et al. [8] inspected the resilience of the LN and showed that removing hubs leads to the collapse of the network into many components, evidence suggesting that this network may be a target for the so-called split attacks. Single-layer LN privacy has recently been studied by Kappos et al. [11], who focused on balance discovery and showed that an attacker running an active attack can easily infer the balance by running nodes and sending forged payments to target nodes. Nowostawski and Ton [15] conducted an initial cross-layer analysis and investigated footprints of the LN on the public BTC blockchain in order to find which transactions in the BTC blockchain are used to open and close LN channels. Our work instead uses the funding and settlement transactions (and more) as input data to investigate for the first time: (i) the link between LN nodes and BTC entities; (ii) clustering of BTC entities allowed by blockchain footprint for the interaction of these entities with the LN; and (iii) the associated security and privacy implications.

3 Dataset

In this section, we present the data we collected for our analysis.

3.1   Off-Chain Data: LN

We used the LN Daemon (LND) software and captured a copy of the LN topology at regular intervals (30 min) via the *describegraph* command since May 21 2019. The off-chain part of our dataset contains $98,431$ channels, $37,996$ of which were still open on September 9, 2020. The most recent channel in our dataset was opened on September 9, 2020, while the oldest was opened on January 12, 2018. We also define the *activity period* of a node as the time that starts with the funding transaction that opened the first public channel in which the node appeared and ends either with the settlement transaction of its last public channel or with 2020-09-09 (the time of preparing the dataset), if the nodes had still public channels open. Finally, we observe that channels in our dataset were established between $10,910$ distinct nodes.

3.2   On-Chain Data: BTC Blockchain

First, for each channel in our off-chain dataset, we used the transaction hash included in the channel's field chpoint for retrieving the *funding transaction*. Then, we checked whether the coins sent to the multisig address were spent or not. If a coin was spent, we fetched the *settlement transaction*, that uses that multisig address as input. We obtained this data by querying the open-source GraphSense API[3] and the Blockstream API[4]. We thereby extracted $98,240$ funding transactions[5] and $60,447$ settlement transactions. Next, we extracted the input addresses of all funding transactions and the output addresses of all settlement transactions and mapped them to funding and settlement entities, as defined in Sect. 2.1. Before clustering entities, we used BlockSci [10] to filter CoinJoin transactions because they would merge addresses of unrelated users. For the same reason, we also made sure that no CoinJoins from Wasabi nor Samourai[6] wallets were in our dataset. On the funding side, we also extracted the *source entities* that were sending coins to funding entities; on the settlement side, we retrieved *destination entities* that received coins from settlement entities. For that purpose, we implemented a dedicated data extraction and analytics job for the GraphSense Platform and executed it on a snapshot of the BTC blockchain up to block $647,529$ (2020-09-09 23:00), amounting for a total of $566,776,778$ transactions and $703,443,739$ addresses clustered into $336,847,691$ entities. After having extracted the BTC entities that were involved in opening and closing payment channels, we attributed them using the Chainalysis API[7] and assigned service categories (e.g., exchange, hosted wallet) to entities.

Table 1 summarizes the number of addresses (*# Addr*) found in funding and settlement transactions as well as the number of resulting entities after applying the co-spending heuristic on these addresses (*# Entities*). We can clearly

---

[3] https://api.graphsense.info/.

[4] https://github.com/Blockstream/esplora/blob/master/API.md.

[5] Some channels were opened with the same funding transaction.

[6] https://github.com/nopara73/WasabiVsSamourai.

[7] https://www.chainalysis.com/.

Table 1. On-chain dataset summary

	Source	Funding	Settlement	Destination
# Addr		170,777	88,166	
# Entities	196,131	96,838	53,371	424,732
# Addr (Exp.)	70,638,581	196,818	2,243,525	107,474,279
# Services	5,812	1	5	67,969
# Relations		203,328	438,725	

observe that the number of distinct source entities (196, 131) is lower than the number of destination entities (424, 732), which is also reflected in the number of relations (# *Relations*) representing monetary flows from source to funding entities and from settlement to destination entities, respectively. These unbalanced numbers might be due to funds going from settlement entities to mixing services, as we discuss later. Since the co-spending heuristic also groups addresses which were not part of our dataset snapshot, we also added the number of expanded addresses (# *Addr (Exp.)*). The difference between the number of addresses and entities on both the source and destination side can be explained by the presence of super-clusters, which are responsible for large transaction inputs and outputs and typically represent service entities such as cryptocurrency exchanges [7]. Finally, this table also lists the number of identified service entities (# *Services*). We only found them in few cases for funding (1) and settlement (5) entities, probably because mostly non-custodial wallets are used when opening and closing channels and known services in our dataset behave only as source and destination entities. Roughly 0.9% of all source entities were categorized, with the majority (0.8%) being exchanges. On the settlement side, we identified 10% of all destination entities as wallets being controlled by services, with the majority (8%) being mixing services. We can not fully account for this strong connection to mixing, but it does suggest that many LN users are privacy-aware. Indeed, there is evidence that the LN is recognized as a privacy technology complementary to mixing. e.g., the well-known mixing wallet Wasabi suggests LN as one way to enhance privacy when using the wallet[8].

3.3   Ground Truth Data: LN Payments

We devised and implemented a simple process that allows us to create a ground truth dataset of entity-node pairs that can then be compared with our linking results as a validation step. We first run our linking algorithms resulting in an initial set of entity-node pairs. We then found a trade-off for selecting the target nodes: some randomly-selected linked nodes for generality purposes and some other nodes with the highest number of settlement transactions as a sign of being very active on the network and reusing funds, a useful aspect for the next

---

[8] https://docs.wasabiwallet.io/using-wasabi.

steps. Next, we managed to open channels, perform payments and close channels with 52 of them. For these nodes that received coins from us, we are able to see their settlement entity, but only 11 nodes further spent the settlement funds in other transactions, necessary for us to capture their spending behaviors with our heuristics. We additionally managed to have channels open to us from 3 LN nodes that provide inbound channels as a service, revealing their funding entities. We performed this activity at the beginning of September 2020 (block 646559) and after waiting some days to let the nodes spend our coins, we run the linking algorithms again on our latest dataset (until block 647,529) so that for these targeted nodes we have both ground truth and heuristically-obtained links to entities. In Sect. 5.3, we compare this ground truth data with our linking results, while a more detailed explanation of the methodology to extract this data is presented in the appendix.

4   Clustering Heuristics

In this section we introduce the on-chain and off-chain clustering heuristics.

4.1   On-Chain BTC Entity Clustering (Layer 1)

LN-blockchain interactions result in monetary flows from source to funding and from destination to settlement entities (see Fig. 1). When analyzing the resulting entity graph abstraction, we observed four patterns (see Fig. 2).

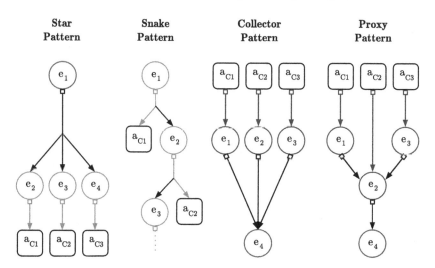

Fig. 2. On-chain clustering heuristics. Following the same notation of Fig. 1, in the star pattern, a source entity e_1 replenishes three different funding entities creating a single cluster (e_1, e_2, e_3, e_4). In the snake pattern, a series of funding transactions are performed using the change address of a previous funding transaction as input and the funding entities can be clustered (e_1, e_2, e_3). In the collector and proxy pattern, multiple settlement entities merge their coins in one single entity and these settlement entities can be clustered (e_1, e_2, e_3, e_4).

First, several funding entities received funds from the same source entities with one source entity transferring coins to several funding entities. This forms a *star-shaped pattern* and reflects a current LN wallet feature, which requires[9] users to transfer funds from an external wallet (source entity) to an internal wallet (funding entity) before opening a channel. If these source entities are not services, which is rarely the case (see Sect. 3), then we can assume:

Definition 1 (Star Heuristic). *If a component contains one source entity that forwards funds to one or more funding entities, then these funding entities are likely controlled by the same user.*

Second, again on the funding side, we observed a *snake-like pattern* in which source entities transfer coins to a funding entity, which then opens a channel and the change from the funding transaction is used to fund another channel, and so on (analogous to the Bitcoin Change-Heuristic [14]).

Definition 2 (Snake Heuristic). *If a component contains one source entity that forwards funds to one or more entities, which themselves are used as source and funding entities, then all these entities are likely controlled by the same user.*

Third, we identified a so-called *collector pattern*, which mirrors the previously described star pattern on the settlement side: a user forwards funds from several settlement entities, which hold the unlocked coins of closed channels in an internal wallet, to the same *destination entity*, which serves as an external *collector* wallet of funds and therefore fulfills a convenience function for the user.

Definition 3 (Collector Heuristic). *If a component contains one destination entity that receives funds from one or more settlement entities, then these settlement entities are likely controlled by the same user.*

Fourth, we found a refined collector pattern, which we call *proxy pattern*: a user first aggregates funds from several settlement transactions in a single settlement entity and then forwards them to a single destination entity.

Definition 4 (Proxy Heuristic). *If a component contains one destination entity that receives funds from one or more entities, which themselves are used as settlement and destination entities, then these entities are likely controlled by the same user.*

We compute the above heuristics as follows: we construct 1-hop ego-networks for the funding and settlement entities and extract funding relations and settlement relations (see Sect. 3). Next, we compute all weakly-connected components in these graphs and filter them by the conditions defined above.

Table 2 shows the number of BTC entities we were able to cluster with each heuristic. When regarding the connected components, we can clearly see the rare

---

[9] We note that this requirement may no longer be there if the "fund-from-external-wallet" functionality, already available in the recent release [19], is widely adopted.

Table 2. On-chain clustering results

	Star (F)	Snake (F)	Collector (S)	Proxy (S)
# Components	52 (0.3%)	5,638 (31%)	1,476 (14%)	989 (9%)
# Entities	139	18,512 (19%)	3,923 (7%)	3,229 (6%)
# Addresses	144	18,556	6,146	12,292

occurrence of the star patterns and the dominance of the snake pattern, which represents 31% of all funding components. On the settlement side, 23% of all components either match the collector or the proxy pattern. Consequently, we were able to group 19.39% (18,651) of all funding entities and 13.40% (7,152) of all settlement entities. This corresponds to 18,700 funding addresses and 18,438 settlement addresses.

Discussion. Our heuristic can, by definition, also yield false positives for two main reasons: first, an entity could represent several users if clustered addresses are controlled by a service (e.g., exchange) on behalf of their users (custodial wallet) or if transactions of several unrelated users are combined in a CoinJoin transaction. Second, users could transfer ownership of BTC wallets off-chain, e.g., by passing a paper wallet. While the second case is hard to filter automatically, we applied countermeasures to the first case: first, we filtered known CoinJoin transactions (see Sect. 3), and second, we filtered all components containing service entities by using Chainalysis, one of the most comprehensive attribution dataset available.

Countermeasures. We suspect that the above patterns reflect a user behavior that is already known to compromise the privacy of transactions: reuse of TXOs (transaction outputs). If outputs of funding transactions are not reused for opening other channels, the snake heuristic would not work; if users refrain from funding channels from a single external source and avoid collecting funds in a single external destination entity, the other heuristics would not yield any significant results. Despite not pervasive on the network, Coinjoins and similar solutions could, in theory (e.g., if used as funding transactions), obfuscate the entity linked to an LN node behind a set of unrelated addresses.

4.2   Off-Chain LN Nodes Clustering (Layer 2)

We have also designed an algorithm to cluster LN nodes based on aliases and IPs reported in the LN, along with their corresponding autonomous systems (AS). If a set of node aliases share a common substring, and they are hosted on the same AS, we cluster them. Similarly, if a set of nodes report the same IP or onion address, we cluster them assuming they are controlled by the same entity. This allows us to cluster 1,251 nodes into 301 clusters. Due to space constraints, we defer the description of this clustering the appendix.

5   Linking LN Nodes and BTC Entities

In this section, we present two algorithms that link LN nodes to the BTC entities that control them. In both of these heuristics, we do not consider settlement transactions with more than two output entities (1.9% of the settlement transactions), as they are not a cooperative close and do not allow us to unambiguously link nodes and output entities. Furthermore, we ignore settlement transactions that involve punishment transactions [2]. Finally, an assumption that we make in both of the following linking algorithms is that if one node in a channel has been linked to a settlement entity and the settlement transaction has two output entities, then the other node can be linked to the other settlement entity.

5.1   Linking Algorithm 1: Coin Reuse

Our linking algorithm builds upon the usage pattern that appears when a payment channel is closed and the user that receives the coins from such channel reuses them to open a new payment channel. An illustrative example of this linking algorithm is included in Fig. 1 where a funding entity e_2 has been used to open a channel c_1 between nodes n_1 and n_2 with the funding transaction tx_{F1}. Later, this channel has been closed in the settlement transaction tx_S, releasing the coins in the channel to the entities e_2 (i.e., the same that was used as input in tx_{F1}) and e_3. Finally, assume that the owner of entity e_2 decides to open a new channel reusing the coins from tx_S performing a new funding transaction tx_{F2} which results in the payment channel c_2 between the aforementioned node n_2 and n_3. In this situation, given that the entity e_2 has appeared in the settlement transaction of c_1 and has been reused to open a new channel in the funding transaction c_2, our heuristic concludes that the entity e_2 controls node n_2.

Definition 5 (Linking Algorithm 1: Coin Reuse). *Assume that a BTC entity e opens an LN channel $c_1 := (\mathsf{chpoint}_1, n_1, n_2)$. If e is used as settlement entity to close the LN channel c_1 and also as funding entity to open a new LN channel $c_2 := (\mathsf{chpoint}_2, n_1, n_3)$, and the nodes n_2 and n_3 have activity period overlap, then the user controlling entity e also controls the LN node n_1 in common to both channels c_1 and c_2.*

We applied the linking algorithm based on coin reuse which resulted in 83 tuples of (funding transaction, settlement transaction, funding transaction) and 22 entities reusing their addresses for opening and closing channels. Once these 22 entities are linked to LN nodes, all the other output entities in the settlement transactions of these 22 entities can be linked to the counter-party nodes in the channels as mentioned earlier. Finally, after these new links are created, our heuristic can iteratively go over the settlement transactions that involve these newly linked entities to find other entity-node pairs.

After 7 iterations, the heuristic yielded $9,042$ entities linked to $2,170$ nodes, thus having cases where a node is linked to multiple entities. In total, considering the number of entities we have in our dataset ($138,457$ overall, both funding and settlement side[10]) the heuristic is able to link 6.53% of them. This result is a lower bound on the possible number of linked entity-node pairs because the linking algorithm mainly relies on channels to be closed (in our dataset only half of them are) and on a specific subset of entities, namely the output entities of settlement transactions with exactly two outputs, one per node. In fact, if we focus only on settlement transactions with two output entities, we have $32,321$ entities, 27.98% of which can be linked, showing thereby that this linking algorithm has a targeted but effective linking effect. Regarding the nodes percentages, we can link 19.89% of the total ($10,910$ overall) and 46.91% of the nodes for which there exists at least one channel that has been closed using a 2-output-entity settlement transaction, confirming the trend we observed with entities.

Discussion. We note that requiring that the same entity is used for all three transactions (i.e., funding and settlement of the first channel as well as funding of the second channel) may be too restrictive and leave out further links of entities and nodes. However, we enforce this restriction to avoid false positives that could be otherwise introduced as we describe next. Assume we control an LN node, n_2, with an associated BTC entity e_1 that funds channel c_1 between node n_2 and n_1 through tx_{F1}. Furthermore, we have an LN wallet with an associated BTC entity, e_3, on our phone provided by a third-party app. This means that there must be another node in the LN, n_3, managed by this third-party app. When we decide to close channel c_1, we specify an address provided by our third-party app, hence belonging to entity e_3, as settlement address to receive the funds back. We finally proceed to use these funds to open a new channel, c_2, again with node n_1 but from node n_3, the third-party node. Without the requirement on the same funding entity, the heuristic would link the node n_1, in common between the two channels, to the entity e_3 reusing the funds, which is false. With the same funding address requirement, instead, this case is ignored. A further condition that needs to be satisfied to strengthen this heuristic is that the nodes not common to the two channels (nodes n_1 and n_3 in Fig. 1) have a time overlap in their activity period. This excludes the unlikely, but not impossible case that one node changes its ID (public key) from n_2 to n_3 keeping the same BTC wallet (and thus entity), which could allow one to open two channels from two different nodes, but to the same node, using the same BTC entity, creating a false-positive case for the heuristic.

Countermeasures. The default functionality of LN wallets followed thus far by virtually all users consists of having a single wallet per node from where to extract the funds to open channels and where to send the coins after channels connected to such node are closed. We conjecture that this setting favors the usage pattern leveraged in the linking algorithm described in this section. As a countermeasure, we advocate for the support of funding and settlement channels of a single node from different (external) BTC wallets, helping thus to diversify

---

[10] Here we do not consider source and destination entities as they do not directly interact with the LN.

the source of funds. We observe that recent versions of the LN wallet *lnd* and *c-lightning* have started to support this functionality [5,19].

5.2 Linking Algorithm 2: Entity Reuse

In this linking algorithm we leverage the usage pattern that appears when a user reuses the same BTC wallet (e.g., the one integrated within the LN wallet) to open several payment channels. Thus, in this linking algorithm we assume that an entity e opened several payment channels with other entities. This common usage pattern in practice can be detected at the blockchain by finding the set of N_C funding transactions that have e in common as the funding entity. We can thus say that e has opened N_C channels. At the LN, if there is only one node n common to all the N_C channels funded by e, we say that e controls n. An illustrative example of this linking algorithm is shown in the appendix.

Definition 6 (Linking Algorithm 2: Entity Reuse). *If there are $N_C > 1$ channels opened by one single funding entity e that have only one LN node n in common, and there are at least two nodes n_x and n_y in these channels with activity period overlap, then the user controlling entity e controls node n too.*

We can link $9,904$ entities to $2,170$ nodes which correspond to 7.15% of all the entities and 22.84% of all the nodes respectively.

Discussion. The way this linking algorithm has been described and implemented so far might yield false entity-node links. As discussed in Sect. 5.1, a user can open a channel from its node n_2 to another node n_1, then close the channel, change its node ID to n_3 keeping the same BTC wallet and finally open a second channel to n_1. For this linking algorithm, this example would cause a false positive because n_1 would be linked to the BTC entity of this user. To prevent this from happening, we add the following condition. Consider the set of nodes appearing in the channels funded by a single funding entity e and exclude from this set the node that has been linked to e with this heuristic. Now, if there is at least one pair of nodes (n_2, n_3 from the example above) in this set that have an activity period overlap, then we discard the false-positive risk as it is not possible for node n_2 to change to n_3 keeping two channels open. When implementing this additional requirement, we discovered that our results do not contain any false positive as there is at least one pair of nodes with an activity period overlap for each entity-node link. To further validate the results of this second linking algorithm, we report that it provides the same entity-node links that are in common with the linking algorithm presented in Sect. 5.1.

Countermeasures. A countermeasure to this heuristic is to not reuse the same funding entity to open multiple channels. This can be achieved either by having multiple unclustered addresses in a wallet or to rely on external wallets [5,19].

5.3 Validation

For the validation of the heuristics presented in this work we use the ground truth dataset presented in Sect. 3. For each of the 11 nodes that received funds from us, we compare their set of ground truth settlement entities with their set of linked entities from our linking algorithms. If there is an intersection between these two sets, we say that the link is validated. In total, we find that 7 nodes (i.e., 63%) are validated. The validation for the 3 nodes that opened channels to us is the same, but uses their ground truth funding entities as set for comparison with the set of linked entities from our linking algorithms. In this case, we can validate 2 nodes. The lack of validation for the other nodes can have several reasons: i) as reported in Sect. 3, we notice that only 11 out of the 52 nodes receiving our coins (by default on newly-generated BTC addresses) also spent them, ii) the coins spent are not merged with funds from other channels or iii) the coins are spent and merged with funds from channels missing in our dataset. Nevertheless, one should note that over time our ground truth data will increase and more nodes could be validated as soon as they spend our funds.

We believe that our small ground truth dataset is a reasonable trade-off between obtaining a representative picture of the LN main net and a responsible and ethical behavior that does not alter the LN properties significantly. We also see our methodology to gather ground truth data as an interesting contribution due to its scalability features: costs are relatively low (two on-chain transactions and LN routing fees for each targeted node) and executable in a programmatic way. We defer a more detailed description of this methodology to the appendix.

6   Assessing Security and Privacy Impact

We merged the results of our clustering algorithms (Sect. 4) and our linking algorithms (Sect. 5), thereby increasing the linking between entities and nodes as shown in Table 3. We defer to the appendix a detailed description of the contribution for each heuristic individually.

6.1   Privacy Impact on BTC Entities (Layer 1)

The linking algorithms and clustering algorithms described in this work allow attributing activity to BTC entities derived from their interaction with the LN. Assume that a cluster is formed by a certain number of BTC entities and LN nodes, then if any of the LN nodes has publicly identifiable information (e.g., alias or IP address), this information can be attributed to the BTC entities as well. In total, we can attribute tagging information to 17,260 different entities that in total account for 50,456 different addresses, which represent 21.19% of our dataset.

This deanonymization is based purely on publicly available data[11] and can be carried out by a low budget, passive adversary that simply downloads the BTC blockchain and the information from the LN. We envision that further impact can be achieved by a more powerful adversary (e.g., a BTC miner). Moreover,

---

[11] We note that Chainalysis attribution data is not strictly necessary for the linking algorithms.

Table 3. Summary results

Linking + Clustering	% addresses linked	% entities linked	% nodes linked
Linking Algorithm 1	18.16	6.53	19.89
Linking Algorithm 1 + all on/off-chain	20.96	8.14	23.64
Linking Algorithm 2	19.19	7.15	22.84
Linking Algorithm 2 + all on/off chain	29.61	12.72	45.97

the possible deanonymization of BTC entities hereby presented shows that it is crucial to consider the privacy of both layers simultaneously instead of one of them at a time as largely done so far in the literature.

6.2   Security and Privacy Impact on the LN (Layer 2)

We have evaluated the implications of our clustering and linking algorithms in the security and privacy of the LN. In summary, we studied how the capacity of the LN is distributed across actors and found that a single actor controls over 24% of the total LN capacity and as few as five actors consisting of 36 nodes control over 33% of the total capacity. Few LN actors are thus in a privileged situation that can be used to diminish the security and privacy of the LN. For instance, we observed that the entity with the highest capacity can render useless over 40% of the channels for a period of time by means of DoS attacks. Similar issues appear from the privacy point of view, where just 5 actors can learn the payment amounts used in up to 60% of the cheapest paths in the LN and determine who pays to whom in up to 16% of the cheapest paths. Due to space constraints, we defer a detailed discussion of our security and privacy assessment to the appendix.

7   Conclusion and Future Work

In this paper, we presented two novel linking algorithms to reveal the ownership of BTC addresses that are controlled by LN nodes using publicly-available data. We also developed four BTC address clustering algorithms and one LN node clustering algorithm that allowed us to link 29.61% of the BTC addresses in our dataset to 45.97% of the public LN nodes, and cluster 1, 251 LN nodes into 301 actors. Finally, we discussed the security and privacy implications of our findings in the LN, where we find that a single actor controls 24% of the overall capacity and a few actors have a large impact on value privacy and payment relationship anonymity. These few actors also have a large overlap with those that would be candidates for high-impact attacks, the success of which can have significant negative effects on payment success and throughput for the entire LN.

Scalability issues appear in a broad range of blockchain applications and layer-2 protocols are increasingly considered as possible solutions. In light of these developments, we find an interesting venue for future work to evaluate whether our heuristics apply to layer-2 protocols other than the LN such as the Raiden Network for Ethereum.

Acknowledgments. This work is partially funded by the European Research Council (ERC) under the European Unions Horizon 2020 research (grant agreement No 771527-BROWSEC), by PROFET (grant agreement P31621), by the Austrian Research Promotion Agency through the Bridge-1 project PR4DLT (grant agreement 13808694); by COMET K1 SBA, ABC, by CoBloX Labs, by the Austrian Science Fund (FWF) through the Meitner program (project agreement M 2608-G27) and by the Austrian security research programme KIRAS of the Federal Ministry of Agriculture, Regions and Tourism (BMLRT) under the project KRYPTOMONITOR (879686). The authors would also like to thank Peter Holzer and Marcel Müller for setting up and starting the LN data collection process.

References

1. Hash time locked contracts. Wiki post. https://en.bitcoin.it/wiki/Hash_Time_Locked_Contracts
2. Community, L.N.: Bitcoin transaction and script formats. https://github.com/lightningnetwork/lightning-rfc/blob/master/03-transactions.md
3. Community, L.N.: Wip: dual funding (v2 channel establishment protocol). Github Issue. https://github.com/lightningnetwork/lightning-rfc/pull/524
4. Decker, C.: Privacy in lightning. Blog post (2018). https://snyke.net/post/privacy-in-lightning/
5. Decker, L.N.C.: New release: c-lightning 0.7.1. Blostream Blog Post. https://medium.com/blockstream/new-release-c-lightning-0-7-1-9fca65debeb2
6. Gudgeon, L., Moreno-Sanchez, P., Roos, S., McCorry, P., Gervais, A.: SoK: layer-two blockchain protocols. In: Bonneau, J., Heninger, N. (eds.) FC 2020. LNCS, vol. 12059, pp. 201–226. Springer, Cham (2020). https://doi.org/10.1007/978-3-030-51280-4_12
7. Harrigan, M., Fretter, C.: The unreasonable effectiveness of address clustering. In: Conferences on Ubiquitous Intelligence & Computing, Advanced and Trusted Computing, Scalable Computing and Communications, Cloud and Big Data Computing, Internet of People, and Smart World Congress (UIC/ATC/ScalCom/CBDCom/IoP/SmartWorld) (2016)
8. Jian-Hong, L., Kevin, P., Tiziano, S., Christian, D., J, T.C.: Lightning network: a second path towards centralisation of the bitcoin economy (2020). https://arxiv.org/abs/2002.02819
9. Jourenko, M., Kurazumi, K., Larangeira, M., Tanaka, K.: SoK: A Taxonomy for Layer-2 Scalability Related Protocols for Cryptocurrencies. Cryptology ePrint Archive, Report 2019/352 (2019). https://eprint.iacr.org/2019/352
10. Kalodner, H., Goldfeder, S., Chator, A., Möser, M., Narayanan, A.: BlockSci: design and applications of a blockchain analysis platform (2017). https://arxiv.org/abs/
11. Kappos, G., et al.: An empirical analysis of privacy in the lightning network (2020). https://arxiv.org/abs/2003.12470
12. Kus Khalilov, M.C., Levi, A.: A survey on anonymity and privacy in bitcoin-like digital cash systems. Commun. Surv. Tutor. **20**(3), 2543–2585 (2018)
13. Martinazzi, S., Flori, A.: The evolving topology of the lightning network: centralization, efficiency, robustness, synchronization, and anonymity. PLOS ONE **15**(1), 1–18 (2020)
14. Meiklejohn, S., et al.: A fistful of bitcoins: characterizing payments among men with no names. In: Internet Measurement Conference (2013)

15. Nowostawski, M., Jardar, T.: Evaluating methods for the identification of off-chain transactions in the lightning network. Appl. Sci. **9**(12), 2519 (2019)
16. Poon, J., Dryja, T.: The Bitcoin Lightning Network (2016). http://lightning. network/
17. Rohrer, E., Malliaris, J., Tschorsch, F.: Discharged payment channels: quantifying the lightning network's resilience to topology-based attacks. In: European Symposium on Security and Privacy Workshops (2019)
18. Seres, I.A., Gulyás, L., Nagy, D.A., Burcsi, P.: Topological analysis of bitcoin's lightning network. In: Pardalos, P., Kotsireas, I., Guo, Y., Knottenbelt, W. (eds.) Mathematical Research for Blockchain Economy. SPBE, pp. 1–12. Springer, Cham (2020). https://doi.org/10.1007/978-3-030-37110-4_1
19. Vu, B.: Announcing lnd v0.10-beta! Lightning Labs Blog Post. https://lightning. engineering/posts/2020-04-30-lnd-v0.10/

The Complex Shape of Anonymity in Cryptocurrencies: Case Studies from a Systematic Approach

Niluka Amarasinghe[✉], Xavier Boyen[✉], and Matthew McKague[✉]

Queensland University of Technology, Brisbane, Australia
{niluka.amarasinghe,xavier.boyen,matthew.mckague}@qut.edu.au

Abstract. The modern financial world has seen a significant rise in the use of cryptocurrencies in recent years, in no small part due to convincing levels of anonymity promised by such schemes. Bitcoin, despite being the most widespread, has significant lapses of anonymity. Several recent constructions aim to bridge some of those gaps. Amid such developments, there have been many attempts to evaluate the anonymity prospects of such schemes, but always with a rather narrow view based on metrics tailored to the schemes being studied.

Here, we employ a common universal framework to characterise the many aspects of anonymity achieved, or not, by any (crypto, digital, or physical) currency schemes, irrespective of the underlying implementation. We focus on a few high-profile practical cases of interest (including Bitcoin, Zcash, Monero, Mimblewimble) and use our common framework to draw detailed and meaningful comparisons.

Keywords: Anonymity · Cryptocurrencies

1 Introduction

Cryptocurrencies are undeniably one of the most attention-grabbing developments in security research of the last decade. They continue to open up new classes of inquiries for the crypto- and distributed-systems communities, while also arguably offering tangible financial benefits as alternatives to traditional fiat currencies.

Thanks to the blockchain technology, *trust*, the grease of financial transactions, can now be *inferential* rather than *axiomatic*. The decentralised nature, ease of conducting cross-border transactions, resistance to censure, and promises (or hopes) of privacy and anonymity, are factors that have contributed towards this popularity. Bitcoin is the first and by far the most widely used *true*[1] cryptocurrency at the time of this writing, and has attracted much attention with respect to its privacy and anonymity aspects.

---

[1] By which we mean: permissionless, fully decentralized, with democratic governance, and transparently operated—in other words, conducive to trust from first principles.

© International Financial Cryptography Association 2021
N. Borisov and C. Diaz (Eds.): FC 2021, LNCS 12674, pp. 205–225, 2021.
https://doi.org/10.1007/978-3-662-64322-8_10

Anonymity broadly means that an entity cannot be uniquely identified in a given setting. This concept has been widely discussed in the context of anonymous communication and information sharing. Consequently, many terminologies [22,30] and theoretical models such as k-anonymity have been developed to model anonymity [10,29]. For better or worse, these available theoretical frameworks have been borrowed for discussing anonymity in cryptocurrencies.

Many traditional currency schemes are centralised systems where customers depend on another party to preserve their privacy. For example, in a banking model, banks are bound by regulation to preserve the confidentiality of customer information. If the transaction history of a particular individual or entity were exposed to an outsider, it could result in many undesirable consequences, from a subjective sense of betrayal, to more concrete abuses such as misuse of information to gain undue advantages in contract bidding. Even worse, if currency units came attached with transaction histories, that could lead to the blacklisting of specific units based on their use in unlawful activities in the past, even though the units may have had only uncontroversial uses afterwards.

Anonymity of cryptocurrencies has received much attention since the current Bitcoin framework is claimed to provide only a form of 'pseudonymity' as transactions are linked to payment addresses in a big graph that is visible to all [9,15]. Detailed analyses of public transaction data, such as the work presented in [6,19,26], have shown that it is possible to uncover behaviour patterns of Bitcoin users and trace their identities in real life.

As a result of this tension between the need for, and the lack of, improved anonymity in cryptocurrencies, a lot of energy has been expended to fulfil that demand. Some solutions are centered around improving the Bitcoin framework (e.g. Zcash) whereas other approaches have sought to revisit the blockchain machinery in the design of new cryptocurrency schemes (e.g. Monero). Despite many such solutions making claims of "anonymity", some studies claim that those could still be subject to deanonymisation [18,20].

As rationalised in [4], despite a large number of studies on cryptocurrency anonymity, no standardised means are available to evaluate the actual level of privacy achieved by different cryptocurrencies. Many studies have been conducted in isolation using various metrics, with the consequence that it is not feasible to compare and benchmark the anonymity landscape in a reliable manner across various schemes. To make matters worse, it turns out that the very notion of anonymity itself, in such complex multi-party systems as decentralized cryptocurrencies, has been until now very poorly understood, and is anything but clear-cut. We discuss the specifics in a separate report [5].

1.1 Our Contribution

The present study was initially motivated by the works of [3,4,9,15], which lifted the veil on the multiplicity of anonymity notions for cryptocurrencies, but stopped short of actually providing a crisp formalism for defining and using those notions. Over the course of this study, we identified a very *fine-grained* structure for the intuitive notion of payment anonymity, parameterised through qualitative distinct definitions that are all sensible and justifiable in appropriate scenarios [5].

Our purpose in this work, is to analyse the multiple precise ways in which a broad notion of anonymity can be envisaged, and we provide a common game-based security template that combines a massive group of explicit attacker scenarios. Indeed, our notions generalise many security notions familiar to cryptographers such as known vs. chosen plaintext, forward security, indistinguishability, active vs. passive adversaries, and so on. The fact that we consider all of these security dimensions simultaneously multiplies the number of definitions, but also allows us to meaningfully understand and compare the anonymity of systems that differ along multiple dimensions. However, it should be noted that we do not intend to address the anonymity of the underlying construction of currency schemes in this work i.e. consensus or communication mechanisms.

Our framework is based around the fundamental notion of *distinguishability*, leading to a security concept of *indistinguishability*, likely familiar to readers from other security definitions. These notions are further particularized to certain subjects such as *transaction value*, *sender*, *recipient* and *metadata*, and parameterised across multiple dimensions based on which information and capabilities are given to the adversary [5].

Our main contribution here is to demonstrate the concrete potential of our model by analysing the anonymity landscape from a few major cryptocurrency implementations. We start with a simple Trusted Third Party scheme as a benchmark and show that it is, as expected, anonymous against all adversaries appropriate to the trusted third party model. We then study Bitcoin, which still receives much criticism in relation to anonymity. In addition, we also examine Zcash, Monero and Mimblewimble; three cryptocurrency schemes with diverse implementations, which have recently become popular due to their claims for improved anonymity.

The take-away message from our effort is that (financial) anonymity is not an all-or-nothing binary property; it is far more subtle. We fully intend that our framework be used to clearly spell out what aspects of privacy a certain coin does or does not satisfy, across diverse implementations. Of course, one could be content with asking for *absolute fungibility* (think: isotopically pure melted gold), but that is likely not to lead us anywhere, as no cryptocurrency in existence comes close to reaching that goal. This only makes the need for a (much) more refined model all the more pressing.

Organisation. Subsequent sections of this paper are organised as follows. We first present a brief summary of related studies where theoretical notions of anonymity have been discussed with reference to cryptocurrencies. We then set forth the preliminaries of our framework, while emphasising its features and relevant anonymity definitions. Next, we present the analysis outcomes followed by a detailed discussion on the significance of this work.

1.2   Other Related Work

As mentioned at the outset, many early studies have focused on quantitative analysis of publicly available Bitcoin transaction data such as payment addresses and values as the Bitcoin blockchain records all transaction details publicly. As claimed in [17,25,26,28], such public transaction data can be used to compromise the anonymity of Bitcoin users by studying behavioural patterns and transaction flows etc. Moving forward, some have attempted to formalise anonymity concepts in a theoretical manner, yet such are not standardised across different constructions. For example, Androulaki et al. [6] conducted an analysis of Bitcoin privacy based on *activity unlinkability* and *profile indistinguishability* with respect to addresses and transactions, which was also used in [21] to analyse Bitcoin network data. Conversely, [33] uses the notion of *unlinkability* with respect to linking different entities as formulated by [22].

More recently, new currency schemes have emerged with more promising anonymity expectations, which has led to more concrete formalisation of anonym- ity concepts. Zcash is one such scheme which offers improved anonymity levels through its 'shielded transactions', which conceal payment addresses and values. Yet, experimental studies in [14,24,34] have shown that it is prone to *linkability* of transactions with corresponding payment addresses.

The Cryptonote protocol, which forms the foundation for several currency systems, is claimed to satisfy anonymity in terms of *unlinkability* and *untraceability* [31]. Their interpretation of *unlinkability* is more specific in that, given two transactions, it should not be possible to identify whether both transactions were intended to the same party. *Untraceability* on the other hand is defined as the inability to identify the corresponding sender for a given transaction. Nevertheless, subsequent studies in [20,32] claim that Monero, which originated from the Cryptonote protocol, is prone to deanonymisation attacks through analyses of public transaction data.

Fungibility, which is the property of every currency unit being identical, is regarded by many as an elementary requirement of any currency scheme, but it is a tall order. It is well accepted that Bitcoin is not fungible [9,27]. Although it has been claimed in [24] that Zcash achieves fungibility through its use of zero-knowledge SNARK proofs, the survey study of [9] makes the countermanding claim that Mimblewimble [23] is the only cryptocurrency scheme to do so. Even so, the original Mimblewimble is insecure, and the fix proposed in [11], by making it preserve a lot more data, reintroduces coin history thereby negating the original fungibility claim.

Methods such as network analysis proposed in [7] and transaction graph-based analysis in [8] provide means for modelling anonymity through experimental analysis, which however may not be possible across different constructions. In comparison, our model deviates from this as our emphasis is on modelling anonymity from first principles in any currency scheme.

With the increasing complexity, comparing anonymity of cryptocurrencies has become a challenge. Surveys conducted in [4,9,15] present independent categorisations of cryptocurrencies based on different anonymity properties such as *untraceability, unlinkability, fungibility, hidden values* and *hidden IP addresses.* In a different approach, [3] provides a systematic grouping of a subset of cryptocurrencies in terms of four privacy tiers; *pseudonymity, set anonymity, full anonymity* and *confidential transactions*, based on unlinkability and hidden user identities. Yet, all such categorisations provide a very high level picture of anonymity levels based on the techniques used by the schemes, which is orthogonal to our work.

Nonetheless, these studies, mostly based on experimental analyses or specific constructions, do not necessarily facilitate the assessment and comparison of cryptocurrencies in terms of a common, *fine-grained, formal* qualitative model of anonymity.

2 Anonymity Framework

Our work is based on an abstract model of a cryptocurrency scheme, depicting the overall functionality of a generic cryptocurrency scheme. We construct an anonymity framework for this scheme through a game-based approach. We chose game-based definitions over the UC (Universal Composability) framework because the former are intuitive and can be agreed upon by non-specialists (much less non-cryptographers). This is essential as a bridge between theory and applications. Further, UC, though a very nice theoretical methodology, is best suited for small primitives whose ideal functionalities may still have a clean description, which is certainly not the case with cryptocurrencies. This abstract anonymity model is formalised in detail in [5]; here we summarise the points of interest for our purposes in this paper of analysing concrete cryptocurrency schemes.

2.1 A Generic Cryptocurrency Scheme

We define a currency scheme in terms of a security parameter $\lambda \in \mathbb{Z}^+$, and a system state consisting of payment addresses, each having a public key (a_{pk}) and a private key (a_{sk}), and transaction history. A transaction takes place between senders and recipients with inputs such as values and other metadata (such as IP addresses). Each transaction comprises private and public parts (t_s and t_p), with the latter being broadcast to the network. A mint operation collects new transactions on the network at any given time and generates a new state. New currency units may be created as a result of minting, as per its underlying implementation. Then an adjudicate operation selects the rightful new state of the system. Accordingly, consecutive states of the scheme form a partial ordering.

It should be noted that we model only the generic functionality of a cryptocurrency scheme in this scheme. Hence, we do not consider the specifics of the underlying consensus mechanism or the communication here.

Further details of the algorithms are included in Appendix A. The full theoretical study in [5] details how correctness and security requirements of this abstract currency scheme are established.

Definition 1. *A cryptocurrency scheme Π, is defined in terms of security parameter $\lambda \in \mathbb{Z}^+$ and with the functionality prescribed by means of a set of algorithms; { Init, CreateAddr, IsValidPubAddr, IsValidSecAddr, GetBalance, CreateTxn, IsValidPubTxn, IsValidSecTxn, ExtractSenderPubAddr, ExtractRecipientPubAddr, ExtractInputVal, ExtractOutputVal, IsMintable, Mint, Adjudicate, IsValidState, IsGenesisState, CreateCheckpointState, RetrieveCheckpointState}.*

2.2 A Comprehensive Adversarial Capability Model

We define a comprehensive adversarial model to include a wide range of capabilities for adversarial power and knowledge, represented by a set of parameters (Table 1). Adversarial knowledge of public/secret keys of senders/recipients, values, metadata and other transaction-related data are modelled by ψ. Here, metadata refers to implementation specific data that appear in a transaction such as IP addresses, while the knowledge of a transaction represents other related information as shown in Table 1. Adversarial power is modelled by the adversary's ability to modify the state (δ), to control state initialisation in the experimental setup (α), and to cause minting to fail during the game (β). This parametrisation accommodates a wide range of adversaries; passive with all parameters equal to '0', static with δ, $\alpha = 1$ and adaptive with parameter values greater than 1. It is assumed that the adversary $(\mathcal{A})$ has oracle access to hidden entities via opaque handles.

Table 1. Parameters of the adversarial capability model

Param. Value	Adversarial knowledge						Adversarial power		
	Sender public/secret keys	Recipient public/secret keys	Transaction value	Transaction meta-data	Transaction	State manipulation	State initialisation	Cause mint to fail
	ψ_{pk_s}/ψ_{sk_s}	ψ_{pk_r}/ψ_{sk_r}	ψ_v	ψ_m	ψ_t	δ	α	β
0	Hidden	Hidden	Hidden	Hidden	Hidden	Hidden	Hidden randomness, honest init	Not allowed
1	Hidden but revealed at the end	Hidden but revealed at the end	Hidden but revealed at the end	Hidden but revealed at the end	t_p is revealed	Can view the state	Public randomness, honest init	Allowed
2	Access public keys through oracle	Access secret keys through oracle	Chosen by Oracle and known	Chosen by oracle and known	t_s is revealed	Can manipulate the state	Public randomness, adversarial init	–
3	$\mathcal{A}$ chooses identity, oracle creates addresses	$\mathcal{A}$ chooses randomness, oracle creates addresses	$\mathcal{A}$ chooses values	$\mathcal{A}$ chooses metadata	Randomness is revealed	-	Hidden randomness, adversarial init	–
4	$\mathcal{A}$ generates address	$\mathcal{A}$ generates address	–	–	$\mathcal{A}$ chooses randomness	–	–	–
5	–	–	–	–	$\mathcal{A}$ creates transaction	–	–	–

$\text{Exp}^{Anonymity}_{\pi,\mathcal{A},\mathcal{O},\omega,\psi,\delta,\alpha,\beta}(\lambda)$

1. Initialises the state based on the parameter α.
2. $\mathcal{A}$ provides inputs based on the capabilities decided by the parameters ψ and δ.
3. $\mathcal{C}$ checks the inputs against the parameters and if there is any discrepancy, $\mathcal{A}$ loses the game.
4. If $\psi_t \neq 5$, $\mathcal{C}$ creates two transactions t_{p_0} and t_{p_1} based on the test variable/s parameterised by ω. $\mathcal{A}$ continues to evolve the state through appropriate oracle calls. If $\beta = 0$, then $\mathcal{A}$ loses the game if any mint operation fails during the execution. If $\psi_t = 5$, $\mathcal{C}$ accepts the transactions provided by the adversary.
5. $\mathcal{C}$ picks a bit $b \in \{0, 1\}$ and mints the transaction t_{p_b}.
6. Based on the parameter values of ψ, corresponding data are revealed to $\mathcal{A}$, but $\mathcal{A}$ is not allowed to create or mint any further transactions.
7. $\mathcal{A}$ makes a guess for the bit and wins the game if the guess is correct.

Fig. 1. Anonymity game

2.3 All-in-one Generic Flexible Anonymity Game

We now formulate a generic game, that captures different attacker scenarios, each depicting a unique aspect of anonymity. We use the variable $\omega = (\omega_s \omega_r \omega_v \omega_m)$ to set the test variable/s (the attacker's goal); sender (s), recipient (r), value (v) and metadata (m). Accordingly, we develop a set of definitions around the fundamental concept of *indistinguishability*, which requires the adversary to distinguish between two known entities in the game. We also define a weaker notion, *unlinkability*, in which case, the two entities to choose between, are not known to the attacker explicitly, but rather by their history in previous transactions. We define the *Anonymity Game* between a challenger $(\mathcal{C})$ and an adversary $(\mathcal{A})$ as given in Fig. 1 and further explained in Appendix A.1.

2.4 Notions of Anonymity

Unsurprisingly, there are around 5,000,000 distinct combinations of ω, ψ, δ, α and β alone, resulting in different attacker scenarios, which reveal the complexity of what it means for a currency scheme to be anonymous. While some notions may not result in apprehensible real world scenarios, others may assist in assessing different aspects of anonymity. Each notion is defined based on a unique adversary, as per the goal, knowledge and power (i.e. GOAL-KNOWL-POWER), which is also given as a unique parameter vector, ω-ψ-(δ, α, β) setting the game. The strongest adversary is assigned the full power (to manipulate the state setup, the state, and minting) and the full knowledge (of secret keys of senders/recipients, values, metadata, transaction), which we call a FULL-FULL adversary. The weakest is named a NIL-NIL adversary, with no power nor knowledge. Others are named accordingly to reveal relevant adversarial capabilities.

3 Analysis

Formally proving consistency and all implications and separations that exist across all resulting flavours of anonymity would be far beyond the scope and space available in this paper (but see [5] for details). Instead, we will focus on specific notions of interest towards our purpose here to demonstrate how our framework can be deployed to very precisely characterise concrete properties of actual cryptocurrencies. We consider *Indistinguishability* (IND) and *Unlinkability* (ULK) notions related to sender (S), recipient (R) and value (V) (not metadata which may be different in each implementation), in a bid to provide a meaningful comparison across real-world currency schemes.

We start by analysing a Trusted Third Party scheme, which has a very high level of anonymity, as a benchmark for comparison. Then, we study the Bitcoin system, followed by Zcash, Monero and Mimblewimble, all three of which claim to have convincing anonymity levels, yet have very diverse implementations.

3.1   A Trusted Third Party (TTP) Scheme

Consider a TTP scheme where a trusted Central Authority (CA) operates a currency scheme. The CA registers users, validates, creates and mints transactions upon request by users. We also assume that the CA communicates with all other parties over authenticated channels and only honours requests from the rightful owners of accounts. A user registers one or more accounts with the CA and maintains funds under those registered identities. No negative fund balances are allowed at any given time. A user can request the CA to create a transaction, and subsequently to mint the transactions and the CA performs corresponding fund transfer/s and creates a transaction record internally. The CA can view the transaction history at any time. With this functionality, there are no public/private keys involved in the scheme and transactions will always be secret, hence the system state is always internal and private.

Adversarial Capabilities. In the TTP model, CA can have its own state variables outside the challenger and the adversary, and thus is not required to accept the adversarial state. Also, the initial state will be an empty list of transactions, accounts etc., allowing any method of state initialisation possible. Hence we can allow the adversary to take any value for δ and α in our model (Table 1). Further, we assume that transactions are encrypted with an asymmetric system using CA's public key, and hence can be revealed in the end without revealing any information. We model user identities in terms of a single address thereby setting $a_{pk} = a_{sk}$ in our model. To enable the adversary to supply sender/recipient addresses to the challenger, we provide access to an additional oracle `DelegateAccess` to transfer the authority of the addresses controlled by the adversary to the challenger. Thus, the challenger is able to create the transactions required for different scenarios. Note that this oracle is only specific to the TTP functionality, and is reminiscent of how ideal functionalities must be augmented with corruption functions in the UC model.

Analysis of Anonymity. First, we consider a FULL power adversary (denoted by $(2_\delta, 3_\alpha, 1_\beta)$), who has the complete knowledge of recipients, value and metadata, but knows senders only by public keys and provides the input transactions to the game (named as PUBS knowledge denoted by $((3,0)_s, (4, 4_r), 3_v, 3_m, 5_t)_\psi)$ against the goal of S-IND. We name this adversary as S-IND-PUBS-FULL, who in this case cannot learn any new information about the sender corresponding to the minted transaction as the state is private, and thus has negligible advantage of winning the Anonymity game (given by the parameter vector $(1_s 000)_\omega\text{-}((\mathbf{3}, \mathbf{0})_\mathbf{s}, (4, 4)_r, 3_v, 3_m, 5_t)_\psi\text{-}(2_\delta, 3_\alpha, 1_\beta))$. Hence, the TTP scheme is secure against S-IND-PUBS-FULL adversary and also against a S-ULK-NILS-FULL adversary having no knowledge of senders (NILS knowledge) represented by $(1_s 000)_\omega\text{-}((\mathbf{0}, \mathbf{0})_\mathbf{s}, (4, 4)_r, 3_v, 3_m, 5_t)_\psi\text{-}(2_\delta, 3_\alpha, 1_\beta)$ by implication. Similar anony-mity notions hold for R and V as well. Accordingly, we can say that the scheme is secure even against an adversary with FULL-FULL capabilities, for all entities; i.e. ALL-IND-FULL-FULL setting, as the scheme does not leak any information to the adversary. This is modelled by the vector $(1111)_\omega\text{-}((4, 4)_s,$ $(4, 4)_r, 3_v, 3_m, 5_t)_\psi\text{-}(2_\delta, 3_\alpha, 1_\beta)$, which depicts '*absolute fungibility*' demonstrating the strongest possible level of anonymity in our model.

3.2   Bitcoin

The Bitcoin peer-to-peer cryptocurrency relies on a public blockchain where transaction data are public. Users are identified via public addresses and they initiate transactions using their private keys to spend funds (unspent transaction outputs). Transaction inputs include references to unspent transaction outputs and a set of new outputs with corresponding values, which later becomes inputs to another transaction. In addition, transactions also contain additional data which help in the verification. Participating network nodes compete to create new blocks (mining) to include new transactions in the blockchain and a qualifying block is accepted by the network based on a Proof-of-Work system.

Adversarial Capabilities. Most parameters in our model directly corresponds to Bitcoin except that there is no secret transaction part of the transaction t_s. Since the scheme does not have a private state, this can be modelled with $\delta \neq 0$ in our model. Similarly, honest state initialisation with hidden randomness is not allowed, and hence we model this by setting $\alpha \neq 0$.

Analysis of Anonymity. As all Bitcoin transaction details are public, any adversary has non-negligible advantage in winning the game against any test variable (i.e. S, R or V), since they can observe the topology of the transaction graph. Adversaries can create a specific set of transactions (through the oracle) chosen in a way that they can correctly identify the graph (by analysing starting balances of inputs etc.). Hence, it is not secure in any adversary with respect to indistinguishability or unlinkability of S, R or V.

Conversely, consider a weak adversary in our game against an empty test variable, who has no information of the transaction (NIL knowledge), but can view the state setup and the state (VIEW power), denoted by NIL-IND-NIL-VIEW and parameterised by $(0000)_\omega\text{-}((0, 0)_s, (0, 0)_r, 0_v, 0_m, 0_t)_\psi\text{-}(1_\delta, 1_\alpha, 0_\beta)$.

Here, the adversary has to distinguish between two identical transactions carrying same data, except with different randomness. Despite the public transaction history, the adversary cannot identify the correct transaction with a substantial probability, thus making the Bitcoin system secure against this attacker. However, if we increase at least one capability, the scheme becomes insecure. Thus, we conclude that Bitcoin only satisfies an extremely weak notion in our model, which only provides anonymity against two identical transactions that only differ in the randomness. It should be noted however that we make this claim subject to the computational and operational assumptions of the Bitcoin construction. In fact, the only way to make the scheme anonymous is to make the state private (i.e. $\delta = 0$), which is impossible with the current Bitcoin construction.

3.3   Zcash

Zcash emerged as a result of the efforts of improving the anonymity of Bitcoin. We consider the Zcash Sapling specification for this study. This scheme consists of shielded and transparent payment addresses where transparent addresses and related transactions operate similar to Bitcoin [12]. Here we only consider the transactions between shielded addresses (referred to as addresses hereafter). Each address has a private spending key that allows the owner to spend the coins (notes) sent to that address. Each note is coupled with a unique nullifier generated using the spending key and a note commitment, which is publicly revealed when the note is created. Without the private key, it is infeasible to link a note commitment to its nullifier. An unspent note in Zcash is a note with a publicly revealed commitment and a hidden nullifier. When a shielded transaction is created, nullifiers of input notes and commitments of output notes are revealed. In addition, the value of a shielded transaction is also hidden, and is revealed through value commitments related to input and output notes, and relevant balancing operations are carried out as homomorphic operations. Further, zk-SNARK primitives are used for functions such as proving the ownership of notes, verifying and validating transactions [12].

Adversarial Capabilities. Similar to Bitcoin, we can model Zcash addresses through the payment addresses a_{pk}, a_{sk} in our model. As the state is public, it can be modelled by setting $\delta \in \{1, 2\}$ and $\alpha \in \{1, 2, 3\}$. In shielded transactions, senders and recipients correspond to the nullifiers of input notes and to the commitments of output notes respectively. Further, the values of input/output notes are also concealed as value commitments. t_p represents nullifiers of input notes, output note commitments and value commitments whereas actual input/output notes and relevant data can be modelled by t_s. The knowledge of secret keys (i.e. ψ_{sk_s}) is required to link the nullifiers of input notes to their owners (senders) and the private keys of recipients (i.e. ψ_{sk_r}) should be known to link the note commitments of output notes to their owners (recipients).

Analysis of Anonymity. We begin by analysing the unlinkability property. Although the linkability of Zcash transactions is explored in literature such as [24] with respect to transactions involving both shielded and transparent addresses, we only consider shielded addresses here. Consider an adversary for S-ULK who has all powers except to cause minting to fail (ACTIVE power), and has full knowledge of recipients, values, metadata and public transaction data (output note commitments), except the senders (NILS-PUBT knowledge) which we capture in a parameter vector $((0,0)_s, (4,4)_r, 3_v, 3_m, 1_t)_\psi\text{-}(2_\delta, 3_\alpha, 0_\beta)$. The adversary cannot obtain any additional knowledge of the transaction as output note commitments do not leak any information about the sender, and thus has a negligible advantage over winning the game. Hence, Zcash scheme is secure in S-ULK-NILS-PUBT-ACTIVE. If the adversary is given more powers to cause minting to fail (i.e. FULL power), then he may gain additional information about account balances etc., making the system insecure against S-ULK-NILS-PUBT-FULL. Further, for any $\psi_t > 1$, the adversary has access to additional knowledge about the transaction which makes the system insecure. Hence, we can also show that Zcash is secure in R-ULK-NILR-PUBT-ACTIVE, but not in R-ULK-NILR-PUBT-FULL.

The scheme also satisfies S-IND-PUBST-ACTIVE security, as the knowledge of senders' public keys and public transaction data (PUBST knowledge) does not reveal any information about the nullifiers of input notes (i.e. $((3,0)_s, (4,4)_r, 3_v, 3_m, 1_t)_\psi\text{-}(2_\delta, 3_\alpha, 0_\beta))$. Yet, with the same reasoning as with S-ULK, Zcash fails in S-IND-PUBST-FULL. Similarly, Zcash is secure in R-IND-PUBRT-ACTIVE, but not in R-IND-PUBRT-FULL.

When testing for the value (i.e. $\omega_v = 1$), the system is secure against a FULL power adversary, having only the knowledge of public keys of senders, recipients and public transaction, but with no knowledge of the values (NILV-PUBSRT knowledge) as in V-ULK-NILV-PUBSRT-FULL (given by $(001_v0)_\omega\text{-}((3,0)_s, (3,0)_r, \mathbf{0}_v, 3_m, 1_t)_\psi\text{-}(2_\delta, 3_\alpha, 1_\beta))$, since failed minting attempts do not reveal any information despite knowing public keys. Hence, the level of anonymity with respect to V depends on the knowledge of secret keys as the value is hidden. Therefore, V-IND property holds only for an adversary with ACTIVE power and PUBSRT knowledge; i.e. V-IND-PUBSRT-ACTIVE notion denoted by $(001_v0)_\omega\text{-}((3,0)_s, (3,0)_r, \mathbf{3}_v, 3_m, 1_t)_\psi\text{-}(2_\delta, 3_\alpha, 0_\beta)$.

Accordingly, we can say that Zcash satisfies the strongest level of anonymity against a PUBSRT-ACTIVE adversary for all test variables given by ALL-IND-PUBSRT-ACTIVE setting and parameterised by $(1111)_\omega\text{-}((3,0)_s, (3,0)_r, 3_v, 3_m, 1_t)_\psi\text{-}(2_\delta, 3_\alpha, 0_\beta)$. Hence, Zcash achieves higher anonymity prospects compared to Bitcoin, and is bounded by the knowledge of secret keys of payment addresses.

3.4 Monero

Monero is another cryptocurrency that claims improved anonymity based on several cryptographic primitives such as ring signatures and stealth addresses to achieve anonymity with respect to senders and recipients [32]. In addition, Ring Confidential Transactions (RingCT) are used to conceal transaction values through value commitments [32]. Each user has two pairs of private/public keys as spend and view keys. A sender creates a one-time public key (stealth address) for each output using recipients' public keys. The sender mixes the actual inputs with a set of additional random public keys (aka mixins) using ring signatures, to produce a signature for the ring of inputs. The one-time public key, the signature and the public keys of inputs (in the ring) are submitted to the network along with other transaction data [2,32]. A sender can include an (optional) pre-agreed, encrypted payment ID, enabling respective recipients to identify the sender using their private keys. The recipients can retrieve outputs using both their private/public view keys and can spend them using the spending keys. Outsiders can only view the public keys in the ring (of probable senders), with each being an equally probable input to the transaction.

Adversarial Capabilities. Similar to others, the Monero Blockchain state is also public, thus we set the parameters $\delta \in \{1, 2\}$ and $\alpha \in \{1, 2, 3\}$ as before. However, most of the transaction data (e.g. actual senders, recipients, values etc.) are hidden from the public. We map public and private keys of both spend and view keys collectively to public/private keys in our model. We represent mixin data by metadata in our model, i.e. ψ_m. The knowledge of secret keys of a sender/recipient is sufficient to identify the respective sender/recipient of a transaction, respectively. Conversely, the knowledge of ψ_{sk_r} alone is not enough to identify the sender, if the transaction does not contain a payment ID.

Analysis of Anonymity. First we look at the unlinkability property of Monero, which is analogous to the notion of traceability of Monero, referred to in [16,32]. We consider the S-ULK-NILS-PUBT-ACTIVE notion as with Zcash, without the knowledge of likely senders (i.e. $((0, 0)_s, (4, 4)_r, 3_v, 3_m, 1_t)_\psi\text{-}(2_\delta, 3_\alpha, 0_\beta))$. The state only reveals the public keys of a possible set of senders, but not the recipients nor the value. Yet, if the adversary chooses the mixins, then he has additional information about the sender as ring participants are public. Thus, Monero cannot be secure if the adversary knows the mixins in the ring. Hence, we define a weaker adversary by setting $\psi_m = 0$ in our model, with an adversary having no knowledge of sender or metadata (NILSM-PUBT knowledge), in which case Monero is secure in S-ULK-NILSM-PUBT-ACTIVE (modelled by $(1_s 000)_\omega\text{-}((0, 0)_s, (4, 4)_r, 3_v, 0_m, 1_t)_\psi\text{-}(2_\delta, 3_\alpha, 0_\beta))$.

With S-IND-PUBSMT-ACTIVE, Monero cannot be secure as the knowledge of mixins along with the public keys of probable senders may leak information about the actual sender. Further, the knowledge of the transaction t_p can also leak information about the mixins. Hence, we consider a weaker adversary with no knowledge of metadata or the transaction (i.e. NILMT-PUBS knowledge) with S-IND-NILMT-PUBS-ACTIVE, represented by $(1_s 000)_\omega\text{-}((3, 0)_s, (4, 4)_r, 3_v, 0_m, 0_t)_\psi\text{-}(2_\delta, 3_\alpha, 0_\beta)$, who fails against Monero. However, these claims may be broken if the mixins are not chosen carefully by the sender.

With recipient anonymity, we can see that Monero complies with R-ULK-NILR-PUBT-ACTIVE as funds are received by stealth addresses which can be claimed only by the recipient with the matching private key. This notion of unlinkability closely relates to the notions described in [16,32]. Similarly, Monero is also secure in R-IND-PUBRT-ACTIVE as the knowledge of recipients' public keys do not reveal anything about the stealth addresses. Further, as values are hidden, Monero's anonymity in V reduces to the knowledge of the secret keys of the senders/recipients similar to Zcash and hence it satisfies V-ULK-NILV-PUBSRT-FULL and V-IND-PUBSRT-ACTIVE notions. As with Zcash, S-IND, S-ULK, R-IND, R-ULK and V-IND goals fail against a FULL power adversary with the information leakage from failed minting. Thus, we can see that the maximal anonymity level satisfied by Monero is the ALL-IND-NILMT-PUBSR-ACTIVE security given by the parameter vector $(1111)_\omega$-$((3,0)_s, (3,0)_r,$ $3_v, 0_m, 0_t)_\psi$-$(2_\delta, 3_\alpha, 0_\beta)$.

3.5 Mimblewimble

The Mimblewimble protocol focuses on improving anonymity and scalability through confidential transactions and transaction aggregation [11,13]. We study the Grin implementation for this analysis [1]. A coin in this is a commitment, $C = vH + rG$ where v is the value, r is the randomness (hence the private key of the coin), and H, G are generators of a discrete logarithm [11]. The opening of the commitment of a coin is necessary to spend that coin, which requires the corresponding secret key (r). The sender sends the input coins (commitments) to the recipient over an authenticated channel, who then adds the commitments to the output coins (by including individual private keys) and a partial signature for the transaction (using a random nonce), which is sent back to the sender. The sender validates the received signature and generates his portion of the signature and broadcasts the transaction on the network, which is verified (via the relevant public key generated through public transaction data) and minted by the network nodes subsequently. Transactions are included in the blockchain, subject to transaction aggregation which hides the actual transaction graph [1]. A typical transaction consists of input/output coins (commitments) and relevant range proofs (proving that values are positive), transaction fee and a signature.

Adversarial Capabilities. As before, the Mimblewimble state is public. However, transactions hide the senders, recipients and the values while revealing only the commitments required to validate a given transaction by any third-party. The knowledge of the secret key (r) of the coins is required to produce a valid signature for a transaction, allowing the rightful owners to spend the coins. Hence we model the knowledge of secret keys of inputs and outputs as ψ_{sk_s} and ψ_{sk_r} respectively in our model. The knowledge of the public key of the transaction can be modelled as ψ_{pk_s} and ψ_{pk_r}. As the sender initiates a transaction by communicating with relevant recipients, when the adversary knows any of the secret keys, there is no anonymity (i.e. when $\psi_{sk_s}, \psi_{sk_r} > 0$ in the model).

Analysis of Anonymity. Consider the S-IND-PUBSRT-ACTIVE notion, which is parameterised by $(1_s000)_\omega$-$((3,0)_s,(3,0)_r,\ 3_v,3_m,1_t)_\psi$-$(2_\delta,3_\alpha,0_\beta)$. Despite lear- ning the value, metadata and public transaction data, the adversary is not able to distinguish between any sender, as secret keys are not known, thus making Mimblewimble secure against this adversary. However, any further leakage of information (i.e. private keys of recipients) would compromise anonymity. Similarly, the notion of S-ULK-NILS-PUBRT-ACTIVE denoted by $(1_s000)_\omega$-$((0,0)_s,(3,0)_r,\ 3_v,3_m,1_t)_\psi$-$(2_\delta,3_\alpha,0_\beta)$ is also satisfied by implication. With a similar argument, we can show that it also satisfies R-IND-PUBSRT-ACTIVE and R-ULK-NILR-PUBST-ACTIVE. With V-IND, we can see that it is secure in V-IND-PUBSRT-ACTIVE as the value is hidden similar to Zcash and Monero, and hence also secure in V-ULK-NILV-PUBSRT-FULL. Thus, we can conclude that Mimblewimble satisfies strongest anonymity with respect to ALL-IND-

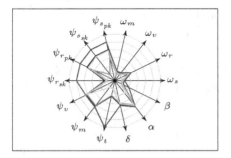

Fig. 2. Maximal anonymity notions satisfied by: TTP (red), Bitcoin(yellow), Zcash(blue), Monero(pink), Mimblewimble(green) (Color figure online)

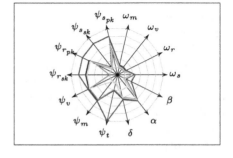

Fig. 3. Sender indistinguishability satisfied by: TTP (red), Bitcoin(yellow), Zcash(blue), Monero(pink), Mimblewimble(green) (Color figure online)

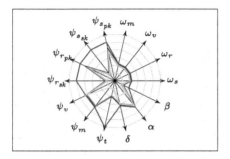

Fig. 4. Recipient indistinguishability satisfied by: TTP (red), Bitcoin(yellow), Zcash(blue), Monero(pink), Mimblewimble(green) (Color figure online)

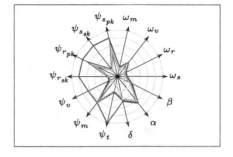

Fig. 5. Value unlinkability satisfied by: TTP (red), Bitcoin(yellow), Zcash(blue), Monero(pink), Mimblewimble(green) (Color figure online)

PUBSRT-ACTIVE, denoted by the vector $(1111)_\omega$-$((3,0)_s, (3,0)_r, 3_v, 3_m, 1_t)_\psi$-$(2_\delta, 3_\alpha, 0_\beta)$.

4   Discussion

While anonymity on the surface looks like an atomic notion, it is evident from the above analysis that it is actually quite quirky and splits apart under a powerful microscope. These findings reveal how minute differences of anonymity exist among the currency schemes studied, as illustrated by the Figs. 2 to 5. Figure 2 compares the schemes with respect to the maximal anonymity notion[2]. Compared to the TTP scheme, the other four schemes show weaker anonymity prospects, proving that they do not meet the criteria for "absolute fungibility". As expected, Bitcoin demonstrates the weakest anonymity of all. Conversely Zcash, Monero and Mimblewimble demonstrate improved anonymity with minor deviations among them. Zcash shows the highest level while Mimblewimble shows weaker anonymity with respect to the participants of a transaction and in Monero, anonymity is compromised when details of the choice of mixins are leaked to the adversary. Nevertheless, the knowledge of the randomness of the coins (i.e. $\psi_t > 1$) hinders the anonymity in all three schemes above. Figures 3 to 5 compare three individual anonymity notions related to S-IND, R-IND and V-ULK, and accordingly Zcash is secure against a stronger adversary, compared to other two. However, we only consider shielded addresses here whereas in reality Zcash users have the option to choose transparent addresses, in which case its anonymity is degraded to that of Bitcoin.

On that account, our work shows the very complex nature of the level of anonymity realised by various currency schemes. Consequently, our analysis demonstrates how one can effectively evaluate anonymity in a unified manner across dissimilar implementations as opposed to different categorisations presented in studies such as [4,9,15]. Hence, claims for anonymity cannot be made lightly in the presence of such granularity.

Therein, we have presented a qualitative recap of anonymity of a subset of real world cryptocurrency schemes as our major contribution in this work. One may wonder why we need such granularity in modelling anonymity in the context of cryptocurrencies, yet the findings of our case studies show how a minute change such as varying one value along a single dimension, could drastically affect the level of anonymity. The study of such impact and the interdependencies can be regarded as a separate study by itself and hence is recommended as a future work in this context.

As noted earlier, this study does not investigate the privacy aspects of the underlying consensus mechanism or the network of a cryptocurrency scheme, which may leak information independently from the currency scheme in which case it may affect the achievable level of anonymity. Our model already provides a way of capturing this leak as an instance of metadata, but the exact mechanisms

---

[2] I.e. where the adversary has to distinguish between two transactions that differ in all aspects: sender, receiver, value and metadata.

by which such leaks occur would have to be studied on a case by case basis and it would be another direction for further study.

5   Conclusion

In this paper, we have demonstrated how anonymity of cryptocurrency schemes can be analysed rigorously by means of a common framework, regardless of the implementation method. Our analysis is centered around an extensive group of anonymity properties based on the fundamental property of indistinguishability, further particularised to varying security subjects and adversarial models. Together, these represent a precise and exhaustive recount of true anonymity achieved by any currency scheme. We are first to be surprised by the richness of this formal financial anonymity landscape, which is unlike other formal notions of security and privacy seen in cryptography. This reality is well demonstrated through the case studies presented in this work.

Acknowledgements. Xavier Boyen is the recipient of an Australian Research Council Future Fellowship and acknowledges generous support from the grant, number FT140101145. Authors also thank the anonymous reviewers for their comments.

Appendix A   Anonymity framework

We provide a summary of the framework here while a comprehensive explanation is available in the report in [5]. We use the notation in Table 2.

Table 2. Notation

Description	Notation
Security parameter	$\lambda : \lambda \in \mathbb{Z}^+$
A tuple of random bit strings	$\rho : \rho \in (\{0,1\}^*)^*$
A system state/Current state, a set of states	p, P
Public key/Private key of a payment address	a_{pk}, a_{sk}
Ordered tuple of one/more addresses (senders/recipients) of secret keys	$\bar{S}, \bar{R}$
Ordered tuple of one/more addresses containing only public keys	S, R
Public and private parts of a transaction	t_p, t_s
Ordered tuples of input and output values of a transaction	V_{old}, V_{new}
Metadata for a transaction	m
Excess value of a transaction (fees + minted value)	V_x
A tuple of addresses of miners	R_m
Return X if y, otherwise return 1	X^y
If $a = \perp$ then return c, else return b	$a?b:c$
If $a = \perp$ then return b, else return a	$a?\_:b$

Table 3. Functions of the framework.

Algorithm	Syntax
Init	$p_0 \leftarrow \texttt{Init}_\pi(1^\lambda)$
CreateAddress	$\perp \vee (a_{pk}, a_{sk}, t_p, t_s) \leftarrow \texttt{CreateAddr}_\pi(p, d; \rho)$
IsValidPubAddr	$\{0,1\} \leftarrow \texttt{IsValidPubAddr}_\pi(a_{pk}, p)$
IsValidSecAddr	$\{0,1\} \leftarrow \texttt{IsValidSecAddr}_\pi(a_{pk}, a_{sk}, p)$
GetBalance	$\perp \vee Bal \leftarrow \texttt{GetBalance}_\pi(a_{pk}, a_{sk}, p)$
CreateTxn	$\perp \vee (t_s, t_p) \leftarrow \texttt{CreateTxn}_\pi(R, V_{new}, \bar{S}, V_{old}, m, p, \rho)$
IsValidPubTxn	$\{0,1\} \leftarrow \texttt{IsValidPubTxn}_\pi(t_p, p)$
IsValidSecTxn	$\{0,1\} \leftarrow \texttt{IsValidSecTxn}_\pi(t_p, t_s, p)$
ExtractSenderPubAddr	$\perp \vee S \leftarrow \texttt{ExtractSenderPubAddr}_\pi(t_p, t_s, p)$
ExtractRecipientPubAddr	$\perp \vee R \leftarrow \texttt{ExtractRecipientPubAddr}_\pi(t_p, t_s, p)$
ExtractInputVal	$\perp \vee V_{old} \leftarrow \texttt{ExtractInputVal}(t_p, t_s, p)$
ExtractOutputVal	$\perp \vee V_{new} \leftarrow \texttt{ExtractOutputVal}(t_p, t_s, p)$
IsMintable	$\{0,1\} \leftarrow \texttt{IsMintable}_\pi(\{t_p\}, p)$
Mint	$\perp \vee (p', V_x) \leftarrow \texttt{Mint}_\pi(\{t_p\}, R_m, p)$
Adjudicate	$p' \in P: \quad p \vee p' \leftarrow \texttt{Adjudicate}_\pi(P, p)$
IsValidState	$\{0,1\} \leftarrow \texttt{IsValidState}_\pi(p, \lambda)$
IsGenesisState	$\{0,1\} \leftarrow \texttt{IsGenesisState}_\pi(p, \lambda)$
RetrieveCheckpointState	$\perp \vee p_c \leftarrow \texttt{RetrieveCheckpointState}_\pi(p)$
CreateCheckpointState	$\perp \vee p_c \leftarrow \texttt{CreateCheckpointState}_\pi(p)$
AdditionalFunctionality	$(outputs) \leftarrow \texttt{AdditionalFunctionality}(inputs)$

Functionality of a Generic Cryptocurrency Scheme. We define the algorithms of the currency scheme in Table 3. There may be additional functionality associated with real world cryptocurrency systems, e.g. Smart contracts with Ethereum. In order to capture such additional features, we define a supplementary function AdditionalFunctionality. This enables us realise the security implications of functionality of a scheme that may be outside our base model.

A.1   Anonymity Game

We present the Anonymity game and required helper functions here. Helper functions check the adversarial conditions of inputs at the start of the game (CheckAdvConditions) and reveals data in the end (RevealData) based on the parameter ψ (Fig. 6). Moreover, the test variable, $\omega = (\omega_s, \omega_r, \omega_v, \omega_m)$ with each $\omega_x \in \{0,1\}$ indicates which entity is being tested in a given instance of the game. The adversarial inputs are crafted based on the ω, ψ, δ, α and β parameters. Figure 7 illustrates the game.

```
RevealData(t_p, ω, ψ, A*_O, T*_O, T_O, p_1)
```

1. $(\psi_{s_{pk}}, \psi_{s_{sk}}, \psi_{r_{pk}}, \psi_{r_{sk}}, \psi_v, \psi_m, \psi_t) \leftarrow \psi;\ (\omega_s, \omega_r, \omega_v, \omega_m) \leftarrow \omega$
2. $t_p \leftarrow \text{LookupPubTxn}(t_p, T*_O)$
3. $t_s \leftarrow \text{AA.Lookup}(t_p, T_O)$
4. $S \leftarrow \text{ExtractSenderPubAddr}_\pi(t_p, t_s, p_1)$
5. $R \leftarrow \text{ExtractRecipientPubAddr}_\pi(t_p, t_s, p_1)$
6. $V_{old} \leftarrow \text{ExtractInputVal}_\pi(t_p, t_s, p_1)$
7. $V_{new} \leftarrow \text{ExtractOutputVal}_\pi(t_p, t_s, p_1)$
8. $m \leftarrow \text{ExtractMetadata}_\pi(t_p, t_s, p_1)$
9. $U_s \leftarrow (S^{\psi_{s_{pk}}}, (\text{LookupSecAddr}(S, A*_O))^{\psi_{s_{sk}}})$
10. $U_r \leftarrow (R^{\psi_{r_{pk}}}, (\text{LookupSecAddr}(R, A*_O))^{\psi_{r_{sk}}})$
11. $U_v \leftarrow ((V_{old}, V_{new})^{\psi_v});\ U_m \leftarrow (m)^{\psi_m}$
12. $U_t \leftarrow (t_p^{\psi_t}, t_s^{(\psi_t=2)}, \rho_t^{(\psi_t=3)})$
13. **return** $(U_s \| U_r \| U_v \| U_m \| U_t)$

```
CheckAdvConditions(ω, ψ, S_0, S_1, R_0, R_1, V_old_0, V_new_0, V_old_1, V_new_1, m_0, m_1, A*_O, A_{O_{jk}}, D*_O)
```

1. $(\omega_s, \omega_r, \omega_v, \omega_m) \leftarrow \Omega;\ (\psi_{pk_s}, \psi_{sk_s}, \psi_{pk_r}, \psi_{sk_r}, \psi_v, \psi_m, \psi_t) \leftarrow \psi$
2. **if** $(\psi_{pk_s} \in \{0,1\}) \wedge (\psi_{sk_s} \in \{0,1\}) \wedge \neg(S_0, S_1 \subseteq A*_O)$, **return** 0
3. **if** $(\psi_{pk_s} \in \{0,1,2\}) \wedge (\psi_{sk_s} \in \{0,1,2\}) \wedge \neg(S_0, S_1 \subseteq \text{AA.keys}(A_{O_{11}}))$, **return** 0
4. **if** $(\psi_{pk_s} = 3) \wedge (\psi_{sk_s} \notin \{3,4\}) \wedge \neg(S_0, S_1 \subseteq \text{AA.keys}(A_{O_{01}}))$, **return** 0
5. **if** $(\psi_{pk_s} \notin \{3,4\}) \wedge (\psi_{sk_s} = 3) \wedge \neg(S_0, S_1 \subseteq \text{AA.keys}(A_{O_{00}}))$, **return** 0
6. **if** $(\psi_{pk_s} = 3) \wedge (\psi_{sk_s} = 3) \wedge \neg(S_0, S_1 \subseteq \text{AA.keys}(A_{O_{10}}))$, **return** 0
7. **if** $(\psi_{pk_r} \in \{0,1\}) \wedge (\psi_{sk_r} \in \{0,1\}) \wedge \neg(R_0, R_1 \subseteq A*_O)$, **return** 0
8. **if** $(\psi_{pk_r} \in \{0,1,2\}) \wedge (\psi_{sk_r} \in \{0,1,2\}) \wedge \neg(R_0, R_1 \subseteq \text{AA.keys}(A_{O_{11}}))$, **return** 0
9. **if** $(\psi_{pk_r} = 3) \wedge (\psi_{sk_r} \notin \{3,4\}) \wedge \neg(R_0, R_1 \subseteq \text{AA.keys}(A_{O_{01}}))$, **return** 0
10. **if** $(\psi_{pk_r} \notin \{3,4\}) \wedge (\psi_{sk_r} = 3) \wedge \neg(R_0, R_1 \subseteq \text{AA.keys}(A_{O_{00}}))$, **return** 0
11. **if** $(\psi_{pk_r} = 3) \wedge (\psi_{sk_r} = 3) \wedge \neg(R_0, R_1 \subseteq \text{AA.keys}(A_{O_{10}}))$, **return** 0
12. **if** $(\psi_m \in \{0,1\}) \wedge \neg(m \in D*_O)$, **return** 0
13. **return** 1

Fig. 6. Additional helper functions for the Anonymity game

```
Exp^{Anonymity}_{π, A, O, ω, ψ, δ, α, β}(λ)
```

1. $A_O, A_{O_{11}}, A_{O_{10}}, A_{O_{01}}, A_{O_{00}}, T_O, T'_O \leftarrow \text{AA.Init}();\ A*_O, T*_O, D*_O \leftarrow ()$
2. $U \leftarrow \emptyset;\ M_O \leftarrow \{\};\ f_O \leftarrow 0$ ▷ Initialise variables
3. $(p_O, r, s) \leftarrow \text{SetupState}_{\pi, O, A}(\lambda, \gamma)\ \langle p_O \neq \bot \rangle$ ▷ State initialisation
4. $(p_O, (S_0, S_1, R_0, R_1, V_{old_0}, V_{new_0}, V_{old_1}, V_{new_1}, T, R_m, m_0, m_1, t_0, t_1, \rho_0, \rho_1), s) \leftarrow$
   $\text{RunAdversary}_{\pi, O}(A_2, p_O, (\emptyset), r, s, \delta)\ \langle p_O \neq \bot \rangle$ ▷ Adversary inputs
5. $(\omega_s, \omega_r, \omega_v, \omega_m) \leftarrow \omega$ ▷ Testing entities
6. $(\psi_{pk_s}, \psi_{sk_s}, \psi_{pk_r}, \psi_{sk_r}, \psi_v, \psi_m, \psi_t) \leftarrow \psi$ ▷ Adversary capabilities
7. **if** $\neg\{\text{CheckAdvConditions}(\omega, \psi, S_0, S_1, R_0, R_1, V_{old_0}, V_{new_0}, V_{old_1}, V_{new_1}, m_0, m_1, A*_O,$
   $A_{O_{jk}}, D_O)\}$ **then return** 0   ▷ Check adversarial conditions on inputs
8. **if** $(\psi_t = 5)$ **then**
9. $(t_{p_0}, t_{s_0}) \leftarrow t_0$ $\langle \text{IsMintable}_\pi(\{t_{p_0}\} \cup T, p_O)^\beta \rangle$
10. $(t_{p_1}, t_{s_1}) \leftarrow t_1$ $\langle \text{IsMintable}_\pi(\{t_{p_1}\} \cup T, p_O)^\beta \rangle$
11. **else**
12. $t_{p_0} \leftarrow O_{txn}(R_0, V_{new_0}, S_0, V_{old_0}, m_0, \psi, p_O, \rho_0)$ $\langle \text{IsMintable}_\pi(\{t_{p_0}\} \cup T, p_O, \rho_1)^\beta \rangle$
13. $t_{p_1} \leftarrow O_{txn}(R_{\omega_r}, V_{new_{\omega_v}}, S_{\omega_s}, V_{old_{\omega_v}}, m_{\omega_m}, \psi, p_O)$ $\langle \text{IsMintable}_\pi(\{t_{p_1}\} \cup T, p_O)^\beta \rangle$
14. $b \xleftarrow{\$} \{0,1\}$ ▷ Challenger picks a bit
15. $(p_1, V_x) \leftarrow \text{Mint}_\pi(\{t_{p_b}\} \cup T, R_m, p_O)$
16. $U \leftarrow \text{RevealData}(t_{p_b}, \psi, \omega, A*_O, T*_O, T_O, p_1)$
17. $(\cdot, b', \cdot) \leftarrow \text{RunAdversary}_{\pi, O}(A_3, p_1, (U), r, s, \delta)\ \langle \beta \vee (f_O \neq 1) \rangle$
18. **return** $b' \overset{?}{=} b$

Fig. 7. Anonymity Game

In this game, we use '$\langle condition \rangle$' notation after an action to check if a valid outcome is obtained and if the condition inside the brackets is false, then the game terminates and the adversary loses the game. Upon submission of valid inputs, the adversary continues to evolve the current state through appropriate oracle queries. If $\psi_t \neq 5$, then the challenger creates two transactions (Fig. 7 - lines 12 and 13), or chooses the transactions provided by the adversary otherwise. Out of the two transactions, only one transaction is minted based on the chosen bit b (line 15). Failed mint operations are not allowed except when $\beta = 1$ and to check this condition, the notation '$\langle \texttt{IsMintable}_\pi(\{t_{p_1}\} \cup T, p_\mathcal{O})^{\bar\beta} \rangle$' is used. In this case, when $\beta = 0$, $\bar\beta = 1$ and the game continues if $\texttt{IsMintable}() = 1$. When $\beta = 1$, $\bar\beta = 0$ and hence $\texttt{IsMintable}()^0 = 1$ always and hence the game proceeds. After revealing the relevant data (line 16), the adversary is not allowed to create any transactions involving revealed addresses. The adversary wins the game if the chosen bit is guessed correctly, subject to the condition $\beta \vee (f_\mathcal{O} \neq 1)$.

A.2   Anonymity Notions

We summarise some useful anonymity notions with their corresponding parameter vectors in Table 4 below. Formal definitions of these notions are given in [5].

Table 4. Some useful anonymity notions

Goal	Adversarial knowledge	Adversarial power	Parameter vector
ALL-IND	FULL	FULL	$(1_s 1_r 1_v 1_m)_\omega\text{-}((4,4)_s,(4,4)_r,3_v,3_m,5_t)_\psi\text{-}(2_\delta,3_\alpha,1_\beta)$
ALL-IND	NILMT-PUBSR	ACTIVE	$(1_s 1_r 1_v 1_m)_\omega\text{-}((3,0)_s,(3,0)_r,3_v,0_m,0_t)_\psi\text{-}(2_\delta,3_\alpha,0_\beta)$
ALL-IND	PUBSRT	ACTIVE	$(1_s 1_r 1_v 1_m)_\omega\text{-}((3,0)_s,(3,0)_r,3_v,3_m,1_t)_\psi\text{-}(2_\delta,3_\alpha,0_\beta)$
S-IND	PUBST	ACTIVE	$(1_s 0_r 0_v 0_m)_\omega\text{-}((3,0)_s,(4,4)_r,3_v,3_m,1_t)_\psi\text{-}(2_\delta,3_\alpha,0_\beta)$
S-IND	NILMT-PUBS	ACTIVE	$(1_s 0_r 0_v 0_m)_\omega\text{-}((3,0)_s,(4,4)_r,3_v,0_m,0_t)_\psi\text{-}(2_\delta,3_\alpha,0_\beta)$
S-ULK	NILS-PUBT	ACTIVE	$(1_s 0_r 0_v 0_m)_\omega\text{-}((3,0)_s,(4,4)_r,3_v,3_m,1_t)_\psi\text{-}(2_\delta,3_\alpha,0_\beta)$
R-IND	PUBRT	ACTIVE	$(0_s 1_r 0_v 0_m)_\omega\text{-}((4,4)_s,(3,0)_r,3_v,3_m,1_t)_\psi\text{-}(2_\delta,3_\alpha,0_\beta)$
R-ULK	NILR-PUBT	ACTIVE	$(0_s 1_r 0_v 0_m)_\omega\text{-}((4,4)_s,(0,0)_r,3_v,3_m,1_t)_\psi\text{-}(2_\delta,3_\alpha,0_\beta)$
V-IND	PUBSRT	ACTIVE	$(0_s 0_r 1_v 0_m)_\omega\text{-}((3,0)_s,(3,0)_r,3_v,3_m,1_t)_\psi\text{-}(2_\delta,3_\alpha,0_\beta)$
V-ULK	NILV-PUBSRT	FULL	$(0_s 0_r 1_v 0_m)_\omega\text{-}((3,0)_s,(3,0)_r,0_v,3_m,1_t)_\psi\text{-}(2_\delta,3_\alpha,1_\beta)$
NIL-IND	NIL	VIEW	$(0_s 0_r 0_v 0_m)_\omega\text{-}((0,0)_s,(0,0)_r,0_v,0_m,0_t)_\psi\text{-}(1_\delta,1_\alpha,0_\beta)$
NIL-IND	NIL	NIL	$(0_s 0_r 0_v 0_m)_\omega\ ((0,0)_s,(0,0)_r,0_v,0_m,0_t)_\psi\text{-}(0_\delta,0_\alpha,0_\beta)$

References

1. Introduction to mimblewimble and grin (August 2020). https://github.com/mimblewimble/grin/blob/master/doc/intro.md
2. Alonso, K.M.: Zero to Monero (2020). https://src.getmonero.org/library/Zero-to-Monero-1-0-0.pdf
3. Alsalami, N., Zhang, B.: SoK: A systematic study of anonymity in cryptocurrencies. In: 2019 IEEE Conference on Dependable and Secure Computing (DSC) (2019)

4. Amarasinghe, N., Boyen, X., McKague, M.: A survey of anonymity of cryptocurrencies. In: Proceedings of the Australasian Computer Science Week Multiconference, pp. 2:1–2:10. ACSW 2019, ACM, New York (2019)

5. Amarasinghe, N., Boyen, X., McKague, M.: The cryptographic complexity of anonymous coins: A systematic exploration. Cryptology ePrint Archive, Report 2021/036 (2021). https://eprint.iacr.org/2021/036

6. Androulaki, E., Karame, G.O., Roeschlin, M., Scherer, T., Capkun, S.: Evaluating user privacy in bitcoin. In: Sadeghi, A.-R. (ed.) FC 2013. LNCS, vol. 7859, pp. 34–51. Springer, Heidelberg (2013). https://doi.org/10.1007/978-3-642-39884-1_4

7. Biryukov, A., Tikhomirov, S.: Deanonymization and linkability of cryptocurrency transactions based on network analysis. In: 2019 IEEE European Symposium on Security and Privacy (EuroS P), pp. 172–184 (June 2019)

8. Cachin, C., De Caro, A., Moreno-Sanchez, P., Tackmann, B., Vukolic, M.: The transaction graph for modeling blockchain semantics. IACR Cryptology ePrint Archive **2017**, 1070 (2017)

9. Conti, M., Kumar, S., Lal, C., Ruj, S.: A survey on security and privacy issues of bitcoin. IEEE Commun. Surv. Tutorials **20**(4), 3416–3452 (2018)

10. Díaz, C., Seys, S., Claessens, J., Preneel, B.: Towards measuring anonymity. In: Dingledine, R., Syverson, P. (eds.) PET 2002. LNCS, vol. 2482, pp. 54–68. Springer, Heidelberg (2003). https://doi.org/10.1007/3-540-36467-6_5

11. Fuchsbauer, G., Orrù, M., Seurin, Y.: Aggregate cash systems: a cryptographic investigation of mimblewimble. In: EUROCRYPT (2019)

12. Hopwood, D., Bowe, S., Hornby, T., Wilcox, N.: Zcash protocol specification version 2020.1.3. Technical Report, Electric Coin Company (2020)

13. Jedusor, T.E.: Mimblewimble (2017). https://scalingbitcoin.org/papers/mimblewimble.txt

14. Kappos, G., Yousaf, H., Maller, M., Meiklejohn, S.: An empirical analysis of anonymity in zcash. CoRR abs/1805.03180 (2018)

15. Khalilov, M.C.K., Levi, A.: A survey on anonymity and privacy in bitcoin-like digital cash systems. IEEE Commun. Surv. Tutorials **3**, 1 (2018)

16. Kumar, A., Fischer, C., Tople, S., Saxena, P.: A traceability analysis of monero's blockchain. In: Foley, S.N., Gollmann, D., Snekkenes, E. (eds.) ESORICS 2017. LNCS, vol. 10493, pp. 153–173. Springer, Cham (2017). https://doi.org/10.1007/978-3-319-66399-9_9

17. Meiklejohn, S., et al.: A fistful of bitcoins: characterizing payments among men with no names. In: Proceedings of the 2013 Conference on Internet Measurement Conference, pp. 127–140. IMC 2013, ACM, New York (2013)

18. Miller, A., Moeser, M., Lee, K., Narayanan, A.: An empirical analysis of linkability in the monero blockchain. arXiv preprint arXiv:1704.04299 (2017)

19. Morris, L.: Anonymity Analysis of Cryptocurrencies. Ph.D. thesis, Rochester Institute of Techology (2015)

20. Möser, M., et al.: Narayanan, A., et al.: An empirical analysis of traceability in the monero blockchain. Proceedings on Privacy Enhancing Technologies (3) (2018)

21. Ober, M., Katzenbeisser, S., Hamacher, K.: Structure and anonymity of the bitcoin transaction graph. Future Internet **5**(2), 237–250 (2013). copyright - Copyright MDPI AG 2013; Last updated - 2014-07-30

22. Pfitzmann, A., Hansen, M.: A terminology for talking about privacy by data minimization: Anonymity, unlinkability, undetectability, unobservability, pseudonymity, and identity management. http://dud.inf.tu-dresden.de/literatur/Anon_Terminology_v0.34.pdf (August 2010), v0.34

23. Poelstra, A.: Mimblewimble (2016). https://scalingbitcoin.org/he/papers/mimblewimble.pdf
24. Quesnelle, J.: An Analysis of Anonymity in the Zcash Cryptocurrency. Master's thesis, University of Michigan-Dearborn (2018)
25. Reid, F., Harrigan, M.: An analysis of anonymity in the bitcoin system. In: Altshuler, Y., Elovici, Y., Cremers, A., Aharony, N., Pentland, A. (eds.) Security and Privacy in Social Networks, pp. 197–223. Springer, New York (2013). https://doi.org/10.1007/978-1-4614-4139-7_10
26. Ron, D., Shamir, A.: Quantitative analysis of the full bitcoin transaction graph. In: Sadeghi, A.-R. (ed.) FC 2013. LNCS, vol. 7859, pp. 6–24. Springer, Heidelberg (2013). https://doi.org/10.1007/978-3-642-39884-1_2
27. Ruffing, T., Moreno-Sanchez, P., et al.: ValueShuffle: mixing confidential transactions for comprehensive transaction privacy in bitcoin. In: Brenner, M. (ed.) FC 2017. LNCS, vol. 10323, pp. 133–154. Springer, Cham (2017). https://doi.org/10.1007/978-3-319-70278-0_8
28. Spagnuolo, M., Maggi, F., Zanero, S.: BitIodine: extracting intelligence from the bitcoin network. In: Christin, N., Safavi-Naini, R. (eds.) FC 2014. LNCS, vol. 8437, pp. 457–468. Springer, Heidelberg (2014). https://doi.org/10.1007/978-3-662-45472-5_29
29. Sweeney, L.: k-anonymity: a model for protecting privacy. Int. J. Uncertainty Fuzziness Knowl.-Based Syst. **10**(05), 557–570 (2002)
30. Tsukada, Y., Mano, K., Sakurada, H., Kawabe, Y.: Anonymity, privacy, onymity, and identity: a modal logic approach. In: 2009 International Conference on Computational Science and Engineering, vol. 3, pp. 42–51 (August 2009)
31. Van Saberhagen, N.: Cryptonote v 2. 0 (2013). https://cryptonote.org/whitepaper.pdf
32. Wijaya, D.A., Liu, J., Steinfeld, R., Liu, D., Yuen, T.H.: Anonymity reduction attacks to monero. In: Guo, F., Huang, X., Yung, M. (eds.) Inscrypt 2018. LNCS, vol. 11449, pp. 86–100. Springer, Cham (2019). https://doi.org/10.1007/978-3-030-14234-6_5
33. Wijaya, D.A., Liu, J.K., Steinfeld, R., Sun, S.-F., Huang, X.: Anonymizing bitcoin transaction. In: Bao, F., Chen, L., Deng, R.H., Wang, G. (eds.) ISPEC 2016. LNCS, vol. 10060, pp. 271–283. Springer, Cham (2016). https://doi.org/10.1007/978-3-319-49151-6_19
34. Zhang, Z., Li, W., Liu, H., Liu, J.: A refined analysis of zcash anonymity. IEEE Access **8**, 31845–31853 (2020)

Secure Multi-party Computation

Improving the Efficiency of AES Protocols in Multi-Party Computation

F. Betül Durak[✉] and Jorge Guajardo[✉]

Robert Bosch LLC — Research and Technology Center, Pittsburgh, USA
{betul.durak,jorge.guajardomerchan}@us.bosch.com

Abstract. The AES is a standardized symmetric block cipher, whose efficiency has been studied widely. This has resulted in very efficient software and hardware implementations of AES, which allow for the encryption of millions of blocks per second. However, AES was not designed with Multi-Party Computation in mind. Though there are many real-world applications of MPC requiring block ciphers, standard ciphers such as AES are far from being efficient for real-world applications of MPC. In this paper, we study how to improve the efficiency of AES modes of operation in the actively secure MPC setting with dishonest majority with precomputation as put forward by SPDZ and its variants. We propose two new protocols. The first one is aimed at improving the efficiency of the Sbox computation, the only non-linear layer in the AES. In particular, we use an (equally secure) inverse Sbox computation instead of the standard forward Sbox. The second protocol improves on the overall AES computation by optimizing the off-line phase and computing special (Beaver)-tuples specifically designed to improve the performance of the Sbox AES computation. Our proposals, result in an overall improvement of 3.33. The on-line phase of the protocols is fully implemented using the MP-SPDZ framework.

1 Introduction

Secure multi-party computation (MPC) was introduced in the seminal work of Yao [26] and follow up work [14,24] more than 30 years ago. MPC has been far from being practical until recently when it has been implemented and tested in various frameworks[1] [5,10,17,22,25]. MPC can come with various flavors in terms of security where we have actively, covertly, and passively secure protocols; in terms of underlying techniques such as garbled circuits or secret sharing; or in terms of adversarial settings such as honest or dishonest majority. Designing protocols which are actively secure in the dishonest majority setting and also efficient remains a challenge. In this work, we will focus on one significant MPC protocol: SPDZ [13]. SPDZ is based on linear secret sharing and achieves active security in the dishonest majority setting. In practice, we use the MP-SPDZ framework [17] as it is commonly used for benchmarks.

---

[1] See [16] for comparisons of various implementations.

© International Financial Cryptography Association 2021
N. Borisov and C. Diaz (Eds.): FC 2021, LNCS 12674, pp. 229–248, 2021.
https://doi.org/10.1007/978-3-662-64322-8_11

Advanced Encryption Standard (AES) and Modes of Operation. The AES is a symmetric-key block cipher that was invented and standardized two decades ago [1]. It is a block cipher accepting 128-bit inputs and outputs using 128-bit, 192-bit and 256-bit keys corresponding to 10, 12 and 14 rounds variants, respectively. All rounds except for the last one include four different layers: (i) a non-linear substitution layer SubBytes or AES Sbox, which is applied to each of the 16 bytes in the AES state each round. This is followed by (ii) the ShiftRows, (iii) the MixColumns, and (iv) the AddRoundKey layers, all of which are linear operations. Before the first round, an AddRoundKey layer is applied. The last round of all variants excludes the MixColumns layer.

In practice, any block cipher such as AES is used in a mode of operation such as CTR, AES-GCM, AES-CCM, etc. We will refer to the operation of encrypting one data block with AES as the forward AES (or forward cipher) computation and similarly, we will refer to the AES "decryption" operation as the inverse AES (or inverse cipher) operation. We refer to encryption and decryption when we talk about mode of operations to encrypt/decrypt data that is longer than a single AES block. We observe that depending on the mode of operation, it is possible to use the forward AES for both encryption and decryption operations (e.g., CTR mode). Alternatively, certain modes of operation require the use of both forward AES for encryption and the inverse AES for decryption (e.g. CBC mode). Notice that the inverse AES requires inverting not only the order of the layers but also the operation in each layer itself. In particular, the SubBytes layer reverses the order of operations given in the Sbox computation; inverting ShiftRows shifts rows to the left instead of shifting them to the right; the inverse of MixColumns uses a different matrix than forward AES to multiply the columns in inverse AES. Finally, the round keys that are added to the internal states need to be read in reverse order from the list of expanded keys.

The AES security and efficiency has been widely studied. As a result, there are many fast standard AES software and hardware implementations in the literature. However, AES was not designed to be efficient in MPC. Among the four AES layers, only the SubBytes layer performs non-linear operations. Since in the MPC setting, the cost for the linear layers is negligible because of their linearity (i.e. they can be implemented without interaction), the focus of this paper is on optimizing the Sbox MPC implementation.

Why an MPC Implementations of AES? Since the main point of MPC is to "distribute" trust among participants of the protocol, one very significant application of MPC is to protect long term secret keys. This allows participants in a computation to manage their secrets without requiring hardware security modules (which tend to be expensive and hard to manage and deploy) or without relying on off-the-shelf secure environments (which have been demonstrated to suffer from major vulnerabilities rendering them unsuitable to keep the confidentiality and integrity cryptographic secret keys [20,21]). In this setting, the secret key is distributed among participants by splitting it into shares such that only a qualified subset of participants can encrypt or decrypt data by running the MPC protocol without ever revealing the key. In this work, we assume that the encryption/decryption mechanism will be the AES.

1.1   Our Contributions

In this work, we study new optimization techniques for MPC evaluation of AES following the SPDZ model [13], which itself is based on the offline/online computation model (proposed by Beaver [4]) combined with information theoretic MACs to achieve security against active malicious adversaries.

The main contribution of our work starts with the observation that in the MPC setting, implementing the inverse AES can be made faster than the forward AES. This is due to the fact that the inverse SubBytes can be modified to require less operations than the (forward) SubBytes operation, while keeping the same functionality and security. We start our study by looking into two different approaches to compute AES: the method in [11], which we denote as AES-BD and it uses bit decomposition to implement the AES Sbox computation and a method called as AES-LT which implements a table look up described in [18]. We choose to work with AES-BD due to the very costly storage requirements of the AES-LT method. More specifically, in AES-LT, *each Sbox* operation requires the pre-computation of a large masked table. We compare the performance of these two methods in Sect. 4. We, then, focus on the implementation of a single Sbox in AES-BD in MP-SPDZ framework to compute the forward AES encryption in $GF(2^{40})$ [11]. Our results indicate that we can achieve about a 50% penalty in latency compared to the AES-LT approach of [18] but our approach requires 20 times less storage. The performance achieved is also about the same as the best semi-honest implementation presented in [8] but we achieve active security.

Our high-level idea relies on the following observations: AES-BD follows a specific order of operations where the protocol has to perform one bit decomposition on the secret input; 7 linear transformations which are all local computations; six secret multiplications; one more bit decomposition; and finally an Sbox affine transformation. Two bit decompositions are necessary because the operations after the first secret bit decomposition results with composition of secret values due to the multiplications. In order to apply the last affine forward Sbox transformation, AES-BD performs a second secret bit decomposition. Secret bit decomposition in MPC is a costly operation. Namely, it requires random values from the offline phase and communication to reveal masked values (as described in detail in Appendix 6.2). Thus, we wish to avoid excessive usage of it. Our specific idea is to avoid the need for the second secret bit decomposition to save communication and merge all the local computations into a single operation. This results in a factor of four performance improvement as well as it allowed us to save communication/storage. We note that this optimization requires no changes to the offline phase of SPDZ protocol. We can indeed take the MP-SPDZ framework as it is and integrate our protocol.

Next, we explore offline phase pre-computation that result in additional online performance improvement. We exploited the fact that bit decomposition in $GF(2^{40})$ is a linear operation and that we can pre-compute *specialized* tuples during the SPDZ offline phase. Observe that the idea of using specialized tuples has been previously described [7,12,13,23] but not in the context of improving the computation of the AES in MPC. Following this approach, we can pre-compute all the secret bit decompositions in the offline phase and reduce the number of full secret multiplications to 2 instead of 6 as forward AES requires. Strictly speaking, all linear functions can be computed by masking and revealing operations. We implemented both of our optimizations and verified the expected theoretical gains for the storage and communication as well as the performance. In particular, we save 33.6 KBytes of storage (resulting in 61% improvement) and 10.17 KBytes of communication (resulting in 55% reduction in communication overhead) compared to the implementation in [11]. The performance improves from 5 msec to 1.5 msec with the proposed protocols resulting in a factor of 3.33 improvement.

Given the fact that the inverse AES operation is more efficient to implement in the MPC setting and that parallelisable and highly efficient modes such as CTR, OFB or CFB only use the forward-AES for encryption and decryption, we also propose to implement such modes of operation with the inverse AES in both encryption and decryption operations, instead. For example, we could implement CTR mode of operation where both encryption and decryption are implemented with only inverse AES for each block. Note that in terms of security, the forward and inverse AES are equivalent [1, Section 5.3.5] [3]. Thus, having a mode of operation encrypting blocks with inverse AES is as secure as the mode of operation encrypting blocks with forward AES.

The remainder of this paper is organized as follows. In Sect. 3, we discuss in detail the performance of previous AES implementations in the active malicious adversary setting using SPDZ as previously proposed in [11,18]. Our new protocols and optimizations are described in Sect. 4. We thoroughly compare our implementation requirements in Sect. 4.5. Here we also include in our analysis implementations in the semi-honest setting [2,8]. To the best of our knowledge the mentioned implementations constitute the fastest and most efficient implementations of AES in each of their corresponding security MPC settings.

2   Preliminaries

Notation. We will denote the secret sharing of a value x as $[\![x]\!]$. It is understood that for n parties $P_i, i = 1 \ldots n$, $x = \sum_i x_i$ where x_i are random shares of x. We will refer to the share x_i also as $[\![x]\!]_i$, so it is also valid to write $x = \sum_i [\![x]\!]_i$.

The SPDZ Protocol. A secret sharing scheme allows a secret value to be shared and computed securely among multiple untrusted parties. We will denote the secret sharing of a value x as $[\![x]\!]$. It is understood that for n parties S_i, where $i = 1 \ldots n$, $x = \sum_i x_i$ where x_i are random shares of x. We use SPDZ which uses linear secret sharing with information theoretic MACs as proposed [12,13]. SPDZ achieves security against active malicious adversaries. In particular, it allows for active adversaries with dishonest majority without abort. It guarantees that the if the protocol terminates then the output received by the honest parties is correct, except with negligible probability. In this paper (as in most previous work), this probability is set to 2^{-40}.

Additive Homomorphic Properties. SPDZ secret sharing offers additive homomorphic properties as follows. Given additive shares $[\![s_1]\!]$ and $[\![s_2]\!]$ and $c \in \mathbb{F}_p$, each party can locally compute the additive share of addition and scalar multiplication as $[\![s_1 + s_2]\!] \leftarrow [\![s_1]\!] + [\![s_2]\!]$ and $[\![cs]\!] \leftarrow c[\![s]\!]$.

Authenticated Homomorphic Multiplication in the Online/Offline Model. We recall the authenticated secret sharing in [13], in which each secret s is augmented with an information-theoretic Message Authenticated Code (MAC) computed as αs, where α is a global MAC key owned by the dealer. We denote the authenticated share of a secret s as $\langle \cdot \rangle$, which contains the additive share of s and the additive share of αs as $\langle s \rangle = ([\![s]\!], [\![\alpha s]\!])$, where $[\![\alpha s]\!]$ is created in the same manner as $[\![s]\!]$. The algorithm to create shares uses the homomorphic multiplication protocol with malicious security from [13,19]. In this setting, each party S_i owns a share of the MAC key $[\![\alpha]\!]_i$. The protocols follows the pre-computation model using Beaver multiplication triples [4] of the form (a, b, c) such that $c = a * b$.

Offline Phase. In the offline phase, all parties harness homomorphic encryption (HE) and zero-knowledge (ZK) protocols [13,19] to compute the authenticated share of the Beaver triple and its MAC in such a way that no party learns about (a, b, c) and α. This is achieved in the pre-computation phase using a somewhat homomorphic encryption (SHE) scheme. To this end, each S_i obtains $(\langle a \rangle_i, \langle b \rangle_i, \langle c \rangle_i)$, where $\langle a \rangle_i = ([\![a]\!]_i, [\![\alpha a]\!]_i)$ and similarly $\langle b \rangle_i = ([\![b]\!]_i, [\![\alpha b]\!]_i)$ and $\langle ab \rangle_i = \langle c \rangle_i = ([\![c]\!]_i, [\![\alpha c]\!]_i) = ([\![ab]\!]_i, [\![\alpha ab]\!]_i)$

Online Phase. In the online phase, several protocols are required to perform online computations. For now, we only describe the multiplication protocol. Throughout the paper, we will use a few additional protocols, which we will describe when they are introduced.

Multiplication (without MAC verification). In order to multiply two secret value $[\![u]\!]$ and $[\![v]\!]$ with multiplication triplets $([\![a]\!], [\![b]\!], [\![c]\!])$, each S_i (locally) computes $[\![\epsilon]\!]_i \leftarrow [\![u]\!]_i - [\![a]\!]_i$, and $[\![\rho]\!]_i \leftarrow [\![v]\!]_i - [\![b]\!]_i$. All parties come together to open ϵ and ρ by broadcasting $[\![\epsilon]\!]_i$ and $[\![\rho]\!]_i$. Finally, each S_i (locally) computes $[\![uv]\!]_i \leftarrow [\![c]\!]_i + \epsilon[\![b]\!]_i + \rho[\![a]\!]_i + \epsilon\rho$.

Verifying the MAC of the multiplication. During the multiplication protocol above, the parties also get $[\![\alpha uv]\!]_i \leftarrow [\![\alpha c]\!]_i + \epsilon[\![\alpha b]\!]_i + \rho[\![\alpha b]\!]_i + \epsilon\rho$. For all (partially) open values they perform a MACCheck protocol [12, Fig. 10] which requires multiple commitment rounds to guarantee synchronicity. In particular, without the commitments, it might be possible that a malicious party broadcasts different σ_i values to different parties in the protocol in such a way that the addition of the σ_i values still is equal to zero even if some of them are incorrect. Full multiplication is the combination of these two protocols.

MPC Framework for AES: MP-SPDZ allows us to implement functions in binary finite field (such as $GF(2^{40})$) as well as prime finite field (as in $\mathbb{Z}_p$). Standard AES arithmetic is defined with Galois field $GF(2^8)$ with a reduction modulus. To satisfy statistical security, [18] requires computations in the binary finite field $\mathsf{GF}(2^{40})$. Therefore, the AES implementation in Keller[2] et al. [18] is also over $\mathsf{GF}(2^{40})$ instead of $\mathsf{GF}(2^8)$. This means that MP-SPDZ needs to define the field $\mathsf{GF}(2^{40})$ with a reduction modulus and an isomorphic embedding from $\mathsf{GF}(2^8)$ elements to $\mathsf{GF}(2^{40})$ elements (these elements form a sub-field of size 2^8). As detailed in [18], the reduction modulus to define $\mathsf{GF}(2^{40})$ is $Q(X) = X^{40} + X^{20} + X^{15} + X^{10} + 1$ and the embedding of X is defined with $X^5 + 1$.

3 Analysis of Previous MPC AES Implementations

In this sections, we will discuss two previous methods to implement AES Sboxes in MPC presented in [11,18]. Reference [11] uses arithmetic circuits (denoted by AES-BD) by taking advantage of the algebraic presentation of the AES Sbox, which uses multiplications and linear transformations. Keller et al. [18] uses table look-ups (denoted by AES-LT). This makes computations very fast but requires pre-computed data during the offline phase. This, in turn, results in additional communication and storage requirements.

Implementation Environment. We have implemented all (online) protocols presented in this paper as well as estimated their offline phase complexity. All numbers reported have been obtained by running our experiments on a standard laptop with an Intel i5-8350U 1.70 GHz processor and 24 GB of RAM. We have also implemented the protocols in [11,18] to be able to provide a meaningful comparison and verify that our estimates are accurate.

Estimates and Complexity. For the Sbox computations, we consider the operations performed during the offline and online phases, separately. For the *offline* phase, we estimate the communication complexity required to generate the tuples needed in the online phase. The online phase requires all the precomputed data to be available to the participants before computation. This communicated data can be stored by each player for later use or used on-the-fly[3]. For the *online* phase, there are three aspects to consider: (i)computation complexity; (ii) storage of the precomputed data from the offline phase consumed during the online phase; and (iii) the communication complexity, which we separate into two parts: amount of data exchange among the parties and the number of rounds. We observe that this distinction might be useful in further optimizations as, in practice, transmitting 1 MByte of data in one round trip will be much faster than transmitting 10 KBytes of data with 100 rounds, thus resulting in potential performance improvements. In our analysis, we report the storage, round trip and

---

[2] This approach has been implemented in the MP-SPDZ library, which we have used for our implementation.

[3] If stored, then it requires storage per player and the amount is equal to the amount transferred during the computation. If the protocol is "on-the-fly", then no storage is required but the pre-computed data has to be available realtime and on request when needed. In practice, it is likely that storage will be required since the offline phase is much slower than the online phase.

communication complexity for full AES by multiplying the complexities for a single Sbox by 160 (16 Sbox computations per round and 10 rounds).

3.1 Complexity of Available SPDZ Modules for AES

As previously mentioned, to achieve security, SPDZ embeds $GF(2^8)$ into $GF(2^{40})$. Thus, we will apply the embedding to the initial states and reverse the embedding after computations. Both embedding and reverse embedding require bit decomposition and it has to be done for full AES regardless of the method used for Sbox computations. Depending on the method used, the SPDZ AES S-box computation requires certain operations which can be classified into 3 different types: reveal used to make a secret value publicly available, bit decomposition of embedded value (denoted by BDEmbed), and multiplication of two secret values (denoted by mult). In the following, we describe these operations in more detail and analyze their communication and storage requirements. Table 1 summarizes these complexities and the actual measured latency and communication complexity in our implementation.

1. reveal: uses no stored data. In theory, revealing one secret $GF(2^{40})$ element, requires a round trip communication of 10 bytes.
2. BDEmbed: uses a tuple $(\langle a \rangle, \langle a_1 \rangle, \ldots, \langle a_7 \rangle)$ where $\langle a_i \rangle$'s are the decomposed bits of a random secret value[4] a. Each bit $\langle a_i \rangle$ needs 40 bits storage, therefore the tuple has $8 \cdot 2 \cdot 40$ bits $= 80$ bytes (as each bit requires a 40-bit MAC). Communication used to reveal a $GF(2^{40})$ element which is 10 bytes per operation.
3. mult: implements multiplication using Beaver triples. Hence, the storage is a triplet of data, i.e. 30 bytes (3*80 bit) and communication is used to reveal two elements, which amounts to 20 bytes per player, per operation.

Table 1. Estimated storage (i.e. data required from the **offline phase**) and communication requirements for three functions (1a) and actual running time and communication requirements in practice averaged over 100 runs (1b). The reported figures are per player.

Operation	storage (bytes)	comm. (bytes)
reveal	0	10
BDEmbed	80	10
mult	30	20

(a) Estimated overhead offline phase

Operation	latency (msec)	comm. (bytes)
reveal	0.0015	9.16
BDEmbed	0.0061	9.16
mult	0.0017	17.6

(b) Implementation online phase

---

[4] A more detailed explaination is given in Sect. 4.2.

3.2   AES-BD Arithmetic Circuits [11]

In [11], the Sbox evaluation of $[\![s]\!]$ first computes the inverse $[\![s^{-1}]\!]$ by $[\![s^{254}]\!]$ followed by the AES affine transformation [1]. For the inverse computation of $[\![s]\!]$, AES-BD method observes that: (1) $[\![s^{254}]\!]$ can be computed with an addition chain using the powers of two: $[\![s^{254}]\!] = ([\![s^2]\!] * [\![s^4]\!]) * ([\![s^8]\!] * [\![s^{16}]\!]) * ([\![s^{32}]\!] * [\![s^{64}]\!]) * [\![s^{128}]\!]$ and (2) that exponentiation by powers of two is a linear operation over any binary finite field. Hence, to generate these 7 powers, AES-BD applies 7 linear transformations.

Protocol 1 defines the full version of the Sbox computation on an input $[\![s]\!]$ using AES-BD. In step 1, the bit decomposition is applied to the secret state. Step 2 computes the powers with linear transformations operating on bits. Step 3 computes $[\![s^{254}]\!]$ using 6 multiplications. The output from Step 3 is actually a $\mathsf{GF}(2^{40})$ value even though the input is the bit decomposition of $[\![s]\!]$. To continue the operations as described in [1], another bit decomposition is required. Step 4 applies the second bit decomposition, the result of which is used in the affine transformation in Step 5. The output from Step 5 is a bit decomposed value (compliant with the AES standard [1]), thus, we compose it back to a $\mathsf{GF}(2^{40})$ element. Note that all the steps include computations in $\mathsf{GF}(2^{40})$.

Input: A secret input as state $\langle s \rangle \in \mathsf{GF}(2^{40})$
Output: Computes $\langle \mathsf{Sbox}(s) \rangle$
1: Apply bit decomposition on $\langle s \rangle = [\langle s_0 \rangle, \langle s_1 \rangle, \cdots, \langle s_7 \rangle]$
2: Compute $\{\langle s^2 \rangle, \ldots, \langle s^{128} \rangle\}$ with linear transformation using $[\langle s_0 \rangle, \langle s_1 \rangle, \cdots, \langle s_7 \rangle]$
3: Compute $\langle y \rangle = \langle s^{254} \rangle = (((\langle s^2 \rangle * \langle s^4 \rangle) * (\langle s^8 \rangle * \langle s^{16} \rangle)) * ((\langle s^{32} \rangle * \langle s^{64} \rangle) * \langle s^{128} \rangle))$
4: Apply bit decomposition on $\langle y \rangle$ as $[\langle y_0 \rangle, \langle y_1 \rangle, \cdots, \langle y_7 \rangle]$
5: Apply Sbox affine transformation to compute the output bits $[\langle x_0 \rangle, \langle x_1 \rangle, \cdots, \langle x_7 \rangle]$
6: Compose $\langle x \rangle$ from its bits
7: **return** $\langle x \rangle$

Protocol 1: One Sbox computation of forward AES-BD method

Offline Phase. We need to generate 16 random bits and 6 triplets for one Sbox. This requires 2560 random bits and 960 triplets for the full AES.

Online Phase. The complexity of the online phase are as follows:

1. **Storage:** tuples are required for the multiplication and bit decomposition operations. Since there are 6 multiplications per Sbox, we store 6*30 bytes. Moreover, we need to store 160 bytes due to the two bit decomposition (see Table 1). Thus, for a single Sbox, the protocol stores 340 bytes. For the full AES, it stores 54.4 Kbytes per player.

2. **Round Trip:** each Sbox operation requires 5 round-trips. Thus, the full AES block requires 800 round-trips.

3. **Communication:** Among the 5 round-trips, two of them consume 10 bytes each and the remaining ones require 120 bytes ($120 = 20*3 + 20*2 + 20*1$). In total, 140 bytes communication per Sbox. For the full AES, data communication is $140*160$ bytes = 20.8 KBytes.

In Appendix 6.1, the look-up table method AES-LT [18] is described. Its performance is compared with AES-BD in Table 2.

4   AES Decryption in MPC

In this section, we describe our core ideas and the protocols that we propose as a new mode of operation. The final optimized protocol for the Sbox computation is the result of several improvements which we describe next as different protocols.

4.1   Optimized **AES-BD** for Inverse AES

Protocol 2 explains the inverse Sbox computation in inverse AES. In Step 1, we apply the bit decomposition on the embedded input state for once and all. This is important to compute the inverse affine transformation as operated in Step 2. The output from Step 2 is still the bit decomposed values, thus we can compute the powers of the state in Step 3 by using 7 linear transformations. The output from Step 3 are now composed values in $GF(2^{40})$. Therefore, to compute the 254th power (i.e. the inverse of the secret state), we apply 6 (secret by secret) multiplications from the output of Step 3 without applying another bit decomposition. This saves 1 bit decomposition operation.

Input: A secret input state $\langle x \rangle \in GF(2^{40})$
Output: Computes $\langle Sbox^{-1}(x) \rangle$
 1: Apply bit decomposition on $\langle x \rangle = [\langle x_0 \rangle, \langle x_1 \rangle, \cdots, \langle x_7 \rangle]$
 2: Apply inverse Sbox affine transformation to compute the output bits $[\langle s_0 \rangle, \langle s_1 \rangle, \cdots, \langle s_7 \rangle]$
    (that forms $\langle s \rangle$) from the bits of $\langle x \rangle$
 3: Compute $\{\langle s^2 \rangle, \ldots, \langle s^{128} \rangle\}$ with linear transformation using $[\langle s_0 \rangle, \langle s_1 \rangle, \cdots, \langle s_7 \rangle]$
 4: Compute $\langle b \rangle = \langle s^{254} \rangle = (((\langle s^2 \rangle * \langle s^4 \rangle) * (\langle s^8 \rangle * \langle s^{16} \rangle))) * (((\langle s^{32} \rangle * \langle s^{64} \rangle) * \langle s^{128} \rangle))$
 5: **return** $\langle b \rangle$

Protocol 2: Single Sbox computation of inverse AES-BD method

The difference between Protocol 1 and Protocol 2 comes from the fact that when we reversed the order of computations, we can do them with one single bit decomposition at the beginning in Protocol 2 (Step 1). In forward AES, we first compute the inverse of the input (Step 3 in Protocol 1) which is a composed value. Therefore, we have to apply one more bit decomposition (Step 4 in Protocol 1) to compute the forward Sbox affine transformation. Therefore, in inverse AES we save 1.6 KBytes of data as well as one bit decomposition operation.

Next, we observe that linear operations can be integrated together to improve the computational complexity further. Indeed, Protocol 2 integrates several steps. More specifically, we integrate the computations in Step 2 and 3 into a set of pre-computed variables. We generate these pre-computed values once for all Sbox computations and we do the multiplication (given in Step 4) with this pre-computed values by skipping Step 2 and 3. The reason this is possible is that Steps 2 and 3 are the affine and linear transformations which operate one after another. This gives us a significant advantage in terms of computational complexity, which we further detail in the next section.

4.2   Performance Optimization of Protocol 2

Sbox in $\mathsf{GF}(2^8)$*:* For a secret state $[\![s]\!]$, the Sbox of this state is computed as $\mathsf{Sbox}([\![s]\!]) = \mathsf{M_{fwd}}([\![s]\!]^{254}) + \mathsf{C_{fwd}}$, where $\mathsf{M_{fwd}}$ is a public matrix of bits, $\mathsf{C_{fwd}}$ is a public vector of bits and $[\![s]\!]^{254}$ is represented with bits. $\mathsf{M_{fwd}}$ and $\mathsf{C_{fwd}}$ are given in [1]. As mentioned previously, $[\![s]\!]^{254}$ is computed with an addition chain using a list of powers $= [2, 4, 8, 16, 32, 64, 128]$. This is shown in (1). Note that one can swap the power and matrix computation due to linearity.

$$\mathsf{Sbox}([\![s]\!]) = \prod_{i=0}^{6} [\mathsf{M_{fwd}}([\![s]\!])]^{\mathsf{powers}[i]} + \mathsf{C_{fwd}}$$

$$= [\mathsf{M_{fwd}}([\![s]\!])]^{\mathsf{powers}[0]} * [\mathsf{M_{fwd}}([\![s]\!])]^{\mathsf{powers}[1]} * \ldots * [\mathsf{M_{fwd}}([\![s]\!])]^{\mathsf{powers}[7]} + \mathsf{C_{fwd}} \quad (1)$$

$$[\![x]\!] = [\mathsf{M_{fwd}}([\![s]\!])]^{254} + \mathsf{C_{fwd}}$$

Inverse Sbox in $\mathsf{GF}(2^8)$*:* For a secret state $[\![x]\!]$, $\mathsf{Sbox}^{-1}([\![x]\!]) = \mathsf{M_{bwd}}(([\![x]\!] + \mathsf{C_{fwd}})^{254})$, where $\mathsf{M_{bwd}}$ is the inverse matrix to compute the inverse Sbox as shown in (2)

$$\mathsf{Sbox}^{-1}([\![x]\!]) = [\mathsf{M_{bwd}}([\![x]\!] + \mathsf{C_{fwd}})]^{254}$$

$$= [\mathsf{M_{bwd}}([\![x]\!] + \mathsf{C_{fwd}})]^{\mathsf{powers}[0]} * \ldots * [\mathsf{M_{bwd}}([\![x]\!] + \mathsf{C_{fwd}})]^{\mathsf{powers}[6]} \quad (2)$$

$$[\![s]\!] = \prod_{i=0}^{6} [\mathsf{M_{bwd}}([\![x]\!] + \mathsf{C_{fwd}})]^{\mathsf{powers}[i]}$$

Inverse Sbox in $\mathsf{GF}(2^{40})$*:* We now describe how to compute inverse Sbox in $\mathsf{GF}(2^{40})$ for an embedded secret input byte $[\![\mathsf{embed\_byte}]\!]$. Before describing the method, we introduce few functions that we will use in the description.

1. ApplyBDEmbed is a function that takes a vector of 8 bits which represents a value in $\mathsf{GF}(2^8)$ and returns the bit embedding in $\mathsf{GF}(2^{40})$.
2. BDEmbed is a function that takes a composite value in $\mathsf{GF}(2^{40})$ and returns the 8 bits of this embedded value for positions $\{0, 5, 10, 15, 20, 25, 30, 35\}$. More precisely, for an input $[\![x]\!]$, BDEmbed outputs $[\![y_0]\!], \ldots, [\![y_7]\!]$ such that $[\![x]\!] = \sum_{i=0}^{7} [\![y_i]\!] * (0x20)^i$. This is due to the fact that the embedding in MP-SPDZ works with a special reduction modulus $Q(X) = X^{40} + X^{20} + X^{15} + X^{10} + 1$ (see Appendix 6.3 for more details).
3. InverseBDEmbed is a function that takes a composite value in $\mathsf{GF}(2^{40})$ and returns the bits of its unembedded value in $\mathsf{GF}(2^8)$.

To better understand BDEmbed and InverseBDEmbed, consider the following example. Let $x \in \mathsf{GF}(2^8)$, x is embedded into $\mathsf{GF}(2^{40})$ as $y = X^5 + 1$, represented by the byte $0x21$. When we apply BDEmbed to the value $y \in GF(2^{40})$, the output is the eight bits $[1, 1, 0, 0, 0, 0, 0, 0]$, where only the 0th and 5th bits are set to 1 and bits $10^{th}, \ldots, 35^{th}$ are set to 0. We can think of this as a function that takes 8 bits of an element in $GF(2^{40})$ and packs them into a byte by returning the bits specified in the function BDEmbed. On the other hand, when y is input to InverseBDEmbed, the output is $[0, 1, 0, 0, 0, 0, 0, 0]$ which is the bit decomposition of $x = 0x02 \in GF(2^8)$.

For the full algorithm, we can take the computations given in (2) and transform all the steps into embedded format. The full algorithm is given in Protocol 3. In Step 1, we add the embedded input $\llbracket \text{embed\_byte} \rrbracket$ to C_{fwd} after embedding C_{fwd}. The output is called $\llbracket x \rrbracket$. In Step 2, we bit decompose $\llbracket x \rrbracket$ and obtain a vector $\llbracket y \rrbracket$. Step 3–5 merges the following operations: first, $\llbracket y \rrbracket$ goes through the affine transformation with matrix M_{bwd} where the matrix M_{bwd} is multiplied with vector $\llbracket y \rrbracket$, the result is $\llbracket s \rrbracket$. The output $\llbracket s \rrbracket$ would be, therefore, a vector of bits, too. Then, it computes $\llbracket s^2 \rrbracket, \ldots, \llbracket s^{128} \rrbracket$ with another linear transformation. These steps are merged with the help of a table named magic. We pause here to explain the computations of the table magic and why Steps 3–5 work.

$$
\begin{aligned}
\llbracket s \rrbracket &= M_{\text{bwd}}(\llbracket x \rrbracket) \\
&= M_{\text{bwd}}\left(\sum_{i=0}^{7} \llbracket y_i \rrbracket * (0x20)^i\right) \\
&= M_{\text{bwd}}(\llbracket y_0 \rrbracket * (0x20)^0 + \ldots + \llbracket y_7 \rrbracket * (0x20)^7) \\
&= \llbracket y_0 \rrbracket * M_{\text{bwd}}((0x20)^0) + \ldots + \llbracket y_7 \rrbracket * M_{\text{bwd}}((0x20)^7)
\end{aligned}
\tag{3}
$$

The last line in (3) is due to the linearity of the operations. Since $\llbracket y_i \rrbracket$'s are bits, they can be taken out and all we are left is to compute the affine transformation of the powers of $(0x20)$ by multiplying with M_{bwd} in the unembedded domain. This is shown in steps 3–4 of Protocol 4. The rest of the steps in Protocol 4 is to merge the linear transformations to compute the powers of two of $\llbracket s \rrbracket$. Notice that the entire procedure in Protocol 4 will be used in Step 3 of Protocol 3. We implicitly apply 7 linear transformations $(L_0, \ldots L_6)$ to compute $M_{\text{bwd}}(\llbracket y \rrbracket + C_{\text{fwd}})^{\text{powers}[i]} \ \forall i \in \{0, \ldots, 6\}$ in the vector mapper from a precomputed table denoted by magic. Protocol 4 describes how to compute the magic table.

4.3 Optimizations with Offline Phase

In this section, we present an additional optimization technique for inverse AES protocol given in Protocol 3. Our technique requires special tuples computed in the offline phase without requiring any changes in the underlying SHE and ZK protocols. The idea of such an optimization comes from the fact that for binary finite fields, the bit decomposition turns out to be a linear operation (as opposed to finite fields with (odd) prime characteristics). This gives us the opportunity to integrate several steps in the beginning where the bit decomposition is performed. We refer to Appendix 6 for in depth and early-stage optimization ideas.

Input: A secret input state $\langle$embed_byte$\rangle \in \mathsf{GF}(2^{40})$
Output: Computes $\langle$Sbox$^{-1}($embed_byte$)\rangle$
1: Compute $\langle x \rangle = $ embed_byte $+$ ApplyBDEmbed(C_{fwd})
2: $\langle y \rangle = $ BDEmbed($\langle x \rangle$)
3: **for** $i \in \{0, \ldots 6\}$ **do**
4:     mapper$[i] = \sum\limits_{j=0}^{7}($magic$[i][j] * \langle y_j \rangle)$ ▷ mapper $= [\langle s^2 \rangle, \ldots, \langle s^{128} \rangle]$
5:
6: **end for**
7: Compute $\langle s^{254} \rangle = (($mapper$[0] * $mapper$[1]) * \cdots * $mapper$[6])$
8: **return** $\langle s^{254} \rangle$

Protocol 3: Optimized Single Sbox Implementation of Protocol 2

Input: Public matrix M_{bwd} and public vector C_{fwd}
Output: Computes a predefined table magic
1: **for** $i \in \{0, \ldots 6\}$ **do**
2:     **for** $j \in \{0, \ldots 7\}$ **do**
3:         $A = $ InverseBDEmbed($0x20^j$)   ▷ return a vector of 8 bits
4:         $B = M_{\mathsf{bwd}} * A$ ▷ matrix*vector multiplication
5:         $C = $ ApplyBDEmbed(B)   ▷ Composes embedded value from its bits
6:         $D = C^{\mathsf{powers}[i]}$ ▷ powers $= [2, 4, 8, 16, 32, 64, 128]$
7:         magic$[i][j] = D$
8:     **end for**
9: **end for**
10: **return** magic

Protocol 4: Computation of magic once for all AES decryption.

Protocol 5 shows the final optimized protocol. In Step 1, one gets 13 secret $\mathsf{GF}(2^{40})$ elements computed in the offline phase. Each function L_i is a linear transformation used to compute 2^{i+1}th power of a secret. This corresponds to 130 bytes of data that needs to be stored in the offline phase. Step 2 performs one reveal, which requires 1 round-trip and 10 bytes of communication. Step 3, 4, 5 and 6 only require local computations. Step 7 is multiplication of two secret values (which is the unaltered SPDZ protocol) computed from the previous step: $\langle L_0(x) * L_1(x) \rangle$ and $\langle L_2(x) * L_3(x) \rangle$ with two reveals, each needing 20 bytes of data. Step 8 is a special multiplication which requires only 1 reveal (10 bytes and 1 round-trip). More specifically, we multiply $\langle L_4(x) * L_5(x) \rangle$ by $\langle L_6(x) \rangle$ using Beaver triplets. Let $\langle L_4(x) * L_5(x) \rangle$ be masked with a secret $\langle b \rangle$, obtained from the offline tuples in Step 1; then $L_4(x) * L_5(x) + b$ is revealed. $L_6(x)$ is masked with $L_6(a)$ where $\langle L_6(x) \rangle + \langle L_6(a) \rangle$ is already revealed. Finally, we use the product of these two masks, $\langle b * L_6(a) \rangle$ in Step 1. Step 8 is a normal SPDZ multiplication which requires 2 reveals (20 bytes and 2 round-trips).

For **a single Sbox** the complete optimization requires 130 bytes of storage to store the special tuples generated in the offline phase, 6 round-trips, and 60 bytes of communication as opposed to 260 bytes storage, 13 round-trips, and 130 bytes of communication with Protocol 3. We implemented our optimization in full AES and report the results in Table 2. Observe that the communication and storage requirements for Protocol 5 is less than half that of Protocol 3.

Input: A secret input state $\langle x \rangle \in \mathsf{GF}(2^{40})$
Output: Computes $\langle \mathsf{Sbox}^{-1}(x) \rangle \in \mathsf{GF}(2^{40})$
1: Receive a tuple with 13 secret $\mathsf{GF}(2^{40})$ values from the offline phase: $\mathsf{T} =$
$(\langle a \rangle, \langle \mathsf{L}_0(a) \rangle, \ldots, \langle \mathsf{L}_6(a) \rangle, \langle \mathsf{L}_0(a) * \mathsf{L}_1(a) \rangle, \langle \mathsf{L}_2(a) * \mathsf{L}_3(a) \rangle, \langle \mathsf{L}_4(a) * \mathsf{L}_5(a) \rangle, \langle b \rangle, \langle b * \mathsf{L}_6(a) \rangle))$ [5]
2: Compute $\langle y \rangle = \langle x \rangle + \langle a \rangle$ and reveal y.
3: Compute $\mathsf{L}_0(y), \ldots, \mathsf{L}_6(y)$, $A = \mathsf{L}_0(y) * \mathsf{L}_1(y)$, $B = \mathsf{L}_2(y) * \mathsf{L}_3(y)$, $C = \mathsf{L}_4(y) * \mathsf{L}_5(y)$
4: Compute $\langle \mathsf{L}_0(x) * \mathsf{L}_1(x) \rangle$ as follows:
$\langle \mathsf{L}_0(x) * \mathsf{L}_1(x) \rangle = A + \mathsf{L}_1(y) * \langle \mathsf{L}_0(a) \rangle + \mathsf{L}_0(y) * \langle \mathsf{L}_1(a) \rangle + \langle \mathsf{L}_0(a) * \mathsf{L}_1(a) \rangle$
5: Compute $\langle \mathsf{L}_2(x) * \mathsf{L}_3(x) \rangle$ as
$\langle \mathsf{L}_2(x) * \mathsf{L}_3(x) \rangle = B + \mathsf{L}_3(y) * \langle \mathsf{L}_2(a) \rangle + \mathsf{L}_2(y) * \langle \mathsf{L}_3(a) \rangle + \langle \mathsf{L}_2(a) * \mathsf{L}_3(a) \rangle$
6: Compute $\langle \mathsf{L}_4(x) * \mathsf{L}_5(x) \rangle$ as
$\langle \mathsf{L}_4(x) * \mathsf{L}_5(x) \rangle = B + \mathsf{L}_5(y) * \langle \mathsf{L}_4(a) \rangle + \mathsf{L}_4(y) * \langle \mathsf{L}_5(a) \rangle + \langle \mathsf{L}_4(a) * \mathsf{L}_5(a) \rangle$
7: Compute $\langle \mathsf{L}_0(x) * \mathsf{L}_1(x) * \mathsf{L}_2(x) * \mathsf{L}_3(x) \rangle$
8: Compute $\langle U \rangle = \langle \mathsf{L}_4(x) * \mathsf{L}_5(x) \rangle + \langle b \rangle$ and reveal U.
9: Compute $V = \mathsf{L}_6(y)$. [6] and $\langle \mathsf{L}_4(x) * \mathsf{L}_5(x) * \mathsf{L}_6(x) \rangle$ as follows:
$U * V + \langle b \rangle * V + \langle \mathsf{L}_6(a) \rangle * U + \langle b * \mathsf{L}_6(a) \rangle$
10: Compute the full product $\langle X \rangle = \langle \mathsf{L}_0(x) * \cdots * \mathsf{L}_6(x) \rangle$
11: **return** $\langle X \rangle$

Protocol 5: Storage and Communication Optimizations of Protocol 3

Table 2. Storage (measured with data required from **offline phase**), round trip and communication requirements for **a full block of inverse** AES compared with forward AES

estimated overhead	storage (KB)	# round trip	comm (KB)		implementation	latency (ms)	comm (KBytes)
AES-BD	54.4	800	20.4		AES-BD	5.026	18.37
Protocol 1					Protocol 1		
AES-LT	410	160	1.6		AES-LT	0.80	3.13
Protocol 7					Protocol 7		
Protocol 3	41.6	640	18.8		Protocol 3	1.642	17.21
Protocol 5	20.8	260	9.6		Protocol 5	1.501	8.20

When we compare Protocol 5 with AES-LT, we observe that AES-LT requires over twenty times as much storage as our protocols, while the latency of AES-LT is almost twice as fast requiring 2.5 times less communication overhead.

4.4 Offline Phase Tuples

In Protocol 5 we assume the availability of special tuples from the offline phase: $\mathsf{T} = (\langle a \rangle, \langle \mathsf{L}_0(a) \rangle, \ldots, \langle \mathsf{L}_6(a) \rangle, \langle \mathsf{L}_0(a) * \mathsf{L}_1(a) \rangle, \langle \mathsf{L}_2(a) * \mathsf{L}_3(a) \rangle, \langle \mathsf{L}_4(a) * \mathsf{L}_5(a) \rangle, \langle b \rangle, \langle b * \mathsf{L}_6(a) \rangle)$. For the computation of such tuples, we refer to the original SPDZ offline phase protocols in [13] (Reshare in Fig. 4, PAngle in Fig. 6, and Triple generation in Fig. 7 from Π_{PREP} [13, eprint version]).

We like to generate $\mathsf{T} = (\langle a \rangle, \langle \mathsf{L}_0(a) \rangle, \ldots, \langle \mathsf{L}_6(a) \rangle, \langle \mathsf{L}_0(a) * \mathsf{L}_1(a) \rangle, \langle \mathsf{L}_2(a) * \mathsf{L}_3(a) \rangle, \langle \mathsf{L}_4(a) * \mathsf{L}_5(a) \rangle, \langle b \rangle, \langle b * \mathsf{L}_6(a) \rangle)$ from two random values a, b. We adapt the SPDZ Triplet protocol to generate them in Protocol 6. Let $C_1 = \mathsf{L}_0(a) * \mathsf{L}_1(a)$, $C_2 = \mathsf{L}_2(a) * \mathsf{L}_3(a)$, $C_3 = \mathsf{L}_4(a) * \mathsf{L}_5(a)$, $b, D = b * \mathsf{L}_6(a)$.

Input: Random a, b.
Output: $\mathsf{T} = (\langle a \rangle, \langle \mathsf{L}_0(a) \rangle, \ldots, \langle \mathsf{L}_6(a) \rangle, \langle C_1 \rangle, \langle C_2 \rangle, \langle C_3 \rangle, \langle b \rangle, \langle D \rangle)$
1: Each player generates a_i and b_i such that $a = \sum_i a_i$ and $b = \sum_i b_i$.
2: Each player broadcasts e_{a_i} and e_{b_i}.
3: Each player invokes Π_{ZKPoPK}.
4: Players set $e_a = \sum_i e_{a_i}$ and $e_b = \sum_i e_{b_i}$.
5: Players set $e_{\mathsf{L}_j(a)} = \mathsf{L}_j(e_a)$ for $j = 0, \ldots, 6$.
6: n players generate $\langle a \rangle \leftarrow \mathsf{PAngle}(a_0, \ldots, a_n, e_a)$, $\langle b \rangle \leftarrow \mathsf{PAngle}(b_0, \ldots, b_n, e_b)$ and
   $\quad \langle \mathsf{L}_j(a) \rangle \leftarrow \mathsf{PAngle}(\mathsf{L}_j(a), e_{\mathsf{L}_j(a)})$ for $j = 0, \ldots, 6$.
7: Players compute $e_D = e_{\mathsf{L}_6(a)} * e_b$ and
$$e_{C_1} = e_{\mathsf{L}_0(a)} * e_{\mathsf{L}_1(a)}$$
$$e_{C_2} = e_{\mathsf{L}_2(a)} * e_{\mathsf{L}_3(a)}$$
$$e_{C_3} = e_{\mathsf{L}_4(a)} * e_{\mathsf{L}_5(a)}$$
8: n players set
$$(D_1, \ldots, D_n, e_D') = \mathsf{ReShare}(e_D, \mathsf{NewCipherText})$$
$$(C_{11}, \ldots, C_{1n}, e_{C_1}') = \mathsf{ReShare}(e_{C_1}, \mathsf{NewCipherText})$$
$$(C_{21}, \ldots, C_{2n}, e_{C_2}') = \mathsf{ReShare}(e_{C_2}, \mathsf{NewCipherText})$$
$$(C_{31}, \ldots, C_{3n}, e_{C_3}') = \mathsf{ReShare}(e_{C_3}, \mathsf{NewCipherText})$$
9: n players generate
$$\langle D \rangle = \mathsf{PAngle}(D_1, \ldots, D_n, e_D')$$
$$\langle C_1 \rangle = \mathsf{PAngle}(C_{11}, \ldots, C_{1n}, e_{C_1}')$$
$$\langle C_2 \rangle = \mathsf{PAngle}(C_{21}, \ldots, C_{2n}, e_{C_2}')$$
$$\langle C_3 \rangle = \mathsf{PAngle}(C_{31}, \ldots, C_{3n}, e_{C_3}')$$
10: **return** $\langle a \rangle, \langle b \rangle, \langle \mathsf{L}_j(a) \rangle$ for $j = 0, \ldots, 6$ from Step 6 and $\langle C_1 \rangle, \langle C_2 \rangle, \langle C_3 \rangle, \langle D \rangle$ from Step 9.

Protocol 6: Adapted Triplet Protocol of [13]

Line 5 in Protocol 6 is the computation of the powers of two with the underlying homomorphic encryption scheme. SPDZ in $\mathsf{GF}(2^{40})$ uses a modified version of BGV [6] protocol as HE in the pre-processing phase. Essentially, we can replace, in BGV, the polynomial ring $\mathsf{R} = \mathbb{Z}[X]/X^d + 1$ with binary coefficients where d is a power of two with a cyclotomic ring with reduction polynomial $\Phi_m(X)$. When $m = 75$, $\Phi_m(X)$ has degree 40, and the cyclotomic ring is isomorphic to $\mathsf{GF}(2^{40})$ [15]. In this ring, for a polynomial $P(X)$, squaring $P^2(X)$ modulo $\Phi_m(X)$ is equivalent to computing $P(X^2) \bmod \Phi_m(X)$ (a.k.a. Frobenius authomorphism). This automorphism is nearly free, meaning that it adds little noise and does not cause to change the "level" in BGV. $\mathsf{L}_0, \ldots, \mathsf{L}_6$ are squaring operations and computing a homomorphic encryption of them as we do in Line 5 can be done with similar parameters and without a performance penalty.

Overall, if we neglect local computation overhead, the cost of tuple generation is what is communicated: Reshare (also called in PAngle), broadcasts, and ZKPoPK. The original Triple protocol from [13] needs 4 Reshare calls. Our adapted version in Protocol 6 needs 17 Reshare calls. In Protocol 5, we observe that the protocol needs 4 pairs of triplets as well as the tuple T from the offline phase. In total, to generate all the data it requires $(17 + 4*2 = 25)$ Reshare calls in the offline phase. On the other hand, Protocol 3 needs BDEmbed which uses 8 Reshare calls and 6 multiplications which requires 4 Reshare calls per multiplication. In total, Protocol 3 makes 32 Reshare calls, whereas Protocol 5 makes 25 such calls per SBox a reduction of more than 20%.

4.5   Comparison with Other AES MPC Implementations

In this section, we briefly compare this work to previous implementations in the literature. We compare latency, security, and storage and bandwidth requirements. Latency refers to the time required to process one single AES block. We have not optimized the implementation reported in this paper for throughput, which refers to the time required to process many such blocks, possibly in parallel and, therefore, we do not discuss this aspect explicitly. Table 3 summarizes the discussion.

Security. From a security perspective, the implementations in [11,18] and this paper provide the strongest type of security (active security against malicious adversaries with a dishonest majority). The works described in [2,8] although only secure in the semi-honest setting with honest majority also offer a privacy guaranteed in the client-server model where clients outsource data to untrusted servers performing the computation. In this setting, [2] shows that their protocol provides privacy as long as the servers do not get information about the output disclosed to the client. This is strictly weaker than the standard malicious security guarantees provided in the SPDZ-based protocols as corretness is not guaranteed. This has been pointed out in [2].

Latency, Storage, and Bandwidth. The AES implementation with the smallest latency is given in [18]. But this latency comes at the cost of considerable storage costs (a factor of more than 20 compared to this work and two orders of magnitude larger than [2,8]). The implementation with the lowest storage costs is the

Table 3. Comparison of distributed (MPC) online single threaded AES implementations (LAN Setting). All performance data is for two parties implementation unless otherwise noted. For SPDZ protocols we use 2^{40} for statistical security. TLU:Table Look-Up; BitDec: BitDecomposition; CR: Correlated Randomness; na: not available

Protocol	Secret sharing	Security	SBox Impl.	Latency per block (msec)	LAN (Gbps)	Storage (KB)	Comm. (KB)
[2]	Replicated 2-out-3 sharing w. CR	Semi honest	Boolean circuit	166	10	na	1 bit per AND gate
AES-BD [11]	SPDZ	Active	BitDec	5.026[†]	1	54.4	20.4
AES-LT [18]	SPDZ w Masked TLU	Active active	TLU	0.80[‡]	1	410	1.6
[8]	Replicated 2-out-3 sharing	Semi-honest	Arithmetic circuit	1.7	10	na	1 bit per AND gate
This work (Protocol 5)	SPDZ	Active	BitDec	1.5	1[*]	20.8	8.2

† Latency reported in [18] is 5.20 msec. Values in this table correspond to own implementation.
‡ Latency reported in [18] is 0.928 msec. Values in this table correspond to own implementation.
∗ Estimated by benchmarking laptop network interface.

works in [2,8] since they only require the online computation of correlated randomness bits. This translates into significantly lower bandwidth requirements, which likely would provide significant gains in throughput (see next paragraph). However, this is at the cost of weaker security guarantees. Among implementations providing active security [11,18], our work seems to strike an interesting trade-off in terms of latency and storage requirements. It appears that table lookup implementations might be best suited to applications in which very little data needs to encrypted or decrypted. In this case, the storage requirements can be ignored. In applications, in which large amounts of data are to be processed, it seems that Protocol 5 would be a very attractive solution achieving smaller latency than [2,8] and having rather modest storage requirements.

Further Optimizations and Throughput. The performance that we have reported does not make use of parallelization potential in the underlying platform (e.g., multi-threading or multi-cores). In practice, each AES round can be implemented with 16 parallel and independent Sbox computations (all internal states go through Sboxes independently), hence reducing communication overhead and bandwidth requirements. Such parallelism will not change the storage or the volume of data to transmit but will increase throughput. In addition, depending on the platform and the mode of operation properties, one can further parallelize by taking advantage of the multiple cores in the platform. This has been used in [8] to achieve their best throughput. As we start to process multiple, blocks in parallel, there will be increased pressure on the network bandwidth. We expect that at some point this will start to affect our throughput and consequently, that [2,8] will still have higher throughput than any current active security implementation. This is because of their almost negligible bandwidth requirements and their ability to use the PRSS trick [2,9], which in the active security setting would have to be adapted.

5   Conclusion

We propose two optimized protocols for AES computations in MPC setting. Our first protocol requires no changes to the offline phase and only takes advantage of flexible Sbox computations. The second protocol proposes to use special tuples generated in the offline phase and utilizes them in order to make more efficient transformations and multiplications required in the online phase of Sbox computation. Our implementation results indicates that we reduce the running time, the storage and communication cost of AES-BD three times with our techniques.

6   Appendix

6.1   **AES-LT** with Masked Table [18]

In a table look-up based implementation of the AES standard, the table representing the Sbox is publicly available. Such look-ups happen securely by the key owner who knows all the internal states.[7] On the other hand, in MPC,

---

[7] Excluding side-channel attacks attacks.

the internal states as well as the secret key are secrets which are distributed among participants and therefore it is not possible to perform a table look-up based on secret state information. The idea in [18] is to generate a pair $(x, \mathsf{MaskedTable})$ such that $x \oplus \mathsf{MaskedTable} = \mathsf{Sbox}$ in the offline phase and distribute it as secret shares to each participant: $([\![x]\!], [\![\mathsf{MaskedTable}]\!])$. Therefore, in MPC, instead of looking up a public entry with a secret internal state, we look up a secret table with a (public) masked internal state. The $\mathsf{MaskedTable}$ generation is described in [18]. We observe that every single Sbox computation requires one pair $([\![x]\!], [\![\mathsf{MaskedTable}]\!])$. Thus, even though the online phase is a lot faster than other methods, it requires a lot more data to be communicated and stored from the offline phase. The online computations of a single Sbox in AES-LT [18] is shown in Protocol 7.

Input: A secret input as state $\langle s \rangle \in \mathsf{GF}(2^{40})$, one pair $(\langle x \rangle, \langle \mathsf{MaskedTable} \rangle)$
Output: Computes $\langle \mathsf{T}[s] \rangle$, where T is the public Sbox table
1: The parties compute $h = x \oplus s$ and reveals h
2: The parties locally compute $\langle \mathsf{T}[s] \rangle = \langle \mathsf{MaskedTable} \rangle [h]$ where $\langle \mathsf{MaskedTable} \rangle [h]$ means the hth component of $\langle \mathsf{MaskedTable} \rangle$
3: **return** $\langle \mathsf{T}[s] \rangle$

Protocol 7: One Sbox computation of AES-LT method

Offline Phase. For 10 rounds and 16 bytes per round, Protocol 7 must prepare 160 $\mathsf{MaskedTable}$ for a block of AES requiring 48 KBytes of communication during the offline phase [18]. Communicating 160 tables for the online phase requires 410 KBytes per party.

Online Phase. The online phase requirements are as follows:

- **Storage:** the protocol needs one masked table per Sbox operation. Each table has 256 $\mathsf{GF}(2^{40})$-elements. Thus, to process one full AES block, 410 KBytes of storage are required per participant.
- **Round trip:** Per Sbox, we need one round trip of communication between players for a reveal. For the whole AES 160 rounds are required.
- **Communication:** Per Sbox, one reveal operation is performed, which requires 10 bytes of communication. Thus, 1600 bytes of communication needed in total for a full AES block.

6.2   Details of **BDEmbed**

In this section, we describe the bit decomposition of an embedded value in MP-SPDZ which is important to understand our optimization techniques given in 4.3. The following algorithm is used to compute BDEmbed of an embedded secret input $[\![x]\!]$. This computation is run in Step 2 in Protocol 3. In total, Protocol 3 requires 13 rounds of communication. This is summarized in Table 4.

1. Take a secret pair $(\langle a \rangle, \langle a' \rangle)$ where $\langle a' \rangle$ is the output of InverseBD Embedding(a) computed during the offline phase.
2. Compute $\langle \bar{x} \rangle = \langle x \rangle + \langle a \rangle$ and reveal $\bar{x}$.
3. Compute the bits of the clear value $\bar{x}$. Call it x'.
4. Compute $\langle y' \rangle = x' + \langle a' \rangle$
5. Return $\langle y \rangle$ which is the composition of $\langle y' \rangle$.

Table 4. Complexity of steps in Protocol 3

	Storage (bytes)	Round trip	Communication (bytes)
Step 2 (1-bit decomposition)	80	1	10
Step 3–5 (transformations)	0	0	0
Step 6 (6 multiplications)	180	13	130

6.3 Regarding The Embedding from $\mathbf{GF(2^8)}$ to $\mathbf{GF(2^{40})}$

We further clarify the notation used in Sect. 4 and some aspects of the embedding used, originally introduced in [11]. As previously mentioned, given an element $x \in GF(2^8)$, one can map this to an element in $GF(2^{40}) \cong GF((2^8)^5)$, using the irreducible polynomial $Q(X) = X^{40} + X^{20} + X^{15} + X^{10} + 1$. Thus, $x \in GF(2^8)$ gets mapped to the element $X^5 + 1 \in GF(2^{40})$. We observe the following equivalences:

$$x^0 \cong (X^5 + 1)^0 = 1; \; x^1 \cong (X^5 + 1)^1 = X^5 + 1, \text{ or } (\mathbf{0x21})_{16}; \; \cdots$$
$$x^7 \cong (X^5 + 1)^7 = X^{35} + X^{30} + X^{25} + X^{15} + X^{10} + X^5 + 1, \text{ or } (\mathbf{0x0842108421})_{16}$$

It has been observed [11,17] that this representation can be used to extract the $GF(2^8)$ element representation by extracting indeces that are a multiple of 5 in the corresponding $GF(2^{40})$ representation. In Sect. 4, we have abused notation and written $\mathbf{0x20}_{16} = (0010\,0000)_2$ to mean $X^5 \in GF(2^{40})$ (as the 5th bit of $\mathbf{0x20}_{16}$ is set to 1).

References

1. The Advanced Encryption Standard, Nov 26, 2001. FIPS PUB 197: Federal Information Processing Standard https://csrc.nist.gov/csrc/media/publications/fips/197/final/documents/fips-197.pdf
2. Araki, T., Furukawa, J., Lindell, Y., Nof, A., Ohara, K.: High-throughput semi-honest secure three-party computation with an honest majority. In: Weippl, E.R., Katzenbeisser, S., Kruegel, C., Myers, A.C., Halevi, S., (eds.), ACM SIGSAC Conference on Computer and Communications Security – CCS 2016, pp. 805–817. ACM, 24–28 October 2016

3. Barkan, E., Biham, E.: In how many ways can you write rijndael? In: Zheng, Y. (ed.) ASIACRYPT 2002. LNCS, vol. 2501, pp. 160–175. Springer, Heidelberg (2002). https://doi.org/10.1007/3-540-36178-2_10

4. Beaver, D.: Efficient multiparty protocols using circuit randomization. In: Feigenbaum, J. (ed.) CRYPTO 1991. LNCS, vol. 576, pp. 420–432. Springer, Heidelberg (1992). https://doi.org/10.1007/3-540-46766-1_34

5. Bogdanov, D., Laur, S., Willemson, J.: Sharemind: a framework for fast privacy-preserving computations. In: Jajodia, S., Lopez, J. (eds.) ESORICS 2008. LNCS, vol. 5283, pp. 192–206. Springer, Heidelberg (2008). https://doi.org/10.1007/978-3-540-88313-5_13

6. Brakerski, Z., Gentry, C., Vaikuntanathan, V.: (Leveled) Fully Homomorphic Encryption without Bootstrapping. ACM Trans. Comput. Theor. 6(3), 1–36 (2014)

7. Chen, H., Kim, M., Razenshteyn, I., Rotaru, D., Song, Y., Wagh, S.: Maliciously secure matrix multiplication with applications to private deep learning. In: Moriai, S., Wang, H. (eds.) ASIACRYPT 2020. LNCS, vol. 12493, pp. 31–59. Springer, Cham (2020). https://doi.org/10.1007/978-3-030-64840-4_2

8. Chida, K., Hamada, K., Ikarashi, D., Kikuchi, R., Pinkas, B.: High-throughput secure AES computation. In: Brenner, M., Rohloff, K., (eds.), 6th Workshop on Encrypted Computing & Applied Homomorphic Cryptography, WAHC@CCS 2018, pp. 13–24. ACM, 19 October 2018

9. Cramer, R., Damgård, I., Ishai, Y.: Share conversion, pseudorandom secret-sharing and applications to secure computation. In: Kilian, J. (ed.) TCC 2005. LNCS, vol. 3378, pp. 342–362. Springer, Heidelberg (2005). https://doi.org/10.1007/978-3-540-30576-7_19

10. Damgård, I., Keller, M.: Secure multiparty AES. In: Sion, R. (ed.) FC 2010. LNCS, vol. 6052, pp. 367–374. Springer, Heidelberg (2010). https://doi.org/10.1007/978-3-642-14577-3_31

11. Damgård, I., Keller, M., Larraia, E., Miles, C., Smart, N.P.: Implementing AES via an actively/Covertly secure dishonest-majority MPC protocol. In: Visconti, I., De Prisco, R. (eds.) SCN 2012. LNCS, vol. 7485, pp. 241–263. Springer, Heidelberg (2012). https://doi.org/10.1007/978-3-642-32928-9_14

12. Damgård, I., Keller, M., Larraia, E., Pastro, V., Scholl, P., Smart, N.P.: Practical covertly secure MPC for dishonest majority – or: breaking the SPDZ limits. In: Crampton, J., Jajodia, S., Mayes, K. (eds.) ESORICS 2013. LNCS, vol. 8134, pp. 1–18. Springer, Heidelberg (2013). https://doi.org/10.1007/978-3-642-40203-6_1

13. Damgård, I., Pastro, V., Smart, N., Zakarias, S.: Multiparty computation from somewhat homomorphic encryption. In: Safavi-Naini, R., Canetti, R. (eds.) CRYPTO 2012. LNCS, vol. 7417, pp. 643–662. Springer, Heidelberg (2012). https://doi.org/10.1007/978-3-642-32009-5_38

14. Chaum, D., Crepeau, C., Damgård, I.: Multiparty unconditionally secure protocols. In: Proceedings of the Twentieth Annual ACM Symposium on Theory of Computing, STOC 1988, New York, ACM (1988)

15. Gentry, C., Halevi, S., Smart, N.P.: Homomorphic evaluation of the AES circuit. In: Safavi-Naini, R., Canetti, R. (eds.) CRYPTO 2012. LNCS, vol. 7417, pp. 850–867. Springer, Heidelberg (2012). https://doi.org/10.1007/978-3-642-32009-5_49

16. Hastings, M., Hemenway, B., Noble, D., Zdancewic, S.: Sok: general purpose compilers for secure multi-party computation. In: 2019 IEEE Symposium on Security and Privacy (SP), pp. 1220–1237 (2019)

17. Keller, M.: MP-SPDZ: a versatile framework for multi-party computation. In: Ligatti, J., Ou, X., Katz, J., Vigna, G., (eds.), 2020 ACM SIGSAC Conference on Computer and Communications Security, CCS. Virtual Event, pp. 1575–1590. ACM (2020)

18. Keller, M., Orsini, E., Rotaru, D., Scholl, P., Soria-Vazquez, E., Vivek, S.: Faster secure multi-party computation of AES and DES using lookup tables. In: Gollmann, D., Miyaji, A., Kikuchi, H. (eds.) ACNS 2017. LNCS, vol. 10355, pp. 229–249. Springer, Cham (2017). https://doi.org/10.1007/978-3-319-61204-1_12

19. Keller, M., Pastro, V., Rotaru, D.: Overdrive: making SPDZ great again. In: Nielsen, J.B., Rijmen, V. (eds.) EUROCRYPT 2018. LNCS, vol. 10822, pp. 158–189. Springer, Cham (2018). https://doi.org/10.1007/978-3-319-78372-7_6

20. Kocher, P., et al.: Spectre attacks: exploiting speculative execution. In: 2019 IEEE Symposium on Security and Privacy, SP 2019, pp. 1–19. IEEE, 19–23 May 2019

21. Lipp, M., et al.: Meltdown: reading kernel memory from user space. In: 27th USENIX Security Symposium, USENIX Security 2018, pp. 973–990. USENIX Association, 15–17 August 2018

22. Malkhi, D., Nisan, N., Pinkas, B., Sella, Y.: Fairplay - secure two-party computation system. In: Proceedings of the 13th USENIX Security Symposium, pp. 287–302. USENIX, 9–13 August 2004

23. Mohassel, P., Zhang, Y.: SecureML: a system for scalable privacy-preserving machine learning. In: 2017 IEEE Symposium on Security and Privacy (SP), pp. 19–38 (2017)

24. Goldreich, O., Micali, S., Wigderson, A.: How to play any mental game. In: Proceedings of the Nineteenth Annual ACM Symposium on Theory of Computing, STOC 1987, New York, ACM (1987)

25. Songhori, E.M., Hussain, S.U., Sadeghi, A.R., Schneider, T., Koushanfar, F.: TinyGarble: highly compressed and scalable sequential garbled circuits. In: 2015 IEEE Symposium on Security and Privacy, pp. 411–428 (2015)

26. Yao, A.C.: Protocols for secure computations. In: 23rd Annual Symposium on Foundations of Computer Science, vol. 1982, pp. 160–164. IEEE (1982)

Rabbit: Efficient Comparison for Secure Multi-Party Computation

Eleftheria Makri[1,5]([✉]), Dragos Rotaru[1,2], Frederik Vercauteren[1], and Sameer Wagh[3,4]

[1] imec-COSIC, Ku Leuven, Leuven, Belgium
emakri@esat.kuleuven.be, frederik.vercauteren@kuleuven.be
[2] Cape Privacy, Leuven, Belgium
dragos@capeprivacy.com
[3] University of California, Berkeley, USA
swagh@berkeley.edu
[4] Princeton University, Princeton, USA
[5] ABRR, Saxion University of Applied Sciences, Enschede, The Netherlands

Abstract. Secure comparison has been a fundamental challenge in privacy-preserving computation, since its inception as Yao's millionaires' problem (FOCS 1982). In this work, we present a novel construction for general n-party private comparison, secure against an active adversary, in the dishonest majority setting. For the case of comparisons over fields, our protocol is more efficient than the best prior work (edaBits: Crypto 2020), with $\sim 1.5\times$ better throughput in most adversarial settings, over $2.3\times$ better throughput in particular in the passive, honest majority setting, and lower communication. Our comparisons crucially eliminate the need for bounded inputs as well as the need for statistical security that prior works require. An important consequence of removing this "slack" (a gap between the bit-length of the input and the MPC representation) is that multi-party computation (MPC) protocols can be run in a field of smaller size, reducing the overhead incurred by privacy-preserving computations. We achieve this novel construction using the commutative nature of addition over rings and fields. This makes the protocol both simple to implement and highly efficient and we provide an implementation in MP-SPDZ (CCS 2020).

Keywords: Secure comparison · Multi-party computation · Unconditional security · Dishonest majority

1 Introduction

After years of active research, both in theoretical results and system building, multi-party computation (MPC) is becoming practical as a paradigm. Recent research results and practical implementations [1,13], deployment of MPC in real-life applications [3], as well as organizations beyond academia offering commercial MPC solutions [26,27,30], confirm that MPC is reaching maturity. However, MPC, just like any other cryptographic primitive deployed to enhance

© International Financial Cryptography Association 2021
N. Borisov and C. Diaz (Eds.): FC 2021, LNCS 12674, pp. 249–270, 2021.
https://doi.org/10.1007/978-3-662-64322-8_12

privacy, comes at a significant efficiency penalty, in terms of computation and communication. While some research focuses on tailoring MPC solutions to a particular problem, to compensate for this efficiency penalty, other works focus on improving the efficiency of fundamental MPC building blocks, which are applicable to a wide variety of problems.

Secure comparison is an important problem in multi-party computation – it involves the comparison of two or more secret values in a privacy-preserving manner. Comparison is a fundamental building block, necessary for the realization of various larger tasks: from online auctions to big data analytics and machine learning. Given the privacy considerations that today's digital infrastructure entails, protocols for secure comparison are a fundamental MPC tool in privacy-preserving applications.

Since the introduction of the secure comparison problem by Andrew Yao in 1982 [34] as the millionaires' problem, research efforts have pushed the frontiers of performance of this primitive. MPC has traditionally been efficient either on linear operations, when it is based on arithmetic circuits, or on non-linear operations, when it is based on Boolean circuits. Recent applications require a combination of linear and non-linear operations, and they are most of the time addressed with solutions based on arithmetic circuits, because these are significantly more efficient than Boolean circuits for the linear part, which presents itself as the bulk of the computation. Given the non-linear nature of the comparison operation, protocols for secure comparison still remain a bottleneck for privacy-preserving computation. Thus, any improvement in this line of work has a compounding impact on improving the overall efficiency of privacy-preserving computations.

In this work, we present a novel comparison protocol that is secure against an active adversary in the dishonest majority setting and holds for general n-party computation. Our work improves upon the state-of-the-art protocol for comparison in dishonest majority in both the total time and communication by a factor of two for the OT-based preprocessing. In addition, our protocol is easy to implement requiring no heavy cryptography. Notably, our protocol is highly conducive to amortization and preprocessing, which makes it attractive for deployment in real-life applications, as these are important considerations in building practical secure systems.

1.1   Our Contribution

We present Rabbit[1], a novel secure comparison protocol, which leverages the commutative nature of addition over rings and fields. Our protocol exploits recent advances in the generation and deployment of *doubly authenticated shared bits* (daBits [25]), which are bits living both in $\mathbb{F}_p$ and in $\mathbb{F}_{2^k}$, as well as *extended doubly authenticated bits* (edaBits [14]), which correspond to shared integers in the arithmetic domain, whose bit decomposition is shared in the binary domain. The proposed comparison is more efficient than previously proposed secure comparison protocols, while at the same time removing the dependence on bounds

---

[1] The name is an extension of the daBit [25], maBit [24] and edaBit [14] line of work.

and statistical parameters. This allows the MPC engines used for our secure comparison to be smaller than the ones required by previous protocols, which has a positive impact on the concrete efficiency of the MPC protocols. Concretely we make the following contributions:

(i) **Novel comparison protocol:** We propose Rabbit, a novel secure comparison protocol based on the commutative nature of addition over rings and fields. Rabbit is a general n-party protocol and crucially eliminates the need for any "slack" – a statistically larger dataspace to ensure security of computations, and thus enables computations over smaller datatypes. For instance, to compute over 64-bits, prior works require the use of 128-bit datatypes, while we can support these computations in standard 64-bit datatypes.

(ii) **Security:** Since we eliminate the slack and keep an exact tab of overflows, our protocols are unconditionally secure even against active adversaries in the dishonest majority setting. In the case of comparison over fields, we do have to account for a statistical security parameter, because of the existing implementation of edaBits [14]. In general, when implemented in a larger body of MPC computation, our comparison inherits the security properties of the platform, such as statistical security when using MP-SPDZ [13].

(iii) **Simplicity and Efficiency:** Our protocol is straightforward to implement. As shown in Fig. 1b, it is merely a few lines of code in MP-SPDZ. This also makes our protocol highly amenable to secure implementation. As for efficiency, the benefits of our work over the state-of-the-art are most pronounced in the case of comparison over fields. In this case, we improve end-to-end computations such as secure evaluation of ResNet-50 up to 2x faster, albeit at a higher communication.

1.2   Technical Overview

Our central focus in this work is to propose novel and efficient protocols for secure comparison. Comparison protocols usually rely on statistical security or bit-decomposition combined with prefix computation to achieve the results. We observe that·

(i) When considering arithmetic secret shares, the bit encoding modulus overflow of secrets enables exact integer relations between the secret, the secret shares, and the modulus.

(ii) Using the commutativity of addition over standard structures, such as rings and fields, we can express a sum in two different ways and thus equate the corresponding constraint equations.

These two observations together enable more efficient protocols for comparisons. More specifically, the core idea behind our comparison protocols lies in our ability to detect when a sum over a particular modulus overflows (i.e., wraps around), and when this happens we can correct it. Observe that given two integers $x, y \in \mathbb{Z}_M$, their sum $x + y \bmod M$ is less than either of the two summands, iff the sum wrapped around the modulus. That is, given a comparison function:

```
# Secure comparison in MP-SPDZ
k = program.bit_length
r, r_bits = sint.get.edabit(k, True)
a = (x+r).reveal()
b = a + M - R

w1 = LTBits(a, r_bits, k)
w2 = LTBits(b, r_bits, k)
w3 = (b < M - R)

movs(s, sint.conv(w1-w2+w3))
return
```

(a) Intuition behind **Rabbit** comparison protocol   (b) **Rabbit** code snippet

Fig. 1. Our protocol relies on the commutative properties of addition over rings/fields as shown in Fig. 1a. This diagram indicates the two different ways we can obtain the value b. The $[\cdot]_M$ notation indicates that the corresponding values or sums are taken modulo M. The horizontal arrows indicate addition of a uniformly random value $r \in \{0, \ldots, M-1\}$, used to mask the secret input of the comparison x (so that we can later open it without information leakage, to perform a comparison). The vertical arrows indicate addition of a known constant $B \in \{0, \ldots, M-1\}$ related to the public quantity to be compared against. These two ways of computing the sum b, are necessary for the comparison protocol between a secret value x and a public constant $M - B$. The code on the right (Fig. 1b) shows the simplicity of implementing our protocol, implemented in this case in the MP-SPDZ codebase [13].

$$\mathsf{LT}(\cdot, \cdot) : \mathbb{Z} \times \mathbb{Z} \to \{0, 1\} \subseteq \mathbb{Z} \ : \ \begin{cases} \mathsf{LT}(x, y) = 1 & \text{if } (x < y); \\ \mathsf{LT}(x, y) = 0 & \text{otherwise,} \end{cases}$$

we can compute the modular sum $x + y \mod M$, by performing computations over the integers as:

$$x + y \mod M = x + y - M \cdot \mathsf{LT}(x + y \mod M, x) = x + y - M \cdot \mathsf{LT}(x + y \mod M, y)$$

This is due to the observation that $\mathsf{LT}(x + y \mod M, x)$ (or $\mathsf{LT}(x + y \mod M, y)$) is true, iff the sum wrapped around. Given that the $\mathsf{LT}(\cdot, \cdot)$ function detects (i.e., outputs true) when a wrap around happens, we can indeed realize the modular sum, while performing computations over the integers, by conditionally subtracting the quantity of the wrap around (i.e., M), when $\mathsf{LT}(\cdot, \cdot)$ returns true.

Notation. We use $[x]_N$ to denote the sharing of a secret x in the ring $\mathbb{Z}_N$. We primarily consider two values of the modulus: $N = M$ and $N = 2$, where M is a fixed constant, set to either a prime p, or a power of two 2^k. The types of sharings are:

(i) $[x]_M$, where the secret is $x \in \mathbb{Z}_M$ or $[b]_2$, where the secret is a bit $b \in \mathbb{F}_2$;
(ii) $[x]_M$ and $[x_0]_2, \ldots [x_{m-1}]_2$ such that $x = \sum_{i=0}^{m-1} x_j \cdot 2^j \pmod{M}$ and $M < 2^m$ (this is also known as an edaBit [14])

Similarly, given a (public) constant value $R \in \mathbb{Z}_M$, we denote by $R_0, \ldots, R_{m-1}$ the bit decomposition of R, and by R_i its individual bits (at the corresponding position i).

2   Comparison Protocols

In this section we present our comparison protocols and their workings on a step-by-step basis. Then, for each presented protocol, we also show correctness. We do not provide any formal proofs of security of our protocols, as these follow trivially from the arithmetic black box functionality paradigm [11]. We present the protocols in the following order:

(i) First, we present the protocol Π_{LTBits} (Fig. 3), which realizes a comparison between a secret bit-decomposed value, and a public value, and outputs a secret bit indicating the result of the comparison. This is a building block that uses prefix computation for comparison.

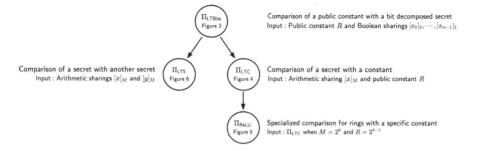

Fig. 2. Proposed comparison protocols, their inputs, and their interdependencies.

(ii) Second, we introduce the protocol Π_{LTC} (Fig. 4), which invokes Π_{LTBits} and performs a comparison between a secret value (without bit-decomposition), and a public value, where the output is a secret bit indicating the result of the comparison.

(iii) Third, we present a specialized comparison protocol, Π_{ReLU} (Fig. 5), that can be applied when the modulus is a power of 2 and the public constant against which we compare is half the modulus. Note that this is an important case, as it corresponds to computation of the ReLU function, which is widely used in machine learning.

(iv) Finally, in Π_{LTS} (Fig. 6), we show how to generalize Π_{LTC} to compare two secret shared values, where once again the output is a secret bit.

Note that given our novel approach of comparison, there is a difference between secret-public constant comparison (Π_{LTC}) and secret-secret comparison (Π_{LTS}), which often comes for free when using standard techniques that require a slack. For more details on this, we refer the reader to Sect. 4. Finally, for all proposed protocols, the output can either be an element of $\mathbb{Z}_M$ or $\mathbb{F}_2$ (depending on the needs of the follow-up computations) indicating the result of the comparison. An overview of all our comparison protocols, their inputs, and their interdependencies is given in Fig. 2.

2.1   Comparison with Bitwise Shared Input – **LTBits** Protocol

The protocol Π_{LTBits}, listed in Fig. 3, follows a standard bit decomposition idea to privately compute a secret bit, indicating the result of a comparison. It is essentially an adaptation of the BIT-LT protocol by Damgård *et al.* [9], which instead of two secret bit-decomposed inputs (that BIT-LT receives), it receives one bitwise secret shared input and a public arithmetic value to compare upon, while its output is a secret Boolean value indicating the result of the comparison. Notably, each component of our bit-decomposed secret lives in $\mathbb{F}_2$, unlike Damgård *et al.*'s [9] construction, where each secret bit lives in $\mathbb{F}_p$. The protocol LTBits computes the following:

1. The XOR of each bit of the secret input $[x_i]_2$ value with the corresponding bit of the public value R_i. This results in a bit-string $[y_0]_2, \ldots [y_{m-1}]_2$ with ones on all positions where the bits of the values to be compared differ.
2. A prefix OR (circuit computes for each position i of a bit vector, the OR between all previous bits in the vector up to position i. - more details in Catrina and de Hoogh [6]) of the previously computed bits $[y_i]_2$, which results in a vector $[z_i]_2$ of 0's followed by 1's with the transition from 0 to 1 occurring at the first bit where the secret and the public value differ.
3. In this step, the previous vector is converted into a vector $[w_i]_2$, $i = 0, \ldots, m-1$ of all 0's and a single 1 at the index of the first differing bit.
4. In the last step, we take the inner product between the vector $\mathbf{w}$ (which is a vector of 0's in all positions, except for the position of the first differing bit of the values to be compared) and the bits of the public value R. This inner product results in 0, if at the position of the differing bit R was 0, which further implies that x is larger than R, and it results in 1 otherwise. We have computed the value $[(x < R)]_2$, but we are actually after $[(R < x)]_2$, thus $1 - [(x < R)]_2$ concludes the protocol.

Less Than Bits $\Pi_{\mathsf{LTBits}}(R, [x_0]_2, \ldots [x_{m-1}]_2)$

Inputs: Secret value x shared bitwise, such that parties hold $[x_0]_2, \ldots [x_{m-1}]_2$, where $x = \sum_{i=0}^{m-1} x_j \cdot 2^j$, and public value R.
Outputs: Compute the Boolean value $[c]_2 = [(R \leqslant x)]_2$.
Protocol: Complete steps 1-3 for all $i \in \{0,1,\ldots,m-1\}$
    1. Parties compute $[y_i]_2 = [x_i]_2 \oplus R_i$.
    2. Parties compute $[z_i]_2 = \vee_{j=i}^{m-1} [y_j]_2$ using **PrefixOR** circuit.
    3. Parties compute $[w_i]_2 = [z_i]_2 - [z_{i+1}]_2$, where $z_m = 0$.
    4. Output $[c]_2 = 1 - [(x<R)]_2$, where $[(x<R)]_2 = \sum_{i=0}^{m-1} R_i \cdot [w_i]_2$.

Fig. 3. Protocol for comparison between an input shared bitwise and a public value.

Correctness of Π_{LTBits}: To see the correctness of Π_{LTBits}, note the following series of observations:

1. To compare two numbers, we start from the most significant bit (MSB) and look for the first bit where the two numbers differ. This is precisely what is computed in Step 1 of Π_{LTBits}. Thus, $y_{m-1}, \ldots, y_0$ contains a series of 0's, followed by a 1, which in turn is followed by bits that are irrelevant to the comparison.

2. As a consequence, $z_{m-1}, \ldots, z_0$ contains a series of 0's followed by 1's starting at the first location where x_i and R_i differ. Let $k \in \{0, \ldots, m-1\}$ be the largest index where $x_i \neq R_i$. Thus, $w_i = 1$ iff $i = k$ and $w_i = 0$ otherwise.

3. Finally, multiplying w_i by R_i ensures the following:

$$\mathsf{output} = \begin{cases} 1 & \text{if } R_k = 1, \ x_k = 0 \ \text{(implying } R > x) \\ 0 & \text{otherwise (implying } R \leqslant x) \end{cases}$$

∎

2.2   Comparison with a Constant – LTC Protocol

The protocol Π_{LTC}, listed in Fig. 4, is a comparison protocol between a shared secret value, and a public constant. Unlike Π_{LTBits}, it does not require the secret input value to be bitwise secret shared, but it invokes the protocol Π_{LTBits} twice. These two invocations can be parallelized, decreasing the total number of rounds of the comparison protocol. Π_{LTC} requires an edaBit as an input. An edaBit is a shared value in the arithmetic domain, accompanied by its own bit decomposition in the binary domain [14]. The core idea behind this comparison protocol is that addition in a ring or field is commutatitve as explained in Fig. 1a.

Less Than Constant $\Pi_{\mathsf{LTC}}([x]_M, R)$

Inputs: Value x secret shared, such that parties hold $[x]_M$, a shared edaBit$([r]_M, [r_0]_2, \ldots, [r_{m-1}]_2)$ and public value R.

Outputs: Compute the Boolean value $[(x < R)]_2$.

Protocol:

1. Parties compute the value $[a]_M = [x+r]_M$ (and $[b]_M = [x+r+M-R]_M$).
2. Parties open the value a ($b \equiv a + M - R$ can be opened locally).
3. Parties compute the following quantities:
   - $[w_1]_2 = \Pi_{\mathsf{LTBits}}(a, [r_0]_2, \ldots, [r_{m-1}]_2)$.
   - $[w_2]_2 = \Pi_{\mathsf{LTBits}}(b, [r_0]_2, \ldots, [r_{m-1}]_2)$.
   - $w_3 = (b < M - R)$.
4. Output $[w]_2 = 1 - ([w_1]_2 - [w_2]_2 + w_3)$ or use one classical daBit to output $[w]_M$.

Fig. 4. Protocol for comparison between *an input shared in* $\mathbb{Z}_M$ *and a public value* R for any modulus M (in particular, M can be 2^k or a prime p).

The Π_{LTC} protocol proceeds as follows:

1. Using the arithmetic value $[r]_M$ of the random edaBit from the input, the parties mask the input value x, computing $[a]$.

2. $[a]$ is opened, without revealing any information about x.
3. The parties then do the following:
   (a) Invoke Π_{LTBits} to compare the masked value $[a]$ against the random edaBit (in bitwise sharing), resulting in $[w_1]_2$.
   (b) Invoke Π_{LTBits} to compare $b = [a + M - R]_M$ against the random edaBit (in bitwise sharing), resulting in $[w_2]_2$.
   (c) Compare in the clear b against the public value $B = M - R$, resulting in w_3.
4. Finally, they conclude the comparison test by computing $[w]_2 = 1 - ([w_1]_2 - [w_2]_2 + w_3)$. This equation follows from the way we exploited the commutative property of addition, and its correctness is explained in the next paragraph. The output at this step is the binary value indicating the result of the comparison, shared in $\mathbb{F}_2$. Depending on the follow-up computations in the larger MPC protocol that uses the comparison, if the next input needs to be arithmetic, a classical daBit [25] can be used to transform the representation of this bit in $\mathbb{Z}_M$.

Correctness of Π_{LTC}: Let us denote by $[x]$ the value of $x \in \mathbb{Z}_M$, i.e., the modular reduction in $\{0, 1, \ldots, M - 1\}$. We are interested in securely computing the Boolean value $(x < R)$, for R a public constant. Furthermore, let $\mathsf{LT}(x, y)$ be defined as follows:

$$\mathsf{LT}(x, y) = \begin{cases} 1 & \text{if } x < y \\ 0 & \text{otherwise} \end{cases} \tag{1}$$

Recall from Sect. 1.2 that the $\mathsf{LT}(x, y)$ function enables writing exact integer relations for the sum of two numbers as follows:

$$\begin{aligned} [x + y] &= [x] + [y] - M \cdot \mathsf{LT}([x + y], [x]) \\ &= [x] + [y] - M \cdot \mathsf{LT}([x + y], [y]) \end{aligned} \tag{2}$$

To be consistent with the notation followed in Fig. 1a, we define $B = M - R$, and $c = [x + B]$. We then use the commutative nature of addition to represent the sum $b = [x + r + B]$ in two different ways, as shown in Fig. 1a. Using Eq. 2 for the two additions in the top path and noting that $a, b, B \in \mathbb{Z}_M$:

$$\begin{aligned} b = [a + B] &= a + B - M \cdot \mathsf{LT}(b, B) \\ &= x + r - M \cdot \mathsf{LT}(a, r) + B - M \cdot \mathsf{LT}(b, B) \end{aligned} \tag{3}$$

Similarly, using Eq. 2 for the two additions on the bottom path , we get:

$$\begin{aligned} b = [c + r] &= c + r - M \cdot \mathsf{LT}(b, r) \\ &= x + B - M \cdot \mathsf{LT}(c, B) + r - M \cdot \mathsf{LT}(b, r) \end{aligned} \tag{4}$$

Equating the RHS of Eq. 3, and Eq. 4, we get:

$$\mathsf{LT}(a, r) + \mathsf{LT}(b, B) = \mathsf{LT}(c, B) + \mathsf{LT}(b, r) \tag{5}$$

Recall that the result we are after is $\mathsf{LT}(x, R)$, which is equivalent to $(1 - \mathsf{LT}(c, B))$, since $B = M - R$, and $c = [x + B]$. Thus, from Eq. 5 we have

$LT(c, B) = 1 - (LT(a, r) + LT(b, B) - LT(b, r))$, which is exactly what we compute in Step 4 of Π_{LTC}. Finally, to complete the proof, we reiterate that $LT(c, B) = 0$ iff $(x < R)$ and that $LT(\cdot, \cdot)$ correctly computes the function defined by Eq. 1. ∎

2.3 Π_{ReLU} – Special Case of Π_{LTC} for $R = 2^{k-1}$, $M = 2^k$

Π_{LTC} is a general comparison protocol for comparing against *any* public value. However, a special case of interest is when the modulus is a power of 2 and the public constant to be compared against is half the modulus. When considering privacy-preserving alternatives to machine learning, the use of fixed-point arithmetic converts the widely used $ReLU(x) = \max(x, 0)$ function to the above comparison, when considering such a special modulus (power of 2). In this case, where $R = 2^{k-1}$ and $M = 2^k$, the protocol can be optimized further to improve performance. We present this optimized protocol in Fig. 5. This comparison setting is useful in a number of privacy-preserving machine learning frameworks [22,32], where fixed point encoding transforms the ReLU function into a comparison with $R = 2^{k-1}$ and $M = 2^k$. In this case, we can simplify our protocol to open the masked value $a = [x + r]$ (Step 1 of the protocol), subtract the mask r from it using a binary circuit in the secret shared domain (Steps 2, 3, 4 of the protocol), and extract the MSB of this result (Step 6). This way we are essentially extracting the MSB of x. This replaces the overhead of two invocations of Π_{LTBits} with a single invocation of a binary addition protocol ($\Pi_{BitAdder}$). The computation in Step 4 can also be used to perform comparisons when $R = 2^{\ell}$ is another power of two, however that would require additional computation over the bits $s_{k-1}, \ldots, s_{\ell}$.

ReLU $\Pi_{ReLU}([x]_{2^k}, 2^{k-1})$

Inputs: Value x secret shared, such that parties hold $[x]_{2^k}$, a shared edaBit $([r]_{2^k}, [r_0]_2, \ldots, [r_{k-1}]_2)$ and the public value 2^{k-1}.
Outputs: Compute shares $[y]_{2^k}$ where $y = x$ if $(x \leqslant 2^{k-1})$ and 0 otherwise.
Protocol:

1. Parties compute the value $[a]_{2^k} = [x + r]_{2^k}$ and open a.
2. Parties locally compute $[t_0]_2, \ldots [t_{k-1}]_2 = [1 - r_0]_2, \ldots, [1 - r_{k-1}]_2$
3. Parties set $a_0, \ldots a_{k-1}$ to be the bits of $(a + 1)$.
4. $[s_0]_2, \ldots, [s_{k-1}]_2, [s_k]_2 = \Pi_{BitAdder}(a_0, \ldots, a_{k-1}, [t_0]_2, \ldots, [t_{k-1}]_2)$.[a]
5. Output $[s_{k-1}]_2$ or use one classical daBit to output $[s_{k-1}]_{2^k}$ if only the derivative of ReLU is required in the computation.
6. Use one multiplication triple and output $y = [x]_{2^k} \cdot [s_{k-1}]_{2^k}$.

---

[a] $\Pi_{BitAdder}$ is a circuit performing addition over bitwise shared values.

Fig. 5. Protocol for comparison between *an input shared in* $\mathbb{Z}_{2^k}$ *and* 2^{k-1}.

Correctness of Π_{ReLU}: Observe that in this special case comparison with the constant 2^{k-1} where the modulus is 2^k, the MSB of the secret input defines the result of the comparison. Our protocol essentially performs a bit decomposition of the input $[x]_{2^k}$ by masking it (using the arithmetic version of the edaBit) and then again subtracting this mask in a binary circuit (using the binary version of the edaBit). This results in the bit decomposition of x, and by extracting its MSB we conclude the comparison, and hence the computation of this ReLU function.

Remark – Optimizing Π_{ReLU}: Note that Step 4 in Figure 5 can be optimized as we only require a single bit $[s_{k-1}]_2$. In particular, this requires $\log_2 k$ rounds and $k \log_2 k$ invocations of bit-triples. This can be reduced to $\log_2 k$ rounds and $2k-2$ bit-triples by simply modifying the MSB values and using a prefix computation protocol Π_{PreOpL} (cf [6]). We modify the most significant bit of the input tuple to be $(1,0)$ before passing to the Π_{PreOpL}. Consequently, the second element of the output tuple of the Π_{PreOpL} protocol is the carry bit $[s_{k-2}]_2$ and thus $[s_{k-1}]_2$ can be computed locally as the XOR of the MSB's of the two bits and the bit $[s_{k-2}]_2$.

2.4 Comparison with Secret – LTS Protocol

While the protocol described in Sect. 2.2 provides an efficient way to compare with a public constant, the protocol described in this section, Π_{LTS}, listed in Fig. 6, enables the comparison of two secret values x and y. In most prior works, due to the use of a slack or bounds on inputs, the corresponding protocols for these two settings are nearly identical. In our case, the elimination of slack

---

Less Than Secret $\Pi_{\mathsf{LTS}}([x]_M, [y]_M)$

Inputs: Values x and y secret shared, such that parties hold $[x]_M$ and $[y]_M$, two shared edaBits$([r]_M, [r_0]_2, ..., [r_{m-1}]_2)$ and $([r']_M, [r'_0]_2, ..., [r'_{m-1}]_2)$.
Outputs: Compute the Boolean value $[(x < y)]_2$.
Protocol:

1. Parties compute the values $[b]_M = [y+r]_M$, $[a]_M = [r'-x]_M$
2. Parties open the values a and b, and compute $T \equiv a+b \pmod{M}$ locally.
3. Parties compute the following quantities:
   - $[w_1]_2 = \Pi_{\mathsf{LTBits}}(b, [r_0]_2, ..., [r_{m-1}]_2)$.
   - $[w_2]_2 = \Pi_{\mathsf{LTBits}}(a, [r'_0]_2, ..., [r'_{m-1}]_2)$.
   - $w_3 = (T < b)$.
   - $[s_0]_2, ..., [s_{m-1}]_2, [s_m]_2 = \Pi_{\mathsf{BitAdder}}([r_0]_2, ..., [r_{m-1}]_2, [r'_0]_2, ..., [r'_{m-1}]_2)$.
   - $[w_4]_2 = [s_m]_2$
   - $[w_5]_2 = \Pi_{\mathsf{LTBits}}(T, [s_0]_2, ..., [s_{m-1}]_2)$.
4. Output $[w]_2 = [w_1]_2 + [w_2]_2 + w_3 - [w_4]_2 - [w_5]_2$, or use one classical daBit and output $[w]_M$.

Fig. 6. Protocol for comparison between *two arithmetic inputs shared in* $\mathbb{Z}_M$, for any modulus M (in particular, M can be 2^k or a prime p).

requires slightly different protocols. We provide a brief discussion on applications of either of these protocols in Sect. 4.2.

Each step of the protocol Π_{LTS} computes the following:

1. Parties mask the input values $[y]$ and $[x]$ using the arithmetic shares of two random edaBits $[r]$ and $[r']$, resulting in shared values $[b]$ and $[a] \in \mathbb{Z}_M$.
2. These masked values are opened (without revealing any information about x or y) and the value $T \equiv a + b \pmod{M}$ is computed locally.
3. The parties then perform the following computations:
   (a) Using Π_{LTBits}, a secret comparison between the open value b and the bitwise sharing of the edaBit r, and store the result $[w_1]_2$.
   (b) A similar comparison between a and the bitwise sharing of r', and store the output in $[w_2]_2$.
   (c) Check in the clear whether $(T < b)$, and store this value in w_3.
   (d) Compute a circuit for bitwise addition of two binary (secret) vectors, where the result is a bitwise secret shared vector of the bits of $(r + r')$.
   (e) Extract the last carry bit from the binary adder (Step 3d) as $[w_4]_2$.
   (f) Finally, using Π_{LTBits}, compare the value T against the bitwise secret sharing of $r + r'$ (computed in Step 3d), and store the output in $[w_5]_2$.
4. In the end, the parties conclude the comparison protocol by computing the output $[w]_2 = [w_1]_2 + [w_2]_2 + w_3 - [w_4]_2 - [w_5]_2$. This final step, similarly to the LTC protocol follows from the way we exploit the commutative nature of addition, and we show correctness subsequently. The final output is the binary sharing of the comparison result, which can be transformed to a shared bit in $\mathbb{Z}_M$ if needed.

Correctness of Π_{LTS}: Following the same notation set-up as in Sect. 2.2 for Π_{LTC}, we denote by $[x]$ the value of $x \in \mathbb{Z}_M$, and the function $\mathsf{LT}(x, y)$ as defined in Eq. 1. We are interested in securely computing the Boolean value $(x < y)$, for x and y two secret shared values in $\mathbb{Z}_M$. The intuition for our protocol is presented in Fig. 7 and follows the same idea as in Π_{LTC}, viz., computing a sum in two different ways and using Eq. 2 to find a constraint between the various wrappings around the modulus.

First note that $[x] < [y]$ iff $\mathsf{LT}([y - x], [y]) = 1$. We then mask the inputs y and $-x$ using the two edaBits: $[b] = [y + r]$, $[a] = [r' - x]$. Finally, we look at computing the value $[T] = [y - x + r + r']$ in two different ways, as the sum of a and b, and as the sum of $y - x$ and $r + r'$. Looking at the addition using the first way, we first open the values a and b, and write the exact integer relation (using Eq. 2):

$$T = b + a - M \cdot \mathsf{LT}(T, b) \tag{6}$$

We can also write similar expressions for b and a,

$$b = [y] + [r] - M \cdot \mathsf{LT}(b, [r])$$
$$a = [-x] + [r'] - M \cdot \mathsf{LT}(a, [r']) \tag{7}$$

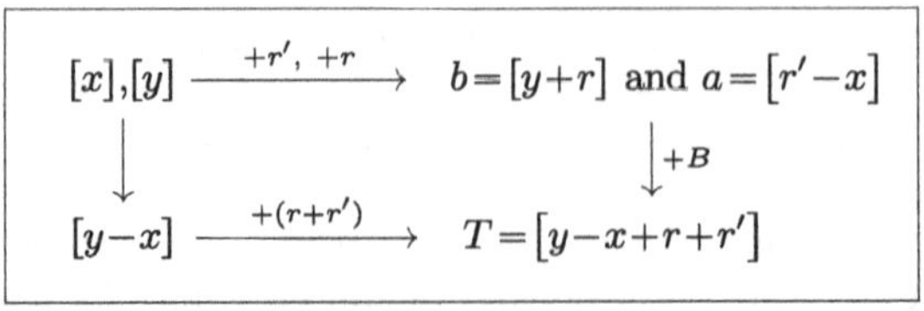

Fig. 7. Intuition behind the comparison protocol for two secret values, once again based on the commutative nature of addition over rings and fields.

Thus the first expression for the sum T is given by (combining Eqs. 6, 7):

$$T = [y] + [r] - M \cdot \mathsf{LT}(b, [r]) + [-x] + [r'] - M \cdot \mathsf{LT}(a, [r']) - M \cdot \mathsf{LT}(T, b) \quad (8)$$

Grouping the terms differently and computing the sum using the latter expression:

$$T = [y - x] + [r + r'] - M \cdot \mathsf{LT}(T, [r + r']) \quad (9)$$

Once again, $[y - x]$ and $[r + r']$ can be expanded using Eq. 2 as:

$$\begin{aligned} [y - x] &= [y] + [-x] - M \cdot \mathsf{LT}([y - x], [y]) \\ [r + r'] &= [r] + [r'] - M \cdot \mathsf{LT}([r + r'], [r]). \end{aligned} \quad (10)$$

Plugging Eq. 10 into Eq. 9, and equating that with the expression in Eq. 8, we get the following expression for $\mathsf{LT}([y - x], [y])$, the quantity of interest:

$$\mathsf{LT}([y - x], [y]) = \mathsf{LT}(b, [r]) + \mathsf{LT}(a, [r']) + \mathsf{LT}(T, b) - \mathsf{LT}([r + r'], [r]) - \mathsf{LT}(T, [r + r'])$$

This completes the correctness proof. To generate an efficient protocol for this expression, the final observation is that $\mathsf{LT}([r + r'], [r])$ is generated as a by-product of the computation required to generate the bit decomposition of $r + r'$ from the bit decompositions of r, r' (to enable a call to Π_{LTBits}). ∎

3 Evaluation

We implement our protocol in the MP-SPDZ Framework [13]. The entire protocol is a handful of lines of python code, as shown in Fig. 1b, and reads directly from the pseudocode; this makes it highly amenable to implementation. We evaluate our protocol over various MPC settings and a brief summary of our experiments is provided below:

(i) **Throughput of Comparisons:** In this experiment, we measure the throughput of comparison operations and compare this with prior art. These results are presented in Sect. 3.1.

(ii) **Private Evaluation of ResNet-50:** We provide benchmarks for evaluating ResNet-50 [17] using dishonest majority privacy-preserving computation. We use the state-of-the-art matrix triple generation algorithm [7] and combine that with our comparison protocol and compare that against the prior art [7,14]. These results are presented in Sect. 3.2.

Set-up Details: We use an MPC set-up similar to prior works [14,24,25]. Each party is run on an Intel(R) Core(TM) i9-9900 CPU @ 3.10 GHz with 128 GB of RAM over a 10 Gb/s network switch with an average round-trip ping time of 1 ms. For the WAN setting we use two or three machines depending on the protocol wich are equipped with Intel(R) Xeon(R) CPU E5-2690 v3 @ 2.60 GHz and 54 GB of RAM while the network capability was slowed down using the Linux **tc** command limiting the bandwidth to 100Mb/s and 100 ms round-trip ping time.

3.1 Throughput of Rabbit comparisons

We conduct experiments in all combinations of the possible adversarial models (active, passive), adversarial settings (honest majority, dishonest majority), and domains (OT-based in $\mathbb{Z}_{2^k}$, OT-based in $\mathbb{F}_p$, HE-based in $\mathbb{F}_p$), and in both the LAN and WAN network settings. Table 1 provides a summary of the primitives used as preprocessing (i.e., offline cost) for a Rabbit comparison, vs. an edaBit comparison [14], their online round complexity, security, and the need for slack, in $\mathbb{Z}_{2^k}$ and in $\mathbb{F}_p$. As in Escudero et al. [14], we benchmark the time required for a million comparisons between two (DM) or three (HM) servers described in the setup above. Table 2, 3 show the number of comparisons per second (throughput) and communication per party (kbits) for a single operation in the LAN and WAN settings respectively. Our protocol improves prior art in runtime and communication by upto 2×, and in all cases, achieves these without any slack.

Communication for Π_{LTC} over $\mathbb{F}_p$. Note that our protocol incurs higher communication cost, when performing comparisons over fields. This is due to the use of a more expensive Prefix OR computation. Prior works encode the data in a larger dataspace and simply extract the MSB for the comparison. In a manner similar to the optimization from Π_{LTC} to Π_{ReLU}, we can extract the MSB to compute a comparison. This operation requires using a prefix computation protocol Π_{PreOpL} (cf [6]), which has a linear overhead of $2(k-1)$ bit-triples in $\log_2 k$ rounds – matching that of edaBits [14]. If a different encoding is used, where positive and negative numbers are determined by comparison with $\lfloor p/2 \rfloor$,

Table 1. Theoretical complexity comparison of exact comparison functionality over $\mathbb{Z}_{2^k}$ and $\mathbb{F}_p$ where k is the bit-size of the datatypes, l is the $\log_2$ bound on the inputs/data, and m refers to the number of bits to be truncated.

Sub-protocols	Rabbit		edaBits Comp. [14]	
	$\mathbb{Z}_{2^k}$	$\mathbb{F}_p$	$\mathbb{Z}_{2^k}$	$\mathbb{F}_p$
edaBits	1:$\{k\}$	1:$\{k\}$	1:$\{l\}$	2:$\{l-m+s, m\}$
daBits	1	1	1	1
ANDs	$3(k-1)$	$k\log_2 k^*$	$3(l-1)$	$2(k-1)$
# Rounds	$2+\log_2 k$	$\log_2 k$	$2\log_2 l$	$2\log_2 k$
Security, slack	Perfect, No	Statistical, No	Statistical, Yes	Statistical, Yes

Table 2. Throughput and communication for running secure comparisons using Rabbit in contrast to prior art *over LAN* for 16 threads, with 2 million comparisons in total.

		Domain	Rabbit		edaBits Comp. [14]	
			Thru.(ops/s)	Comm.(kb)	Thru.(ops/s)	Comm.(kb)
Dishonest majority	Active	2^k (OT)	2936	1252.4	3038	1252.2
		p (OT)	1537	2847.0	1056	4458.6
		p (HE)	1495	1678	1495	1635.99
	Passive	2^k (OT)	165368	39.5	172211	38.3
		p (OT)	73947	87.8	51478	132.2
		p (HE)	65750	67.63	41175	41.71
Honest majority	Active	2^k	117607	5.62	116616	5.54
		p	88780	9.43	41028	19.62
	Passive	2^k	5706569	0.5	5600265	0.5
		p	1421412	0.96	472316	1.58

the same protocol can be used with statistical correctness, determined by the specific choice of prime (with a small gap between p and 2^k). A suitable choice of prime p would also further lower the prepossessing time, when performed using HE.

3.2 Neural Network Evaluation

In this section, we provide benchmarks for using our approach for comparison on evaluating the ResNet-50 architecture [17]. In our experiments, we consider neural network inference over 64-bit datatypes and compare the offline and online performance of our protocol with the state-of-the-art protocols with active security in the dishonest majority setting. For prior art, we use the recent protocol for matrix triple generation [7] in conjunction with our Π_{LTC} comparison protocol. The results are summarized below.

The work of Chen *et al.* [7] requires the plaintext modulus to be 128-bits, due to the slack required in the comparison. In this work, we eliminate that slack and hence only require generation of matrix triples using homomorphic encryption (HE) with a plaintext space of 64-bits. While Chen *et al.* [7] require a 128-bit modulus and $N = 2^{15}$ (degree of the cyclotomic polynomial), we can generate 64-bit triples. This enables us to run the algorithm with lower HE parameters (and consequently better performance). We use $N = 2^{14}$, a plaintext modulus of 64-bits and a ciphertext modulus of 480. With a conservative analysis this leaves enough room for 40-bits of statistical security. We set the block size to 64 instead of 128 and thus pack 4 matrices in a single ciphertext (compared to 2 in Chen *et al.* [7]). We list the sizes of matrices required for the computations in ResNet-50 and then measure the time required (and communication overhead) for matrix triple generations using these different set-ups. We run the protocols on a similar set-up as Chen *et al.* [7], using a 5 Gb/s LAN bandwidth and about 300 Mbps WAN bandwidth. Hence, just for the triple generation, our communication complexity reduces by about 60% and the total time by about 40% of [7] for the same set of triple generations (LAN and WAN settings are fairly similar

Table 3. Throughput and communication for running secure comparisons using Rabbit in contrast to prior art *over WAN*. All numbers were produced using 2 million comparisons with 8 threads, except in the active security, dishonest majority field cases where we used only 32,000 comparisons due to time constraints. Note that for the active security, dishonest majority field case with HE preprocessing, the 54 GB RAM machines ran out of memory due to the large ciphertexts kept in memory by MP-SPDZ - for Rabbit there were no memory issues as the memory footprint is reduced to half due to ciphertexts that only need to accommodate 64-bits plaintexts.

		Domain	Rabbit		edaBits Comp. [14]	
			Thru.(ops/s)	Comm.(kb)	Thru.(ops/s)	Comm.(kb)
Dishonest Majority	Active	2^k (OT)	33	1237	33	1237
		p (OT)	1.37	29646	0.37	112594
		p (HE)	2	19089	N/A	N/A
	Passive	2^k (OT)	596	39.26	604	38.18
		p (OT)	366	87.59	245	131
		p (HE)	427	67.01	431	41.71
Honest Majority	Active	2^k	5444	5.54	5488	5.52
		p	1639	16.96	1463	19.53
	Passive	2^k	15096	0.49	15182	0.49
		p	11492	0.96	7640	1.53

as the protocols are compute dominated). Furthermore, our computational burden for the matrix triple computations reduces from about 72 GB to 9.3 GB – a critical improvement for systems based on HE.

We also run the offline and online computations for the comparisons in ResNet-50 and compare the total time. Our protocol takes about 11 h and 2883.3 GB of communication. When compared to prior art of Chen *et al.* [7], they evaluate the same network in about 24hrs with 2036 GB (using improved comparisons using edaBits). Thus, our work is 2× faster albeit uses slightly more communication due to the communication gap for Rabbit and edaBit for dishonest majority within a characteristic p field. Thus, our comparison protocol, combined with the improvement in the triple generation phase due to slack elimination, provides a significant throughput improvement over state-of-the-art MPC protocols for neural network evaluation.

4 Discussion

In this section, we provide a deeper discussion on the following aspects of this work. We (1) elaborate on our central contribution of removing the slack and how it enables computation over smaller data types; (2) we discuss applications of these protocols; and (3) provide an analysis of the statistical security provided by our protocol along with the choice of modulus for the case of fields.

4.1   Elimination of "Slack" in Comparisons

One important contribution of this work is the elimination of a "slack" between the inputs (in other words the computable part of the data) and the actual size of the datatypes used in the MPC engines. Note that prior work in the dishonest majority setting requires a slack to accommodate for the statistical parameter. Commonly, this statistical parameter, which is necessary to ensure security, is at least 40-bits. This implies that the actual datatypes used in the MPC are at least 40-bits longer than the values we need to compute upon. As a consequence, prior work requires 128-bit datatypes for the MPC, necessary to support 64-bit computations. On the contrary, our comparison protocol achieves exact comparison without the need for any slack and thus operates on smaller, 64-bit datatypes. As shown in Sect. 3.2, when the slack removal is combined with recent advances such as the contributions of the work of Chen *et al.* [7], the smaller MPC datatypes enable faster triple generation, reduce the communication and computational overhead and increase the overall efficiency of the MPC computations, beyond secure comparisons.

4.2   Applications to Machine Learning and Beyond

Privacy-preserving machine learning, which is of increasing interest in the field of MPC, often relies on efficient protocols for computing ReLU, a non-linear function that is given by $\mathsf{ReLU}(x) = \max(x,0)$. Using fixed-point encoding, computation of the ReLU function reduces to a comparison with an encoding of 0 (i.e., a constant). Given that this non-linear function is the bottleneck of many state-of-the-art secure machine learning protocols [18,21], our proposed protocol improves this entire line of work.

The thresholding operation is yet another application where we require a comparison with a public constant. In image processing and computer vision, threasholding is used for segmenting images (e.g., turn a grayscale image into a binary one). In particular, it replaces a pixel with a black (resp. white) pixel, if the image intensity is less (resp. greater) than a fixed constant. In yet another application, Cryptography for #metoo [19], the system heavily relies on the use of public value thresholding. In adversarial machine learning, algorithms for robustness that work over privacy-preserving computation also require thresholdings with small public values. In all these applications, the functionality can be efficiently achieved using our comparison with constant protocol. Thus, our efficient comparison with constant protocol, Π_{LTC} (Sec. 2.2), is deployable on several application scenarios.

On the other hand, there are applications, where secure comparisons with a constant do not suffice, but a comparison between two values that are both secret is required. In such cases, our comparison with secret protocol, Π_{LTS} (Sect. 2.4) can be deployed. Applications in this line of work go as far in the past as the first instance of the problem: Yao's millionaires' problem [34], and include amongst others also secure auctions [4], and secure linear programming [28].

4.3 Statistical Security

We remark that the protocols Π_{LTBits}, Π_{LTC}, Π_{ReLU} and Π_{LTS} are all inherently information theoretically secure. However, when combined with a larger MPC platform, the overall security is set by the weaker between the MPC platform and the protocol, and hence when using protocols such as SPDZ [12], BDOZa [2], SPDZ2^k [10], our security reduces to statistical. The current implementation has a small statistical security due to the use of edaBits [14]. The protocol for edaBit generation produces shares:

$$[r]_M \text{ and } \{[r_i]_2\}_{i=0}^{m-1} \text{ such that } r \equiv \sum_{i=0}^{m-1} r_i \cdot 2^i \pmod{M} \qquad (11)$$

In particular, for the correctness of Π_{LTC} in Sec. 2.2, we require that $r = \sum r_i \cdot 2^i$, and this condition is different from Eq. 11 in a subtle yet important way. In the case where $M = 2^m$, this does not raise an issue. However, in all other cases, in particular including the field case, we have $2^{m-1} < M < 2^m$, and so we can have $r = (\sum r_i \cdot 2^i) - M$. In this case, the correctness of Π_{LTC} does not hold, as the set of sharings $\{[r_i]_2\}_{i=0}^{m-1}$ does not correspond to the bit decomposition of r. To address this issue, we note that this failure probability depends on the size of the gap between the modulus and the bounding power of 2 in relation to the modulus. The failure probability is given by:

$$\text{Failure probability } = \frac{2^m - M}{2^m} \qquad (12)$$

which is simply the probability that r is between M and 2^m. Thus, if $\delta = 2^m - M$, the failure probability can be made small for suitable choice of $\delta/2^m$. Thus, in practice, we choose the largest 64-bit prime $p = 2^{64} - 59$ for our implementation. This gives our protocol a failure probability of less than 2^{-59}. However, from a security point of view, for statistical hiding, we use the fact that $r \leftarrow R\{0, 1, \cdots, 2^m - 1\}$ when reduced modulo M is still close to uniform in $\mathbb{Z}_M$ (to ensure the masked value is hidden). If the former distribution is D_1 and the latter is D_2, then this statistical distance can be computed exactly as given in Eq. 13. Thus, the statistical closeness can also be made negligible by a suitable choice of $\delta/2^m$. A union bound over the two expressions (Eq. 12 and 13) allows us to achieve both correctness and privacy with a statistical parameter close to 58-bits.

$$\text{Statistical closeness } = \text{Distance}(D_1, D_2)$$
$$= \frac{1}{2} \left[\left(\sum_{i=0}^{\delta-1} \frac{2}{2^m} - \frac{1}{M} \right) + \left(\sum_{i=\delta}^{2^m-1} \frac{1}{M} - \frac{1}{2^m} \right) \right] \qquad (13)$$
$$= \frac{\delta \cdot (M - \delta)}{M \cdot 2^m} \leqslant \frac{\delta}{2^m}$$

Furthermore, we note that one can use rejection sampling as follows: run Π_{LTBits} over the bit decomposition of r and the modulus M to check if $r \geqslant M$. If this is the case then reject the sample. This way we can eliminate such edaBits and note that the rejections happen with probability similar to the expression in Eq. 12 and is thus ideal once again when the prime p is close to a power of 2.

As an aside, the closer the prime is to the power of two, the lower is the failure probability. However, when combining with other protocols, such as those mentioned in Sect. 3.2, there are other considerations in choosing the prime. For instance, for efficiency reasons BFV [5,15] requires special prime modulus, where $p-1$ has a large factor (around 2^{14} - 2^{16}). One such prime is $p = 2^{64} - 83$, where $33196 \mid p-1$ and $\phi(33196) = 16128$ (with ϕ the Euler's Totient function), which would be secure given the 16k degree and appropriately chosen modulus q.

5   Comparison with Related Work

After the seminal work of Yao [34], which operates in the two-party setting, and is based on garbled circuits, many works studied the problem of secure comparisons, both in the two-party [8,29,35], as well as in the multi-party setting [6,9,20,23]. In this work, we focus on the general n-party setting. Damgård et al. [9] were the first to tackle the challenge of secure, constant-round bit decomposition of secret shared inputs, which is a necessary building block for most comparison protocols. In the same work [9], they extend and apply their bit-decomposition protocol to develop a secure comparison protocol (amongst other applications). Their comparison protocol works in the general n-party setting, with any underlying linear secret sharing scheme (LSSS), and provides unconditional security against active adversaries (assuming that the multiplication protocol of the LSSS is also actively secure), in the honest majority setting.

Improving upon the complexity of Damgård et al.'s [9] bit decomposition, comparison, equality, and interval test protocols, Nishide and Ohta [23] provide new, simplified protocols. In addition, Nishide and Ohta [23] construct new secure comparison, equality, and interval test protocols, which do not rely on bit decomposition. For their deterministic equality test protocol that is independent of bit decomposition, Nishide and Ohta [23] apply a masking technique similar to the one we use in our comparison protocol: they use a random shared value that the parties possess both in its $\mathbb{F}_p$ and in its bit decomposed form to mask and afterwards open the secret shared input of the equality test.

In an attempt to design comparison protocols with concrete efficiency instead of asymptotic, Catrina and de Hoogh [6] propose several versions of secure equality and comparison tests. Their protocols run in logarithmic number of rounds, in the bit-length of the values to be compared, but also with logarithmic communication cost (instead of the usually linear communication cost). The efficiency of these protocols comes also at the cost of statistical, instead of unconditional security and have been adopted and implemented in a number of MPC platforms (e.g., [1,13]). Our comparison protocol, in combination with the recent advances in the generation of daBits [25], and edaBits [14] performs concretely better than the one of Catrina and de Hoogh [6], while offering unconditional (instead of statistical) security in $\mathbb{Z}_{2^k}$.

Lipmaa and Toft [20] propose three different comparison protocols. Only one of these comparison protocols works for the general n-party setting with active security, and while it offers sublinear online communication complexity, it is not constant-round and it has linear offline communication cost. Like other protocols in the literature [8, 29], the core of [20] lies in the idea of splitting the two strings to be compared into smaller, equal length blocks, and perform the comparison on the first block where they differ. This way the problem of comparison only needs to be addressed on smaller strings (the blocks), and equality testing can be applied to the larger strings (to allow for the necessary reduction of the size of the blocks on which comparison is to be performed). Other recent concretely-efficient comparison protocols such as [16, 31–33] also eliminate the need for a slack but operate in fixed adversarial models and are tied to a 3-party MPC setting.

Table 4. Comparison of the related work in the n-party setting in terms of offline, and online communication and computation complexity; in terms of rounds; in terms of security; and in terms of adversarial model and adversarial settings supported. In the context of adversarial setting HM stands for honest majority, while DM stands for dishonest majority. *perfect security holds only when the underlying secret sharing scheme operates over $\mathbb{Z}_{2^k}$.

Protocol	Communication		Computation		Rounds	Security	Adversary	Setting
	Offline	Online	Offline	Online				
[9]	–	$\mathcal{O}(\ell \log \ell)$	–	$\mathcal{O}(\ell \log \ell)$	$\mathcal{O}(1)$	Perfect	Active	HM
[23]	–	$\mathcal{O}(\ell)$	–	$\mathcal{O}(\ell)$	$\mathcal{O}(1)$	Perfect	Passive	HM
[6]	–	$\mathcal{O}(\log \ell)$	–	$\mathcal{O}(\log \ell)$	$\mathcal{O}(\log \ell)$	Statistical	Passive	HM
[20]	$\mathcal{O}(\ell)$	$\mathcal{O}(\log \ell)$	$\mathcal{O}(\log \ell)$	$\mathcal{O}(\log \ell)$	$\mathcal{O}(\log \ell)$	Statistical	Active	HM
Rabbit	$\mathcal{O}(\ell)$	$\mathcal{O}(\ell \log \ell)$	$\mathcal{O}(\ell)$	$\mathcal{O}(\ell)$	$\mathcal{O}(\log \ell)$	Perfect*	Active	DM

In Table 4 we detail the asymptotic costs and security features of the related work in secure comparisons for the general n-party setting. It is important to remark that most prior secure comparison protocols require the values to be compared to be smaller than the space where the comparison takes place. Although this may result in efficient protocols for the particular comparison operations, it also requires a larger MPC engine to perform all (other) computations. Essentially, this means that all adjacent computations should be performed in a larger space, and all values to be communicated throughout the protocol need to be larger by a factor proportional to the necessary slack for the secure comparison. Our protocol crucially overcomes this limitation.

6 Conclusion

In this work, we propose novel comparison protocols for general n-party computation. Our protocols enjoy perfect security, when we operate over $\mathbb{Z}_{2^k}$, and crucially eliminate the need for "slack" – a larger dataspace to compute secure comparisons, enabling computations over smaller datatypes. In terms of concrete efficiency, our protocols improve prior art by twice for most adversary structures, while keeping a smaller communication complexity. Given that comparisons are a fundamental secure computation primitive, many MPC applications can benefit from our protocols.

Acknowledgements. This work was supported in part by the Research Council KU Leuven grant C14/18/067, and by CyberSecurity Research Flanders with reference number VR20192203, and by ERC Advanced Grant ERC-2015-AdG-IMPaCT.

References

1. Aly, A.: SCALE-MAMBA v1.2: Documentation (2018)
2. Bendlin, R., Damgård, I., Orlandi, C., Zakarias, S.: Semi-homomorphic encryption and multiparty computation. In: Paterson, K.G. (ed.) EUROCRYPT 2011. LNCS, vol. 6632, pp. 169–188. Springer, Heidelberg (2011). https://doi.org/10.1007/978-3-642-20465-4_11
3. Bogetoft, P., et al.: Secure multiparty computation goes live. In: Dingledine, R., Golle, P. (eds.) FC 2009. LNCS, vol. 5628, pp. 325–343. Springer, Heidelberg (2009). https://doi.org/10.1007/978-3-642-03549-4_20
4. Bogetoft, P., Damgård, I., Jakobsen, T., Nielsen, K., Pagter, J., Toft, T.: A practical implementation of secure auctions based on multiparty integer computation. In: Di Crescenzo, G., Rubin, A. (eds.) FC 2006. LNCS, vol. 4107, pp. 142–147. Springer, Heidelberg (2006). https://doi.org/10.1007/11889663_10
5. Brakerski, Z.: Fully homomorphic encryption without modulus switching from classical GapSVP. In: Safavi-Naini, R., Canetti, R. (eds.) CRYPTO 2012. LNCS, vol. 7417, pp. 868–886. Springer, Heidelberg (2012). https://doi.org/10.1007/978-3-642-32009-5_50
6. Catrina, O., de Hoogh, S.: Improved primitives for secure multiparty integer computation. In: Garay, J.A., De Prisco, R. (eds.) SCN 2010. LNCS, vol. 6280, pp. 182–199. Springer, Heidelberg (2010). https://doi.org/10.1007/978-3-642-15317-4_13
7. Chen, H., Kim, M., Razenshteyn, I., Rotaru, D., Song, Y., Wagh, S.: Maliciously secure matrix multiplication with applications to private deep learning. In: Moriai, S., Wang, H. (eds.) ASIACRYPT 2020. LNCS, vol. 12493, pp. 31–59. Springer, Cham (2020). https://doi.org/10.1007/978-3-030-64840-4_2
8. Couteau, G.: New protocols for secure equality test and comparison. In: Preneel, B., Vercauteren, F. (eds.) ACNS 2018. LNCS, vol. 10892, pp. 303–320. Springer, Cham (2018). https://doi.org/10.1007/978-3-319-93387-0_16
9. Damgård, I., Fitzi, M., Kiltz, E., Nielsen, J.B., Toft, T.: Unconditionally secure constant-rounds multi-party computation for equality, comparison, bits and exponentiation. In: Halevi, S., Rabin, T. (eds.) TCC 2006. LNCS, vol. 3876, pp. 285–304. Springer, Heidelberg (2006). https://doi.org/10.1007/11681878_15
10. Damgård, I., Keller, M., Larraia, E., Pastro, V., Scholl, P., Smart, N.P.: Practical covertly secure mpc for dishonest majority – or: breaking the SPDZ limits. In: Crampton, J., Jajodia, S., Mayes, K. (eds.) ESORICS 2013. LNCS, vol. 8134, pp. 1–18. Springer, Heidelberg (2013). https://doi.org/10.1007/978-3-642-40203-6_1

11. Damgård, I., Nielsen, J.B.: Universally composable efficient multiparty computation from threshold homomorphic encryption. In: Boneh, D. (ed.) CRYPTO 2003. LNCS, vol. 2729, pp. 247–264. Springer, Heidelberg (2003). https://doi.org/10.1007/978-3-540-45146-4_15
12. Damgård, I., Pastro, V., Smart, N., Zakarias, S.: Multiparty computation from somewhat homomorphic encryption. In: Safavi-Naini, R., Canetti, R. (eds.) CRYPTO 2012. LNCS, vol. 7417, pp. 643–662. Springer, Heidelberg (2012). https://doi.org/10.1007/978-3-642-32009-5_38
13. Data61. MP-SPDZ: Versatile Framework for Multi-party Computation (2019). https://github.com/data61/MP-SPDZ
14. Escudero, D., Ghosh, S., Keller, M., Rachuri, R., Scholl, P.: Improved Primitives for MPC over Mixed Arithmetic-Binary Circuits. Cryptology ePrint Archive, Report 2020/338 (2020). https://eprint.iacr.org/2020/338
15. Fan, J., Vercauteren, F.: Somewhat Practical Fully Homomorphic Encryption. Cryptology ePrint Archive, Report 2012/144 (2012). https://eprint.iacr.org/2012/144
16. Fujii, W., Iwamura, K., Inamura, M.: Secure comparison and interval test protocols based on three-party MPC. In: 6th International Conference on Information Systems Security and Privacy, ICISSP 2020, pp. 698–704. SciTePress (2020)
17. He, K., Zhang, X., Ren, S., Sun, J.: Deep residual learning for image recognition. In: Proceedings of the IEEE Conference on Computer Vision and Pattern Recognition, pp. 770–778 (2016)
18. Juvekar, C., Vaikuntanathan, V., Chandrakasan, A.: GAZELLE: a low latency framework for secure neural network inference. In: 27th USENIX Security Symposium (USENIX Security 18), pp. 1651–1669 (2018)
19. Kuykendall, B., Krawczyk, H., Rabin, T.: Cryptography for# metoo. In: Privacy Enhancing Technologies Symposium (PETS) (2019)
20. Lipmaa, H., Toft, T.: Secure equality and greater-than tests with sublinear online complexity. In: Fomin, F.V., Freivalds, R., Kwiatkowska, M., Peleg, D. (eds.) ICALP 2013. LNCS, vol. 7966, pp. 645–656. Springer, Heidelberg (2013). https://doi.org/10.1007/978-3-642-39212-2_56
21. Liu, J., Juuti, M., Lu, Y., Asokan, N.: Oblivious neural network predictions via MiniONN transformations. In: Proceedings of the 2017 ACM SIGSAC Conference on Computer and Communications Security, pp. 619–631 (2017)
22. Mohassel, P., Zhang, Y.: SecureML: a system for scalable privacy-preserving machine learning. In: IEEE Symposium on Security and Privacy (S&P) (2017)
23. Nishide, T., Ohta, K.: Multiparty computation for interval, equality, and comparison without bit-decomposition protocol. In: Okamoto, T., Wang, X. (eds.) PKC 2007. LNCS, vol. 4450, pp. 343–360. Springer, Heidelberg (2007). https://doi.org/10.1007/978-3-540-71677-8_23
24. Rotaru, D., Smart, N.P., Tanguy, T., Vercauteren, F., Wood, T.: Actively Secure Setup for SPDZ. Cryptology ePrint Archive, Report 2019/1300 (2019). https://eprint.iacr.org/2019/1300
25. Rotaru, D., Wood, T.: MArBled circuits: mixing arithmetic and boolean circuits with active security. In: Hao, F., Ruj, S., Sen Gupta, S. (eds.) INDOCRYPT 2019. LNCS, vol. 11898, pp. 227–249. Springer, Cham (2019). https://doi.org/10.1007/978-3-030-35423-7_12
26. Sepior. https://sepior.com/ (2020)
27. Sharemind. https://sharemind.cyber.ee/ (2020)

28. Toft, T.: Solving linear programs using multiparty computation. In: Dingledine, R., Golle, P. (eds.) FC 2009. LNCS, vol. 5628, pp. 90–107. Springer, Heidelberg (2009). https://doi.org/10.1007/978-3-642-03549-4_6
29. Toft, T.: Sub-linear, secure comparison with two non-colluding parties. In: Catalano, D., Fazio, N., Gennaro, R., Nicolosi, A. (eds.) PKC 2011. LNCS, vol. 6571, pp. 174–191. Springer, Heidelberg (2011). https://doi.org/10.1007/978-3-642-19379-8_11
30. Unbound. https://www.unboundtech.com/ (2020)
31. Wagh, S.: New Directions in Efficient Privacy Preserving Machine Learning. PhD thesis, Princeton University (2020)
32. Wagh, S., Gupta, D., Chandran, N.: SecureNN: 3-party secure computation for neural network training. In: Privacy Enhancing Technologies Symposium (PETS) (2019)
33. Wagh, S., Tople, S., Benhamouda, F., Kushilevitz, E., Mittal, P., Rabin, T.: FALCON: honest-majority maliciously secure framework for private deep learning. In: Privacy Enhancing Technologies Symposium (PETS) (2021)
34. Yao, A.C.: Protocols for Secure Computations. In: 23rd Annual Symposium on Foundations of Computer Science (sfcs 1982), pp. 160–164. IEEE (1982)
35. Yu, C.-H., Yang, B.-Y.: Probabilistically correct secure arithmetic computation for modular conversion, zero test, comparison, MOD and exponentiation. In: Visconti, I., De Prisco, R. (eds.) SCN 2012. LNCS, vol. 7485, pp. 426–444. Springer, Heidelberg (2012). https://doi.org/10.1007/978-3-642-32928-9_24

Efficient Noise Generation to Achieve Differential Privacy with Applications to Secure Multiparty Computation

Reo Eriguchi[1,2]([⊠]), Atsunori Ichikawa[3], Noboru Kunihiro[4], and Koji Nuida[1,2]

[1] The University of Tokyo, Tokyo, Japan
{reo_eriguchi,nuida}@mist.i.u-tokyo.ac.jp
[2] National Institute of Advanced Industrial Science and Technology, Tokyo, Japan
[3] NTT Secure Platform Laboratories, Tokyo, Japan
atsunori.ichikawa.nf@hco.ntt.co.jp
[4] University of Tsukuba, Ibaraki, Japan
kunihiro@cs.tsukuba.ac.jp

Abstract. This paper studies the problem of constructing secure multiparty computation protocols whose outputs satisfy differential privacy. We first provide a general framework for multiparty protocols generating shares of noise drawn from distributions capable of achieving differential privacy. Then, using this framework, we propose two kinds of protocols based on secret sharing. The first one is a constant-round protocol which enables parties to jointly generate shares of noise drawn from the discrete Laplace distribution. This protocol always outputs shares of noise while the previously known protocol fails with non-zero probability. The second protocol allows the parties to non-interactively obtain shares of noise following the binomial distribution by predistributing keys for pseudorandom functions in the setup phase. As a result, the parties can compute a share of noise enough to provide the computational analogue of ϵ-differential privacy with communication complexity independent of ϵ. It is much more efficient than the previous protocols which require communication complexity proportional to ϵ^{-2} to achieve (information-theoretic) (ϵ, δ)-differential privacy for some $\delta > 0$.

Keywords: Secure multiparty computation · Differential privacy · Laplace distribution · Binomial distribution

1 Introduction

There is an increasing demand for services aggregating private data from a large number of parties and providing some statistical analysis of them. A typical example is computing histograms of customer information held by banks [9] or medical data stored on servers [25]. Secure multiparty computation (MPC) is a cryptographic technique which enables the parties to compute a function on their data without revealing any information on them to an adversary. Assume that

© International Financial Cryptography Association 2021
N. Borisov and C. Diaz (Eds.): FC 2021, LNCS 12674, pp. 271–290, 2021.
https://doi.org/10.1007/978-3-662-64322-8_13

there are n parties holding their private inputs x_i, $i \in [n] := \{1, 2, \ldots, n\}$. Let g be a function to compute on their inputs. In an MPC protocol based on secret sharing [31], (1) the parties share their inputs among the other parties, (2) they obtain a share of $g(\boldsymbol{x})$ via interaction, and (3) a designated party reconstructs $g(\boldsymbol{x})$, where $\boldsymbol{x} = (x_1, \ldots, x_n)$. The privacy requirement is that an adversary who corrupts at most t parties learns nothing about the inputs of the other parties beyond what follows from the inputs of the corrupted parties and the output.

However, standard MPC protocols output an exact calculation result and cannot prevent the adversary from learning what follows from the result. For example, the exact result of a statistical survey can be used to find out whether a specific individual actually participates in that survey, which may make individuals less motivated about pooling their information. To deal with this problem, differentially private mechanisms [2, 18, 21, 26] add noise drawn from an appropriate distribution to the calculation result and make the distributions of the outputs for two "similar" inputs approximately the same. Nevertheless, since the parties' inputs are typically sensitive, it is not appropriate to assume a trusted party who aggregates their data and applies the mechanism to them, and hence it is necessary to do that task in a distributed setting.

From this point of view, several studies have proposed MPC protocols combined with differential privacy [11, 17, 19, 33]. In [17], the parties compute a share of noise r so that a noisy output $g(\boldsymbol{x})+r$ achieves differential privacy. Technically, the authors in [17] devise methods to jointly generate shares of noise following the binomial distribution of parameter $1/2$ and the discrete Laplace distribution.

That task is not straightforward in that it is necessary to guarantee differential privacy even against an adversary that has access to the internal states of the corrupted parties. Particularly, it cannot be solved by a simple protocol in which a designated party samples noise from a certain distribution and shares it among the other parties. An alternative solution may be to let each party add noise r_i to his share of $g(\boldsymbol{x})$ and then reconstruct $g(\boldsymbol{x}) + \sum_{i \in [n]} r_i$. However, to ensure that $\sum_{i \in [n]} r_i$ is distributed according to our target distribution, we require that the distribution has the reproductive property, which does not hold in the case of the Laplace distribution. Furthermore, since the adversary can subtract the noise generated by the corrupted parties, each honest party has to add more noise and as a result, the noisy output loses its utility.

Although the contributions of [17] are helpful and well suited to our motivations introduced above, there is still room for improvement with respect to the communication and round complexity. First, the protocols for the binomial distribution must generate many uniform random bits, which requires communication complexity proportional to ϵ^{-2} to achieve (ϵ, δ)-differential privacy (see Sect. 2.3 for its definition) for some $\delta > 0$. Secondly, the protocol for the discrete Laplace distribution is essentially based on securely evaluating a Boolean circuit generating biased bits. Hence, it requires round complexity proportional to the depth approximately $\log \log \delta^{-1}$. Moreover, it fails to generate noise with non-zero probability, that is, there is no outcome of the protocol with a certain probability and therefore the parties should re-run it again. Since the probability is determined by a level of differential privacy, the only solution to making it negligible with the same level of privacy is to run the protocol several times.

1.1 Our Results

A General Framework for Distributed Noise Generation. Our first contribution is that we reduce distributed noise generation to secure computation of a function h with input domain S^n for some finite set S such that on a uniform random input $s = (s_i)_{i \in [n]} \in S^n$, the output $h(s)$ is according to a certain distribution capable of providing differential privacy. More precisely, assume that for $T \subseteq [n]$ of size at most t, the distribution of $h(s)$ conditioned on $(s_i)_{i \in T}$ being fixed provides (ϵ, δ)-differential privacy. Then we can obtain a protocol that is (ϵ, δ)-differentially private against an adversary who corrupts at most t parties by combining a (non-differentially private) protocol for computing $g(x)$ on the parties' private inputs x and a protocol for computing $h(s)$ on random inputs s. A more formal statement is given in Sect. 3. Using this framework, we can concentrate on the task of obtaining the noise generator function h and its compact representation, e.g., an arithmetic circuit of small size. We emphasize that our framework completely separates secure computation of h from that of g. Therefore, the level of differential privacy and utility that our noise generation protocol provides and the communication and round complexity of the protocol are all independent of the complexity or functionality of g though being dependent on the sensitivity.

A Novel Protocol for Discrete Laplace Noise Generation. As an instantiation of h, we propose a function h such that $h(s)$ follows a finite-range discrete Laplace distribution if s is uniformly selected. It has two advantages over [17]: (1) it can be represented as a constant-depth arithmetic circuit and (2) it always outputs an appropriate value. Hence, we can obtain a constant-round and error-free protocol for sampling noise from the finite-range discrete Laplace distribution. As a drawback, our protocol requires more communication complexity than [17]. Nevertheless, we show an example parameter setting in which the difference in the communication complexity between [17] and ours is not significant. A more detailed comparison is given in Sect. 6.1.

A Novel Protocol for Binomial Noise Generation. In addition, we consider a function h such that the distribution of $h(s)$ for uniformly selected s is given by $Z - N/2$, where Z follows the binomial distribution of size N and parameter $1/2$. To construct a protocol for h, we make use of pseudorandom secret sharing [14], which enables the parties to locally compute shares of a pseudorandom number using predistributed keys. At the cost of precommunication, our protocol allows the parties to non-interactively obtain shares of binomial noise and significantly reduces the communication complexity of [17]. As a drawback, due to the use of pseudorandom functions, our protocol only satisfies the computational analogue of differential privacy [28]. Moreover, the mean squared error between the output of our protocol and the exact calculation result is $\binom{n}{t}$ times larger than that of [17]. Nevertheless, our protocol works in the client-server model, in which the number n of servers is quite small, e.g., $n = 3$, while a lot of inputs can be dealt with. In Sect. 6.2, we provide a more detailed comparison.

1.2   Related Work

Eigner et al. [19] present an architecture for computing a share of noise following the Laplace distribution. Wu et al. [33] give a necessary and sufficient condition for a protocol to securely realize a differentially private mechanism and construct protocols for Gaussian and Laplace mechanisms. The protocols in [19,33] make black-box use of MPC primitives for operations over real numbers [3,10]. However, [19,33] lack a rigorous analysis of the impact of the finite-precision implementations on differential privacy, which is undesirable in that differentially private mechanisms are vulnerable to the inexact computations [20,27]. On the other hand, our protocols evaluate arithmetic circuits over a prime field and hence, we can rigorously analyze an achievable level of differential privacy.

The authors in [11] propose an efficient method to jointly generate many biased bits and improve the amortized communication complexity of [17]. However, the method is based on oblivious data structures and is not directly applicable to MPC protocols based on secret sharing.

There are two major models of MPC combined with differential privacy: the central model and the local model. In the former, a trusted party aggregates all the parties' inputs, generates noise following a certain distribution, and publishes the result perturbed by the noise. Our protocols can be regarded as solutions to efficiently implementing central-model mechanisms without the trusted party. In the local model, every party locally randomizes his input and sends it to a designated party, who then collects the data and publishes the result. However, local-model mechanisms require a careful analysis of accumulated noise and are proposed only for a limited class of simple functions [1,18,32]. Thus, they do not fit in our setting, where functions to compute are possibly much more complex. It is also shown in [7,12] that the accuracy of noisy outputs is limited to some extent in the local model. Although an intermediate model called the shuffled model has been introduced recently [13], known mechanisms are still applicable only for simple functions such as summation [5,13] and histograms [4].

2   Preliminaries

2.1   Notations

For $n \in \mathbb{N}$, $[n]$ denotes $\{z \in \mathbb{Z} : 1 \leq z \leq n\}$ and $[0..n)$ denotes $\{z \in \mathbb{Z} : 0 \leq z \leq n - 1\}$. A function $f : \mathbb{N} \to \mathbb{R}$ is negligible if for any $c > 0$, there exists $N \in \mathbb{N}$ such that $0 \leq f(\lambda) < 1/\lambda^c$ for any $\lambda \geq N$. Let R and R' be two random variables with range U. We define the statistical distance $\mathrm{SD}(R, R')$ between R and R' as $\mathrm{SD}(R, R') = (1/2) \sum_{u \in U} |\mathrm{Pr}\,[R = u] - \mathrm{Pr}\,[R' = u]|$. It holds that

$SD((R_1, R_2), (R'_1, R'_2)) \leq SD(R_1, R'_1) + SD(R_2, R'_2)$ for random variables R_1, R_2, R'_1, R'_2 and that $SD(F(R), F(R')) \leq SD(R, R')$ for any randomized function F. If s is sampled from a probability distribution $\mathcal{D}$, we write $s \sim \mathcal{D}$. If $\mathcal{D}$ is the uniform distribution over a finite set S, we simply write $s \leftarrow_s S$. For $T \subseteq [n]$ and a vector $\boldsymbol{x} \in S^n$, we denote by $\boldsymbol{x}_T \in S^{|T|}$ the sub-vector obtained by restricting the indices to T. We assume that q is an odd prime and identify the prime field $\mathbb{Z}_q$ of size q with $\{z \in \mathbb{Z} : -q/2 < z < q/2\}$.

2.2   Secure Multiparty Computation

We briefly provide the security definition of MPC protocols only for n-input/1-output deterministic functionalities. See [22] for a more general case of n-input/n-output randomized functionalities. Assume that there are n parties each of which holds an input x_i, $i \in [n]$ from a finite set X_i. Let Y be a finite set and $f : \prod_{i \in [n]} X_i \to Y$ be a deterministic function. Let Π be a protocol between the parties for computing f. We assume that an adversary is passive, that is, a set $T \subseteq [n]$ of corrupted parties reveals their internal information to the adversary although they do not deviate from the protocol Π. For $T \subseteq [n]$ and $\boldsymbol{x} \in \prod_{i \in [n]} X_i$, define $\text{View}_T^{\Pi}(\boldsymbol{x})$ as the random variable containing the inputs of the parties in T, their random inputs, and the messages including an output received by them during the execution of Π with inputs $\boldsymbol{x}$. We say that the protocol Π t-securely computes f if there exists a probabilistic polynomial-time (PPT) algorithm Sim such that for every $T \subseteq [n]$ with $|T| \leq t$, the distribution of $\text{View}_T^{\Pi}(\boldsymbol{x})$ is identical to that of $\text{Sim}(T, \boldsymbol{x}_T, f(\boldsymbol{x}))$.

Secret Sharing. Let $[\![a]\!]_i$ be the i-th share of the (t, n)-Shamir secret sharing scheme [31] for a secret $a \in \mathbb{Z}_q$, where $q > n$, that is, $[\![a]\!]_i = p(i)$ for a random polynomial p of degree at most t such that $p(0) = a$. We simply write $[\![a]\!]$ if the index i is clear from the context. In this paper, we always assume $t < n/2$. Then, a protocol MULT securely computes the multiplication of two shared secrets [8,16]. Since the addition can be locally done, for any function $y : \mathbb{Z}_q^n \to \mathbb{Z}_q$ represented by an arithmetic circuit, there is a protocol Π_g that enables the parties to securely compute $([\![g(\boldsymbol{x})]\!]_i)_{i \in [n]}$. We measure the communication complexity of a protocol Π based on secret sharing by the number $\text{Mult}(\Pi)$ of invocations of MULT and measure the round complexity by the number of sequential rounds of MULT invocations since it is a dominant factor of the complexity.

Primitives. We explain several protocols for specific functions which are constant-round independent of the number of inputs. See [6,15,29] for the details and the exact round complexity of the protocols. A protocol MULT* allows the parties to obtain $[\![\prod_{i \in [\ell]} a_i]\!]$ from $[\![a_i]\!]$, $i \in [\ell]$ for $a_i \in \mathbb{Z}_q \setminus \{0\}$. It has communication complexity equivalent to $5\ell + 1$ invocations of MULT. A protocol PRE$_\vee$ securely computes ℓ shares $[\![\vee_{k=1}^j a_k]\!]$, $j \in [\ell]$ from $[\![a_k]\!]$, $k \in [\ell]$ if $q > 2\ell$. The communication complexity is 17ℓ. When $b_i \in \{0, 1\}$, $i \in [\ell]$ are shared, a protocol

XOR* securely computes $[\![\oplus_{i\in[\ell]}b_i]\!]$ with communication complexity 5ℓ. By computing the XOR of their local random bits, the parties realize the functionality $\mathcal{F}_{\text{Bit}}$ for generating a uniform share of a uniform random bit. Another protocol RAN₂ [15] realizes $\mathcal{F}_{\text{Bit}}$ with 2 invocations of MULT but it fails with probability q^{-1}.

Pseudorandom Secret Sharing. We explain pseudorandom secret sharing [14], which allows the parties to non-interactively share pseudorandom values in $\mathbb{Z}_q$ with predistributed keys.

A pseudorandom function [23] with length parameters $s, \ell : \mathbb{N} \to \mathbb{N}$ is a collection of functions $\{\psi_r : \{0,1\}^{s(\lambda)} \to \{0,1\}^{\ell(\lambda)}\}_{r\in\{0,1\}^*}$, where $\{0,1\}^*$ denotes the set of all the bit strings of arbitrary length and λ is the bit length of r, such that (efficient evaluation) $\psi_r(a)$ can be computed in polynomial time from $r \in \{0,1\}^\lambda$ and $a \in \{0,1\}^{s(\lambda)}$ and (pseudorandomness) for every PPT oracle machine M which has access to outputs of a function on inputs of its choice, it holds that $|\Pr[\mathsf{M}^{\psi_{U_\lambda}}(1^\lambda) = 1] - \Pr[\mathsf{M}^{F_\lambda}(1^\lambda) = 1]| = \mathsf{negl}(\lambda)$, where $U_\lambda \leftarrow_\$ \{0,1\}^\lambda$ and F_λ is a uniformly selected map from $\{0,1\}^{s(\lambda)}$ to $\{0,1\}^{\ell(\lambda)}$.

Let $\mathcal{A}$ be the collection of all the subsets of $n - t$ parties, i.e., $\mathcal{A} = \{A \subseteq [n] : |A| = n - t\}$ and $\mathcal{A}_i = \{A \in \mathcal{A} : i \in A\}$ for $i \in [n]$. Note that $|\mathcal{A}| = \binom{n}{t}$ and $|\mathcal{A}_i| = \binom{n-1}{t}$. For $A \in \mathcal{A}$, let $f_A \in \mathbb{Z}_q[X]$ be the unique polynomial such that $f_A(0) = 1$, $f_A(i) = 0$ for any $i \in [n]\setminus A$, and $\deg(f_A) = t$. Assume that the parties in A agree on a key $r_A \in \{0,1\}^\lambda$ and let $a \in \{0,1\}^{s(\lambda)}$ be a public input. Each party $i \in [n]$ locally computes $r_i = \sum_{A\in\mathcal{A}_i} \psi_{r_A}(a)f_A(i)$ by embedding $\{0,1\}^{\ell(\lambda)}$ into $\mathbb{Z}_q$. It can be verified that r_i is the i-th share for $\sum_{A\in\mathcal{A}} \psi_{r_A}(a) \in \mathbb{Z}_q$.

2.3 Differential Privacy

Two vectors $\boldsymbol{x} = (x_1, \ldots, x_n), \boldsymbol{x}' = (x'_1, \ldots, x'_n) \in \prod_{i\in[n]} X_i$ are called T-neighboring if there is exactly one index $i \in [n]\setminus T$ such that $x_i \neq x'_i$, and simply called neighboring if they are $\emptyset$-neighboring. The sensitivity Δ of $f : \prod_{i\in[n]} X_i \to \mathbb{R}$ is defined as $\Delta = \max\{|f(\boldsymbol{x}) - f(\boldsymbol{x}')| : \boldsymbol{x} \text{ and } \boldsymbol{x}' \text{ are neighboring}\}$.

Let $\mathcal{M}$ be a randomized algorithm with domain $\prod_{i\in[n]} X_i$ and range Y. We say that $\mathcal{M}$ is (ϵ, δ)-differentially private if for all neighboring vectors $\boldsymbol{x}, \boldsymbol{x}' \in \prod_{i\in[n]} X_i$ and for every distinguisher D, it holds that

$$\Pr[\mathsf{D}(\mathcal{M}(\boldsymbol{x})) = 1] \leq \exp(\epsilon) \cdot \Pr[\mathsf{D}(\mathcal{M}(\boldsymbol{x}')) = 1] + \delta.$$

Focusing on computationally bounded distinguishers, we obtain the computational analogue of differential privacy. Let λ be a security parameter. The algorithm $\mathcal{M}$ is computationally ϵ-differentially private [28] if for all neighboring $\boldsymbol{x}$, $\boldsymbol{x}'$ and for every PPT distinguisher D, it holds that

$$\Pr[\mathsf{D}(\mathcal{M}(\boldsymbol{x})) = 1] \leq \exp(\epsilon) \cdot \Pr[\mathsf{D}(\mathcal{M}(\boldsymbol{x}')) = 1] + \mathsf{negl}(\lambda).$$

A protocol Π between n parties is called $(t; \epsilon, \delta)$-differentially private (resp. computationally $(t; \epsilon)$-differentially private) [7] if for any $T \subseteq [n]$ of size at most

t, the mechanism $\text{View}_T^\Pi(\cdot)$ is (ϵ, δ)-differentially private (resp. computationally ϵ-differentially private) for any pair of T-neighboring vectors.

Since we mainly focus on integer data, we consider the discrete analogue of the Laplace distribution $\mathrm{DL}(p)$. For $0 < p < 1$, the probability distribution of $L \sim \mathrm{DL}(p)$ is $\Pr[L = k] = p^{|k|}(1 - p)/(1 + p)$ for $k \in \mathbb{Z}$ [24]. Noise sampled from $\mathrm{DL}(p)$ provide $(\epsilon, 0)$-differential privacy for a function with sensitivity Δ if $p = \exp(-\epsilon/\Delta)$ [21]. In Sect. 4, we show that a finite-range discrete Laplace distribution can also provide differential privacy.

The binomial distribution is also useful to construct a differentially private mechanism [2]. For $N, M \in \mathbb{N}$ and $f : \prod_{i \in [n]} X_i \to \mathbb{R}$ with sensitivity Δ, consider a mechanism $\mathcal{M}_f^{\mathrm{Bin}, N, M}(\boldsymbol{x}) = f(\boldsymbol{x}) + (1/M) \cdot (Z - N/2)$, where Z is a random variable following $\mathrm{Bin}(N, 1/2)$, i.e., $\Pr[Z = k] = \binom{N}{k} 2^{-N}$ for $k = 0, 1, \ldots, N$. Suppose that N, M satisfy $N/4 \geq \max\{23 \log(10/\delta), 2\Delta M\}$ for some $\delta > 0$. Then $\mathcal{M}_f^{\mathrm{Bin}, N, M}$ is (ϵ, δ)-differentially private for any ϵ such that

$$\epsilon \geq \epsilon(\delta, N, M, \Delta) := \Delta \left(c_1(\delta) \frac{M}{\sqrt{N}} + c_2(\delta) \frac{M}{N} \right), \tag{1}$$

where $c_1(\delta) = \mathcal{O}\left(\sqrt{\log \delta^{-1}} \right)$ and $c_2(\delta) = \mathcal{O}\left((\log \delta^{-1})^2 \right)$. Furthermore, for any $\boldsymbol{x} \in \prod_{i \in [n]} X_i$ it holds that $\mathbb{E}\left[|\mathcal{M}_f^{\mathrm{Bin}, N, M}(\boldsymbol{x}) - f(\boldsymbol{x})|^2 \right] = N/4M^2$.

3   A General Framework for Distributed Noise Generation

It is known that if a protocol t-securely realizes an (ϵ, δ)-differentially private mechanism, then it is $(t; \epsilon, \delta)$-differentially private [7,33]. However, it is often complicated to formally prove that a protocol securely realizes a given randomized functionality. Instead, we decompose the mechanism into a function to compute on the parties' private inputs $\boldsymbol{x}$ and a function generating noise from their random inputs $\boldsymbol{s}$. Specifically, assume that the mechanism is represented as $f(\boldsymbol{x}; \boldsymbol{s}) = g(\boldsymbol{x}) + h(\boldsymbol{s})$ using some deterministic functions $g : \mathbb{Z}_q^n \to \mathbb{Z}_q$, $h : S^n \to \mathbb{Z}_q$. Furthermore, assume that for any $T \subseteq [n]$ of size at most t, the mechanism $f(\cdot; \boldsymbol{s})$ for $\boldsymbol{s} \leftarrow_\$ S^n$ satisfies (ϵ, δ)-differential privacy even when the random inputs $\boldsymbol{s}_T$ of the parties in T are fixed. Then, we show that the adversary's view during the execution of a protocol computing the deterministic function f on $\boldsymbol{x} \in \mathbb{Z}_q^n$ and $\boldsymbol{s} \leftarrow_\$ S^n$ satisfies (ϵ, δ)-differential privacy.

Proposition 1. *Let S be a finite set. Let $g : \mathbb{Z}_q^n \to \mathbb{Z}_q$ and $h : S^n \to \mathbb{Z}_q$ be deterministic functions and define $f(\boldsymbol{x}; \boldsymbol{s}) = g(\boldsymbol{x}) + h(\boldsymbol{s})$ for $\boldsymbol{x} \in \mathbb{Z}_q^n$ and $\boldsymbol{s} \in S^n$. Let Π_g (resp. Π_h) be a protocol which takes $\boldsymbol{x} \in \mathbb{Z}_q^n$ (resp. $\boldsymbol{s} \in S^n$) as inputs and securely computes $(\llbracket g(\boldsymbol{x}) \rrbracket_i)_{i \in [n]}$ (resp. $(\llbracket h(\boldsymbol{s}) \rrbracket_i)_{i \in [n]}$). Let $T \subseteq [n]$ be any subset of size t, $\boldsymbol{x}, \boldsymbol{x}' \in \mathbb{Z}_q^n$ be any pair of T-neighboring vectors, and $\boldsymbol{a} \in S^t$. Assume that for any distinguisher D*

$$\Pr[\mathsf{D}(\boldsymbol{x}_T, \boldsymbol{s}_T, f(\boldsymbol{x}; \boldsymbol{s})) = 1 \mid \boldsymbol{s}_T = \boldsymbol{a}]$$
$$\leq \exp(\epsilon) \cdot \Pr[\mathsf{D}(\boldsymbol{x}_T', \boldsymbol{s}_T, f(\boldsymbol{x}'; \boldsymbol{s})) = 1 \mid \boldsymbol{s}_T = \boldsymbol{a}] + \delta, \tag{2}$$

where the probabilities are taken over the randomness of D *and the random choice of* s. *Then the protocol* Π *(described in Fig. 1)* t-*securely computes* $f(x; s)$ *and if* s *is uniformly selected from* S^n, *it is* $(t; \epsilon, \delta)$-*differentially private.*

PROTOCOL Π
Input: $x \in \mathbb{Z}_q^n, s \in S^n$.
Output: $z = g(x) + h(s) \in \mathbb{Z}_q$.
The protocol:
    1. The parties run Π_g with inputs x and obtain $\llbracket g(x) \rrbracket$.
    2. The parties run Π_h with inputs s and obtain $\llbracket h(s) \rrbracket$.
    3. The parties compute $\llbracket z \rrbracket = \llbracket g(x) \rrbracket + \llbracket h(s) \rrbracket$.
    4. The parties reconstruct and output z.

Fig. 1. The protocol for computing a differentially private output

Proof. Let $T \subseteq [n]$ be any subset of size t. The security of Π_g, Π_h and the composition theorem [22] imply that there exists a simulator Sim such that the distribution of $\mathsf{View}_T^{\Pi}(x; s)$ is the same as $\mathsf{Sim}(T, x_T, s_T, f(x; s))$ for all fixed $x \in \mathbb{Z}_q^n$ and $s \in S^n$. In particular, Π t-securely computes $f(x; s)$.

We prove that Π is $(t; \epsilon, \delta)$-differentially private if s is uniformly selected from S^n. Let $x, x' \in \mathbb{Z}_q^n$ be any pair of T-neighboring vectors. First, from the condition (2), we have that for any distinguisher D,

$$\Pr\left[s \leftarrow_{\$} S^n : \mathsf{D}(x_T, s_T, f(x; s)) = 1\right]$$

$$= \sum_{a \in S^t} \Pr\left[s_T = a\right] \Pr\left[\mathsf{D}(x_T, s_T, f(x; s)) = 1 \mid s_T = a\right]$$

$$\leq \exp(\epsilon) \sum_{a \in S^t} \Pr\left[s_T = a\right] \Pr\left[\mathsf{D}(x_T', s_T, f(x'; s)) = 1 \mid s_T = a\right] + \delta$$

$$= \exp(\epsilon) \cdot \Pr\left[s \leftarrow_{\$} S^n : \mathsf{D}(x_T', s_T, f(x'; s)) = 1\right] + \delta. \tag{3}$$

The condition (3) means that $(x_T, s_T, f(x; s))$ is (ϵ, δ)-differentially private if $s \leftarrow_{\$} S^n$. Recall that $\mathsf{View}_T^{\Pi}(x; s)$ is identical to $\mathsf{Sim}(T, x_T, s_T, f(x; s))$ for all fixed x and s. Since differential privacy is immune to post-processing, $\mathsf{View}_T^{\Pi}(\cdot; s)$ with $s \leftarrow_{\$} S^n$ is also (ϵ, δ)-differentially private. $\square$

If we only consider computationally bounded distinguishers, we obtain an analogous result in the computational setting.

Proposition 2. *Let* λ *be a security parameter and suppose that* $\log q, \log |S|, n \in$ $\mathsf{poly}(\lambda)$. *Continuing with the notation in Proposition 1, assume that for any PPT distinguisher* D, *it holds that*

$$\Pr\left[\mathsf{D}(x_T, s_T, f(x; s)) = 1 \mid s_T = a\right]$$

$$\leq \exp(\epsilon) \cdot \Pr\left[\mathsf{D}(x_T', s_T, f(x'; s)) = 1 \mid s_T = a\right] + \mathsf{negl}(\lambda), \tag{4}$$

where the probabilities are taken over the randomness of D *and the random choice of* s. *Then the protocol* Π *t-securely computes* $f(\boldsymbol{x}; \boldsymbol{s})$ *in an information-theoretic sense and if* $\boldsymbol{s}$ *is uniformly selected from* S^n, *then it is computationally* $(t; \epsilon)$-*differentially private.*

In view of Propositions 1 and 2, a construction of differentially private protocols for an aggregate function g can be reduced to securely computing a deterministic function h for which the condition (2) or (4) holds.

4   A Novel Protocol for Discrete Laplace Noise Generation

In this section, we construct a protocol for securely sampling noise from a finite-range discrete Laplace distribution. As we mentioned above, the discrete Laplace distribution $DL(p)$ can be used to construct a differentially private mechanism. However, noise sampled from $DL(p)$ takes an arbitrarily large integer, which is inconvenient if data from a finite interval $\mathbb{Z}_q$ are dealt with. Accordingly, we introduce a finite-range distribution $FDL(p, N)$ defined as

$$\Pr[L = k] = \begin{cases} p^{|k|}(1-p)/(1+p), & \text{if } |k| < N, \\ p^N/(1+p), & \text{if } |k| = N, \\ 0, & \text{otherwise.} \end{cases}$$

We show that $FDL(p, N)$ can be used to make a mechanism differentially private.

Proposition 3. *Let* Δ *be the sensitivity of a function* $f : \prod_{i \in [n]} X_i \to \mathbb{Z}$ *and set* $p = \exp(-\epsilon/\Delta)$. *Let* N *be a positive integer such that* $N \geq \Delta$ *and* $p^N(1 + p^{-\Delta})/(1 + p) \leq \delta$. *Define* $\mathcal{M}_f^{FDL(p,N)}(\boldsymbol{x}) = f(\boldsymbol{x}) + L$ *for* $\boldsymbol{x} \in \prod_{i \in [n]} X_i$, *where* $L \sim FDL(p, N)$. *Then* $\mathcal{M}_f^{FDL(p,N)}$ *is* (ϵ, δ)-*differentially private. Furthermore, for any* $\boldsymbol{x} \in \prod_{i \in [n]} X_i$

$$\mathbb{E}\left[|\mathcal{M}_f^{FDL(p,N)}(\boldsymbol{x}) - f(\boldsymbol{x})|^2\right] = \frac{2p}{(1-p)^2} - \frac{2(2(1-p)N + (1+p))p^{N+1}}{(1+p)(1-p)^2}.$$

Proof. We simply write $\mathcal{M} = \mathcal{M}_f^{FDL(p,N)}$. It is straightforward to calculate the mean squared error and we omit it here. Let $\boldsymbol{x}, \boldsymbol{x}'$ be neighboring vectors and $S \subseteq \mathbb{Z}$. Suppose that $f(\boldsymbol{x}) \leq f(\boldsymbol{x}')$. Note that $0 \leq f(\boldsymbol{x}') - f(\boldsymbol{x}) \leq \Delta \leq N$. Let $S_1 = \{k \in S : f(\boldsymbol{x}') - N < k < f(\boldsymbol{x}) + N\}$ and $S_2 = S \setminus S_1$. It follows from the definition of $FDL(p, N)$ that $\Pr[\mathcal{M}(\boldsymbol{x}) \in S_1] \leq \exp(\epsilon)\Pr[\mathcal{M}(\boldsymbol{x}') \in S_1]$. Since $f(\boldsymbol{x}') - f(\boldsymbol{x}) \leq \Delta$, it holds that $\Pr[\mathcal{M}(\boldsymbol{x}) \in S_2] \leq \Pr[N - \Delta \leq L < N] + \Pr[|L| = N] \leq \delta$. Therefore, we have $\Pr[\mathcal{M}(\boldsymbol{x}) \in S] \leq \exp(\epsilon)\Pr[\mathcal{M}(\boldsymbol{x}') \in S] + \delta$. A similar argument works when $f(\boldsymbol{x}) \geq f(\boldsymbol{x}')$. $\square$

4.1   The Bernoulli Distribution

We first show a protocol for sampling a biased bit that has statistical distance at most 2^{-d} from a Bernoulli random variable $b \sim \text{Ber}(\alpha)$, i.e., $\Pr[b = 1] = \alpha$ and $\Pr[b = 0] = 1 - \alpha$. Let α be $0 < \alpha < 1$ and for $\ell \in [d]$, α_ℓ be the ℓ-th most significant bit in the binary expansion of α. The protocol is based on the folklore method: Generate d random bits $u_1, \ldots, u_d$, compute the minimum index j such that $u_j \neq \alpha_j$, and then output $b = 1 - u_j$. To realize it in the multiparty setting, let $q > 2d$ and $h_d^{\text{Ber}(\alpha)} : (\{0,1\}^d)^n \to \mathbb{Z}_q$ be a deterministic function defined by $h_d^{\text{Ber}(\alpha)}((s_{i1}, \ldots, s_{id})_{i \in [n]}) = 1 - u_j$, where $u_\ell = \oplus_{i \in [n]} s_{i\ell}$ for $\ell \in [d]$, $u_{d+1} = 0$, and j is the smallest index such that $u_j \neq \alpha_j$ (we set $j = d + 1$ if there is no such index). Note that the statistical distance between $\text{Ber}(\alpha)$ and $h_d^{\text{Ber}(\alpha)}(s)$ for $s \leftarrow_\$ (\{0,1\}^d)^n$ is at most 2^{-d}. The protocol $\Pi_d^{\text{Ber}(\alpha)}$ (described in Fig. 2) t-securely computes a share of $h_d^{\text{Ber}(\alpha)}(s)$ and $\text{Mult}(\Pi_d^{\text{Ber}(\alpha)}) = 5nd + 19d = \mathcal{O}(nd)$. Note that in Step 3, $[\![u_\ell \oplus \alpha_\ell]\!]$ can be locally computed from $[\![u_\ell]\!]$ since α_ℓ is a public parameter.

PROTOCOL $\Pi_d^{\text{Ber}(\alpha)}$

Input: $s = (s_{i1}, \ldots, s_{id})_{i \in [n]} \in (\{0,1\}^d)^n$.

Output: $([\![h_d^{\text{Ber}(\alpha)}(s)]\!]_i)_{i \in [n]}$.

The protocol:
1. Each party $i \in [n]$ shares $s_{i\ell}$, $\ell \in [d]$.
2. The parties run XOR* with inputs $([\![s_{i\ell}]\!])_{i \in [n]}$ and obtain $[\![u_\ell]\!] = [\![\oplus_{i \in [n]} s_{i\ell}]\!]$ for $\ell \in [d]$.
3. Each party locally computes $[\![c_\ell]\!] = [\![u_\ell \oplus \alpha_\ell]\!]$ for $\ell \in [d]$.
4. The parties run PRE$_\vee$ with inputs $[\![c_\ell]\!]$, $\ell \in [d]$ and obtain $[\![e_\ell]\!] = [\![\vee_{k=1}^\ell c_k]\!]$, $\ell \in [d]$.
5. Each party locally computes $[\![f_\ell]\!] = [\![e_\ell]\!] - [\![e_{\ell-1}]\!]$ for $\ell \in [d]$, where $e_0 = 0$.
6. The parties run MULT with inputs $[\![f_\ell]\!]$ and $[\![u_\ell]\!]$ and obtain $[\![f_\ell u_\ell]\!]$ for $\ell \in [d]$.
7. The parties compute $[\![b]\!] = 1 - \sum_{\ell=1}^d [\![f_\ell u_\ell]\!]$ and output $[\![b]\!]$.

Fig. 2. The protocol for generating noise drawn from $\text{Ber}(\alpha)$

4.2   The Discrete Laplace Distribution

We show a protocol which converts biased bits to noise following $\text{FDL}(p, N)$. For $0 < p < 1$, set $p_0 = (1-p)/(1+p)$ and $p_1 = 1 - p$. Define $\alpha_0 = p_0$ and $\alpha_i = p_1$ for $i \in [N-1]$. If $\sigma \leftarrow_\$ \{-1, +1\}$ and $b_i \sim \text{Ber}(\alpha_i)$, $i \in [0..N)$, then $\sigma\ell \sim \text{FDL}(p, N)$, where ℓ is the smallest index such that $b_\ell = 1$ (we set $\ell = N$ if there is no such index). Indeed, $\Pr[\sigma\ell = 0] = p_0$, $\Pr[\sigma\ell = k] = (1/2)(1-p_0)(1-p_1)^{|k|-1} p_1 = p^{|k|}(1-p)/(1+p)$ if $0 < |k| < N$, and $\Pr[\sigma\ell = k] = (1/2)(1-p_0)(1-p_1)^N = p^N/(1+p)$ if $|k| = N$. Let $q > 2N$ and $h_d^{\text{FDL}(p,N)} : (\{0,1\}^{dN} \times \{-1, +1\})^n \to$

$\mathbb{Z}_q$ be a function defined by $h_d^{\mathrm{FDL}(p,N)}(((s_{j1}^{(i)}, \ldots, s_{jd}^{(i)})_{i \in [0..N]}, \sigma_j)_{j \in [n]}) = \sigma\ell$, where $\sigma = \prod_{j \in [n]} \sigma_j$, $b_i = h_d^{\mathrm{Ber}(\alpha_i)}((s_{j1}^{(i)}, \ldots, s_{jd}^{(i)})_{j \in [n]})$ for $i \in [0..N]$, and ℓ is the smallest index such that $b_\ell = 1$. The statistical distance between $\mathrm{FDL}(p, N)$ and $h_d^{\mathrm{FDL}(p,N)}(s)$ for uniform random s is at most $N2^{-d}$. The protocol $\Pi_d^{\mathrm{FDL}(p,N)}$ (described in Fig. 3) t-securely computes a share of $h_d^{\mathrm{FDL}(p,N)}(s)$ and $\mathrm{Mult}(\Pi_d^{\mathrm{FDL}(p,N)}) = (5n + 19)Nd + 17N + 5n + 3 = \mathcal{O}(Nd)$.

PROTOCOL $\Pi_d^{\mathrm{FDL}(p,N)}$

Input: $s = ((s_{j1}^{(i)}, \ldots, s_{jd}^{(i)})_{i \in [0..N]}, \sigma_j)_{j \in [n]}$.

Output: $([\![h_d^{\mathrm{FDL}(p,N)}(s)]\!]_j)_{j \in [n]}$.

The protocol:

1. The parties run $\Pi_d^{\mathrm{Ber}(\alpha_i)}$ with inputs $s_i = (s_{j1}^{(i)}, \ldots, s_{jd}^{(i)})_{j \in [n]}$ and obtain $[\![b_i]\!] = [\![h_d^{\mathrm{Ber}(\alpha_i)}(s_i)]\!]$ for $i \in [0..N]$.
2. The parties run $\mathrm{PRE}_\vee$ with inputs $[\![b_i]\!]$, $i \in [0..N]$ and obtain $[\![c_i]\!] = [\![\vee_{k=1}^i b_k]\!]$ for $i \in [0..N]$.
3. Each party locally computes $[\![\ell]\!] = N - \sum_{i=0}^{N-1} [\![c_i]\!]$.
4. Each party $j \in [n]$ shares σ_j.
5. The parties run MULT^* with inputs $[\![\sigma_j]\!]$, $j \in [n]$ and obtain $[\![\sigma]\!] = [\![\prod_{j \in [n]} \sigma_j]\!]$.
6. The parties output $[\![k]\!] = [\![\sigma\ell]\!]$ by running MULT with inputs $[\![\sigma]\!]$ and $[\![\ell]\!]$.

Fig. 3. The protocol for generating noise drawn from $\mathrm{FDL}(p, N)$

Instantiating Π_h in Proposition 1 with $\Pi_d^{\mathrm{FDL}(p,N)}$, we obtain Theorem 1.

Theorem 1. *Let d, N be parameters and $S = \{0,1\}^{dN} \times \{-1,+1\}$. Let $g : \mathbb{Z}_q^n \to \mathbb{Z}_q$ be a deterministic function with sensitivity Δ. Let $M = \max_x |g(x)|$ and $p = \exp(-\epsilon/\Delta)$. Assume that $N \geq \Delta$, $q > 2N + 2M$, and*

$$p^N \cdot \frac{1 + p^{-\Delta}}{1 + p} + N2^{-d}(1 + \exp(\epsilon)) \leq \delta. \tag{5}$$

Then, there is a protocol which t-securely computes $g(x) + h_d^{FDL(p,N)}(s)$ for $x \in \mathbb{Z}_q^n$ and $s \in S^n$. Furthermore, if $s \leftarrow_{\$} S^n$, then it is $(t; \epsilon, \delta)$-differentially private. The communication complexity is $\mathcal{O}(Mult(\Pi_g) + ndN)$ multiplications.

Proof. We define $f(x; s) = g(x) + h_d^{\mathrm{FDL}(p,N)}(s)$ for $x \in \mathbb{Z}_q^n$ and $s \in S^n$. Let $\delta_0 = p^N(1 + p^{-\Delta})/(1 + p)$. For all neighboring vectors x, x' and any $U \subseteq \mathbb{Z}_q$,

$$\Pr[s \leftarrow_{\$} S^n : f(x; s) \in U] \leq \Pr\left[\mathcal{M}_g^{\mathrm{FDL}(p,N)}(x) \in U\right] + N2^{-d}$$

$$\leq \exp(\epsilon) \cdot \Pr\left[\mathcal{M}_g^{\mathrm{FDL}(p,N)}(x') \in U\right] + \delta_0 + N2^{-d}$$

$$\leq \exp(\epsilon) \cdot \Pr[s \leftarrow_{\$} S^n : f(x'; s) \in U] + \delta. \tag{6}$$

Observe that $h_d^{\mathrm{FDL}(p,N)}(((s_{j1}^{(i)},\ldots,s_{jd}^{(i)})_{i\in[0..N]},\sigma_j)_{j\in[n]})$ only depends on $\sigma = \prod_{j\in[n]}\sigma_j$ and $u_\ell^{(i)} = \oplus_{j\in[n]}s_{j\ell}^{(i)}$ for $\ell \in [d]$ and $i \in [0..N]$. In addition, for any $T \subseteq [n]$ with $|T| \le t$, σ (resp. $u_\ell^{(i)}$) are both uniformly distributed on $\{-1,+1\}$ (resp. $\{0,1\}$) even conditioned on $\{(s_{j1}^{(i)},\ldots,s_{jd}^{(i)})_{i\in[0..N]} : j \in T\}$ (resp. $\{\sigma_j : j \in T\}$) being fixed. Therefore, the distribution of $h_d^{\mathrm{FDL}(p,N)}(s)$ induced by $s \leftarrow_\$ S^n$ does not change even when the random inputs of the parties in T are fixed. Therefore, together with the condition (6), we can see that the condition (2) in Proposition 1 holds for f, from which Theorem 1 follows. $\qquad\square$

5   A Novel Protocol for Binomial Noise Generation

We provide a protocol which allows the parties to non-interactively obtain a share of binomial noise. Let λ be a security parameter. We restrict ourselves to the family $\{\psi_r : \{0,1\}^{s(\lambda)} \to \{0,1\}^{\ell(\lambda)}\}_{r\in\{0,1\}^\lambda}$ of pseudorandom functions with key length of λ and simply write $s = s(\lambda)$ and $\ell = \ell(\lambda)$. In Sect. 2.2, we have defined $\mathcal{A}$ and $\mathcal{A}_i$ for $i \in [n]$ as $\mathcal{A} = \{A \subseteq [n] : |A| = n - t\}$ and $\mathcal{A}_i = \{A \in \mathcal{A} : i \in A\}$. We assume that $\ell|\mathcal{A}|$ is even. Observe that for $r \leftarrow_\$ \{0,1\}^\lambda$, the number $\ell_r(a)$ of 1's in $\psi_r(a) \in \{0,1\}^\ell$ is supposed to follow $\mathrm{Bin}(\ell,1/2)$.

By using pseudorandom secret sharing, we obtain a share of $\sum_{A\in\mathcal{A}}\ell_{r_A}(a)$ from predistributed keys r_A. Specifically, we define $S = \{0,1\}^{\lambda\cdot\binom{n-1}{t}}$,

$$U = \{((r_{A,i})_{A\in\mathcal{A}_i})_{i\in[n]} \in S^n : r_{A,i} = r_{A,j} \text{ for all } i,j\},$$

and $U_T = \{s_T \in S^t : s \in U\}$ for $T \subseteq [n]$ of size t. Note that we can augment any $u = ((r_A)_{A\in\mathcal{A}_i})_{i\in T} \in U_T$ to $s = ((r_A)_{A\in\mathcal{A}_i})_{i\in[n]} \in U$ such that $u = s_T$ by appending $r_J \in \{0,1\}^\lambda$, where $J = [n] \setminus T$. Since $s \in U$ can be written as $s = ((r_A)_{A\in\mathcal{A}_i})_{i\in[n]}$ for some $r_A \in \{0,1\}^\lambda$, it is possible to define $h : U \to \mathbb{Z}_q$ as $h(s) = \sum_{A\in\mathcal{A}}\ell_{r_A}(a) - \ell|\mathcal{A}|/2$ for $q > \ell|\mathcal{A}|/2$. The protocol Π_h (described in Fig. 4) non-interactively and hence t-securely computes a share of $h(s)$ for $s \in U$.

PROTOCOL Π_h
Parameter: $a \in \{0,1\}^s$.
Input: $s = ((r_A)_{A\in\mathcal{A}_i})_{i\in[n]} \in U$.
Output: $([\![h(s)]\!]_i)_{i\in[n]}$.
The protocol:
    1. Each party $i \in [n]$ locally computes the number $\ell_{r_A}(a)$ of 1's in $\psi_{r_A}(a)$.
    2. Each party $i \in [n]$ outputs $\ell_i = \sum_{A\in\mathcal{A}_i}\ell_{r_A}(a)f_A(i) - \ell|\mathcal{A}|/2$.

Fig. 4. The protocol for generating noise drawn from the binomial distribution

Theorem 2. *Let λ be a security parameter and assume a pseudorandom function $\{\psi_r : \{0,1\}^s \to \{0,1\}^{\ell}\}_{r \in \{0,1\}^{\lambda}}$. Let $M \in \mathbb{N}$, $a \in \{0,1\}^s$, $\delta \in \lambda^{-\omega(1)}$, and $\epsilon \in \mathcal{O}(\log \lambda)$. Let $g : \mathbb{Z}_q^n \to \mathbb{Z}_q$ be a deterministic function with sensitivity Δ and define $Mg : \mathbb{Z}_q^n \to \mathbb{Z}_q$ as $(Mg)(\boldsymbol{x}) = M \cdot g(\boldsymbol{x})$. Assume that $\ell |\mathcal{A}|$ is even, $q > 2(M \cdot \max_{\boldsymbol{x}} |g(\boldsymbol{x})| + \ell |\mathcal{A}|)$, and $\epsilon \geq \epsilon(\delta, \ell, M, \Delta)$. Then, there is a protocol Π (described in Fig. 5) which t-securely computes $f(\boldsymbol{x}; \boldsymbol{s}) = g(\boldsymbol{x}) + (1/M) \cdot h(\boldsymbol{s})$ for $\boldsymbol{x} \in \mathbb{Z}_q^n$ and $\boldsymbol{s} \in U$ and if $\boldsymbol{s} \leftarrow_s U$, then it is computationally $(t; \epsilon)$-differentially private. The communication complexity is $\mathcal{O}\left(\text{Mult}(\Pi_{Mg})\right)$ multiplications.*

Theorem 2 follows from Proposition 2 with the following two exceptions: the parties run Π_{Mg} rather than Π_g and then divide the recovered secret $Mg(\boldsymbol{x}) + h(\boldsymbol{s})$ by a public parameter M to avoid an arithmetic operation over $\mathbb{R}$; and the random inputs of the parties are supposed to be uniformly selected from $U \subseteq S^n$ rather than from S^n. For completeness, we formally describe the protocol Π.

PROTOCOL Π
Parameter: $M \in \mathbb{N}, a \in \{0,1\}^s$.
Input: $\boldsymbol{x} \in \mathbb{Z}_q^n, \boldsymbol{s} \in U$.
Output: $z = g(\boldsymbol{x}) + (1/M)h(\boldsymbol{s}) \in \mathbb{R}$.
The protocol:
   1. The parties run Π_{Mg} with inputs $\boldsymbol{x}$ and obtain $[\![Mg(\boldsymbol{x})]\!]$.
   2. The parties run Π_h with inputs $\boldsymbol{s}$ and obtain $[\![h(\boldsymbol{s})]\!]$.
   3. The parties compute $[\![y]\!] = [\![Mg(\boldsymbol{x})]\!] + [\![h(\boldsymbol{s})]\!]$.
   4. The parties reconstruct y and output $z = y/M$.

Fig. 5. The protocol for computing a differentially private output based on the binomial distribution

Proof (of Theorem 2). Fix a set $T \subseteq [n]$ of t corrupted parties and let $J = [n] \setminus T \in \mathcal{A}$. The output of Π has the form of $\mathcal{M}_g^{\text{Bin}, \ell |\mathcal{A}|, M}(\boldsymbol{x})$. However, the adversary knows all but one keys r_A, $A \neq J$ and the only noise unknown to him is $\ell_{r_J}(a)$. Therefore, a level of differential privacy that the adversary's view satisfies deteriorates to that of $\mathcal{M}_g^{\text{Bin}, \ell, M}$.

More formally, we prove that Π is computationally $(t; \epsilon)$-differentially private. In view of Proposition 2, it is sufficient to show that $f(\cdot; \boldsymbol{s})$ is computationally ϵ-differentially private even when the random inputs $\boldsymbol{s}_T$ are fixed. Note that $\boldsymbol{s}_T$ includes all the components of $\boldsymbol{s} = ((r_A)_{A \in \mathcal{A}_i})_{i \in [n]}$ except r_J.

First, define a randomized function $\widetilde{f}_J$ as $\widetilde{f}_J(\boldsymbol{x}; \boldsymbol{u}) = f_J(\boldsymbol{x}; \boldsymbol{u}) + (1/M) \cdot (\widetilde{\ell}_J - \ell/2)$ for $\boldsymbol{x} \in \mathbb{Z}_q^n$ and $\boldsymbol{u} = ((r_A)_{A \in \mathcal{A}_i})_{i \in T} \in U_T$, where $f_J(\boldsymbol{x}; \boldsymbol{u}) = g(\boldsymbol{x}) + (1/M) \cdot \sum_{A \in \mathcal{A} \setminus \{J\}} (\ell_{r_A}(a) - \ell/2)$ and $\widetilde{\ell}_J \sim \text{Bin}(\ell, 1/2)$. In other words, $\widetilde{f}_J$ is defined by replacing pseudorandom binomial noise $\ell_{r_J}(a)$ in $f(\boldsymbol{x}; \boldsymbol{s})$ with $\widetilde{\ell}_J$ properly sampled from $\mathrm{Bin}(\ell, 1/2)$. For fixed $\boldsymbol{u} \in U_T$, $\widetilde{f}_J(\cdot; \boldsymbol{u})$ is equivalent to the (ϵ, δ)-differentially private mechanism $\mathcal{M}^{\mathrm{Bin}, \ell, M}_{f_J(\cdot; \boldsymbol{u})}$ and hence for every distinguisher D, for all T-neighboring vectors $\boldsymbol{x}, \boldsymbol{x}'$, and for every $\boldsymbol{u} \in U_T$,

$$\Pr\left[\boldsymbol{s} \leftarrow_\$ U : \mathsf{D}(\boldsymbol{x}_T, \boldsymbol{s}_T, \widetilde{f}_J(\boldsymbol{x}; \boldsymbol{s}_T)) = 1 \mid \boldsymbol{s}_T = \boldsymbol{u}\right]$$

$$\leq \exp(\epsilon) \cdot \Pr\left[\boldsymbol{s} \leftarrow_\$ U : \mathsf{D}(\boldsymbol{x}'_T, \boldsymbol{s}_T, \widetilde{f}_J(\boldsymbol{x}'; \boldsymbol{s}_T)) = 1 \mid \boldsymbol{s}_T = \boldsymbol{u}\right] + \delta. \quad (7)$$

Next, we show that for any but fixed $\boldsymbol{x} \in \mathbb{Z}_q^n$ and $\boldsymbol{u} = ((r_A)_{A \in \mathcal{A}_i})_{i \in T} \in U_T$, the distribution of $\widetilde{f}_J(\boldsymbol{x}; \boldsymbol{u})$ and that of $f(\boldsymbol{x}; ((r_A)_{A \in \mathcal{A}_i})_{i \in [n]}) = f_J(\boldsymbol{x}; \boldsymbol{u}) + (1/M) \cdot (\ell_{r_J}(a) - \ell/2)$ induced by $r_J \leftarrow_\$ \{0, 1\}^\lambda$ are computationally indistinguishable. Assume otherwise that there are a PPT distinguisher D which can distinguish $(\boldsymbol{x}_T, \boldsymbol{u}, f(\boldsymbol{x}; ((r_A)_{A \in \mathcal{A}_i})_{i \in [n]}))$ from $(\boldsymbol{x}_T, \boldsymbol{u}, \widetilde{f}_J(\boldsymbol{x}; \boldsymbol{u}))$ with non-negligible advantage for some $\boldsymbol{x} \in \mathbb{Z}_q^n$ and $\boldsymbol{u} = ((r_A)_{A \in \mathcal{A}_i})_{i \in T} \in U_T$. We construct a PPT oracle machine Alg for $\{\psi_r : \{0, 1\}^s \to \{0, 1\}^\ell\}_{r \in \{0, 1\}^\lambda}$ as follows. First, Alg invokes the oracle to receive $\xi^b \in \{0, 1\}^\ell$, and sets ℓ_J^b as the number of 1's in ξ^b. Here, the oracle flips a bit $b \leftarrow_\$ \{0, 1\}$ and sets $\xi^b = \psi_{r_J}(a)$ for $r_J \leftarrow_\$ \{0, 1\}^\lambda$ if $b = 1$ or else $\xi^b = F(a)$ for a uniformly selected map $F : \{0, 1\}^s \to \{0, 1\}^\ell$. Next, Alg computes $z^b = f_J(\boldsymbol{x}; \boldsymbol{u}) + (1/M) \cdot (\ell_J^b - \ell/2)$. Note that z^0 (resp. z^1) has the same distribution as $\widetilde{f}_J(\boldsymbol{x}; \boldsymbol{u})$ (resp. $f(\boldsymbol{x}; ((r_A)_{A \in \mathcal{A}_i})_{i \in [n]})$, where $r_J \leftarrow_\$ \{0, 1\}^\lambda$). Then, Alg gives $(\boldsymbol{x}_T, \boldsymbol{u}, z^b)$ to D and receives a guess $b' \in \{0, 1\}$ from D. Finally, it outputs b'. Then, $\Pr[b' = b] - 1/2$ is non-negligible, which contradicts the indistinguishability of ψ. Therefore, together with the condition (7) applied to a PPT distinguisher D, we can see that the condition (2) in Proposition 1 holds for f since $\delta \in \lambda^{-\omega(1)}$ and $\epsilon \in \mathcal{O}(\log \lambda)$. This concludes the proof. $\qquad \square$

The parties have to agree on a tuple $\boldsymbol{s} = ((r_A)_{A \in \mathcal{A}_i})_{i \in [n]}$ of keys for the pseudorandom function. In other words, they cannot select their random inputs independent of the others. This problem is solved by obtaining a share of a uniform random element via a replicated secret sharing scheme as in [14]. An alternative solution is assuming a trusted party which provides the parties with random keys ahead of the protocol execution.

Finally, we remark on the mean squared error. For fixed $a \in \{0, 1\}^s$ and $r_A \leftarrow_\$ \{0, 1\}^\lambda$, $\ell_{r_A}(a)$ is supposed to follow $\mathrm{Bin}(\ell, 1/2)$. Thus, we suppose the mean squared error between the output z of Π and $g(\boldsymbol{x})$ is $\ell|\mathcal{A}|/4M^2 = \ell\binom{n}{t}/4M^2$.

6 Comparison

6.1 The Discrete Laplace Distribution

First, we compare our protocols with the one in [17], which draws noise from a finite-range discrete Laplace distribution slightly different from ours. Technically, let N be a power of 2 and $L \sim \mathrm{TDL}(p, N)$ be the truncated discrete Laplace distribution, i.e., $\Pr[L = k] = Cp^{|k|}(1 - p)/(1 + p)$, $-N < k < N$, where $C =$

$(1 + p)/(1 + p - 2p^N)$ is a normalizing constant. As in Proposition 3, it can be shown that $\mathrm{TDL}(p, N)$ provides (ϵ, δ)-differential privacy for a function with sensitivity Δ if $p = \exp(-\epsilon/\Delta)$ and $p^N(p^{-\Delta} - 1)/(1 + p - 2p^N) \leq \delta$. Due to the lack of space, we only show the performance of the protocol [17]. See [17, Section 4] or Appendix A.1 for the detailed description.

In Table 1, we do the comparison based on the MPC primitives given in [15,29]. If we perform all the sub-protocols in parallel as much as possible, then our protocol always produces a sample from $\mathrm{FDL}(p, N)$ in 7 rounds, which is independent of a level of differential privacy. On the other hand, the protocol [17] needs to evaluate a certain Boolean circuit for generating biased bits. The authors of [30] propose such a circuit of size $7d-3$ and depth $2\lceil \log d \rceil + 2$ to sample biased bits with statistical difference at most 2^{-d}. Therefore, the total round complexity is $2\lceil \log d \rceil + 12 = \mathcal{O}(\log d)$, which is approximately proportional to $\log \log \delta^{-1}$ since the statistical distance should be incorporated to δ.

Moreover, according to [11], the protocol [17] needs to discard a certain bad sample in order to obtain noise correctly drawn from $\mathrm{TDL}(p, N)$, which incurs the probability of failure $(1 - p)/2$. Since $p = \exp(-\epsilon/\Delta)$, that probability depends only on the level of differential privacy, which cannot decrease no matter how we choose other parameters q, N, and d. Thus, the only solution to making it negligible with the same privacy budget is to run the protocol several times.

As a drawback, the communication complexity and the statistical distance are proportional to N in our protocol while they are to $\log N$ in [17]. The protocol [17] evaluates the above Boolean circuit $c = \lceil \log N \rceil$ times and then invokes an equality test to ensure that the output is not a bad sample. Thus, the communication complexity of [17] is $(5n+7)cd+162 \log q-3c+5n+5 = \mathcal{O}(nd \log N + \log q)$, where the equality test is instantiated with the protocol given in [29]. We remark that it is possible to reduce the communication complexity of the protocol [17] and ours by a multiplicative factor of n by generating random bits with RAN_2 rather than XOR^* or MULT^*. Although that modification incurs the probability of failure Ndq^{-1}, we can make it arbitrarily small by choosing a large q.

To emphasize the advantage of our protocol, we provide an example parameter setting. Let g be a function to compute with sensitivity $\Delta = 1$, e.g., a counting function $g(x) = |\{i \subset [n] : x_i \in I\}|$ where $I \subseteq \mathbb{Z}_q$. We choose $q = 2^{61} - 1$ and $\delta = 2^{-40}$ and consider two privacy budgets $\epsilon = 0.5$ and $\epsilon = 1$. Since the number of parties n is subject to change depending on applications, we do the comparison replacing each invocation of XOR^* and MULT^* with RAN_2 so that the number of multiplications does not depend on n. If $\epsilon = 0.5$, then, choosing $N = 75$ and $d = 50$, our protocol and [17] both achieve (ϵ, δ)-differential privacy. The round complexity of [17] is $2\lceil \log d \rceil + 12 = 24$ while ours only needs 7 rounds. The number of multiplications of our protocol is at most 7 times as large as the protocol of [17] (excluding multiplications necessary to evaluate g). Note that since it fails with probability $(1 - p)/2 \approx 0.2$, the latter protocol requires 1.25 times more multiplications on average. Similarly, if $\epsilon = 1$, we can choose $N = 30$ and $d = 50$ to achieve (ϵ, δ)-differential privacy and then [17] needs 24 rounds.

Our protocol requires roughly 2.7 times more multiplications but since [17] fails with probability ≈ 0.3, the difference is reduced to $2.7 \times 0.7 < 2$ on average.

Table 1. Comparison of protocols sampling noise from finite-range discrete Laplace distributions. $d \in \mathbb{N}$ is an arbitrarily chosen parameter.

Reference	Communication	Round	Prob. failure	Distribution	Stat. distance
[17]	$\mathcal{O}\left(nd \log N + \log q\right)$	$\mathcal{O}\left(\log d\right)$	$(1-p)/2$	TDL(p, N)	$2^{-d} \log N$
Ours	$\mathcal{O}\left(ndN\right)$	$\mathcal{O}\left(1\right)$	0	FDL(p, N)	$2^{-d} N$

Finally, we compare our protocol with the ones in [19,33]. Our protocol only performs secure arithmetic computations in $\mathbb{Z}_q$. The protocols in [19,33] make black-box use of MPC primitives for complex operations over real numbers (e.g., square root, logarithm, and division). There is no rigorous analysis of the impact of the finite-precision implementations on the level of differential privacy that the protocols achieve. Moreover, our protocol exceeds these protocols in efficiency since secure computation on real numbers is much more costly than on integers in both terms of communication and round complexity [3].

6.2   The Binomial Distribution

As shown in Table 2, the first protocol in [17] needs to jointly generate ℓ random bits to obtain a share of $(1/M)(Z - \ell/2)$, $Z \sim \mathrm{Bin}(\ell, 1/2)$. The communication complexity of the second protocol is still proportional to ℓ although decreasing the number of random bits by a multiplicative factor of n, which comes at a cost: the achievable region of ϵ is more limited. In view of the condition (1), the protocols in [17] require communication proportional to ϵ^{-2}. See [17, Section 3] or Appendix A.2 for the details. In our protocol, once keys for a pseudorandom function are distributed, the parties can non-interactively compute a share of noise following $\mathrm{Bin}(\ell m, 1/2)$ by using the keys m times (if overflow does not occur).

As a drawback, the mean squared error between the output and $g(\boldsymbol{x})$ is $\binom{n}{t}$ times larger than [17]. Nevertheless, we should also consider the client-server model for practical applications. Our protocol is available and even suitable for this model since n corresponds to the number of servers and is typically small.

We provide an example parameter setting. Consider the client-server model and set $n = 3$ and $t = 1$. Let g be a function to compute with sensitivity $\Delta = 1$. We choose $q = 2^{61} - 1$ and a security parameter as $\lambda = 128$. We use the pseudorandom function based on AES-128 $\{\mathsf{Enc}(k, \cdot) : \{0, 1\}^{128} \to \{0, 1\}^{128}\}_{k \in \{0,1\}^{128}}$. Our protocol requires interaction only when distributing keys for the pseudorandom function and hence just needs to communicate $(n - t)\binom{n}{t}\lambda = 768$ bits independent of parameters regarding differential privacy. To compare it with [17], we consider a privacy budget $\epsilon = 1$ and set $\delta = 2^{-80} < \lambda^{-\log \lambda} \in \lambda^{-\omega(1)}$. To achieve (ϵ, δ)-differential privacy, it is necessary to choose m and M such that

$\epsilon \geq \epsilon(\delta, 128m, M, \Delta)$. For example, we choose $m = 2^{15}$ and to keep the mean squared error $\ell/4M^2$ as small as possible, we choose $M = 79$ as the maximum number satisfying $\epsilon \geq \epsilon(\delta, 128 \times 2^{15}, M, \Delta)$. Then, the numbers of multiplications of [17] are both proportional to $\ell = 128 \times 2^{15} = 2^{22}$. Finally, the mean squared error of [17] is $\ell/4M^2 \approx 168$ while that of our protocol is $\binom{n}{t}\ell/4M^2 \approx 504$.

Table 2. Comparison of protocols generating noise $(1/M)(Z - \ell/2)$, $Z \sim \text{Bin}(\ell, 1/2)$. We denote by Δ the sensitivity of a function to be perturbed. Π_{Bit} is a protocol jointly generating a uniform random bit.

Reference	Communication	Round	Differential privacy	MSE
[17]	$\mathcal{O}\left(\ell\text{Mult}(\Pi_{\text{Bit}})\right)$	$\mathcal{O}(1)$	(ϵ, δ)-DP for $\epsilon \geq \epsilon(\delta, \ell, M, \Delta)$	$\ell/4M^2$
[17]	$\mathcal{O}(\ell/n)$	$\mathcal{O}(1)$	(ϵ, δ)-DP for $\epsilon \geq \epsilon(\delta, \ell(1 - t/n), M, \Delta)$	$\ell/4M^2$
Ours	$\mathcal{O}(1)$	$\mathcal{O}(1)$	Computational ϵ-DP for $\epsilon \geq \epsilon(\delta, \ell, M, \Delta)$, where $\delta \in \lambda^{-\omega(1)}$	$\binom{n}{t}\ell/4M^2$

Acknowledgments. This research was partially supported by JSPS KAKENHI Grant Numbers JP20J20797 and JP19K22838, JST CREST Grant Numbers JPMJCR14D6 and JPMJCR19F6, Japan, and the Ministry of Internal Affairs and Communications SCOPE Grant Number 182103105.

A   Appendix

A.1   The Protocol for Discrete Laplace Noise Generation [17]

The authors of [17] show that sampling an integer g from the truncated geometric distribution with support $\{z \in \mathbb{Z} : 0 \leq z < N\}$ is reduced to generating $\log N$ independent biased bits. They implicitly show the following lemma. Define $\mathbb{Z}_{\geq c} = \{z \in \mathbb{Z} : z \geq c\}$ for $c \in \mathbb{Z}$. Let $0 < p < 1$ and $t_i = (1 + p^{-2^i})^{-1}$ for $i \in \mathbb{Z}_{\geq 0}$.

Lemma 1. *Let X_i be the random variable with $Ber(t_i)$. Then $G := \sum_{i \in \mathbb{Z}_{\geq 0}} X_i 2^i$ has the geometric distribution $Geo(p)$, i.e., $\Pr[G = g] = (1 - p)p^g$ for $g \geq 0$.*

To obtain a concrete protocol, we provide the probability distribution of the truncated sum of the X_i's. Let $c \in \mathbb{N}$ and $N = 2^c$. It follows from the above lemma that $\sum_{i \in [0..c)} X_i 2^i$ follows the truncated geometric distribution, i.e., $\Pr\left[\sum_{i \in [0..c)} X_i 2^i = g\right] = D(1 - p)p^g$ for $g \in [0..N)$, where $D = (1 - p^N)^{-1}$. Indeed, the lemma implies that for every finite set $I \subseteq \mathbb{Z}_{\geq 0}$,

$$\Pr[X_i = 1 \ (\forall i \in I) \land X_i = 0 \ (\forall i \in (\mathbb{Z}_{\geq 0} \setminus I))] = (1 - p)p^{y(I)},$$

where we define $y(I) = \sum_{i \in I} 2^i$. Let $g \in [0..N)$ and $I \subseteq [0..c)$ be such that $g = y(I)$.

$$\Pr\left[\sum_{i \in [0..c)} X_i 2^i = g \right] = \Pr\left[X_i = 1 \ (\forall i \in I) \wedge X_i = 0 \ (\forall i \in ([0..c) \setminus I)) \right]$$

$$= \sum_{J \subseteq \mathbb{Z}_{\geq c}} (1-p) p^{y(I \cup J)}$$

$$= (1-p) p^g \sum_{J \subseteq \mathbb{Z}_{\geq c}} p^{y(J)}.$$

Since $\sum_{g \in [0..N)} \Pr\left[\sum_{i \in [0..c)} X_i 2^i = g \right] = 1$, we have $\sum_{J \subseteq \mathbb{Z}_{\geq c}} p^{y(J)} = (\sum_{g \in [0..N)} (1-p) p^g)^{-1} = D$.

Then, according to [11], $L := \sigma G$ conditioned on $(G, \sigma) \neq (0, -1)$ follows $\mathrm{TDL}(p, N)$ if $\sigma \leftarrow_\$ \{-1, +1\}$ and $G = \sum_{i \in [0..c)} X_i 2^i$ for $X_i \sim \mathrm{Ber}(t_i)$.

The protocol [17] evaluates a certain Boolean circuit to generate biased bits X_i. It also needs to invoke an equality test protocol to verify $(\sigma, g) \neq (0, -1)$ and hence it fails with probability $\Pr\left[(\sigma, g) = (0, -1) \right] = (1-p)/2$. The statistical distance between $\mathrm{TDL}(p, N)$ and the output is at most $2^{-d} \log N$.

A.2   The Protocol for Binomial Noise Generation [17]

First, the authors in [17] propose a protocol, in which the parties jointly ℓ random bits b_k, $k \in [\ell]$ and securely compute a share of $(1/M) \cdot (\sum_{k \in [\ell]} b_k - \ell/2)$. For a function with sensitivity Δ, the protocol achieves (ϵ, δ)-differential privacy for $\epsilon \geq \epsilon(\delta, \ell, M, \Delta)$ and the mean squared error is given by $\ell/4M^2$. The protocol requires the communication complexity $\mathcal{O}(\ell \mathrm{Mult}(\Pi_{\mathrm{Bit}}))$ if the functionality $\mathcal{F}_{\mathrm{Bit}}$ is realized by a protocol Π_{Bit}. As we mentioned in Sect. 2.2, if we implement Π_{Bit} with XOR* (resp. RAN2), then $\mathrm{Mult}(\Pi_{\mathrm{Bit}})$ is $\mathcal{O}(n)$ (resp. $\mathcal{O}(1)$).

In addition, a protocol simultaneously flipping n bits is proposed in [17]. Technically, each party $i \in [n]$ shares his local random bit s_i among the other parties and then the parties obtain n shares $[\![s_i]\!]$, $i \in [n]$. This can reduce the communication complexity to $\mathcal{O}(\ell/n)$. However, since $t\ell/n$ out of the ℓ bits are revealed to the adversary, the modified protocol is (ϵ, δ)-differentially private only for $\epsilon \geq \epsilon(\delta, \ell(1 - t/n), M, \Delta)$.

References

1. Acar, A., Celik, Z.B., Aksu, H., Uluagac, A.S., McDaniel, P.: Achieving secure and differentially private computations in multiparty settings. In: 2017 IEEE Symposium on Privacy-Aware Computing (PAC), pp. 49–59 (2017)
2. Agarwal, N., Suresh, A.T., Yu, F.X.X., Kumar, S., McMahan, B.: cpSGD: communication-efficient and differentially-private distributed SGD. In: Advances in Neural Information Processing Systems, pp. 7564–7575 (2018)

3. Aliasgari, M., Blanton, M., Zhang, Y., Steele, A.: Secure computation on floating point numbers. In: NDSS (2013)
4. Balcer, V., Cheu, A.: Separating local & shuffled differential privacy via histograms. In: 1st Conference on Information-Theoretic Cryptography (ITC 2020). Leibniz International Proceedings in Informatics (LIPIcs), vol. 163, pp. 1:1–1:14 (2020)
5. Balle, B., Bell, J., Gascón, A., Nissim, K.: The privacy blanket of the shuffle model. In: Boldyreva, A., Micciancio, D. (eds.) CRYPTO 2019. LNCS, vol. 11693, pp. 638–667. Springer, Cham (2019). https://doi.org/10.1007/978-3-030-26951-7_22
6. Bar-Ilan, J., Beaver, D.: Non-cryptographic fault-tolerant computing in constant number of rounds of interaction. In: Proceedings of the Eighth Annual ACM Symposium on Principles of Distributed Computing, pp. 201–209 (1989)
7. Beimel, A., Nissim, K., Omri, E.: Distributed private data analysis: simultaneously solving how and what. In: Wagner, D. (ed.) CRYPTO 2008. LNCS, vol. 5157, pp. 451–468. Springer, Heidelberg (2008). https://doi.org/10.1007/978-3-540-85174-5_25
8. Ben-Or, M., Goldwasser, S., Wigderson, A.: Completeness theorems for non-cryptographic fault-tolerant distributed computation. In: Proceedings of the Twentieth Annual ACM Symposium on Theory of Computing, pp. 1–10 (1988)
9. Bogdanov, D., Talviste, R., Willemson, J.: Deploying secure multi-party computation for financial data analysis. In: Keromytis, A.D. (ed.) FC 2012. LNCS, vol. 7397, pp. 57–64. Springer, Heidelberg (2012). https://doi.org/10.1007/978-3-642-32946-3_5
10. Catrina, O., Saxena, A.: Secure computation with fixed-point numbers. In: Sion, R. (ed.) FC 2010. LNCS, vol. 6052, pp. 35–50. Springer, Heidelberg (2010). https://doi.org/10.1007/978-3-642-14577-3_6
11. Champion, J., Shelat, A., Ullman, J.: Securely sampling biased coins with applications to differential privacy. In: Proceedings of the 2019 ACM SIGSAC Conference on Computer and Communications Security, pp. 603–614 (2019)
12. Chan, T.-H.H., Shi, E., Song, D.: Optimal lower bound for differentially private multi-party aggregation. In: Epstein, L., Ferragina, P. (eds.) ESA 2012. LNCS, vol. 7501, pp. 277–288. Springer, Heidelberg (2012). https://doi.org/10.1007/978-3-642-33090-2_25
13. Cheu, A., Smith, A., Ullman, J., Zeber, D., Zhilyaev, M.: Distributed differential privacy via shuffling. In: Ishai, Y., Rijmen, V. (eds.) EUROCRYPT 2019. LNCS, vol. 11476, pp. 375–403. Springer, Cham (2019). https://doi.org/10.1007/978-3-030-17653-2_13
14. Cramer, R., Damgård, I., Ishai, Y.: Share conversion, pseudorandom secret-sharing and applications to secure computation. In: Kilian, J. (ed.) TCC 2005. LNCS, vol. 3378, pp. 342–362. Springer, Heidelberg (2005). https://doi.org/10.1007/978-3-540-30576-7_19
15. Damgård, I., Fitzi, M., Kiltz, E., Nielsen, J.B., Toft, T.: Unconditionally secure constant-rounds multi-party computation for equality, comparison, bits and exponentiation. In: Halevi, S., Rabin, T. (eds.) TCC 2006. LNCS, vol. 3876, pp. 285–304. Springer, Heidelberg (2006). https://doi.org/10.1007/11681878_15
16. Damgård, I., Nielsen, J.B.: Scalable and unconditionally secure multiparty computation. In: Menezes, A. (ed.) CRYPTO 2007. LNCS, vol. 4622, pp. 572–590. Springer, Heidelberg (2007). https://doi.org/10.1007/978-3-540-74143-5_32
17. Dwork, C., Kenthapadi, K., McSherry, F., Mironov, I., Naor, M.: Our data, ourselves: privacy via distributed noise generation. In: Vaudenay, S. (ed.) EUROCRYPT 2006. LNCS, vol. 4004, pp. 486–503. Springer, Heidelberg (2006). https://doi.org/10.1007/11761679_29

18. Dwork, C., McSherry, F., Nissim, K., Smith, A.: Calibrating noise to sensitivity in private data analysis. In: Halevi, S., Rabin, T. (eds.) TCC 2006. LNCS, vol. 3876, pp. 265–284. Springer, Heidelberg (2006). https://doi.org/10.1007/11681878_14

19. Eigner, F., Kate, A., Maffei, M., Pampaloni, F., Pryvalov, I.: Differentially private data aggregation with optimal utility. In: Proceedings of the 30th Annual Computer Security Applications Conference, pp. 316–325 (2014)

20. Gazeau, I., Miller, D., Palamidessi, C.: Preserving differential privacy under finite-precision semantics. Theoret. Comput. Sci. **655**, 92–108 (2016)

21. Ghosh, A., Roughgarden, T., Sundararajan, M.: Universally utility-maximizing privacy mechanisms. SIAM J. Comput. **41**(6), 1673–1693 (2012)

22. Goldreich, O.: Foundations of cryptography: volume 2, basic applications. Cambridge University Press (2009)

23. Goldreich, O., Goldwasser, S., Micali, S.: How to construct random functions. J. ACM **33**(4), 792–807 (1986)

24. Inusah, S., Kozubowski, T.J.: A discrete analogue of the laplace distribution. J. Stat. Plann. Inference **136**(3), 1090–1102 (2006)

25. Kimura, E., et al.: Evaluation of secure computation in a distributed healthcare setting. Stud. Health Technol. Inf. **228**, 152–156 (2016)

26. McSherry, F., Talwar, K.: Mechanism design via differential privacy. In: 48th Annual IEEE Symposium on Foundations of Computer Science (FOCS 2007), pp. 94–103 (2007)

27. Mironov, I.: On significance of the least significant bits for differential privacy. In: Proceedings of the 2012 ACM Conference on Computer and Communications Security, pp. 650–661 (2012)

28. Mironov, I., Pandey, O., Reingold, O., Vadhan, S.: Computational differential privacy. In: Halevi, S. (ed.) CRYPTO 2009. LNCS, vol. 5677, pp. 126–142. Springer, Heidelberg (2009). https://doi.org/10.1007/978-3-642-03356-8_8

29. Nishide, T., Ohta, K.: Multiparty computation for interval, equality, and comparison without bit-decomposition protocol. In: Okamoto, T., Wang, X. (eds.) PKC 2007. LNCS, vol. 4450, pp. 343–360. Springer, Heidelberg (2007). https://doi.org/10.1007/978-3-540-71677-8_23

30. Park, K., Park, H., Jeun, W.C., Ha, S.: Boolean circuit programming: a new paradigm to design parallel algorithms. J. Discrete Algorithms **7**(2), 267–277 (2009)

31. Shamir, A.: How to share a secret. Commun. ACM **22**(11), 612–613 (1979)

32. Shi, E., Chan, T.H., Rieffel, E., Chow, R., Song, D.: Privacy-preserving aggregation of time-series data. In: NDSS, vol. 2 (2011)

33. Wu, G., He, Y., Wu, J., Xia, X.: Inherit differential privacy in distributed setting: Multiparty randomized function computation. In: 2016 IEEE Trustcom/BigDataSE/ISPA, pp. 921–928 (2016)

System and Application Security

Specfuscator: Evaluating Branch Removal as a Spectre Mitigation

Martin Schwarzl[1]([✉]), Claudio Canella[1], Daniel Gruss[1], and Michael Schwarz[2]

[1] Graz University of Technology, Graz, Austria
martin.schwarzl@iaik.tugraz.at
[2] CISPA Helmholtz Center for Information Security, Saarbrücken, Germany

Abstract. Attacks exploiting speculative execution, known as Spectre attacks, have gained substantial attention in the scientific community and in industry with a broad range of defense techniques proposed. In particular, in-software defenses for commodity systems attempt to leave the program structure as is, but defuse every potential Spectre gadget by, e.g., stopping the speculation, or limiting value ranges. While these mitigations disrupt the program flow on every conditional branch, they still contain every single conditional branch instruction.

In this paper, we show that one dimension of Spectre mitigations has been overlooked entirely. We explore a novel principled Spectre mitigation that sits at the other end of the scale: the absence of conditional and indirect branches. Our mitigation is based on automatically linearizing the program flow through a special compiler pass, eliminating **all** conditional and indirect branches. We show that our Spectre mitigation has very clear security guarantees. We explore the feasibility of this unorthodox approach and evaluate its performance in comparison to the more conservative approaches presented so far. We observe that the performance overhead can be low, e.g., 5 %, for certain use cases, being on-par with state-of-the-art mitigations, but very high for other use cases, e.g., and overhead factor of 1000. Our results demonstrate the feasibility of Spectre defenses that eliminate branches and indicate good performance-security trade-offs for Spectre defenses can be achieved by sticking to neither of the extremes.

1 Introduction

Speculative execution is a significant factor in the performance of modern processors. Instead of waiting for a branch decision or branch target to be architecturally determined, the processor takes an educated guess based on behavior observed in the past. From a pipeline perspective, this linearizes the execution of instructions as the branch decision is omitted in the speculative execution flow and only subsequently validated. Spectre attacks [31] induce incorrect speculative execution flows into a victim context by manipulating the branch predictors. During this speculative execution, the attacker can make the victim access secrets and encode them into the microarchitectural state. Using a side-channel attack, e.g., Flush+Reload [54], the secrets can then be recovered.

© International Financial Cryptography Association 2021
N. Borisov and C. Diaz (Eds.): FC 2021, LNCS 12674, pp. 293–310, 2021.
https://doi.org/10.1007/978-3-662-64322-8_14

Previous countermeasures [11,12,36] either attempt to thwart successful covert-channel transmission during speculation [27,28,53], abort the speculative execution before secrets can be accessed [1,3,13,21,22,39,41,50], or ensure that secrets cannot be accessed during speculative execution [43,44,56]. Amit et al. [4] tried to increase the performance of indirect branches by rewriting them into two direct branches. However, from the perspective of branches in a program, all these countermeasures remain in the same range of the scale, namely all conditional and indirect branches remain in the program, in some cases even with additional branches added. This raises an important scientific question:

Can the (substantial) reduction of branches, in particular the elimination of all vulnerable branches, be a viable Spectre mitigations? Can such Spectre mitigations maintain a reasonable overhead in certain use cases?

In this paper, we answer both questions in the affirmative. To answer these scientific questions, we explore a novel Spectre mitigation at the other end of the scale: the elimination of all conditional and indirect branches. While this may sound impractical at first, it has been used for years to implement cryptographic algorithms in constant time [7]. We demonstrate the feasibility of this approach with our new mitigation, Specfuscator. Specfuscator is based on the movfuscator [14] tool that automatically linearizes the program flow through a special compiler pass. In contrast to *M/o/Vfuscator*, we do not replace all operations, but just control-flow manipulating instructions, effectively eliminating **all** conditional branches. To improve the performance of *M/o/Vfuscator*, we bring back ALU operations, the cmp instruction and exploit the x86 addressing mode. In comparison to the *M/o/Vfuscator* we increase the runtime up to a factor of 50 and decrease the binary size by 30 % and compile time up to 46 %. We show that our Spectre mitigation is a principled approach with respect to security, following the simple argument that if there are no conditional or indirect branches, no branches can be mispredicted.

For our evaluation we analyzed Specfuscator in comparison with a set of other compilers: the related *M/o/Vfuscator* and LCC, a patched clang with lfence protections on all conditional branches, and an unpatched clang without any Spectre mitigations. We evaluate the performance of our unorthodox approach and discover that the overhead can be as low as 5 %, being on-par with state-of-the-art mitigations, but also much higher, up to factor 1000, performing clearly worse than state-of-the-art mitigations. Thus, for some use cases, the elimination of conditional and indirect branches is nearly as efficient as state-of-the-art mitigations but with a stronger security argument. This indicates that the space between the two extremes, all conditional and indirect branches and no conditional and indirect branches, should receive more attention for the design of future countermeasures.

Our key contributions are:

- We explore a previously unexplored mitigation space against Spectre: the absence of conditional and indirect branches.
- We present a solution based on a linearized control-flow with very clear and strong security guarantees.

- We evaluate our approach and observe that the performance overhead can be lower than state-of-the-art mitigations in some use cases, but also significantly higher in others.
- Our results shed light on a new direction for performance-security trade-offs for Spectre defenses.

The remainder of this paper is organized as follows. In Sect. 2, we provide background information. In Sect. 3, we discuss the landscape of existing Spectre defenses and point out blank spots. In Sect. 4, we present Specfuscator, our Spectre defense mechanism. In Sect. 5, we evaluate the performance and security of Specfuscator. In Sect. 6, we discuss the context and implications of our work. We conclude in Sect. 7.

2 Background

This section provides some background information about speculative execution attacks and the internals of the *M/o/Vfuscator*.

2.1 Speculative Execution Attacks

Modern CPUs extensively use out-of-order execution and prediction mechanisms to increase performance. Speculative execution uses branch predictions to advance the control flow speculatively. Branch prediction mechanisms are implemented via different structures, such as the Branch History Buffer (BHB) [8,31], the Branch Target Buffer (BTB) [16,31,33], the Pattern History Table (PHT) [17,31], and the Return Stack Buffer (RSB) [17,32,34].

Mispredicted branches are reverted on the architectural level, but not on the microarchitectural level [31]. Hence, code that should not have been executed architecturally still leaves microarchitectural traces, e.g., in various caches. By leveraging traditional side-channel attacks, these microarchitectural traces can be brought into the architectural domain, potentially recovering data that was not supposed to be accessed, *i.e.*, secrets.

Kocher et al. [31] first discussed transient-execution attacks [12] using speculative execution and demonstrated that conditional branches and indirect jumps can be exploited to leak data. Subsequent work has then shown that the idea can be extended to function returns [32,34] and store-to-load forwarding [20]. Canella et al. [12] then systematically analyzed the field and demonstrated that the necessary mistraining can be done in the same and a different address space due to some predictors being shared across hyperthreads. Additionally, they also showed that many of the proposed countermeasures are ineffective and do not target the root cause of the problem. While the cache has been predominantly exploited for the transmission of the secret data [12,31,32,34], other channels have also been shown to be effective, *i.e.*, execution port contention [9].

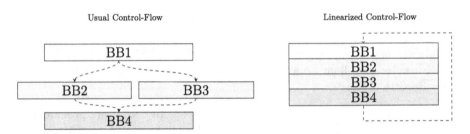

Fig. 1. Branch instructions typically split up the control flow. Constant-time cryptographic algorithms avoid branches (left) and instead linearize the control flow (right), e.g., square-and-always-multiply [15], turning the security-critical branches and basic blocks into one large basic block. *M/o/Vfuscator* follows the same idea of linearizing the control-flow and uses one main execution loop, turning the program into one large basic block.

To mitigate all these attacks, various proposals have been made by industry and academia. Canella et al. [11] analyzed the differences between countermeasures proposed by academia and by industry, highlighting that academia proposes more radical countermeasures compared to industry. In general, the proposed mitigations either require significant changes to the hardware [27,28,53], require a developer to annotate secrets [19,40,44], introduce data dependencies [13,39], or reduce the accuracy of timers [35,42,49,51].

2.2 *M/o/Vfuscator*

Turing completeness is a part of computability theory that describes a set of rules or instructions that can be simulated on a single-taped Turing machine. Dolan [48] showed that the x86 mov instruction is Turing-complete. Based on this observation, Domas [14] invented the single-instruction compiler *M/o/Vfuscator*. The *M/o/Vfuscator* patches the Little C compiler (LCC) to use an emitter that only emits mov instructions. *M/o/Vfuscator* is an x86 32-bit compiler and also only supports 32-bit arithmetic operations.

The compiled program runs in a virtual machine, which basically runs like a Turing machine. The entire program is branch-free and thus executed as a single basic block, leading to a linearized control flow graph. Figure 1 illustrates the linearized control flow graph. Thus, the program is always executed from start to end in a loop. To ensure the correctness of the program, a flag specifies whether an instruction should compute on the target location or a dummy *discard* location. All instructions that are not relevant for a specific iteration are discarded using this discard location. Hence, although the instruction is executed, it has no impact on the current behavior of the program. This technique is the same that is used to ensure constant-time implementations of, e.g., cryptographic algorithms [15].

Note that this is similar to constant-time cryptographic algorithms, e.g., square-and-always-multiply [15], the program executes both branches and, thus, always runs the algorithm from start to end in a loop.

Arithmetic operations, *i.e.*, additions, multiplications, divisions, bitwise-operations, are implemented using two-dimensional lookup tables. To save memory. 32-bit operations are split into two 16-bit operations, and, thus, only 16-bit lookup tables are required. By exploiting the addressing modes of x86-mov, the first mov looks up the row for the first operand, the second mov looks up the corresponding column for the second operand, and the value is reported as result.

M/o/Vfuscator handles internal jumps to specific parts of the code using a target register. *M/o/Vfuscator* installs two signal handlers for SIGSEGV and SIGILL to enable branching [14]. At the end of the program, an illegal instruction is emitted to trigger the SIGILL handler and jump back to the start of the program. To perform external library calls, *i.e.*, calling libc functions such as printf, segmentation faults are used [14]. To adhere to the x86 calling convention, the function's arguments are pushed onto the stack.

As the name indicates, *M/o/Vfuscator* can also be used as an obfuscation technique. However, as Kirsch et al. [29] demonstrated, it is possible to deobfuscate this technique with taint analysis.

3   Blank Spots in the Spectre Defense Landscape

Most Spectre countermeasures attempt to break different phases of Spectre attacks [11,12]. These phases are described in previous work as *preparation, misspeculation, access, encoding, leakage,* and *decoding.*

Preparation. Preventing the preparation phase can often be seen as equivalent to disabling performance optimizations in the CPU. By disabling either microarchitectural states or speculation at all, an attacker is unable to prepare a Spectre attack. While disabling speculation has been suggested as a mitigation [31], modern CPUs do not support disabling speculative execution. Moreover, it can be expected that disabling speculative execution results in a considerable slowdown. Similarly, disabling the cache also has an unacceptable performance overhead as every memory access has to be served from memory. Additionally, other microarchitectural elements could be used as side channel in the absence of the cache [9,12,45].

Misspeculation and Preventing Access. Most focus so far was on the main cause of Spectre attacks, the misspeculation phase, or the transient access of secrets following the misspeculation. Intel, AMD, and ARM [3,5,23] prevent Spectre-BTB and Spectre-RSB by restricting how an attacker can influence the predictors. For Spectre-PHT, serializing instructions are recommended to stop speculation at security-critical branches [23]. However, this means that branches have to be identified and separately patched.

Furthermore, it could be that memory barrier instructions are not fully serializing [2]. To entirely protect an application, speculation barriers are required for each branch that could be followed by cache fetches. Adding memory barriers for each conditional branch can lead to runtime overheads of up to 440 % [39].

Additional to that performance overhead, Schwarz et al. [45] have shown that speculation barriers for each branch do not suffice as other channels can be used to leak data, such as the AVX unit or the TLB, as these barriers do not prevent interaction with these microarchitectural elements.

Oleksenko et al. [39] introduced data dependencies to branch conditions and the following instructions to force a stall if the branch cannot be decided yet. Similarly, Carruth [13] proposed to use branchless code to check loads, ensuring that the load is executed along a valid control-flow path. One pre-requisite for this approach is that the hardware supports branchless and unpredicted conditional updates of register values.

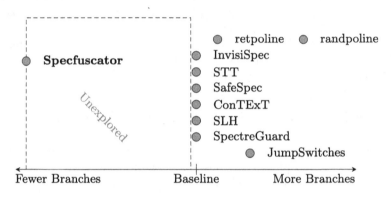

Fig. 2. Previous Spectre defenses were either not changing the number of conditional branches, but possibly adding more (direct) branches to a program. The space of eliminating branches is largely unexplored.

Schwarz et al. [44] and Fustos et al. [19] propose to annotate secrets and propagate these annotations to the CPU to ensure that secrets are inaccessible during transient execution. Speculative taint tracking (STT) [56] uses light-weight taint tracking to taint not yet committed data and delay instructions that use it. Similarly, NDA [52] prevents the execution of potentially leaking instructions if they depend on a not yet retired operation.

All of these mitigations keep the number of branches identical but ensure that no leakage occurs by breaking the link between the *misspeculation* phase and the subsequent *access* or *encoding* phases.

Other solutions attempt to add branches that are potentially less easy to exploit [4]. Google proposed *retpoline* [50], a code sequence replacing indirect branches with return instructions, to prevent Spectre-BTB. While *retpoline* also adds more jumps to the program, these are direct jumps and, thus, likely unexploitable. Hence, the total number of branches increases, although potentially fewer are exploitable. Branco [10] proposed a probabilistic alternative to *retpoline*, called *randpoline*, which is compatible with Intel Control-flow Enforcement Technology (CET). This alternative introduces a large number of indirect branches and randomly chooses one of them, reducing the chance that an attacker can mistrain the actually executed branch.

Encoding, Leakage, and Decoding. In these phases, the secret was already accessed transiently. Preventing exploitation in these phases would require ensuring that no covert channel exists between the transient and the architectural domain. However, the way modern CPUs work, it is unrealistic to assume that covert channels can be entirely prevented. While proposals exist to limit the resolution of timers [51] or to build microarchitectural shadow structures [27,53] to squash the results on mispredictions and leave no microarchitectural traces in the cache. However, these mitigations are typically incomplete [12].

Classification. While these defenses have different security properties, depending on the phase they target, they have in common that specific branches are either transformed into other branches, or that the flow from mispredicted branch to leakage is interrupted. We classify the existing Spectre defenses, as illustrated in Fig. 2. From this figure, it becomes apparent that most solutions sit in the same range of keeping the number of branches identical, and some defenses increase the number of branches.

Existing software-based countermeasures try to surgically modify conditional branches or subsequent data access to prevent the exploitation of misspeculation. However, as an alternative to preventing speculative execution of conditional branches entirely [31], another possibility is to *eliminate* conditional branches. In this work, we analyze this largely unexplored mitigation technique of removing conditional branches, thus also eliminating the root cause of Spectre attacks.

4   Specfuscator

In this section, we introduce the design of Specfuscator in the first part. Then we discuss the security guarantees of Specfuscator and outline the implementation.

4.1   Design of Specfuscator

Specfuscator is based on the work by Dolan [48] showing that the x86 mov instruction is Turing complete. Hence, it is always possible to transform a regular application into an application that consists only of mov instructions, and thus *no conditional branches*. This approach has been implemented by Domas [14] as *M/o/Vfuscator* with the goal of obfuscating applications and making them difficult to reverse engineer.

The main idea is always to execute both code paths of every conditional branch, similar to the constant-time square-and-always-multiply algorithm for RSA [15]. Per conditional branch, a flag decides whether the calculated results are kept and committed to the program state, or discarded by specifying a dummy location as the target. Such an approach is also considered secure for implementing side-channel resilient cryptographic algorithms [15,38,55]. The advantage of this approach is that it can be fully automated in the compiler.

M/o/Vfuscator leverages the code generation of the LCC compiler but replaces the emitter for single instructions by a special emitter, generating the corresponding assembly code. *M/o/Vfuscator* labels all branches and uses a software-emulated target register to decide which of the branches is currently executed. If the execution flag is set, all operations are performed as specified in the program code. Conversely, if the flag is not set, the results of the operations are discarded, similar as square-and-always-multiply [15].

Branching is emulated using branch-free comparison using subtraction and logical operations. Depending on the result of the comparison, the corresponding flags (zero flag, signed flag, carry flag, and overflow flag) are set, and the target location is selected. A flag specific to this approach is the execution flag that can be changed by compare instructions. After disabling the execution flag, the results of the subsequent instructions are stored to a scratch location. If the instruction pointer (EIP) reaches the target basic block, the execution is enabled again, and the results are again made architectural.

Similar to the square-and-always-multiply loop [15], the code is always executed in its entirety in a loop. Hence, the execution speed suffers while secret-dependent operations, secret-dependent branches, and secret-leaking misspeculation are eliminated. This design leads to a linearization of the program flow. Therefore, the CPU does not need to predict the outcome of branch instructions. If there are no branches in the program, there can be no mispredictions and resulting pipeline stalls [25].

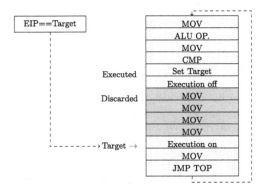

Fig. 3. Branching is handled via a target value for each basic block. If the target is reached, the execution flag is toggled, and the results modify the program's state. Conversely, until the target does not match, the results are written to scratch locations.

While the mov-based approach is already secure against Spectre attacks, it introduces a considerable performance overhead. Arithmetic operations are implemented via extensive use of two-dimensional arithmetic lookup tables. For instance, a 32-bit addition requires 50 x86 mov instructions, which use 16-bit lookup tables. To increase the performance of Specfuscator, we do not solely rely on the mov instruction. As we only aim to prevent Spectre attacks, we do not implement arithmetic operations using movs. Instead, we rely on the native x86 arithmetic instructions, as they cannot be exploited using Spectre. In addition, we exploit the x86 addressing modes to operate directly in memory instead of moving both operands into registers. This optimization saves one additional mov instruction per memory operation.

Another instruction that is safe with respect to Specter is the cmp instruction. Thus, Specfuscator directly uses the cmp instruction instead of a subtraction for comparing two values. The required flag, e.g., the execution flag, is then set via arithmetic and logic instructions. Figure 3 illustrates how Specfuscator emits branch-free code using mov instructions.

The only jump instruction in Specfuscator is the jump from the end of the program to the top of the execution loop. In *M/o/Vfuscator*, this was solved using an illegal instruction and a corresponding exception handler. However, this causes a considerable performance overhead and might even lead to mis-speculation in the interrupt handler [46]. Hence, as a Spectre attack cannot exploit a direct, unconditional jump, the illegal instruction can be replaced via a direct jump to the top of the execution loop.

4.2   Security of Specfuscator

Specfuscator is a defense against Spectre attacks that exploit control-flow mis-prediction, *i.e.*, Spectre-PHT [31], Spectre-BTB [31], and Spectre-RSB [32,34], as classified by Canella et al. [12]. Straightline Spectre [6] is a special case of Spectre-BTB and Spectre-RSB, where the CPU speculatively skips a branch and continue with the instruction directly after the branch. Another Spectre variant, Spectre-STL [20], is a separate mechanism that relies on incorrect speculations for store-to-load forwarding, *i.e.*, it is a data-flow misprediction.

The idea of Specfuscator is that none of the control-flow mispredicting Spectre variants (Spectre-PHT [31], Spectre-BTB [31], and Spectre-RSB [32,34], including Straightline Spectre [6]), work if the corresponding control-flow modifying instructions are not used at all. Specfuscator strictly avoids these instructions and only permits direct, unconditional control flow changes. As the only emitted branch is the unconditional branch at the end of the program, adding a memory fence after this jump prevents Straightline Spectre. Due to the unconditional nature of the branch, this memory fence is never executed architecturally, and has therefore no performance impact. Hence, programs compiled with Specfuscator, by design, cannot be susceptible to the above Spectre variants as the corresponding instructions are not present in the binary. This is a very clear and strong security guarantee that most other defenses cannot provide [12,31].

Specfuscator is a software-only solution and does not require hardware mod-ifications like other proposed Spectre defense mechanisms [27,28,44]. Thus, it can even work in environments where other mitigations cannot be applied, e.g., because lfence instructions are not serializing [2], or patches are unavailable for other reasons.

4.3   Implementation of Specfuscator

Specfuscator is a modification to the LCC C compiler [18]. The reason we chose LCC and not gcc or clang is that we base the implementation of Specfuscator on the open-source *M/o/Vfuscator*, as this compiler already generates a branch-free binary based on the technique from Dolan [48]. *M/o/Vfuscator* itself is a patch to the current version (September 2020) of LCC. However, we require several custom changes, as outlined in Sect. 4.1. In contrast to *M/o/Vfuscator*, Specfuscator can use a broader range of native instructions without sacrificing security. By relying on arithmetic and logic operations, as well as complex addressing modes, the amount of mov instructions is reduced heavily, *i.e.*, for the addition, we now have 3 instructions instead of 50 mov instruction. For example, in a tiny AES program, the number of instructions is reduced from 222 935 to 127 631, *i.e.*, a reduction of about 43 %, when compiling with Specfuscator instead of *M/o/Vfuscator*.

As all of our changes are in the code emitter of the compiler, this could also be ported to a different compiler, such as clang. As Specfuscator is based on *M/o/Vfuscator*, we can already adopt the control-flow-linearization code from *M/o/Vfuscator* but also emit arithmetic and logic operations. Divisions and modulo operations require additional handling, as they can cause floating-point exceptions in case of a division by zero. We handle those special cases using conditional mov (cmov) instructions to ensure that we do not introduce conditional branches. The conditional mov instructions, e.g., cmov, are not affected by Spectre, as they are never predicted [24].

For comparisons, we cannot merely emit the x86 instructions instead of the mov-based constructs, as *M/o/Vfuscator* uses its own internal representation of CPU flags to select whether the computation results of a branch are stored or discarded. Hence, to ensure correct branching with e.g., , the cmp instruction, we need to update the internal flags in a branch-free way. We achieve this by transferring the CPU flags to an unused general-purpose register via the stack and using binary masks to extract the required bits.

In total, we changed (added, removed, or replaced) 437 lines of code of *M/o/Vfuscator*, which is about 10 % of the *M/o/Vfuscator* codebase.

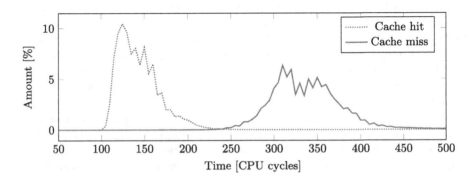

Fig. 4. Flush+Reload within a Specfuscator-compiled program works successfully as intended.

5   Evaluation

In this section, we first verify the security of Specfuscator by compiling and executing Spectre-PHT, Spectre-BTB, and Spectre-RSB gadgets. Furthermore, we evaluate the performance of Specfuscator and compare it to the original *M/o/Vfuscator*, LCC, and a modified clang version, which emits lfences for each conditional branch, and a basic clang compiler without Spectre mitigations activated. We compare each compiler on a set of benchmark programs and compare the averaged runtime performance, binary size, and compile time. The results of this evaluation are given in Table 1 and Table 2. Our test system was equipped with Ubuntu 20.04 (5.4.0-42-lowlatency) running on an Intel i5-8250U CPU.

5.1   Security Evaluation

We demonstrate that it is impossible to successfully use an existing Spectre proof-of-concept attack on Specfuscator compiled code. To verify that the *misspeculation* is indeed prevented, we separately validate all other Spectre attack steps. We add additional functionality to the compiled binaries to obtain accurate time measurements with rdtsc and enable flushing of a virtual address using the clflush instruction. This allows us to accurately verify the cache encoding of the Spectre attack with a Flush+Reload side-channel.

We verify that the cache covert channel in a compiled binary works exactly as in a regular Spectre attack by creating a histogram of cached and uncached data. Figure 4 shows that it is still possible to distinguish between cached and uncached data in a program compiled with Specfuscator. Therefore, cache-based side-channel attacks are still possible in Specfuscator-compiled programs.

To validate whether Spectre is still possible, we use the 15 sample Spectre gadgets from Kocher [30]. First, we evaluate that these gadgets indeed sucessfully show Spectre attacks. We compile them using the unmodified LCC and execute each gadget 100 000 times. For all gadgets, we successfully leak data using Spectre.

For the security evaluation, we compile all sample gadgets using Specfuscator. We again execute each gadget 100 000 times on our test device, and check whether the secret is leaked. As we do not observe any leakage on our test device using any of the gadgets, we practically confirm that our mitigation that should work in theory due to the absence of misspeculation, also works in practice.

In addition, we port a Spectre-BTB and Spectre-RSB proof-of-concept to 32-bit and evaluate it on our unmitigated clang. Again, as expected, these proof-of-concepts work on an unmitigated clang. When the programs are compiled with Specfuscator, no indirect jumps, calls, or return instructions are emitted. To experimentally show that Specfuscator indeed stops the leakage for these attacks, we again compile them using our defense. We execute the proof-of-concept implementations 100 000 times and do not observe any leakage for either Spectre-BTB or Spectre-RSB.

5.2 Performance Evaluation

For the evaluation, we extend LLVM 10.0.1 with a new compiler pass that runs just before the final code is emitted. In this pass, we analyze every conditional branch using the `analyzeBranch` function and insert an `lfence` instruction if this instruction is not already present. To mitigate speculation on both sides of a conditional branch, we also emit an `lfence` instruction in its fall-through basic block if this code path is not already fenced. This compiler pass required changing or adding 125 lines of code across 4 files. In addition to enabling our fencing pass, we enable the `retpoline` mitigation for `clang` by adding the –mretpoline flag. As a result, speculative execution is stopped for all conditional branches and jumps, as e.g., , suggested by Intel [23].

For our evaluation, we compare different programs, including cryptographic implementations and real-world applications [14]. We compile each program as a 32-bit binary since our Specfuscator proof-of-concept only supports 32-bit. However, while we showcase our compiler for this architecture, our approach is generic and is equally applicable to other architectures as well.

We compile the same benchmark program in 5 different configurations. Each test case is compiled with `clang` without any Spectre mitigations, `clang` with `lfences` and `retpoline` active, the LCC, the unmodified *M/o/Vfuscator*, and Specfuscator. To get stable benchmarking results, we fixed the CPU frequency to 3.4 GHz and ran our test program on an isolated core.

Run Time

We use the runtime of the `clang`-compiled programs without mitigations as a baseline to compute the runtime overhead. To measure the runtime of the programs, we use the `perf` command-line tool. We run each test case 1000 times. For the individual test cases, we observe standard deviations between 0.1 % and, for some cases, 3 %. The maximum value of 3 % was observed in the case of clang. The reason for this higher standard deviation might be speculative execution.

As shown in Table 1, the runtime overhead factor strongly depends on the different tasks being executed. We gained a runtime speedup in comparison to *M/o/Vfuscator* by a runtime factor of up to 50. For our benchmark programs, we observe that the LCC has a runtime overhead between 3% and an overhead factor of 26 over `clang`. The overhead of *M/o/Vfuscator* is substantially higher, and the overhead of Specfuscator is in between. We observe the highest performance penalties in terms of runtime for a tiny program that calculates the square root of 2. Also, the modified clang reaches a maximum runtime overhead factor of 20.89. The performance of *M/o/Vfuscator* and Specfuscator deteriorates, particularly on programs where small amounts of code are executed a large number of times, as the whole program has to be completely executed for each iteration.

We leave it as future work to further optimize Specfuscator optimizing the way how branches are performed. Partial control flow linearization could be integrated as compiler optimization with a similar approach proposed by Moll et al. [37]. The partial control flow linearization improved the performance of the overall program by a factor of 146 % [37]. Furthermore, we leave it as future work to extend Specfuscator to 64-bit architecture or integrating a similar approach to LLVM. As LLVM has significantly better optimizations than LCC, as can be seen in the benchmarks, porting Specfuscator to LLVM will also improve its performance.

Table 1. Average runtime overhead factor of our benchmarks for the different compilers compared to our baseline (clang). The baseline is given in milliseconds on the right for the unmodified `clang`

Test program	M/o/Vfuscator	Specfuscator	Clang (fences)	LCC	Clang (baseline)
aes	424.17	221.53	1.31	1.17	1.13 ms
arcfour	36.86	5.18	1.01	1.14	0.81 ms
base64	27.12	8.95	1.19	1.15	0.80 ms
blowfish	129.41	40.79	1.26	1.14	1.10 ms
des	1046.20	520.47	1.15	1.04	0.93 ms
md2	85.57	62.73	1.07	1.20	0.82 ms
md5	18.30	4.71	1.03	1.13	0.80 ms
rot-13	2.20	1.46	1.02	1.24	0.76 ms
arithmetic	1.25	1.05	1.05	1.03	0.96 ms
crc32	7.80	3.45	1.24	1.17	0.88 ms
hello	1.10	1.11	1.00	1.04	0.89 ms
maze	310.03	88.98	1.10	1.13	0.97 ms
mersenne	4.12	1.31	1.02	1.13	0.80 ms
sqm	1.33	1.25	1.02	1.15	0.80 ms
nqueens	319.84	234.46	1.99	4.99	1.89 ms
prime	980.27	161.59	1.93	0.96	1.65 ms
s2	46085.82	981.20	20.89	26.64	0.71 ms
sudoku	656.91	149.69	2.15	1.17	1.13 ms

In addition to the runtime, we evaluate the binary size and compile time of the different compilers. For this purpose, we compile each program 1000 times for our 5 compilers and measure the compilation time using the `perf` command-line tool. Table 2 illustrates the averaged overhead factor in terms of binary size and compilation time.

Compile-time

Table 2 lists the compile-time and the binary size of our benchmark programs. In comparison to *M/o/Vfuscator*, we reduce the compile time by up to 46 %. The compile-time of *M/o/Vfuscator* and Specfuscator depends on a part in how many instructions are needed to generate the assembler. Thus, with the use of fewer instructions per operation, the compile-time is halved in most cases for Specfuscator in comparison to the original *M/o/Vfuscator*. As the results of Table 2 show, the compile-time is about two times higher than with the `clang` compiler.

For small programs, the compile-time appears to be relatively constant for the *M/o/Vfuscator* and also Specfuscator. While this is not problematic for smaller binaries, compiling large software projects such as browsers or web servers would take substantial amounts of time with Specfuscator. We note that our approach of eliminating all conditional branches is extreme. Still, it shows that solutions that eliminate conditional branches are not infeasible, and less extreme solutions in this direction could maintain higher performance levels.

Binary Size
Stripping the binary reduces the binary size by 50%, as it removes debugging information. Hence, for a fair comparison, we strip all the binaries to only compare the actual code footprint. Compared to *M/o/Vfuscator*, Specfuscator reduces the binary size by roughly 30% This reduction was achieved by removing most of the two-dimensional lookup tables used for arithmetic operations. The binary size could additionally be reduced by decreasing the size of the virtual stack, which is currently constant at 1.68 MB. As can be seen from Table 2, the binary size is about 280 times larger for Specfuscator than for binaries compiled with clang and for *M/o/Vfuscator* even 398 times. Again, this overhead is due to our extreme solution, but it shows that solutions eliminating conditional branches are not infeasible. Surprisingly, the programs compiled with LCC are smaller than the programs compiled with the unmodified clang.

6 Discussion

The goal of our paper is to clearly demonstrate the feasibility of branch reduction up to complete elimination as a Spectre mitigation. While we demonstrated the feasibility, we also identified the limitations of our extreme approach. Due to these limitations, we do not consider Specfuscator a real-world solution, but an important contribution as an explorational study that yields interesting insights. Eliminating all branches to reduce the susceptibility to Spectre has not been explored so far. Our solution inherits the performance overheads of the underlying compiler (LCC and its modification *M/o/Vfuscator*) that falls far behind the state of the art performance-wise. The fact that it can still achieve on-par performance for specific programs protected with state-of-the-art mitigations with a state-of-the-art compiler shows that the elimination or reduction of branches is a strategy to defeat Spectre that must be examined in more detail. In particular, we see potential synergies with the compiler community that explored the question of branch elimination in the past for performance reasons. For instance, Moll et al. [37] developed a technique to partially linearize the program flow by removing branches, improving performance by 146%. Exploring related techniques, even if they incur a subtle performance overhead, may yield more efficient Spectre mitigations in future compilers. Software-based solutions are especially important as there is a lot of hardware without in-silicon fixes, and existing software-workarounds are often expensive. While Intel recommends keeping the number of branches as low as possible to achieve the highest possible runtime performance [25], actually reducing branches is a complex task. Although branch elimination can boost the program's performance, it might also be exploited, as it has been demonstrated in the JavaScript engine V8 [26,47]. Another direction of research is to investigate the susceptibility to control-flow hijacking attacks. Future work should evaluate whether branch-less binaries, like those compiled with Specfuscator, or branch-reduced binaries, could realistically mitigate such attacks and, thus, provide control-flow integrity.

Table 2. Average compile time in ms and binary size in kB overhead factor for *M/o/V-fuscator*, Specfuscator, and `clang` with active mitigations compared to `clang` without active mitigations (rightmost column).

Test program	M/o/Vfuscator		Specfuscator		Clang (fences)		LCC		Clang (baseline)	
	Time	Size	Time	Size	Time	Size	Time	Size	Time	Size
hello	2.23	388.28	1.86	279.18	1.07	1.01	0.71	0.89	38.36 ms	13.62 kB
maze	3.93	394.09	2.12	274.96	1.05	1.01	0.63	0.86	46.80 ms	13.82 kB
mersenne	3.00	396.28	1.83	279.84	1.02	1.01	0.70	0.89	41.90 ms	13.63 kB
nqueens	2.39	386.75	2.05	278.22	1.17	1.01	0.75	0.88	40.19 ms	13.64 kB
prime	2.39	389.97	1.81	279.47	1.06	1.01	0.62	0.89	39.02 ms	13.64 kB
s2	2.87	395.22	1.89	279.72	1.00	1.01	0.78	0.89	39.34 ms	13.62 kB
sudoku	3.47	398.10	2.05	280.39	1.10	1.01	0.68	0.91	37.76 ms	14.00 kB
aes	4.80	218.69	2.95	151.15	1.20	1.00	0.53	1.01	101.89 ms	33.21 kB

7 Conclusion

Speculative execution attacks, known as Spectre attacks, have gained substantial attention both in the scientific community and in industry with a broad range of defense techniques proposed. In particular, in-software defenses for commodity systems attempt to leave the program structure as is, but defuse every potential Spectre gadget, e.g., by stopping the speculation, or limiting value ranges. While these mitigations disrupt the program flow on every conditional branch, they still contain every single conditional branch instruction. In this work, we explore a new possibility of mitigating Spectre attacks by using a branch-free compiler. Our mitigation is based on automatically linearizing the program flow through a special compiler pass, eliminating **all** conditional and indirect branches. We showed the security guarantees of this approach and evaluated the feasibility by evaluating its performance in terms of its runtime. In addition, we discussed the compile-time and the binary size of this approach. Furthermore, we verified that existing Spectre-PHT, Spectre-BTB, and Spectre-RSB proof-of-concepts compiled with Specfuscator do not leak secret data anymore. We observe that the performance overhead can be very low, e.g., 5%, for specific use cases, being on-par with state-of-the-art mitigations. However, we also observed very high overheads of factor 1000 for other use cases. Our results indicate that the best performance-security trade-off for Spectre defenses can be achieved by sticking to neither of the extremes.

Acknowledgments. This project has received funding from the European Research Council (ERC) under the European Union's Horizon 2020 research and innovation program (grant agreement No 681402). Funding was provided by generous gifts from Cloudflare, from Intel, Red Hat and from ARM. Any opinions, findings, and conclusions or recommendations expressed in this paper are those of the authors and do not necessarily reflect the views of the funding parties.

References

1. Vulnerability of Speculative Processors to Cache Timing Side-Channel Mechanism (2018). https://developer.arm.com/support/arm-security-updates/speculative-processor-vulnerability
2. x86/cpu/AMD: Make LFENCE a serializing instruction (2018). https://git.kernel.org/pub/scm/linux/kernel/git/stable/linux.git/commit/?id=e4d0e84e490790798691aaa0f2e598637f1867ec
3. Advanced Micro Devices Inc.: Software Techniques for Managing Speculation on AMD Processors (2018). Accessed 7 Oct 2018
4. Amit, N., Jacobs, F., Wei, M.: Jumpswitches: restoring the performance of indirect branches in the era of spectre. In: USENIX ATC (2019)
5. ARM: Cache Speculation Side-channels (2018). version 2.4
6. ARM: Straight-line Speculation (2020). version 1.0
7. Bernstein, D.J.: Cache-Timing Attacks on AES (2005). http://cr.yp.to/antiforgery/cachetiming-20050414.pdf
8. Bhattacharya, S., Maurice, C.M.T.N., Bhasin, S., Mukhopadhyay, D.: Template Attack on Blinded Scalar Multiplication with Asynchronous perf-ioctl Calls. Cryptology ePrint Archive, Report 2017/968 (2017)
9. Bhattacharyya, A., et al.: SMoTherSpectre: exploiting speculative execution through port contention. In: CCS (2019)
10. Branco, R., Hu, K., Sun, K., Kawakami, H.: Efficient mitigation of side-channel based attacks against speculative execution processing architectures (2019). uS Patent App. 16/023,564
11. Canella, C., Pudukotai Dinakarrao, S.M., Gruss, D., Khasawneh, K.N.: Evolution of defenses against transient-execution attacks. In: GLSVLSI (2020)
12. Canella, C., et al.: A systematic evaluation of transient execution attacks and defenses. In: USENIX Security Symposium (2019). Extended classification tree and PoCs at https://transient.fail/
13. Carruth, C.: RFC: Speculative Load Hardening (a Spectre variant #1 mitigation) (2018)
14. Domas, C.: M/o/Vfuscator (2015). https://github.com/xoreaxeaxeax/movfuscator
15. Coron, J.S.: Resistance against differential power analysis for elliptic curve cryptosystems. In: CHES (1999)
16. Evtyushkin, D., Ponomarev, D., Abu-Ghazaleh, N.: Jump over aslr: attacking branch predictors to bypass aslr. In: MICRO (2016)
17. Fog, A.: The microarchitecture of Intel. An optimization guide for assembly programmers and compiler makers, AMD and VIA CPUs (2016)

18. Fraser, C.W., Hanson, D.R.: A retargetable C compiler: design and implementation (1995)
19. Fustos, J., Farshchi, F., Yun, H.: SpectreGuard: an efficient data-centric defense mechanism against spectre attacks. In: DAC (2019)
20. Horn, J.: speculative execution, variant 4: speculative store bypass (2018)
21. Intel: Intel Analysis of Speculative Execution Side Channels (2018). revision 4.0
22. Intel: Retpoline: A Branch Target Injection Mitigation (2018). revision 003
23. Intel: Speculative Execution Side Channel Mitigations (2018). revision 3.0
24. Intel: Intel 64 and IA-32 Architectures Optimization Reference Manual (2019)
25. Intel: Avoiding the Cost of Branch Misprediction (2020). https://software. intel.com/content/www/us/en/develop/articles/avoiding-the-cost-of-branch-misprediction.html
26. Fetiveau, J.: Circumventing Chrome Typer Bugs (2020). https://doar-e.github.io/blog/2019/05/09/circumventing-chromes-hardening-of-typer-bugs/
27. Khasawneh, K.N., Koruyeh, E.M., Song, C., Evtyushkin, D., Ponomarev, D., Abu-Ghazaleh, N.: SafeSpec: banishing the spectre of a meltdown with leakage-free speculation. In: DAC (2019)
28. Kiriansky, V., Lebedev, I., Amarasinghe, S., Devadas, S., Emer, J.: DAWG: a defense against cache timing attacks in speculative execution processors. In: MICRO (2018)
29. Kirsch, J., Jonischkeit, C., Kittel, T., Zarras, A., Eckert, C.: Combating control flow linearization. In: 32nd International Conference on ICT Systems Security and Privacy Protection (IFIP SEC) (2017). https://www.sec.in.tum.de/i20/publications/combating-control-flow-linearization/@@download/file/CFL.pdf
30. Kocher, P.: Spectre Mitigations in Microsoft's C/C++ Compiler (2018)
31. Kocher, P., et al.: Spectre attacks: exploiting speculative execution. In: S&P (2019)
32. Koruyeh, E.M., Khasawneh, K., Song, C., Abu-Ghazaleh, N.: Spectre Returns! WOOT, Speculation Attacks using the Return Stack Buffer. In (2018)
33. Lee, S., Shih, M., Gera, P., Kim, T., Kim, H., Peinado, M.: Inferring fine-grained control flow inside SGX enclaves with branch shadowing. In: USENIX Security Symposium (2017)
34. Maisuradze, G., Rossow, C.: ret2spec: speculative execution using return stack buffers. In: CCS (2018)
35. Microsoft: Mitigating speculative execution side-channel attacks in Microsoft Edge and Internet Explorer (2018)
36. Miller, M.: Mitigating speculative execution side channel hardware vulnerabilities (2018)
37. Moll, S., Hack, S.: Partial control-flow linearization. In: Proceedings of the 39th Conference on Programming Language Design and Implementation, pp. 543–556. ACM (2018)
38. Molnar, D., Piotrowski, M., Schultz, D., Wagner, D.: The program counter security model: automatic detection and removal of control-flow side channel attacks. In: International Conference on Information Security and Cryptology (2005)
39. Oleksenko, O., Trach, B., Reiher, T., Silberstein, M., Fetzer, C.: You shall not bypass: employing data dependencies to prevent Bounds Check Bypass (2018). arXiv:1805.08506
40. Palit, T., Monrose, F., Polychronakis, M.: Mitigating data leakage by protecting memory-resident sensitive data. In: ACSAC (2019)
41. Pardoe, A.: Spectre mitigations in MSVC (2018)
42. Pizlo, F.: What Spectre and Meltdown mean for WebKit (2018)

43. Reis, C., Moshchuk, A., Oskov, N.: Site isolation: process separation for web sites within the browser. In: USENIX Security Symposium (2019)
44. Schwarz, M., Lipp, M., Canella, C., Schilling, R., Kargl, F., Gruss, D.: ConTExT: a generic approach for mitigating spectre. In: NDSS (2020)
45. Schwarz, M., Schwarzl, M., Lipp, M., Gruss, D.: NetSpectre: read arbitrary memory over network. In: ESORICS (2019)
46. Schwarzl, M., Schwarz, M., Schuster, T., Gruss, D.: It's not prefetch: speculative dereferencing of registers (2020). (in submission)
47. Sense Post: v8 - Documentation (2020). https://sensepost.com/blog/2020/intro-to-chromes-v8-from-an-exploit-development-angle/
48. Dolan, S.: MOV is Turing-complete (2013). https://drwho.virtadpt.net/files/mov.pdf
49. The Chromium Projects: Actions required to mitigate Speculative Side-Channel Attack techniques (2018)
50. Turner, P.: Retpoline: a software construct for preventing branch-target-injection (2018). https://support.google.com/faqs/answer/7625886
51. Wagner, L.: Mitigations landing for new class of timing attack (2018)
52. Weisse, O., Neal, I., Loughlin, K., Wenisch, T.F., Kasikci, B.: NDA: preventing speculative execution attacks at their source. In: MICRO (2019)
53. Yan, M., Choi, J., Skarlatos, D., Morrison, A., Fletcher, C.W., Torrellas, J.: InvisiSpec: making speculative execution invisible in the cache hierarchy. In: MICRO (2018)
54. Yarom, Y., Falkner, K.: Flush+Reload: a high resolution, low noise, L3 cache side-channel attack. In: USENIX Security Symposium (2014)
55. Yu, J., Hsiung, L., El Hajj, M., Fletcher, C.W.: Data oblivious ISA extensions for side channel-resistant and high performance computing. In: NDSS (2019)
56. Yu, J., Yan, M., Khyzha, A., Morrison, A., Torrellas, J., Fletcher, C.W.: Speculative taint tracking (stt) a comprehensive protection for speculatively accessed data. In: MICRO (2019)

Speculative Dereferencing:
Reviving Foreshadow

Martin Schwarzl[1]([✉]), Thomas Schuster[1], Michael Schwarz[2], and Daniel Gruss[1]

[1] Graz University of Technology, Graz, Austria
martin.schwarzl@iaik.tugraz.at
[2] CISPA Helmholtz Center for Information Security, Saarbrücken, Germany

Abstract. In this paper, we provide a systematic analysis of the root cause of the prefetching effect observed in previous works and show that its attribution to a prefetching mechanism is incorrect in all previous works, leading to incorrect conclusions and incomplete defenses. We show that the root cause is speculative dereferencing of user-space registers in the kernel. This new insight enables the first end-to-end Foreshadow (L1TF) exploit targeting non-L1 data, despite Foreshadow mitigations enabled, a novel technique to directly leak register values, and several side-channel attacks. While the L1TF effect is mitigated on the most recent Intel CPUs, all other attacks we present still work on all Intel CPUs and on CPUs by other vendors previously believed to be unaffected.

1 Introduction

For security reasons, operating systems hide physical addresses from user programs [34]. Hence, an attacker requiring this information has to leak it first, e.g., with the *address-translation attack* by Gruss et al. [17, §3.3 and §5]. It allows user programs to fetch arbitrary kernel addresses into the cache and thereby to resolve virtual to physical addresses. As a mitigation against e.g., the address-translation attack, Gruss et al. [16,17] proposed the KAISER technique.

Other attacks observed and exploited similar prefetching effects. Meltdown [41] practically leaks memory that is not in the L1 cache. Xiao et al. [73] show that this relies on a prefetching effect that fetches data from the L3 cache into the L1 cache. However, Van Bulck et al. [67] observe no such effect for Foreshadow.

We systematically analyze the root cause of the prefetching effect exploited in these works. We show that, despite the sound approach of these papers, the attribution of the root cause, *i.e.*, why the kernel addresses are cached, is incorrect in all cases. The root cause is unrelated to software prefetch instructions or hardware prefetching effects due to memory accesses and instead is caused by speculative dereferencing of user-space registers in the kernel. While there are many speculative code paths in the kernel, we focus on code paths with Spectre [6,35] gadgets that can be reliably triggered on both Linux and Windows.

© International Financial Cryptography Association 2021
N. Borisov and C. Diaz (Eds.): FC 2021, LNCS 12674, pp. 311–330, 2021.
https://doi.org/10.1007/978-3-662-64322-8_15

These new insights correct several wrong assumptions from previous works, also leading to new attacks. Most significantly, the difference that Meltdown can leak from L3 or main memory [41] but Foreshadow (L1TF) can only leak from L1 [67, Appendix A], was never a limitation in practice. The same effect that allowed Meltdown to leak data from L3, enables our slightly modified Foreshadow attack to leak data from L3 as well, *i.e.*, L1TF was in practice never restricted to the L1 cache. Worse still, we show that for the same reason Foreshadow mitigations [67,70] are still incomplete. We reveal that Foreshadow attacks are unmitigated on many kernel versions even with all mitigations and even on the most recent kernel versions. However, retpoline affects the success rate, but it is only enabled on some kernel versions and some microarchitectures.

We present a new technique that uses dereferencing gadgets to directly leak data without an encoding attack step. We show that we can leak data from registers, e.g., cryptographic key material, from SGX and that the assumptions in previous works were incorrect, making certain attacks only reproducible on kernels susceptible to speculative dereferencing, including, e.g., results from Gruss et al. [17, §3.3 and §5], Lipp et al. [41, §6.2], and Xiao et al. [73, §4-E]. This also allowed us to improve the performance of address-translation attacks and to mount them in JavaScript [17]. We demonstrate that the address-translation attack also works on recent Intel CPUs with the latest hardware mitigations with all mitigations enabled. Finally, we also demonstrate the attack on CPUs previously believed to be unaffected by the prefetch address-translation attack, *i.e.*, ARM, IBM Power9, and AMD CPUs.

Contributions. The main contributions of this work are:

1. We discover an incorrect attribution of the root cause in previous works to prefetching effects [17,41,73].
2. We show that the root cause is speculative execution, leaving CPUs from other vendors equally affected and the effect exploitable from JavaScript.
3. We discover a novel way to exploit speculative dereferences, enabling direct leakage data in registers.
4. We show that this effect, responsible for Meltdown from non-L1 data, can be adapted to Foreshadow and show that Foreshadow attacks on data from the L3 cache are possible, even with Foreshadow mitigations enabled.

Outline. Section 2 provides background. Section 3 analyzes the root cause. Section 4 improves and extends the attacks. Section 5 presents cross-VM data leakage. Section 6 presents a new leakage method. Section 7 presents a JavaScript-based attack. Section 8 discusses implications. Section 9 concludes.

2   Background and Related Work

In this section, we provide relevant details regarding virtual memory, CPU caches, Intel SGX, and transient execution attacks and defenses.

Virtual Memory. In modern systems, each process has its own virtual address space, divided into user and kernel space. Many operating systems map physical memory directly into the kernel [30, 39], e.g., to access paging structures. Thus, every user page is mapped at least twice: in user space and in the kernel direct-physical map. Access to virtual-to-physical address information requires root privileges [34]. The prefetch address-translation attack [17, §3.3 and §5] obtains the physical address for any user-space address via a side-channel attack.

Caches and Prefetching. Modern CPUs have multiple cache levels, hiding latency of slower memory levels. Software prefetch instructions hint the CPU that a memory address should already be fetched into the cache early to improve performance. Intel and AMD x86 CPUs have 5 software prefetch* instructions.

Prefetching Attacks. Gruss et al. [17] observed that software prefetches appear to succeed on inaccessible memory. Using this effect on the kernel direct-physical map enables the user to fetch arbitrary physical memory into the cache. The attacker guesses the physical address for a user-space address, tries to prefetch the corresponding address in the kernel's direct-physical map, and then uses Flush+Reload [74] on the user-space address. On a cache hit, the guess was correct. Hence, the attacker can determine the exact physical address for any virtual address, re-enabling various mircorarchitectural attacks [32, 43, 50, 61].

Intel SGX. Intel SGX is a trusted execution mechanism enabling the execution of trusted code in a separate protected area called an enclave [26]. Although enclave memory is mapped in the virtual address space of the host application, the hardware prevents access to the code or data of the enclave from any source other than the enclave code itself [27]. However, as has been shown in the past, it is possible to exploit SGX via memory corruption [37, 54], ransomware [59], side-channel attacks [5, 55], and transient-execution attacks [52, 56, 67, 68].

Transient Execution. Modern CPUs execute instructions *out of order* to improve performance and then retire *in order* from reorder buffers. Another performance optimization, speculative execution, predicts control flow and data flow for not-yet resolved conditional control- or data-flow changes. Intel CPUs have several branch predictors [25], e.g., the Branch History Buffer (BHB) [3, 35], Branch Target Buffer (BTB) [12, 35, 38], Pattern History Table (PHT) [13, 35], and Return Stack Buffer (RSB) [13, 36, 42]. Instructions executed out-of-order or speculatively but not architecturally are called *transient instructions* [41].

These *transient instructions* can have measurable side effects, e.g., modification of TLB and cache state, that can be exploited to extract secrets in so-called transient-execution attacks [6, 28]. Spectre-type attacks [7, 19, 33, 35, 36, 42, 58] exploit misspeculation in a victim context. By executing along the misspeculated path, the victim inadvertently leaks information to the attacker. To mitigate Spectre-type attacks several mitigations were developed [24], such as retpoline [23], which replaces indirect jump instructions with ret instructions.

In Meltdown-type attacks [41], such as Foreshadow [67], an attacker deliberately accesses memory across isolation boundaries, which is possible due to deferred permission checks in out-of-order execution. Foreshadow exploits a cleared present bit in the page table-entry to leak data from the L1 cache or the line fill buffer [52,56]. A widely accepted mitigation is to flush the L1 caches and line fill buffers upon context switches and to disable hyperthreading [22].

3   From Address-Translation Attack to Foreshadow-L3

In this section, we systematically analyze the properties of the address-translation attack erroneously attributed to the software prefetch instructions [17, §3.3 and §5]. We identify the root cause to be unmitigated misspeculation in the kernel, leading to a new Foreshadow-L3 attack that works despite mitigations [67].

```
1  41 0f 18 06    prefetchnta (%r14)  ; replace with nop for testing, r14 = direct phys. addr.
2  41 0f 18 1e    prefetcht2 (%r14)   ; replace with nop for testing, r14 = direct phys. addr.
```

Listing 1. Disassembly of the prefetching in the address-translation attack.

In the address-translation attack [17] the attacker tries to find a direct physical map address $\bar{p}$ for a virtual address p. The attacker flushes the user-space address p, and prefetches the inaccessible direct physical map address $\bar{p}$. If Flush+Reload [74] determines that p was reloaded via $\bar{p}$, the physical address of p is $\bar{p}$ minus the known direct-physical-map offset. We measure the attack performance in *fetches per second*, i.e., how often per second p was cached via $\bar{p}$.

The prefetching component of the original attack's proof-of-concept [20] runs a loop, `for (size_t i = 0; i < 3; ++i) { sched_yield(); prefetch(direct_phys_map_addr); }`. The compiled and disassembled code can be found in Listing 1. We extracted the following hypotheses (H1–H5) from the original attack (cf. Appendix A for quotes):

H1 the `prefetch` instruction (to instruct the prefetcher to prefetch);

H2 the value stored in the register used by the `prefetch` instruction (to indicate which address the prefetcher should prefetch);

H3 the `sched_yield` syscall (to give time to the prefetcher);

H4 the use of the `userspace_accessible` bit (as kernel addresses could otherwise not be translated in a user context);

H5 an Intel CPU – other CPU vendors are claimed to be unaffected.

We test each of the above hypotheses in this section.

3.1   H1: Prefetch Instruction Required

The first hypothesis is that the `prefetch` instruction is necessary for the address-translation attack. We replace the `prefetch` instructions in the original code [20] with same-size `nops` (cf. Listing 1). Surprisingly, we observe no change in the number of cache fetches, i.e., we measure 60 cache fetches per second (i7-8700K,

Ubuntu 18.10, kernel 4.15.0-55), without any prefetch instruction. We also exclude the hardware prefetcher by disabling them via the model-specific register 0x1a4 [69] during the experiment. We still observe ≈60 cache fetches per second.

> Documented prefetchers are not required for the address-translation attack.

3.2 H2: Values in Registers Required

The second hypothesis is that providing the direct-physical map address via the register is necessary. The registers that must be used vary across kernel versions. We identified the registers r12,r13,r14 (Ubuntu 18.10, kernel 4.18.0-17), r9,r10 (Debian 8, kernel 4.19.28-2 and Kali Linux, kernel 5.3.9-1kali1) and rdi,rdx (Linux Mint 19, kernel 4.15.0-52). Gruss et al. [17] used recompiled binaries that used different registers for the kernel address (cf. Appendix A).

> A referenced location is only fetched into the cache if the absolute virtual address is stored in one of these registers.

We additionally verified that only the absolute virtual address causes this effect. Any other addressing mode for the prefetch instruction does not leak. By loading the address into most general-purpose registers, we observe leakage across all Linux versions, even with KPTI enabled, meaning that the KAISER technique [16] never protected against this attack. Instead, the implementation merely changed the required registers, hiding the effect for a specific binary-kernel combination. On an Intel Xeon Silver 4208 CPU with in-silicon patches against Meltdown [41], Foreshadow [67], and ZombieLoad [56], we still observe about 30 cache fetches per second on Ubuntu 19.04 (kernel 5.0.0-25). On Windows 10 (build 1803.17134), which has no direct physical map, we fill all registers with a kernel address and perform the syscall SwitchToThread. We observe ≈15 cache fetches per second for our kernel address.

3.3 H3: sched_yield Required

The third hypothesis is that the sched_yield syscall is required. We observe that other syscalls e.g., gettid, expose a similar number of cache fetches. This shows that sched_yield is not required and can be replaced with other syscalls. To test whether syscalls in the main attack loop are required, we run a address-translation attack without context switches or interrupts and without sched_yield on an isolated core. Here, we do not observe any cache fetches (i7-8700K, kernel 4.15.0-55) when running this attack for 10 h. However, when inducing a large number of context switches using interrupts, we observe about 15 cache fetches per second if the process filling the registers gets interrupted continuously. These hits occur during speculative execution in the interrupt handler, as we validated manually via code changes and fencing in interrupt handlers.

> We conclude that the essential part is performing syscalls or interrupts while specific registers are filled with an attacker-chosen address.

```
1 ;<do_syscall_64+106>                          ; with retpoline
2 => 0xffffffff81802000: jmpq    *%rax         callq  0xffffffff8180200c
3 => 0xffffffff8180200c:                        mov    %rax,(%rsp)
4 => 0xffffffff81802010:                        retq
```

Listing 2. The kernel performs indirect jumps, e.g., to syscall handlers. With retpoline [64], the kernel uses a `retq` instead of the indirect jump.

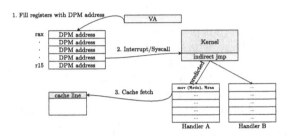

Fig. 1. The kernel speculatively dereferences the direct-physical map address. Flush+Reload detects cache hits on the corresponding user-space address.

3.4 H4: userspace_accessible Bit Required

The fourth hypothesis is that user-mapped kernel pages are required, *i.e.*, access is prevented via the `userspace_accessible` bit. We constructed an experiment where we allocate several pages of memory. We choose cache lines A and B on different pages. In a loop, we dereference a register pointing to A and use Flush+Reload to detect whether A was cached. In the last loop iteration, we speculatively exchange the register value to point to either B or the direct-physical map address of B. Hence, both the architectural and speculative dereferences happen at the same instruction pointer value and in the same register. With a register-value-based hardware prefetcher, we would expect B to be cached. When dereferencing the direct-physical-map address of B architecturally, B is usually cached after the loop. However, when we dereference the register with its value speculatively changed from A to either B or the direct-physical map address of B, B is never cached after the final run. In a second experiment, we show that the effect originates from the kernel. While prefetching direct-physical-map addresses works, user-space addresses are only fetched when SMAP (supervisor-mode access prevention) is disabled. Thus, the root cause of the address-translation attack adheres to SMAP.

> Hence, we can conclude that the root cause is code execution in the kernel.

3.5 H5: Effect only on Intel CPUs

The fifth hypothesis is that the "prefetching" effect only occurs on Intel CPUs. We run our experiments (cf. Sect. 3.4) on an AMD Ryzen Threadripper 1920X (Ubuntu 17.10, kernel `4.13.0-46generic`), an ARM Cortex-A57 (Ubuntu 16.04.6 LTS, kernel `4.4.38-tegra`), and an IBM Power9 (Ubuntu

18.04, kernel `4.15.0-29`). On the AMD Ryzen Threadripper 1920X, we achieve up to 20, on the Cortex-A57 up to 5, and on the IBM Power9 up to 15 speculative fetches per second.

> Any Spectre-susceptible CPU is also susceptible to speculative dereferencing.

3.6 Speculative Execution in the Kernel

From the previous analysis, we conclude that the leakage is due to speculative execution in the kernel. While this might not be surprising with the knowledge of Spectre, Spectre was only discovered one year after the original prefetch paper [17] was published. We show that the primary leakage is caused by Spectre-BTB-SA-IP (training in same address space, and in-place) [6].

```
1 movzbl (%rax,%rdi,1),%eax
2 <op> (%rcx,%rax,1),%dl
3 ; gadget in Linux kernel
4 98d4be:        0f b6 34 06        movzbl (%rsi,%rax,1),%esi
5 98d4c2:        45 01 3c b3        add    %r15d,(%r11,%rsi,4)
```

Listing 3. If the attacker controls three register values, it is possible to leak arbitrary kernel memory.

During a syscall, the kernel performs multiple indirect jumps (cf. Listing 2), which are generally susceptible to Spectre-BTB-SA-IP. The address-translation attack succeeds because misspeculated branch targets dereference registers without sanitization. With retpoline, the kernel uses a `retq` instead of the indirect jump to trap the speculative execution to a fixed branch. Thus, during speculative execution, the CPU might use an incorrect prediction from the branch-target buffer (BTB) and speculate into the wrong syscall while registers contain attacker-chosen addresses (cf. Fig. 1). In the misspeculated syscall, registers containing attacker-chosen addresses are used. On recent kernels (4.19 or newer), retpoline eliminates the leakage. We provide a full analysis of the `sched_yield` gadget causing speculative dereferences in Appendix B. Even worse, cloud providers still use older kernel versions (e.g., the first option on AWS at the time of writing is Amazon Linux 2 AMI with kernel 4.14) where retpoline does *not* fully eliminate the leakage. On the other hand, recent systems such as Ice Lake do not use retpoline anymore due to improved hardware mitigations, which unfortunately have *no* effect on our speculative dereferencing attack. Hence, our attack remains unmitigated on many systems, and is most importantly not mitigated by KAISER (KPTI) [16], or LAZARUS [14] as claimed in previous works. The Spectre-BTB-SA-IP leak from Listing 2 is only one of many, e.g., we still observe ≈ 15 speculative fetches per second on an i5-8250U (kernel `5.0.0-20`) if we eliminate this specific leak. However, any prefetch gadget [6], based on PHT, BTB, or RSB mispredictions, can be used for an address-translation attack [17] and thus would also re-enable Foreshadow-VMM attacks [67,70]. Concurrent work showed that there are kernel gadgets to fetch data into the L1D cache in Xen [72] and an artificial gadget was exploited by Stecklina for that purpose [63].

We also analyzed the interrupt handling in the Linux kernel version 4.19.0 and observed that the register values from r8–r15 are cleared but stored on the stack and restored after the interrupt. In between, stack dereferences in mis-speculated branches can still access these values. On recent Ice Lake processors, retpoline is replaced by enhanced IBRS. Unfortunately, this is a security regression, re-enabling Spectre-BTB in-place attacks and, thus, moves our focus on a set of previously overlooked gadgets, where the user only controls certain register values in the transient domain. We measure the performance of our attack by exploiting such a Spectre-BTB gadget in a kernel module and evaluate it on our Ice Lake CPU. Listing 3 illustrates an eIBRS-bypassing Spectre-BTB gadget containing only two instructions, where the attacker controls, e.g., three registers. The smallest eIBRS-bypassing Spectre-BTB gadget we found contains only 7 bytes.

We demonstrate that on Ice Lake, this regression re-enables transient leakage of kernel memory like the original Spectre attack paper described [35], *i.e.*, measured by leaking a 1024 B secret key. We observe a completely noise-free leakage rate of 30 B/s ($n = 1000, \sigma_{\bar{x}} = 0.1429$). By shifting the byte *i.e.*, binary searching via two consecutive cache lines, we then can recover the exact byte value [35]. We analyzed the Linux kernel 5.4.0-48 (vmlinux binary) and looked for similar opcodes and found a gadget at offset 0x984dbe (see Listing 3 line 3 and 4).

3.7   Meltdown-L3 and Foreshadow-L3

The speculative dereferencing was noticed but also misattributed to the prefetcher in subsequent work. The Meltdown paper [41] reports that data is fetched from L3 into L1 while mounting a Meltdown attack. Van Bulck et al. [67] confirmed the effect for Meltdown but did not observe this prefetching effect for Foreshadow. Based on this observation, further works also mentioned this effect without analyzing it thoroughly [6,31,47,52]. Xiao et al. [73] state that a Meltdown-US attack causes data to be repeatedly prefetched from L1 to L3 [73].

We used similar Meltdown-L3 setups as SPEECHMINER [73] (kernel 4.4.0-134 with boot flags nopti,nokaslr and Meltdown [41] (Ubuntu 16.10, kernel 4.8.0, no mitigations existed back then). In our Meltdown-L3 experiment, one physical core constantly accesses a secret to ensure that the value stays in the L3, as the L3 is shared across all physical cores. On a different physical core, we run Meltdown on the direct-physical map. On recent Linux kernels with full Spectre v2 mitigations implemented, we could not reproduce the result. With the nospectre_v2 flag, our Meltdown-L3 attack works again by triggering the prefetch gadget in the kernel on the direct-physical map address. In the SPEECH-MINER [73] and Meltdown [41] experiment, no mitigation (including retpoline) eliminates the leakage fully. Without our new insights that the prefetching effect is caused by speculative execution, it is almost inevitable to not misdesign these experiments, inevitably leading to incomplete or incorrect observations and conclusions on Meltdown and Foreshadow and their mitigations. We confirmed with the authors that their experiment design was not robust to our new insight and therefore lead to wrong conclusions. Foreshadow-L3, The same prefetching effect can be used to perform Foreshadow [67]. If a secret is present in the L3 cache and the direct-physical map address is dereferenced in the hypervisor kernel, data can be fetched into the L1. This reenables Foreshadow even with Foreshadow mitigations enabled. We demonstrate this attack in KVM in Sect. 5.

4   Improving the Leakage Rate

We can leverage our insights to increase the leakage by using syscalls other than sched_yield, and executing additional syscalls to mistrain the branch predictor.

Setup. We tested our attacks on an Intel i5-8250U (Linux kernel 4.15.0-52), an i7-8700K (Linux kernel 4.15.0-55), an ARM Cortex-A57 (Linux kernel 4.4.38-tegra), and an AMD Threadripper 1920X (Linux kernel 4.13.0-46). As retpoline is not available on all machines, we run the tests without retpoline. By performing syscalls before filling the registers with the direct-physical map address, we can mistrain the BTB, triggering the CPU to speculatively execute this syscall. The mistraining analysis of sched_yield can be seen in the extended version of the paper [60].

Evaluation. We evaluated different syscalls for branch prediction mistraining by executing a single syscall before and after filling the registers with the target address. We observe that effects occur for different syscalls and both on AMD and ARM CPUs, with similar success rates (extended version Appendix G) [60]. Alternating syscalls additionally mistrains the branch prediction and increases the success rate, e.g., with syscalls like stat, sendto, or geteuid. However, not every additional syscall increases the number of cache fetches. On recent Linux kernels (version 5), we observe that the number of speculative cache fetches decreases, due to a change in syscall handling. Our results show that the pipe syscall much more reliably triggers speculative dereferencing ($\geq$99.9%), but the execution time of sched_yield is much lower and thus despite the lower success rate (around 66.4% in the most basic case) it yields a higher attack performance.

Capacity Measurement in a Cross-Core Covert Channel. We measure the capacity of our attack in a covert channel by using the speculative dereferencing effect ('1'-bit) or not ('0'-bit). The receiver uses Flush+Reload to measure whether the cache state of cache line dereferenced in the kernel. We evaluated the covert channel on random data and across physical CPU cores. Our test system was equipped with an Intel i7-6500U CPU Linux 4.15.0-52 with the nospectre_v2 boot flag. We achieved the highest capacity at a transmission rate of 10 bit/s. At this rate, the standard error is, on average, 0.1%. This result is comparable to related work in similar scenarios [50,71]. To achieve an error-free transmission, error-correction techniques [43] can be used. I/O interrupts, *i.e.*, syncing the NVMe device, create additional speculative dereferences and can thus further improve the capacity.

5   Speculative Dereferences and Virtual Machines

In this section, we examine speculative dereferencing in virtual machines. We demonstrate a successful end-to-end attack using interrupts from a virtual-machine guest running under KVM on a Linux host [10]. We leak data (e.g., cryptographic keys) from other virtual machines and the hypervisor, like the original Foreshadow attack. We do not observe any speculative dereferencing of guest-controlled registers in Microsoft's Hyper-V HyperClear Foreshadow mitigation which additionally uses retpoline, or on more recent kernel versions with retpoline. We provide a thorough analysis of this negative result. However, the attack succeeds even with the recommended Foreshadow mitigations enabled and with kernel versions before 4.18 (e.g., as used by default on AWS Amazon Linux 2 AMI) with all default mitigations enabled, *i.e.*, including retpoline. We investigate whether speculative dereferencing also exists in hypercalls. The attacker targets a specific host-memory location where the host virtual address and physical address are known but inaccessible.

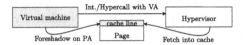

Fig. 2. If a guest-chosen address is speculatively fetched into the cache during a hyper-call or interrupt and not flushed before the virtual machine is resumed, the attacker can perform a Foreshadow attack to leak the fetched data.

Foreshadow Attack on Virtualization Software. If an address from the host is speculatively fetched into the L1 cache on a hypercall from the guest, it has a similar speculative-dereferencing effect. With the speculative memory access in the kernel, we can fetch arbitrary memory from L2, L3, or DRAM into the L1 cache. Consequently, Foreshadow can be used on arbitrary memory addresses provided the L1TF mitigations in use do not flush the entire L1 data cache [63,65,72]. Figure 2 illustrates the attack using hypercalls or interrupts and Foreshadow. The attacking guest loads a host virtual address into the registers used as hypercall parameters and then performs hypercalls. If there is a prefetch-ing gadget in the hypercall handler and the CPU misspeculates into this gadget, the host virtual address is fetched into the cache. The attacker then performs a Foreshadow attack and leaks the value from the loaded virtual address.

5.1   Foreshadow on Patched Linux KVM

Concurrent work showed that prefetching gadgets in the kernel, in combination with L1TF, can be exploited on Xen and KVM [63,72]. The default setting on Ubuntu 19.04 (kernel `5.0.0-20`) is to only conditionally flush the L1 data cache upon VM entry via KVM [65], which is also the case for Kali Linux (kernel

5.3.9-1kali1). The L1 data cache is only flushed in nested VM entry scenarios or in situations where data from the host might be leaked. Since Linux kernel 4.9.81, Linux's KVM implementation clears all guest clobbered registers to prevent speculative dereferencing [11]. In our attack, the guest fills all general-purpose registers with direct-physical-map addresses from the host.

End-to-End Foreshadow Attack via Interrupts. In Sect. 3.3, we observed that context switches triggered by interrupts can also cause speculative cache fetches. We use the example from Sect. 3.3 to verify whether the "prefetching" effect can also be exploited from a virtualized environment. In this setup, we virtualize Linux buildroot (kernel 4.16.18) on a Kali Linux host (kernel 5.3.9-1kali1) using qemu (4.2.0) with the KVM backend. In our experiment, the guest constantly fills a register with a direct-physical-map address and performs the sched_yield syscall. We verify with Flush+Reload in a loop on the corresponding host virtual address that the address is indeed cached. Hence, we can successfully fetch arbitrary hypervisor addresses into the L1 cache on kernel versions before the patch, *i.e.*, with Foreshadow mitigations but incomplete Spectre-BTB mitigations. We observe about 25 speculative cache fetches per minute using NVMe interrupts on our Debian machine. The attacker, running as a guest, can use this gadget to prefetch data into the L1. Since data is now located in the L1, this reenables a Foreshadow attack [67], allowing guest-to-host memory reads. 25 fetches per minute means that we can theoretically leak up to $64 \cdot 25 = 1600$ bytes per minute (or 26.7 bytes per second) with a Foreshadow attack despite mitigations in place. However, this requires a sophisticated attacker who avoids context switches once the target cache line is cached. We develop an end-to-end Foreshadow-L3 exploit that works despite enabled Foreshadow mitigations. In this attack the host constantly performs encryptions using a secret key on a physical core, which ensures it remains in the shared L3 cache. We assign one isolated physical core, consisting of two hyperthreads, to our virtual machine. In the virtual machine, the attacker fills all registers on one logical core (hyperthread) and performs the Foreshadow attack on the other logical core. Note that this is different from the original Foreshadow attack where one hyperthread is controlled by the attacker and the sibling hyperthread is used by the victim. Our scenario is more realistic, as the attacker controls both hyperthreads, *i.e.*, both hyperthreads are in the same trust domain. With this proof-of-concept attack implementation, we are able to leak 7 bytes per minute successfully[1]. Note that this can be optimized further, as the current proof-of-concept produces context switches regardless of whether the cache line is cached or not. Our attack clearly shows that the recommended Foreshadow mitigations alone are not sufficient to mitigate Foreshadow attacks, and retpoline must be enabled to fully mitigate our Foreshadow-L3 attack.

No Prefetching Gadget in Hypercalls in KVM. We track the register values in hypercalls and validate whether the register values from the guest system are speculatively fetched into the cache. We neither observe that the

---

[1] Demonstration video can be found here: https://streamable.com/8ke5ub.

direct-physical-map address is still located in the registers nor that it is speculatively fetched into the cache. However, as was shown in concurrent work [63,72], prefetch gadgets exist in the kernel that can be exploited to fetch data into the cache, and these gadgets can be exploited using Foreshadow.

5.2   Negative Result: Foreshadow on Hyper-V HyperClear

We examined whether the same attack also works on Windows 10 (build 1803.17134), which includes the latest patch for Foreshadow. As on Linux, we disabled retpoline and tried to fetch hypervisor addresses from guest systems into the cache. Microsoft's Hyper-V HyperClear Mitigation [45] for Foreshadow claims to only flush the L1 data cache when switching between virtual cores. Hence, it should be susceptible to the same basic attack we described at the beginning of this section. For our experiment, the attacker passes a known virtual address of a secret variable from the host operating system for all parameters of a hypercall. However, we could not find any exploitable timing difference after switching from the guest to the hypervisor. The extended version discusses the negative result in Appendix F [60].

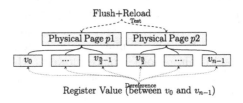

Fig. 3. Leaking the value of an x86 general-purpose register using *Dereference Trap* and Flush+Reload on two different physical addresses. v_0 to v_{n-1} represent the memory mappings on one of the shared memory regions.

6   Leaking Values from SGX Registers

In this section, we present a novel method, *Dereference Trap*, to leak register contents via speculative register dereference. Leaking the values of registers is useful, e.g., to extract parts of keys from cryptographic operations.

6.1   Dereference Trap

The setup for *Dereference Trap* is similar as in Sect. 3.6. We exploit transient code paths inside an SGX enclave that speculatively dereference a register containing a secret value. Such a gadget is easily introduced in an enclave, e.g., when using polymorphism in C++. The extended version contains a minimal example of such a gadget (Appendix C, Listing 5) [60]. However, there are also many different causes for such gadgets [23], e.g., function pointers or (compiler-generated) jump tables. The basic idea of *Dereference Trap* is to ensure that the entire virtual address space of the application is mapped. Thus, if a register containing a secret is speculatively dereferenced, the corresponding virtual address is cached. The attacker can detect which virtual address is cached and infer the secret. However, it is infeasible to back every virtual address with unique physical pages and mount Flush+Reload on every cache line, as that takes 2 days on a 4 GHz CPU [54].

Instead of mapping every page in the virtual address space to its own physical pages, we only map 2 physical pages $p1$ and $p2$, as illustrated in Fig. 3. By leveraging shared memory, we can map one physical page multiple times into the virtual address space. The maximum number of mappings per page is $2^{31} - 1$, which makes it possible to map $1/16^{th}$ of the user-accessible virtual address space. If we only consider 32-bit secrets, $i.e.$, secrets which are stored in the lower half of 64-bit registers, 2^{20} mappings are sufficient. Out of these, the first 2^{10} virtual addresses map to physical page $p1$ and the second 2^{10} addresses map to page $p2$. Consequently the majority of 32-bit values are now valid addresses that either map to $p1$ or $p2$. Thus, after a 32-bit secret is speculatively dereferenced inside the enclave, the attacker only needs to probe the 64 cache lines of each of the two physical pages. A cache hit reveals the most-significant bit (bit 31) of the secret as well as bits 6 to 11, which define the cache-line offset on the page. To learn the remaining bits 12 to 30, we continue in a fashion akin to binary-search. We unmap all mappings to $p1$ and $p2$ and create half as many mappings as before. Again, half of the new mappings map to $p1$ and half of the new mappings map to $p2$. From a cache hit in this setup, we can again learn one bit of the secret. We can repeat these steps until all bits from bit 6 to 31 of the secret are known. As the granularity of Flush+Reload is one cache line, we cannot leak the least-significant 6 bits of the secret. On our test system, we recovered a 32-bit value (without the least-significant 6 bits) stored in a 64-bit register within 15 min with *Dereference Trap*.

6.2   Generalization of Dereference Trap

Dereference Trap is a generic technique that applies to any scenario where the attacker can set up the hardware and address space accordingly. *Dereference Trap* applies to all Spectre variants. Many in-place Spectre-v1 gadgets that are not the typical encoding array gadget are still entirely unprotected with no plans to change this. For instance, Intel systems before Haswell and AMD systems before Zen do not support SMAP, and more recent systems may have SMAP disabled. On these systems, we can also mmap memory regions and the kernel will dereference 32-bit values misinterpreted as pointers (into user space). Using this technique the attacker can reliably leak a 32-bit secret which is speculatively dereferenced by the kernel. Cryptographic implementations often store keys in the lower 32 bits of 64bit registers ($i.e.$, OpenSSL AES round key u32 *rk) [48]. Hence, these implementations might be susceptible to *Dereference Trap*. We evaluated the same experiment on an Intel i5-8250U, ARM Cortex-A57, and AMD ThreadRipper 1920X with the same result of 15 min to recover a 32-bit secret (without the least-significant 6 bits). Thus, retpoline and SMAP must remain enabled to mitigate attacks like *Dereference Trap*.

7   Leaking Physical Addresses from JavaScript Using WebAssembly

In this section, we present an attack that leaks the physical address (cacheline granularity) of a JavaScript variable. This shows that the "prefetching" effect is much simpler than described in the original paper [17], *i.e.*, *it does not require native code execution*. The only requirement for the environment is that it can keep a 64-bit register filled with an attacker-controlled 64-bit value. In contrast to the original paper's attempt to use native code in browser, we create a JavaScript-based attack to leak physical addresses from Javascript variables and evaluate its performance in Firefox. We demonstrate that it is possible to fill 64-bit registers with an attacker-controlled value via WebAssembly.

Attack Setup. JavaScript encodes numbers as 53-bit double-precision floating-point values [46]. It is not possible to store a full 64-bit value into a register with vanilla JavaScript. Hence, we leverage WebAssembly, a binary instruction format which is precompiled for the JavaScript engine and not further optimized [66]. On our test system (i7-8550U, Debian 8, kernel 5.3.9-1kali1) registers r9 and r10 are speculatively dereferenced in the kernel. Hence, we fill these registers with a guessed direct-physical-map address of a variable. The WebAssembly method load_pointer (Appendix F [60]) takes two 32-bit values that are combined into a 64-bit value and populated into as many registers as possible. To trigger interrupts, we use web requests, as shown by Lipp et al. [40]. Our attack leaks the direct-physical-map address of a JavaScript variable. The attack works analogously to the native-code address-translation attack [17].

1. Guess a physical address p for the variable and compute the corresponding direct-physical map address $d(p)$.
2. Load $d(p)$ into the required registers (load_pointer) in an endless loop, e.g., using endless-loop slicing [40].
3. The kernel fetches $d(p)$ into the cache when interrupted.
4. Use Evict+Reload on the target variable. On a cache hit, the physical address guess p from Step 1 was correct. Otherwise, continue with the next guess.

Attack from Within Browsers. We mount an attack in an unmodified Firefox 76.0 by injecting interrupts via web requests. We observe up to 2 speculative fetches per hour. If the logical core running the code is constantly interrupted, e.g., due to disk I/O, we achieve up to 1 speculative fetch per minute. As this attack leaks parts of the physical and virtual address, it can be used to implement various microarchitectural attacks [15,18,35,49,50,53,57]. Hence, the address-translation attack is possible with JavaScript and WebAssembly, without requiring the NaCl sandbox as in the original paper [17]. Upcoming JavaScript extensions expose syscalls to JavaScript [8]. Hence, as the second part of our evaluation, we investigate whether a syscall-based attack would also yield the same performance as in native code. To simulate the extension, we expose the sched_yield syscall to JavaScript. We observe the same performance of 20 speculative fetches per second with the syscall function.

Limitations of the Attack. We conclude that the bottleneck of this attack is triggering syscalls. In particular, there is currently no way to directly perform a single syscall via Javascript in browsers without high overhead. We traced the syscalls of Firefox using strace. We observed that syscalls such as sched_yield, getpid, stat, sendto are commonly performed upon window events, e.g., opening and closing pop-ups or reading and writing events on the JavaScript console. However, the registers r9 and r10 get overwritten before the syscall is performed. Thus, whether the registers are speculatively dereferenced while still containing the attacker-chosen values strongly depends on the engine's register allocation and on other syscalls performed. As Jangda et al. [29] stated, not all registers are used in JIT-generated native code [29].

8   Discussion

The "prefetching" effect was first observed by Gruss et al. [17] in 2016. In May 2017, Jann Horn discovered that speculative execution can be exploited to leak arbitrary data, later on published in the Spectre [35] paper. Our results indicate that the address-translation attack was the first inadvertent exploitation of speculative execution, albeit in a much weaker form where only metadata, *i.e.*, information about KASLR, is leaked rather than real data as in a full Spectre attack. Even before the address-translation attack, speculative execution was well known [51] and documented [26] to cause cache hits on addresses that are not architecturally accessed. Currently, the address-translation attack and our variants are mitigated on both Linux and Windows using the retpoline technique to avoid indirect branches. Another possibility upon a syscall is to save user-space register values to memory, clear the registers to prevent speculative dereferencing, and later restore the user-space values after execution of the syscall. However, as has been observed in the interrupt handler, there might still be some speculative cache accesses on values from the stack. The retpoline mitigation for Spectre-BTB introduces a large overhead for indirect branches. The performance overhead can in some cases be up to 50% [62]. This is particularly problematic in large scale systems, e.g., cloud data centers, that have to compensate for the performance loss and increased energy consumption. Furthermore, retpoline breaks CET and CFI technologies and might thus also be disabled [4]. As an alternative, randpoline [4] could be used to replace the mitigation with a probabilistic one, again with an effect on Foreshadow mitigations. And indeed, mitigating memory corruption vulnerabilities may be more important than mitigating Foreshadow in certain use cases. Cloud computing concepts that do not rely on traditional isolation boundaries are already being explored [1,9,21,44]. On current CPUs, retpoline must remain enabled, which is not the default in many cases. Other Spectre-BTB mitigations, including enhanced IBRS, do not mitigate our attack. On newer kernels for ARM Cortex-A CPUs, the branch prediction results can be discarded, and on certain devices branch prediction can be entirely disabled [2]. Our results suggest that these mechanisms are required for context switches or interrupt handling. Additionally, the L1TF mitigations must be applied on affected CPUs to prevent Foreshadow. Otherwise, we can still fetch arbitrary hypervisor addresses into the cache. Finally, our attacks also show that SGX enclaves must be compiled with the retpoline flag. Even with LVI mitigations, this is currently not the default setting, and thus all SGX enclaves are potentially susceptible to *Dereference Trap*.

9   Conclusion

We showed that the underlying root cause of prefetching effects was misattributed in previous works [6,16,31,41,47,52,67] and speculative dereferencing of a user-space register in the kernel actually causes the leakage. As a result, we were able to mount a Foreshadow (L1TF) attack on data from the L3 cache, even with the latest mitigations enabled. Furthermore, we were able to improve the performance of the original attack, apply it to AMD, ARM, and IBM and exploit the effect via JavaScript in browsers. Our novel technique, *Dereference Trap*, leaks the values of registers used in SGX (or privileged contexts) via speculative dereferencing.

Acknowledgments. We want to thank Moritz Lipp, Clémentine Maurice, Anders Fogh, Xiao Yuan, Jo Van Bulck, and Frank Piessens of the original papers for reviewing and providing feedback to drafts of this work and for discussing the technical root cause with us. Furthermore, we want to thank Intel and ARM for valuable feedback on an early draft. This project has received funding from the European Research Council (ERC) under the European Union's Horizon 2020 research and innovation program (grant agreement No. 681402). Additional funding was provided by generous gifts from Cloudflare, Intel and Red Hat. Any opinions, findings, and conclusions or recommendations expressed in this paper are those of the authors and do not necessarily reflect the views of the funding parties.

A   Extracting Hypotheses from Previous Works

The hypotheses are extracted from previous works as detailed in this section. The footnotes for each hypothesis provide the exact part of the previous work that we reference.

H1 the `prefetch` instruction (to instruct the prefetcher to prefetch);[2]
H2 the value stored in the register used by the `prefetch` instruction (to indicate which address the prefetcher should prefetch);[3]

---

[2] "Our attacks are based on weaknesses in the hardware design of prefetch instructions" [17].

[3] "2. Prefetch (inaccessible) address $\bar{p}$. 3. Reload p. [...] the *prefetch of $\bar{p}$ in step 2 leads to a cache hit* in step 3 with a high probability." [17] with emphasis added.

H3 the `sched_yield` syscall (to give time to the prefetcher);[4]

H4 the use of the `userspace_accessible` bit (as kernel addresses could otherwise not be translated in a user context);[5]

H5 an Intel CPU – the "prefetching" effect only occurs on Intel CPUs, and other CPU vendors are not affected.[6]

The original paper also describes that "delays were introduced to lower the pressure on the prefetcher" [17]. In fact, this was done via recompilation. Note that recompilation with additional code inserted may have side effects such as a different register allocation, which we find to be an important influence factor to the attack.

B   Actual Spectre V2 gadget in Linux kernel

We analyzed the Linux kernel 4.16.18 and used the GNU debugger (GDB) to debug our kernel. As our target syscall we analyzed the path of the `sched_yield` syscall. We used the same experiment, which fills all general-purpose registers with the corresponding DPM address, perform `sched_yield` and verify the speculative dereference with Flush+Reload. We repeat this experiment 10 000 000 times. We analyzed each indirect branch in this code path and replaced the indirect call/jump with a retpolined version. Furthermore, we analyzed all general-purpose registers and traced their content if the DPM-address is still valid in some registers. By systematically retpolining the indirect branches, we observed that the indirect call `current->sched_class->yield_task(rq)`; in the function `sys_sched_yield` causes the main leakage. We set a breakpoint to this function and observed that four general-purpose registers (`%rcx,%rsi,%r8,%r9`) still contain the kernel address we set in our experiment.

In the function `put_prev_task_fair`, the `%rsi` register is dereferenced. To check whether this dereference cause the leakage, we add an `lfence` instruction at the beginning of the function. We run the same experiment again and observe almost no cache fetches on our address. The `%rsi` register is dereferenced in line 48.

References

1. Amazon AWS: AWS Lambda@Edge (2019). https://aws.amazon.com/lambda/edge/

---

4 "[...] delays were introduced to lower the pressure on the prefetcher." [17]. These delays were implemented using a different number of `sched_yield` system calls, as can also be seen in the original attack code [20].

5 "Prefetch can fetch inaccessible privileged memory into various caches on Intel x86." [17] and corresponding NaCl results.

6 "[...] we were not able to build an address-translation oracle on [ARM] Android. As the prefetch instructions do not prefetch kernel addresses [...]" [17] describing why it does not work on ARM-based Android devices.

2. ARM: ARM: Whitepaper Cache Speculation Side-channels (2018). https://developer.arm.com/support/arm-security-updates/speculative-processor-vulnerability/download-the-whitepaper
3. Bhattacharya, S., Maurice, C., Bhasin, S., Mukhopadhyay, D.: Template Attack on Blinded Scalar Multiplication with Asynchronous perf-ioctl Calls. Cryptology ePrint Archive, Report 2017/968 (2017)
4. Branco, R., Hu, K., Sun, K., Kawakami, H.: Efficient mitigation of side-channel based attacks against speculative execution processing architectures (2019). US Patent App. 16/023,564
5. Brasser, F., Müller, U., Dmitrienko, A., Kostiainen, K., Capkun, S., Sadeghi, A.R.: Software grand exposure: SGX cache attacks are practical. In: WOOT (2017)
6. Canella, C., et al.: A Systematic evaluation of transient execution attacks and defenses. In: USENIX Security Symposium (2019). Extended classification tree and PoCs at https://transient.fail/
7. Chen, G., Chen, S., Xiao, Y., Zhang, Y., Lin, Z., Lai, T.H.: SgxPectre attacks: stealing Intel secrets from SGX enclaves via speculative execution. In: EuroS&P (2019)
8. Chromium: Mojo in Chromium (2020). https://chromium.googlesource.com/chromium/src.git/+/master/mojo/README.md
9. Cloudflare: Cloudflare Workers (2019). https://www.cloudflare.com/products/cloudflare-workers/
10. KVM Contributors: Kernel-based Virtual Machine (2019). https://www.linux-kvm.org
11. Elixir bootlin (2018). https://elixir.bootlin.com/linux/latest/source/arch/x86/kvm/svm.c#L5700
12. Evtyushkin, D., Ponomarev, D., Abu-Ghazaleh, N.: Jump over ASLR: attacking branch predictors to bypass ASLR. In: MICRO (2016)
13. Fog, A.: The microarchitecture of Intel. An optimization guide for assembly programmers and compiler makers, AMD and VIA CPUs (2016)
14. Gens, D., Arias, O., Sullivan, D., Liebchen, C., Jin, Y., Sadeghi, A.R.: LAZARUS: practical side-channel resilient kernel-space randomization. In: RAID (2017)
15. Gras, B., Razavi, K., Bosman, E., Bos, H., Giuffrida, C.: ASLR on the line: practical cache attacks on the MMU. In: NDSS (2017)
16. Gruss, D., Lipp, M., Schwarz, M., Fellner, R., Maurice, C., Mangard, S.: KASLR is dead: long live KASLR. In: ESSoS (2017)
17. Gruss, D., Maurice, C., Fogh, A., Lipp, M., Mangard, S.: Prefetch side-channel attacks: bypassing SMAP and Kernel ASLR. In: CCS (2016)
18. Gruss, D., Maurice, C., Mangard, S.: Rowhammer.js: a remote software-induced fault attack in JavaScript. In: DIMVA (2016)
19. Horn, J.: Speculative execution, variant 4: speculative store bypass (2018)
20. IAIK: Prefetch Side-Channel Attacks V2P (2016). https://github.com/IAIK/prefetch/blob/master/v2p/v2p.c
21. IBM (2019). https://cloud.ibm.com/functions/
22. Intel: Intel Analysis of Speculative Execution Side Channels (2018). Revision 4.0
23. Intel: Retpoline: A Branch Target Injection Mitigation (2018). Revision 003
24. Intel: Speculative Execution Side Channel Mitigations (2018). Revision 3.0
25. Intel: Intel 64 and IA-32 Architectures Optimization Reference Manual (2019)
26. Intel: Intel 64 and IA-32 Architectures Software Developer's Manual, Volume 3 (3A, 3B & 3C): System Programming Guide (2019)
27. Intel Corporation: Software Guard Extensions Programming Reference, Rev. 2 (2014)

28. Intel Corporation: Refined Speculative Execution Terminology (2020). https://software.intel.com/security-software-guidance/insights/refined-speculative-execution-terminology
29. Jangda, A., Powers, B., Berger, E.D., Guha, A.: Not so fast: analyzing the performance of webassembly vs. native code. In: USENIX ATC (2019)
30. kernel.org: Virtual memory map with 4 level page tables (x86_64) (2009). https://www.kernel.org/doc/Documentation/x86/x86_64/mm.txt
31. Kim, T., Shin, Y.: Reinforcing meltdown attack by using a return stack buffer. IEEE Access **7**, 186065–186077 (2019)
32. Kim, Y., et al.: Flipping bits in memory without accessing them: an experimental study of DRAM disturbance errors. In: ISCA (2014)
33. Kiriansky, V., Waldspurger, C.: Speculative buffer overflows: attacks and defenses. arXiv:1807.03757 (2018)
34. Shutemov, K.A.: Pagemap: Do Not Leak Physical Addresses to Non-Privileged Userspace (2015). https://git.kernel.org/cgit/linux/kernel/git/torvalds/linux.git/commit/?id=ab676b7d6fbf4b294bf198fb27ade5b0e865c7ce
35. Kocher, P., et al.: Spectre attacks: exploiting speculative execution. In: S&P (2019)
36. Koruyeh, E.M., Khasawneh, K., Song, C., Abu-Ghazaleh, N.: Spectre returns! speculation attacks using the return stack buffer. In: WOOT (2018)
37. Lee, J., et al.: Hacking in Darkness: Return-oriented Programming against Secure Enclaves. In: USENIX Security Symposium (2017)
38. Lee, S., Shih, M., Gera, P., Kim, T., Kim, H., Peinado, M.: Inferring fine-grained control flow inside SGX enclaves with branch shadowing. In: USENIX Security Symposium (2017)
39. Levin, J.: Mac OS X and IOS Internals: To the Apple's Core. Wiley, Hoboken (2012)
40. Lipp, M., Gruss, D., Schwarz, M., Bidner, D., Maurice, C., Mangard, S.: Practical keystroke timing attacks in sandboxed JavaScript. In: ESORICS (2017)
41. Lipp, M., et al.: Meltdown: reading kernel memory from user space. In: USENIX Security Symposium (2018)
42. Maisuradze, G., Rossow, C.: ret2spec: speculative execution using return stack buffers. In: CCS (2018)
43. Maurice, C., et al.: Hello from the other side: SSH over robust cache covert channels in the Cloud. In: NDSS (2017)
44. Microsoft: Azure serverless computing (2019). https://azure.microsoft.com/en-us/overview/serverless-computing/
45. Microsoft Techcommunity: Hyper-V HyperClear Mitigation for L1 Terminal Fault (2018). https://techcommunity.microsoft.com/t5/Virtualization/Hyper-V-HyperClear-Mitigation-for-L1-Terminal-Fault/ba-p/382429
46. Mozilla: Javascript data structures (2019). https://developer.mozilla.org/en-US/docs/Web/JavaScript/Data_structures
47. Nilsson, A., Nikbakht Bideh, P., Brorsson, J.: A Survey of Published Attacks on Intel SGX (2020)
48. OpenSSL: OpenSSL: The Open Source toolkit for SSL/TLS (2019). http://www.openssl.org
49. Oren, Y., Kemerlis, V.P., Sethumadhavan, S., Keromytis, A.D.: The Spy in the sandbox: practical cache attacks in JavaScript and their implications. In: CCS (2015)
50. Pessl, P., Gruss, D., Maurice, C., Schwarz, M., Mangard, S.: DRAMA: exploiting DRAM addressing for cross-CPU attacks. In: USENIX Security Symposium (2016)

51. Rebeiro, C., Mukhopadhyay, D., Takahashi, J., Fukunaga, T.: Cache timing attacks on Clefia. In: International Conference on Cryptology in India. Springer, Heidelberg (2009)

52. van Schaik, S.: RIDL: rogue in-flight data load. In: S&P (2019)

53. Schwarz, M., Canella, C., Giner, L., Gruss, D.: Store-to-leak forwarding: leaking data on meltdown-resistant CPUs. arXiv:1905.05725 (2019)

54. Schwarz, M., et al.: Automated detection, exploitation, and elimination of double-fetch bugs using modern CPU features. In: AsiaCCS (2018)

55. Schwarz, M., Gruss, D., Weiser, S., Maurice, C., Mangard, S.: Malware guard extension: using SGX to conceal cache attacks. In: DIMVA (2017)

56. Schwarz, M., et al.: ZombieLoad: cross-privilege-boundary data sampling. In: CCS (2019)

57. Schwarz, M., Maurice, C., Gruss, D., Mangard, S.: Fantastic timers and where to find them: high-resolution microarchitectural attacks in JavaScript. In: FC (2017)

58. Schwarz, M., Schwarzl, M., Lipp, M., Gruss, D.: NetSpectre: read arbitrary memory over network. In: ESORICS (2019)

59. Schwarz, M., Weiser, S., Gruss, D.: Practical enclave malware with Intel SGX. In: DIMVA (2019)

60. Schwarzl, M., Schuster, T., Schwarz, M., Gruss, D.: Speculative dereferencing of registers: reviving foreshadow (2021). https://martinschwarzl.at/media/files/spec_deref_extended.pdf

61. Seaborn, M., Dullien, T.: Exploiting the DRAM rowhammer bug to gain kernel privileges. In: Black Hat Briefings (2015)

62. Slashdot EditorDavid: Two Linux Kernels Revert Performance-Killing Spectre Patches (2019). https://linux.slashdot.org/story/18/11/24/2320228/two-linux-kernels-revert-performance-killing-spectre-patches

63. Stecklina, J.: An demonstrator for the L1TF/Foreshadow vulnerability (2019). https://github.com/blitz/l1tf-demo

64. Turner, P.: Retpoline: a software construct for preventing branch-target-injection (2018). https://support.google.com/faqs/answer/7625886

65. Ubuntu Security Team: L1 Terminal Fault (L1TF) (2019). https://wiki.ubuntu.com/SecurityTeam/KnowledgeBase/L1TF

66. V8 team: v8 - Adding BigInts to V8 (2018). https://v8.dev/blog/bigint

67. Van Bulck, J., et al.: Foreshadow: extracting the keys to the intel SGX kingdom with transient out-of-order execution. In: USENIX Security Symposium (2018)

68. Van Bulck, J., et al.: LVI: hijacking transient execution through microarchitectural load value injection. In: S&P (2020)

69. Viswanathan, V.: Disclosure of hardware prefetcher control on some intel processors. https://software.intel.com/en-us/articles/disclosure-of-hw-prefetcher-control-on-some-intel-processors

70. Weisse, O., et al.: Foreshadow-NG: Breaking the Virtual Memory Abstraction with Transient Out-of-Order Execution (2018). https://foreshadowattack.eu/foreshadow-NG.pdf

71. Wu, Z., Xu, Z., Wang, H.: Whispers in the hyper-space: high-bandwidth and reliable covert channel attacks inside the cloud. ACM Trans. Netw. **23**, 603–614 (2014)

72. xenbits: Cache-load gadgets exploitable with L1TF (2019). https://xenbits.xen.org/xsa/advisory-289.html

73. Xiao, Y., Zhang, Y., Teodorescu, R.: SPEECHMINER: a framework for investigating and measuring speculative execution vulnerabilities. In: NDSS (2020)

74. Yarom, Y., Falkner, K.: Flush+Reload: a high resolution, low noise, L3 cache side-channel attack. In: USENIX Security Symposium (2014)

Sigforgery: Breaking and Fixing Data Authenticity in Sigfox

Loïc Ferreira[(✉)]

Applied Crypto Group, Orange Labs, Caen, France
loic.ferreira@orange.com

Abstract. Sigfox is a popular communication and security protocol which allows setting up low-power wide-area networks for the Internet of Things. Currently, Sigfox networks operate in 72 countries, and cover 1.3 billion people. In this paper, we make an extensive analysis of the security mechanisms used to protect the radio interface in Sigfox. We describe news attacks against data authenticity, which is the only mandatory security property in Sigfox. Namely we describe how to replay frames, and how to compute forgeries. In addition, we highlight a flaw in the (optional) data encryption procedure. Our attacks do not exploit implementation or hardware bugs, nor do they imply a physical access to any equipment (e.g., legitimate end-device). They rely only on the peculiarities of the Sigfox security protocol. Our analysis is supported by practical experiments made in interaction with the Sigfox back-end network. These experiments validate our findings. Finally, we present efficient counter-measures which are likely straightforward to implement.

Keywords: Sigfox · Security protocol · Internet of things · Low-power wide-area network · Cryptanalysis

1 Introduction

1.1 Context

Sigfox is a communication system used in the Internet of Things (IoT). It allows establishing a low-power wide-area (LPWA) network between a set of remote end-devices and a central back-end network (see Sect. B, Fig. 3). The back-end network, owned by the Sigfox company, is an intermediary between a service provider and its fleet of end-devices (e.g., sensors, actuators). The messages sent by an end-device is received on the Sigfox's back-end network where they are made available to the service provider. Conversely, the service provider can send messages to its end-device through the back-end network managed by Sigfox. Different kind of subscriptions are proposed by Sigfox, from the "One" subscription (which allows 1–2 daily uplink messages, 0 downlink message), up to the "Platinum" subscription (101–140 daily uplink messages, 4 downlink messages).

© International Financial Cryptography Association 2021
N. Borisov and C. Diaz (Eds.): FC 2021, LNCS 12674, pp. 331–350, 2021.
https://doi.org/10.1007/978-3-662-64322-8_16

The Sigfox system enables different services such as asset tracking, geolocation, sensitive site monitoring, smart home, smart metering, healthcare. Sigfox uses free but regulated frequency bands (e.g., 868–869 MHz in Europe, 902-905 MHz in North America, 922–923 MHz in Japan and South Korea). Supplied with an autonomous battery, a Sigfox end-device is supposed to communicate through several kilometers. Its lifespan is expected to be up to five or ten years. With respect to the radio specificities, Sigfox can be compared, up to some point, to LoRaWAN [8, 18] and NB-IoT.

Currently, Sigfox operates in more than 72 countries on all continents [15]. The multiple networks cover 1.3 billion people, and represent 56 million daily messages from 17 million IoT devices.

1.2   Related Work

Prior to the public release of the official specification by Sigfox [16] several analyses have been conducted based on practical experiments and reverse engineering.

Lifchitz [7] and Euchner [5] have observed that, since the frame's counter cnt is allowed to wrap around, the ability to replay clear uplink frames is "natural" in Sigfox. Once the counter cnt reaches its highest value, it is set to 0. Hence all previous frames become cryptographically valid anew. We note that such a replay is also possible with downlink frames. Moreover, in Sect. 3.2, we explain how the same can be done with *encrypted* downlink frames.

When an uplink frame is received by the back-end network, the latter verifies, among other parameters, the frame's counter with respect to an acceptance interval. Euchner [5] and Coman, Malarski, Petersen, and Ruepp [1] describe two denial of service (DoS) attacks. In the first scenario the adversary uses a previous frame which counter belongs to the current acceptance interval, and is as high as possible. Upon reception of this replayed frame (which is valid anew), the back-end network takes its counter as the new reference to verify subsequent uplink frames. Therefore, the frames sent by the legitimate end-device are discarded until its counter exceeds the value used by the adversary. Depending on the type of subscription, the duration of this DoS attack may be rather long (several days up to several months). Coman et al. present a variant of Euchner's attack, and a second scenario. The latter is based on a previous definition of the acceptance interval (which was static) used during the verification of the frame counter [9]. This attack is now thwarted by the use of an evolving interval (see the full version of this paper [6]).

Euchner [5] observes that, since the MAC tag size may be low (down to 2 bytes), it may be possible to forge valid (clear) uplink frames. The complexity of this attack is exponential in the tag size. In contrast, we describe in Sect. 3.1 an attack against data authenticity, targeting clear and encrypted uplink frames, which complexity is $O(1)$.

1.3   Contributions

In this paper we present new flaws and attacks that are practicable against Sigfox, and describe counter-measures that are straightforward to implement. More precisely, our contributions are the following.

New Attacks Against Sigfox. We present a flaw in the Sigfox encryption procedure, and two news attack against Sigfox. These two attacks break data authenticity.

The flaw in the encryption procedure allows to passively get access to the plaintext data in a specific case when encryption is activated.

Regarding the attacks, we first explain how to replay previous downlink encrypted frames to an end-device (even once encryption is deactivated). Then, we describe how to forge a valid uplink frame (i.e., with a correct MAC tag) from a genuine uplink frame. We describe how to forge such frames with encrypted and clear frames. The complexity of this attack is $O(1)$, and it allows deceiving the back-end network.

The attacks that we propose do not exploit potential implementation or hardware bugs. They do not imply a physical access to any equipment (in particular a legitimate end-device). They are independent of the means used to protect the secret parameters (e.g., a secure element in the end-device). These attacks depend exclusively on the peculiarities of the Sigfox MAC and encryption functions. The adversary needs only to act on the air interface (i.e., to eavesdrop on legitimate frames, and to send the forged frame to the back-end network).

Table 1 summarises the different attacks presented in this paper.

Practical Experiments. We have validated the MAC tag forgeries that we describe in two ways. First "offline", with the librenard library developed by Euchner [3], which implements the same cryptographic functions as a legitimate Sigfox end-device. Secondly, we have made real-life experiments, and we have observed that the forged frames have been accepted on the Sigfox back-end network.

Efficient Counter-Measures. Finally, we present efficient counter-measures which are likely straightforward to implement. They allow thwarting all the aforementioned attacks.

Table 1. New attacks against Sigfox. The context indicates if the frames are encrypted ("ENC") or not ("MAC only"). The direction indicates if the uplink frames ("UL") or the downlink frames ("DL") are targeted.

Attack	Security property	Context	Direction
MAC tag forgery (Sect. 3.1)	Data authenticity	MAC only, ENC	UL
Frame replay (Sect. 3.2)	Data authenticity	ENC	DL
Lack of encryption (Sect. 3.3)	Data confidentiality	ENC	UL

1.4   Responsible Disclosure

We reported our findings to Sigfox (August 19, 2020). Sigfox acknowledged receipt of our paper. At the time of submitting the camera-ready version, and despite new messages sent to Sigfox, we have received no further news.

2   Description of the Sigfox Security Protocol

On the radio interface, Sigfox provides data authenticity (mandatory) for the uplink and downlink messages, and data confidentiality (optional). The security mechanisms are based on the AES block cipher, and a 128-bit static symmetric key called "Network Access Key" (NAK) shared between the end-device and the back-end network.

A partial description of the security and cryptographic mechanisms used in Sigfox can be found in the official specification [16]. To the best of our knowledge, there exists no official specification describing the Sigfox encryption function which is publicly available. Pinault has presented this encryption function [12]. We have corrected the latter through the reverse engineering of the X-CUBE-SFOX package [19] done with the Ghidra tool [10]. Our findings have been validated with practical experiments made in interaction with the back-end network.

2.1   Frame Format

Uplink Frame. The format of an uplink frame (i.e., sent by the end-device to the back-end network) is the following (length in bit)

$$\text{ft } (13)\|\text{hdr } (48)\|\text{payload } (0\text{-}96)\|\text{mac } (16\text{-}40)\|\text{crc } (16)$$

where hdr corresponds to

$$\text{li } (2)\|\text{bf } (1)\|\text{rep } (1)\|\text{cnt } (12)\|\text{devid } (32)$$

The frame type ft depends mainly on the nature of the frame (application, control), and its length. The payload field carries the (optionally encrypted) data, which size ranges from 0 to 12 bytes, or is 1-bit long (in such a case the data is carried in the header hdr, and payload is empty). The field mac carries the frame's MAC tag (which length ranges from 2 to 5 bytes), and crc carries the CRC tag.

In the hdr field, the parameter li is used to indicate the size of the MAC tag (which is variable), or to carry the 1-bit data. The parameter bf indicates if a downlink frame is expected in response to the uplink frame. rep is always set to 0. The parameter cnt is a frame counter, incremented each time a new uplink frame is sent. Although, the length of the cnt field is 12 bits, the maximum value of this parameter is $2^i - 1$, $i \in \{7, \ldots, 12\}$. When cnt reaches its maximum value, it *must* be set to 0 (i.e., cnt wraps around). Presumably, i depends on the Sigfox subscription (i.e., the maximum of allowed daily uplink frames). The parameter devid corresponds to the end-device's identifier (encoded in little endian format).

Downlink Frame. The format of a downlink frame is the following (length in bit)

$$\mathsf{ft}\ (13)\|\mathsf{ecc}\ (32)\|\mathsf{payload}\ (64)\|\mathsf{mac}\ (16)\|\mathsf{crc}\ (8)$$

The frame type ft is constant. The parameter ecc is an error correction code computed over $\mathsf{payload}\|\mathsf{mac}\|\mathsf{crc}$. The (optionally encrypted) data is carried in $\mathsf{payload}$. The fields mac and crc carry respectively the frame's MAC tag and CRC tag.

2.2 Encryption Function

The format of encrypted and clear frames is the same. Encryption is (de)activated on the back-end side, upon request of the end-device's owner. Encryption cannot be done on a per frame basis. That is, either all the frames are encrypted or none. Then, the back-end acts accordingly. This implies in particular that, if encryption is activated, the downlink frames are also encrypted.

The encryption of a frame is made with AES-CTR. From the NAK key K, and two 16-byte values V_0, V_1, an encryption key K_e and a value W for the counter mode are computed.

The value V_b, $b \in \{0,1\}$, is the concatenation of the bit b, followed by the 4-byte end-device's identifier devid, and 95 zero bits:

$$V_0 = 0\|\mathsf{devid}\|0\cdots 0$$
$$V_1 = 1\|\mathsf{devid}\|0\cdots 0$$

The encryption key K_e and the value W are computed as

$$K_e = \mathsf{AES}(K, V_0)$$
$$W = \mathsf{AES}(K, V_1)$$

A counter ctr is computed by concatenating the first 104 bits of W, a 4-bit direction value dir, the 1-byte counter rc, and the 12 bit frame counter cnt:

$$ctr = \mathsf{msb}(W, 104)\|dir\|\mathsf{rc}\|\mathsf{cnt}$$

where msb denotes the most significant bits.

The parameter rc is an implicit counter which is incremented any time cnt wraps around. The value dir indicates the direction: if uplink, then $dir = 0$, otherwise $dir = 1$.

Let $ptxt$ be some n-bit plaintext data ($n \le 96$) to be sent in a frame corresponding to counter cnt. The encryption of $ptxt$ is done as follows:

1. $msk = \mathsf{msb}(\mathsf{AES}(K_e, ctr), n)$
2. $ctxt = msk \oplus ptxt$

The encrypted data $ctxt$ is carried in the $\mathsf{payload}$ field.

2.3   MAC Function

The message authentication code (MAC) is based on AES in CBC-MAC mode with a null IV. The key used to compute a MAC tag is the static NAK key K. The MAC function outputs a tag which length (ranging from 2 to 5 bytes) depends on the size of the input data.

In order to get an input which length is a multiple of 16 bytes, the data to be authenticated is padded with itself. For instance, if the data corresponds to 7 bytes $B_0\|\cdots\|B_6$, the input to the inner CBC-MAC computation is then $B_0\|\cdots\|B_6\|B_0\|\cdots\|B_6\|B_0\|B_1$. If the length of the data is a multiple of 16 bytes, then the data is unchanged.

Let $data$ be a byte string. Let selfpad be the function that pads the input byte string with itself, and outputs a byte string which length is a multiple of 16 bytes. A MAC tag t (carried in the field mac) is computed as follows:

1. $\widetilde{data} = \mathsf{selfpad}(data)$
2. $C = \mathsf{AES\text{-}CBC\text{-}MAC}(K, \widetilde{data})$
3. $t = \mathsf{msb}(C, n)$

with $n \in \{16, 24, 32, 40\}$.

The MAC tag of an uplink frame is computed with the following $data$ as input:

- $\mathsf{hdr}\|\mathsf{payload} = \mathsf{li}\|\mathsf{bf}\|\mathsf{rep}\|\mathsf{cnt}\|\mathsf{devid}\|\mathsf{payload}$ if the Sigfox encryption function is not used;
- $\mathsf{rc}\|\mathsf{hdr}\|\mathsf{payload} = \mathsf{rc}\|\mathsf{li}\|\mathsf{bf}\|\mathsf{rep}\|\mathsf{cnt}\|\mathsf{devid}\|\mathsf{payload}$ if the Sigfox encryption function is used (then payload carries the encrypted data).

The MAC tag of a downlink frame is computed with the following $data$ as input (length in bit):

$$\mathsf{devid}\ (32)\|\mathsf{lsb}(\mathsf{cnt}, 8)\|\mathsf{0b0000}\ (4)\|\mathsf{msb}(\mathsf{cnt}, 4)\|\mathsf{payload}\ (64)\|\mathsf{msb}(\mathsf{devid}, 16)$$

where devid is encoded in little endian format, lsb denotes the least significant bits, and 0b0000 corresponds to four 0 bits.

3   New Attacks Against Sigfox

In this section we present two new attacks against Sigfox, and highlight a flaw in the encryption procedure.

The attacks that we present break data authenticity, and allow deceiving the end-device or the back-end network. The first attack allows forging uplink (clear or encrypted) frames. The second attack allows replaying downlink encrypted frames.

3.1   MAC Tag Forgery

In this section we present a scenario that allows an adversary to forge valid uplink frames (encrypted or not). This attack relies upon the fact that the data length in an uplink frame is variable, and also on the design of the Sigfox MAC function. The complexity of this attack is $O(1)$. We describe unconditional and conditional forgeries. This attack scenario does not apply to downlink frames because they all have the same fixed size.

We have experimentally validated the MAC tag forgeries first with the librenard library provided by Euchner [3]. Secondly, we have validated the forgeries with real-life experiments done in interaction with the back-end network.

Issue. The MAC tag is computed in CBC-MAC mode (with AES). This mode is insecure for variable length inputs, and yet, in Sigfox, the data to be authenticated in an uplink frame may have different sizes (in a downlink frame, the length of the data is fixed to 8 bytes).

In order to pad the input data up to a multiple of 16 bytes, the data is padded with itself. That is, if the input to the MAC function corresponds to seven bytes $m = B_0\|\cdots\|B_6$, the data in input to the inner CBC-MAC computation is then $B_0\|\cdots\|B_6\|B_0\|\cdots\|B_6\|B_0\|B_1$ (16 bytes). Now, if the input to the MAC function corresponds to the following 14 bytes $m' = B_0\|\cdots\|B_6\|B_0\|\cdots\|B_6$, then, after padding, the data in input to the inner CBC-MAC computation is $B_0\|\cdots\|B_6\|B_0\|\cdots\|B_6\|B_0\|B_1$. That is, the same data as for m. Consequently, the MAC tag of m' is equal to that of m. This allows completion attacks against the MAC function in Sigfox.

Due to the constraints that bind the data length, the MAC tag length, and the value of the parameter li (cf. Table 2), not all kinds of modification are possible. Nonetheless, several are doable.

Table 2. li values and MAC tag sizes for an uplink frame (source: [16])

data	$\|\mathsf{hdr}\|\mathsf{payload}\|$ (byte) (clear frame)	$\|\mathsf{rc}\|\mathsf{hdr}\|\mathsf{payload}\|$ (byte) (encrypted frame)	li	$\|\mathsf{mac}\|$ (byte)
0b0	6	7	0b10	2
0b1	6	7	0b11	2
(empty)	6	7	0b00	2
1 byte	7	8		
4 bytes	10	11		
8 bytes	14	15		
12 bytes	18	19		
3 bytes	9	10	0b01	3
7 bytes	13	14		
11 bytes	17	18		
2 bytes	8	9	0b10	4
6 bytes	12	13		
10 bytes	16	17		
5 bytes	11	12	0b11	5
9 bytes	15	16		

Overview. The goal of the adversary is to forge an uplink frame with a valid MAC tag. To do so, the adversary reuses an existing valid uplink frame. Such a frame can be picked from the set of previous frames when they can be replayed (this excludes an encrypted frame), or can be a fresh uplink frame eavesdropped and blocked by the adversary (i.e., not received by the back-end network). In the latter case, the frame used can be encrypted or not. There are two cases: when the frame is encrypted and when it is not (clear frame). Table 3 summarises the different forgeries that we present next.

Table 3. Summary of the forgeries for uplink frames. The "Cond." field indicates if some (probabilistic) condition must be fulfilled in order for the forgery to be possible. The sizes are given in byte.

Type of frame	Original frame	Forged frame		Cond	$(\mathsf{li}, \|\mathsf{mac}\|)$
Clear	$\|pld\| = 1$	$pld' = pld\|hdr\|pld$	$\|pld'\| = 8$	no	$(0\mathsf{b}00, 2)$
Clear	$\|pld\| = 2$	$pld' = pld\|hdr\|pld$	$\|pld'\| = 10$	no	$(0\mathsf{b}10, 4)$
Clear	$\|pld\| = 6$	$pld' = pld\|hdr[0\cdots 3]$	$\|pld'\| = 10$	no	$(0\mathsf{b}10, 4)$
Encrypted	(empty)	$pld' = rc\|hdr\|rc$	$\|pld'\| = 8$	no	$(0\mathsf{b}00, 2)$
Encrypted	$\|pld\| = 1$	$pld' = pld\|rc\|hdr$	$\|pld'\| = 8$	yes	$(0\mathsf{b}00, 2)$
Encrypted	$\|pld\| = 4$	$pld' = pld\|rc\|hdr[0\cdots 2]$	$\|pld'\| = 8$	yes	$(0\mathsf{b}00, 2)$
Encrypted	$\|pld\| = 5$	$pld' = pld\|rc\|hdr[0\cdots 2]$	$\|pld'\| = 9$	no	$(0\mathsf{b}11, 5)$

Clear Frame. Let us consider first how the adversary can produce a forgery from a non-encrypted uplink frame.

The sizes $\|\mathsf{hdr}\|\mathsf{payload}\| \in \{7, 8, 12\}$ corresponding to $\|\mathsf{payload}\| \in \{1, 2, 6\}$ are of interest to the adversary.

Type "clear_1". Let us first consider a genuine frame

$$frame = \mathsf{ft}\|\mathsf{hdr}\|\mathsf{payload}\|\mathsf{mac}\|\mathsf{crc}$$
$$= ft\|hdr\|pld\|mac\|crc$$

such that $\|\mathsf{payload}\| = \|pld\| = 1$ byte (ft, hdr, etc., correspond respectively to the current values of the parameters ft, hdr, etc.).

From $frame$, the adversary computes

$$frame' = \mathsf{ft}\|\mathsf{hdr}\|\mathsf{payload}\|\mathsf{mac}\|\mathsf{crc}$$
$$= ft'\|hdr'\|pld'\|mac'\|crc'$$

as follows:

1. $hdr' = hdr$
2. $pld' = pld\|hdr\|pld$ (and $\|pld'\| = 8$ bytes)
3. The frame type ft' is chosen in accordance with $\|pld'\|$.
4. $mac' = mac$
5. The adversary computes crc' from $hdr'\|pld'\|mac'$.

Since $|pld| = 1$ byte, we have that $(\mathsf{li}, |\mathsf{mac}|) = (\mathsf{0b00}, 2)$ in $frame$. Since $|pld'| = 8$ bytes, $(\mathsf{li}, |\mathsf{mac}|)$ in $frame'$ must be, and is indeed, equal to $(\mathsf{0b00}, 2)$ (because $hdr' = hdr$).

The MAC tag $mac' = mac$ is a valid tag for $frame'$. Indeed this tag is valid for $frame$. This means that the data used as input to the inner CBC-MAC computation for $frame$ is (size in byte)

$$hdr\ (6)\|pld\ (1)\|hdr\ (6)\|pld\ (1)\|\|hdr[0\cdots 1]\ (2)$$

where $hdr[0\cdots 1]$ indicates the two first bytes of hdr.

In turn, the data used as input to the inner CBC-MAC computation in order to verify the MAC tag mac' in $frame'$ is

$$hdr'\ (6)\|pld'\ (8)\|hdr'[0\cdots 1]\ (2)$$
$$=$$
$$hdr\ (6)\|pld\ (1)\|hdr\ (6)\|pld\ (1)\|\|hdr[0\cdots 1]\ (2)$$

Since the MAC tag is computed with the same key, and the same input data in either case ($frame$ and $frame'$), we have that $mac' = mac$ is a valid MAC tag for $frame'$. Hence, $frame'$ is a valid uplink frame forged by the adversary.

Type "clear_2". The same holds with a genuine frame $frame = ft\|hdr\|pld\|mac\|crc$ with $|pld| = 2$ bytes. The adversary forges a frame $frame'$ carrying a payload (size in byte)

$$pld'\ (10) = pld\ (2)\|hdr\ (6)\|pld\ (2)$$

(with the corresponding frame type and CRC value). The frame $frame'$ is a valid frame for the MAC tag $mac' = mac$. Indeed, $(\mathsf{li}, |\mathsf{mac}|) = (\mathsf{0b10}, 4)$ in $frame$ and $frame'$ (because $hdr' = hdr$), and

$$hdr'\ (6)\|pld'\ (10) = hdr\ (6)\|pld\ (2)\|hdr\ (6)\|pld\ (2)$$

This corresponds to the data in input to the inner CBC-MAC computation for $frame'$ and $frame$.

Type "clear_6". Another forgery is possible with an original frame $frame = ft\|hdr\|pld\|mac\|crc$ such that $|pld| = 6$ bytes. The adversary forges a frame $frame'$ carrying a payload (size in byte)

$$pld'\ (10) = pld\ (6)\|hdr[0\cdots 3]\ (4)$$

(with the corresponding frame type and CRC value). The frame $frame'$ is a valid frame for the MAC tag $mac' = mac$. Indeed, $(\mathsf{li}, |\mathsf{mac}|) = (\mathsf{0b10}, 4)$ in $frame$ and $frame'$, and

$$hdr'\ (6)\|pld'\ (10) = hdr\ (6)\|pld\ (6)\|hdr[0\cdots 3]\ (4)$$

which is the data in input to the inner CBC-MAC computation for $frame'$ and $frame$.

Encrypted Frame. Now let us consider how the adversary can produce a forgery from an encrypted uplink frame.

Unconditional Forgeries. We present first two unconditional forgeries.

Type "encrypted_5". Let us first consider a genuine encrypted frame

$$frame = ft\|hdr\|pld\|mac\|crc$$

with $|pld| = 5$ bytes. The MAC tag mac is computed with the following input data to the inner CBC-MAC function (size in byte)

$$rc\ (1)\|hdr\ (6)\|pld\ (5)\|rc\ (1)\|hdr[0\cdots2]\ (3)$$

where rc is the current value of the counter rc.

The adversary computes $frame' = ft'\|hdr'\|pld'\|mac'\|crc'$ with $hdr' = hdr$, $pld' = pld\|rc\|hdr[0\cdots2]$ (and $|pld'| = 9$ bytes), and $mac' = mac$. The frame type ft' is chosen in accordance with $|pld'|$. The adversary computes crc' from $hdr'\|pld'\|mac'$.

In order to verify the MAC tag mac', the data used as input to the inner CBC-MAC function is

$$rc\ (1)\|hdr'\ (6)\|pld'\ (9) = rc\ (1)\|hdr\ (6)\|pld\ (5)\|rc\ (1)\|hdr[0\cdots2]\ (3)$$

Moreover, $(li, |mac|) = (0b11, 5)$ in $frame$ and $frame'$. Therefore $mac' = mac$ is a valid MAC tag for $frame'$. Hence $frame'$ is a valid encrypted frame forged by the adversary.

Type "encrypted_empty". Let us consider an original empty encrypted frame $frame = ft\|hdr\|mac\|crc$. In such a case $(li, |mac|) = (0b00, 2)$, and the data in input to the inner CBC-MAC function is (size in byte)

$$rc\ (1)\|hdr\ (6)\|rc\ (1)\|hdr\ (6)\|rc\ (1)\|hdr[0]\ (1)$$

The adversary computes $frame' = ft'\|hdr'\|pld'\|mac'\|crc'$ with $hdr' = hdr$, and $pld' = rc\|hdr\|rc$. The values ft' and crc' are computed in accordance with the other fields of $frame'$. The payload pld' is 8-byte long, which corresponds also to $(li, |mac|) = (0b00, 2)$.

The data used as input to the inner CBC-MAC function in order to verify mac' is

$$rc\ (1)\|hdr'\ (6)\|pld'\ (8)\|rc\ (1) = rc\ (1)\|hdr\ (6)\|rc\ (1)\|hdr\ (6)\|rc\ (1)\|rc\ (1)$$

Hence, $mac' = mac$ is a valid MAC tag for $frame'$ if $hdr[0] = rc$.

The first byte of the header hdr corresponds to (length in bit)

$$li\ (2)\|bf\ (1)\|rep\ (1)\|msb(cnt, 4)$$

Since $frame$ carries no data, $li = 0b00$. The parameter bf can be equal to 0 (unidirectional procedure) or 1 (bidirectional procedure), and rep is always equal to 0. Therefore $rc = hdr[0]$ implies that

$$rc$$
$$=$$

li	bf	rep	$\mathsf{msb}(cnt, 4)$
$b_7\ b_6$	b_5	b_4	$b_3\ b_2\ b_1\ b_0$

$$=$$

0 0	·	0	· · · ·

where cnt, li, bf, rep are respectively the current values of the message counter cnt, the li, bf, and rep parameters in $frame$.

Therefore, the adversary can forge a valid frame $frame'$ with any original frame $frame$ which fulfils the following characteristics:

- $frame$ carries an empty payload (i.e., $li = \mathsf{0b00}$), and
- $cnt = j \times 2^8 + i$, and
- $rc = bf \times 2^5 + j$,

with $(i, j) \in \{0, \ldots, 255\} \times \{0, \ldots, 15\}$, and $bf \in \{0, 1\}$.

The number of such encrypted uplink frames that the adversary can forge for a given end-device is at most $2^4 \times 2^8 = 2^{12}$ (bf takes only one value in $\{0, 1\}$ for each possible value $rc\|cnt$). This figure does not take into account the number of times the counter cnt is reset, which multiplies in proportion the number of usable uplink frames.

Conditional Forgeries. Now we describe two conditional forgeries.

Type "encrypted_1". The first conditional possibility is the following. From a genuine encrypted frame $frame$ with $|pld| = 1$ byte, the adversary computes $frame' = ft'\|hdr'\|pld'\|mac'\|crc'$ with $hdr' = hdr$, and $pld' = pld\|rc\|hdr$. The values ft' and crc' are computed in accordance with the other fields of $frame'$. We have that $|pld| = 1$ byte and $|pld'| = 8$ bytes, which both correspond to $(li, |mac|) = (\mathsf{0b00}, 2)$. The MAC tag mac in $frame$ is computed with the following input data to the inner CBC-MAC function (size in byte)

$$rc\ (1)\|hdr\ (6)\|pld\ (1)\|rc\ (1)\|hdr\ (6)\|pld\ (1)$$

The MAC tag mac' in $frame'$ is verified with the following input data to the inner CBC-MAC function

$$rc\ (1)\|hdr'\ (6)\|pld'\ (8)\|rc\ (1) = rc\ (1)\|hdr\ (6)\|pld\ (1)\|rc\ (1)\|hdr\ (6)\|rc\ (1)$$

Therefore, $mac' = mac$ is a valid MAC tag for $frame'$ if $pld = rc$. Since pld corresponds to encrypted data, the probability of success in this case is roughly 2^{-8}.

Type "encrypted_4". From a genuine encrypted frame $frame$ with $|pld| = 4$ bytes, the adversary computes $frame' = ft'\|hdr'\|pld'\|mac'\|crc'$ with $hdr' = hdr$, and $pld' = pld\|rc\|hdr[0 \cdots 2]$. The values ft' and crc' are computed in accordance with the other fields of $frame'$. We have that $|pld| = 4$ bytes and $|pld'| = 8$ bytes. Both cases correspond to $(\mathsf{li}, |\mathsf{mac}|) = (0\mathsf{b}00, 2)$. The MAC tag mac in $frame$ is computed with the following input data to the inner CBC-MAC function

$$rc\ (1)\|hdr\ (6)\|pld\ (4)\|rc\ (1)\|hdr[0\cdots 3]\ (4)$$

The MAC tag mac' in $frame'$ is verified with the following input data to the inner CBC-MAC function (size in byte)

$$rc\ (1)\|hdr'\ (6)\|pld'\ (8)\|rc\ (1)$$

$$=$$

$$rc\ (1)\|hdr\ (6)\|pld\ (4)\|rc\ (1)\|hdr[0\cdots 2]\ (3)\|rc\ (1)$$

Therefore, $mac' = mac$ is a valid MAC tag for $frame'$ if $rc = hdr[3] = devid[1]$, where $devid$ is the value of the (targeted) end-device's identifier (encoded in little endian format).

For each end-device, the adversary can forge as many uplink encrypted frame as distinct values for cnt (unless rc wraps around). For instance, with respect to the "Platinum" subscription, the number of forgeries is 2^{12}.

Other Types of Forgery. Other kinds of forgery are possible but with stronger constraints (i.e., equality between two bit strings which length is higher than 8 bits), hence lower probability of success.

Experiments. We have validated the MAC tag forgeries that we describe in two ways.

"Offline" Experiments. The librenard library, developed by Euchner [3], implements the Sigfox cryptographic functions (we have completed librenard in order to support encryption). We have used librenard to successfully validate all the MAC tag forgeries that we describe.

Real-life Experiments. Secondly, we have conducted experiments in real conditions of use in interaction with the Sigfox back-end network. For each forgery type, we have generated several genuine uplink (clear or encrypted) frames with the NAK key corresponding to our legitimate end-device. From these frames, we have computed forgeries (without the NAK key). Each forged frame has been transmitted to the back-end network. The latter has accepted all the forged frames.

The only forgery type that we have not been able to test in interaction with the back-end network is the "encrypted_4" type (i.e., from a 4-byte genuine encrypted payload). Indeed, in order for this forgery to be possible, it must hold that $rc = devid[1]$. In order for rc to be equal to some value x, the counter cnt must wrap around x times. That is, $x \times 2^{12}$ uplink frames must be sent (for a "Platinum" subscription with at most 140 daily uplink messages). This corresponds to $x \times 2^{12}/140$ days at least. Given the $devid$ value attributed to our end-device, this would have taken too long in order to reach the corresponding value for rc. Nonetheless, we stress that even this forgery type has been successfully validated with librenard.

Experiment Bench. The experiments have been done with a laptop Dell Latitude E6430 running Debian 10.5 with the (completed) librenard library installed on it. The radio communication has been managed with the module HackRF One [11], and the renard-phy scripts from Euchner [4] (cf. Sect. A).

3.2 Frame Replay

As explained in previous analyses [5,7], Sigfox allows "naturally" frame replays because the message counter cnt is rather short, and wraps around when it reaches its maximum value. Nonetheless, when encryption is activated, an additional 8-bit counter rc is involved in the MAC tag computation of an uplink frame. However, according to the Sigfox specification, the parameter rc is *not* involved in the MAC tag computation of a downlink frame even when it is encrypted (cf. [16, Section 4.3]). Consequently, downlink encrypted frames can be replayed as well. In addition, such encrypted frames can be replayed even if encryption is later deactivated. Indeed, the MAC tag is then valid (anew), and the encrypted data will be accepted as clear data. In such a case, this may lead the end-device to adopt an incoherent (possibly harmful) behaviour because what is then taken as plaintext data is essentially random data.

According to Euchner [2], Sigfox claims that activating encryption thwarts frame replays with the use of the implicit counter rc, which extends the frame's counter from 12 to 20 bits. We observe that the way downlink encrypted frames are computed contradicts this argument raised by Sigfox.

3.3 Lack of Encryption

Variable length data can be transmitted in an uplink frame: 1 to 12 bytes, and 1 bit. If the length is 1-byte long at least, data is carried in the payload field. If the data is 1-bit long (single-bit case), the payload field is empty, and data is carried in the "length indicator" ll field, which is located in the frame's header. When encryption is activated, data is encrypted if it is carried in the payload. However, our experiments show that, in the single-bit case (i.e., empty payload, and 1-bit data in the header hdr), data is *not* encrypted. Therefore, in the single-bit case the plaintext data remains accessible to a passive eavesdropper. That is, in such a case, Sigfox does not achieve the intended security level.

4 Counter-Measures

In this section we present counter-measures in order to thwart the attacks described in Sect. 3. In addition, these counter-measures are also efficient against attacks presented in previous analyses [1,5,7]. Table 4 summarises the different counter-measures.

Table 4. Proposed counter-measures

Attack	Counter-measure
MAC tag forgery	CMAC mode
Frame replay	Extended (implicit) message counter
Lack of encryption	Encryption

4.1 MAC Tag Forgery

The attack described in Sect. 3.1 is possible because the end-device uses the same static NAK key, and the Sigfox MAC function is based on the CBC-MAC mode, which is insecure for variable length inputs. This issue can be easily fixed. Instead of using the CBC-MAC mode, the MAC function can rely upon the CMAC mode [17]. CMAC is built upon the same underlying CBC operation as CBC-MAC but is secure for variable length inputs.

4.2 Frame Replay

The frame replay presented in Sect. 3.2 is possible because the maximum value for the cnt counter can be rather low. A simple way to fix this issue is to extend this counter. To do so, we can use the rc counter. First we recommend that the parameter rc be involved in the MAC tag computation in any case (i.e., be the frame encrypted or not). That is, the input data to the Sigfox MAC function is prepended with rc, and becomes

- for an uplink frame: rc∥hdr∥payload = rc∥li∥bf∥rep∥cnt∥devid∥payload;
- for a downlink frame:
  - rc∥devid∥lsb(cnt, 8)∥0b0000∥msb(cnt, 4)∥payload∥msb(devid, 16), or
  - lsb(rc, 4)∥devid∥lsb(cnt, 8)∥msb(rc, 4)∥msb(cnt, 4)∥payload∥msb(devid, 16).

Now we estimate how long the size of rc must be. Let us assume that the bit length of cnt goes with the maximum amount c of daily uplink frames. That is, we can have $(|\text{cnt}|, c) = (12, 140)$ at most ("Platinum" subscription), or $(|\text{cnt}|, c) = (7, 2)$ at least ("One" subscription), but not $(|\text{cnt}|, c) = (7, 140)$. Let n be the lifespan of an end-device. Then, the maximum number of uplink messages an end-device may send during its whole lifetime is $n \times c$. Therefore we must have $2^{|\text{rc}|+|\text{cnt}|} \geq n \times c$. That is, $|\text{rc}| \geq \log_2(n \times c) - |\text{cnt}|$. With $n = 10$ years, this implies

- $|\text{rc}| \geq 7$ if $(|\text{cnt}|, c) = (12, 140)$,
- $|\text{rc}| \geq 6$ if $(|\text{cnt}|, c) = (7, 2)$.

The current size of rc (8 bits) seems then already sufficient. But this assumes that the end-device respects the limitation in the number of daily uplink frames. Yet, we can not exclude that an adversary succeed in forcing an end-device to send uplink frames at will. That is, possibly at a frequency higher than $c = 140$ frames per day.

Let v be the minimum time to transmit one uplink frame that an adversary may impose to an end-device. The number of uplink frames is then at most n/v. For instance, if $n = 10$ years and $v = 112/600$ second (corresponding to the shortest uplink frame, and the highest allowed speed), then $n/v < 2^{31}$. In such a case, $|\mathsf{rc}| = 31 - |\mathsf{cnt}| \in \{19, \ldots, 24\}$.

Note that this counter-measure is also an efficient mitigation against previous (clear) frame replay attacks [5,7], and DoS attacks [1,5] (which are also based on the ability to replay frames).

4.3   Lack of Encryption

When encryption is activated, in the single-bit case (i.e., empty payload with 1-bit data in the frame's header), data must be encrypted in the same way as when data is carried in the payload field.

5   Conclusion

Sigfox is a communication and security protocol which allows setting up low-power wide-area networks for the IoT. Currently, Sigfox operates in 72 countries on all continents. The multiple networks cover 1.3 billion people, and represent 56 million daily messages from 17 million IoT devices.

In this paper we have made an extensive security analysis of the radio interface in Sigfox. We have presented new attacks against Sigfox. First, we have described how to replay downlink encrypted frames, and forge valid (encrypted or clear) uplink frames. These attacks break data authenticity with complexity $O(1)$ (in contrast to previous attacks against Sigfox), and allow deceiving the end-device or the back-end network.

We have validated the MAC tag forgeries that we describe with practical real-life experiments made in interaction with the Sigfox back-end network.

In addition, we have presented a flaw that affects the encryption procedure, and is detrimental to data confidentiality.

The attacks that we have described do not exploit potential implementation or hardware bugs. They do not imply a physical access to any equipment (in particular a legitimate end-device). They depend exclusively on the peculiarities of the Sigfox security protocol. The adversary needs only to act on the air interface.

Finally, we have presented efficient counter-measures which are likely straightforward to implement. They allow thwarting all the aforementioned attacks.

Acknowledgment. We thank Florian Euchner and Paul Pinault for their previous work on Sigfox.

A   Practical Experiments

Figure 2 corresponds to screen shots made, from top to bottom, of two forged frames of type "clear_6" (the first original frame is made of 6 zero bytes, the second one of random bytes), and two forged frames of type "encrypted_5" (the first original frame is made of 5 zero bytes, the second one of random bytes) received on the back-end network. Table 5 lists an example of each forgery type (Fig. 1).

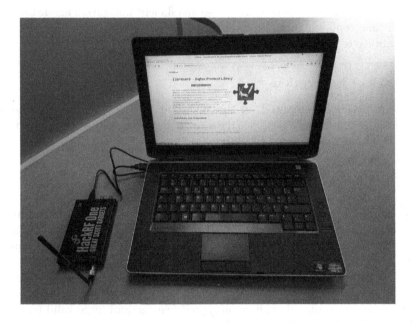

Fig. 1. Experiment bench

sigfox		DEVICE	DEVICE TYPE	USER	GROUP

Device 1415E89 - Messages

INFORMATION
LOCATION
MESSAGES
EVENTS
STATISTICS
EVENT CONFIGURATION

2020-08-15 11:24:53	76	000000000000804c895e
2020-08-14 18:25:58	50	c24415cbf3448032895e
2020-08-17 18:04:46	99	0000000000e4bd138d
2020-08-14 17:37:33	10	8d25312e2d9a7b06ca

Fig. 2. Screen shots of forged frames accepted by the Sigfox back-end network. From top to bottom, the two pairs of frames correspond to the forgery types "clear_6" and "encrypted_5". For each forgery type, the pair of genuine frames corresponds respectively to zero bytes and random bytes in the payload.

Table 5. Samples of forged frames. If the uplink frame is encrypted, the data received on the back-end is first decrypted, and then stored. The type "encrypted_4" has not been tested in real-life experiments.

Forgery type
Genuine frame
Forged frame
Data stored on the back-end network
clear_1
08d0046895e410100f9b12ac8
6110046895e4101000046895e410100f9b1dff7
000046895e410100
clear_2
35f8049895e41010000b9a169493c11
94c8049895e410100008049895e41010000b9a169493657
00008049895e41010000
clear_6
611804c895e4101000000000000a749be547739
94c804c895e4101000000000000804c895ea749be5448f3
000000000000804c895e
encrypted_empty
06b0001895e4101adcf6d5f
6110001895e4101000001895e410100adcfe183
81879dc719010339
encrypted_1
08d0014895e4101006ddc072e
6110014895e410100000014895e41016ddccbe0
731180c554618155
encrypted_4
[35f0001895e4101e20095ebbb465029]
[6110001895e4101e20095eb5e000189bb463b0d]
[00000000697f3bd5]
encrypted_5
611e063895e410182d8c8538ff49fb6d41c149e
94ce063895e410182d8c8538f00e06389f49fb6d41c4356
0000000000e4bd138d

B   Sigfox Architecture

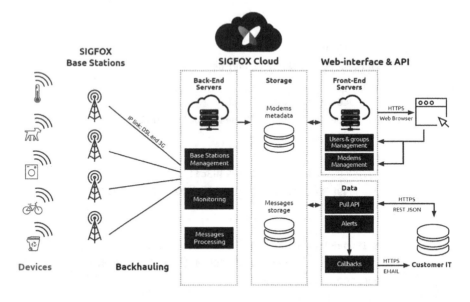

Fig. 3. Sigfox architecture (source: [13])

C   Sigfox Coverage in Several Geographic Areas

See (Fig. 4).

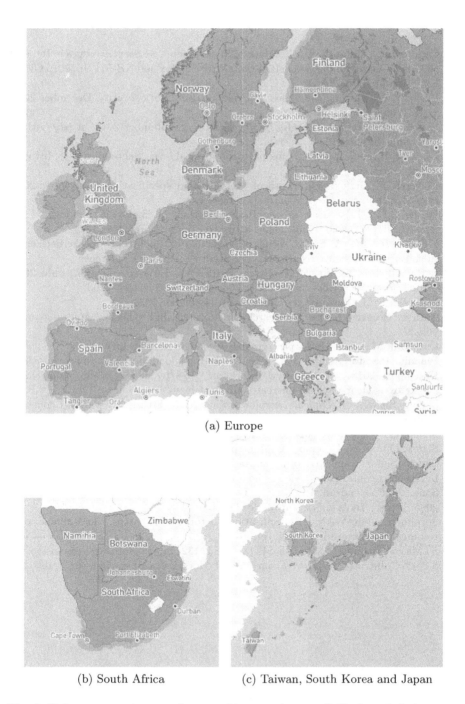

(a) Europe

(b) South Africa   (c) Taiwan, South Korea and Japan

Fig. 4. Sigfox coverage in several geographic areas (source: [14]). Actual deployments appear in blue, ongoing deployments appear in purple. (Color figure online)

References

1. Coman, F.L., Malarski, K.M., Petersen, M.N., Ruepp, S.: Security issues in Internet of Things: Vulnerability analysis of LoRaWAN, Sigfox and NB-IoT. In: 2019 Global IoT Summit (2019)
2. Euchner, F.: Hunting the Sigfox - Wireless IoT network security, December 2018. https://jeija.net/renard-slides/
3. Euchner, F.: librenard - Sigfox protocol library, September 2018. https://github.com/Jeija/librenard
4. Euchner, F.: renard-phy - Sigfox protocol physical layer, September 2018. https://github.com/Jeija/renard-phy
5. Euchner, F.: Sigfox radio protocol overview and specifications, December 2018. https://github.com/Jeija/renard-spec/releases
6. Ferreira, L.: (In)security of the Radio Interface in Sigfox. Cryptology ePrint Archive, Report 2020/1575 (2020). https://eprint.iacr.org/2020/1575
7. Lifchitz, R.: IoT & Sigfox security, November 2016. https://speakerdeck.com/rlifchitz/iot-and-sigfox-security, Cyber Security Alliance Conference
8. LoRa Alliance Technical committee: LoRaWAN 1.0.3 specification, July 2018. https://lora-alliance.org/resource-hub/lorawanr-specification-v103
9. Malarski, K.M.: Personal communication, December 2020
10. National Security Agency's Research Directorate: Ghidra. https://ghidra-sre.org/, v9.1.2
11. Ossmann, M.: HackRF. https://greatscottgadgets.com/hackrf/
12. Pinault, P.: Stop telling me Sigfox is clear payload, for real you're just lazy, December 2018. https://www.disk91.com/2018/technology/sigfox/stop-telling-me-sigfox-is-clear-payload-for-real-youre-just-lazy/
13. Sigfox: Sigfox - Technical overview, May 2017. https://www.disk91.com/wp-content/uploads/2017/05/4967675830228422064.pdf
14. Sigfox: Coverage, July 2020. https://www.sigfox.com/en/coverage
15. Sigfox: Our story, December 2020. https://www.sigfox.com/en/sigfox-story
16. Sigfox: Sigfox connected objects: Radio specifications, February 2020. https://build.sigfox.com/sigfox-device-radio-specifications, ref. EP-SPECS, rev. 1.5
17. Song, J., Poovendran, R., Lee, J., Iwata, T.: The AES-CMAC algorithm, June 2006. https://tools.ietf.org/html/rfc4493, RFC 4493
18. Sornin, N.: LoRaWAN 1.1 specification, October 2017. https://lora-alliance.org/resource-hub/lorawantm-specification-v11
19. STMicroelectronics: X-CUBE-SFOX - STM32 Sigfox software expansion for STM32Cube. https://www.st.com/en/embedded-software/x-cube-sfox.html

Short Paper: Terrorist Fraud in Distance Bounding: Getting Around the Models

David Gerault[(✉)]

University of Surrey, Guildford, UK
`david.gerault@surrey.ac.uk`

Abstract. Terrorist fraud is an attack against distance bounding protocols, whereby a malicious prover allows an adversary to authenticate on their behalf without revealing their secret key. In this paper, we propose new attack strategies that lead to successful terrorist frauds on proven-secure protocols.

Keywords: Distance bounding · RFID authentication · Terrorist fraud

1 Introduction

The problem of secure authentication is fundamental in cryptography, and constitutes a basic building block for a wide range of applications. Authentication is overwhelmingly performed by proving the knowledge of a secret key, typically embedded in a device such as a card. A major inconvenience with secret key authentication is that, since we authenticate the secret key of a device (the prover) rather than an individual, it can be difficult to guarantee that the correct person is authenticated. This problem is at the root of relay attacks, whereby an adversary passively relays the messages between a legitimate distant prover and a verifier, effectively impersonating each of these parties to the other.

A countermeasure to relay attacks, distance bounding protocols [9], provides the verifier with a way to estimate an upper bound for its respective distance to the prover, based on the round-trip time of the messages.

The primary objective of distance bounding protocols is to combine authentication and relay attack protection. However, other threats are considered. Mafia Fraud (MF), is a generalisation of relay attacks, in which a pair of adversaries can not only passively relay the messages, but also actively forge, modify, or delete messages, acting as a man-in-the-middle. In addition, distance bounding protocols aim at resisting attempts by dishonest provers to make the verifier believe that they are in close range when they are, in fact, far away. Such attacks can be Distance Frauds (DF) when only the prover and a verifier are involved, Distance Hijackings (DH) when honest provers are located near the verifier, or Terrorist Frauds (TF) when an accomplice of the dishonest prover is located near the verifier.

© International Financial Cryptography Association 2021
N. Borisov and C. Diaz (Eds.): FC 2021, LNCS 12674, pp. 351–359, 2021.
https://doi.org/10.1007/978-3-662-64322-8_17

In this paper, we propose novel views on terrorist fraud. In particular, we present a new attack strategy based on unicast messages that enables terrorist frauds on several proven secure protocols. In addition, we present a generic terrorist fraud strategy, based on temper-proof clones of the prover, that effectively affects all protocols of the litterature.

Distance Bounding and Terrorist Fraud. Among the 40+ published distance bounding protocols protocols [3], most rely on a similar structure: the prover and verifier agree on a response vector r. Then, in n timed rounds, the verifier issues challenge, and receives a respons from the prover. The saga of terrorist fraud resistance started with Desmedt's seminal paper [12], where he described how a terrorist (let us call her Alice) could enter a country if identities are verified through an authentication scheme implemented in passports. The attack relies on a third party, Bob, giving Alice his responses to the terminal's challenges in real time. Terrorist fraud resistance mechanisms were introduced by Bussard and Bagga [11], and included in virtually all protocols that attempt to resist terrorist fraud, *e.g.* [17] [19] [20]. The proposed solution relies on a fundamental assumption: **Bob does not want Alice to be able to impersonate him in further sessions.** Therefore, distance bounding protocols are considered to be terrorist-fraud resistant if helping Alice to authenticate forces Bob to give her his secret material. This design principle is illustrated in Fig. 1: the prover and the verifier agree on a response two response vectors r^0 and r^1, such that the prover's key x can be retrieved from r^0 and r^1. During the timed exchanges, the verifier issues n binary challenges, to which the prover replies either with a bit of r^0 or a bit of r^1. In a terrorist fraud attempt, the timing measurements prevent Alice from querrying Bob in real time, so that Alice needs to know both r^0 and r^1, and therefore x, to authenticate succesfully.

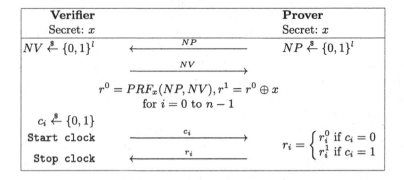

Fig. 1. The classical countermeasure against terrorist fraud.

Recently, Ahmadhi [2] proposed a directional terrorist fraud against anonymous protocols such as SPADE [10] and TREAD [4], where the initial message of the prover contains an encrypted session key. Ahmadhi proposed that Bob could send the encrypted session key to the verifier using a *directional antenna*, effectively making this message unicast. This strategy prevents Alice from using the session key in later authentication, and therefore, breaks the terrorist fraud resistance of the protocols.

Our first attack is similar in nature, but uses directional antennas during the timed exchanges rather than the for the initial messages, and works on most distance bounding protocols of the litterature, rather than only the anonymous protocols.

2 New Strategies for Terrorist Fraud

In this section, we present a novel attack strategy, which applies to most terrorist fraud resistant protocols having single-bit challenges and responses, including (non-exhaustive list): FO [13], Hitomi [18], Swiss-knife [17], Proprox [20]. The aforementioned protocols are prominent protocols, and to the exception of Hitomi, proven to be terrorist fraud resistant. We then present a generic terrorist fraud startegy that applies to all but one protocol of the litterature.

2.1 Notations and Assumptions

In this session, we consider protocols using the terrorist fraud resistance mechanism of Fig. 1. We denote the challenge at round i c_i, and the two possible responses r_i^0, r_i^1. The secret key used during the challenge response exchanges is denoted by xdb, and is such that $r_i^0 \oplus r_i^1 = xdb_i$, where xdb_i is the ith bit of xdb. The distinction between xdb and the actual secret key is introduced for the sake of clarity: in most cases, they are identical, but in some protocols, xdb a session key, or a second key.

In ome protocols, such as FO [13] or SPADE [10], not all key bits are necessary to authenticate: the knowledge of $n - t$ bits (with t a treshold) is sufficient (as part of a mechanism for provable terrorist fraud resistance). This mechanism does not deter our attack.

We assume that dishonest parties can use directional antennas to effectively send unicast messages, such that only the intended target party receives the message sent through this antenna. It is also crucial to our attack that the very fact a message was sent (though the directional antenna) is undetectable by other parties than the intending receiving party. We also assume that, when receiving more than one response to a challenge, the verifier only keeps the first one and discard the following responses as noise. Finally, we assume that dishonest provers know the value of their key xdb (as usual in a terrorist fraud resistance context), and that the secret keys follow a uniform distribution. In our analysis, we omit the (negligible) advantage of the adversary against the primitives (e.g., PRF) used to generate the responses r^j for the sake of readability.

2.2   Our Attack

The key observation to our attack is the following: due to the uniform distribution of xdb, it holds that $\Pr[xdb_i = 0] = \frac{1}{2}$. Therefore, for half the rounds on average, we have $r_i^0 \oplus r_i^1 = xdb_i = 0$, and thus, $r_i^0 = r_i^1$. Let us denote the set of these rounds by $\mathcal{I}^{EQ}$, and the other rounds by $\mathcal{I}^{DIFF}$. In other words, let

$$\mathcal{I}^{EQ} = \{i : r_i^0 = r_i^1, i \in [1; n]\},$$

$$\mathcal{I}^{DIFF} = \{i : r_i^0 \neq r_i^1, i \in [1; n]\}$$

For the rounds in $\mathcal{I}^{EQ}$, Bob does not need the value of the challenge to compute the correct response (since both are equal); he can therefore send his response r_i at an appropriate time for the verifier to receive r_i within the time bound. Furthermore, by using a directional antenna and careful timing, Bob can calibrate his send in such a way that (1) the verifier receives Bob's response before receiving Alice's, and (2) Alice does not receive Bob's message, nor know that Bob even sent a message. In our attack, Bob exploits these two points by giving Alice the correct responses for the rounds in $\mathcal{I}^{DIFF}$, and random responses for the rounds in $\mathcal{I}^{EQ}$. During the challenge response exchanges, depending on which set the round belongs to, Bob either sends his response in the setting defined by (1) and (2), or does nothing. More formally, our attack goes as follows:

1. Bob runs the untimed exchanges himself, sends a help bit-vector H to Alice, and instruct her to send a response at each round using H;
2. During the timed challenge-response part of the protocol, at round i:
   (a) If $i \in \mathcal{I}^{DIFF}$: Bob does nothing;
   (b) If $i \in \mathcal{I}^{EQ}$: Bob sends the response $r_i = r_i^0 = r_i^1$ to the verifier through a directional antenna. Bob times his send so that the verifier receives Bob's message first, and ignores Alice's message;
3. If the protocol has final message exchanges, Bob performs them.

If H permits Alice to send the correct responses for all rounds in $\mathcal{I}^{DIFF}$, then the authentication is accepted. To have a valid terrorist fraud, we further need to show that Alice does not obtain enough information to authenticate on her own in further sessions. To that end, H needs to be chosen carefully.

The choice of H. The help vector H given by Bob to Alice must satisfy two conditions for the attack to be valid: (1) it must contain sufficient information for Alice to respond correctly to the rounds in $\mathcal{I}^{DIFF}$ and (2) it must not contain enough information for Alice to be able to extract Bob's key with non negligible probability. Remember that we make the assumption that Alice does not see when Bob sends a message through the directional antenna: she does not know to which rounds her response is overwritten by Bob.

Strategy 1. A first choice is to give Alice exactly the set of responses she needs, *i.e.*, $H = \{(r_i^0, r_i^1) : i \in \mathcal{I}^{DIFF}\}$. In this case, condition (1) is satisfied. One could argue that condition (2) is also satisfied, as Alice only receives on average half of the key bits (by computing $r^0 \oplus r^1$), and would therefore need to guess the remaining $2^{\frac{n}{2}}$ bits to authenticate. However, in reality, the additional information that the authentication succeeds is enough for Alice to make an educated guess on the strategy employed by Bob, deduce that she received the responses to $\mathcal{I}^{DIFF}$, and therefore guess that the remaining bits of xdb are 0.

Strategy 2. A natural way to fix strategy one would be to add random responses to the help vector, *i.e.*, give Alice the correct responses for the rounds in $\mathcal{I}^{DIFF}$, and two random bits for each round in $\mathcal{I}^{EQ}$. Under this strategy, by XOR-ing r^0 and r^1, Alice obtains a bitstring xdb' that has, on average, 75% of its bits in common with xdb. For many protocols, this is enough to qualify as an attack. However, protocols relying a backdoor mechanism for provable terrorist-fraud resistance, such as FO, allow an adversary knowing a bitstring "close" to the actual xdb, up to a predefined threshold, to authenticate. Therefore, if the threshold is chosen to be approximately 75%, xdb' is sufficient for Alice to authenticate on her own with it: the attack is invalid.

Strategy 3. The downfall of Strategy 2 is that the noise vector provided for $\mathcal{I}^{EQ}$ still has a probability $\frac{1}{2}$ of resulting in the correct bit of x for each round. To counter that, we propose that Bob gives Alice $H = \{(r_i^0, r_i^0 \oplus 1) : i \in [1; n]\}$. In other words, Bob gives Alice r_i^0 and its complement, thus effectively leaking no information about x in an information theoretic sense (remember that we abstract away the advantage of Alice against the primitive used to generate r): by XORing these two vectors, Alice obtains nothing but a string of 1s. On the other hand, she does have all the necessary information to respond to the rounds of $\mathcal{I}^{DIFF}$, where by definition, $r_i^1 = r_i^0 \oplus 1$. Therefore, at the end of the session, Alice is authenticated, but learnt no information about the value xdb.

Strategy 3 effectively counters backdoor mechanisms that permit to authenticate with $n - t$ bits of the secret: by XORing the two response vectors, Alice obtains a string with hamming distance $\frac{n}{2}$ to the secret, *i.e.*, the same as what a random bitstring would have. Allowing a party holding such a string to bypass authentication would therefore effectively grant access to outsiders.

Protocols That Resist our Attack. Notice that the protocols we mentioned so far have a binary challenges and responses. To the best of our knowledge, among the protocols that attempt to resist terrorist fraud, only a few $m > 2$-bit challenges/responses, the most prominent being:

- TDB [5]: TDB is a protocol that uses secret sharing as a means to defeat terrorist fraud. In particular, for each round i, $m > 2$ different challenge values are possible, and each reponse r_i^j constitutes a share, such that $\bigoplus_{j=0}^{m-1} r_i^j = x_i$;
- SKI, DBopt [6] [7]: These protocols have variants with $m > 2$.

In these protocols, the number of rounds in $\mathcal{I}^{EQ}$ is lower than 50%, and our attack does not apply directly. Therefore, protocols with $m > 2$ seem to effectively prevent our attack. We suspect considering a noise resistance threshold could make our attack feasible, but leave this analysis to future work.

In addition to these protocols, PUFDB [15], which relies on physically uncloneable functions, and the protocols described in [16], which add randomized timings to DBopt, resist our attack. Finally, Poxy [1] uses two challenges, one to select the response vector, and one that is XORed to the response, which counters our strategies.

Our Attack Within Formal Models. There are two main families of formalisms for terrorist fraud: DFKO [13] and BMV [8]. The main difference between these two approaches is the number of times Alice recieves help. In DFKO, the key of Bob must leak after a single authentication by Alice for the protocol to be secure, whereas in BMV, Alice is allowed to be helped by Bob several times. Interestingly, if Alice is helped several times, then our attack may not apply.

Assume Alice is helped by Bob not once, but n times, and she is aware of Bob's strategy. She can recover one bit of xdb in each session, by refusing to answer the corresponding challenge. If the authentication is denied, she concludes that Bob did not send a response, so that the corresponding key bit is 1; otherwise, it is 0.

This strategy points to two unexplored areas in the terrorist fraud resistance litterature: (1) Alice knowing/infering what strategy Bob is using, and (2) Alice actively deviating from the instructions of Bob.

It is interesting to observe that, after so many years of intense scrutiny, some aspects of terrorist fraud resistance are still left completely unexplored.

A Note on Practical Application of our Attack. Our attack relies on very strong assumption, and is therefore probably unfeasible in short range distance bounding such as contactless payment as of today. On the other hand, in applications where the measured distances are larger, it may apply. Overall, the main interest of this attack at the time being is theoretical, as it exhibits hidden spots that are not considered in current formal models.

2.3   Attack of the Clones

Protocols that aim at being terrorist fraud resistant consider that provers have access to their secret key. In fact, the very notion of terrorist-fraud needs whitebox access to provers to make sense. If the prover devices, for instance, payment cards, are black-box, then Bob can not learn more information by querrying his device than Alice could obtain by querrying it. Therefore, in a black-box context, terrorist fraud adversaries are no stronger than mafia fraud adversaries, so that considering terrorist fraud becomes irrelevant.

In applications where security is important, the devices are often blackbox. For instance, for payment applications, the cards are designed to be temper-proof, and thwart attempts to recover the secret material they embbed.

Arguably, in such applications, if a dishonest prover manages to extract their secret key, them being able to perform a terorrist fraud is probably not the biggest issue. On the other hand, for applications where security is less critical, or on specific platforms such as smartphones, a dishonest participant may be able to extract their secret material.

Let us now assume that Bob knows his secret key. In a terrorist fraud scenario, Bob wants Alice to be able to authenticate, but not to impersonate him. We argue that he can always do that, providing temper-proof devices exist, by applying the following strategy, which we call "attack of the clones":

1. Clone his device into a temper-proof *oracle* device
2. Give the oracle device to Alice
3. Let Alice authenticate, using the oracle device.

Of course, this strategy alone is not sufficient, as Alice would be able to use the oracle device in further authentications. Therefore, we propose to include a secure remote activation mechanism within the oracle device, such that it only performs authentication when Bob decides to activate it. Furthermore, Bob can include instruction within the oracle device's algorithm, so that it erases its memory after one successful authentication. In practice, what we call an oracle device in this attack corresponds to the notion of one-time program [14]. We argue that this constitutes a universal terrorist fraud attack, in that it applies to all protocols the security of which only relies on cryptographic keys (as opposed to using additional biometric verification, or physically uncloneable functions). As such, to the best of our knowledge, only pufDB [15] resists this attack.

In essence, our attack amounts to an intricate way for Bob to lend his access card to Alice, while making sure she only uses it once. We believe that this type of simple strategies are too often overlooked in terrorist-fraud resistance models. There are indeed protocols in which Bob can provide response vectors to Alice without exposing his secret, which, in an ideal world, should not be possible. However, forcing Bob to expose his secret if he choses to apply this attack strategy does not seem to fix the problem.

3 Conclusion

In this paper, we present two attack strategies that circumvent formal models, and permit to perform terrorist frauds on proven secure protocols. We discuss blind spots in the terrorist fraud resistance litterature, in particular the possibility that Alice deviates from the strategy Bob asked her to follow, in order to extract more information. These new research directions show that, after more than 25 years of research, our understanding and formalisms for terrorist fraud resistance are still lacking. Including such considerations in formal models, and integrating noise resistance in the analysis, is left to future work.

References

1. Ahmadi, A., Safavi-Naini, R.: Directional distance-bounding identification. In: Mori, P., Furnell, S., Camp, O. (eds.) ICISSP 2017. CCIS, vol. 867, pp. 197–221. Springer, Cham (2018). https://doi.org/10.1007/978-3-319-93354-2_10
2. Ahmadi, H., Safavi-Naini, R.: Secure distance bounding verification using physical-channel properties. CoRR abs/1303.0346 (2013)
3. Avoine, G., et al.: Security of distance-bounding: a survey. ACM Comput. Surv. **51**, 1–33 (2017)
4. Avoine, G., et al.: A terrorist-fraud resistant and extractor-free anonymous distance-bounding protocol. In: Proceedings of ASIA CCS '17, pp. 800–814. ACM (2017)
5. Avoine, G., Lauradoux, C., Martin, B.: How secret-sharing can defeat terrorist fraud. In: Proceedings of the Fourth ACM Conference on Wireless Network Security, WiSec '11, pp. 145–156. ACM, New York (2011)
6. Boureanu, I., Mitrokotsa, A., Vaudenay, S.: Practical and provably secure distance-bounding. J. Comput. Secur. **23**(2), 229–257 (2015)
7. Boureanu, I., Vaudenay, S.: Optimal proximity proofs. In: Lin, D., Yung, M., Zhou, J. (eds.) Inscrypt 2014. LNCS, vol. 8957, pp. 170–190. Springer, Cham (2015). https://doi.org/10.1007/978-3-319-16745-9_10
8. Boureanu, I., Mitrokotsa, A., Vaudenay, S.: Practical and provably secure distance-bounding. In: Desmedt, Y. (ed.) ISC 2013. LNCS, vol. 7807, pp. 248–258. Springer, Cham (2015). https://doi.org/10.1007/978-3-319-27659-5_18
9. Brands, S., Chaum, D.: Distance-bounding protocols. In: Helleseth, T. (ed.) EURO-CRYPT 1993. LNCS, vol. 765, pp. 344–359. Springer, Heidelberg (1994). https://doi.org/10.1007/3-540-48285-7_30
10. Bultel, X., Gambs, S., Gérault, D., Lafourcade, P., Onete, C., Robert, J.M.: A prover-anonymous and terrorist-fraud resistant distance-bounding protocol. In: WISEC 2016. ACM, New York (2016)
11. Bussard, L., Bagga, W.: Distance-bounding proof of knowledge to avoid real-time attacks. In: Sasaki, R., Qing, S., Okamoto, E., Yoshiura, H. (eds.) SEC 2005. IAICT, vol. 181, pp. 223–238. Springer, Boston, MA (2005). https://doi.org/10.1007/0-387-25660-1_15
12. Desmedt, Y.: Major security problems with the 'unforgeable' (feige)-fiat-shamir proofs of identity and how to overcome them. In: SecuriCom, pp. 15–17. SEDEP Paris, France (1988)
13. Fischlin, M., Onete, C.: Terrorism in distance bounding: modeling terrorist-fraud resistance. In: Jacobson, M., Locasto, M., Mohassel, P., Safavi-Naini, R. (eds.) ACNS 2013. LNCS, vol. 7954, pp. 414–431. Springer, Heidelberg (2013). https://doi.org/10.1007/978-3-642-38980-1_26
14. Goldwasser, S., Kalai, Y.T., Rothblum, G.N.: One-time programs. In: Wagner, D. (ed.) CRYPTO 2008. LNCS, vol. 5157, pp. 39–56. Springer, Heidelberg (2008). https://doi.org/10.1007/978-3-540-85174-5_3
15. Igier, M., Vaudenay, S.: Distance bounding based on PUF. In: Foresti, S., Persiano, G. (eds.) CANS 2016. LNCS, vol. 10052, pp. 701–710. Springer, Cham (2016). https://doi.org/10.1007/978-3-319-48965-0_48
16. Kılınç, H., Vaudenay, S.: Optimal proximity proofs revisited. In: Malkin, T., Kolesnikov, V., Lewko, A.B., Polychronakis, M. (eds.) ACNS 2015. LNCS, vol. 9092, pp. 478–494. Springer, Cham (2015). https://doi.org/10.1007/978-3-319-28166-7_23

17. Kim, C.H., Avoine, G., Koeune, F., Standaert, F.-X., Pereira, O.: The swiss-knife RFID distance bounding protocol. In: Lee, P.J., Cheon, J.H. (eds.) ICISC 2008. LNCS, vol. 5461, pp. 98–115. Springer, Heidelberg (2009). https://doi.org/10.1007/978-3-642-00730-9_7

18. Peris-Lopez, P., Hernandez-Castro, J., Dimitrakakis, C., Mitrokotsa, A., Tapiador, J.E.: Shedding light on rfid distance bounding protocols and terrorist fraud attacks (2009). arXiv: Cryptography and Security

19. Reid, J., Nieto, J.M.G., Tang, T., Senadji, B.: Detecting relay attacks with timing-based protocols. In: Proceedings of ASIACCS 2007, pp. 204–213. ACM Press (2007)

20. Vaudenay, S.: Sound proof of proximity of knowledge. In: Au, M.-H., Miyaji, A. (eds.) ProvSec 2015. LNCS, vol. 9451, pp. 105–126. Springer, Cham (2015). https://doi.org/10.1007/978-3-319-26059-4_6

SoK: Securing Email—A Stakeholder-Based Analysis

Jeremy Clark[1(✉)], P. C. van Oorschot[2], Scott Ruoti[3], Kent Seamons[4], and Daniel Zappala[4]

[1] Concordia University, Montreal, Canada
j.clark@concordia.ca
[2] Carleton University, Ottawa, Canada
paulv@scs.carleton.ca
[3] University of Tennessee, Knoxville, USA
ruoti@utk.edu
[4] Brigham Young University, Provo, USA
{seamons,zappala}@cs.byu.edu

Abstract. While email is the most ubiquitous and interoperable form of online communication today, it was not conceived with strong security guarantees, and the ensuing security enhancements are, by contrast, lacking in both ubiquity and interoperability. This situation motivates our research. We begin by identifying a variety of stakeholders who have an interest in the current email system and in efforts to provide secure solutions. We then use the tussle among stakeholders to explain the evolution of fragmented secure email solutions undertaken by industry, academia, and independent developers, and to draw the conclusion that a one-size-fits-all solution is unlikely. We highlight that vulnerable users are not well served by current solutions. We also account for the failure of PGP, and argue secure messaging, while complementary, is not a fully substitutable technology.

1 Introduction

Email has been called *"probably the most valuable service on the Internet"* [14]. It has evolved over its 50-year history to become a pillar of seamless interoperability—if you know someone's email address, you can send email to them [114] across a diverse range of desktop, mobile, and web client software. As an indication of its near-universal acceptance, an email address is often required to create online accounts and to make online purchases. As of 2020, there were an estimated 4 billion users of email sending over 306 billion email messages per day [120]. Despite its ubiquity, email was not created the security desirable for its ensuing wide deployment.

Work to provide security for email, in various forms, has been ongoing for over three decades. Early efforts focused on the confidentiality, authenticity, and integrity of email messages, with efforts to develop PEM [96] leading to work on S/MIME [119] and then, as a reaction, PGP [46]. However, as measured in

© International Financial Cryptography Association 2021
N. Borisov and C. Diaz (Eds.): FC 2021, LNCS 12674, pp. 360–390, 2021.
https://doi.org/10.1007/978-3-662-64322-8_18

Table 1. Stakeholders with an interest in email and secure email.

Stakeholder	Description
Email Service Providers	Organizations that provide email services to industry and the public
Enterprise Organizations	Large organizations in both government and industry
Privacy Enthusiasts	Users with strong privacy preferences who believe email should offer strong protection from corporate or government surveillance
Vulnerable Users	Users who deal with strongly sensitive information that could induce personal safety risks, including journalists, dissidents, whistleblowers, informants, and undercover agents; we also include criminals as part of this stakeholder (due to aligned goals, despite ethical differences)
Secure Mailbox Providers	Organizations that provide secure email services to the public
Typical Users	Users of standard, plaintext email services
Enforcement	National security, intelligence, and law enforcement

recent years, email is only sometimes transmitted over an encrypted connection, with limited protection from passive network eavesdropping and active network attacks [37,45,69,101]. Meanwhile, S/MIME has only seen limited uptake within enterprises and experts are abandoning PGP.[1] Greater attention has focused on spam, malware, and phishing as they became problems for everyday users. While spam filtering by many email providers has significantly improved, extensive email archives are typically stored in plaintext and vulnerable to hacking, and fraud through phishing and spear phishing remain problematic [123]. It is within this context that we set out to systematically understand what went wrong with email security, how email security can theoretically be improved, and how tussling between stakeholders can lead to inaction.

Contributions and Methodology. To better understand the current state of affairs and identify where future research and development efforts should focus, we conduct a stakeholder-based analysis of secure email systems. Our initial deliverable was a framework to evaluate secure email systems (preserved in the full version [25]), allowing us to map out the landscape of solutions and compare how they satisfy a set of security, utility, deployability, and usability properties. Ensuing discussion and review of this framework encouraged us to look specifically at

---

[1] Including Phil Zimmermann [46], the creator of PGP; Moxie Marlinspike [99], who called PGP a *"glorious experiment that has run its course,"* and Filippo Valsorda [148], who bemoans the challenges of maintaining long-term PGP keys.

how the actions and interests of a set of stakeholders (Table 1) helps to explain the history of failures and successes in secure email, leading to the current patchwork of partial secure email solutions. Using this new orientation for the paper, we systemize the academic literature on email, relevant IETF standards, industry solutions and software projects. For each, we consider which stakeholder is behind the proposal, determine how it furthers the goals of the stakeholder, and infer how these goals compose with the goals of other stakeholders. This allows us to identify incompatibilities, illustrate how different solutions have evolved to meet their needs, and show which stakeholders are under-served.

While we did not follow a standard or formal methodology for identifying research literature, our approach was as follows. We (i) examined the proceedings of top ranked security, cryptography, and measurements venues; (ii) expanded the research set by contemplating other work that was cited in the papers we identified; and (iii) relied on our personal experience (which, for some, dates back to the early 1990s) and our acquired knowledge of the literature. Similarly, the stakeholder groups were extracted from the literature through experience and discussion. It is likely that a different set of authors would end up with a somewhat different set of papers and categorizations, but this seems to be true of nearly all SoKs at top security venues.

Rise of Secure Instant Messaging. The relatively low level of adoption of secure email is often contrasted with the wider success of secure messaging applications. WhatsApp and Facebook Messenger have over a billion users, while iMessage, Signal, Telegram, Line, and Viber have millions. The best of these provide forward secrecy and message deniability [17,116] in addition to end-to-end encryption. Unger et al. [147] have an excellent systematization of secure messaging. Yet, despite some calls to abandon secure email in favor of Signal [148], there are important reasons to not give up on email. Email is an open system, in contrast to messaging's walled gardens, giving it fundamentally different uses, often involving longer messages, archival, search, and attachments. There is no indication email is going away anytime soon. As such, there is still an important need to increase the security and privacy of email-based communication.

2   Preliminaries

A series of protocols are used to send email, transfer it from the sender's email provider to the recipient's provider, and then retrieve it. Figure 1 shows the most basic steps involved, in steps marked (1) through (3). When a user initiates sending an email, their client may use SMTP [85] to submit the message to their organization's mail server (also called a mail transfer agent or MTA [29,71]). The sender's MTA uses DNS to locate the mail MTA for the recipient's domain, then uses SMTP to transfer the message. Finally, the recipient retrieves the message from their own organization's MTA, possibly using POP or IMAP. If either the sender or receiver is using webmail, then step (1) or step (3) may use HTTPS instead. Note also that the version of SMTP used to submit a message in step (1) is modified from the version of SMTP used to transfer messages [55].

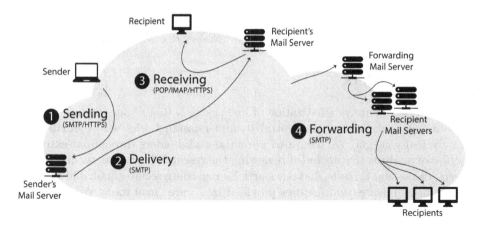

Fig. 1. Overview of email operation and protocols. (1) Sending email generally uses SMTP or HTTPS between a client and its mail server. (2) Delivery of email between mail servers uses SMTP. (3) Receiving email generally uses POP, IMAP, or HTTPS. (4) Any mail server receiving email may forward it to other servers. This happens when a user asks to forward their email to a different account, or when a user sends to a mailing list.

This sequence of events is complicated somewhat by additional features supported by email as shown in step (4). First, a receiving MTA can be configured to forward email for a recipient on to another MTA; *e.g.,* forwarding email from bob@company.org to bob@gmail.com. This can repeat an arbitrary number of times. Second, a destination email address may correspond to a mailing list server which forwards the email to all subscribers on the list (a potentially large number). This adds numerous other recipient MTAs to the process.

An email message itself consists of two parts: the envelope and the body. The envelope contains SMTP commands that direct MTAs regarding how the message should be delivered. In particular, the envelope specifies the sender's email address (MAIL FROM) and the recipient's email address (RCPT TO). The message body has a separate format, including the familiar *From, To, CC,* and *Subject* header fields. Email clients generally display the sender's email address shown in the *From* header in the body, rather than the one in the SMTP envelope.

Why Email is Insecure. Every aspect of email was initially designed, specified, and developed without foreseeing the need for security protection that would later be recognized given how universal email has become. Security issues persist today despite decades of work to fix them. The original designs of protocols used to send, receive, and deliver email among clients and servers contained no protections for integrity or confidentiality. All messages were transmitted in the clear and could be intercepted and modified by anyone able to act as a man-in-the-middle. The original specifications contain nothing that validates the MAIL FROM command or prevents forgery of the *From* header. The ease of forging emails did nothing to inhibit the emergence of unsolicited email. Email never easily faciliated network-level anonymity, message deniability, or untraceability.

3 Stakeholders

The premise of our systematization of knowledge is that understanding the tussles among stakeholders are central to understanding why secure email lacks a universal solution. We identified potential stakeholders through an extensive period of analysis that included reviewing the research literature; reading online posts, discussion threads, and news articles regarding secure email; and by looking at press releases and features provided by secure email tools. We then carefully distilled the set to *key* stakeholders who: (1) reflect unique preferences, and (2) are important to the history of research and development in this area (see Table 1).

An example of a stakeholder that is not a key stakeholder within our framework would be a company that produces client email software, as these companies tend to reflect the preferences of their customers—customers that are already key stakeholders like *enterprise organizations*, *typical users*, and *privacy enthusiasts*. Another example is government which is multifaceted. Many government departments operate like *enterprise organizations*, while others are captured by *enforcement*. But even within national security, law enforcement and intelligence agents and assets themselves have the preferences of *privacy enthusiasts* or *vulnerable users*. In this section, we align various efforts toward secure email with the appropriate stakeholders and in Sect. 4 discuss the trade-offs.

3.1 Email Service Providers

An email service (or mailbox) provider [29] is focused on retaining its customers for business and personal use. Providers have adopted several technologies to improve the security of email, including link encryption, domain authentication, and sender authentication. Providers often require access to plaintext so they can scan incoming emails for spam and malware. We review current and planned efforts, the protection they offer, and assessments of their effectiveness.

Link Encryption. Providers have adopted methods for encrypting email while it is in transit between MTAs or between an MTA and a client. Such 'link' encryption is designed to prevent eavesdropping and tampering by third parties that may own untrusted routers along the path that email is being delivered [67], however messages are not protected from inspection or modification at each MTA. While more privacy invasive than end-to-end encryption (encryption between the email sender and recipient), link encryption enables providers to scan for malicious email attachments, classify potential spam or phishing attacks, modify email tracking links, and provide other services.

Mail transferred with SMTP between MTAs is by default plaintext, and an MTA can use the STARTTLS command [67] to negotiate an encrypted channel.

However, an active adversary between the MTAs can corrupt or strip START-TLS, downgrading the connection to plaintext [37]. A recent initiative (currently called MTA-STS [98]) provides a way for an MTA to advertise a strict transport security (STS) policy stating that they always require STARTTLS. The policy is trusted on first use (TOFU) or authenticated using the certificate authority (CA) system. Should DNSSEC become widely deployed, policies can be directly advertised by the MTA in its DNS record [12,68]. Even with link encryption, SMTP reveals significant metadata about email messages—some proposed mitigations have been drafted [95,143].

Recall that email client software most often uses IMAP (or the older POP3) to retrieve mail and SMTP to send messages. STARTTLS is supported across each of these protocols [111] and is often required by the mail server. Users of webmail typically access their mail client using HTTPS. Under the link encryption paradigm, end users can ensure encryption to their mail server but have no control over (or even visibility of) the use of encryption for the transport of their emails.

Authentication. Consider the case when Alice receives an email from bob@gmail.com. *Domain authentication* indicates that the email was sent by a server authorized to send email from gmail.com, while *sender authentication* validates the user account bob@gmail.com originated the mail. The final level of authentication is *user authentication*, which occurs when Alice ensures that a human, such as Bob Smith owns the bob@gmail.com account. While user authentication is ideal, it taps into a public key infrastructure that email providers have avoided, settling instead for *domain authentication*, which has a long history rooted in identifying spam and filtering malware [5,43,84,88].

Domain Authentication. The primary protocol for domain authentication is DomainKeys Identified Mail (DKIM) [30,87]. The server originating email for a particular domain will generate a digital signature key pair, advertise the public key in the DNS record for the same domain, and sign all outbound email, with the appropriate validation data added to a header field in the email. A well-positioned adversary can modify a recipient's retrieval of the public key from DNS—DNSSEC can mitigate this threat [6]. DKIM signatures are fragile to any modification to the message body or header fields.

Using the same principle of advertising through DNS records, Sender Policy Framework (SPF) [84] allows a domain to specify which IP addresses are allowed to originate email for their domain, while Domain Message Authentication, Reporting, and Conformance (DMARC) [88] enables specification of which services (DKIM, SPF) they support, along with a policy indicating what action should be taken if authentication fails. DMARC has many additional features around reporting misconfigurations and abuse, but importantly it also requires identifier alignment. For SPF, this means that the domain in the envelope MAIL FROM address (which is authenticated with SPF) must match the domain in the *From* header field. For DKIM, this means that the domain used for signing must match the domain in the *From* header field. This links the authentication or signature verification done by SPF and DKIM to the *From* address seen by the user.

Security extensions like SPF and DKIM were developed at different times for different purposes. DMARC is intended to cover gaps between SPF and DKIM. Such a patchwork approach to security is often susceptible to vulnerabilities, particularly when the protocols are implemented across different client and server software components that need to interoperate. A recent study on the composition of SPF, DKIM, and DMARC identifies 18 attack vectors and finds that all tested mail providers and email clients were vulnerable to at least one [24].

Sender Authentication. There is no wide support for sender authentication. Most mailbox providers do authenticate their users [66]. For example, if the sender is using webmail, then she may authenticate by logging into her webmail account. If the sender is using a desktop client, the mail domain can authenticate her with SMTP Authentication, which provides several methods that enable the sender to authenticate with the MTA by a username and password [139–141]. However, the measures a domain uses to authenticate a sender are not communicated to the recipient of an email message, nor can they be verified by the recipient.

Reducing the Fragility of Authentication. Authenticated Received Chain (ARC) [5,77] extends email authentication to handle cases when messages are potentially modified when being forwarded, such as by a mailing list. With ARC, authentication checks are accumulated by forwarders in a message header field [86] as well as a signature on the email as received (these header fields are sealed with an additional signature by each forwarder, creating a chain). The protocol is intended for broad use by all email handlers along a transmission path, not just perimeter MTAs, and it is designed to allow handlers to safely extend the chain even if when they are certain they have not modified the message. When all email handlers are trusted by the recipient, ARC enables any modifications to the message to be attributed, and for DKIM, SPF, and DMRAC results to be validated on the pre-modified message. However, a malicious handler is not prevented from altering messages or removing ARC headers.

Mitigating Email Misuse. Mailbox providers have invested significant effort in spam, phishing, and malware filtering. In the early 2010s, a successful malicious email campaign might see a spammer employ a botnet of 3,000 compromised machines to send 25 billion emails to 10 million addresses [75]. Each aspect of the pipeline—from the compromised machines to the email list to the software tools—might be sold by specialists [93], and the campaign itself is typically run by third-party advertisers earning pay-per-click revenue for directing traffic to a third-party site (*e.g.,* storefronts for unregulated pharmaceuticals constitute over a third of spam) [102].

Spam filtering has evolved from IP address blacklists to highly sophisticated classifiers that examine content, meta-information including origin, user reports, and protocol details such as SMTP header fingerprints [145]. Malware filtering is often performed by comparing email attachments to signatures of known malware. Spammers use a variety of evasion techniques, including sending from the IP addresses of malware-compromised computers [47], spoofing sender addresses, and encoding text as images. An esoteric proposal for spam prevention is requiring the sender to compute a costly function to send an email [9, 38]—an approach that never caught on [90].

Measurement Studies of Adoption and Effectiveness. In 2015–2018, several papers were published [37,45,69,73,101] that measured the level of adoption and effectiveness of the encryption and domain authentication used by email providers. The general picture they paint is that top email providers encrypt messages with STARTTLS and use SPF and DKIM for authentication, but there is a long tail of organizations that are lagging in deploying these mechanisms. However, even when protection methods within email are deployed, they are often compromised by insecure practices, such as acceptance of: self-signed certificates[2] (when CA-signed certificates were expected), expired certificates, or broken chains, all of which cause the validation of the certificate to fail. Email traffic often uses weak cipher suites, weak cryptographic primitives and parameters, weak keys, or password authentication over unencrypted connections. Of the techniques that rely on DNS, basic attacks such as DNS hijacking, dangling DNS pointers [97], and modifying non-DNSSEC lookups can enable circumvention. Stripping attacks can compromise STARTTLS, with Durumeric et al. [37] illustrating how these attacks caused 20% of inbound Gmail messages to be sent in cleartext for seven countries. Use of SPF is common, but enforcement is limited, and DNS records often are not protected with DNSSEC. There is little use of DKIM, and few servers reject invalid DKIM signatures [45]. Many implementations also lack security indicators for communicating SPF/DKIM/DMARC failures to users in a way that is effective at increasing secure behaviour [73].

As Mayer et al. [101] conclude, *"the global email system provides some protection against passive eavesdropping, limited protection against unprivileged peer message forgery, and no protection against active network-based attacks."*

3.2   Enterprise Organizations

Enterprises have overlapping interests with email service providers (like reducing email misuse) but often prefer stronger (end-to-end) encryption and authentication, at least within their internal boundaries. Enterprises played a role in developing standards that could meet their needs, starting with PEM [11,78,82,83,96] and leading to S/MIME [28,118,119]. Another issue that is highly relevant to enterprises is mitigating carefully targeted social engineering attacks against its employees, often conducted through email.

End-to-End Encryption and Authentication. The primary goals of PEM [11,78, 82,83,96] were end-to-end email security with confidentiality, data origin authentication, connectionless integrity (order not preserved), non-repudiation with

---

[2] With the advent of free domain certificates with Let's Encrypt, it is possible that more providers are using verifiable certificates since these measurements were conducted in 2015–2016.

proof of origin, and transparency to providers and to SMTP. PEM was distinguished by interoperability with non-PEM MTAs, and a hierarchical X.509 public key infrastructure (PKI) with revocation that largely precludes rogue certificate issues haunting later PKI systems. A contributing factor cited [113] in PEM's demise was its slow progress in evolving for Multipurpose Internet Mail Extensions (MIME) [48], the standard for including attachments, multi-part bodies, and non-ASCII character sets. Industry support moved to S/MIME, while privacy advocates favored PGP (see Sect. 3.3) because it was free from the restrictions imposed by PEM's centralized and hierarchical organization.

S/MIME [118] is a standards suite for securing MIME data with both encryption and digital signatures. It was originally developed during the early 1990s by RSA Data Security, then later adopted by the IETF, resulting in standards in 1999 [28,118,119]. S/MIME's Cryptographic Message Syntax (CMS) [70] has origins in PEM and PKCS. S/MIME has wide support on major platforms and products [113, p.60–62]. S/MIME clients use *certificate directories* to look up X.509v3 certificates.[3] S/MIME does not mandate a hierarchy with a single root certificate authority (CA) and any organization can act as an independent, trusted root for its certificates—the most common usage today. Interoperability between organizations is limited or non-existent.

Several works have examined usability deficiencies with S/MIME implementations, noting difficulties knowing which CAs to trust [81], difficulties with certificate management [49], and inconsistency in handling certificates [113, p.60–67]. Automatically creating and distributing signing and encryption keys at account creation is considered good practice [50].

Private Key Escrow. Enterprises often use *private key escrow* in conjunction with S/MIME, which enables the organization to decrypt emails and scan for spam, malware, fraud, and insider trading, as well as archiving messages for regulatory reasons and enabling recovery if a client loses its private key. The suitability of S/MIME's centralized certificate management for enterprises and government has led to large, but siloed, deployments [21]. Some providers simplify S/MIME deployment using *hosted S/MIME* [62], where an enterprise uploads user private keys to an email provider, and the provider automatically uses S/MIME for some emails (*e.g.,* to other users of the same provider). Encryption in this case is only *provider-to-provider* rather than end-to-end.

As an alternative to S/MIME, some enterprise email solutions rely on identity-based encryption (IBE) [138]. IBE uses a trusted server to store a master private key and generate individual private keys for users. The trusted server also advertises a master public key, which clients can use to derive a public key for any email address. Users can validate their ownership of an email address with the IBE server to retrieve their generated private key. IBE simplifies key management for clients but leaves the IBE server with persistent access to each

---

[3] Of note, S/MIME uses a supporting suite of certificate management protocols, including RFC 5280 [28], which defines an IETF subset of X.509v3 certificates.

user's private key, and also substantially complicates revocation [16].[4] Ruoti et al. [128,130] integrated IBE into a webmail system, demonstrating how automating interactions with key management results in successful task completion and positive user feedback.

Transparent Email Encryption. A distinct approach to making interactions with PKI transparent to users is to layer encryption and signing below client software. Levien et al. [94] places this functionality between the email client software and the MTA, while Wolthusen [155] uses the operating system to intercept all network traffic and then automatically apply email encryption. Currently, several companies (*e.g.*, Symantec) offer automated encryption of emails by intercepting them as they traverse a corporate network.

Spear Phishing. Social engineering may be crafted as a generic attack but is often a targeted attack against specific enterprise employees. The openness of email enables direct contact with targets and an opportunity to mislead the target through the content of the email, a spoofed or look-alike send address, and/or a malicious file attachment [63,107]. As an illustration, the company RSA was breached through a sophisticated attack that started with a targeted email impersonating an employee and a corrupted spreadsheet attachment [123]. Employee training [20] and email filtering are important countermeasures, however spam filters are typically trained to detect *bulk* email delivery and classifying bespoke spear phishing emails remains a challenge [89].

3.3 Privacy Enthusiasts

Privacy enthusiasts prefer end-to-end encrypted email to avoid government surveillance or commercial use of their data generally. They differ from vulnerable users (see Sect. 3.4) in that there is not an immediate personal safety risk driving their usage of secure email. Privacy enthusiasts have historically favored PGP, which was developed as "public key cryptography for the masses" and "guerrilla cryptography" to counter authorities [160]. The difficulty with PGP has always been finding a suitable alternative to the centralized trust model of S/MIME.

End-to-End Encryption and Authentication. PGP's history is a fascinating 25-year tale of controversy, architectural zig-zags, name ambiguity, and patent disputes, with changes in algorithms, formats and functionality; commercial vs. non-commercial products; corporate brand ownership; and circumvention of U.S.

---

[4] Revocation of a compromised private key can be supported by having versions of the key. The result of obtaining an incorrect key version is comparable to obtaining a compromised key. The trust model of IBE is tantamount to a trusted public key server.

crypto export controls.[5] The current standard for the PGP message format is OpenPGP [19,39], a patent-unencumbered variation. Despite evolving formats or encryption algorithms, PGP enthusiasts until recently have largely remained faithful to PGP's distinguishing concepts:

- **PGP key packets and lightweight certificates:** PGP key packets hold bare keys (public or private). Public keys are kept in *lightweight certificates* (*cf.* [160]), which are not signed certificates in the X.509 sense, but instead contain keys and a User ID (username and email address). To help client software determine which keys to trust, PGP also includes *transferable public keys* [19], which include one or more *User ID packets* each followed by zero or more *signature packets*. The latter attest the signing party's belief that the public key belongs to the user denoted by the User ID. Users typically store private keys on their local device, often encrypted with a password, though hardware tokens are also available.
- **PGP's web of trust:** The web of trust (WoT) is a model in which users personally decide whether to trust public keys of other users, which may be acquired through personal exchanges or from public servers, and which may be endorsed by other users they explicitly designate to be *trusted introducers* [159].
- **PGP key packet servers:** Users publish their public key to either closed or publicly accessible key packet servers, which contain a mapping of email address to the public key. Clients query to locate the public key associated with an email address.

Problems with PGP. PGP's design around the web of trust has allowed quick deployment in small groups without bureaucracy or costs of formal Certification Authorities [103], but leads to other significant obstacles:

- **Scalability beyond small groups:** Zimmerman notes [160, p.23] that *"PGP was originally designed to handle small personal keyrings"*. Scaling PGP requires acquiring large numbers of keys, along with a manual trust decision for each key, plus manual management of key storage and the key lifecycle.
- **Design failure to address revocation:** Zimmermann writes [160, p.31], *"If your secret key is ever compromised...you just have to spread the word and hope everyone hears about it"*. PGP does have methods to revoke keys, but distribution of these to others is ad hoc.
- **Usability by non-technical users:** Zimmerman [160, p.31] says *"PGP is for people who prefer to pack their own parachutes"*. There is no system help or recovery if users fail to back up their private key or forget their passphrase. Furthermore, users must understand the nuances of generating and storing

---

[5] PGP was distributed as freeware on the Internet in 1991, leading to an investigation of Zimmermann by the United States Customs Office for allegedly violating U.S. export laws. He published the PGP source code in book form in 1995 [158], and the case was subsequently dropped in 1996 [91].

keys, trusting public keys, endorsing a public key for other users, and designating others as trusted introducers. The poor usability of PGP has received significant attention [126, 153].

- **Trust model mismatch:** Zimmerman notes [160, p.25] that *"PGP tends to emphasize [an] organic decentralized non-institutional approach"* reflecting personal social interaction rather than organizational relationships. The PGP web of trust was designed to model social interaction, rather than decision-making processes in governments and large enterprises. It is thus not a one-size-fits-all trust model.

Trust-on-First-Use (TOFU). An alternative to PGP's web of trust is to exchange keys in-band and have clients trust them on first use. This has been the subject of several research projects [51, 100, 125]. Since 2016, the developer community has been integrating TOFU into PGP implementations in the MailPile, PEP [15], LEAP [143], and Autocrypt [8] projects. A common critique of TOFU is that users cannot distinguish valid key changes from an attack. Recent work by developers in the PEP and LEAP projects is aiming to address this problem with additional methods to authenticate public encryption keys, such as using a trusted public key server, auditing public key servers, and the fraught procedure of asking the user to compare key fingerprints [33, 72].

Public Key Servers and Logs. Another web of trust alternative—applicable to (and aligned with) S/MIME's trust model—is introducing a trusted public key server. Recent work [7, 129] showed that automated servers have high usability when integrated into a PGP-based email system. Bai et al. [10] found users prefer key servers to manual key exchange, even after being taught about the security limitations of a key server.

A compromise between TOFU and a fully trusted server is to allow key assertions from users but ensuring they are published publicly in untrusted logs, allowing monitors to examine a history of all certificates or key packets that a key server has made available for any entity [13, 104, 133]. This enables detection of rogue keys and server equivocation.

Social Authentication. Another way to disseminate public keys is to associate them with public social media accounts. The Keybase project[6] helps users to post a signed, cryptographic proof to their account, simultaneously demonstrating ownership of a public key and ownership of the account. By aggregating proofs across multiple social media accounts for the same person, a client can establish evidence that ties a public key to an online persona, under the assumption that it is unlikely that a person's social media accounts are all compromised simultaneously. The Confidante email system leverages Keybase for distribution of encryption public keys, with a study finding it was usable for lawyers and journalists [92].

---

[6] https://keybase.io.

Short-Lived Keys and Forward Secrecy. Schneier and Hall [136] explored the use of short-term private keys to minimize the damage resulting from the compromise of a private key. Brown and Laurie [18] discuss timeliness in destroying a short-lived key and how short-lived keys complicate usability by requiring more frequent key dissemination.

3.4   Vulnerable Users

Vulnerable users deal with strongly sensitive information that could induce personal safety risks. Using email from a malware-infected device is a primary concern [22,64], as well as risks due to the design and common practices of email.

Pseudonymity. One concern for vulnerable users is the inability to forgo leaking personally identifiable meta-information: *i.e.,* unlink the contents of the email from their true email address, their IP address, and/or the identity of their mail server. Technically inclined vulnerable users generally opt for pseudonymity [60] where more than one email sent from the same pseudonymous account can be established as having the same origin, but no further information is known.

Historically, PEM accommodated anonymous users with *persona certificates,* which could provide assurances of continuity of a pseudonymous user ID but does not prevent network level traceability. Today, *layered encryption* is used in which messages are routed through multiple non-colluding servers, with each server unwrapping a layer of encryption until the message is delivered to its destination, with the same happening for replies in reverse. This idea was championed by the cypherpunk movement [109,110] and adapted to the email protocol with remailers like mixminion and others [31,57–59]. Pseudonymity is realized as indistinguishability from a set of plausible candidates—the set of other users at the time of use [35]—which may be small, depending on the system and circumstances.[7]

A simpler approach is to register a webmail account under a pseudonymous email address, optionally using Tor [36] to access the mailbox. Satoshi Nakamoto, the inventor of Bitcoin [108], corresponded over webmail for many months while remaining anonymous.

Traceability, Deniability, and Ephemerality. Email senders for some time have abused the browser-like features of modern email clients to determine when recipients view an email, when a links are clicked, and (via third-party trackers) what other collected information is known about the recipient [40]. Email service provider interventions can interfere with domain authentication (DKIM).

Deniability considers a case where the recipient wants to authenticate the sender, but the sender does not want the evidence to be convincing to anyone

---

[7] To illustrate, a student emailed a bomb threat to Harvard's administration via webmail accessed over Tor [36]. The suspect was found to be the only individual accessing Tor on Harvard's network at the time the email was sent—while strictly circumstantial, the suspect confessed [61].

else. Cryptographers have suggested new signature types [23,76,122] to provide deniability, but these typically require trusted third parties and/or a robust PKI and have near-zero deployment.

Once sent, a sender loses control over an email and the extent to which its contents will be archived. In order to automate a shorter retention period, emails might contain a link to the message body which is deposited with and automatically deleted by a trusted service provider or a distributed network [54, 154].

3.5   Secure Mailbox Providers

A secure mailbox provider offers end-to-end encryption and authentication between users of their service. Providers like ProtonMail [117], Hushmail [74], and Tutanota [146] have millions of users combined. Users' private keys are password-protected client-side and then stored with the provider, preventing provider access (assuming the password is strong [44]) while allowing cross-device access. However, providers are trusted in other regards: inter-user encryption and authentication is generally blackbox and not independently verifiable,[8] and the model relies on client-side scripting where malicious (first or third-party) scripts would compromise security. Additional methods are needed to provide code signing and privilege separation for JavaScript in the browser [106,149]. Generally, email sent to outside users are encrypted client-side with a one-time use passphrase, deposited in message repository with an access link sent as the original email (the passphrase is communicated between the sender and recipient out-of-band).

A second approach is to use a browser extension to overlay signed and encrypted email on an existing mailbox provider. Initiatives here include automating PGP key management tasks (Mailvelope and FlowCrypt), providing automated S/MIME-based encryption and signing (Fossa Guard), encryption with a symmetric key held by the service (Virtru), or encryption using a password shared out of band (SecureGmail). Google developed E2EMail to integrate OpenPGP with Gmail in Chrome but the project has been inactive for several years.

3.6   Typical Users

Some work has examined the question of why most people do not use encrypted email. Renaud et al. [121] found support for four reasons for non-adoption—lack of concern, misconceptions about threats, not perceiving a significant threat, and not knowing how to protect themselves. An earlier survey of 400+ respondents by Garfinkel et al. [50] found that half indicated they didn't use encrypted email because they didn't know how, while the rest indicated they didn't think it was necessary, didn't care, or thought the effort would be wasted. Other work reports

---

[8] Fingerprint comparison is common with secure messaging applications, but the feature is often ignored by users [137].

that users are unsure about when they would need secure email [127] and are skeptical that any system can secure their information [32,131]. It is not clear that users want to use digital signatures or encryption for daily, non-sensitive messages [42,53]. Overall, work in this area demonstrates that usability is not the only obstacle to adoption, and that users don't perceive significant risk with email, lack knowledge about effective ways to mitigate risk, and don't have self-confidence about their ability to effectively use secure systems.

The usable security and privacy community is increasingly utilizing new approaches to address broader questions of adoption of security and privacy practices. Users are often rational when making decisions about whether to follow security advice; Herley [65] makes the case that users sometimes understand risks better than security experts, that worst-case harm is not the same as actual harm, and that user effort is not free. Sasse [135] has likewise warned against scaring or bullying people into doing the "right" thing. As a result, effort is being made to understand users' mental models [41,80,152,157] when they interact with secure software and using risk communication techniques to better understand adoption or non-adoption of secure software [144,156], among other methods.

3.7 Enforcement

We broaden the term enforcement to encompass police and law enforcement agencies, as well as national security and intelligence services. Law enforcement prioritizes access to plaintext communications, either through broad surveillance or exceptional access such as with a warrant. This need for access to plaintext communications has led to calls for so-called encryption back doors, leading to regular debates on whether this is desirable or feasible. This debate originally surfaced in the U.S. in the 1990s concerning email and has been rekindled regularly, now with greater emphasis on instant messaging which has seen better success than email at deploying end-to-end encryption to regular users. Proponents cite fears that widespread use of end-to-end encryption will enable criminals and terrorists to "go dark" and evade law enforcement. In response, privacy advocates decry growing mass surveillance, point to a history of abuses of wiretapping [34], and suggest that market forces will ensure there is plenty of unencrypted data for use by law enforcement regardless [52].

A 2015 paper from Abelson et al. [2] highlights risks of regulatory requirements in this area, reiterating many issues discussed in their earlier 1997 report [1]. Identified risks include reversing progress made in deploying forward secrecy, leading to weaker privacy guarantees when keys are compromised; substantial increases to system complexity, making systems more likely to contain exploitable flaws; and the concentration of value for targeted attacks. Their report also highlights jurisdictional issues that create significant complexity in a global Internet. More broadly, whenever service providers have access to keys that can decrypt customer email, this allows plaintext to be revealed due to incompetent or untrustworthy service providers, by disillusioned employees, by government subpoena, or by regulatory coercion.

4 Stakeholder Priorities

In the previous section, we aligned past efforts in securing email with their appropriate stakeholders. In Table 2, we establish 17 priorities that are important to at least one stakeholder. These priorities are a result of extensive discussion among the authors using our literature review and current practices as evidence for our ratings. The precise definition of each priority can be found in the full version of this paper [25].

For each stakeholder, a given priority can be a high, low, or a non-priority. In some cases, we rate a stakeholder as highly valuing partial support of a property. We also identify several cases where a stakeholder has a high priority that the property is *not* met, meaning it is antithetical to their goals. We lightly clustered the stakeholders into three groups. Enforcement has unique priorities for the

Table 2. Stakeholder priorities.

Stakeholder	Security								Utility				Deploy.			Usab.	
	S1	S2	S3	S4	S5	S6	S7	S8	T1	T2	T3	T4	D1	D2	D3	U1	U2
Enforcement				☠		☠											
Email Service Providers	░	░							█	█	░	░	░	⚔	█		
Typical Users	░	░		⚔					█	░							
Enterprise Organizations	█	█		☠					█	█	█						
Secure Mailbox Providers	█	█															█
Privacy Enthusiasts	█	⚔								⚔							
Vulnerable Users											☠	⚔					░

Legend: ■ high priority for full support   ▓ high priority for partial support   ░ low priority   □ a non-priority or not applicable
⚔ there is disagreement within the stakeholder group about the priority of this property   ☠ high priority for no support

S1: Protection from eavesdropping
S2: Protection from tampering and injection
S3: Private keys only accessible to user
S4: Prevents exceptional access
S5: Responsive public key revocation
S6: Provides a public key audit trail
S7: Supports sender pseudonymity
S8: Easy to detect phishing
T1: Supports user choice of email providers
T2: Supports user choice of identity provider
T3: Supports server-side content processing
T4: Provides persistent access to email
D1: No client software modifications needed
D2: No email server modifications needed
D3: No infrastructure modifications needed
U1: Effortless same system encryption key discovery
U2: Effortless encryption/signing key validation

targets of their investigation; priorities are to backdoor completely confidential and anonymous communication. The second cluster generally prioritizes utility and deployability, while the third prefers security. We accept that the reader may disagree with some rankings but believe the framework enables a useful discussion of tradeoffs that are often otherwise glossed over.

We call particular attention to instances where a stakeholder strongly opposes a property (marked ☠). One might think that no stakeholder would be opposed to increase security, utility, deployability, or usability. However, enforcement prefers a system where exceptional access is granted (S4), as do enterprises, because analyzing plaintext is essential to their operation. (One could argue that enforcement prefers when most traffic is not encrypted at all.) Enforcement likewise prioritizes attribution and thus opposes sender pseudonymity (S7). Vulnerable users are opposed to server-side content processing (T3) and systems that provide persistent access (T4) since they cannot trust their safety to others.

There are several cases where we found disagreement within a stakeholder group regarding the priority of a given property (marked ☠☠). An example is preventing exceptional access to email (S4)—typical email users are divided between those who advocate for government surveillance of email and who are willing to accept government access to email on presentation of a warrant, and those who strongly prefer end-to-end encryption that would prevent exceptional access. Likewise, privacy enthusiasts are split on whether there is a high priority on ensuring that private keys are accessible only to users (S3), with a minority placing a high priority on this property but others accepting password-protected cloud storage of a private key. Privacy enthusiasts are also split on whether persistent access to email is a high priority (T4), along similar lines. Finally, while many email service providers place a high priority on not being required to deploy new email-related servers to support a given technology (D2), this is likely not a high priority for larger providers. For example, large providers have shown a willingness to adopt best practices such as STARTTLS and DKIM more rapidly.

In several cases, stakeholders have a high priority for partial support of a property but do not want it fully (or universally) supported (marked ▦). All stakeholders, aside from enforcement, prefer that emails are protected from eavesdropping by third parties (S1). However certain stakeholders want read capabilities for some email. For example, an enterprise may want to run automated services on their employees' plaintext emails—for security, compliance or other reasons—but do not want the emails accessible in plaintext by anyone outside of the enterprise, or even anyone within the enterprise that is not a party to the email. Similarly, enterprises and service providers may want the ability to modify email messages (S2) to protect their users (remove malware or insert a phishing warning) without disrupting message authentication. Users may want this protection as well.

As a final example of partial support, secure mailbox providers offer users the ability to control their own signing and encryption keys (S3) but balance this with some usability features. For example, storing password-protected decryption keys in the cloud allows users to check their email from new devices without transferring their keys, while it limits the provider's access to their users' decryption keys. This is in contrast to a (normal) email service provider that, if it supported encryption and signatures at all, would give customers the additional usability feature of backing up their private decryption keys, enabling key recovery and the ability to read past encrypted emails. Note that private keys for signing do not require backup as users can generate new ones, although the old public signature keys should be maintained for verification of past emails (or revoked if the signing key is stolen as opposed to lost).

Table 2 illustrates the reality that there are significant disagreements between stakeholders in the secure email space and that no single solution will satisfy them all. The strongest disagreements happen in columns where at least one stakeholder fully supports a property (marked ■) while another strongly opposes it (marked 🐾). The four high conflict properties are exceptional access (S4), sender pseudonymity (S7), server-side content-processing (T3), and persistent access (T4).

The conflict between enforcement and other stakeholders over exceptional access (S4) and sender pseudonymity (S7) is well-known in both secure email and other technical domains: web browsing, network traffic, server IP addresses and locations, and payment systems. We emphasize again that the enforcement stakeholder category captures enforcement's preferences for the targets of their investigations and actions, while the agents themselves are better aligned with privacy enthusiasts, and agents could use (or create) vulnerable users through their investigations.

High conflict also exists over server-side content-processing (T3) for spam, malware filtering, classification, or automatic replies; and persistent access (T4) which indicates that the user can recover their access and archive after losing their authentication credentials. This conflict illustrates an important result: some of the most fundamental disagreements occur over the utility properties of a secure email system. Email service providers, typical users, and enterprise organizations all place a high value on content processing and persistent access. Yet, these are mostly low priorities for the other stakeholders and, in some cases, antithetical to the principles held by vulnerable users who prioritize exclusive access to their email with no backdoors. Even if it means managing a secret value that only they know, they accept the risk of key loss being permanent.

The tussles among stakeholders help explain the history of how this space has evolved. The needs of typical users are largely met by email service providers; these two stakeholders disagree mainly on deployment properties that affect only the service provider (D2, D3), along with a tussle over exceptional access (S4). Privacy enthusiasts have a demonstrated history of highly valuing end-to-end encryption (hence the development of PGP and person-to-person key exchange), but it is not a priority for email service providers and typical users, and this explains why it is not pursued more broadly. The needs of some enterprise organizations to deploy secure email explains why they often adopt S/MIME based products. They need encryption within the organization, plus escrow of private keys and content processing. They also have the IT budget to provide a seamless user experience.

Privacy enthusiasts overlap significantly with enterprise organizations, but disagreements on private key storage (S3), server-side content processing (T3) and persistent access (T4) make finding common ground difficult. Privacy enthusiasts also overlap with vulnerable users but vulnerable users will tolerate poor usability and a lack of features to maximize security. To our knowledge, no major commercial provider currently meets the needs of vulnerable users.

Most email service providers prioritize opportunistic encryption with TLS. Secure email providers have emerged, with priorities that mostly match those of privacy enthusiasts, some of whom may previously have used PGP-based services. Some privacy enthusiasts would prefer the private key is only accessible to themselves (S3), but due to the loss of grass-roots support for PGP, the only apparent feasible alternative is password-protected keys used in secure webmail. The services offered by secure email providers have supported vastly more users of secure email than PGP ever did. However their business model naturally means some deployment properties cannot be met, hence requiring users to use new email software.

5   Further Discussion

After extensively reviewing the history of email, academic literature, and discussing stakeholder priorities, we highlight several critical points in understanding the state of secure email today.

A One-Size-Fits-All Solution is Unlikely. It is clear from Table 2 that stakeholders have conflicting priorities and that the needs of different stakeholders dictate diverging solutions. As such, it is unlikely that any single secure email system will be suitable for all users and their divergent use cases. Furthermore, no single party controls the email ecosystem, and widespread deployment of secure email needs cooperation of numerous stakeholders. No one stakeholder has the capability to build (or the ability to demand) a secure email system that provides seamless interoperability for the billions of email users and supports email's many diverse uses. This means that even in the best case, with different solutions being adopted by different parties, there will almost surely be interoperability challenges that act as natural roadblocks and will require significant investment to overcome, if this is even possible.

The PGP Web of Trust Remains Unsuccessful After 25 Years. The web of trust that is central to the original design of PGP—including manual key exchange and trusted introducers—has largely failed. Its use is generally limited to isolated, small communities. Its appeal is that it allows quick, interoperable deployment in small groups without bureaucracy or costs of formal Certification Authorities, but in practice the downside is poor usability and lack of responsive revocation.

Arguably, the resulting product indecision and non-interoperability has negatively impacted the deployment of secure email in general.

Incremental Improvement is Still Possible. Most email users trust their mailbox providers with plaintext email. While link encryption and domain authentication are available, vulnerabilities to active attacks and a lack of adoption leave email in transit subject to eavesdropping and message forgery. Providers could create an interoperable hosted S/MIME standard to automate provider-to-provider confidentiality and integrity, while still working within the threat model of a trusted mailbox provider. Unlike end-to-end encryption, server-based search, content-filtering, and persistent/portable mailbox access would be supported. Easy-to-deploy tools are needed to ensure the solution is not a barrier to entry for small providers.

Secure Messaging is Only a Partial Answer. Messaging protocols are walled gardens, allowing proprietary protocols that are interactive and supported by central servers. This enables automated encryption for users, including automatic key exchange via a trusted key server and automatic end-to-end encryption of messages [147]. Using a trusted key server means that users may be unaware of the security and usability tradeoffs they are making. Users of secure messaging applications are typically only warned to check the encryption keys if they change, and numerous studies have shown that these applications fail to help users understand how to do this successfully [3,137,151]. Security experts recommend encrypting all messages, however some applications make encryption optional, resulting in many users failing to turn encryption on [150].

Further, email's open nature gives it fundamentally different uses than messaging, including easily communicating with strangers, sending long, content-rich messages, permanently archiving messages, searching past conversations, and attaching files. While email's additional features are part of the reason ubiquitous end-to-end encryption is so elusive, they are also why email is likely to continue to be a primary form of communication on the Internet for years to come.

Vulnerable Users are Not Well Served. Aside from vulnerable users, every stakeholder represents a class of user that has their needs met by at least one system available today. Typical users are served by current offerings from email service providers. Enterprises (and their employees) are served by corporate S/MIME, which provides a combination of security, utility, and usability that matches their priorities. Deployment cost are likely what hinders its broader adoption among enterprises. Privacy enthusiasts are served by secure webmail services, with their stronger emphasis on end-to-end encryption and good usability, while sacrificing utility to meet these priorities. In contrast, there is no system that clearly serves vulnerable users well. PGP is perhaps the best option, given its use by investigative journalists [124], but it does not meet all the security priorities of vulnerable users. No system except for remailers provides sender pseudonymity, and these do not typically meet other security properties important to vulnerable users.

The small size and desire for anonymity among members of this stakeholder group (journalists, dissidents, whistleblowers, survivors of violence, informants, under-cover agents, and even criminals) does not lend itself to commercial solutions, and volunteer organizations in this area have historically struggled.

6   Research and Development Directions

Improving the security of email is important to us. In this section, we briefly outline several avenues for future research and development.

Interoperability. Interoperability among secure email systems is a complex topic. Email evolved into an open system decades ago, allowing anybody to email anyone else. Thus, a justifiable user expectation is that secure email should likewise be open. However, we are far from achieving this today with secure mailbox providers (recall Sect. 3.5), since the primary secure systems in use are walled gardens, as either online services and/or dedicated software clients. Using standardized cryptographic suites is a small step but systems should also allow key (and key server) discovery between services (*e.g.,* ProtonMail-esque mailboxes to enterprise S/MIME certificate directories).

Interoperability introduces challenging issues around privacy, spam, and trust. Enterprises and providers are unwilling to expose the public keys of their users to outside queries. Encrypted spam, and other kinds of malicious email, can evade standard content filtering techniques that work on plaintext. Different systems operate under different trust models. While the web has built a system based on global trust, this requires only one-way trust of the web server, whereas secure email involves two-way trust between individuals and organizations. Simply adopting the web's CA trust model would be unlikely to yield a workable system, given the challenges that remain still largely unsolved with this model [26]. Technically a system based on a CA alternative (*e.g.,* trust-on-first-use) could interoperate with a different system (*e.g.,* certificate directory) but typical users are unlikely to comprehend the difference in trust even if communicated to them, and the entire system could end up with weakest link security. Even if formats and protocols were universally agreed upon, it is not clear whether interoperability is always desired or meaningful. Finally, opening any system to interoperability means users will need help deciding which organizations or providers to trust to provide correct public keys. We argue it is both infeasible and unnecessary to expect that every individual or organization can be globally trusted by the others.

We advise future work on a much more limited goal of establishing trust among communicating parties when they need it. Any individual user or organization has a relatively small set of other users or organizations that it needs to trust. Developing infrastructure and protocols with this end in mind would appear to be necessary to leverage any gains made in technical interoperability.

Content Inspection on Encrypted Email. Another major problem for secure email is coping with spam and malware. Even if interoperability was a solved problem, authentication of an email sender is not the same as authorization to send email [14], and building a system that provides the former but not the latter simply means users will get authenticated spam and phishing emails. End-to-end encryption systems without sufficient spam prevention for users are impractical, since both email providers and users lack an incentive to use such a system.

One possibility is to try to work around this problem. A secure email client could accept encrypted email only from regular or accepted contacts; rejecting encrypted email from unapproved senders could serve as a viable substitute for spam and malware filtering. Spam and malware could still be propagated by compromising accounts and spreading it to others who have approved those users, but the attack surface would be significantly limited. However, email providers are not likely to embrace such a system since it arguably offers less spam and malware protection for users than current practice.

A better alternative might be to build secure email systems that allow for server-side content processing even when private keys are only accessible to users. One possibility is to develop improved methods for processing on data that is encrypted [56,79,142]. Alternatively, clients could send encrypted email and a decryption key to a trusted cloud computing environment [115,134], perhaps based on trusted execution platforms where the email could be decrypted and filtered for malware and spam. Likewise, a trusted computing environment could be used for storing and searching archives. Another possibility is to move email storage to edge devices owned by an end-user where content processing can be performed, with encrypted backup in the cloud to provide fault tolerance and portability.

Auditing Identity Providers. Providing an auditable certificate directory or key server enables a system to provide a public key audit trail, responsive public key revocation, and effortless public key verification. However, additional work is needed to ensure such a system can meet its goals. For example, consider auditing systems like Certificate Transparency and CONIKS [13,104,133]. When it is a user's personal public key that is audited in such a system, the system must also then provide a usable method for users to monitor the public keys being advertised. In the case that a client's system notices that an unauthorized key is advertised for them, the system needs a method for the user to whistleblow and have the offending key revoked. Additionally, if the user's own identity provider has equivocated, then the user needs a method for being informed of this in a trustworthy manner and then being guided on choosing a new identity provider. If the identity provider is also their email provider, then they will also need to choose a new email provider. These auditing systems are promising and would benefit from further development and study to the point where we can be confident that it will be easy for users to accomplish these tasks.

Increasing Trust. Recent work has shown that even with the proliferation of secure messaging applications, there is still a gap in how users perceive the effectiveness of security technology [4,32]. Users overestimate the capabilities of attackers and underestimate the strength of encryption technology, resulting in a lack of trust in applications that claim to protect their privacy. It is debatable whether this lack of trust is misplaced—the best cryptography cannot protect against errors in implementations or breaches that expose data that is stored unencrypted. Users have a healthy skepticism of general software and technology when they pay attention to highly publicized security failures. This is further complicated by 'snake-oil' security and encryption tools that do not offer concrete benefits. Nevertheless, users are better off using encryption if they are going to communicate sensitive data online. Thus, user lack of trust in encryption is a major obstacle to overcome.

Trust is a longstanding challenge in computing [27]. Secure messaging is only secure if you trust WhatsApp, for example, to exchange keys properly, or if you know enough to verify exchanged keys manually, or if you trust your messaging partners not to reveal the content of your messages. Yet the biggest success to date in getting users to adopt secure communication—the use of secure messaging applications—is not due to users choosing security or privacy but because users migrate to applications with large user bases and convenient functionality, which happen to use end-to-end encryption [4]. It is not clear how email can follow the same path. Getting users to adopt secure email services may require gains in user understanding of risks and trust in solutions that mitigate those risks. The field of risk communication which has been used successfully for many years in public health, may offer a path toward helping users understand and cope with online security risks [112,156].

Removing Private Key Management Barriers. There are numerous open questions regarding how typical (non-enterprise) users [132] will manage the full key life cycle, which includes private key storage, expiration, backup, and recovery [105, §13.7]. These questions are complicated by issues such as whether to use separate keys for encrypting email during transmission, as opposed to those for long-term storage [21]. Storing keys in trusted hardware where they cannot be exfiltrated solves some storage issues, but also requires users to create backup hardware keys and revoke keys stored in lost or stolen devices. It is worth noting that major browsers and operating systems now support synchronizing passwords across user devices (under a user account with the provider), and one part of solving key management problems may involve using similar techniques to synchronize private keys.

Addressing Archive Vulnerability. One of the consequences of high-profile phishing attacks in recent years has been the digital theft of the extensive information stored in long-term email archives of various individuals, companies, and organizations. It is ironic that the most active areas of research into securing email are largely orthogonal to the email security issues reported in the news. While data leaks might be categorized as a general data security issue, the way email products and architectures are designed (*e.g.,* emails archived by default, mail servers accessible by password) are inculpatory factors. Research on technical solutions, revised social norms about email retention, and other approaches could be helpful in addressing this issue.

7   Concluding Remarks

Deployment and adoption of end-to-end encrypted email continue to face many technical challenges, particularly related to key management. Our analysis indicates that conflicting interests among stakeholders explains the fragmented nature of existing secure email solutions and the lack of widespread adoption. This suggests it is time to acknowledge that a one-size-fits-all (*i.e.,* for all target scenarios, environments, and user classes) solution or architecture will not emerge. In particular, we find the strongest conflicts among stakeholders over exceptional access, sender pseudonymity, server-side content-processing, and persistent access (T4). In each case, at least one stakeholder strongly prioritizes one of these properties while another strongly opposes it.

In this light, a significant barrier to progress is opposition to any new product or service that does not meet one stakeholder's particular needs, though it works well for others. A path forward is to acknowledge the need for alternate approaches and support advancement of alternatives in parallel. Divided communities and differing visions can lead to paralysis if we insist on a single solution, but it can also be a strength if we agree that multiple solutions can co-exist.

Full Version. In the full version of this paper [25], we provide a detailed evaluation framework for secure email systems. Using the same properties as our stakeholder analysis, we evaluate existing secure email systems. The definition of each property is given, along with an explanation of how a given secure email system is rated to have full support, partial support, or no support in terms of meeting this property. This analysis shows how different secure email systems line up with the needs of each stakeholder. Highlighting the properties that are important to a stakeholder reveals which solutions serve them well or poorly.

Acknowledgments. We are grateful to the reviewers for spirited feedback, and the final version was highly reshaped based on their suggestions. J. Clark acknowledges funding from the NSERC/Raymond Chabot Grant Thornton/Catallaxy Industrial Research Chair and his Discovery Grant. P.C. van Oorschot acknowledges NSERC funding for both his Canada Research Chair and a Discovery Grant. K. Seamons and D. Zappala acknowledge support by the National Science Foundation Grant No. CNS-1816929.

References

1. Abelson, H., et al.: The risks of key recovery, key escrow, and trusted third-party encryption. World Wide Web J. **2**(3), 241–257 (1997)
2. Abelson, H., et al.: Keys under doormats: mandating insecurity by requiring government access to all data and communications. J. Cybersecurity **1**(1) (2015)
3. Abu-Salma, R., et al.: The security blanket of the chat world: an analytic evaluation and a user study of Telegram. In: European Workshop on Usable Security (EuroUSEC 2017). Internet Society (2017)

4. Abu-Salma, R., Sasse, M.A., Bonneau, J., Danilova, A., Naiakshina, A., Smith, M.: Obstacles to the adoption of secure communication tools. In: IEEE Symposium on Security & Privacy (2017)
5. Andersen, K., Long, B., Blank, S., Kucherawy, M.: Authenticated Received Chain (ARC) protocol. RFC 8617, IETF, July 2019
6. Arends, R., Austein, R., Larson, M., Massey, D., Rose, S.: DNS security introduction and requirements. RFC 4033, March 2005
7. Atwater, E., Bocovich, C., Hengartner, U., Lank, E., Goldberg, I.: Leading Johnny to water: Designing for usability and trust. In: SOUPS (2015)
8. Autocrypt Team: Autocrypt level 1 specification, release 1.1.0, April 2019
9. Back, A.: Hashcash - A Denial of service counter-measure. Technical report, hashcash.org (2002). http://www.hashcash.org/hashcash.pdf
10. Bai, W., Namara, M., Qian, Y., Kelley, P.G., Mazurek, M.L., Kim, D.: An inconvenient trust: User attitudes toward security and usability tradeoffs for key-directory encryption systems. In: SOUPS (2016)
11. Balenson, D.: Privacy enhancement for Internet electronic mail: Part III: Algorithms, modes, and identifiers. RFC 1423, February 1993
12. Barnes, R.L.: DANE: taking TLS authentication to the next level using DNSSEC. IETF J. **7**(2) (2011)
13. Basin, D., Cremers, C., Kim, T.H.J., Perrig, A., Sasse, R., Szalachowski, P.: ARPKI: attack resilient public-key infrastructure. In: CCS (2014)
14. Bellovin, S.M.: A look back at "security problems in the TCP/IP protocol suite". In: ACSAC (2004)
15. Birk, V., Marques, H., Shelburn, Koechli, S.: pretty Easy privacy (pEp): Privacy by default. Internet-Draft draft-birk-pep-06, IETF, November 2020. https://datatracker.ietf.org/doc/html/draft-birk-pep-06, work in progress
16. Boldyreva, A., Goyal, V., Kumar, V.: Identity-based encryption with efficient revocation. In: CCS (2008)
17. Borisov, N., Goldberg, I., Brewer, E.: Off-the-record communication, or, why not to use PGP. In: WPES (2004)
18. Brown, I., Laurie, B.: Security against compelled disclosure. In: ACSAC (2000)
19. Callas, J., Donnerhacke, L., Finney, H., Shaw, D., Thayer, R.: OpenPGP message format. RFC 4880, November 2007
20. Caputo, D.D., Pfleeger, S.L., Freeman, J.D., Johnson, M.E.: Going spear phishing: Exploring embedded training and awareness. IEEE S&P Mag. **12**(1) (2014)
21. Chandramouli, R., Garfinkel, S.L., Nightingale, S.J., Rose, S.W.: Trustworthy email. Special Publication NIST SP 800-177 Rev.1, 26 Feb 2019
22. Chatterjee, R., et al.: The spyware used in intimate partner violence. In: 2018 IEEE Symposium on Security and Privacy, SP 2018, Proceedings, 21–23 May 2018, pp. 441–458 (2018)
23. Chaum, D.: Designated confirmer signatures. In: De Santis, A. (ed.) EUROCRYPT 1994. LNCS, vol. 950, pp. 86–91. Springer, Heidelberg (1995). https://doi.org/10.1007/BFb0053427
24. Chen, J., Paxson, V., Jiang, J.: Composition kills: A case study of email sender authentication. In: USENIX Security (2020)
25. Clark, J., van Oorschot, P.C., Ruoti, S., Seamons, K.E., Zappala, D.: Sok: Securing email–a stakeholder-based analysis. Technical report 1804.07706, arXiv v2, 25 October 2020
26. Clark, J., van Oorschot, P.C.: SSL and HTTPS: revisiting past challenges and evaluating certificate trust model enhancements. In: IEEE Symposium on Security & Privacy (2013)

27. Computing Researach Association: Four grand challenges in trustworthy computing (2003)
28. Cooper, D., Santesson, S., Farrell, S., Boeyen, S., Housley, R., Polk, W.: Internet X.509 public key infrastructure certificate and certificate revocation list (CRL) profile. RFC 5280, May 2008
29. Crocker, D.: Internet mail architecture. RFC 5598, IETF (2009)
30. Crocker, D., Hallam-Baker, P., Hansen, T.: DomainKeys Identified Mail (DKIM) service overview. RFC 5585, July 2009
31. Danezis, G., Dingledine, R., Mathewson, N.: Mixminion: design of a type iii anonymous remailer protocol. In: 2003 Symposium on Security and Privacy, 2003, pp. 2–15 (2003)
32. Dechand, S., Naiakshina, A., Danilova, A., Smith, M.: In encryption we don't trust: the effect of end-to-end encryption to the masses on user perception. In: EuroS&P 2019 (2019)
33. Dechand, S., et al.: An empirical study of textual key-fingerprint representations. In: USENIX Security (2016)
34. Diffie, W., Landau, S.: Privacy on the Line: The Politics of Wiretapping and Encryption. The MIT Press, second edition 2007 (472 pages), first edition 1998 (352 pages)
35. Dingledine, R., Mathewson, N.: Anonymity loves company: usability and the network effect. In: WEIS (2006)
36. Dingledine, R., Mathewson, N., Syverson, P.: Tor: The second-generation onion router. In: USENIX Security (2004)
37. Durumeric, Z., et al.: Neither snow nor rain nor MITM...: An empirical analysis of email delivery security. In: IMC (2015)
38. Dwork, C., Naor, M.: Pricing via processing or combatting junk mail. In: Brickell, E.F. (ed.) CRYPTO 1992. LNCS, vol. 740, pp. 139–147. Springer, Heidelberg (1993)
39. Elkins, M., Torto, D.D., Levien, R., Roessler, T.: MIME security with OpenPGP. RFC 3156, August 2001
40. Englehardt, S., Han, J., Narayanan, A.: I never signed up for this: privacy implications of email tracking. PETS (2018)
41. Fagan, M., Khan, M.M.H.: Why do they do what they do?: a study of what motivates users to (not) follow computer security advice. In: SOUPS (2016)
42. Farrell, S.: Why don't we encrypt our email? IEEE Internet Computing, vol. 13(1) (2009)
43. Fenton, J.: Analysis of threats motivating DomainKeys Identified Mail (DKIM). RFC 4686, September 2006
44. Florêncio, D., Herley, C., van Oorschot, P.C.: An administrator's guide to Internet password research. In: USENIX LISA (2014)
45. Foster, I.D., Larson, J., Masich, M., Snoeren, A.C., Savage, S., Levchenko, K.: Security by any other name: on the effectiveness of provider based email security. In: CCS (2015)
46. Franceschi-Bicchierai, L.: Even the inventor of PGP doesn't use PGP. motherboard.vice.com, September 2015. https://motherboard.vice.com/en_us/article/vvbw9a/even-the-inventor-of-pgp-doesnt-use-pgp
47. Franklin, J., Perrig, A., Paxson, V., Savage, S.: An inquiry into the nature and causes of the wealth of Internet miscreants. In: CCS (2007)
48. Freed, N., Borenstein, N.S.: Multipurpose Internet Mail Extensions (MIME) Part one: Format of Internet message bodies. RFC 2045, November 1996

49. Fry, A., Chiasson, S., Somayaji, A.: Not sealed but delivered: the (un) usability of S/MIME today. In: ASIA (2012)
50. Garfinkel, S.L., Margrave, D., Schiller, J.I., Nordlander, E., Miller, R.C.: How to make secure email easier to use. In: CHI (2005)
51. Garfinkel, S.L., Miller, R.C.: Johnny 2: A user test of key continuity management with S/MIME and Outlook Express. In: SOUPS (2005)
52. Gasser, U., et al.: Don't panic: Making progress on the "going dark" debate. Berkman Center for Internet & Society at Harvard Law School (2016)
53. Gaw, S., Felten, E.W., Fernandez-Kelly, P.: Secrecy, flagging, and paranoia: adoption criteria in encrypted email. In: CHI (2006)
54. Geambasu, R., Kohno, T., Levy, A.A., Levy, H.M.: Vanish: increasing data privacy with self-destructing data. In: USENIX Security Symposium (2009)
55. Gellens, R., Klensin, J.: Message submission for mail. RFC 6409, November 2011
56. Gentry, C.: A fully homomorphic encryption scheme. Ph.D. thesis, Stanford University (2009)
57. Goldberg, I., Wagner, D., Brewer, E.: Privacy-enhancing technologies for the Internet. In: IEEE COMPCON. Digest of Papers, February 1997. https://doi.org/10.1109/CMPCON.1997.584680
58. Goldberg, I.: Privacy-enhancing technologies for the Internet, II: Five years later. In: PETS (2003)
59. Goldberg, I.: Privacy enhancing technologies for the Internet III: Ten years later. In: Acquisti, A., Gritzalis, S., Lambrinoudakis, C., De Capitani di Vimercati, S. (eds.) Digital Privacy: Theory, Technologies and Practices. Auerbach Press (2007)
60. Goldberg, I.A.: A Pseudonymous Communications Infrastructure for the Internet. Ph.D. thesis, UC Berkeley (2000)
61. Goodin, D.: Use of Tor helped FBI ID suspect in bomb hoax case. Ars Technica, December 2013
62. Google: Hosted S/MIME by Google provides enhanced security for Gmail in the enterprise (2019). https://security.googleblog.com/2017/02/hosted-smime-by-google-provides.html
63. Hadnagy, C.: Social Engineering: The Art of Human Hacking. Wiley (2010)
64. Havron, S., Freed, D., Chatterjee, R., McCoy, D., Dell, N., Ristenpart, T.: Clinical computer security for victims of intimate partner violence. In: USENIX Security (2019)
65. Herley, C.: So long, and no thanks for the externalities: the rational rejection of security advice by users. In: NSPW (2009)
66. Hoffman, P.: Allowing relaying in SMTP: A series of surveys. Internet Mail Consortium Report 16 (2002)
67. Hoffman, P.E.: SMTP service extension for secure SMTP over Transport Layer Security. RFC 3207, February 2002
68. Hoffman, P.E., Schlyter, J.: The DNS-Based Authentication of Named Entities (DANE) Transport Layer Security (TLS) Protocol: TLSA. RFC 6698, August 2012
69. Holz, R., Amann, J., Mehani, O., Wachs, M., Kaafar, M.A.: TLS in the wild: an Internet-wide analysis of TLS-based protocols for electronic communication. In: NDSS (2016)
70. Housley, R.: Cryptographic Message Syntax (CMS). RFC 5652, September 2009
71. Houttuin, J.: A tutorial on gatewaying between x.400 and internet mail. RFC 1506, IETF (2016)
72. Hsiao, H.C., et al.: A study of user-friendly hash comparison schemes. In: ACSAC (2009)

73. Hu, H., Wang, G.: End-to-end measurements of email spoofing attacks. In: USENIX Security (2018)
74. Hushmail (2019). https://www.hushmail.com/
75. Iedemska, J., Stringhini, G., Kemmerer, R., Kruegel, C., Vigna, G.: The tricks of the trade: what makes spam campaigns successful? In: SPW (2014)
76. Jakobsson, M., Sako, K., Impagliazzo, R.: Designated verifier proofs and their applications. In: EUROCRYPT (1996)
77. Jones, S.M., Rae-Grant, J., Adams, J.T., Andersen, K.: Recommended Usage of the Authenticated Received Chain (ARC). Internet-draft, IETF, May 2020
78. Kaliski, B.: Privacy enhancement for Internet electronic mail: Part IV: Key certification and related services. RFC 1424, February 1993
79. Kamara, S.: Encrypted search. XRDS **21**(3), 30–34 (2015). https://doi.org/10.1145/2730908
80. Kang, R., Dabbish, L., Fruchter, N., Kiesler, S.: "My data just goes everywhere:" user mental models of the Internet and implications for privacy and security. In: SOUPS (2015)
81. Kapadia, A.: A case (study) for usability in secure email communication. IEEE S&P Mag. **5**(2) (2007)
82. Kent, S.: Privacy enhancement for Internet electronic mail: Part II: Certificate-based key management. RFC 1422, February 1993
83. Kent, S.T.: Internet privacy enhanced mail. CACM **36**(8) (1993)
84. Kitterman, D.S.: Sender Policy Framework (SPF) for authorizing use of domains in email, version 1. RFC 7208, April 2014
85. Klensin, J.C.: Simple Mail Transfer Protocol. RFC 5321, October 2008
86. Kucherawy, M.: Simple Mail Transfer Protocol. RFC 8601, IETF, May 2019
87. Kucherawy, M., Crocker, D., Hansen, T.: DomainKeys Identified Mail (DKIM) signatures. RFC 6376, September 2011
88. Kucherawy, M., Zwicky, E.: Domain-based Message Authentication, Reporting, and Conformance (DMARC). RFC 7489, March 2015
89. Laszka, A., Vorobeychik, Y., Koutsoukos, X.D.: Optimal personalized filtering against spear-phishing attacks. In: AAAI (2015)
90. Laurie, B., Clayton, R.: Proof-of-work proves not to work; version 0.2. In: WEIS (2004)
91. Lauzon, E.: The Philip Zimmermann investigation: the start of the fall of export restrictions on encryption software under first amendment free speech issues. Syracuse L. Rev. **48**, 1307 (1998)
92. Lerner, A., Zeng, E., Roesner, F.: Confidante: usable encrypted email: a case study with lawyers and journalists. In: IEEE EuroS&P (2017)
93. Levchenko, K., et al.: Click trajectories: end-to-end analysis of the spam value chain. In: IEEE Symposium on Security & Privacy (2011)
94. Levien, R., McCarthy, L., Blaze, M.: Transparent Internet e-mail security. In: NDSS (1996)
95. Levison, L.: Dark Internet Mail Environment architecture and specifications, March 2015. https://darkmail.info/downloads/dark-internet-mail-environment-march-2015.pdf
96. Linn, J.: Privacy enhancement for Internet electronic mail: Part I: Message encryption and authentication procedures. RFC 1421, February 1993
97. Liu, D., Hao, S., Wang, H.: All your DNS records point to us: understanding the security threats of dangling DNS records. In: CCS (2016)
98. Margolis, D., et al.: SMTP MTA Strict Transport Security. RFC 8461, IETF (2018)

99. Marlinspike, M.: GPG and me. moxie.org, February 2015. https://moxie.org/2015/02/24/gpg-and-me.html

100. Masone, C., Smith, S.W.: ABUSE: PKI for real-world email trust. In: Martinelli, F., Preneel, B. (eds.) EuroPKI 2009. LNCS, vol. 6391, pp. 146–162. Springer, Heidelberg (2010)

101. Mayer, W., Zauner, A., Schmiedecker, M., Huber, M.: No need for black chambers: testing TLS in the e-mail ecosystem at large. In: IEEE ARES (2016)

102. McCoy, D., et al.: PharmaLeaks: understanding the business of online pharmaceutical affiliate programs. In: USENIX Security Symposium (2012)

103. McGregor, S.E., Watkins, E.A., Al-Ameen, M.N., Caine, K., Roesner, F.: When the weakest link is strong: secure collaboration in the case of the Panama papers. In: USENIX Security Symposium (2017)

104. Melara, M.S., Blankstein, A., Bonneau, J., Felten, E.W., Freedman, M.J.: CONIKS: bringing key transparency to end users. In: USENIX Security Symposium (2015)

105. Menezes, A.J., van Oorschot, P.C., Vanstone, S.A.: Handbook of Applied Cryptography. CRC Press (1996)

106. Meyerovich, L., Livshits, B.: ConScript: specifying and enforcing fine-grained security policies for JavaScript in the browser. In: IEEE Symposium on Security & Privacy (2010)

107. Mitnick, K.D., Simon, W.L.: The Art of Deception: Controlling the Human Element of Security. John Wiley & Sons (2011)

108. Nakamoto, S.: Bitcoin: A peer-to-peer electionic cash system. Unpublished (2008). https://bitcoin.org/bitcoin.pdf

109. Narayanan, A.: What happened to the crypto dream?, Part 1. IEEE S&P Magazine 11 (2013)

110. Narayanan, A.: What happened to the crypto dream?, Part 2. IEEE S&P Magazine 11 (2013)

111. Newman, C.: Using TLS with IMAP, POP3 and ACAP. RFC 2595, June 1999

112. Nurse, J.R., Creese, S., Goldsmith, M., Lamberts, K.: Trustworthy and effective communication of cybersecurity risks: a review. In: Workshop on Socio-Technical Aspects in Security and Trust (STAST 2011). IEEE (2011)

113. Orman, H.: Encrypted Email: The History and Technology of Message Privacy. Springer (2015). https://doi.org/10.1007/978-3-319-21344-6

114. Partridge, C.: The technical development of Internet email. IEEE Ann. History Comput. 30(2), 3–29 (2008)

115. Pasquier, T.F.M., Singh, J., Eyers, D., Bacon, J.: Camflow: managed data-sharing for cloud services. IEEE Trans. Cloud Comput. 5(3), 472–484 (2017)

116. Perrin, T., Marlinspike, M.: Double ratchet algorithm, revision 1. signal.org (2016)

117. Protonmail (2019). https://protonmail.com/

118. Ramsdell, B., Turner, S.: Secure/Multipurpose Internet Mail Extensions (S/MIME) version 3.2 message specification. RFC 5751, January 2010

119. Ramsdell, B.C.: S/MIME version 3 message specification. RFC 2633, June 1999

120. The Radicati Group: Email statistics report, 2020–2024 (2019)

121. Renaud, K., Volkamer, M., Renkema-Padmos, A.: Why doesn't Jane protect her privacy? In: PETS (2014)

122. Rivest, R.L., Shamir, A., Tauman, Y.: How to leak a secret. In: ASIACRYPT (2001)

123. Rivner, U.: Anatomy of an attack. RSA blog, 1 April 2011. http://web.archive.org/web/20110413224418/blogs.rsa.com:80/rivner/anatomy-of-an-attack/

124. Romera, P., Gallego, C.S.: How ICIJ deals with massive data leaks like the Panama Papers and Paradise Papers, 3 July 2018. https://www.icij.org/blog/2018/07/how-icij-deals-with-massive-data-leaks-like-the-panama-papers-and-paradise-papers/
125. Roth, V., Straub, T., Richter, K.: Security and usability engineering with particular attention to electronic mail. Int. J. Hum.-Comput. Stud. **63**(1), 51–73 (2005)
126. Ruoti, S., et al.: A usability study of four secure email tools using paired participants. ACM Trans. Privacy Secur. **22**(2), 22–29 (2019)
127. Ruoti, S., et al.: "We're on the same page": a usability study of secure email using pairs of novice users. In: CHI (2016)
128. Ruoti, S., Andersen, J., Hendershot, T., Zappala, D., Seamons, K.: Private webmail 2.0: Simple and easy-to-use secure email. In: UIST (2016)
129. Ruoti, S., Andersen, J., Monson, T., Zappala, D., Seamons, K.: A comparative usability study of key management in secure email. In: SOUPS (2018)
130. Ruoti, S., Kim, N., Burgon, B., Van Der Horst, T., Seamons, K.: Confused Johnny: when automatic encryption leads to confusion and mistakes. In: SOUPS (2013)
131. Ruoti, S., Monson, T., Wu, J., Zappala, D., Seamons, K.: Weighing context and trade-offs: how suburban adults selected their online security posture. In: SOUPS (2017)
132. Ruoti, S., Seamons, K.: Johnny's journey toward usable secure email. IEEE Secur. Privacy **17**(6), 72–76 (2019)
133. Ryan, M.D.: Enhanced certificate transparency and end-to-end encrypted mail. In: NDSS (2014)
134. Santos, N., Gummadi, K.P., Rodrigues, R.: Towards trusted cloud computing. HotCloud **9**(9), 3 (2009)
135. Sasse, A.: Scaring and bullying people into security won't work. IEEE S&P Magazine 13(3) (2015)
136. Schneier, B., Hall, C.: An improved e-mail security protocol. In: ACSAC (1997)
137. Schröder, S., Huber, M., Wind, D., Rottermanner, C.: When SIGNAL hits the fan: on the usability and security of state-of-the-art secure mobile messaging. In: EuroUSEC (2016)
138. Shamir, A.: Identity-based cryptosystems and signature schemes. In: Crypto (1984)
139. Siemborski, R., Gulbrandsen, A.: IMAP extension for Simple Authentication and Security Layer (SASL) initial client response. RFC 4959, September 2007
140. Siemborski, R., Melnikov, A.: SMTP service extension for authentication. RFC 4954, July 2007
141. Siemborski, R., Menon-Sen, A.: The Post Office Protocol (POP3) Simple Authentication and Security Layer (SASL) authentication mechanism. RFC 5034, July 2007
142. Song, D.X., Wagner, D., Perrig, A.: Practical techniques for searches on encrypted data. In: IEEE Symposium on Security & Privacy (2000)
143. Sparrow, E., Halpin, H., Kaneko, K., Pollan, R.: LEAP: a next-generation client VPN and encrypted email provider. In: CANS (2016)
144. Stewart, G., Lacey, D.: Death by a thousand facts: criticising the technocratic approach to information security awareness. Information Management & Computer Security 20(1) (2012)
145. Stringhini, G., Egele, M., Zarras, A., Holz, T., Kruegel, C., Vigna, G.: B@bel: leveraging email delivery for spam mitigation. In: USENIX Security Symposium (2012)

146. Tutanota (2019). https://tutanota.com/
147. Unger, N., et al.: SoK: secure messaging. In: IEEE Symposium on Security & Privacy (2015)
148. Valsorda, F.: Op-ed: I'm throwing in the towel in PGP, and I work in security. Ars Technica, December 2016
149. Van Acker, S., De Ryck, P., Desmet, L., Piessens, F., Joosen, W.: WebJail: least-privilege integration of third-party components in web mashups. In: ACSAC (2011)
150. Vaziripour, E., Wu, J., Farahbakhsh, R., Seamons, K., O'Neill, M., Zappala, D.: A survey of the privacy preferences and practices of iranian users of telegram. In: Workshop on Usable Security (USEC) (2018)
151. Vaziripour, E., et al.: Is that you, Alice? a usability study of the authentication ceremony of secure messaging applications. In: SOUPS (2017)
152. Wash, R.: Folk models of home computer security. In: SOUPS (2010)
153. Whitten, A., Tygar, J.D.: Why Johnny can't encrypt: a usability evaluation of PGP 5.0. In: USENIX Security Symposium (1999)
154. Wolchok, S., et al.: Defeating Vanish with low-cost sybil attacks against large DHTs. In: NDSS (2010)
155. Wolthusen, S.D.: A distributed multipurpose mail guard. In: IAW (2003)
156. Wu, J., Gatrell, C., Howard, D., Tyler, J., Vaziripour, E., Seamons, K., Zappala, D.: "Something isn't secure, but I'm not sure how that translates into a problem": promoting autonomy by designing for understanding in Signal. In: SOUPS (2019)
157. Wu, J., Zappala, D.: When is a tree really a truck? exploring mental models of encryption. In: SOUPS (2018)
158. Zimmermann, P.: PGP Source Code and Internals. MIT Press, Boston (1995)
159. Zimmermann, P.: PGP marks 10th anniversary, 5 June 2001
160. Zimmermann, P.R.: The Official PGP User's Guide. MIT Press, Cambridge (1995)

Zero-Knowledge Proofs

Zero-Knowledge Proofs for Set Membership: Efficient, Succinct, Modular

Daniel Benarroch[1], Matteo Campanelli[2], Dario Fiore[3], Kobi Gurkan[4],
and Dimitris Kolonelos[3,5](✉)

[1] QEDIT, Tel Aviv-Yafo, Israel
daniel@qed-it.com
[2] Aarhus University, Aarhus, Denmark
matteo@cs.au.dk
[3] IMDEA Software Institute, Madrid, Spain
dario.fiore@imdea.org
[4] Ethereum Foundation and cLabs, Netanya, Israel
me@kobi.one
[5] Universidad Politécnica de Madrid, Madrid, Spain
dimitris.kolonelos@imdea.org

Abstract. We consider the problem of proving in zero knowledge that an element of a public set satisfies a given property without disclosing the element, i.e., for some u, "$u \in S$ and $P(u)$ holds". This problem arises in many applications (anonymous cryptocurrencies, credentials or whitelists) where, for privacy or anonymity reasons, it is crucial to hide certain data while ensuring properties of such data.

We design new *modular* and *efficient* constructions for this problem through new *commit-and-prove zero-knowledge systems for set membership*, i.e. schemes proving $u \in S$ for a value u that is in a public commitment c_u. We also extend our results to support *non-membership proofs*, i.e. proving $u \notin S$. Being commit-and-prove, our solutions can act as plug-and-play modules in statements of the form "$u \in S$ and $P(u)$ holds" by combining our set (non-)membership systems with any other commit-and-prove scheme for $P(u)$. Also, they work with Pedersen commitments over prime order groups which makes them compatible with popular systems such as Bulletproofs or Groth16.

We implemented our schemes as a software library, and tested experimentally their performance. Compared to previous work that achieves similar properties—the clever techniques combining zkSNARKs and Merkle Trees in Zcash—our solutions offer more flexibility, shorter public parameters and 3.7×–30× faster proving time for a set of size 2^{64}.

1 Introduction

The problem of proving set membership—that a given element x belongs to some set S—arises in many applications, including governmental white-lists to prevent terrorism or money-laundering, voting and anonymous credentials, among others. More recently, this problem also appears at the heart of currency transfer

The full version of the paper can be found at https://eprint.iacr.org/2019/1255.pdf.
N. Borisov and C. Diaz (Eds.): FC 2021, LNCS 12674, pp. 393–414, 2021.
https://doi.org/10.1007/978-3-662-64322-8_19

and identity systems over blockchains. In this setting, parties can first publicly commit to sets of data (through the blockchain itself) and then, by proving set membership, can claim ownership of assets or existence of identity attributes, while ensuring privacy.

A naive approach to check if an element is in a set is to go through all its entries. The complexity of this approach, however, is unacceptable in many scenarios. This is especially true for blockchains, where most of the parties (the verifiers) should run quickly.

How to efficiently verify set membership then? Cryptographic *accumulators* [5] provide a nice solution to this problem. They allow a set of elements to be compressed into a short value (the accumulator) and to generate membership proofs that are short and fast to verify. For security, they require that it should be computationally infeasible to generate a false membership proof.

As of today, we can divide constructions for accumulators into three main categories: Merkle Trees [32]; RSA-based [3,7,11,28]; pairing-based [10,19,34,42]. Approaches based on Merkle Trees[1] allow for short (i.e., $O(1)$) public parameters and accumulator values, whereas the witness for membership proofs is of size $\log(n)$, where n is the size of the set. In RSA-based constructions (which can be actually generalized to any group of unknown order [30], including class groups) both the accumulator and the witness are each a single element in a relatively large hidden-order group $\mathbb{G}$,[2] and thus of constant-size. Schemes that use pairings in elliptic curves such as [10,34] offer small accumulators and small witnesses (which can each be a single element of a prime order bilinear group, e.g., 256 bits) but require large parameters (approximately $O(n)$) and a trusted setup.

In anonymous cryptocurrencies, e.g. Zerocash [4] (but also in other applications such as Anonymous Credentials [14] and whitelists), we also require *privacy*. That is, parties in the system would not want to disclose *which* element in the set is being used to prove membership. Phrased differently, one desires to prove that $u \in S$ without revealing u, or: the proof should be *zero-knowledge* [24] for u. As an example, in Zerocash users want to prove that a coin exists (i.e. belongs to the set of previously sent coins) without revealing which coin it is that they are spending.

In practice it is common that this privacy requirement goes beyond proving membership. In fact, these applications often require proving further properties about the accumulated elements, e.g., that for some element u in the set, property $P(u)$ holds. And this without leaking any more information about u other than what is entailed by P. In other words, we desire zero-knowledge for the statement $R^*(S, u) :=$ "$u \in S$ and $P(u)$".

One way to solve the problem, as done in Zerocash, is to directly apply general-purpose zero-knowledge proofs for R^*, e.g., [25,37]. This approach, how-

---

[1] We can include under this class currently known lattice-based accumulators such as [29,36].

[2] The group $\mathbb{G}$ is typically $\mathbb{Z}_N^*$ where N is an RSA modulus. The size of an element in this group for a standard 128-bit security parameter is of 3072 bits.

ever, tends to be expensive and ad-hoc. One question we aim to tackle is: how to design a more efficient proof system for set membership relations that is also modular?

Specifically, as observed in [12], the design of practical proof systems can benefit from a more modular vision. A modular framework such as the one in [12] not only allows for separation of concerns, but also increases reusability and compatibility in a plug-and-play fashion: the same proof system is designed once and can be reused for the same sub-problem regardless of the context;[3] it can be replaced with a component for the same sub-problem at any time. Also, as [12] shows, this can have a positive impact on efficiency since designing a *special-purpose* proof system for a *specific* relation can lead to significant optimizations. Finally, this compositional approach can also be leveraged to build general-purpose proof systems.

In this work we focus on applying this modular vision to designing *succinct zero-knowledge proofs for set membership*. Following the abstract framework in [12] we investigate how to apply commit-and-prove techniques [13] to our setting. Our approach uses commitments for composability as follows. Consider an efficient zero-knowledge proof system Π for property $P(u)$. Let us also assume it is commit-and-prove, i.e. the verifier can test $P(u)$ by simply holding a commitment $c(u)$ to u. Such Π could be for example a commit-and-prove NIZK such as Bulletproofs [8] or a commit-and-prove zkSNARK such as LegoGroth16 from [12] that are able to operate on Pedersen commitments $c(\cdot)$ over elliptic curves. In order to obtain a proof gadget for set membership, all one needs to design is a commit-and-prove scheme for the relations "$u \in S$" where *both* u and S are committed: u through $c(u)$ and S through some other commitment for sets, such as an accumulator.

Our main contribution is to propose a formalization of this approach and new constructions of succinct zero-knowledge commit-and-prove systems for set membership. In addition, as we detail later, we extend our results to capture proofs of *non-membership*, i.e., to show that $u \notin S$. For our constructions we focus on designing schemes where $c(u)$ is a Pedersen commitment in a prime order group $\mathbb{G}_q$. We focus on linking through Pedersen commitments as these can be (re)used in some of the best state-of-the-art zero-knowledge proof systems for general-purpose relations that offer for example the shortest proofs and verification time (see, e.g., [25] and its efficient commit-and-prove variant [12]), or transparent setup and logarithmic-size proofs [8].

Before describing our results in more detail, we review existing solutions and approaches to realize commit-and-prove zkSNARKs for set membership.

Existing Approaches for Proving Set Membership for Pedersen Commitments. The accumulator of Nguyen [34], by the simple fact of having a succinct pairing-based verification equation, can be combined with standard zero-knowledge proof techniques (e.g., Sigma protocols or the celebrated Groth-Sahai

---

[3] For instance, one can plug a proof system for matrix product $C = A \cdot B$ in any larger context of computation involving matrix multiplication. This regardless of whether, say, we then hash C or if A, B are in turn the output of a different computation.

proofs [26]) to achieve a succinct system with reasonable proving and verification time. The main drawbacks of [34], however, are the large public parameters (i.e. requiring as many prime group elements as the elements in the set) and a high cost for updating the accumulator, to add or remove elements (essentially requiring to recompute the accumulator from scratch).

By using general-purpose zkSNARKs one can obtain a solution with constant-size proofs based on Merkle Trees: prove that there exists a valid path which connects a given leaf to the root; this requires proving correctness of about $\log n$ hash function computations (e.g., SHA256). This solution yields a constant-size proof and requires $\log n$-size public parameters if one uses pre-processing zkSNARKs such as [25,37]. On the other hand, often when proving a relation such as $R^*(S,u) :=$ "$u \in S$ and $P(u)$" the bulk of the work stems from the set membership proof. This is the case in Zcash or Filecoin where the predicate $P(\cdot)$ is sufficiently small.

Finally, another solution that admits constant-size public parameters and proofs is the protocol of [11]. Specifically, Camenisch and Lysyanskaya showed how to prove in zero-knowledge that an element u committed in a Pedersen commitment over a prime order group $\mathbb{G}_q$ is a member of an RSA accumulator. In principle this solution would fit the criteria of the gadget we are looking for. Nonetheless, its concrete instantiations show a few limitations in terms of efficiency and flexibility. The main problem is that, for its security to hold, we need a prime order group (the commitment space) and the primes (the message space) to be quite large, for example[4] $q > 2^{519}$. But having such a large prime order group may be undesirable in practice for efficiency reasons. In fact the group $\mathbb{G}_q$ is the one that is used to instantiate more proof systems that need to interact and be linked with the Pedersen commitment.

1.1 Our Contributions

We investigate the problem of designing commit-and-prove zero-knowledge systems for set membership and non-membership that can be used in a modular way and *efficiently* composed with other zero-knowledge proof systems for potentially arbitrary relations. Our main results are the following.

First, building upon the view of recent works on composable proofs [2,12], we define a formal framework for commit-and-prove zkSNARKs (CP-SNARKs) for set (non-)membership. The main application of this framework is a compiler that, given a CP-SNARK $\mathsf{CP_{mem}}$ for set membership and any other CP-SNARK CP_R for a relation R, yields a CP-SNARK CP for the composed relation "$u \in S \wedge \exists \omega : R(u, \omega)$". As a further technical contribution, our framework extends the one in [12] in order to work with commitments from multiple schemes (including set commitments, e.g., accumulators).

Second, we propose new efficient constructions of CP-SNARKs for set membership and non-membership, in which elements of the accumulated set can be

---

[4] More specifically: the elements of a set need to be prime numbers in a range (A, B) such that $q/2 > A^2 - 1 > B \cdot 2^{2\lambda_{st}+2}$. If aiming at 128 bits of security level one can meet this constraint by choosing for example $A = 2^{259}$, $B = 2^{260}$ and $q > 2^{519}$.

committed with a Pedersen commitment in a prime order group $\mathbb{G}_q$—a setting that, as argued before, is of practical relevance due to the widespread use of these commitments and of proof systems that operate on them. In more detail, we propose: four schemes (two for set membership and two for non-membership) that enjoy constant-size public parameters and are based on RSA accumulators for committing to sets, and a scheme over pairings that has public parameters linear in the size of the set, but where the set can remain hidden.

Finally, we implement our solutions in a software library and experimentally evaluate their performance; see below for details.

Like the recent works [2] and [12], our work can be seen as showing yet another setting—set membership—where the efficiency of SNARKs can benefit from a modular design.

RSA-Based Constructions. Our first scheme, a CP-SNARK for set membership based on RSA accumulators, supports a large domain for the set of accumulated elements, represented by binary strings of a given length η. Our second scheme, also based on RSA accumulators, supports elements that are prime numbers of exactly μ bits (for a given μ). Neither scheme requires an a-priori bound on the cardinality of the set. Both schemes improve the proof-of-knowledge protocol by Camenisch and Lysyanskaya [11]: (i) we can work with a prime order group $\mathbb{G}_q$ of "standard" size, e.g., 256 bits, whereas [11] needs a much larger $\mathbb{G}_q$ (see above). We note that the size of $\mathbb{G}_q$ affects not only the efficiency of the set membership protocol but also the efficiency of any other protocol that needs to interact with commitments to alleged set members; (ii) we can support flexible choices for the size of set elements. For instance, in the second scheme, we could work with primes of about 50 or 80 bits,[5] which in practice captures virtually unbounded sets and can make the accumulator operations 4–5× faster compared to using $\approx$ 256-bits primes as in [11].

Our main technical contribution here involves a new way to link a proof of membership for RSA accumulators to a Pedersen commitment in a prime order group, together with a careful analysis showing this can be secure under parameters *not requiring a larger prime order group* (as in [11]). See Sect. 4 for further details.

Pairing-Based Construction. Our pairing-based scheme for set membership supports set elements in $\mathbb{Z}_q$, where q is the order of bilinear groups, while the sets are arbitrary subsets of $\mathbb{Z}_q$ of cardinality less than a fixed a-priori bound n. This scheme has the disadvantage of having public parameters linear in n, but has other advantages in comparison to previous schemes with a similar limitation (and in comparison to the RSA-based schemes above): it supports commitments to the set that are hiding and extractable; it works entirely in a single "group setup", that of the bilinear group $\mathbb{Z}_q$. The scheme is based on the EDRAX Vector Commitment [15] for the set commitment combined with the verifiable

---

[5] When prime representation is suitable for the application, distinct primes can be generated without a hash fuction (e.g. even sequential primes).

polynomial delegation scheme of zk-vSQL [41]. Our construction appears in the full version [6].

Extensions to Set Non-membership. We propose extensions of both our CP-SNARK framework and RSA constructions to deal with proving *set non-membership*, namely proving in zero-knowledge that $u \notin S$ with respect to a commitment $c(u)$ and a committed set S. Our two RSA-based schemes for non-membership have the same features as the analogous membership schemes mentioned above: the first scheme supports sets whose elements are strings of length η, the second one supports elements that are prime numbers of μ bits, and both work with elements committed using Pedersen in a prime order group and sets committed with RSA accumulators. A byproduct of sharing the same parameters is that we can easily compose the set-membership and non-membership schemes, via our framework, in order to prove statements like $u \in S_1 \wedge u \notin S_2$. Our technical contribution in the design of these schemes is a zero-knowledge protocol for non-membership witnesses of RSA accumulators that is linked to Pedersen commitments in prime order groups.

Implementation and Experiments. We have implemented our RSA-based[6] schemes for membership and non-membership as a Rust library which is publicly available [1]. Our library is implemented in a modular fashion to work with any elliptic curve from **libzexe** [38] and Ristretto from **curve25519-dalek** [31]. This choice enables everyone to easily and efficiently combine our CP-SNARKs in a modular way with other CP-SNARKs implemented over these elliptic curves, such as Bulletproofs [8] and LegoGroth16 [12].

We evaluated our RSA-based constructions and compared them against highly optimized solutions based on Merkle Trees.[7] Our schemes achieve significantly better performance in proving time while slightly compromising on proof size and verification time. Our implementation is fast, yet we have not heavily optimized it and thus expect the results can be further improved. See appendix for further details.

Our solutions supporting sets of arbitrary elements achieve a proving time that is up to[8] 3.7× faster for set membership (309 ms vs. 1.14 s). and up to 7× faster for set non-membership (325 ms vs. 2.28 s)[9]

Our solutions where set elements are large prime numbers (i.e., of 252-bit size) offer even better results: our proving time is 4.5×–23.5× faster for membership and 6.8×–36× faster for non-membership (depending on the depth of the Merkle tree used in the comparison). We also show an optimization that, at the price

---

[6] For the implementation we focused on schemes where the public parameters do not depend on the set size; hence, we did not implement the pairing-based solutions.

[7] For our experiments we consider Merkle Trees using Pedersen Hash over JubJub [27].

[8] We stress the proving time for our construction does not vary when the set grows. On the other hand this time varies for solutions based on Merkle trees.

[9] These ratios refer to a comparison against Interval Merkle Trees which require opening two paths to prove non-membership. When compared against Sparse Merkle Trees, our solutions show similar improvement ratios.

	P_{time}	V_{time}	$|crs|$	$|\Pi|$	P_{memory}
Merkle trees through [25] zkSNARK					
Pedersen - depth 16	356	2.8	5023	0.192	35
Pedersen - depth 32	607	2.8	10047	0.192	49
Pedersen - depth 64	1135	2.8	20094	0.192	79
SHA256 - depth 16	2563	2.8	82430	0.192	196
SHA256 - depth 32	5066	2.8	164737	0.192	423
SHA256 - depth 64	10005	2.8	329352	0.192	913
	ms	ms	KB	KB	MB
Our Solutions					
Our 1st scheme - 252bit primes	309.10	31.44	6852	4.4	45
Our 2nd scheme - 252bit primes	48.14	29.10	86	4.4	5
Our 2nd scheme - 63bit primes	43.91	27.49	86	4.4	5
	ms	ms	KB	KB	MB

Fig. 1. Set Membership benchmarks. The columns refer to prover time (P_{time}), verifier time (V_{time}), size of the common reference string ($|crs|$), size of the proof ($|\Pi|$) and memory consumed for the proof (P_{memory}) respectively.

of achieving computational (instead of statistical) zero-knowledge, is 2x faster (see full version). Sets of prime numbers can for example capture the case of sets made of hiding commitments that are prime numbers. In Sect. 5 we discuss how this can be relevant for a slight variant of the Zerocash protocol where commitments can be made prime numbers.

In the table of Fig. 1 we show our benchmarks for our two schemes described above(we benchmark the second for prime element of 252 and 63 bits resp.) and for set membership proofs using Merkle trees of different depths-using Pedersen and SHA256 hash functions resp.- and [25]. The details of the experiments are in the full version [6].

Transparent Instantiations. In the full version of our paper, we generalize our building blocks for RSA groups to any hidden-order group. As a consequence, we obtain variants of our RSA-based schemes with *transparent setup* through class groups and a transparent CP-NIZK such as Bulletproofs. Class groups are more expensive than traditional RSA groups; in this setting we still obtain performance (proving time 12 s; $|\Pi| = 6.4$ KB) outperforming other transparent solution for large Merkle trees, roughly 2^{64} leaves (see [40, Fig. 5] which summarizes performances of transparent SNARKs used to prove Merkle tree computations using SHA256 as hash). These potential gains come at the price of a relatively longer verification (compared to other solutions): 6.4 s.

1.2   Other Related Work

Ozdemir et al. [35] recently proposed a solution to scale operations on RSA accumulators inside a SNARK. In particular, their approach scales when these operations are *batched* (i.e., when proving membership of many elements at the same time); for example, they surpass a 2^{20}-large Merkle tree when proving batches of at least 600 elements. This approach is attractive in settings where we can delegate a *large* quantity of these checks to an untrusted server as there is a high constant proving cost. In contrast, our approach can achieve faster proving time than Merkle trees already for a single membership check. It is an interesting open problem to adapt our techniques for modular set (non-)membership for the case of batched membership while keeping the tested elements hidden.

1.3   Organization

We give basic definitions in Sect. 2. In Sect. 3 we formalize commit-and-prove zkSNARKs for set membership, and then we describe our main constructions based on RSA accumulators in Sect. 4. Finally, in Sect. 5 we discuss applications. For lack of space, technical details, the RSA-based scheme for non-membership, the pairing-based construction, and our experimental results are in the full version of the paper [6].

2   Preliminaries

We recall basic cryptographic notions used by our schemes; details are in the full version.

Type-Based Commitments. We shall use type-based commitments [20] which allow one to commit to values from different domains under a single commitment key. Through this notion we can formalize commit-and-prove NIZKs that work with commitments from different groups and schemes. Here is a brief description of the syntax: – $\mathsf{Setup}(1^\lambda) \to \mathsf{ck}$ returns a commitment key ck; – $\mathsf{Commit}(\mathsf{ck}, \mathsf{t}, u) \to (c, o)$ produces a commitment/opening pair of type t for value u; – $\mathsf{VerCommit}(\mathsf{ck}, \mathsf{t}, c, u, o) \to b$ verifies that commitment c of type t opens to value u given opening o, and accepts $(b = 1)$ or rejects $(b = 0)$. Security properties of the scheme, i.e., *binding*—a commitment cannot be opened to two different values—and *hiding*—commitment leaks nothing about the value it opens to—should hold with respect to a certain type. In our constructions we will assume two main types: $\mathsf{t_{set}}$, through which we can commit to a set (we can think of a commitment of this type roughly as an accumulator for a set U) , and $\mathsf{t_{elm}}$ through which we can commit to elements. In the remainder of this work we will assume commitment schemes that are binding for both types $\mathsf{t_{set}}$ and $\mathsf{t_{elm}}$, but hiding only for the latter: we should be able to hide specific committed elements in a set but it is acceptable to leak the set itself. Given two commitment schemes C and C' respectively for types $\mathsf{t_{set}}$ and $\mathsf{t_{elm}}$, we denote by $\mathsf{C} \bullet \mathsf{C}'$ the commitment scheme over both types $\mathsf{t_{set}}$ and $\mathsf{t_{elm}}$ obtained by the natural composition, i.e., a scheme able to commit to both sets and to elements in them.

Commit-and-Prove NIZKs. A *commit-and-prove NIZK* (CP-NIZK) is essentially a non-interactive zero-knowledge argument for a specific family of relations augmented with a commitment opening verification. In a standard NIZK, a verifier would have access to a public input x and to a proof that a witness w exists for that specific input, i.e. that $R(x, w)$ holds for a fixed relation R. In a CP-NIZK the public input also includes ℓ commitments $c_1, \ldots, c_\ell$ to ℓ "parts" of the witness $u_1, \ldots, u_\ell$ (not necessarily disjoint). Informally, in a CP-NIZK for relation R, the verifier is now checking the conjunction of two facts: *(i)* that the original relation holds, i.e., $R(x, u_1, \ldots, u_\ell, \omega)$, where ω is the non-committed part of the witness; *(ii)* that for each $j \in [\ell]$, c_j opens to u_j (with respect to the type of c_j).

We denote a CP-NIZK as a tuple of algorithms $\mathsf{CP} = (\mathsf{KeyGen}, \mathsf{Prove}, \mathsf{VerProof})$ with the following explicit syntax for CP's algorithms: – $\mathsf{KeyGen}(\mathsf{ck}, R) \to \mathsf{crs} := (\mathsf{ek}, \mathsf{vk})$ produces a structured reference string (evaluation/verification key) for the CP version of R (NB: KeyGen takes as input a commitment key generated by $\mathsf{CS.Setup}$ for a commitment scheme CS). – $\mathsf{Prove}(\mathsf{ek}, x, (c_j)_{j \in [\ell]}, (u_j)_{j \in [\ell]}, (o_j)_{j \in [\ell]}, \omega) \to \pi$ produces a proof given the public input, commitments, witness and their openings $o_1, \ldots, o_\ell$. – $\mathsf{VerProof}(\mathsf{vk}, x, (c_j)_{j \in [\ell]}, \pi) \to b \in \{0, 1\}$ verifies a proof for a public input x and commitments $c_1, \ldots, c_\ell$. For security properties of CP-NIZKs, see the appendix.

CP-SNARKs. In brief, a CP-SNARK is a CP-NIZK that additionally satisfies *succinctness*, i.e., the running time of $\mathsf{VerProof}$ is $\mathsf{poly}(\lambda + |x| + \log |w|)$ and the proof size is $\mathsf{poly}(\lambda + \log |w|)$.

3   CP-SNARKs for Set Membership

In this section we discuss a specialization of CP-SNARKs for a specific NP relation: membership of an element in a set;[10] a similar formalization is possible for non-membership as well. For formal details we refer to the full version of the paper.

Set Membership Relations. Let $\mathcal{D}_{\mathsf{elm}}$ be some domain for set elements, and let $\mathcal{D}_{\mathsf{set}} \subseteq 2^{\mathcal{D}_{\mathsf{elm}}}$ be a set of possible sets over $\mathcal{D}_{\mathsf{elm}}$. We define the set membership relation $R_{\mathsf{mem}} : \mathcal{D}_{\mathsf{set}} \times \mathcal{D}_{\mathsf{elm}}$ as $R_{\mathsf{mem}}(U, u) = 1 \iff u \in U$.

CP-SNARKs for Set Membership. Intuitively, a commit-and-prove SNARK for set membership allows one to commit to a set U and to an element u, and then to prove in zero-knowledge that $R_{\mathsf{mem}}(U, u) = 1$. If $\mathsf{Com}_{S \cup \mathsf{elm}}$ is a type-based commitment scheme that allows one to commit to either an element of $\mathcal{D}_{\mathsf{elm}}$ (with type $\mathsf{t}_{\mathsf{elm}}$) or to a set of values of $\mathcal{D}_{\mathsf{elm}}$ (with type $\mathsf{t}_{\mathsf{set}}$), then a CP-SNARK for set membership is a zkSNARK for relation $\mathbf{R}_{\mathsf{mem}}^{\mathsf{ck}} = (\mathsf{ck}, R_{\mathsf{mem}})$, the CP version of R_{mem}, such that $\mathbf{R}_{\mathsf{mem}}^{\mathsf{ck}}(c_U, c_u, U, u, o_U, o_u) = 1 \iff R_{\mathsf{mem}}(U, u) = 1 \wedge \mathsf{VerCommit}(\mathsf{ck}, \mathsf{t}_{\mathsf{set}}, c_U, U, o_U) = 1 \wedge \mathsf{VerCommit}(\mathsf{ck}, \mathsf{t}_{\mathsf{elm}}, c_u, u, o_u) = 1$.

---

[10] As discussed in the introduction, CP-SNARKs for set membership are a different lens on accumulators that support (non-)membership proofs on committed values. In the full version we formally construct a CP-SNARK for set membership from any accumulator scheme that has a zero-knowledge proof for committed values. This formalization captures existing schemes, such as [11] and [34].

Notice that for the relation R_{mem} it is relevant for the proof system to be succinct so that proofs can be at most polylogarithmic (or constant) in the size of the set (that is part of the witness). This is why for set membership we are mostly interested in designing CP-SNARKs.

4 CP-SNARKs for Set Membership with Short Parameters

In this section we describe CP-SNARKs for set membership in which the elements of the sets can be committed using a Pedersen commitment scheme defined in a prime order group, and the sets are committed using an RSA accumulator. Since RSA accumulators are not extractable commitments, these schemes are secure in a model where the commitment to the set is assumed to be checked at least once, namely they are knowledge-sound with partial opening[11] of the set commitment.

A bit more in detail, we propose two CP-SNARKs. Our first scheme, called MemCP$_{RSA}$, works for set elements that are arbitrary strings of length η, i.e., $\mathcal{D}_{elm} = \{0,1\}^{\eta}$, and for sets that are any subset of $\mathcal{D}_{elm}$, i.e., $\mathcal{D}_{set} = 2^{\mathcal{D}_{elm}}$. Our second scheme, MemCP$_{RSAPrm}$, instead works for set elements that are prime numbers of exactly μ bits, and for sets that are any subset of such prime numbers. This second scheme is a simplified variant of the first one that requires more structure on the set elements (they must be prime numbers). On the other hand it is more efficient and thus preferable in those applications that can work with prime elements.

An High-Level Overview of Our Constructions. We provide the main idea behind our scheme, and to this end we use the simpler scheme MemCP$_{RSAPrm}$ in which set elements are prime numbers in $(2^{\mu-1}, 2^{\mu})$. The commitment to the set $P = \{e_1, \ldots, e_n\}$ is an RSA accumulator [3,5] that is defined as $\mathsf{Acc} = G^{\prod_{e_i \in P} e_i}$ for a random quadratic residue $G \in \mathsf{QR}_N$. The commitment to a set element e is instead a Pedersen commitment $c_e = g^e h^{r_q}$ in a group $\mathbb{G}_q$ of prime order q, where q is of ν bits and $\mu < \nu$. For public commitments Acc and c_e, our scheme allows to prove in zero-knowledge the knowledge of e committed in c_e such that $e \in P$ and $\mathsf{Acc} = G^{\prod_{e_i \in P} e_i}$. A public coin protocol for this problem was proposed by Camenisch and Lysyanskaya [11]. Their protocol however requires various restrictions. For instance, the accumulator must work with at least 2λ-bit long primes, which slows down accumulation time, and the prime order group must be more than 4λ-bits (e.g., of 512 bits), which is undesirable for efficiency reasons, especially if this prime order group is used to instantiate more proof systems to create other proofs about the committed element. In our scheme the goal is instead to keep the prime order group of "normal" size (say, 2λ bits), so that it can be for example a prime order group in which we can efficiently

---

[11] Briefly, this means the CP-SNARK extractor is not required to extract the set from its commitment, as this is assumed to be opened by the adversary (see the full version for a formal definition).

instantiate another CP-SNARK that could be composed with our MemCP$_{\text{RSAPrm}}$. And we can also allow flexible choices of the primes size that can be tuned to the application so that applications that work with moderately large sets can benefit in efficiency.

A bit more technically: in [11] the accumulated primes lie in a pre-specified interval: $e \in (A, B)$. Their protocol can ensure that $|e| < B2^{\lambda_z + \lambda_s + 2}$, for the (knowledge) extracted e. In order to ensure that e represents exactly *one* accumulated element we need that $B2^{\lambda_z + \lambda_s + 2} < A^2 - 1$. We also need to ensure that it is non-trivial ($e = \pm 1$); therefore, we move to a prime-order group and prove the statement $e \neq \pm 1$ there (this also requires an equality proof "between the two groups"). This results in the constraint $A^2 - 1 < q/2$ (q: order of the prime-order group) for proof of equality to hold, otherwise "collisions" attacks may happen in the prime order group (more details about this issue are below). Our observation is this: if we fix our primes to be of specific bit size (say μ) and ensure this to the verifier, then *(i)* we wouldn't need the $\neq \pm 1$ proof, and *(ii)* we can eliminate the "collisions" so that we can adopt a smaller (and more standard) prime-order group size; see below for the analysis. To ensure this we apply a very cheap range proof (only 1-bit long) in the prime order group.

In order to achieve these goals, our idea to create a membership proof is to compute the following:

- An accumulator membership witness $W = G^{\prod_{e_i \in P \setminus \{e\}} e_i}$, and an integer commitment to e in the RSA group, $C_e = G^e H^r$.
- A ZK proof of knowledge (CP$_{\text{Root}}$) of a committed root for Acc, i.e. of (e, W) such that $W^e = $ Acc and $C_e = G^e H^r$. This guarantees that C_e commits to $e \in \mathbb{Z}$ accumulated in Acc (at this point, however, e may be a trivial root, i.e., 1).
- A ZK proof CP$_{\text{modEq}}$ that C_e and c_e commit to the same value modulo q.
- A ZK proof CP$_{\text{Range}}$ that c_e commits to an integer in the range $\left(2^{\mu-1}, 2^{\mu}\right)$.

From the combination of the above proofs we would like to conclude that the integer committed in c_e is in P. Without further restrictions, however, this may not be the case; in particular, since for the value committed in C_e we do not have a strict bound it may be that the integer committed in c_e is another e_q such $e = e_q \pmod{q}$ but $e \neq e_q$ over the integers. In fact, the proof CP$_{\text{Root}}$ does not guarantee us that C_e commits to a single prime number e, but only that e divides $\prod_{e_i \in P} e_i$, namely e might be a product of a few primes in P or the corresponding negative value, while its residue modulo q may be some value that is not in the set—what we call a "collision". We solve this problem by taking in consideration that e_q is guaranteed by CP$_{\text{Range}}$ to be in $\left(2^{\mu-1}, 2^{\mu}\right)$ and by enhancing CP$_{\text{Root}}$ to also prove a bound on e: roughly speaking $|e| < 2^{2\lambda_s + \mu}$ for a statistical security parameter λ_s. Using this information we develop a careful analysis that bounds the probability of such collisions for a malicious e (see Sect. 4.2 for additional intuitions).

In the following section we describe the type-based commitment scheme supported by our CP-SNARK and the building blocks we use, and then we present the MemCP$_{RSA}$ CP-SNARK. The MemCP$_{RSAPrm}$ scheme and the instantiations of our building blocks are in the appendix.

Remark 4.1. Although we describe our protocols for RSA groups, we generalize them to work over any Hidden Order Group with slight modifications (see full version).

4.1   Preliminaries and Building Blocks

Notation. Given a set $U = \{u_1, \ldots, u_n\} \subset \mathbb{Z}$ of cardinality n we denote compactly with $\mathsf{prod}_U := \prod_{i=1}^n u_i$ the product of all its elements. We use capital letters for elements in an RSA group $\mathbb{Z}_N^*$, e.g., $G, H \in \mathbb{Z}_N^*$. Conversely, we use small letters for elements in a prime order group $\mathbb{G}_q$, e.g., $g, h \in \mathbb{G}_q$. Following this notation, we denote a commitment in a prime order group as $c \in \mathbb{G}_q$, while a commitment in an RSA group as $C \in \mathbb{Z}_N^*$.

Commitment Schemes. Our first CP-SNARK, called MemCP$_{RSA}$, is for a family of relations $R_{mem} : \mathcal{D}_{elm} \times \mathcal{D}_{set}$ such that $\mathcal{D}_{elm} = \{0,1\}^\eta$, $\mathcal{D}_{set} = 2^{\mathcal{D}_{elm}}$, and for a type-based commitment scheme that is the canonical composition SetCom$_{RSA}$ • PedCom of the two commitment schemes given in Fig. 2. PedCom is essentially a classical Pedersen commitment scheme in a group $\mathbb{G}_q$ of prime order q such that $q \in (2^{\nu-1}, 2^\nu)$ and $\eta < \nu$.[12] PedCom is used to commit to set elements and its type is t_q. SetCom$_{RSA}$ is a (non-hiding) commitment scheme for sets of η-bit strings, that is built as an RSA accumulator [3,5] to a set of μ-bit primes, each derived from an η-bit string by a deterministic hash function H$_{prime}$: $\{0,1\}^\eta \rightarrow$ Primes $(2^{\mu-1}, 2^\mu)$. SetCom$_{RSA}$ is computationally binding under the factoring assumption[13] and the collision resistance of H$_{prime}$. Its type for sets is t_U.

Hashing to Primes. The problem of mapping arbitrary values to primes in a collision-resistant manner has been studied in the past, see e.g., [9,17,23], and in [21] a method to generate random primes is presented. Although the main idea of our scheme would work with any instantiation of H$_{prime}$, for the goal of significantly improving efficiency, our construction considers a specific class of H$_{prime}$ functions that work as follows. Let H : $\{0,1\}^\eta \times \{0,1\}^\iota \rightarrow \{0,1\}^{\mu-1}$ be a collision-resistant function, and define H$_{prime}(u)$ as the function that starting with $j = 0$, looks for the first $j \in [0, 2^\iota - 1]$ such that the integer represented by the binary string $1|H(u, j)$ is prime. In case it reaches $j = 2^\iota - 1$ it failed to find a prime and outputs $\perp$.[14]

---

[12] The restriction $\eta < \nu$ is for simplicity; in the full version we discuss how to avoid it.

[13] Here is why: finding two different sets of primes $P, P', P \neq P'$ such that $G^{\mathsf{prod}_P} = $ Acc $= G^{\mathsf{prod}_{P'}}$ implies finding an integer $\alpha = \mathsf{prod}_P - \mathsf{prod}_{P'} \neq 0$ such that $G^\alpha = 1$. This is known to lead to an efficient algorithm for factoring N.

[14] For specific instantiations of H, ι can be set so that $\perp$ is returned with negligible probability.

Setup(1^λ) : Choose $\mathbb{G}_q$ of prime order $q \in (2^{\nu-1}, 2^\nu)$, generators $g, h \leftarrow_\$ \mathbb{G}_q$. Return
ck $:= (\mathbb{G}_q, g, h)$
Commit(ck, t_q, u) : sample $r \leftarrow_\$ \mathbb{Z}_q$; return $(c, o) := (g^u h^r, r)$.
VerCommit(ck, t_q, c, u, r) : Output 1 if $c = g^u h^r$; output 0 o.w.

(a) PedCom

Setup($1^\lambda, 1^\mu$) : Let $N \leftarrow$ GenSRSAmod(1^λ), $F \leftarrow_\$ \mathbb{Z}_N^*$, $\mathsf{H_{prime}} \leftarrow_\$ \mathcal{H}$; compute $G \leftarrow F^2 \bmod N \in \mathsf{QR}_N$. Return ck $:= (N, G, \mathsf{H_{prime}})$.
Commit(ck, t_U, U) : $P := \{\mathsf{H_{prime}}(u)\}_{u \in U}$. Acc $\leftarrow G^{\mathsf{prod} P}$. Return $(c, o) := (\mathsf{Acc}, \varnothing)$.
VerCommit(ck, t_U, Acc, $U, \varnothing$) : Define P as above. Accept iff Acc $= G^{\mathsf{prod} P} \bmod N$.

(b) SetCom$_{\mathsf{RSA}}$

Fig. 2. RSA Accumulator and Pedersen commitment schemes for MemCP$_{\mathsf{RSA}}$.

CP-NIZK for H Computation and PedCom. We use a CP-NIZK CP$_{\mathsf{HashEq}}$ for the relation $R_{\mathsf{HashEq}} : \{0,1\}^\mu \times \{0,1\}^\eta \times \{0,1\}^\iota$ defined as

$$R_{\mathsf{HashEq}}(u_1, u_2, \omega) = 1 \iff u_1 = (1|\mathsf{H}(u_2, \omega))$$

and for the commitment scheme PedCom. Essentially, with this scheme one can prove that two commitments c_e and c_u in $\mathbb{G}_q$ are such that $c_e = g^e h^{r_q}$, $c_u = g^u h^{r_u}$ and there exists j such that $e = (1|\mathsf{H}(u, j))$. In the security proof we observe we do not have to prove all the iterations of H until finding j such that $(1|\mathsf{H}(u, j)) = \mathsf{H_{prime}}(u)$ is prime, which saves significantly on the complexity of this CP-NIZK.

Integer Commitments. We use a scheme for committing to arbitrarily large integer values in RSA groups introduced by Fujisaki and Okamoto [22] and later improved in [18]. We briefly recall the commitment scheme. Let $\mathbb{Z}_N^*$ be an RSA group. The commitment key consists of two randomly chosen generators $G, H \in \mathbb{Z}_N^*$; to commit to any $x \in \mathbb{Z}$ one chooses randomly an $r \leftarrow_\$ [1, N/2]$ and computes $C \leftarrow G^x H^r$; the verifier checks whether or not $C = \pm G^x H^r$. This commitment is statistically hiding and computationally binding under the hardness of factoring in $\mathbb{Z}_N^*$. Furthermore, a proof of knowledge of an opening was presented in [18], its knowledge soundness was based on the strong RSA assumption, and later found to be reducible to the plain RSA assumption in [16]. We denote this commitment scheme as IntCom.

RSA Accumulators. As observed earlier, our commitment scheme for sets is an RSA accumulator Acc computed on the set of primes P derived from U through the map to primes, i.e., $P := \{\mathsf{H_{prime}}(s)|s \in U\}$. In our construction we use the accumulator's feature for computing succinct membership witnesses, which we recall works as follows. Given Acc $= G^{\prod_{e_i \in P} e_i} := G^{\mathsf{prod} P}$, the membership witness for e_k is $W_k = G^{\prod_{e_i \in P \setminus \{e_k\}} e_i}$, which can be verified by checking if $W_k^{e_k} = $ Acc.

Argument of Knowledge of a Root. We make use of a zero-knowledge non-interactive argument of knowledge of a root of a public RSA group element $\mathsf{Acc} \in \mathsf{QR}_N$. This NIZK argument is called $\mathsf{CP}_\mathsf{Root}$. More precisely, it takes in an integer commitment to a $e \in \mathbb{Z}$ and then proves knowledge of an e-th root of Acc, i.e., of $W = \mathsf{Acc}^{\frac{1}{e}}$. More formally, $\mathsf{CP}_\mathsf{Root}$ is a NIZK for the relation $R_\mathsf{Root} : (\mathbb{Z}_N^* \times \mathsf{QR}_N \times \mathbb{N}) \times (\mathbb{Z} \times \mathbb{Z} \times \mathbb{Z}_N^*)$ defined as $R_\mathsf{Root} ((C_e, \mathsf{Acc}, \mu), (e, r, W)) = 1$ iff $C_e = \pm G^e H^r \bmod N \wedge W^e = \mathsf{Acc} \bmod N \wedge |e| < 2^{\lambda_z + \lambda_s + \mu + 2}$ where λ_z and λ_s are the statistical zero-knowledge and soundness security parameters respectively of the protocol $\mathsf{CP}_\mathsf{Root}$. $\mathsf{CP}_\mathsf{Root}$ is obtained by applying the Fiat-Shamir transform to a public-coin protocol that we propose based on ideas from the protocol of Camenisch and Lysysanskaya for proving knowledge of an accumulated value [11]. In [11], the protocol ensures that the committed integer e is in a specific range, different from 1 and positive. In our $\mathsf{CP}_\mathsf{Root}$ protocol we instead removed these constraints and isolated the portion of the protocol that only proves knowledge of a root. We present the $\mathsf{CP}_\mathsf{Root}$ protocol in the full version; its interactive public coin version is knowledge sound under the RSA assumption and statistical zero-knowledge.

Proof of Equality of Commitments in $\mathbb{Z}_N^*$ and $\mathbb{G}_q$. Our last building block, called $\mathsf{CP}_\mathsf{modEq}$, proves in ZK that two commitments, a Pedersen commitment in a prime order group and an integer commitment in an RSA group, open to the same value modulo the prime order $q = \mathsf{ord}(\mathbb{G})$. This is a conjunction of a classic Pedersen Σ-protocol and a proof of knowledge of opening of an integer commitment [18], i.e. for the relation $R_\mathsf{modEq} ((C_e, c_e), (e, e_q, r, r_q))$ which is true iff $e = e_q \bmod q \wedge C_e = \pm G^e H^r \bmod N \wedge c_e = g^{e_q \bmod q} h^{r_q \bmod q}$.

4.2 Our CP-SNARK MemCP$_\mathsf{RSA}$

We are now ready to present our CP-SNARK MemCP$_\mathsf{RSA}$ for set membership. The scheme is fully described in Fig. 3 and makes use of the building blocks presented in the previous section.

The KeyGen algorithm takes as input the commitment key of Com_1 and a description of R_mem. It then samples a random generator $H \leftarrow_\$ \mathsf{QR}_N$ so that (G, H) define a key for the integer commitment, and generates a CRS $\mathsf{crs}_\mathsf{HashEq}$ of the $\mathsf{CP}_\mathsf{HashEq}$ CP-NIZK. The approach behind proof generation is similar to that informally described at the beginning of Sect. 4 for the case when set elements are prime numbers. In order to support sets U of arbitrary strings the main differences are the following: (i) we use $\mathsf{H}_\mathsf{prime}$ in order to derive a set of primes P from U, (ii) given a commitment c_u to an element $u \in \{0,1\}^\eta$, we commit to $e = \mathsf{H}_\mathsf{prime}(u)$ in c_e; (iii) we use the previously mentioned ideas to prove that c_e commits to an element in P (that is correctly accumulated), except that we replace the range proof π_Range with a proof π_HashEq that c_u and c_e commits to u and e respectively, such that $\exists j : e = (1|\mathsf{H}(u, j))$.

The correctness of MemCP$_\mathsf{RSA}$ can be checked by inspection: essentially, it follows from the correctness of all the building blocks and the condition that $\eta, \mu < \nu$. For succinctness, we observe that the commitments C_U, c_u and all the

KeyGen(ck, $R^\in$) : parse ck := $((N, G, \mathsf{H_{prime}}), (\mathbb{G}_q, g, h))$ as the commitment keys of
SetCom$_{\mathsf{RSA}}$ and PedCom respectively. Sample random generator H;
Generate the crs for CP$_{\mathsf{HashEq}}$: crs$_{\mathsf{HashEq}}$ $\leftarrow$\$ CP$_{\mathsf{HashEq}}$.KeyGen$(((\mathbb{G}_q, g, h), R_{\mathsf{HashEq}})$;
Return crs := $(N, G, H, \mathsf{H_{prime}}, \mathbb{G}_q, g, h, \mathsf{crs_{HashEq}})$.
Define crs$_{\mathsf{Root}}$:= (N, G, H), crs$_{\mathsf{modEq}}$:= $(N, G, H, \mathbb{G}_q, g, h)$.

Prove(crs, $(C_U, c_u), (U, u), (\varnothing, r_u))$: Compute prime $e \leftarrow \mathsf{H_{prime}}(u) = (1|\mathsf{H}(u,j))$;
$(c_e, r_q) \leftarrow$ Com$_1$.Commit(ck, t$_q$, e); $(C_e, r) \leftarrow$ IntCom.Commit$((G, H), e)$;
$P \leftarrow \{\mathsf{H_{prime}}(u) : u \in U\}$; $W = G^{\Pi_{e_i \in P \setminus \{e\}} e_i}$;
$\pi_{\mathsf{Root}} \leftarrow$ CP$_{\mathsf{Root}}$.Prove(crs$_{\mathsf{Root}}$, $(C_e, C_U, \mu), (e, r, W))$;
$\pi_{\mathsf{modEq}} \leftarrow$ CP$_{\mathsf{modEq}}$.Prove(crs$_{\mathsf{modEq}}$, $(C_e, c_e), (e, e, r, r_q))$;
$\pi_{\mathsf{HashEq}} \leftarrow$ CP$_{\mathsf{HashEq}}$.Prove(crs$_{\mathsf{HashEq}}$, $(c_e, c_u), (e, u), (r_q, r_u), j)$;
Return $\pi := (C_e, c_e, \pi_{\mathsf{Root}}, \pi_{\mathsf{modEq}}, \pi_{\mathsf{HashEq}})$.

VerProof(crs, $(C_U, c_u), \pi)$: Return 1 whenever it holds
CP$_{\mathsf{Root}}$.VerProof(crs$_{\mathsf{Root}}$, $(C_e, C_U, \mu), \pi_{\mathsf{Root}}) = 1 \wedge$
CP$_{\mathsf{modEq}}$.VerProof(crs$_{\mathsf{modEq}}$, $(C_e, c_e), \pi_{\mathsf{modEq}}) = 1\wedge$
CP$_{\mathsf{HashEq}}$.VerProof(crs$_{\mathsf{HashEq}}$, $(c_e, c_u), \pi_{\mathsf{HashEq}}) = 1$.

Fig. 3. MemCP$_{\mathsf{RSA}}$ CP-SNARK for set membership

three proofs have size that does not depend on the cardinality of the set U, which is the only portion of the witness whose size is not fixed a-priori.

The requirements of security are slightly different according to the setting of parameters as we will see below, so we state two separate theorems, one for each case. Due to space restrictions, we provide a (semi-formal) proof intuition for the first, while for the second we refer to the full version For ease of exposition we let $d = 1 + \lfloor \frac{\lambda_z + \lambda_s + 2}{\mu} \rfloor$.

Theorem 4.1. *Let* PedCom, SetCom$_{\mathsf{RSA}}$ *and* IntCom *be computationally binding commitments,* CP$_{\mathsf{Root}}$, CP$_{\mathsf{modEq}}$ *and* CP$_{\mathsf{HashEq}}$ *be knowledge-sound NIZK arguments, and assume that the Strong RSA assumption hold, and that* H *is collision resistant. If* $d\mu + 2 \leq \nu$, *then* MemCP$_{\mathsf{RSA}}$ *is knowledge-sound with partial opening of the set commitments* C_U

Theorem 4.2. *Let* PedCom, SetCom$_{\mathsf{RSA}}$ *and* IntCom *be computationally binding commitments,* CP$_{\mathsf{Root}}$, CP$_{\mathsf{modEq}}$ *and* CP$_{\mathsf{HashEq}}$ *be knowledge-sound NIZK arguments, and assume that the Strong RSA assumption hold, and that* H *is collision resistant. If* $d\mu + 2 > \nu$, $d = O(1)$ *is a small constant,* $2^{\mu - \nu} \in$ negl(λ) *and* H *is modeled as a random oracle, then* MemCP$_{\mathsf{RSA}}$ *is knowledge-sound with partial opening of the set commitments* C_U.

Proof of Theorem 4.1. We provide an intuition about the security of our construction. A formal proof appears in the full version of the paper.

Recall that the goal is to prove in ZK that c_u is a commitment to an element $u \in \{0,1\}^\eta$ that is in a set U committed in C_U. Intuitively, we obtain the security of our scheme from the conjunction of proofs for relations $R_{\text{Root}}, R_{\text{modEq}}$ and R_{HashEq}: (i) π_{HashEq} gives us that c_e commits to $e_q = (1|\text{H}(u, j))$ for some j and for u committed in c_u. (ii) π_{modEq} gives that C_e commits to an integer e such that $e \bmod q = e_q$ is committed in c_e. (iii) π_{Root} gives us that the integer e committed in C_e divides prod_P, where $C_U = G^{\text{prod}_P}$ with $P = \{\text{H}_{\text{prime}}(u_i) : u_i \in U\}$.

By combining these three facts we would like to conclude that $e_q \in P$ that, together with π_{HashEq}, should also guarantee $u \in U$. A first problem to analyze, however, is that for e we do not have guarantees of a strict bound in $(2^{\mu-1}, 2^\mu)$; so it may in principle occur that $e = e_q \pmod q$ but $e \neq e_q$ over the integers. Indeed, the relation R_{Root} does not guarantee us that e is a single prime number, but only that e divides the product of primes accumulated in C_U. Assuming the hardness of Strong RSA we may still have that e is the product of a few primes in P or even is a negative integer. Consider the simple attack that could arise from this: an adversary can find a product of primes from the set P, let it call e, such that $e = e_q \pmod q$ but $e \neq e_q$ over the integers. Since e is a legitimate product of members of P, the adversary can efficiently compute the e-th root of C_U and provide a valid π_{Root} proof. This is what we informally call a "collision". Another simple attack would be that an adversary takes a single prime e and then commits to its opposite $e_q \leftarrow -e \bmod q$ in the prime order group. Again, since $e \in P$ the adversary can efficiently compute the e-th root of C_U, $W^e = C_U$, and then the corresponding $-e$-th root of C_U, $(W^{-1})^{-e} = C_U$. This is a second type of attack to achieve a "collision". With a careful analysis we show that with appropriate parameters the probability that such collisions occur can be either 0 or negligible.

One key observation is that R_{Root} does guarantee a lower and an upper bound, $-2^{\lambda_z+\lambda_s+\mu+2}$ and $2^{\lambda_z+\lambda_s+\mu+2}$ respectively, for e committed in C_e. From these bounds (and that $e \mid \text{prod}_P$) we get that an adversarial e can be the product of at most $d = 1 + \lfloor \frac{\lambda_z+\lambda_s+2}{\mu} \rfloor$ primes in P (or their corresponding negative product). Then, if $2^{d\mu} \leq 2^{\nu-2} < q$, or $d\mu + 2 \leq \nu$, we get that $e < 2^{d\mu} < q$. In case $e > 0$ and since q is prime, $e = e_q \bmod q \wedge e < q$ implies that $e = e_q$ over $\mathbb{Z}$, namely no collision can occur at all. In the other case $e < 0$ we have $e > -2^{d\mu}$ and $e = e_q \pmod q$ implies $e = -q + e_q < -2^{\nu-1} + 2^\mu < -2^{\nu-1} + 2^{\nu-2} = -2^{\nu-2}$. Therefore, $-2^{d\mu} < -2^{\nu-2}$, a contradiction since we assumed $d\mu + 2 \leq \nu$, so this type of collision cannot happen.

If on the other hand we are in a parameters setting where $d\mu > \nu - 2$, we give a concrete bound on the probability that such collisions occur. More precisely, for this case we need to assume that the integers returned by H are random, i.e., H is a random oracle, and we also use the implicit fact that R_{HashEq} guarantees that $e_q \in (2^{\mu-1}, 2^\mu)$. Then we give a concrete bound on the probability that the product of d out of $\text{poly}(\lambda)$ random integers lies in a specific range $(2^{\mu-1}, 2^\mu)$, which turns out to be negligible when d is constant and $2^{\mu-\nu}$ is negligible.

4.3   A CP-SNARK for Set Non-membership with Short Parameters

Here we describe two CP-SNARKs for set non-membership that work in a setting identical to the one of Sect. 4. Namely, the set is committed using an RSA accumulator, and the element (that one wants to prove not to belong to the set) is committed using a Pedersen commitment scheme. As in the previous section, we propose two protocols for non-membership, called NonMemCP$_{\mathsf{RSA}}$ and NonMemCP$_{\mathsf{RSAPrm}}$, in complete analogy to MemCP$_{\mathsf{RSA}}$ and MemCP$_{\mathsf{RSAPrm}}$. In the former, the elements of the set are arbitrary bit-strings of length η, $\mathcal{D}_{\mathsf{elm}} = \{0,1\}^\eta$, while in the latter the elements are primes of length μ. The schemes are fully described in the full version.

An High-Level Overview of the Constructions. The main idea of NonMemCP$_{\mathsf{RSA}}$ is similar to the one of the corresponding membership protocol, MemCP$_{\mathsf{RSA}}$. It uses in the same modular way the modEq and HashEq protocols. The only difference lies in the third protocol: instead of using Root it uses a new protocol Coprime. In a similar manner, NonMemCP$_{\mathsf{RSAPrm}}$ uses modEq, Range and Coprime.

Let us explain the need of the Coprime protocol and what it does. First, recall how a non-membership proof is computed in RSA Accumulators [28]. Let P be a set of primes to be accumulated and prod the corresponding product. For any prime element $e \notin P$ it holds that $\gcd(e, \mathsf{prod}) = 1$, while for any member $e \in P$ it is $\gcd(e, \mathsf{prod}) = e \neq 1$. Thus, proving that $\gcd(e, \mathsf{prod}) = 1$ would exhibit non-membership of e in P. Recall, also, that using the extended Euclidean algorithm one can efficiently compute coefficients (a, b) such that $a \cdot e + b \cdot \mathsf{prod} = \gcd(e, \mathsf{prod})$. A non-membership proof for an element e w.r.t. an accumulator $\mathsf{Acc} = G^{\mathsf{prod}}$ consists of a pair $(D = G^a, b)$, where a, b are such that $a \cdot e + b \cdot \mathsf{prod} = 1$. The verification is $D^e \mathsf{Acc}^b = G$, which ensures that e and prod are coprime, i.e. $\gcd(e, \mathsf{prod}) = 1$. Therefore, the goal of the Coprime protocol is to prove knowledge of an element e committed in an integer commitment C_e that satisfies this relation. A more formal definition of Coprime is given below.

Argument of Knowledge for a Coprime Element. We make use of a non-interactive argument of knowledge of a non-membership witness of an element such that the verification equation explained above holds. More formally CP$_{\mathsf{Coprime}}$, is a NIZK for the relation: $R_{\mathsf{Coprime}} : (\mathbb{Z}_N^* \times \mathsf{QR}_N) \times (\mathbb{Z} \times \mathbb{Z} \times \mathsf{QR}_N \times \mathbb{Z})$ defined as
$R_{\mathsf{Coprime}} ((C_e, \mathsf{Acc}), (e, r, D, b)) = 1$ iff

$$C_e = \pm G^e H^r \bmod N \ \wedge \ D^e \mathsf{Acc}^b = G \wedge |e| < 2^{\lambda_z + \lambda_s + \mu + 2}$$

An instantiation of a protocol for the above relation is in the full version.

5 Applications

As one can note, in our solutions the set of committed elements is public and not hidden to the verifier. Nevertheless, our solutions can still capture applications in which the "actual" data in the set is kept private. This is for example the case of anonymous cryptocurrencies like Zerocash. In this scenario, the public set of elements to be accumulated, U, is derived by creating a commitment to the underlying data, X, e.g., $u = COMM(x)$. To support this setting, we can use our solutions for arbitrary elements (so supporting virtually any commitment scheme). Interestingly, though, we can also use our (more efficient) solution for sets of primes if commitments are prime numbers. This can be done by using for example the *hash-to-prime* method described in Sect. 4.1 or another method for Pedersen commitments that we explain below in the context of Zerocash.

We now discuss concrete applications for which our constructions are suitable, both for set-membership and set non-membership. Below we discuss applications to Zerocash, financial identities, and Zerocoin; more applications to *asset governance* and *anonymous broadcast* can be found in the full version. In particular all these are applications in which: (1) the prover time must be small; (2) the size of the state (i.e.: the accumulator value and commitments) must be small (potentially constant); (3) the verifier time should be small; and (4) the time to update the accumulator—adding or deleting an element—should be fast. As we discuss below, our RSA-based constructions are suitable candidate for settings with these constraints.

ZEROCASH. Zerocash [4] is a UTXO-type (Unspent Transaction Output) cryptocurrency protocol which extends Bitcoin with privacy-preserving (*shielded*) transactions. When performing a shielded transaction users need to prove they are spending an output note from a token they had previously received. Users concerned with privacy should not reveal which note they are spending, else their new transaction could be linked to the original note that contained the note commitment. This would reveal information *both to the public and the sender of the initial transaction, and hence partially reveal the transaction graph.* In order to keep transactions unlinkable, the protocol uses zkSNARKs to prove a set membership relation, namely that a note commitment is in a publicly known set of "usable" note commitments.

Zcash is a full-fledged digital currency using Zerocash as the underlying protocol. In its current deployment, Sapling [27], it employs Pedersen commitments of the notes and makes a zero-knowledge set membership proof of these commitments using a Pedersen-Hash-based Merkle tree approach. This is the part of the protocol that can be replaced by one of our RSA-based solutions in order to obtain a speedup in proving time. In particular, we could slightly modify the note commitments in order to enable the use of our scheme MemCP$_{\mathsf{RSAPrm}}$ for sets of prime numbers, which gives the best efficiency. We can proceed as follows. Let us recall that the note commitments are represented by their x coordinates in the underlying elliptic curve group. We can then modify them so that the sender chooses a blinding factor such that the commitment representation of a note is a prime number, and we can add a consensus rule that enforces this check. With this change, we can achieve a solution that is significantly more efficient than that currently used in Zcash. Currently Zcash uses a Merkle Tree whose depth is 32. In this setting, *we would be able to reduce proving time of set-membership from* 1.12 s *to* 48.14 ms, trading it for larger proof sizes. We note that in this application, the set-membership proof about $u \in S$ is accompanied by another predicate $P(u)$. In the proof statement of the Zcash protocol, proving that $P(u)$ is satisfied takes considerably less time than the membership proof, hence this is why our solution would improve the overall proving time considerably, albeit the proof having more components. Another interesting comment is that our solution significantly reduces the size of the circuit, hence the need of a succinct proof system is reduced and one may even consider instantiations with other proof systems, such as Bulletproofs, that would offer transparency at the price of larger proofs and verification time.

ZEROCOIN VULNERABILITY. Another specific application of our RSA-based constructions is that of solving the security vulnerability of the implementation of the Zerocoin protocol [33] used in the Zcoin cryptocurrency [39]. The vulnerability in a nutshell: when proving equality of values committed under the RSA commitment and the prime-order group commitment, the equality may not hold over the integers, and hence one could easily produce collisions in the prime order group. Our work can provide different ways to solve this problem by generating a proof of equality over the integers.

Acknowledgements. Research leading to these results has been partially supported by the Spanish Government under projects SCUM (ref. RTI2018-102043-B-I00), CRYPTOEPIC (ref. EUR2019-103816), and SECURITAS (ref. RED2018-102321-T), by the Madrid Regional Government under project BLOQUES (ref. S2018/TCS-4339), and by research grants from Protocol Labs, and Nomadic Labs and the Tezos Foundation. Matteo Campanelli worked on this project as a post-doc at the IMDEA Software Institute.

References

1. Cpsnarks-set. https://github.com/kobigurk/cpsnarks-set
2. Agrawal, S., Ganesh, C., Mohassel, P.: Non-interactive zero-knowledge proofs for composite statements. In: Shacham, H., Boldyreva, A. (eds.) CRYPTO 2018. LNCS, vol. 10993, pp. 643–673. Springer, Cham (2018). https://doi.org/10.1007/978-3-319-96878-0_22
3. Barić, N., Pfitzmann, B.: Collision-free accumulators and fail-stop signature schemes without trees. In: Fumy, W. (ed.) EUROCRYPT 1997. LNCS, vol. 1233, pp. 480–494. Springer, Heidelberg (1997). https://doi.org/10.1007/3-540-69053-0_33
4. Ben-Sasson, E., et al.: Zerocash: decentralized anonymous payments from bitcoin. In: 2014 IEEE Symposium on Security and Privacy, pp. 459–474. IEEE Computer Society Press, May 2014
5. Benaloh, J.C., de Mare, M.: One-way accumulators: a decentralized alternative to digital sinatures (extended abstract). In: Helleseth, T. (ed.) EUROCRYPT'93. LNCS, vol. 765, pp. 274–285. Springer, Heidelberg (1994)
6. Benarroch, D., Campanelli, M., Fiore, D., Gurkan, K., Kolonelos, D.: Zero-knowledge proofs for set membership: efficient, succinct, modular. Cryptology ePrint Archive, Report 2019/1255, 2019. https://eprint.iacr.org/2019/1255
7. Boneh, D., Bünz, B., Fisch, B.: Batching techniques for accumulators with applications to iops and stateless blockchains. IACR Cryptology ePrint Archive **2018**, 1188 (2018)

8. Bünz, B., Bootle, J., Boneh, D., Poelstra, A., Wuille, P., Maxwell, G.: Bulletproofs: short proofs for confidential transactions and more. In: 2018 IEEE Symposium on Security and Privacy, pp. 315–334. IEEE Computer Society Press, May 2018

9. Cachin, C., Micali, S., Stadler, M.: Computationally private information retrieval with polylogarithmic communication. In: Stern, J. (ed.) EUROCRYPT 1999. LNCS, vol. 1592, pp. 402–414. Springer, Heidelberg (1999). https://doi.org/10.1007/3-540-48910-X_28

10. Camenisch, J., Kohlweiss, M., Soriente, C.: An accumulator based on bilinear maps and efficient revocation for anonymous credentials. In: Jarecki, S., Tsudik, G. (eds.) PKC 2009. LNCS, vol. 5443, pp. 481–500. Springer, Heidelberg (2009). https://doi.org/10.1007/978-3-642-00468-1_27

11. Camenisch, J., Lysyanskaya, A.: Dynamic accumulators and application to efficient revocation of anonymous credentials. In: Yung, M. (ed.) CRYPTO 2002. LNCS, vol. 2442, pp. 61–76. Springer, Heidelberg (2002). https://doi.org/10.1007/3-540-45708-9_5

12. Campanelli, M., Fiore, D., Querol, A.: Legosnark: modular design and composition of succinct zero-knowledge proofs. To appear at ACM CCS 2019. IACR Cryptology ePrint Archive (2019)

13. Canetti, R., Lindell, Y., Ostrovsky, R., Sahai, A.: Universally composable two-party and multi-party secure computation. In: 34th ACM STOC, pp. 494–503. ACM Press, May 2002

14. Chaum, D.: Security without identification: transaction systems to make big brother obsolete. Commun. ACM **28**(10), 1030–1044 (1985)

15. Chepurnoy, A., Papamanthou, C., Zhang, Y.: Edrax: a cryptocurrency with stateless transaction validation (2018)

16. Couteau, G., Peters, T., Pointcheval, D.: Removing the strong RSA assumption from arguments over the integers. In: Coron, J.-S., Nielsen, J.B. (eds.) EUROCRYPT 2017. LNCS, vol. 10211, pp. 321–350. Springer, Cham (2017). https://doi.org/10.1007/978-3-319-56614-6_11

17. Cramer, R., Shoup, V.: Signature schemes based on the strong RSA assumption. In: Motiwalla, J., Tsudik, G. (eds.) ACM CCS 99, pp. 46–51. ACM Press, Nov. (1999)

18. Damgård, I., Fujisaki, E.: A statistically-hiding integer commitment scheme based on groups with hidden order. In: Zheng, Y. (ed.) ASIACRYPT 2002. LNCS, vol. 2501, pp. 125–142. Springer, Heidelberg (2002). https://doi.org/10.1007/3-540-36178-2_8

19. I. Damgård and N. Triandopoulos. Supporting non-membership proofs with bilinear-map accumulators. Cryptology ePrint Archive, Report 2008/538, 2008. http://eprint.iacr.org/2008/538

20. Escala, A., Groth, J.: Fine-tuning groth-sahai proofs. In: Krawczyk, H. (ed.) PKC 2014. LNCS, vol. 8383, pp. 630–649. Springer, Heidelberg (2014). https://doi.org/10.1007/978-3-642-54631-0_36

21. Fouque, P.-A., Tibouchi, M.: Close to uniform prime number generation with fewer random bits. In: Esparza, J., Fraigniaud, P., Husfeldt, T., Koutsoupias, E. (eds.) ICALP 2014. LNCS, vol. 8572, pp. 991–1002. Springer, Heidelberg (2014). https://doi.org/10.1007/978-3-662-43948-7_82

22. Fujisaki, E., Okamoto, T.: Statistical zero knowledge protocols to prove modular polynomial relations. In: Kaliski, B.S. (ed.) CRYPTO 1997. LNCS, vol. 1294, pp. 16–30. Springer, Heidelberg (1997). https://doi.org/10.1007/BFb0052225

23. Gennaro, R., Halevi, S., Rabin, T.: Secure hash-and-sign signatures without the random oracle. In: Stern, J. (ed.) EUROCRYPT 1999. LNCS, vol. 1592, pp. 123–139. Springer, Heidelberg (1999). https://doi.org/10.1007/3-540-48910-X_9
24. Goldwasser, S., Micali, S., Rackoff, C.: The knowledge complexity of interactive proof systems. SIAM J. Comput. **18**(1), 186–208 (1989)
25. Groth, J.: On the size of pairing-based non-interactive arguments. In: Fischlin, M., Coron, J.-S. (eds.) EUROCRYPT 2016. LNCS, vol. 9666, pp. 305–326. Springer, Heidelberg (2016). https://doi.org/10.1007/978-3-662-49896-5_11
26. Groth, J., Sahai, A.: Efficient non-interactive proof systems for bilinear groups. In: Smart, N. (ed.) EUROCRYPT 2008. LNCS, vol. 4965, pp. 415–432. Springer, Heidelberg (2008). https://doi.org/10.1007/978-3-540-78967-3_24
27. Hopwood, D., Bowe, S., Hornby, T., Wilcox, N.: Zcash protocol specification. Technical report 2016–1.10. Zerocoin Electric Coin Company, Tech. Rep. (2016). https://github.com/zcash/zips/blob/master/protocol/sapling.pdf
28. Li, J., Li, N., Xue, R.: Universal accumulators with efficient nonmembership proofs. In: Katz, J., Yung, M. (eds.) ACNS 2007. LNCS, vol. 4521, pp. 253–269. Springer, Heidelberg (2007). https://doi.org/10.1007/978-3-540-72738-5_17
29. Libert, B., Ling, S., Nguyen, K., Wang, H.: Zero-knowledge arguments for lattice-based accumulators: logarithmic-size ring signatures and group signatures without trapdoors. In: Fischlin, M., Coron, J.-S. (eds.) EUROCRYPT 2016. LNCS, vol. 9666, pp. 1–31. Springer, Heidelberg (2016). https://doi.org/10.1007/978-3-662-49896-5_1
30. Lipmaa, H.: Secure accumulators from euclidean rings without trusted setup. In: Bao, F., Samarati, P., Zhou, J. (eds.) ACNS 2012. LNCS, vol. 7341, pp. 224–240. Springer, Heidelberg (2012). https://doi.org/10.1007/978-3-642-31284-7_14
31. Lovecruft, I.A., de Valence, H.: curve25519-dalek: a pure-rust implementation of group operations on ristretto and curve25519. https://github.com/dalek-cryptography/curve25519-dalek
32. Merkle, R.C.: A digital signature based on a conventional encryption function. In: Pomerance, C. (ed.) CRYPTO 1987. LNCS, vol. 293, pp. 369–378. Springer, Heidelberg (1988). https://doi.org/10.1007/3-540-48184-2_32
33. Miers, I., Garman, C., Green, M., Rubin, A.D.: Zerocoin: anonymous distributed E-cash from Bitcoin. In: 2013 IEEE Symposium on Security and Privacy, pp. 397–411. IEEE Computer Society Press, May 2013
34. Nguyen, L.: Accumulators from bilinear pairings and applications. In: Menczcs, A. (ed.) CT-RSA 2005. LNCS, vol. 3376, pp. 275–292. Springer, Heidelberg (2005). https://doi.org/10.1007/978-3-540-30574-3_19
35. Ozdemir, A., Wahby, R.S., Whitehat, B., Boneh, D.: Scaling verifiable computation using efficient set accumulators. Cryptology ePrint Archive, Report 2019/1494 (2019). https://eprint.iacr.org/2019/1494
36. Papamanthou, C., Shi, E., Tamassia, R., Yi, K.: Streaming authenticated data structures. In: Johansson, T., Nguyen, P.Q. (eds.) EUROCRYPT 2013. LNCS, vol. 7881, pp. 353–370. Springer, Heidelberg (2013). https://doi.org/10.1007/978-3-642-38348-9_22
37. Parno, B., Howell, J., Gentry, C., Raykova, M.: Pinocchio: nearly practical verifiable computation. In: 2013 IEEE Symposium on Security and Privacy, pp. 238–252. IEEE Computer Society Press, May 2013
38. SCIPR Lab. Zexe (zero knowledge execution). https://github.com/scipr-lab/zexe
39. Yap, R.: Cryptographic description of zerocoin attack (2019). https://zcoin.io/cryptographic-description-of-zerocoin-attack/

40. Zhang, J., Xie, T., Zhang, Y., Song, D.: Transparent polynomial delegation and its applications to zero knowledge proof. In: IEEE Symposium on Security and Privacy (2020)

41. Zhang, Y., Genkin, D., Katz, J., Papadopoulos, D., Papamanthou, C.: A zero-knowledge version of vSQL. Cryptology ePrint Archive, Report 2017/1146 (2017). https://eprint.iacr.org/2017/1146

42. Zhang, Y., Katz, J., Papamanthou, C.: An expressive (zero-knowledge) set accumulator. In: 2017 IEEE European Symposium on Security and Privacy (EuroS P), pp. 158–173, April 2017

Generic Plaintext Equality and Inequality Proofs

Olivier Blazy[1] , Xavier Bultel[2] , Pascal Lafourcade[3] ,
and Octavio Perez Kempner[4,5(✉)]

[1] Université de Limoges, XLIM, Limoges, France
olivier.blazy@unilim.fr
[2] INSA Centre Val de Loire, LIFO Lab, Blois, France
xavier.bultel@insa-cvl.fr
[3] University Clermont Auvergne, LIMOS, Clermont-Ferrand, France
pascal.lafourcade@uca.fr
[4] DIENS, École normale supérieure, CNRS, PSL University, Paris, France
octavio.perez.kempner@ens.fr
[5] be-ys Research, Paris, France

Abstract. Given two ciphertexts generated with a public-key encryption scheme, the problem of plaintext equality consists in determining whether the ciphertexts hold the same value. Similarly, the problem of plaintext inequality consists in deciding whether they hold a different value. Previous work has focused on building new schemes or extending existing ones to include support for plaintext equality/inequality. We propose generic and simple zero-knowledge proofs for both problems, which can be instantiated with various schemes. First, we consider the context where a prover with access to the secret key wants to convince a verifier, who has access to the ciphertexts, on the equality/inequality without revealing information about the plaintexts. We also consider the case where the prover knows the encryption's randomness instead of the secret key. For plaintext equality, we also propose sigma protocols that lead to non-interactive zero-knowledge proofs. To prove our protocols' security, we formalize notions related to malleability in the context of public-key encryption and provide definitions of their own interest.

Keywords: Public-key encryption · Generic plaintext equality · Generic plaintext inequality · Zero-knowledge proofs

1 Introduction

The problem of proving whether two given ciphertexts encrypt the same or different messages is known as plaintext equality (or inequality) proofs. Considering public-key encryption (PKE), there are scenarios in which deciding equality can easily be done. For instance, if both ciphertexts were generated using the same key and the encryption scheme is deterministic or if access to a trusted third

© International Financial Cryptography Association 2021
N. Borisov and C. Diaz (Eds.): FC 2021, LNCS 12674, pp. 415–435, 2021.
https://doi.org/10.1007/978-3-662-64322-8_20

party, who knows the private key, is provided. However, in practical scenarios, where a prover needs to convince a verifier of the equality or inequality of plaintexts, require stronger guarantees (*i.e.*, the verifier must learn no additional information than the yes or no answer to the problem).

Well-known examples include the use of such proofs in voting protocols [15,35,36], reputation systems [16,23] and cloud-based applications [34]. Additionally, protocols with broadcasting phases where one of the parties needs to broadcast encrypted messages under different keys to several parties can also benefit from these proofs. A less common example involves a client which needs to regularly store encrypted information in a backup server (or in a distributed database such as blockchain), while being able to convince any third party of minimal claims about it. Furthermore, in settings where online interaction between the parties is not desirable or public verifiability is preferred, non-interactive variants can also be very useful.

Sometimes equality or inequality proofs are used as subroutines and need to be integrated with other software. Therefore, having flexible alternatives (*e.g.*, without relying on specific constructions that require particular configurations or specific hardware) is essential to overcome possible conflicts Thus, generic protocols that can be implemented with different PKE schemes, making them more flexible than their customized variants and more suitable to be integrated into different settings, are proposed.

We focus on two-party protocols, where two ciphertexts and auxiliary inputs are given. The prover attempts to convince a verifier on either the plaintext equality or inequality of the ciphertexts. The prover and the verifier share a common input consisting of a set of public keys and ciphertexts generated with those keys. The prover also knows the corresponding set of secret keys or the randomness used to encrypt the plaintexts. As previously mentioned, our aim is to design generic plaintext equality or inequality protocols in this setting.

Contributions. Using randomization properties of PKE schemes, we build secure generic zero-knowledge protocols from standard techniques. Our first contribution introduces different notions related to the concept of malleability in public-key encryption and their formalization. To that end, we make a clear distinction between how a ciphertext can be randomized (*e.g.* the ciphertext alone, the plaintext message or concerning the corresponding key). As a result, we characterize PKE schemes in terms of generic randomizable encryption properties, which we use to build our protocols. Our second contribution is the construction of two interactive zero-knowledge protocols, Π_{PEQ} and Π_{PINEQ}, for plaintext equality and inequality. These protocols are secure against malicious verifiers. For each of them we first present a weaker variant (Π_{HPEQ} and Π_{HPINEQ} respectively) which is only secure against honest verifiers. The protocol Π_{PEQ} requires the PKE scheme to allow the randomization of both, the ciphertext and the corresponding plaintext message. In contrast, the protocol Π_{PINEQ} only requires the former one. Our third contribution is plaintext equality protocols based on proofs of knowledge of the secret key (protocols Π_{MATCHPEQ} and Π_{SIGPEQ}), or of the randomness used for the encryption (protocol Π_{RSPEQ}). Either case admits non-interactive versions applying the Fiat-Shamir transform, but both require schemes with less common properties. The schemes need to be key-randomizable or random coin decryptable. We base our protocols on simple properties, making them independent of a particular scheme and therefore generic. To support this claim, we list various schemes indicating the relation with our definitions and protocols.

Finally, we also see an added value of our contributions in terms of serving as a pedagogical tool to present zero-knowledge protocols (ZKP). Usual examples to introduce ZKP are graph 3-coloring or graph isomorphism. Although such protocols can be explained without requiring any advanced cryptographic knowledge, they are not used in real-world applications. On the contrary, the protocols that we present are very intuitive, can easily be explained without requiring advanced cryptographic knowledge outside the concept of public key encryption, and are also useful for real-world applications of ZKP. For this reason, we think our protocols can serve as a convincing pedagogical example to explain ZKP to a larger audience who has little mathematical background. With this in mind, as a side contribution, we present a physical protocol using simple objects (boxes and padlocks) to explain how our first proof of plaintext inequality works.

Related Work. Jakobsson et al. [26] introduced the concept of distributed plaintext equality test (PETs), which allows $n > 1$ parties to determine whether two ElGamal ciphertexts encrypt the same or different message without learning it, but given knowledge of the secret key and assuming at least one of the parties is honest. Very recently, McMurtry et al. [28] showed that several follow up works based on the PET from [26] are flawed (because they use it as if no trusting assumptions where needed), and showed how to fix it. Choi et al. [12] proposed zero-knowledge equality/inequality proofs for boolean ElGamal ciphertexts with knowledge of the secret key. In their work, the randomness used to produce the two ciphertexts is required. Parkes et al. [30] proposed zero-knowledge equality/inequality proofs for Paillier ciphertexts given access to the randomness used to produce the ciphertexts or access to the plaintexts. In [4], Blazy et al. introduced a generic approach to prove a non-membership concerning some language in non-interactive zero-knowledge. They showed how to prove plaintext inequality of two ElGamal ciphertexts, given that the prover knows the plaintext and the randomness used to produce one of the ciphertexts. More recently, Blazy et al. [5] introduced a generic technique for non-interactive zero-knowledge plaintext equality/inequality proofs in which the prover is given two ciphertexts and trapdoor information. In such a scenario, none of the parties has access to the secret key nor the randomness used to produce the ciphertexts. While being *generic*, those constructions [4,5] require a specific kind of zero-knowledge proofs. More precisely, they need to build a zero-knowledge proof showing that a zero-knowledge proof was computed honestly. While this design works elegantly with pairing-based cryptography (as Groth-Sahai proofs [22] allows to prove in zero-knowledge a pairing-product equation, while also being verifiable with a pairing product equation), this often fails (or requires ad-hoc constructions that are far from being efficient) in other settings. For example, when considering Schnorr [37] proofs, the random oracle prevents any kind of chaining. Therefore, another design is required to allow such functionality. Extensions for PKE schemes such that given a plaintext, a ciphertext and a public key, it is universally possible to check whether the ciphertext encrypts the plaintext under the key also exists. Such an extension has been proposed by Canard et al. [9] under the name of Plaintext Checkable Encryption. There are also different works proposing schemes to support plaintext equality tests from user-specified authorization. For instance, in [38], two users who have their keys can issue tokens to a proxy to authorize it to perform the plaintext equality test for their ciphertexts. Yang et al. [39] constructed a probabilistic scheme that allows anyone provided with two ciphertexts to check if they encrypt the same message, considering that the ciphertexts may not have been generated with the same key. They do this achieving a weak form of ind-cca.

Previous work rests on specific constructions, which do not allow the scheme to be separated from the protocol's requirements. Our approach is different because we first seek to define protocols independently of the scheme and then to present, which are the necessary conditions for a scheme to instantiate them. As a result and unlike prior work, we present many protocols which can be integrated with existing pieces of software just as if they were templates allowing one to switch from one scheme to another more easily. To compare the efficiency of our protocols with custom variants, we discuss the case of ElGamal.

Outline. Section 2 provides the required background. Sect. 3 defines new notions for generic randomizable encryption. In Sect. 4, we present generic interactive protocols for both, plaintext equality and inequality. In Sect. 5, under different assumptions, we present generic protocols for plaintext equality and discuss how to define non-interactive versions in the random oracle model. Before concluding, we discuss the efficiency of our protocols in Sect. 6.

2   Cryptographic Background

Definition 1 (Public-key encryption scheme [32]). *A public-key encryption (PKE) scheme* $\Pi = (\mathsf{KGen}, \mathsf{Enc}, \mathsf{Dec})$ *is a triple of (possibly randomized) efficient algorithms that verifies the following:*

1. $\mathsf{KGen}(1^k)$ *is a p.p.t algorithm that on input the security parameter* k, *produces a key pair* $(\mathsf{pk}, \mathsf{sk})$.
2. $\mathsf{Enc}_{\mathsf{pk}}(\mathsf{m}; \mathsf{r})$ *is a p.p.t algorithm that given a message* m, *a random coin* r *and* pk *produces a ciphertext* c.
3. $\mathsf{Dec}_{\mathsf{sk}}(\mathsf{c})$ *is a deterministic algorithm that given a ciphertext* c *and* sk *produces a message* m.
4. Correctness: *The triple should be such that the following holds for every valid message defined in the message space and every security parameter:*

$$Pr\left[(\mathsf{pk}, \mathsf{sk}) \xleftarrow{\$} \mathsf{KGen}(1^k) : \mathsf{Dec}_{\mathsf{sk}}(\mathsf{Enc}_{\mathsf{pk}}(\mathsf{m})) = \mathsf{m}\right] = 1.$$

By convention, we denote the set of the plaintexts (resp. public keys, random coins, ciphertexts) by $\mathcal{M}$ (resp. $\mathcal{K}$, $\mathcal{R}$, $\mathcal{C}$).

Definition 2 (Random Coin Decryptable PKE (RCD-PKE) [7]). *A probabilistic PKE scheme is Random Coin Decryptable if there exists a polynomial-time algorithm CDec such that for any public key $pk \in \mathcal{K}$, any $m \in \mathcal{M}$, and any random coin σ, the following equation holds:* $CDec_\sigma(Enc_{pk}(m; \sigma), pk) = m$.

For interactive machines $\mathcal{P}$ (the prover) and $\mathcal{V}$ (the verifier), we denote as in [31] that $\langle \mathcal{P}(y), \mathcal{V}(z) \rangle (x)$ is the random variable representing $\mathcal{V}$'s output when interacting with $\mathcal{P}$ on common input x, when the random input to each machine is uniformly and independently chosen with z and y being auxiliary inputs. We also denote a witness relation for a language $L \in \mathcal{NP}$ as R_L and say that y is a witness for the membership $x \in L$ if $(x, y) \in R_L$.

Definition 3 (Interactive Proof System [19,31]). *Let ϵ_c, $\epsilon_s \colon \mathbb{N} \to [0, 1)$ such that both are computable in poly(ℓ)-time and $\epsilon_c(\ell) + \epsilon_s(l) < 1 - poly(\ell)^{-1}$. $(\mathcal{P}, \mathcal{V})$ is called an interactive proof system for the language L with completeness and soundness errors ϵ_c and ϵ_s, if $\mathcal{V}$ is p.p.t and the following conditions hold:*

- *Completeness: For every $x \in L$ there exists a (witness) string y such that for every auxiliary input $z \in \{0, 1\}^* : Pr[\langle \mathcal{P}(y), \mathcal{V}(z) \rangle (x) = 1] = 1 - \epsilon_c(|x|)$.*
- *Soundness: For every $x \notin L$, every interactive machine $\mathcal{B}$, and every $y, z \in \{0, 1\}^* : Pr[\langle \mathcal{B}(y), \mathcal{V}(z) \rangle (x) = 1] \leq \epsilon_s(|x|)$.*

If $\epsilon_c \equiv 0$, we say the system has perfect completeness. *If the soundness condition is required to hold only with respect to a computationally bounded prover $\mathcal{B}$, $(\mathcal{P}, \mathcal{V})$ is called an interactive* argument *system.*

Definition 4 (Sigma protocol [24]). *An interactive proof system $(\mathcal{P}, \mathcal{V})$ is said to be a sigma protocol for the relation R_L when it uses the following pattern: $\mathcal{P}$ sends a commitment C, $\mathcal{V}$ sends a challenge b, $\mathcal{P}$ sends a response r after which $\mathcal{V}$ accepts or rejects the proof, and the following requirement holds:*

- *Special soundness: There exists a polynomial-time algorithm $\mathcal{E}$ that given any x and any pair of accepting transcripts $(t, t') = ((C, b, r), (C, b', r'))$ for x such that $b \neq b' : Pr[y \leftarrow \mathcal{E}(x, t, t') : (x, y) \in R_L]$ is overwhelming.*

In [27], Lindell extends the definition of special soundness to proofs of knowledge that are not sigma protocols. We now recall it using the formalism introduced in [6], where t is a transcript of the protocol execution and s represents the state of $\mathcal{P}^*$ including its random tape.

Definition 5 (Statistical Witness-Extended Emulation [6]). *An interactive proof system $(\mathcal{P}, \mathcal{V})$ has statistical witness-extended emulation if for all deterministic polynomial-time $\mathcal{P}^*$, there exists an expected polynomial-time emulator $\mathcal{E}$ such that for all interactive adversaries $\mathcal{A}$:*

Experiment $\mathbf{Exp}^{Hiding}_{\Gamma,\mathcal{A}}(k)$
ck $\xleftarrow{\$}$ Setup(1^k)
$(m_0, m_1, state) \leftarrow \mathcal{A}_1(ck)$
$b \xleftarrow{\$} \{0,1\}; (c,d) \leftarrow \text{Commit}_{ck}(m_b)$
$b' \leftarrow \mathcal{A}_2(c, state)$
return $b = b'$

Experiment $\mathbf{Exp}^{Binding}_{\Gamma,\mathcal{A}}(k)$
ck $\xleftarrow{\$}$ Setup(1^k)
$(c, d, d') \leftarrow \mathcal{A}_1(ck)$
$m \leftarrow \text{Open}(c, d); m' \leftarrow \text{Open}(c, d')$
if ($m = \bot$ or $m' = \bot$) then return 0
else return $m \neq m'$

Fig. 1. Experiments defining Hiding and Binding respectively.

$$\Pr\left[(y,s) \leftarrow \mathcal{A}(1^k); t \leftarrow \langle \mathcal{P}^*(y,s), \mathcal{V}(y)\rangle; b \leftarrow \mathcal{A}(t) : b = 1\right] \approx$$
$$\Pr\left[\begin{array}{l}(y,s) \leftarrow \mathcal{A}(1^k); (t, x) \leftarrow \mathcal{E}^{\langle \mathcal{P}^*(y,s), \mathcal{V}(y)\rangle}(y); b \leftarrow \mathcal{A}(t): \\ b = 1 \text{ and if } t \text{ is accepting then } (x, y) \in L\end{array}\right]$$

where the oracle called by $\mathcal{E}^{\langle \mathcal{P}^*(y,s), \mathcal{V}(y)\rangle}(y)$ permits rewinding to a specific point and resuming with fresh randomness for the verifier from this point onwards.

Definition 6 (Zero-Knowledge [31]). *An interactive proof system $(\mathcal{P}, \mathcal{V})$ is zero-knowledge if for every p.p.t interactive machine $\mathcal{V}^*$ there exists a probabilistic expected polynomial-time algorithm $\mathcal{S}$ (called simulator) such that the following two ensembles are computationally indistinguishable (when the distinguishing gap is a function in $|x|$) : $\{\langle \mathcal{P}(y), \mathcal{V}^*(z)\rangle(x)\}_{z \in \{0,1\}^*, x \in L}$ for an arbitrary $y \in R_L(x)$ and $\{\mathcal{S}(x, z)\}_{z \in \{0,1\}^*, x \in L}$. That is, for every probabilistic algorithm $\mathcal{D}$ running in time polynomial in the length of its first input, every polynomial p, all $(x, y) \in R_L$ and all auxiliary inputs $z, z' \in \{0,1\}^*$ it holds that: $|Pr[\mathcal{D}(x, z', \langle \mathcal{P}(y), \mathcal{V}^*(z)\rangle(x)) = 1] - Pr[D(x, z', \mathcal{S}(x, z)) = 1]| < p(|x|)^{-1}$.*

The term "perfect zero-knowledge" refers to proof systems where the two ensembles are identically distributed. Furthermore, a weaker variant called *Honest Verifier Zero-Knowledge* (HVZK) is usually considered as well. Only a single verifier $\mathcal{V} = \mathcal{V}^*$ that always follows the protocol is assumed in this variant.

Definition 7 (Commitment Scheme). *A non-interactive commitment scheme $\Gamma = $ (Setup, Commit, Open) on a message space $\mathcal{M}$ is a tuple that verifies:*

1. *ck $\leftarrow$ Setup(1^k) generates a commitment key ck.*
2. *$\forall\, m \in \mathcal{M} : (c, d) \leftarrow \text{Commit}_{ck}(m)$ is the commitment/opening pair for m.*
3. *A commitment can be opened to $m' \in \mathcal{M} \cup \bot$ with $m' \leftarrow \text{Open}(c, d)$, where $\bot$ is returned if c is not a valid commitment to any message.*
4. *Correctness : $\forall\, m \in \mathcal{M} : \text{Open}(\text{Commit}_{ck}(m)) = m$.*

Commitment schemes are required to have two security properties: binding and hiding. Binding states that it should be infeasible for any party to come up with an opening that would reveal a different value than the one initially committed. Hiding states that it should be infeasible for any party to reveal a commitment without the corresponding opening. If a scheme is perfectly binding, it can only be computationally hiding or the other way round.

Definition 8 (Hiding and Binding). *A commitment scheme Γ has the hiding security property if the advantage of any p.p.t algorithm $\mathcal{A} = (\mathcal{A}_1, \mathcal{A}_2)$ defined by $\mathbf{Adv}_{\Gamma,\mathcal{A}}^{Hiding}(k) := 2 \cdot Pr\left[\mathbf{Exp}_{\Gamma,\mathcal{A}}^{Hiding}(k) \Rightarrow \text{true}\right] - 1$ is negligible, where $\mathbf{Exp}_{\Gamma,\mathcal{A}}^{Hiding}(k)$ is the experiment shown in Fig. 1 (left side).*

A commitment scheme Γ has the binding security property if the advantage of any p.p.t algorithm $\mathcal{A}$ defined by $\mathbf{Adv}_{\Gamma,\mathcal{A}}^{Binding}(k) := Pr\left[\mathbf{Exp}_{\Gamma,\mathcal{A}}^{Binding}(k) \Rightarrow \text{true}\right] - 1$ is negligible, where $\mathbf{Exp}_{\Gamma,\mathcal{A}}^{Binding}(k)$ is the experiment shown in Fig. 1 (right side).

3   Generic Randomizable Encryption

In this section we propose several definitions to characterize the kinds of randomizations that PKE schemes can support.

To begin with, we present a definition of *re-randomizability* [33], which has also been introduced under different names or variants [10,18,21,25]. Unlike previous work, we include the notion of *derandomizability*, and omit the distinction with universal re-randomizability from [33], which we consider implicit unless otherwise said. Informally speaking, a scheme that is randomizable and derandomizable supports not only the generation of fresh ciphertexts but also the "rollback" process. Furthermore, we will say that a scheme achieves perfect randomizability when no adversary can distinguish between a fresh encryption of the original message and a randomization of the ciphertext.

Definition 9 (Randomizable PKE scheme (Rand-PKE) [33]). *Given a PKE scheme $\Pi = (\mathsf{KGen}, \mathsf{Enc}, \mathsf{Dec})$, we say that Π is randomizable if there exists a polynomial-time algorithm Rand such that:*

1. Rand *takes $c \in \mathcal{C}$, $r \in \mathcal{R}$ and returns $c' \in \mathcal{C}$.*
2. $\forall$ $(\mathsf{pk}, \mathsf{sk}) \xleftarrow{\$} \mathsf{KGen}(1^k)$, $r \in \mathcal{R}$ *and* $c \in \mathcal{C}$: $\Pr[\mathsf{Dec}_{\mathsf{sk}}(\mathsf{Rand}(c,r)) = \mathsf{Dec}_{\mathsf{sk}}(c)] = 1$.

Moreover, we say that Π is derandomizable if for any $c \subset \mathcal{C}$ and $r \in \mathcal{R}$, there exists an efficiently computable r^* such that: $\Pr[c = \mathsf{Rand}(\mathsf{Rand}(c,r), r^*)] = 1$.

Definition 10 (Computational and perfect randomizability [33]). *We say that a Rand-PKE scheme is computationally randomizable if for any k, $(\mathsf{pk}, \mathsf{sk}) \leftarrow \mathsf{KGen}(1^k)$, $m \in \mathcal{M}$, $r \in \mathcal{R}$, $c = \mathsf{Enc}_{\mathsf{pk}}(m; r)$ and any polynomial-time distinguisher $\mathcal{D}$, there exists a negligible function $\epsilon(\cdot)$ such that:*

$$\left| \Pr\left[\begin{array}{l} r' \xleftarrow{\$} \mathcal{R}; \\ c' \leftarrow \mathsf{Enc}_{\mathsf{pk}}(m; r'); : b = 1 \\ b \leftarrow \mathcal{D}(\mathsf{pk}, c, c'); \end{array} \right] - \Pr\left[\begin{array}{l} r' \xleftarrow{\$} \mathcal{R}; \\ c' \leftarrow \mathsf{Rand}(c, r'); : b = 1 \\ b \leftarrow \mathcal{D}(\mathsf{pk}, c, c'); \end{array} \right] \right| \leq \epsilon(k).$$

We say that the scheme is perfectly randomizable when $\epsilon(k) = 0$.

We now introduce the following definitions that specify how the random coins used to produce fresh encryptions and randomizations can relate together. We will say that a PKE scheme is strongly randomizable when it also supports efficient algorithms to compute such relationship.

Definition 11 (Strong Randomizable PKE scheme). *Given a PKE scheme* $\Pi = (\mathsf{KGen}, \mathsf{Enc}, \mathsf{Dec})$, *we say that* Π *is* strongly randomizable *if it is a* Rand-PKE *and there exist a polynomial-time algorithm* RandR *such that:*

1. RandR *takes* r *and* $r' \in \mathcal{R}$ *and returns* $r'' \in \mathcal{R}$.
2. $\forall$ (pk, sk) $\overset{\$}{\leftarrow}$ $\mathsf{KGen}(1^k)$, $m \in \mathcal{M}$ *and* $r'' \leftarrow \mathsf{RandR}(r, r')$, *the following equation holds:* $\mathsf{Rand}(\mathsf{Enc}_{\mathsf{pk}}(m; r), r') = \mathsf{Enc}_{\mathsf{pk}}(m; r'')$.

Moreover, we say that Π *is* random-extractable *if there exists a a polynomial-time algorithm* RandExt *such that for any* $(r, r', r'') \in \mathcal{R}^3$:

$$\Pr\left[r = \mathsf{RandExt}(r', r'') : r'' \leftarrow \mathsf{RandR}(r, r')\right] = 1.$$

Definition 12 (Computational and perfect strong randomizability). *We say that a* Rand-PKE *scheme is* computationally *strongly randomizable if for any* k, (pk, sk) $\leftarrow$ $\mathsf{KGen}(1^k)$, $m \in \mathcal{M}$, $r \in \mathcal{R}$, $c = \mathsf{Enc}_{\mathsf{pk}}(m; r)$ *and any polynomial-time distinguisher* $\mathcal{D}$, *there exists a negligible function* $\epsilon(\cdot)$ *such that:*

$$\left| \Pr\left[\begin{matrix} r' \overset{\$}{\leftarrow} \mathcal{R}; \\ c' \leftarrow \mathsf{Enc}_{\mathsf{pk}}(m; r'); \\ b \leftarrow \mathcal{D}(\mathsf{pk}, r, c, r', c'); \end{matrix} : b = 1 \right] - \Pr\left[\begin{matrix} r'' \overset{\$}{\leftarrow} \mathcal{R}; \\ r' \leftarrow \mathsf{RandR}(r, r''); \\ c' \leftarrow \mathsf{Rand}(c, r''); \\ b \leftarrow \mathcal{D}(\mathsf{pk}, r, c, r', c'); \end{matrix} : b = 1 \right] \right| \le \epsilon(k).$$

We say that the scheme is perfectly *strongly randomizable when* $\epsilon(k) = 0$.

We now define the notions of *message-randomizability* and *key-randomizability*. For message-randomizability, we consider three different algorithms. The first one computes the plaintext's randomization, the second compute it on the ciphertext, and the third one computes the randomness given two messages.

Definition 13 (Message-randomizable PKE scheme (MsgRand-PKE)). *Given a PKE scheme* $\Pi = (\mathsf{KGen}, \mathsf{Enc}, \mathsf{Dec})$, *we say that* Π *is* message-randomizable *if there exists a set* $\mathcal{R}_{\mathsf{M}}$ *and two polynomial-time algorithms* MsgRandM *and* MsgRandC *such that:*

1. MsgRandM *takes* $m \in \mathcal{M}$, $r \in \mathcal{R}_{\mathsf{M}}$ *and returns* $m' \in \mathcal{M}$. *Moreover, the function* $f_r : \mathcal{M} \Rightarrow \mathcal{M}$ *defined by* $f_r(m) = \mathsf{MsgRandM}(m, r)$, *is bijective.*
2. MsgRandC *takes* $c \in \mathcal{C}$, $r \in \mathcal{R}_{\mathsf{M}}$ *and returns* $c' \in \mathcal{C}$.
3. $\forall$ (pk, sk) $\overset{\$}{\leftarrow}$ $\mathsf{KGen}(1^k)$, $m \in \mathcal{M}$, $r' \in \mathcal{R}$, $r \in \mathcal{R}_{\mathsf{M}}$ *and* $c = \mathsf{Enc}(m; r')$: $\Pr\left[\mathsf{Dec}_{\mathsf{sk}}(\mathsf{MsgRandC}(c, r)) = \mathsf{MsgRandM}(m, r)\right] = 1$.

Moreover, we say that Π is message-derandomizable *if for any $m \in \mathcal{M}$ and $r \in \mathcal{R}_M$, there exists a unique efficiently computable r^* such that:*

$$\Pr\left[m = \mathsf{MsgRandM}(\mathsf{MsgRandM}(m, r), r^*)\right] = 1.$$

Finally, we say that Π is message-random-extractable *if there exists a p.p.t algorithm* $\mathsf{MsgRandExt}$ *such that for any $m \in \mathcal{M}$ and $r \in \mathcal{R}_M$:*

$$\Pr\left[r = \mathsf{MsgRandExt}(m, \mathsf{MsgRandM}(m, r))\right] = 1.$$

Note that we require $\mathsf{MsgRandM}$ to be bijective. This property is implicity required for the message-derandomizability. Indeed, if a randomized message can be obtained using different messages but the same random, then it could also be derandomized in several ways, which contradicts our definition.

Definition 14 (Computational and perfect message-randomizability). *We say that a $\mathsf{MsgRand}$-PKE scheme is* computationally *message-randomizable if for any k, $(\mathsf{pk}, \mathsf{sk}) \leftarrow \mathsf{KGen}(1^k)$, $m \in \mathcal{M}$, $r \in \mathcal{R}$, $c = \mathsf{Enc}_{\mathsf{pk}}(m; r)$ and any polynomial-time distinguisher $\mathcal{D}$, there exists a negligible function $\epsilon(\cdot)$ such that:*

$$\left| \Pr\left[\begin{array}{l} m' \xleftarrow{\$} \mathcal{M}; \\ c' \leftarrow \mathsf{Enc}_{\mathsf{pk}}(m'; r); : b = 1 \\ b \leftarrow \mathcal{D}(\mathsf{pk}, c, c'); \end{array} \right] - \Pr\left[\begin{array}{l} r_m \xleftarrow{\$} \mathcal{R}_M; \\ c' \leftarrow \mathsf{MsgRandC}(c, r_m); : b = 1 \\ b \leftarrow \mathcal{D}(\mathsf{pk}, c, c'); \end{array} \right] \right| \leq \epsilon(k).$$

We say that the scheme is perfectly *message-randomizable when $\epsilon(k) = 0$.*

For key-randomizability, we consider three algorithms as well. The first one randomizes the public key, the second one the secret key, and the third one randomizes a ciphertext given a randomized public key.

Table 1. PKE schemes and their properties.

						Perfect ZK			ZKPoK	
Scheme	Security	RCD	Rand	MsgRand	KeyRand	Π_{PEQ}	Π_{PINEQ}	Π_{MATCHPEQ}	Π_{SIGPEQ}	Π_{RSPEQ}
ElGamal [17]	IND-CPA	✓	✓	✓	✓	✓	✓	✓	✓	✓
Paillier [29]	IND-CPA	✓	✓	✓		✓	✓	✓		✓
GM [20]	IND-CPA		✓	✓		✓	✓	✓		
DEG [14]	IND-CCA1	✓	✓	✓	✓	✓	✓	✓	✓	✓
CS-lite [13]	IND-CCA1	✓	✓	✓		✓	✓			✓
DSCS [33]	RCCA	✓	✓				✓			

Definition 15 (Key-randomizable PKE scheme ($\mathsf{KeyRand}$-PKE)). *Given a PKE scheme $(\mathsf{KGen}, \mathsf{Enc}, \mathsf{Dec})$, we say that Π is* key-randomizable *if there exists a set $\mathcal{R}_K$ and three polynomial-time algorithms such that:*

1. KeyRandPk *takes a public key* pk, $r \in \mathcal{R}_K$ *and returns* pk$'$.
2. KeyRandSk *takes a secret key* sk, $r \in \mathcal{R}_K$ *and returns* sk$'$.
3. KeyRandC *takes* $c \in \mathcal{C}$, $r \in \mathcal{R}_K$ *and returns* $c' \in \mathcal{C}$.
4. $\forall$ (pk, sk) $\overset{\$}{\leftarrow}$ KGen(1^k), $m \in \mathcal{M}$, $r \in \mathcal{R}$, $r_k \in \mathcal{R}_K$ *and* $c = $ Enc$(m; r)$:

$$\Pr \left[\begin{array}{l} (\mathsf{Dec}_{\mathsf{sk}}(c) = \mathsf{Dec}_{\mathsf{KeyRandSk}(\mathsf{sk},r_k)}(\mathsf{KeyRandC}(c, r_k))) \\ \wedge (\mathsf{Dec}_{\mathsf{KeyRandSk}(\mathsf{sk},r_k)}(\mathsf{Enc}_{\mathsf{KeyRandPk}(\mathsf{pk},r_k)}(m;r)) = m) \end{array} \right] = 1.$$

Moreover, we say that Π is key-derandomizable if for any secret key sk *and* $r_k \in \mathcal{R}_K$, *there exists an efficiently computable r_k^* such that:*

$$\Pr\left[\mathsf{sk} = \mathsf{KeyRandSk}(\mathsf{KeyRandSk}(\mathsf{sk}, r_k), r_k^*) \right] = 1.$$

Definition 16 (Computational and perfect key-randomizability). *We say that a* KeyRand-PKE *scheme is computationally key-randomizable if for any k, (pk, sk) $\overset{\$}{\leftarrow}$ KGen(1^k), $m \in \mathcal{M}$, $r \in \mathcal{R}$, $c = $ Enc$_{\mathsf{pk}}(m;r)$ and any polynomial-time distinguisher $\mathcal{D}$, there exists a negligible function $\epsilon(\cdot)$ such that:*

$$\left| \Pr \left[\begin{array}{l} (\mathsf{pk}', \mathsf{sk}') \overset{\$}{\leftarrow} \mathsf{KGen}(1^k); \\ c' \leftarrow \mathsf{Enc}_{\mathsf{pk}'}(m;r); \quad : b = 1 \\ b \leftarrow \mathcal{D}(\mathsf{sk}, \mathsf{pk}, c', \mathsf{sk}', \mathsf{pk}'); \end{array} \right] - \Pr \left[\begin{array}{l} r_k \overset{\$}{\leftarrow} \mathcal{R}_K; \\ \mathsf{pk}' = \mathsf{KeyRandPk}(\mathsf{pk}, r_k); \\ \mathsf{sk}' = \mathsf{KeyRandPk}(\mathsf{sk}, r_k); \quad : b = 1 \\ c' = \mathsf{KeyRandC}(c, r_k); \\ b \leftarrow \mathcal{D}(\mathsf{sk}, \mathsf{pk}, c', \mathsf{sk}', \mathsf{pk}'); \end{array} \right] \right| \leq \epsilon(k).$$

We say that the scheme is perfectly key-randomizable *when $\epsilon(k) = 0$.*

In Table 1, we list some well-known PKE schemes and their relationship with our definitions and protocols. We stress that although fully homomorphic schemes such as those based on lattices could also be used to instantiate our protocols, partial homomorphic properties presented in the scheme can be used to implement the different algorithms as well. Nonetheless, as shown with the DSCS scheme [33], we note that being partially homomorphic is not necessary to achieve re-randomizability. We refer the reader to Appendix A for examples of how our protocols can be instantiated with ElGamal and Paillier.

Prover P(sk, pk, c_0, c_1)	**Verifier** V(pk, c_0, c_1)
	if (pk, $c_0, c_1) \notin \mathcal{K} \times \mathcal{C}^2$ then **Abort**
	$r \overset{\$}{\leftarrow} \mathcal{R}; \ b \overset{\$}{\leftarrow} \{0, 1\}$
if $\mathsf{Dec}_{\mathsf{sk}}(c_b') = \mathsf{Dec}_{\mathsf{sk}}(c_0) \xleftarrow{\ c_b'\ } c_b' \leftarrow \mathsf{Rand}(c_b, r)$	
then $z = 0$ **else** $z = 1 \xrightarrow{\ z\ }$ if $(z = b)$ then **Accept else** Reject	

Fig. 2: One round of the protocol Π_{HPINEQ} (repeated k times).

Fig. 2. One round of the protocol Π_{HPINEQ} (repeated k times).

4   Interactive Protocols

This section presents protocols for proving plaintext equality and inequality where the common input consists of a public key and two ciphertexts generated with it. As private input, the prover will have the corresponding private key. For plaintext inequality protocols we will require the scheme to be randomizable whereas for plaintext equality we will also require it to be message-randomizable.

In both cases, we first introduce an HVZK variant, which we then modify to achieve zero-knowledge in the presence of malicious verifiers. Complete security proofs for all protocols in this work are given in the extended version [3].

4.1   Plaintext Inequality

Let us first introduce our protocol Π_{HPINEQ} (Fig. 2). It starts with the verifier randomly choosing $r \xleftarrow{\$} \mathcal{R}$ and $b \in \{0, 1\}$. Then it computes $c_b' \leftarrow \mathsf{Rand}(c_b, r)$ and sends c_b' to the prover. At this stage, the prover receives a ciphertext that cannot link without decryption to c_0 or c_1. Since the verifier is honest, the prover either decrypts c_b' to m_0 or m_1 and can determine b and send it back to the verifier. The verifier accepts if and only if it receives b as expected.

Theorem 1. *Let Π be a PKE scheme, which is (computationally) randomizable. If Π is used in Π_{HPINEQ}, then Π_{HPINEQ} is complete, computationally sound and perfect HVZK.*

The idea of this protocol can easily be explained to a large audience replacing the ciphertexts with closed boxes using a padlock. Consider two identical closed boxes that contain a white card and a black card respectively. The prover has a key that allows him to open both boxes, and wants to prove the verifier that the boxes contains different things without revealing anything else. The verifier secretly chooses one of the two boxes and challenges the prover to guess which box he picked. The prover secretly opens the box and deduces which one it was from the color of the card. He then tells the verifier which was the box and if the verifier agrees, they repeat the protocol k times. If the two identical boxes contain the same card, then the prover has no information about the box he receives and fails one of the rounds with probability $1/2^k$.

Protocol Π_{PINEQ} (Fig. 3), is an amendment of Π_{HPINEQ} that uses a commitment scheme. Without it, a malicious verifier could send a ciphertext that is not a randomization of c_0 or c_1 and check whether it encrypts the same value. The commitment scheme protects the prover from such verifiers. To this end, the verifier first randomizes the ciphertext and then sends it to the prover, which computes z and commits to the resulting value. Then, the verifier reveals the randomness used at the first stage and the prover opens the commitment if and only if these values are consistent with the ciphertext obtained from the verifier.

Prover $P(\mathsf{sk}, \mathsf{pk}, c_0, c_1)$	**Verifier** $V(\mathsf{pk}, c_0, c_1)$

$$\qquad\qquad\qquad\qquad\qquad\qquad\text{if } (\mathsf{pk}, c_0, c_1) \notin \mathcal{K} \times \mathcal{C}^2 \text{ then } \mathsf{Abort}$$

$z = \neg(\mathsf{Dec}_{\mathsf{sk}}(c_0) = \mathsf{Dec}_{\mathsf{sk}}(c_b')) \qquad \xleftarrow{\quad c_b' \quad} r \xleftarrow{\$} \mathcal{R}; b \xleftarrow{\$} \{0,1\}; c_b' \leftarrow \mathsf{Rand}(c_b, r)$

$(\mathsf{comm}, \mathsf{op}) \leftarrow \mathsf{Commit}(z) \qquad \xrightarrow{\quad \mathsf{comm} \quad}$

$\qquad\qquad\qquad\qquad\qquad\qquad \xleftarrow{\quad r, b \quad}$

$\text{if } c_b' \neq \mathsf{Rand}(c_b, r) \text{ then } \mathsf{op} := \perp \xrightarrow{\quad \mathsf{op} \quad} z' \leftarrow \mathsf{Open}(\mathsf{comm}, \mathsf{op})$

$\qquad\qquad\qquad\qquad\qquad\qquad \text{if } (z' = b) \text{ then } \mathsf{Accept} \text{ else } \mathsf{Reject}$

Fig. 3. One round of the protocol Π_{PINEQ} (repeated k times).

Prover $P(\mathsf{sk}, \mathsf{pk}, c_0, c_1)$	**Verifier** $V(\mathsf{pk}, c_0, c_1)$

$$\qquad\qquad\qquad\qquad\qquad\qquad\text{if } (\mathsf{pk}, c_0, c_1) \notin \mathcal{K} \times \mathcal{C}^2 \text{ then } \mathsf{Abort}$$

$\qquad\qquad\qquad\qquad\qquad\qquad r \xleftarrow{\$} \mathcal{R}; r_m \xleftarrow{\$} \mathcal{R}_M; b \xleftarrow{\$} \{0,1\}$

$\qquad\qquad\qquad\qquad\qquad\qquad c_b' \leftarrow \mathsf{Rand}(c_b, r)$

$m' \leftarrow \mathsf{Dec}_{\mathsf{sk}}(c_b''); m \leftarrow \mathsf{Dec}_{\mathsf{sk}}(c_0) \xleftarrow{\quad c_b'' \quad} c_b'' \leftarrow \mathsf{MsgRandC}(c_b', r_m)$

$z \leftarrow \mathsf{MsgRandExt}(m', m) \qquad \xrightarrow{\quad z \quad} \text{if } (z = r_m) \text{ then } \mathsf{Accept} \text{ else } \mathsf{Reject}$

Fig. 4. One round of the protocol Π_{HPEQ} (repeated k times).

Theorem 2. *Let Π be a PKE scheme, which is perfectly strong randomizable and derandomizable. Let Γ be a commitment scheme, which is computationally binding and perfectly hiding. If Π and Γ are used in the protocol Π_{PINEQ}, then Π_{PINEQ} is complete, computationally sound and perfect zero-knowledge.*

4.2 Plaintext Equality

As before, we begin explaining our protocol Π_{HPEQ} (Fig. 4). First, the verifier randomly chooses $r \in \mathcal{R}$, $r_m \in \mathcal{R}_M$ and $b \in \{0,1\}$. Then it computes $c_b' \leftarrow \mathsf{Rand}(c_b, r)$ and $c_b'' \leftarrow \mathsf{MsgRandC}(c_b', r_m)$ to send c_b'' to the prover. At this stage, the prover receives a ciphertext that cannot be linked to c_0 nor to c_1. The prover decrypts c_b'' obtaining a message m', which corresponds to a message-randomization of either the message decrypted by c_0 or by c_1. The prover computes $z = \mathsf{MsgRandExt}(m', m)$ and sends it to the verifier. The verifier accepts if and only if $z = r_m$. Since both ciphertexts, c_0 and c_1, belong to $\mathsf{Enc}_{\mathsf{pk}}(m)$, the prover can always compute z correctly. If this is not the case, then a cheating prover can only correctly guess the bit b with probability at most $1/2$.

Prover P(sk, pk, c_0, c_1)		Verifier V(pk, c_0, c_1)

$$\text{if } (\mathsf{pk}, c_0, c_1) \notin \mathcal{K} \times \mathcal{C}^2 \text{ then } \textbf{Abort}$$

$$r \xleftarrow{\$} \mathcal{R}; \ r_m \xleftarrow{\$} \mathcal{R}_M; \ b \xleftarrow{\$} \{0, 1\}$$

$$c'_b \leftarrow \mathsf{Rand}(c_b, r)$$

$m' \leftarrow \mathsf{Dec}_{\mathsf{sk}}(c''_b); m \leftarrow \mathsf{Dec}_{\mathsf{sk}}(c_0) \quad \xleftarrow{\ c''_b\ } \quad c''_b \leftarrow \mathsf{MsgRandC}(c'_b, r_m)$

$z \leftarrow \mathsf{MsgRandExt}(m', m)$

$(\mathsf{comm}, \mathsf{op}) \leftarrow \mathsf{Commit}(z) \qquad \xrightarrow{\ \mathsf{comm}\ }$

$\text{if } \mathsf{MsgRandC}(\mathsf{Rand}(c_b, r), r_m) \neq c''_b \xleftarrow{\ (r, r_m, b)\ }$

$\quad \textbf{then } \mathsf{op} := \bot \qquad\qquad \xrightarrow{\ \mathsf{op}\ } \quad z' \leftarrow \mathsf{Open}(\mathsf{comm}, \mathsf{op})$

$$\text{if } (z' = r_m) \textbf{ then Accept else Reject}$$

Fig. 5. One round of the protocol Π_{PEQ} (repeated k times).

Theorem 3. *Let Π be a PKE scheme, which is (computationally) randomizable, (computationally) message-randomizable and message-random-extractable. If Π is the scheme used in Π_{HPEQ}, then Π_{HPEQ} is complete, computationally sound and perfect HVZK.*

Figure 5 shows our last variant, which makes use of a commitment scheme. Without one, a malicious verifier could send a ciphertext c^* for which he knows the corresponding message m^*. Once z is received from the prover, the malicious verifier will gain information about the relation of (m, m^*, z) and could eventually compute m. By relying on the commitment scheme's hiding property, the prover first commits to the value z. Then, it checks whether the verifier has correctly randomized the messages or not to open the commitment.

Theorem 4. *Let Π be a PKE scheme, which is perfectly strong randomizable and derandomizable, perfectly message-randomizable and message-derandomizable and message-random-extractable. Let Γ be the commitment scheme, which is computationally binding and perfectly hiding. If Π and Γ are used in the protocol Π_{PEQ}, then Π_{PFQ} is complete, computationally sound and perfect zero-knowledge.*

Note that in Theorems 2 and 4 zero-knowledge can be computational if the randomization conditions are computational instead of perfect or if the commitment scheme being used has only computational hiding.

5 ZKPoK for Plaintext Equality

We switch our attention to protocols that are Zero-Knowledge Proofs of Knowledge (ZKPoK) for plaintext equality. In Sect. 5.1 we focus on ZKPoK of the secret key whereas in Sect. 5.2 we focus on ZKPoK of the randomness used to generate the ciphertexts. The application is not the same because if the prover knows the secret key, the use case to consider is when the prover acts as a receiver of those ciphertexts. On the other hand, if the prover knows the randomness used to generate the ciphertexts, the use case to consider is when the prover acts as a sender. Finally, we outline how non-interactive variants can be defined in Sect. 5.3.

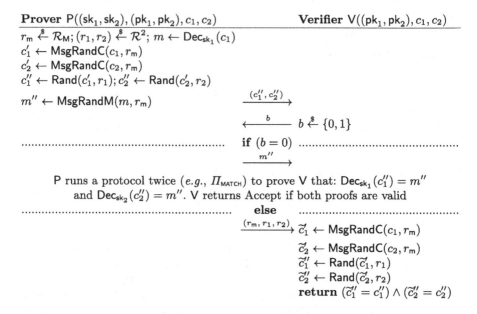

Fig. 6. One round of the protocol Π_{MATCHPEQ} (repeated k times).

5.1 Protocols Based on Knowledge of the Secret Key

Protocols in this section additionally require the scheme to be key-randomizable. We present a protocol called Π_{MATCHPEQ} (Fig. 6), which relies on a ZKP to prove that the decryption of a given ciphertext matches a given message. Such proofs are known for numerous encryption schemes (e.g., [14,17,20,29]). Then, we introduce an auxiliary protocol called Π_{MATCH} (Fig. 7), that meets the requirement of Π_{MATCHPEQ} (its a proof system for the above mentioned). We also present here a third protocol called Π_{SIGPEQ} (Fig. 8) that merges the two previous ones. It requires a randomizable, message-randomizable and key-randomizable scheme, but it does not require any other protocol as a subroutine, which makes it more efficient that Π_{MATCHPEQ} instantiated with Π_{MATCH}. An interesting additional property of Π_{MATCHPEQ} and Π_{SIGPEQ} is that both can also be used to prove plaintext equality of two ciphertexts encrypted under different keys.

In protocol Π_{MATCHPEQ} the prover sends two message-randomizations to the verifier who then challenges it on these ciphertexts. If both ciphertexts encrypt message-randomizations of the same message, then the prover can either prove that it correctly did the message-randomizations or that both ciphertexts encrypt the same message.

Prover $\mathsf{P}(\mathsf{sk}, \mathsf{pk}, c, m)$ **Verifier** $\mathsf{V}(\mathsf{pk}, c, m)$

$r_\mathsf{k} \xleftarrow{\$} \mathcal{R}_\mathsf{K};\ \mathsf{pk}' \leftarrow \mathsf{KeyRandPk}(\mathsf{pk}, r_\mathsf{k})$

$\mathsf{sk}' \leftarrow \mathsf{KeyRandSk}(\mathsf{sk}, r_\mathsf{k});\ r \xleftarrow{\$} \mathcal{R}$

$c'' \leftarrow \mathsf{Rand}(c', r);\ c' \leftarrow \mathsf{KeyRandC}(c, r_\mathsf{k})\ \xrightarrow{\ (\mathsf{pk}', c'')\ }$

$\xleftarrow{\quad b \quad}\ b \xleftarrow{\$} \{0, 1\}$

if $(b = 0)$ **then** $z = \mathsf{sk}'$ **else** $z = (r, r_\mathsf{k})\ \xrightarrow{\quad z \quad}$ **if** $b = 1$ **then**

$\widetilde{\mathsf{pk}}' \leftarrow \mathsf{KeyRandPk}(\mathsf{pk}, r_\mathsf{k})$

$\widetilde{c}' \leftarrow \mathsf{KeyRandC}(c, r_\mathsf{k})$

$\widetilde{c}'' \leftarrow \mathsf{Rand}(\widetilde{c}', r)$

return $(\widetilde{c}'' = c'') \wedge (\widetilde{\mathsf{pk}}' = \mathsf{pk}')$

else return $(m = \mathsf{Dec}_{sk'}(c''))$

Fig. 7. One round of the protocol Π_{MATCH} (repeated k times).

Theorem 5. *Let Π be the PKE scheme used in Π_{MATCHPEQ}. If Π is perfectly randomizable and derandomizable, perfectly message-randomizable and message-derandomizable, and if the proof in step three is instantiated by a sigma protocol that is correct, special sound, and perfectly zero-knowledge, then Π_{MATCHPEQ} is complete, has statistical witness-extended emulation, and perfect zero-knowledge.*

For Π_{MATCH}, we consider a setting in which the verifier has access to the pk, the ciphertext c, the message m and challenges the prover to prove that c is an encryption of m. This protocol's intuition is that if the scheme is randomizable and key-randomizable, the prover can generate a new ciphertext for the same message but under different keys. The verifier is then allowed to check that 1) the prover can generate a new ciphertext c'' which decrypts to the same message and 2) by decrypting c'' to m conclude that the original ciphertext c is also an encryption of m.

Theorem 6. *Let Π be the PKE scheme used in Π_{MATCH}. If Π is perfectly randomizable, perfectly key-randomizable and key-derandomizable, then Π_{MATCH} is complete, special sound, and perfect zero-knowledge.*

To conclude this section, we present the protocol Π_{SIGPEQ}, a sigma protocol for plaintext equality of two ciphertexts built upon the previous ones. In this protocol, the prover performs a message-randomization on the ciphertexts and a key-randomization to obtain new ciphertexts. These ciphertexts decrypt to the same message m' but under a different key. Once the prover sends the public keys and the new ciphertexts to the verifier, the verifier challenges the prover. The intuition behind the challenge is that if the two ciphertexts obtained by

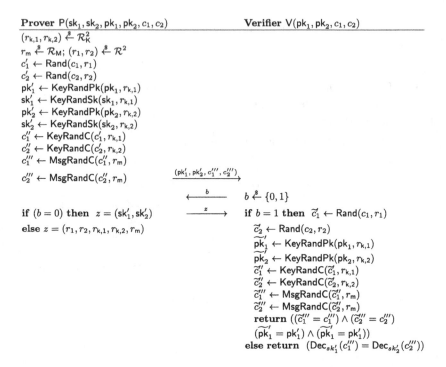

Fig. 8. One round of the protocol Π_{SIGPEQ} (repeated k times).

the verifier are message-randomizations of the same message, then the prover should be able to provide either the corresponding secret key to confirm it or the randomness used to verify the procedure. This protocol is more efficient because it requires exactly k rounds, while Π_{MATCHPEQ} requires k rounds times the number of rounds of Π_{MATCH}.

Theorem 7. *Let Π be the PKE scheme used in Π_{SIGPEQ}. If Π is perfectly randomizable, perfectly message-randomizable and perfectly key-randomizable, then Π_{SIGPEQ} is complete, special sound, and perfect zero-knowledge.*

5.2 Protocols Based on Knowledge of the Encryption Randomness

Based on the previous ideas, we present in this section the protocol Π_{RSPEQ}, which requires the PKE scheme to be random coin decryptable, strong randomizable and message-randomizable. The intuition behind this protocol (Fig. 9) is the same as in Π_{SIGPEQ}; the verifier challenges the prover to either provide the randomizers or to allow it to check the procedure.

Theorem 8. *Let Π be the PKE scheme used in Π_{RSPEQ}. If Π is perfectly strong randomizable, random-extractable, perfectly message-randomizable and random coin decryptable, then Π_{RSPEQ} is complete, special sound, and perfect zero-knowledge.*

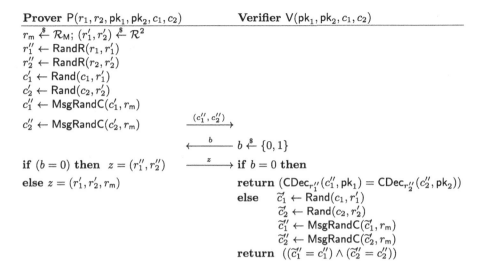

Fig. 9. One round of the protocol Π_{RSPEQ} (repeated k times).

5.3 Non-interactive Variants

Considering that sigma protocols are invariant under parallel composition, for protocols Π_{SIGPEQ} and Π_{RSPEQ}, one can apply the strong Fiat-Shamir transformation [2] and obtain a Non-Interactive Zero-Knowledge Proof, which is secure in the random oracle model. In other words, the prover should generate k commitments $(r_1, ..., r_k)$, calculate $c \in \{0, 1\}^k \leftarrow \mathcal{H}(r_1 || r_2...r_k || \text{public\_parameters})$, and finally compute the responses z_i for all r_i using the i-th bit of c. This way, the soundness error $(1/2)$ is amplified to $1/2^k$.

6   Efficiency

In order to compare the efficiency of our protocols with custom ones, we provide here an efficiency analysis and implementation details using ElGamal.

Comparison with Custom Variants. Our generic protocols Π_{PEQ}, Π_{RSPEQ}, and Π_{PINEQ} are perfect zero-knowledge and do not rely on the random oracle model. We compare the efficiency of our protocols with the best (as far as we know) custom protocols for ElGamal that achieve the same security properties. Note that more efficient protocols exist under weaker hypothesis: HVZK proofs can be done using Shnorr-like protocols [37], non-interactive protocols can be done in the random oracle model replacing the challenge by the hash of the commitment, and non-interactive but computationaly zero-knowlege proofs can be done using the Groth-Sahai construction from pairings [22].

Proving the equality of two ElGamal plaintexts (m_1, m_2) given two ciphertexts $c_1 = \mathsf{Enc}_{\mathsf{pk}}(m_1; r_1) = (g^{r_1}, \mathsf{pk}^{r_1} m_1)$ and $c_2 = \mathsf{Enc}_{\mathsf{pk}}(m_2; r_2) = (g^{r_2}, \mathsf{pk}^{r_2} m_2)$ is equivalent to prove that $(g^\alpha, g^{r_1-r_2}, g^{\alpha(r_1-r_2)})$ is a Diffie-Hellman tuple, which

Table 2. Number of exp. and rounds for plaintext equality/inequality proofs.

	Equality proofs			Inequality proofs	
	Using [11]	Π_{PEQ}	Π_{RSPEQ}	Using [8]	Π_{PINEQ}
Prover	2	6	4	6	6
Verifier	2	4	4	4	4
Rounds	3	4	3	3	4

Table 3. Running times in ms for different protocols using ElGamal.

Protocol	Π_{HPEQ}	Π_{PEQ}	Π_{HPINEQ}	Π_{PINEQ}	Π_{RSPEQ}	Π_{SIGPEQ}
Avg. time	27.47	70.31	26.13	68.75	62.12	112.98
Deviation	0.21	1.28	0.15	0.6	2.06	3.70

can be efficiently done with the Chaum-Pedersen protocol [11] (using either the secret key or the randomness as the witness). Similarly, proving the inequality of the two plaintexts is equivalent to prove that $(g^\alpha, g^{r_1-r_2}, g^{\alpha(r_1-r_2)}m_1/m_2)$ is not a Diffie-Hellman tuple, which can be efficiently done with the Camenisch-Shoup protocol [8]. These protocols must be repeated k times for a security parameter k, like ours. Table 2 gives the number of exponentiations (the dominant operation in all the considered protocols) and rounds for a single run of each protocol. This comparison suggests that our generic protocols' cost is reasonable for perfect zero-knowledge protocols in the standard model.

Implementation. We implemented the protocols Π_{HPEQ}, Π_{PEQ}, Π_{HPINEQ}, Π_{PINEQ}, Π_{RSPEQ} and Π_{SIGPEQ} in Rust using the dalek library [1]. Although the implementation was done for academic purposes and simulating the interaction between a prover and a verifier (it is not production-ready), it serves to demonstrate the practicality of our protocols. More in detail, we show on Table 3 the average running times using a regular laptop (Macbook Pro from 2015) with no extra optimizations and considering a security parameter of 128. Therefore, the times shown consist of 128 *repetitions* for each protocol run so to achieve the desired soundness error. This information was gathered using the external crate *bencher*.

7   Conclusion

We characterized malleability in terms of randomizability, message-randomizability and key-randomizability for public-key encryption. Based on those notions, we defined and presented interactive and non-interactive zero-knowledge protocols for plaintext equality and inequality. As a result, we obtained generic protocols that can be instantiated with different encryption schemes. We provided examples of PKE schemes, which have different properties and that are secure under different security models to support the claim. As future work, we first want to design non-interactive protocols for plaintext inequality. We also would like to propose protocols that do not require k rounds from a generic encryption scheme. Another idea is to construct generic "plaintext inequality test" to prove that the ciphertext's plaintext is smaller or greater than another plaintext.

Acknowledgements. We would like to thank Travis Mayberry for his useful suggestions and comments to improve this work. Olivier Blazy was supported by the French ANR Project IDFIX (ANR-16-CE39-004). The European Commission partially supported Octavio Perez Kempner's work as part of the CUREX project (H2020-SC1-FA-DTS-2018-1 under grant agreement No 826404).

A   Instantiation

Based on the literature review, we found that ElGamal and Paillier were the most used schemes to implement plaintext equality/inequality proofs. For this reason, we present here examples of how to instantiate a subset of our protocols using these schemes

Let us first note that PKE schemes whose set of random coins and messages are cyclic groups $(\mathbb{G}_1, *)$ and $(\mathbb{G}_2, *)$ with identity elements e_1 and e_2 and which are homomorphic for $*$ (*i.e.* $\mathsf{Enc}(m, r) * \mathsf{Enc}(m', r') = \mathsf{Enc}(m * m', r * r'))$, are randomizable and message-randomizable. To randomize a ciphertext $\mathsf{Enc}(m, r)$ with r' one can compute $\mathsf{Enc}(m, r) * \mathsf{Enc}(e_1, r') = \mathsf{Enc}(m, r * r')$, and to randomize the plaintext with m' one can compute $\mathsf{Enc}(m, r) * \mathsf{Enc}(m', e_2) = \mathsf{Enc}(m * m', r)$. We show that ElGamal and Pailler verify this property. Considering two ElGamal ciphertexts $(g^{r_1}, \mathsf{pk}^{r_1} \cdot m_1)$ and $(g^{r_2}, \mathsf{pk}^{r_2} \cdot m_2)$, we define the operation $*$ as $(g^{r_1}, \mathsf{pk}^r \cdot m_1) * (g^{r_2}, \mathsf{pk}^r \cdot m_2) = (g^{r_1} \cdot g^{r_2}, \mathsf{pk}^{r_1} \cdot m_1 \cdot \mathsf{pk}^{r_2} \cdot m_2) = (g^{(r_1+r_2)}, \mathsf{pk}^{(r_1+r_2)} \cdot (m_1 \cdot m_2))$. Considering two Pailler ciphertexts $((1 + n)^{m_1} \cdot r_1^n \mod n^2)$ and $((1+n)^{m_2} \cdot r_2^n \mod n^2)$, we define the operation $*$ as $((1+n)^{m_1} \cdot r_1^n \mod n^2) * ((1+n)^{m_2} \cdot r_2^n \mod n^2) = ((1+n)^{m_1} \cdot r_1^n \cdot (1+n)^{m_2} \cdot r_2^n \mod n^2) = ((1+n)^{m_1} \cdot (1+n)^{m_2} \cdot r_1^n \cdot r_2^n \mod n^2) = ((1+n)^{(m_1+m_2)} \cdot (r_1 \cdot r_2)^n \mod n^2)$. It follows that ElGamal and Pailler can instantiate the protocols Π_{PEQ}, Π_{PINEQ} and Π_{RSPEQ}.

References

1. Protocols' implementation in Rust. https://github.com/oblazy/proofofeq
2. Bernhard, D., Pereira, O., Warinschi, B.: How not to prove yourself: pitfalls of the Fiat-Shamir heuristic and applications to Helios. In: Wang, X., Sako, K. (eds.) ASIACRYPT 2012. LNCS, vol. 7658, pp. 626–643. Springer, Heidelberg (2012). https://doi.org/10.1007/978-3-642-34961-4_38
3. Blazy, O., Bultel, X., Lafourcade, P., Kempner, O.P.: Generic plaintext equality and inequality proofs (extended version) (2021). https://fc21.ifca.ai/papers/79.pdf
4. Blazy, O., Chevalier, C., Vergnaud, D.: Non-interactive zero-knowledge proofs of non-membership. In: Nyberg, K. (ed.) CT-RSA 2015. LNCS, vol. 9048, pp. 145–164. Springer, Cham (2015). https://doi.org/10.1007/978-3-319-16715-2_8
5. Blazy, O., Derler, D., Slamanig, D., Spreitzer, R.: Non-interactive plaintext (In-)Equality proofs and group signatures with verifiable controllable linkability. In: Sako, K. (ed.) CT-RSA 2016. LNCS, vol. 9610, pp. 127–143. Springer, Cham (2016). https://doi.org/10.1007/978-3-319-29485-8_8

6. Bootle, J., Cerulli, A., Chaidos, P., Groth, J., Petit, C.: Efficient zero-knowledge arguments for arithmetic circuits in the discrete log setting. In: Fischlin, M., Coron, J.-S. (eds.) EUROCRYPT 2016. LNCS, vol. 9666, pp. 327–357. Springer, Heidelberg (2016). https://doi.org/10.1007/978-3-662-49896-5_12

7. Bultel, X., Lafourcade, P.: A posteriori openable public key encryption. In: Hoepman, J.-H., Katzenbeisser, S. (eds.) SEC 2016. IAICT, vol. 471, pp. 17–31. Springer, Cham (2016). https://doi.org/10.1007/978-3-319-33630-5_2

8. Camenisch, J., Shoup, V.: Practical verifiable encryption and decryption of discrete logarithms. In: Boneh, D. (ed.) CRYPTO 2003. LNCS, vol. 2729, pp. 126–144. Springer, Heidelberg (2003). https://doi.org/10.1007/978-3-540-45146-4_8

9. Canard, S., Fuchsbauer, G., Gouget, A., Laguillaumie, F.: Plaintext-checkable encryption. In: Dunkelman, O. (ed.) CT-RSA 2012. LNCS, vol. 7178, pp. 332–348. Springer, Heidelberg (2012). https://doi.org/10.1007/978-3-642-27954-6_21

10. Canetti, R., Krawczyk, H., Nielsen, J.B.: Relaxing chosen-ciphertext security. In: Boneh, D. (ed.) CRYPTO 2003. LNCS, vol. 2729, pp. 565–582. Springer, Heidelberg (2003). https://doi.org/10.1007/978-3-540-45146-4_33

11. Chaum, D., Pedersen, T.P.: Wallet databases with observers. In: Brickell, E.F. (ed.) CRYPTO 1992. LNCS, vol. 740, pp. 89–105. Springer, Heidelberg (1993). https://doi.org/10.1007/3-540-48071-4_7

12. Choi, S.G., Elbaz, A., Juels, A., Malkin, T., Yung, M.: Two-party computing with encrypted data. In: Kurosawa, K. (ed.) ASIACRYPT 2007. LNCS, vol. 4833, pp. 298–314. Springer, Heidelberg (2007). https://doi.org/10.1007/978-3-540-76900-2_18

13. Cramer, R., Shoup, V.: A practical public key cryptosystem provably secure against adaptive chosen ciphertext attack. In: Krawczyk, H. (ed.) CRYPTO 1998. LNCS, vol. 1462, pp. 13–25. Springer, Heidelberg (1998). https://doi.org/10.1007/BFb0055717

14. Damgård, I.: Towards practical public key systems secure against chosen ciphertext attacks. In: Feigenbaum, J. (ed.) CRYPTO 1991. LNCS, vol. 576, pp. 445–456. Springer, Heidelberg (1992). https://doi.org/10.1007/3-540-46766-1_36

15. Damgård, I., Jurik, M., Nielsen, J.B.: A generalization of Paillier's public-key system with applications to electronic voting. Int. J. Inf. Secur. 9(6), 371–385 (2010)

16. Dimitriou, T., Michalas, A.: Multi-party trust computation in decentralized environments in the presence of malicious adversaries. Ad Hoc Netw. 15, 53–66 (2014)

17. ElGamal, T.: A public key cryptosystem and a signature scheme based on discrete logarithms. In: Blakley, G.R., Chaum, D. (eds.) CRYPTO 1984. LNCS, vol. 196, pp. 10–18. Springer, Heidelberg (1985). https://doi.org/10.1007/3-540-39568-7_2

18. Faonio, A., Fiore, D., Herranz, J., Ràfols, C.: Structure-preserving and re-randomizable RCCA-secure public key encryption and its applications. In: Galbraith, S.D., Moriai, S. (eds.) ASIACRYPT 2019. LNCS, vol. 11923, pp. 159–190. Springer, Cham (2019). https://doi.org/10.1007/978-3-030-34618-8_6

19. Goldreich, O., Teichner, L.: Super-Perfect Zero-Knowledge Proofs. Springer International Publishing, Cham (2020)

20. Goldwasser, S., Micali, S.: Probabilistic encryption and how to play mental poker keeping secret all partial information. In: Proceedings of the Fourteenth Annual ACM Symposium on Theory of Computing, pp. 365–377. STOC 1982. Association for Computing Machinery, New York, NY, USA (1982)

21. Golle, P., Jakobsson, M., Juels, A., Syverson, P.: Universal re-encryption for mixnets. In: Okamoto, T. (ed.) CT-RSA 2004. LNCS, vol. 2964, pp. 163–178. Springer, Heidelberg (2004). https://doi.org/10.1007/978-3-540-24660-2_14

22. Groth, J., Sahai, A.: Efficient non-interactive proof systems for bilinear groups. In: Smart, N. (ed.) EUROCRYPT 2008. LNCS, vol. 4965, pp. 415–432. Springer, Heidelberg (2008). https://doi.org/10.1007/978-3-540-78967-3_24

23. Hasan, O., Brunie, L., Bertino, E., Shang, N.: A decentralized privacy preserving reputation protocol for the malicious adversarial model. IEEE Trans. Inf. Forensics Security **8**(6), 949–962 (2013)

24. Hazay, C., Lindell, Y.: Efficient Secure Two-Party Protocols: Techniques and Constructions. Springer-Verlag, 1st edn. (2010). https://doi.org/10.1007/978-3-642-14303-8

25. Hirt, M., Sako, K.: Efficient receipt-free voting based on homomorphic encryption. In: Preneel, B. (ed.) EUROCRYPT 2000. LNCS, vol. 1807, pp. 539–556. Springer, Heidelberg (2000). https://doi.org/10.1007/3-540-45539-6_38

26. Jakobsson, M., Juels, A.: Mix and match: secure function evaluation via ciphertexts. In: Okamoto, T. (ed.) ASIACRYPT 2000. LNCS, vol. 1976, pp. 162–177. Springer, Heidelberg (2000). https://doi.org/10.1007/3-540-44448-3_13

27. Lindell, Y.: Parallel coin-tossing and constant-round secure two-party computation. In: Kilian, J. (ed.) CRYPTO 2001. LNCS, vol. 2139, pp. 171–189. Springer, Heidelberg (2001). https://doi.org/10.1007/3-540-44647-8_10

28. McMurtry, E., Pereira, O., Teague, V.: When is a test not a proof? In: Chen, L., Li, N., Liang, K., Schneider, S. (eds.) ESORICS 2020. LNCS, vol. 12309, pp. 23–41. Springer, Cham (2020). https://doi.org/10.1007/978-3-030-59013-0_2

29. Paillier, P.: Public-key cryptosystems based on composite degree residuosity classes. In: Stern, J. (ed.) EUROCRYPT 1999. LNCS, vol. 1592, pp. 223–238. Springer, Heidelberg (1999). https://doi.org/10.1007/3-540-48910-X_16

30. Parkes, D., Rabin, M., Shieber, S., Thorpe, C.: Practical secrecy-preserving, verifiably correct and trustworthy auctions. In: ICEC 2006 (2006)

31. Pass, R.: Alternative Variants of Zero-Knowledge Proofs. Techical report, KTH Royal Institute of Technology (2004)

32. Pass, R., Shelat, A.: A course in Cryptography (2010). http://www.cs.cornell.edu/courses/cs4830/2010fa/lecnotes.pdf

33. Prabhakaran, M., Rosulek, M.: Rerandomizable RCCA encryption. In: Menezes, A. (ed.) CRYPTO 2007. LNCS, vol. 4622, pp. 517–534. Springer, Heidelberg (2007). https://doi.org/10.1007/978-3-540-74143-5_29

34. Reinert, M.: Cryptographic Techniques for Privacy and Access Control in Cloud-Based Applications. Ph.D. thesis, Saarland University, Saarbrücken, Germany (2018)

35. Ryan, P.Y.A.: Prêt à Voter with Paillier encryption. Math. Comput. Model. **48**(9–10), 1646–1662 (2008)

36. Ryan, P.Y.A., Schneider, S.A.: Prêt à voter with re-encryption mixes. In: Gollmann, D., Meier, J., Sabelfeld, A. (eds.) ESORICS 2006. LNCS, vol. 4189, pp. 313–326. Springer, Heidelberg (2006). https://doi.org/10.1007/11863908_20

37. Schnorr, C.P.: Efficient identification and signatures for smart cards. In: Brassard, G. (ed.) Advances in Cryptology – CRYPTO 1989 Proceedings (1990)

38. Tang, Q.: Public key encryption supporting plaintext equality test and user-specified authorization. Sec. and Commun. Netw. **5**(12), 1351–1362 (2012)

39. Yang, G., Tan, C.H., Huang, Q., Wong, D.S.: Probabilistic public key encryption with equality test. In: Pieprzyk, J. (ed.) CT-RSA 2010. LNCS, vol. 5985, pp. 119–131. Springer, Heidelberg (2010). https://doi.org/10.1007/978-3-642-11925-5_9

Somewhere Statistically Binding Commitment Schemes with Applications

Prastudy Fauzi[1], Helger Lipmaa[1,2], Zaira Pindado[3], and Janno Siim[2(✉)]

[1] Simula UiB, Bergen, Norway
[2] University of Tartu, Tartu, Estonia
`janno.siim@ut.ee`
[3] Universitat Pompeu Fabra, Barcelona, Spain

Abstract. We define a new primitive that we call a *somewhere statistically binding* (SSB) commitment scheme, which is a generalization of dual-mode commitments but has similarities with SSB hash functions (Hubacek and Wichs, ITCS 2015) without local opening. In (existing) SSB hash functions, one can compute a hash of a vector v that is statistically binding in one coordinate of v. Meanwhile, in SSB commitment schemes, a commitment of a vector v is statistically binding in some coordinates of v and is statistically hiding in the other coordinates. The set of indices where binding holds is predetermined but known only to the commitment key generator. We show that the primitive can be instantiated by generalizing the succinct Extended Multi-Pedersen commitment scheme (González et al., Asiacrypt 2015). We further introduce the notion of functional SSB commitment schemes and, importantly, use it to get an efficient quasi-adaptive NIZK for arithmetic circuits and efficient oblivious database queries.

Keywords: Commitment scheme · Oblivious transfer · QA-NIZK · SSB

1 Introduction

Commitment schemes are one of the most useful primitives in cryptography. In essence, a commitment to a value binds the value to the commitment, but hides the value from other parties. Commitment schemes are naturally used in zero-knowledge proofs, where one often proves statements about a committed value while keeping the value hidden. For instance, to complete a digital transaction a party may need to prove he has available funds in his account without actually revealing his exact balance. Such proofs on committed values are very efficient due to Bulletproofs [4], and are used in many privacy-preserving cryptocurrency designs such as Mimblewimble [19,35] and Quisquis [18].

Dual-mode commitment schemes [6,9,10] are an interesting variant where the commitment key can be set up in one of two modes: binding or hiding. In the binding mode, the commitment can only be opened to one valid value.

© International Financial Cryptography Association 2021
N. Borisov and C. Diaz (Eds.): FC 2021, LNCS 12674, pp. 436–456, 2021.
https://doi.org/10.1007/978-3-662-64322-8_21

Meanwhile, in the hiding mode, a commitment hides the committed value even to unbounded adversaries. For this definition to make sense, one should not be able to guess which mode is being used based on the commitment key, i.e., the commitment key hides the mode. Dual-mode commitments are an essential tool in Groth-Sahai proofs [28] which is a framework for constructing non-interactive zero-knowledge (NIZK) proofs for algebraic relations.

In the case of committing to a vector, the two modes of a dual-mode commitment can be seen to be two extremes: the commitment is either binding in all positions in the vector, or in none of them. A natural way to generalize the notion would be to have multiple modes of commitment, specifying that the commitment is binding in some positions in the vector of values. A similar generalization for hash functions is known as somewhere statistically binding hash [29,33], in which one can compute a hash of a vector v such that the computed hash is statistically binding in one coordinate of v.

A generalization of dual-mode commitments would lead to interesting applications in NIZK arguments. In a typical zero-knowledge succinct argument of knowledge (zk-SNARK) for Circuit-SAT [11,20,26,32], the prover commits to the witness (i.e., all the inputs to a circuit), and the proof of (knowledge) soundness involves using a non-falsifiable assumption to extract the whole committed vector which is then used to check each gate to establish where exactly the prover cheated; based on the knowledge of the witness one then breaks a computational assumption. One can get a more efficient extraction under falsifiable assumptions if the commitment was binding only on the values corresponding to the inputs and outputs of a specific gate: one then only needs to check the extracted values against a randomly chosen gate. As a caveat, the technique will lead to a security loss linear in the number of gates.

In fact, the above extraction technique has been done before [12,25] using a generalization of the Pedersen commitment scheme called *Extended Multi-Pedersen* [23,24] and resulting in efficient NIZK arguments under falsifiable assumptions. However, the above results are not zk-SNARKs: they are *quasi-adaptive* NIZK (QA-NIZK) arguments which means the CRS may depend on the relation, and while the argument is succinct, the commitment is not.[1] Moreover, previous work did not formalize which properties of a commitment scheme would be required to enable efficient NIZK arguments.

In the above construction, we need a succinct *somewhere statistically binding* property that guarantees that the chosen coordinate is statistically binding while the remaining coordinates can be computationally binding. On the other hand, to get zero-knowledge, the commitment needs to be *almost-everywhere statistically hiding*, that is, computationally hiding at the chosen coordinate, and statistically hiding at any other coordinates. We also need *index-set hiding*, which means an adversary that is given the commitment key does not know which particular coordinate is statistically binding.

---

[1] One cannot construct zk-SNARKs in a black-box way from falsifiable assumptions [21], hence any black-box construction from falsifiable assumptions will not be fully succinct.

Our Contributions. Formalizing the properties of the *Extended Multi-Pedersen* (EMP) commitment scheme [23,24], we define a *somewhere statistically binding (SSB) commitment scheme* to n-dimensional vectors. In the commitment key generation phase of an SSB commitment scheme one chooses an index-set $S \subseteq [1..n]$ of size at most $q \leq n$ and defines a commitment key ck that depends on n, q and S. A commitment to an n-dimensional vector x will be statistically binding and extractable at coordinates indexed by S and perfectly hiding at all other coordinates. Moreover, commitment keys corresponding to any two index-sets S_1 and S_2 of size at most q must be computationally indistinguishable. Thus, an *SSB commitment scheme* is required to be SSB, *somewhere statistically extractable* (SSE), *almost everywhere statistically hiding* (AESH), and *index-set hiding* (ISH). An SSB commitment scheme generalizes dual-mode commitment schemes (where $n = q = 1$ and $|S| \in \{0,1\}$ determines the mode) and the EMP commitment scheme (where $q = 1$ and n is arbitrary).

In Sect. 4, we define algebraic commitment schemes (ACS), where the commitments keys are matrices. We prove that the distribution of key matrices defines which properties of SSB commitments hold in each coordinate and show that these commitments are suitable for working with QA-NIZK arguments. This is because they behave like linear maps and the properties of SSB commitments can be expressed in terms of membership to linear subspaces. Next, we generalize the EMP commitment scheme to work with arbitrary values of q. Importantly, a single EMP commitment consists of $q + 1$ group elements and is thus succinct given small q. We prove that EMP satisfies the mentioned security requirements under a standard Matrix DDH assumption [16].

In Sect. 5, we define *functional SSB* commitments, which are statistically binding on some components that are outputs of some functions $S = \{f_i\}_i$ where $|S| \leq q$. It is a generalization of SSB commitments, where the extracted values are the result of some linear functions of the committed values, instead of the values themselves. We show that results which hold for SSB commitments also naturally hold for functional SSB commitments. The notion of functional SSB commitments for families of linear functions was already used indirectly in prior work [12]; however, they were not formally defined and their security properties were not analyzed. We also see that a minor modification of EMP works as a functional SSB commitment if we consider only linear functions.

We provide some applications of functional SSB commitments. In Sect. 6.1 we propose a novel (but natural) application that we call oblivious database queries (ODQ), where a sender has a private database x and a receiver wants to query the database to learn $f_1(x), \ldots, f_q(x)$ without revealing the functions f_i. In Sect. 6.2 we present a QA-NIZK for Square Arithmetic Programs (SAP, [27]) that follows a similar strategy to prior work [12] but can be used for arithmetic circuit satisfiability instead of Boolean circuit satisfiability. Our QA-NIZK has comparable efficiency and also under falsifiable assumptions.

Relation to Other Primitives. The SSB requirement makes the EMP commitment scheme look similar to SSB hash functions [29,33], but there are obvious differences. SSB hash has the local opening property, where the committer can efficiently open just one coordinate of the committed vector, but SSB commitments do not[2]. Meanwhile, we need hiding while SSB hash does not. This is, intuitively, a natural distinction and corresponds to the difference between collision-resistant hash families and statistically hiding commitment schemes. Also, we allow ck to be long, but require commitments to be succinct.

SSB commitments are directly related to two-message oblivious transfer (OT) protocols as defined in [1]. Essentially, SSB commitments are non-interactive analogs of such protocols: the commitment key corresponds to the first OT message ot_1 and the commitment corresponds to the second OT message ot_2. Importantly, while in OT, the ot_1 generator is always untrusted, in our applications, it is sufficient to consider a trusted ck generator. This allows for more efficient constructions.

We discuss the relation to existing primitives in more detail in the full version of our paper [17].

2 Preliminaries

For a set S, let $\mathbb{P}(S)$ denote the power set (i.e., the set of subsets) of S, and let $\mathbb{P}(S, q)$ denote the set of q-size subsets of S. For an n-dimensional vector $\boldsymbol{\alpha}$ and $i \in [1 .. n]$, let α_i be its ith coefficient. Let $\boldsymbol{e}_i$ be the ith unit vector of implicitly understood dimension. For a tuple $\mathcal{S} = (\sigma_1, \ldots, \sigma_q)$ with $\sigma_i < \sigma_{i+1}$, let $\boldsymbol{\alpha}_{\mathcal{S}} = (\alpha_{\sigma_1}, \ldots, \alpha_{\sigma_q})$. Let $\boldsymbol{\alpha}_{\emptyset}$ be the empty string.

Let PPT denote probabilistic polynomial-time and let $\lambda \in \mathbb{N}$ be the security parameter. All adversaries will be stateful. Let $\mathsf{RND}_\lambda(\mathcal{A})$ denote the random tape of the algorithm $\mathcal{A}$ for a fixed λ. We denote by $\mathsf{negl}(\lambda)$ an arbitrary negligible function, and by $\mathsf{poly}(\lambda)$ an arbitrary polynomial function. Functions f, g are negligibly close, denoted $f \approx_\lambda g$, if $|f - g| = \mathsf{negl}(\lambda)$. Distribution families $\mathcal{D}^0 = \{\mathcal{D}_\lambda^0\}_\lambda$ and $\mathcal{D}^1 = \{\mathcal{D}_\lambda^1\}_\lambda$ are *computationally indistinguishable*, if $\forall$ PPT $\mathcal{A}$, $\Pr[x \leftarrow_\$ \mathcal{D}_\lambda^0 : \mathcal{A}(x) = 1] \approx_\lambda \Pr[x \leftarrow_\$ \mathcal{D}_\lambda^1 : \mathcal{A}(x) = 1]$.

2.1 Bilinear Groups

In the case of groups, we will use additive notation together with the bracket notation [16], that is, for $\iota \subset \{1, 2, T\}$ we define $[a]_\iota := a[1]_\iota$, where $[1]_\iota$ is a fixed generator of the group $\mathbb{G}_\iota$. A *bilinear group generator* $\mathsf{Pgen}(1^\lambda)$ returns $(p, \mathbb{G}_1, \mathbb{G}_2, \mathbb{G}_T, \hat{e}, [1]_1, [1]_2)$, where p (a large prime) is the order of cyclic Abelian groups $\mathbb{G}_1$, $\mathbb{G}_2$, and $\mathbb{G}_T$. Moreover, $\hat{e} : \mathbb{G}_1 \times \mathbb{G}_2 \to \mathbb{G}_T$ is an efficient non-degenerate bilinear pairing, such that $\hat{e}([a]_1, [b]_2) = [ab]_T$. Denote $[a]_1[b]_2 := \hat{e}([a]_1, [b]_2)$, and $[1]_T := [1]_1[1]_2$. We use matrix-vector notation freely, writing say $[\boldsymbol{M}_1]_1[\boldsymbol{M}_2]_2 = [\boldsymbol{M}_1 \boldsymbol{M}_2]_T$ for any compatible matrices $\boldsymbol{M}_1$ and $\boldsymbol{M}_2$.

We use F-extraction notation to mean extraction of the function F. E.g., if F is exponentiation then we have $[\cdot]_\iota$-extraction, where we extract elements in

---

[2] The properties of SSB and local opening are orthogonal: it is possible to construct efficient SSB hashes without local opening [33] and efficient vector commitments [5, 31] (which have a local opening) without the SSB property.

the group $\mathbb{G}_\iota$. Several of our cryptographic primitives have their own parameter generator Pgen. In all concrete instantiations of the primitives, we instantiate Pgen with the bilinear group generator, which is then denoted Pgen_{bg}.

The Matrix DDH (MDDH) Assumption. Let $\ell, k \in \mathbb{N}$, with $\ell \geq k$, be small constants. Let p be a large prime. Following [16], we call $\mathcal{D}_{\ell k}$ a *matrix distribution* if it outputs, in polynomial time, matrices A in $\mathbb{Z}_p^{\ell \times k}$ of full rank k. We denote $\mathcal{D}_{k+1,k}$ by $\mathcal{D}_k$. Let $\mathcal{U}_{\ell k}$ denote the uniform distribution over $\mathbb{Z}_p^{\ell \times k}$.

Let Pgen be as before, and let $\iota \in \{1, 2\}$. $\mathcal{D}_{\ell k}$-*MDDH*$_{\mathbb{G}_\iota}$ [16] holds relative to Pgen, if $\forall$ PPT $\mathcal{A}$, $\mathsf{Adv}_{\mathcal{A},\mathcal{D}_{\ell k},\iota,\mathsf{Pgen}}^{\mathrm{mddh}}(\lambda) := |\varepsilon_{\mathcal{A}}^0(\lambda) - \varepsilon_{\mathcal{A}}^1(\lambda)| \approx_\lambda 0$, where

$$\varepsilon_{\mathcal{A}}^\beta(\lambda) := \Pr\left[\begin{array}{l} p \leftarrow \mathsf{Pgen}(1^\lambda); A \leftarrow_\$ \mathcal{D}_{\ell k}; w \leftarrow_\$ \mathbb{Z}_p^k; \\ y_0 \leftarrow_\$ \mathbb{Z}_p^\ell; y_1 \leftarrow Aw : \mathcal{A}(p, [A, y_\beta]_\iota) = 1 \end{array}\right].$$

Common distributions for the MDDH assumption are $\mathcal{U}_k := \mathcal{U}_{k+1,k}$ and the linear distribution $\mathcal{L}_k$ over $A = \left(\begin{smallmatrix} A' \\ 1 \cdots 1 \end{smallmatrix}\right)$, where $A' \in \mathbb{Z}_p^{k \times k}$ is a diagonal matrix with $a'_{ii} \leftarrow_\$ \mathbb{Z}_p$.

2.2 Quasi-Adaptive NIZK

A quasi-adaptive non-interactive zero-knowledge (QA-NIZK) proof [30] enables one to prove membership in a language defined by a relation $\mathcal{R}_\rho$, which is determined by some parameter ρ sampled from a distribution $\mathcal{D}_{\mathsf{gk}}$. A distribution $\mathcal{D}_{\mathsf{gk}}$ is *witness-sampleable* if there exists an efficient algorithm that samples (ρ, ω_ρ) from a distribution $\mathcal{D}_{\mathsf{gk}}^{\mathsf{par}}$ such that ρ is distributed according to $\mathcal{D}_{\mathsf{gk}}$, and membership of ρ in the *parameter language* $\mathcal{L}_{\mathsf{par}}$ can be efficiently verified by using this witness ω_ρ.

A tuple of algorithms $(\mathsf{K}_0, \mathsf{K}_1, \mathsf{P}, \mathsf{V})$ is called a *QA-NIZK proof system* for witness-relations $\mathcal{R}_{\mathsf{gk}} = \{\mathcal{R}_\rho\}_{\rho \in \sup(\mathcal{D}_{\mathsf{gk}})}$ with parameters sampled from a distribution $\mathcal{D}_{\mathsf{gk}}$ over associated parameter language $\mathcal{L}_{\mathsf{par}}$, if there exists a probabilistic polynomial time simulator $(\mathsf{S}_1, \mathsf{S}_2)$, such that for all non-uniform PPT adversaries $\mathcal{A}_1, \mathcal{A}_2, \mathcal{A}_3$ we have:

Quasi-Adaptive Completeness:

$$\Pr\left[\begin{array}{l} \mathsf{gk} \leftarrow \mathsf{K}_0(1^\lambda); \rho \leftarrow \mathcal{D}_{\mathsf{gk}}; \mathsf{crs} \leftarrow \mathsf{K}_1(\mathsf{gk}, \rho); (x, w) \leftarrow \mathcal{A}_1(\mathsf{gk}, \mathsf{crs}); \\ \pi \leftarrow \mathsf{P}(\mathsf{crs}, x, w) : \mathsf{V}(\mathsf{crs}, x, \pi) = 1 \text{ if } \mathcal{R}_\rho(x, w) \end{array}\right] = 1.$$

Computational Quasi-Adaptive Soundness:

$$\Pr\left[\begin{array}{ll} \mathsf{gk} \leftarrow \mathsf{K}_0(1^\lambda); \rho \leftarrow \mathcal{D}_{\mathsf{gk}}; & \mathsf{V}(\mathsf{crs}, x, \pi) = 1 \text{ and} \\ \mathsf{crs} \leftarrow \mathsf{K}_1(\mathsf{gk}, \rho); (x, \pi) \leftarrow \mathcal{A}_2(\mathsf{gk}, \mathsf{crs}) & : \neg(\exists w : \mathcal{R}_\rho(x, w)) \end{array}\right] \approx 0.$$

Computational Strong Quasi-Adaptive Soundness:

$$\Pr\left[\begin{array}{l} \mathsf{gk} \leftarrow \mathsf{K}_0(1^\lambda); (\rho, \omega_\rho) \leftarrow \mathcal{D}_{\mathsf{gk}}^{\mathsf{par}}; \mathsf{crs} \leftarrow \mathsf{K}_1(\mathsf{gk}, \rho); \\ (x, \pi) \leftarrow \mathcal{A}_2(\mathsf{gk}, \mathsf{crs}, \omega_\rho) : \mathsf{V}(\mathsf{crs}, x, \pi) = 1 \text{ and } \neg(\exists w : \mathcal{R}_\rho(x, w)) \end{array}\right] \approx 0.$$

Perfect Quasi-Adaptive Zero-Knowledge:

$$\Pr[\mathsf{gk} \leftarrow \mathsf{K}_0(1^\lambda); \rho \leftarrow \mathcal{D}_{\mathsf{gk}}; \mathsf{crs} \leftarrow \mathsf{K}_1(\mathsf{gk}, \rho) : \mathcal{A}_3^{\mathsf{P}(\mathsf{crs}, \cdot, \cdot)}(\mathsf{gk}, \mathsf{crs}) = 1]$$
$$= \Pr[\mathsf{gk} \leftarrow \mathsf{K}_0(1^\lambda); \rho \leftarrow \mathcal{D}_{\mathsf{gk}}; (\mathsf{crs}, \tau) \leftarrow \mathsf{S}_1(\mathsf{gk}, \rho) : \mathcal{A}_3^{\mathsf{S}(\mathsf{crs}, \tau, \cdot, \cdot)}(\mathsf{gk}, \mathsf{crs}) = 1]$$

where (i) $\mathsf{P}(\mathsf{crs}, \cdot, \cdot)$ emulates the actual prover. It takes input (x, w) and outputs a proof π if $(x, w) \in \mathcal{R}_\rho$. Otherwise, it outputs $\perp$. (ii) $\mathsf{S}(\mathsf{crs}, \tau, \cdot, \cdot)$ is an oracle that takes input (x, w). It outputs a simulated proof $\mathsf{S}_2(\mathsf{crs}, \tau, x)$ if $(x, w) \in \mathcal{R}_\rho$ and $\perp$ if $(x, w) \notin \mathcal{R}_\rho$.

We assume that crs contains an encoding of ρ, which is thus available to V.

3   SSB Commitment Schemes

In an SSB commitment scheme, the commitment key (i.e., the CRS) depends on n, q, and an index-set $\mathcal{S} \subseteq [1 .. n]$ of cardinality $\leq q$ (in the case of Groth-Sahai commitments [28], $n = q = 1$ while in the current paper $n = \mathsf{poly}(\lambda)$ and $q \geq 1$ is a small constant). At coordinates described by $\mathcal{S}$, an SSB commitment scheme must be *statistically binding* and *F-extractable* [2] for a well-chosen function F, while at all other coordinates it must be *statistically hiding* and *trapdoor*. Moreover, it must be index-set hiding, i.e., commitment keys corresponding to any two index-sets $\mathcal{S}_1$ and $\mathcal{S}_2$ of size $\leq q$ must be computationally indistinguishable.

The Groth-Sahai commitments correspond to a *bimodal* setting where either all coefficients are statistically hiding or statistically binding, and these two extremes are indistinguishable. SSB commitments correspond to a more fine-grained *multimodal* setting where some $\leq q$ coefficients are statistically binding and other coefficients are statistically hiding, and all possible selections of statistically binding coefficients are mutually indistinguishable. Our terminology is inspired by [29,33] who defined SSB hashing; however, the consideration of the hiding property makes the case of SSB commitments sufficiently different.

3.1   Formalization and Definitions

An *F-extractable SSB commitment scheme* COM = (Pgen, KC, Com, tdOpen, Ext$_F$) consists of the following polynomial-time algorithms:

Parameter generation: Pgen(1^λ) returns parameters p (e.g., description of a bilinear group).

Commitment key generation: for parameters p, $n \in \mathsf{poly}(\lambda)$, $q \in [1 .. n]$, and a tuple $\mathcal{S} \subseteq [1 .. n]$ with $|\mathcal{S}| \leq q$, KC(p, n, q, $\mathcal{S}$) outputs a commitment key ck and a trapdoor td = (ek, tk) consisting of an *extraction key* ek, and a *trapdoor key* tk. Also, ck implicitly specifies p, n, q, the message space MSP, the randomizer space RSP, the extraction space ESP, and the commitment space CSP, such that $F(\mathsf{MSP}) \subseteq \mathsf{ESP}$. For invalid input, KC outputs (ck, td) = $(\perp, \perp)$.

Commitment: for p $\in$ Pgen(1^λ), ck $\neq \perp$, a message $\boldsymbol{x} \in \mathsf{MSP}^n$, and a randomizer $r \in \mathsf{RSP}$, Com(ck; $\boldsymbol{x}$; r) outputs a commitment $c \in \mathsf{CSP}$.

Table 1. Properties of an SSB commitment scheme

Abbreviation	Property	Definition
ISH	Index-set hiding	The commitment key reveals nothing about the index-set $\mathcal{S}$
SSB	Somewhere statistically binding	A commitment to x statistically binds the values $x_\mathcal{S}$
AESH	Almost everywhere statistically hiding	The commitment is statistically hiding in the indices outside the set $\mathcal{S}$
F-SSE	Somewhere statistical F-extractability	Given a commitment to x and the extraction key, one can extract the values $F(x_\mathcal{S})$

Trapdoor opening: for $\mathsf{p} \in \mathsf{Pgen}(1^\lambda)$, $\mathcal{S} \subseteq [1..n]$ with $|\mathcal{S}| \leq q$, $(\mathsf{ck}, (\mathsf{ek}, \mathsf{tk})) \in \mathsf{KC}(\mathsf{p}, n, q, \mathcal{S})$, two messages $x_0, x_1 \in \mathsf{MSP}^n$, and a randomizer $r_0 \in \mathsf{RSP}$, $\mathsf{tdOpen}(\mathsf{p}, \mathsf{tk}; x_0, r_0, x_1)$ returns a randomizer $r_1 \in \mathsf{RSP}$.

Extraction: for $\mathsf{p} \in \mathsf{Pgen}(1^\lambda)$, $\mathcal{S} = (\sigma_1, \ldots, \sigma_{|\mathcal{S}|}) \subseteq [1..n]$ with $1 \leq |\mathcal{S}| \leq q$, $(\mathsf{ck}, (\mathsf{ek}, \mathsf{tk})) \in \mathsf{KC}(\mathsf{p}, n, q, \mathcal{S})$, $F : \mathsf{MSP} \to \mathsf{ESP}$ and $c \in \mathsf{CSP}$, $\mathsf{Ext}_F(\mathsf{p}, \mathsf{ek}; c)$ returns a tuple $(y_{\sigma_1}, \ldots, y_{\sigma_{|\mathcal{S}|}}) \in \mathsf{ESP}^{|\mathcal{S}|}$. We allow F to depend on p.

Note that SSB commitment schemes are non-interactive and work in the CRS model; the latter is needed to achieve trapdoor opening and extractability. With the current definition, *perfect completeness* is straightforward: to verify that C is a commitment of x with randomizer r, one just recomputes $C' \leftarrow \mathsf{Com}(\mathsf{ck}; x; r)$ and checks whether $C = C'$.

An F-extractable SSB commitment scheme COM is *secure* if it satisfies the following security requirements. (See Table 1 for a brief summary.)

Index-Set Hiding (ISH): $\forall \lambda$, PPT $\mathcal{A}$, $n \in \mathsf{poly}(\lambda)$, $q \in [1..n]$, $\mathsf{Adv}^{\mathsf{ish}}_{\mathcal{A}, \mathsf{COM}, n, q}(\lambda) := 2 \cdot |\varepsilon^{\mathsf{ish}}_{\mathcal{A}, \mathsf{COM}, n, q}(\lambda) - 1/2| \approx_\lambda 0$, where $\varepsilon^{\mathsf{ish}}_{\mathcal{A}, \mathsf{COM}, n, q}(\lambda) :=$

$$\Pr \left[\begin{array}{l} \mathsf{p} \leftarrow \mathsf{Pgen}(1^\lambda); (\mathcal{S}_0, \mathcal{S}_1) \leftarrow \mathcal{A}(\mathsf{p}, n, q) \text{ s.t. } \forall i \in \{0, 1\}, \mathcal{S}_i \subseteq [1..n] \wedge |\mathcal{S}_i| \leq q; \\ \beta \leftarrow\!\$ \{0, 1\}; (\mathsf{ck}_\beta, \mathsf{td}_\beta) \leftarrow \mathsf{KC}(\mathsf{p}, n, q, \mathcal{S}_\beta) : \mathcal{A}(\mathsf{ck}_\beta) = \beta \end{array} \right].$$

Somewhere Statistically Binding (SSB): $\forall \lambda$, unbounded $\mathcal{A}$, $n \in \mathsf{poly}(\lambda)$, $q \in [1..n]$, $\mathsf{Adv}^{\mathsf{ssb}}_{\mathcal{A}, \mathsf{COM}, n, q}(\lambda) \approx_\lambda 0$, where $\mathsf{Adv}^{\mathsf{ssb}}_{\mathcal{A}, \mathsf{COM}, n, q}(\lambda) :=$

$$\Pr \left[\begin{array}{l} \mathsf{p} \leftarrow \mathsf{Pgen}(1^\lambda); \mathcal{S} \leftarrow \mathcal{A}(\mathsf{p}, n, q) \text{ s.t. } \mathcal{S} \subseteq [1..n] \wedge |\mathcal{S}| \leq q; \\ (\mathsf{ck}, \mathsf{td}) \leftarrow \mathsf{KC}(\mathsf{p}, n, q, \mathcal{S}); (x_0, x_1, r_0, r_1) \leftarrow \mathcal{A}(\mathsf{ck}) : \\ x_{0, \mathcal{S}} \neq x_{1, \mathcal{S}}; \mathsf{Com}(\mathsf{ck}; x_0; r_0) = \mathsf{Com}(\mathsf{ck}; x_1; r_1) \end{array} \right].$$

COM is *somewhere perfectly binding* (SPB) if $\mathsf{Adv}^{\mathsf{ssb}}_{\mathcal{A}, \mathsf{COM}, n, q}(\lambda) = 0$.

Almost Everywhere Statistically Hiding (AESH): $\forall \lambda$, unbounded adversary $\mathcal{A}$, $n \in \mathsf{poly}(\lambda)$, $q \in [1..n]$, $\mathsf{Adv}^{\mathsf{aesh}}_{\mathcal{A}, \mathsf{COM}, n, q}(\lambda) := 2 \cdot |\varepsilon^{\mathsf{aesh}}_{\mathcal{A}, \mathsf{COM}, n, q}(\lambda) - 1/2| \approx_\lambda 0$, where $\varepsilon^{\text{aesh}}_{\mathcal{A},\text{COM},n,q}(\lambda) :=$

$$\Pr \begin{bmatrix} \mathsf{p} \leftarrow \text{Pgen}(1^\lambda); \mathcal{S} \leftarrow \mathcal{A}(\mathsf{p},n,q) \text{ s.t. } \mathcal{S} \subseteq [1..n] \wedge |\mathcal{S}| \leq q; \\ (\text{ck},\text{td}) \leftarrow \text{KC}(\mathsf{p},n,q,\mathcal{S}); (\boldsymbol{x}_0,\boldsymbol{x}_1) \leftarrow \mathcal{A}(\text{ck}) \text{ s.t. } \boldsymbol{x}_{0,\mathcal{S}} = \boldsymbol{x}_{1,\mathcal{S}}; \\ \beta \leftarrow_{\$} \{0,1\}; r \leftarrow_{\$} \text{RSP} : \mathcal{A}(\text{Com}(\text{ck};\boldsymbol{x}_\beta;r)) = \beta \end{bmatrix}.$$

COM is *almost everywhere perfectly hiding* (AEPH) if $\text{Adv}^{\text{aesh}}_{\mathcal{A},\text{COM},n,q}(\lambda) = 0$.
If $\mathcal{A}$ is PPT, COM is *almost everywhere computationally hiding* (AECH).

Somewhere Statistical F-Extractability (F-SSE): $\forall \lambda$, $n \in \text{poly}(\lambda)$, $q \in [1..n]$, $\mathcal{S} = (\sigma_1,\ldots,\sigma_{|\mathcal{S}|})$ with $|\mathcal{S}| \leq q$, $(\text{ck},(\text{ek},\text{tk})) \leftarrow \text{KC}(\mathsf{p},n,q,\mathcal{S})$, and PPT $\mathcal{A}$, $\text{Adv}^{\text{sse}}_{\mathcal{A},F,\text{COM},n,q}(\lambda) :=$

$$\Pr\left[\boldsymbol{x},r \leftarrow \mathcal{A}(\text{ck}) : \text{Ext}_F(\mathsf{p},\text{ek};\text{Com}(\text{ck};\boldsymbol{x};r)) \neq (F(x_{\sigma_1}),\ldots,F(x_{\sigma_{|\mathcal{S}|}})) \right] \approx_\lambda 0.$$

Additionally, an SSB commitment scheme can but does not have to be *trapdoor*.

Almost Everywhere Statistical Trapdoor (AEST): $\forall \lambda$, $n \in \text{poly}(\lambda)$, $q \in [1..n]$, and unbounded $\mathcal{A}$, $\text{Adv}^{\text{aest}}_{\mathcal{A},\text{COM},n,q}(\lambda) \approx_\lambda 0$, where $\text{Adv}^{\text{aest}}_{\mathcal{A},\text{COM},n,q}(\lambda) =$

$$\Pr \begin{bmatrix} \mathsf{p} \leftarrow \text{Pgen}(1^\lambda); \mathcal{S} \leftarrow \mathcal{A}(\mathsf{p},n,q) \text{ s.t. } \mathcal{S} \subseteq [1..n] \wedge |\mathcal{S}| \leq q; \\ (\text{ck},\text{td} = (\text{ek},\text{tk})) \leftarrow \text{KC}(\mathsf{p},n,q,\mathcal{S}); (\boldsymbol{x}_0,r_0,\boldsymbol{x}_1) \leftarrow \mathcal{A}(\text{ck}) \text{ s.t. } \boldsymbol{x}_{0,\mathcal{S}} = \boldsymbol{x}_{1,\mathcal{S}}; \\ r_1 \leftarrow \text{tdOpen}(\mathsf{p},\text{tk};\boldsymbol{x}_0,r_0,\boldsymbol{x}_1) : \text{Com}(\text{ck};\boldsymbol{x}_0;r_0) \neq \text{Com}(\text{ck};\boldsymbol{x}_1;r_1) \end{bmatrix}.$$

It is *almost everywhere perfect trapdoor (AEPT)* if $\text{Adv}^{\text{aest}}_{\text{COM},n,q}(\lambda) = 0$.

It is important to consider the case $|\mathcal{S}| \leq q$ instead of only $|\mathcal{S}| = q$. For example, when $q = n$, the perfectly binding (PB) commitment key ($|\mathcal{S}| = n$) has to be indistinguishable from the perfectly hiding (PH) commitment key ($|\mathcal{S}| = 0$). Moreover, in the applications to construct QA-NIZK argument systems [12,23, 24], one should not be able to distinguish between the cases $|\mathcal{S}| = 0$ and $|\mathcal{S}| = q$.

F-extractability [2] allows one to model the situation where $x_i \in \mathbb{Z}_p$ but we can only extract the corresponding bracketed value $[x_i]_\iota \in \mathbb{G}_\iota$; similar limited extractability is satisfied say by the Groth-Sahai commitment scheme for scalars [28]. Note that in this case, F depends on p. Interestingly, extractability implies SSB, see the full version of the paper for a proof [17].

Lemma 1 (F-SSE & F is injective $\Rightarrow$ SSB). *Let* COM *be an SSB commitment scheme. Fix n and q. Assume F is injective. For all PPT $\mathcal{A}$, there exists a PPT $\mathcal{B}$ such that $\text{Adv}^{\text{ssb}}_{\mathcal{A},\text{COM},n,q}(\lambda) \leq 2 \cdot \text{Adv}^{\text{sse}}_{\mathcal{B},F,\text{COM},n,q}(\lambda)$.*

If $q = 0$ then AESH is equal to the standard statistical hiding (SH) requirement, and AEST is equal to the standard statistical trapdoor requirement. If $q = n$ then SSB is equal to the standard statistical binding (SB) requirement, and F-SSE is equal to the standard statistical F-extractability requirement. We will show that any secure SSB commitment scheme must also be computationally hiding and binding in the following sense.

Computational Binding (CB): $\forall$ PPT $\mathcal{A}$, $n \in \mathsf{poly}(\lambda)$, $q \in [1..n]$, where $\mathsf{Adv}^{\mathsf{cb}}_{\mathcal{A},\mathsf{COM},n,q}(\lambda) :=$

$$\Pr\left[\begin{array}{l}\mathsf{p} \leftarrow \mathsf{Pgen}(1^\lambda); \mathcal{S} \leftarrow \mathcal{A}(\mathsf{p},n,q): \mathcal{S} \subseteq [1..n] \wedge |\mathcal{S}| \leq q; \\ (\mathsf{ck},\mathsf{td}) \leftarrow \mathsf{KC}(\mathsf{p},n,q,\mathcal{S}); (\boldsymbol{x}_0, \boldsymbol{x}_1, r_0, r_1) \leftarrow \mathcal{A}(\mathsf{ck}) \\ \text{s.t. } \boldsymbol{x}_0 \neq \boldsymbol{x}_1; \mathsf{Com}(\mathsf{ck}; \boldsymbol{x}_0; r_0) = \mathsf{Com}(\mathsf{ck}; \boldsymbol{x}_1; r_1)\end{array}\right] \approx_\lambda 0 \ .$$

Computational Hiding (CH): $\forall$ PPT $\mathcal{A}$, $n \in \mathsf{poly}(\lambda)$, $q \in [1..n]$, $\mathsf{Adv}^{\mathsf{ch}}_{\mathcal{A},\mathsf{COM},n,q}(\lambda) := 2 \cdot |\varepsilon^{\mathsf{ch}}_{\mathcal{A},\mathsf{COM},n,q}(\lambda) - 1/2| \approx_\lambda 0$, where $\varepsilon^{\mathsf{ch}}_{\mathcal{A},\mathsf{COM},n,q}(\lambda) :=$

$$\Pr\left[\begin{array}{l}\mathsf{p} \leftarrow \mathsf{Pgen}(1^\lambda); \mathcal{S} \leftarrow \mathcal{A}(\mathsf{p},n,q) \text{ s.t. } \mathcal{S} \subseteq [1..n] \wedge |\mathcal{S}| \leq q; \\ (\mathsf{ck},\mathsf{td}) \leftarrow \mathsf{KC}(\mathsf{p},n,q,\mathcal{S}); (\boldsymbol{x}_0, \boldsymbol{x}_1) \leftarrow \mathcal{A}(\mathsf{ck}); \beta \leftarrow_\$ \{0,1\}; \\ r \leftarrow_\$ \mathsf{RSP}: \mathcal{A}(\mathsf{Com}(\mathsf{ck}; \boldsymbol{x}_\beta; r)) = \beta\end{array}\right] \ .$$

Theorem 1. *Let* COM *be an SSB commitment scheme. Fix n and q.*

(i) *(ISH + SSB $\Rightarrow$ CB) For all PPT $\mathcal{A}$, there exist PPT $\mathcal{B}_1$ and unbounded $\mathcal{B}_2$, such that* $\mathsf{Adv}^{\mathsf{cb}}_{\mathcal{A},\mathsf{COM},n,q}(\lambda) \leq \mathsf{Adv}^{\mathsf{ish}}_{\mathcal{B}_1,\mathsf{COM},n,q}(\lambda) + n/(q - 4 \cdot \mathsf{Adv}^{\mathsf{ish}}_{\mathcal{B}_1,\mathsf{COM},n,q}(\lambda)) \cdot \mathsf{Adv}^{\mathsf{ssb}}_{\mathcal{B}_2,\mathsf{COM},n,q}(\lambda)$.

(ii) *(ISH + AESH $\Rightarrow$ CH) For all PPT $\mathcal{A}$, there exist PPT $\mathcal{B}_1$ and unbounded $\mathcal{B}_2$, such that* $\mathsf{Adv}^{\mathsf{ch}}_{\mathcal{A},\mathsf{COM},n,q}(\lambda) \leq \mathsf{Adv}^{\mathsf{ish}}_{\mathcal{B}_1,\mathsf{COM},n,q}(\lambda) + \mathsf{Adv}^{\mathsf{aesh}}_{\mathcal{B}_2,\mathsf{COM},n,q}(\lambda)$.

The full proof of this theorem is deferred to the full version [17].

4   Constructing SSB Commitment Schemes

In this section we generalize the notion of algebraic commitment schemes to general matrix distributions. We show that they work nicely with QA-NIZK arguments and that certain matrix distributions give us an SSB commitment scheme. We focus on the particular case of EMP in Sect. 4.2, where we propose a general version of EMP and prove that it is an SSB commitment scheme.

4.1   Algebraic Commitment Schemes

Ràfols and Silva [36] defined the notion of *algebraic commitment schemes (ACSs)*, where the commitment keys are matrices, already used implicitly in other works [7,8]. Since they behave like linear maps, it is very natural to work with them. We give a more general definition in the following where the matrices are sampled from general distributions.

Definition 1. *Let $\iota \in \{1,2\}$, and let n, m, k be small integers. Let $\mathcal{D}_1$ be a distribution of matrices from $\mathbb{G}^{k \times n}_\iota$ and let $\mathcal{D}_2$ be a distribution of matrices from $\mathbb{G}^{k \times m}_\iota$. A commitment scheme COM is a $(\mathcal{D}_1, \mathcal{D}_2)$-algebraic commitment scheme (ACS) for vectors in $\mathbb{Z}^n_p$, if for commitment key $\mathsf{ck} = [\boldsymbol{U}_1, \boldsymbol{U}_2]_\iota \leftarrow_\$ \mathcal{D}_1 \times \mathcal{D}_2$ the commitment of a vector $\boldsymbol{x} \in \mathbb{Z}^n_p$ is computed as a linear map of $\boldsymbol{x}$ and randomness $\boldsymbol{r} \leftarrow_\$ \mathbb{Z}^m_p$, i.e., $\mathsf{Com}_{\mathsf{ck}}(\boldsymbol{x}, \boldsymbol{r}) := [\boldsymbol{U}_1]_\iota \boldsymbol{x} + [\boldsymbol{U}_2]_\iota \boldsymbol{r} \in \mathbb{G}^k_\iota$.*

Ràfols and Silva mention that given different commitment key matrices, their distributions are computationally indistinguishable under the MDDH assumption, and each concrete distribution defines which coordinates of the commitments are SB or SH. We prove in the full version [17] that it also gives a characterization of the coordinates of the key matrices for the different SSB properties (AECH, ISH, SPB, SPE) based on linear dependency. In the full version, we also prove that to extract n elements from an ACS we need at least $n + 1$ rows.

4.2   The EMP Commitment Scheme

Extended Multi-Pedersen (EMP) [23,24] is a variant of the standard vector Pedersen commitment scheme [34]. In this section, we will depict a general version of the EMP commitment scheme[3] in group $\mathbb{G}$. We redefine EMP by using a division of the generator matrix g as a product of two matrices R and M; this representation results in very short security proofs for EMP. To simplify notation, we will write Ext instead of $\mathrm{Ext}_{[\cdot]}$. We use a distribution $\mathcal{D}_{q+1}^{p,n,\mathcal{S}}$ that outputs $n + 1$ vectors $g^{(i)}$, such that if $i \in \mathcal{S}' = \mathcal{S} \cup \{n + 1\}$ then $g^{(i)}$ is distributed uniformly over $\mathbb{Z}_p^{q+1}$, and otherwise $g^{(i)}$ is a random scalar multiple of $g^{(n+1)}$.[4]

Definition 2. *Let $p = p(\lambda)$, $n = \mathsf{poly}(\lambda)$, and let $q \leq n$ be a small positive integer. Let $\mathcal{S} \subseteq [1..n]$ with $|\mathcal{S}| \leq q$. Then the distribution $\mathcal{D}_{q+1}^{p,n,\mathcal{S}}$ is defined as the first part of $\mathcal{D}_{gen}(p,n,\mathcal{S},q)$ in Fig. 1 (i.e., just g, without the associated extraction key or trapdoor).*

Note that [24] uses a distribution $\mathcal{D}_{q+1,k}$ instead of the uniform distribution $\mathcal{U}_{q+1}$ over $\mathbb{Z}_p^{q+1}$, which means that taking a larger k gives a weaker security assumption but with worse efficiency. Our version of EMP also works with a general distribution, but for ease of presentation we only use $\mathcal{U}_{q+1}$.

$$
\begin{array}{|l|}
\hline
\mathcal{D}_{gen}(p,n,\mathcal{S},q) \\
\hline
\mathcal{S}' \leftarrow \mathcal{S} \cup \{n+1\}; \quad /\!\!/ \ \mathcal{S}' = \{\sigma_1,\dots,\sigma_{q+1}\} \\
R \leftarrow_\$ \mathbb{Z}_p^{(q+1)\times(q+1)}; M \leftarrow \mathbf{0}_{(q+1)\times(n+1)}; M_{q+1,n+1} \leftarrow 1; \\
\textbf{for } j = 1 \textbf{ to } n \textbf{ do} \\
\quad \textbf{if } j \notin \mathcal{S}' \textbf{ then } M_{q+1,j} = \delta_j \leftarrow_\$ \mathbb{Z}_p; \\
\quad \textbf{else let } i \text{ be such that } j = \sigma_i; M_{i,\sigma_i} \leftarrow 1; \\
g \leftarrow RM; \mathrm{tk} \leftarrow (\delta_j)_{j\in[1..n]\setminus\mathcal{S}}; \quad /\!\!/ \ g \in \mathbb{Z}_p^{(q+1)\times(n+1)}; \\
\textbf{return } (g, R, \mathrm{tk}); \\
\hline
\end{array}
$$

Fig. 1. Generating $\mathcal{D}_{q+1}^{p,n,\mathcal{S}}$, with associated extraction key R and trapdoor tk

---

[3] González *et al.* [24] mostly considered the case $q = 1$; they also did not formalize its security by using notions like ISH.

[4] We add +1 to the dimension (e.g., $q + 1$) to accommodate the randomizer in EMP.

$$
\begin{array}{l}
\hline
\mathsf{KC}(\mathsf{p}, n, q, \mathcal{S}) \quad /\!/ \ \mathcal{S} \subseteq \{1, 2, \ldots, n\} \text{ with } |\mathcal{S}| \leq q \\
\hline
\text{Sample } (\boldsymbol{g}, \boldsymbol{R}, \mathsf{tk}_\iota) \leftarrow\!\!\$ \, \mathcal{D}_{gen}(\mathsf{p}, n, \mathcal{S}, q) \text{ s.t. } \boldsymbol{R} \text{ has full rank;} \\
\mathsf{ck} \leftarrow [\boldsymbol{g}]; \mathsf{ek} \leftarrow \boldsymbol{R}; \quad /\!/ \ \boldsymbol{g} \in \mathbb{Z}_p^{(q+1) \times (n+1)}, \, \boldsymbol{R} \in \mathbb{Z}_p^{(q+1) \times (q+1)} \\
\mathsf{td} \leftarrow (\mathsf{ek}, \mathsf{tk}); \mathbf{return} \ (\mathsf{ck}, \mathsf{td}); \\
\hline
\end{array}
$$

$\mathsf{tdOpen}(\mathsf{p}, \mathsf{tk}_\iota; \boldsymbol{x}_0, r_0, \boldsymbol{x}_1)$	$\mathsf{Ext}(\mathsf{p}, \mathsf{ek}; [\boldsymbol{c}])$
$r_1 \leftarrow \sum_{i \in [1..n] \setminus \mathcal{S}} (x_{0,i} - x_{1,i}) \delta_i + r_0;$	$[\boldsymbol{x}'] \leftarrow \boldsymbol{R}^{-1}[\boldsymbol{c}];$
$\mathbf{return} \ r_1;$	$\mathbf{return} \ [\boldsymbol{x}_{\mathcal{S}}] \leftarrow [\boldsymbol{x}'_{[1..|\mathcal{S}|]}];$

$$
\begin{array}{l}
\hline
\mathsf{Com}(\mathsf{ck}; \boldsymbol{x} \in \mathbb{Z}_p^n; r \in \mathbb{Z}_p) \\
\hline
\mathbf{return} \ [\boldsymbol{g}] \binom{\boldsymbol{x}}{r}; \quad /\!/ = \sum_{j=1}^n x_j[\boldsymbol{g}^{(j)}] + r[\boldsymbol{g}^{(n+1)}] \in \mathbb{G}^{q+1} \\
\hline
\end{array}
$$

Fig. 2. The EMP commitment scheme COM

Example 1. In the Groth-Sahai commitment scheme, $n = q = 1$, so $\mathcal{D}_{gen}$ first samples $\boldsymbol{R} = \left(\begin{smallmatrix} r_{11} & r_{12} \\ r_{21} & r_{22} \end{smallmatrix} \right) \leftarrow\!\!\$ \, \mathbb{Z}_p^{2 \times 2}$. If $\mathcal{S} = \{1\}$ then $\boldsymbol{M} = \left(\begin{smallmatrix} 1 & 0 \\ 0 & 1 \end{smallmatrix} \right)$ and $\boldsymbol{g} = \boldsymbol{R}\boldsymbol{M} = \left(\begin{smallmatrix} r_{11} & r_{12} \\ r_{21} & r_{22} \end{smallmatrix} \right)$. On the other hand, if $\mathcal{S} = \emptyset$ then $\boldsymbol{M} = \left(\begin{smallmatrix} 0 & 0 \\ \delta_1 & 1 \end{smallmatrix} \right)$ and $\boldsymbol{g} = \boldsymbol{R}\boldsymbol{M} = \left(\begin{smallmatrix} \delta_1 r_{12} & r_{12} \\ \delta_1 r_{22} & r_{22} \end{smallmatrix} \right)$ for $\delta_1 \leftarrow\!\!\$ \, \mathbb{Z}_p$.

Consider the case $n = 3$, $q = 2$, and $\mathcal{S} = \{3\}$. Then

$$
\boldsymbol{M} = \begin{pmatrix} 0 & 0 & 1 & 0 \\ 0 & 0 & 0 & 0 \\ \delta_1 & \delta_2 & 0 & 1 \end{pmatrix}, \ \boldsymbol{g} = \boldsymbol{R}\boldsymbol{M} = \begin{pmatrix} \delta_1 r_{13} & \delta_2 r_{13} & r_{11} & r_{13} \\ \delta_1 r_{23} & \delta_2 r_{23} & r_{21} & r_{23} \\ \delta_1 r_{33} & \delta_2 r_{33} & r_{31} & r_{33} \end{pmatrix}, \text{ for } \delta_1, \delta_2 \leftarrow\!\!\$ \, \mathbb{Z}_p, \boldsymbol{R} \leftarrow\!\!\$ \, \mathbb{Z}_p^{3 \times 3} \ .
$$

The following lemma shows that distributions $[\mathcal{D}_{q+1}^{p,n,\mathcal{S}}]$ for different sets $\mathcal{S}$ are indistinguishable under the MDDH assumption. See the full version [17] for a proof.

Lemma 2. *Let $\iota \in \{1, 2\}$. Let $p = p(\lambda)$ be created by $\mathsf{Pgen}(1^\lambda)$, $n = \mathsf{poly}(\lambda)$, and let $q \leq n$ be a positive integer. Let $\mathcal{S} \subseteq [1..n]$ with $|\mathcal{S}| \leq q$. The distribution families $\mathcal{D}^0 := \{[\mathcal{D}_{q+1}^{p,n,\mathcal{S}}]\}_\lambda$ and $\mathcal{D}^1 := \{[\mathcal{D}_{q+1}^{p,n,\emptyset}]\}_\lambda$ are computationally indistinguishable under the $\mathcal{U}_{q+1}$-MDDH$_{\mathbb{G}_\iota}$ assumption relative to Pgen: for any PPT $\mathcal{A}$, there exists a PPT $\mathcal{B}$, such that $\mathsf{Adv}_{\mathcal{A}, \mathcal{D}^0, \mathcal{D}^1}^{\mathrm{indist}}(\lambda) \leq |\mathcal{S}| \cdot \mathsf{Adv}_{\mathcal{B}, \mathcal{U}_{q+1}, \mathsf{Pgen}}^{\mathrm{mddh}}(\lambda)$.*

We define EMP in Fig. 2. We claim that it is indeed an SSB commitment scheme in the following Theorem, see the full version for a proof.

Theorem 2. *Let Pgen_{bg} be a bilinear group generator. Fix λ, n, and q. The EMP commitment scheme is (i) ISH under the $\mathcal{U}_{(q+1) \times (n+1)}$-MDDH$_{\mathbb{G}_\iota}$ assumption, (ii) F-SSE for $F = [\cdot]$ (thus, F depends on p), (iii) AEPT, (iv) SPB, (v) AEPH, (vi) CB and CH under the $\mathcal{U}_{(q+1) \times (n+1)}$-MDDH$_{\mathbb{G}_\iota}$ assumption.*

Alternative Constructions. One can also construct a SSB commitment from any IND-CPA secure cryptosystem if both the message space and the randomness space are additively homomorphic, i.e., $\mathsf{Enc}_{\mathsf{pk}}(m_1; r_1) + \mathsf{Enc}_{\mathsf{pk}}(m_2; r_2) =$

$\mathsf{Enc_{pk}}(m_1 + m_2; r_1 + r_2)$ for any public key pk, messages m_1, m_2 and randomness $r_1, r_2 \in \mathcal{R}$. For simplicity, consider the case when $q = 1$ and the i-th index is binding. We can set $\mathsf{ck} = (\mathsf{pk}, \boldsymbol{c} := (\mathsf{Enc_{pk}}(e_{i,1}; r_1), \dots, \mathsf{Enc_{pk}}(e_{i,n}; r_n)), \mathsf{tk} = \mathsf{sk}$ where e_i is the i-th unit vector. In order to commit to $\boldsymbol{x}$, we compute $\boldsymbol{c} \cdot \boldsymbol{x} + \mathsf{Enc_{pk}}(0; r) = \mathsf{Enc_{pk}}(x_i, r + \sum_{i=1}^{n} r_i)$ for $r \leftarrow_{\$} \mathcal{R}$. Now, ISH follows directly from the IND-CPA security, SSB and F-SSE follow from the correctness of the cryptosystem, and AESH follows since $\mathsf{Enc_{pk}}(x_i, r + \sum_{i=1}^{n} r_i)$ only depends on x_i. However, we obtain a less efficient construction than EMP. E.g., if we instantiate with lifted Elgamal we would have a commitment size of $2q$ group elements, whereas EMP has $q + 1$.

The above is similar to the technique of obtaining 2-message oblivious transfer (OT) from additively homomorphic cryptosystems [1] and this is no coincidence. SSB commitments can indeed be constructed from OT, and we can conversely construct OT from SSB commitments. Hence there are various alternative constructions of SSB, but in this paper we concentrate on EMP due to the applications we are interested in. See the full version for more details.

5   Functional SSB Commitments

We generalize the notion of SSB commitments from being statistically binding on an index-set $\mathcal{S} \subseteq [1 \mathinner{.\,.} n]$ to being statistically binding on outputs of the functions $\{f_i\}_{i=1}^{q}$ from some function family $\mathcal{F}$. We construct a functional SSB commitment scheme for the case when $\mathcal{F}$ is the set of linear functions. In particular, this covers functions $f_j(\boldsymbol{x}) = x_j$ and hence we also have the index-set functionality of EMP commitment.

In our definition, given a family of functions $\mathcal{F}$ we require that the commitment key ck will hide the functions $\{f_i\}_{i=1}^{q} \subset \mathcal{F}$ and given a commitment $\mathsf{Com}(\mathsf{ck}; \boldsymbol{x}; r)$ and an extraction key ek it is possible to F-extract $f_i(\boldsymbol{x})$ for $i \in [1 \mathinner{.\,.} q]$, i.e. if F is the exponentiation function in the group, $[f_i(\boldsymbol{x})]_{\iota}$. The commitment uniquely determines the outputs of the functions (due to the SSB property) and commitments to messages which produce equal function outputs are statistically indistinguishable (due to the AESH property). Our definition is similar to Döttling et al.'s [13] definition for trapdoor hash functions for a family of predicates $\mathcal{F}$.

Definition of Functional SSB. An F-*extractable functional SSB commitment scheme* $\mathsf{COM} = (\mathsf{Pgen}, \mathsf{KC}, \mathsf{Com}, \mathsf{tdOpen}, \mathsf{Ext}_F)$ for a function family $\mathcal{F}$ follows the definitions of SSB commitments in Sect. 3.1, but with the following changes: (i) $\mathcal{S}$ is now a set of functions rather than a set of indices. (ISH then becomes function-set hiding (FSH)). (ii) For $\mathcal{S} = \{f_i\}_{i=1}^{q} \subseteq \mathcal{F}$ and vector $\boldsymbol{x}$ we redefine $\boldsymbol{x}_{\mathcal{S}} := (f_1(\boldsymbol{x}), \dots, f_q(\boldsymbol{x}))$. The complete definitions are given in the the full version [17]. Relations that hold between properties of SSB commitments also hold for functional SSB commitments; the proofs are very similar.

$\mathsf{KC}_\iota(\mathsf{p}, n, q, [\boldsymbol{M}]_\iota \in \mathbb{G}_\iota^{q \times n})$:

Set implicitly $\mathsf{MSP} = \mathsf{RSP} = \mathbb{Z}_p^n$ and $\mathsf{CSP} = \mathbb{G}_\iota^{q+1}$;

Sample $\boldsymbol{R} \leftarrow\!\!\$\, \mathbb{Z}_p^{(q+1) \times (q+1)}$ so that it has full rank; Sample $\boldsymbol{\varrho} \leftarrow\!\!\$\, \mathbb{Z}_p^n$;

Set $\boldsymbol{M}' \leftarrow \left[\begin{smallmatrix} \boldsymbol{M} & 0 \\ \boldsymbol{\varrho}^\mathsf{T} & 1 \end{smallmatrix}\right]_\iota \in \mathbb{G}_\iota^{(q+1) \times (n+1)}$;

Set $\mathsf{ck} \leftarrow [\boldsymbol{R}\boldsymbol{M}']_\iota \in \mathbb{G}_\iota^{(q+1) \times (n+1)}$, $\mathsf{td} \leftarrow (\mathsf{ek} \leftarrow \boldsymbol{R}^{-1}, \mathsf{tk} \leftarrow \boldsymbol{\varrho})$;

return $(\mathsf{ck}, \mathsf{td})$;

$\mathsf{Com}(\mathsf{ck}; \boldsymbol{x} \in \mathbb{Z}_p^n; r \in \mathbb{Z}_p)$	$\mathsf{tdOpen}(\mathsf{p}, \mathsf{tk}; \boldsymbol{x}_0, r_0, \boldsymbol{x}_1)$	$/\!/$ $[\boldsymbol{M}]_\iota \boldsymbol{x}_0 = [\boldsymbol{M}]_\iota \boldsymbol{x}_1$

return $\mathsf{ck}(\begin{smallmatrix} \boldsymbol{x} \\ r \end{smallmatrix})$;   **return** $r_1 \leftarrow \displaystyle\sum_{i \in [1 .. n]} (x_{0,i} - x_{1,i}) \mathsf{tk}_i + r_0$;

$\mathsf{Ext}(\mathsf{p}, \mathsf{ek}; [\boldsymbol{c}]_\iota)$

---

return $\mathsf{ek}[\boldsymbol{c}]_\iota$ without the last component;

Fig. 3. Functional SSB commitment for linear functions

Linear EMP. We construct a functional SSB commitment for a family of linear functions. Our construction follows the ideas in [12] which only dealt with some concrete functions and never formalized the ideas.

We represent q linear functions by a matrix $\boldsymbol{M} \in \mathbb{Z}_p^{q \times n}$ where each row contains coefficients of one function. From a commitment to vector $\boldsymbol{x} \in \mathbb{Z}_p^n$, our construction allows to extract $[\boldsymbol{M}\boldsymbol{x}]_\iota$. In particular, if we take $\boldsymbol{M} = (\boldsymbol{e}_{i_1} | \ldots | \boldsymbol{e}_{i_q})^\mathsf{T}$ where $\boldsymbol{e}_{i_j} \in \mathbb{Z}_p^n$ is the i_jth unit vector, then $[\boldsymbol{M}\boldsymbol{x}]_\iota = [x_{i_1}, \ldots, x_{i_q}]_\iota^\mathsf{T}$. A detailed construction is given in Fig. 3.

We want to note that the matrix $[\boldsymbol{M}]_\iota$ is extended into one row to place the randomness vector $\boldsymbol{\varrho}$ and one column to place the randomizator of the commitment, r, to perfectly hide the secret vector $\boldsymbol{x}$ when we extract. Concretely, in the extraction phase we obtain $\left[\begin{smallmatrix} \boldsymbol{M} & 0 \\ \boldsymbol{\varrho}^\mathsf{T} & 1 \end{smallmatrix}\right]_\iota \left[\begin{smallmatrix} \boldsymbol{x} \\ r \end{smallmatrix}\right]_\iota = \left[\begin{smallmatrix} \boldsymbol{M}\boldsymbol{x} \\ \boldsymbol{\varrho}^\mathsf{T}\boldsymbol{x}+r \end{smallmatrix}\right]_\iota$ from multiplying the commitment by the inverse matrix of $\boldsymbol{R}$. The first q rows contain the functions of $\boldsymbol{x}$ in the group that we want and the last component contains a combination of $\boldsymbol{x}$ with $\boldsymbol{\varrho}$ that is completely masked by r.

Moreover, if we take an ACS (Definition 1), the commitment key is $\mathsf{ck} = [\boldsymbol{U}_1, \boldsymbol{U}_2]_\iota \in \mathbb{G}_\iota^{(q+1) \times n} \times \mathbb{G}_\iota^{(q+1) \times 1}$, which is optimal size for extraction in q coordinates, as proven in the full version [17]. The main differences with the EMP construction in Sect. 4.2 is that in EMP $\boldsymbol{M}$ is a matrix in reduced row echelon form (with multiples of the column vector $(0, \ldots, 0, 1)^T$ possibly inserted in between). We prove security of linear EMP in the full version.

6 Applications of Functional SSB Commitments

We present three applications of functional SSB commitments. In Sect. 6.1 we have two straightforward applications for linear EMP commitments: Oblivious Database Queries (ODQ) and Oblivious Linear Function Evaluation (OLE) [14, 15, 22]. OLE allows the receiver to learn $f(\boldsymbol{x})$ where $\boldsymbol{x}$ is the receiver's private vector and f is the sender's private linear function. ODQ essentially switches the roles of receiver and sender: the receiver wants to learn $f(\boldsymbol{x})$ where $\boldsymbol{x}$ is the sender's private database and f is the receiver's linear query function. In Sect. 6.2 we present a new QA-NIZK argument for SAP relations that uses linear EMP commitments as a technical tool in the security proof.

6.1   ODQ and OLE

A very straight-forward application of linear EMP is oblivious database queries (ODQ). We consider a scenario where the sender knows a private database $\boldsymbol{x}$ and the receiver knows a set of private linear functions $f_i(X_1, \ldots, X_n) = b_i + \sum_{j=1}^{n} a_{i,j} X_j$ for $i \in [1 .. q]$ that he wants to evaluate on that database.

Our ODQ protocol works as follows:

- Receiver defines matrices $\boldsymbol{A} = (a_{ij}) \in \mathbb{Z}_p^{q \times n}$, $\boldsymbol{B} = \mathrm{diag}(b_1, \ldots, b_q) \in \mathbb{Z}_p^{q \times q}$, and $\boldsymbol{M} = (\boldsymbol{A} \mid \boldsymbol{B}) \in \mathbb{Z}_p^{q \times (n+q)}$. Following the KC algorithm it creates the commitment key ck, the extraction key ek, and sends ck to the sender.
- Sender has $\boldsymbol{x} \in \mathbb{Z}_p^n$ and ck as input. It sets $\boldsymbol{x}' = \left(\begin{smallmatrix} x \\ 1_q \end{smallmatrix}\right)$, picks random $r \leftarrow_\$ \mathbb{Z}_p$ and sends $\mathsf{COM} = \mathsf{ck}\left(\begin{smallmatrix} x' \\ r \end{smallmatrix}\right)$ to the receiver.
- Receiver extracts $[\boldsymbol{M} \cdot \boldsymbol{x}']$ from COM using the Ext algorithm with ek.

Privacy and Correctness. We follow privacy and correctness definitions proposed by Döttling et al. [13] (see Sect. 5.1 of their paper for full definitions). From the SSE property we know that the receiver can recover $[\boldsymbol{M} \left(\begin{smallmatrix} x \\ 1_q \end{smallmatrix}\right)]_\iota = [\boldsymbol{A}\boldsymbol{x} + \boldsymbol{b}]_\iota$ and thus correctness holds. Receiver's (computational) privacy follows directly from the FSH property, that is, any two function-sets of size at most q are indistinguishable. Sender's privacy is defined through simulatability of the protocol transcript given only receiver's input $\boldsymbol{M}$ and receiver's output $[\boldsymbol{M}\boldsymbol{x}']$ to the simulator. Simulatability is slightly stronger than the AEPH property but still holds for linear EMP. As a first message, the simulator can generate ck with $\boldsymbol{M}$ and store $\boldsymbol{R}$. An honestly computed second message has the form $[\boldsymbol{R}\left(\begin{smallmatrix} M & 0 \\ r^\top & 1 \end{smallmatrix}\right)]\left(\begin{smallmatrix} x' \\ r \end{smallmatrix}\right) = \boldsymbol{R}\left[\begin{smallmatrix} Mx' \\ x'^\top r + r \end{smallmatrix}\right]$ and therefore we can simulate it by sampling $r^* \leftarrow_\$ \mathbb{Z}_p$ and computing $\boldsymbol{R}\left(\begin{smallmatrix} [Mx'] \\ r^* \end{smallmatrix}\right)$. Thus sender's privacy also holds.

Efficiency. We define download rate as the ratio between output size and sender's message and total rate as the ratio between output size and total transcript size. The total rate of our protocol is $\|[\boldsymbol{M}\boldsymbol{x}']\|/(|\mathsf{ck}| + |\mathsf{COM}|) = q/((n + q + 2)(q + 1))$. However, we achieve very good download rate $\|[\boldsymbol{M}\boldsymbol{x}']\|/|\mathsf{COM}| = q/(q + 1)$ which tends to 1. This is similar to Döttling et al. [13] where they achieve an optimal download rate but sub-optimal total rate.

OLE. We can achieve OLE in a very similar way. Suppose that now the sender has a function $f(X_1, \ldots, X_n) = b + \sum_{i=1}^{n} a_i X_i$ and the receiver has $\boldsymbol{x}$. Then the receiver can send a commitment key with $M = (x_1, \ldots, x_n, 1)$ and the sender responds with a commitment to $(a_1, \ldots, a_n, b)$. The receiver extracts to obtain $[f(x)]_\iota$. The proof is identical to the ODQ case. However, the resulting OLE is less efficient with download rate $1/2$ and total rate $1/(2n + 4)$.

6.2   QA-NIZK Argument for Quadratic Equations

We present a QA-NIZK argument which uses linear EMP commitments as an important technical tool in the security proof, inspired by Daza et al. [12] who presented a commit-and-prove QA-NIZK argument for Square Span Programs (SSP, [11]) which can be used to encode the Boolean circuit satisfiability language. Their construction uses a specific setting of linear EMP commitments without explicitly formalizing it. Our QA-NIZK is for Square Arithmetic Programs (SAP) [27] which can be used to encode the arithmetic circuit satisfiability language, has roughly the same complexity as the argument in [12] and follows a similar overall strategy. However, we use linear EMP commitments as a black-box and thus have a more compact and clear presentation.

A rough intuition of our commit-and-prove QA-NIZK is as follows. The statement of our language $\mathscr{L}_{\mathsf{SAP,ck}}$ contains a linear-length perfectly binding (and $[\cdot]_1$-extractable) commitment $[c]_1$ of the SAP witness. Note that the commitment is only computed once but can be reused for many different SAP relations. For simplicity, we use ElGamal encryption in this role and the commitment key ck as a parameter of the language. The argument itself is succinct and contains the following elements:

- a succinct SNARK-type argument $[V, H, W]_1, [V]_2$ for the SAP relation,
- a succinct linear EMP commitment $[\tilde{c}]_2$ that commits to the SAP witness and to the randomness of the SNARK,
- a succinct linear subspace argument bls [23] that shows that commitments open to consistent values (see bls argument below). I.e., it guarantees that the opening of $[c]_1$ is also used in the SNARK and in $[\tilde{c}]_2$.

Below, we go over some of the technical background and then finally present our QA-NIZK argument for SAP.

Perfectly Binding Commitment. We use ElGamal encryption as our perfectly binding commitment. In particular, the commitment key is $\mathsf{ck} = [u]_1 = [1, u]_1^\top$ where $u \leftarrow_\$ \mathbb{Z}_p$ and $\mathsf{Com}_{\mathsf{ck}}(a \in \mathbb{Z}_p^n; r \in \mathbb{Z}_p^n) = [c]_1 := ([r]_1, [a]_1 + r[u]_1)$. In matrix form $[c_i]_1 = a_i[e_2]_1 + r_i[u]_1$. To $[\cdot]_1$-extract the message, we can simply decrypt each individual ciphertext, that is $[a_i]_1 = [c_{i,2}]_1 - u[c_{i,1}]_1$ where $[c_i]_1 = [c_{i,1}, c_{i,2}]_1^\top$.

Square Arithmetic Program (SAP). A square arithmetic program is a tuple $\mathsf{SAP} = (\mathsf{p}, n, d, \mathbf{V} \in \mathbb{Z}_p^{n \times d}, \mathbf{W} \in \mathbb{Z}_p^{n \times d})$. We define a commit-and-prove language for SAP as the following language with n variables and d quadratic equations

$$\mathscr{L}_{\mathsf{SAP},\mathsf{ck}} = \left\{ [c]_1 \in \mathbb{G}_1^{2n} \middle| \begin{array}{l} \exists a, r \in \mathbb{Z}_p^n \colon [c]_1 = \mathsf{Com}_{ck}(a, r) \land \\ \left\{ (a^\top v_j)^2 - a^\top w_j = 0 \right\}_{j=1}^d \end{array} \right\}$$

where Com_{ck} is a perfectly binding commitment scheme, v_j is j-th column of the matrix V and w_j is the j-th column of the matrix W.

SNARK for SAP. Let $\chi_1, \ldots, \chi_d \in \mathbb{Z}_p$ be unique interpolation points. We define

$$v(X) = \sum_{i=1}^n a_i v_i(X), \quad w(X) = \sum_{i=1}^n a_i w_i(X) \tag{1}$$

where $v_i(X)$, $w_i(X)$ are polynomials of degree less than d such that $v_i(\chi_j) = v_{ij}$ and $w_i(\chi_j) = -w_{ij}$. Moreover, let us define $p(X) = v(X)^2 - w(X)$ and $t(X) = \prod_{j=1}^d (X - \chi_j)$. We have that $p(\chi_j) = (a^\top v_j)^2 - a^\top w_j$ and thus the j-th SAP equation is satisfied exactly when χ_j is a root of $p(X)$. In particular, when all interpolation points are roots of $p(X)$, then $t(X)$ divides $p(X)$ and all the SAP equations are satisfied.

We can use these polynomial representations to construct a SNARK. Our CRS will contain $\{ [s^i]_{1,2} \}_{i=1}^d$ where $s \leftarrow\$ \mathbb{Z}_p$ is a secret point. The prover will compute $[V]_{1,2} = [V(s)]_{1,2}$, $[W]_1 = [W(s)]_1$ and $[H]_1 = [H(s)]_1$ where $V(X) = v(X) + \delta_v t(X)$, $W(X) = w(X) + \delta_w t(X)$, and $H(X) = (V(X)^2 - W(X))/t(X)$. Elements δ_v and δ_w are picked randomly to hide the witness. The verifier checks that the equation $[V]_1[V]_2 - [W]_1[1]_2 = [H]_1[t(s)]_2$ is satisfied. Intuitively, we can use this to show that $t(X)$ divides $P(X) := V(X)^2 - W(X)$. It is easy to see that if $t(X) \mid P(X)$ then also $t(X) \mid p(X)$ and thus the SAP relation is satisfied.

BLS Argument. As a subargument, we use a QA-NIZK argument for membership in linear spaces ($\mathsf{K}_{\mathsf{bls}}, \mathsf{P}_{\mathsf{bls}}, \mathsf{V}_{\mathsf{bls}}$) defined in [23] for the bilateral linear subspace (bls) language $\mathcal{L}_{[N_1]_1,[N_2]_2} := \{ ([x]_1, [y]_2) \mid \exists w \in \mathbb{Z}_p^t \colon x = N_1 w \land y = N_2 w \}$ for $N_1 \in \mathbb{Z}_p^{n \times t}$, $N_2 \in \mathbb{Z}_p^{m \times t}$. We use it to prove that commitments in different groups open to the same value. It has perfect completeness, strong quasi-adaptive soundness under the SKerMDH assumption, and perfect zero-knowledge. The proof size is 2 elements in $\mathbb{G}_1$ and 2 elements in $\mathbb{G}_2$. We refer the reader to the original paper for more details. We leave it as an open question if the slightly more efficient construction by Ràfols and Silva [36] can be used.

New Target Assumption. The q-target strong Diffie-Hellman (q-TSDH) assumption [3] says that given $\{ [s^i]_{1,2} \}_{i=1}^q$ for a random s, it is computationally hard to find $[\nu]_T = [1/(s - r)]_T$ for any $r \in \mathbb{Z}_p$. We generalize this assumption and intuitively say that it is hard to compute $[\nu]_T = [c/(s - r)]_T$ where $r \in \mathbb{Z}_p$ and c is a constant independent of s. In order to satisfy the latter requirement, we include a challenge value $[z]_2$ and let the adversary additionally output $[c]_1$ and $[c']_2$ such that $zc = c'$. Intuitively, then c cannot depend on s^i since otherwise c' should depend on zs^i which is not a part of the challenge. For technical reasons, c in our assumption has a slightly more structured form $\beta_1^2 - \beta_2$.

Definition 3 (q-SATSDH). *The q-Square Arithmetic Target Strong Diffie-Hellman assumption holds relative to* Pgen, *if $\forall$ PPT adversaries $\mathcal{A}$,*

$$\Pr\left[\begin{array}{c} \mathsf{p} \leftarrow \mathsf{Pgen}(1^\lambda); s, z \leftarrow_\$ \mathbb{Z}_p; \\ \left(r, [\beta_1, \beta_2]_1, [\tilde{\beta}_1, \tilde{\beta}_2]_2, [\nu]_T\right) \leftarrow \mathcal{A}\left(\mathsf{p}, \{[s^i]_{1,2}\}_{i=1}^q, [z]_2\right) : \\ \tilde{\beta}_1 = z\beta_1 \wedge \tilde{\beta}_2 = z\beta_2 \wedge \beta_1^2 \neq \beta_2 \wedge \nu = \frac{\beta_1^2 - \beta_2}{s - r} \end{array}\right] \approx_\lambda 0.$$

In the full version, we show that SATSDH is a falsifiable assumption and that assuming a certain (previously known) knowledge assumption, SATSDH and TSDH are equivalent. Alternatively, it is also possible to prove that SATSDH is secure in the generic group model.

QA-NIZK Argument Scheme. Given $n, d \in \mathbb{N}$ we construct a QA-NIZK argument for $\mathscr{L}_{\mathsf{SAP,ck}}$.

- $\mathsf{K}_0(\lambda)$ returns $\mathsf{p} \leftarrow \mathsf{Pgen}(1^\lambda)$.
- $\mathcal{D}_\mathsf{p}(n, d)$ returns a commitment key $\mathsf{ck} = [u]_1 = [1, u]_1^\top$ where $u \leftarrow_\$ \mathbb{Z}_p$.
- $\mathsf{K}_1(\mathsf{p}, n, d, \mathsf{ck})$ picks $s \leftarrow_\$ \mathbb{Z}_p$, then sets $q_v = 4$, $n' = n + 1$, $\boldsymbol{M} = \boldsymbol{0} \in \mathbb{Z}_p^{q_v \times n'}$ (i.e., $S_v = \emptyset$) and generates a linear EMP key $\mathsf{ck}' = [\boldsymbol{K}]_2 \leftarrow \mathsf{KC}_2(\mathsf{p}, n', q_v, \boldsymbol{M}) \in \mathbb{G}_2^{5 \times (n+2)}$. Finally, it runs $(\mathsf{crs_{bls}}, \mathsf{td_{bls}}) \leftarrow \mathsf{K_{bls}}([\boldsymbol{N}_1]_1 \in \mathbb{G}_1^{(2n+2) \times (2n+3)}, [\boldsymbol{N}_2]_2 \in \mathbb{G}_2^{5 \times (2n+3)})$ for

$$[\boldsymbol{N}_1]_1 = \left[\begin{array}{ccc|ccc|ccc} e_2 & & & u & & & & & \\ & \ddots & & & \ddots & & & \boldsymbol{0} & \\ & & e_2 & & & u & & & \\ \hline v_1(s) \dots v_n(s) & & & & \boldsymbol{0} & & t(s) & 0 & 0 \\ w_1(s) \dots w_n(s) & & & & & & 0 & t(s) & 0 \end{array}\right]_1,$$

$$[\boldsymbol{N}_2]_2 = \left[\begin{array}{c|c|ccc} v_1(s) \dots v_n(s) & & t(s) & 0 & 0 \\ \boldsymbol{K}^{(1)} \dots \boldsymbol{K}^{(n)} & \boldsymbol{0} & \boldsymbol{K}^{(n+1)} & 0 & \boldsymbol{K}^{(n+2)} \end{array}\right]_2.$$

Return the CRS $\mathsf{crs} = (\mathsf{p}, \mathsf{ck}, \mathsf{ck}', \{[s^i]_{1,2}\}_{i=1}^d, \mathsf{crs_{bls}})$ with trapdoor $(s, \mathsf{td_{bls}})$.
- The prover P receives an input $(\mathsf{crs}, ([\boldsymbol{c}]_1, \boldsymbol{V}, \boldsymbol{W}), (\boldsymbol{a}, \boldsymbol{r}))$. Let $v_i(X)$ and $w_i(X)$ be the interpolation polynomials at some points $\{\chi_j\}_j$ for the i-th column of $\boldsymbol{V}$ and $\boldsymbol{W}$ respectively for $i \in [1 .. n]$, and set $t(X) = \prod_{i=j}^d (X - \chi_j)$. The prover picks $\delta_v, \delta_w, r_v \leftarrow_\$ \mathbb{Z}_p$ and defines:

$$\begin{array}{ll} V(X) := \sum_{i=1}^n a_i v_i(X) + \delta_v t(X), & W(X) := \sum_{i=1}^n a_i w_i(X) + \delta_w t(X) \\ P(X) := V(X)^2 - W(X) & H(X) := P(X)/t(X) \end{array} \quad (2)$$

The prover computes group elements $[V]_{1,2} = [V(s)]_{1,2}$, $[W]_1 = [W(s)]_1$, $[H]_1 = [H(s)]_1$ and a linear EMP commitment $[\tilde{\boldsymbol{c}}]_2 = \mathsf{Com}(\mathsf{ck}'; (\boldsymbol{a}, \delta_v), r_v)$. The prover also computes a bls argument ψ for the statement $\mathsf{x_{bls}} := ([\boldsymbol{c}]_1, [V]_1, [W]_1, [V]_2, [\tilde{\boldsymbol{c}}]_2)^\top \in \mathbf{Im}\left(\begin{bmatrix} [\boldsymbol{N}_1]_1 \\ [\boldsymbol{N}_2]_2 \end{bmatrix}\right)$ with witness $(\boldsymbol{a}, \boldsymbol{r}, \delta_v, \delta_w, r_v)^\top \in \mathbb{Z}_p^{2n+3}$. Finally, it outputs the argument $\pi := \left([H]_1, [V]_{1,2}, [W]_1, [\tilde{\boldsymbol{c}}]_2, \psi\right)$.

– The verifier V with input $(\mathsf{crs}, [c]_1, \mathbf{V}, \mathbf{W}, \pi)$ returns 1 iff $[V]_1[V]_2 - [W]_1[1]_2 = [H]_1[t(s)]_2$ and $V_{\mathsf{bls}}(\mathsf{crs}_{\mathsf{bls}}, x_{\mathsf{bls}}, \psi) = 1$.

SSB Functionality in the Security Proof. The security proof of the argument uses similar techniques as [12] but simplified because we rely on the properties of SSB commitments. Intuitively, in the security reduction we need to compute some elements of the form $[\sum_i a_i y_i]_2$ where $(a_1, \ldots, a_n)$ is the witness and $[y_1, \ldots, y_n]_2$ are elements that can be computed from the challenge of some falsifiable assumption or public elements. The actual reduction requires us to extract multiple such linear combinations.

If an adversary wins the soundness game, its argument passes verification but at least one SAP equation does not hold. In the security proof, the soundness game is first changed by randomly picking one of the SAP equations $(\mathbf{a}^\top \mathbf{v}_{j^*})^2 - \mathbf{a}^\top \mathbf{w}_{j^*} = 0$ for some $j^* \in [1..d]$. To complete the proof, we have to check the equation and break a computational assumption. For the former, since our perfectly binding commitment is only $[\cdot]_1$-extractable, we can at best extract $[a_i]_1$ which is not enough to check the j^*-th equation, even if $\mathbf{v}_{j^*}$ and $\mathbf{w}_{j^*}$ are public. We need a square of $\mathbf{a}$, so it suffices to extract $\sum [a_i]_2 v_{j^*,i}$ in $\mathbb{G}_2$ and prove the equation in the target group. For the latter, we break the d-SATSDH assumption that is a version of the d-TSDH (Target Strong Diffie-Hellman) assumption [3] with some extra elements that are linear combinations of the witness.

Next, we switch the EMP commitment key that is in perfectly hiding mode in the honest proof $(\mathcal{S} = \emptyset)$ to the mode that encodes the functions $f(a_1, \ldots, a_n) = \sum_i a_i [y_i]_2$ that we need. Then, from $[\tilde{c}]_2$ we can extract $[\sum_i a_i v_{j^*,i}]_2$, and so check the equation in $\mathbb{G}_T$, and also the linear combinations to break the assumption.

The *FSH* property guarantees that the adversary cannot learn the index j^* and thus the j^*-th SAP equation is not satisfied with probability $\geq 1/d$. The $[\cdot]_2$-*SSE* property allows us to extract some linear combinations of the claimed witness and break the d-SATSDH assumption. Zero-knowledge is straightforwardly guaranteed by the *AEPH* property. The full security proof and more intuition of it are deferred to the full version.

Efficiency. The proof size in the original construction in [12] is 4 elements in $\mathbb{G}_1$ and 6 elements in $\mathbb{G}_2$, while our construction's proof size is 5 elements in $\mathbb{G}_1$ and 8 elements in $\mathbb{G}_2$.

Acknowledgments. We would like to thank Carla Ràfols and Janno Veeorg for useful discussions. The authors were supported by the Estonian Research Council grant (PRG49) and by Dora Plus Grant funded by the European Regional Development Fund, Republic of Estonia and Archimedes Foundation. Janno Siim was additionally supported by the European Union's Horizon 2020 research and innovation programme under grant agreement No. 780477 (project PRIViLEDGE). Part of this work was done while Janno Siim was affiliated with the University of Edinburgh.

References

1. Aiello, B., Ishai, Y., Reingold, O.: Priced oblivious transfer: how to sell digital goods. In: Pfitzmann, B. (ed.) EUROCRYPT 2001. LNCS, vol. 2045, pp. 119–135. Springer, Heidelberg (2001). https://doi.org/10.1007/3-540-44987-6_8
2. Belenkiy, M., Chase, M., Kohlweiss, M., Lysyanskaya, A.: P-signatures and non-interactive anonymous credentials. In: Canetti, R. (ed.) TCC 2008. LNCS, vol. 4948, pp. 356–374. Springer, Heidelberg (2008). https://doi.org/10.1007/978-3-540-78524-8_20
3. Boneh, D., Boyen, X.: Secure identity based encryption without random oracles. In: Franklin, M. (ed.) CRYPTO 2004. LNCS, vol. 3152, pp. 443–459. Springer, Heidelberg (2004). https://doi.org/10.1007/978-3-540-28628-8_27
4. Bünz, B., Bootle, J., Boneh, D., Poelstra, A., Wuille, P., Maxwell, G.: Bulletproofs: short proofs for confidential transactions and more. In: 2018 IEEE Symposium on Security and Privacy, pp. 315–334 (2018)
5. Catalano, D., Fiore, D.: Vector commitments and their applications. In: Kurosawa, K., Hanaoka, G. (eds.) PKC 2013. LNCS, vol. 7778, pp. 55–72. Springer, Heidelberg (2013). https://doi.org/10.1007/978-3-642-36362-7_5
6. Catalano, D., Visconti, I.: Hybrid trapdoor commitments and their applications. In: Caires, L., Italiano, G.F., Monteiro, L., Palamidessi, C., Yung, M. (eds.) ICALP 2005. LNCS, vol. 3580, pp. 298–310. Springer, Heidelberg (2005). https://doi.org/10.1007/11523468_25
7. Chase, M., Ganesh, C., Mohassel, P.: Efficient zero-knowledge proof of algebraic and non-algebraic statements with applications to privacy preserving credentials. In: Robshaw, M., Katz, J. (eds.) CRYPTO 2016. LNCS, vol. 9816, pp. 499–530. Springer, Heidelberg (2016). https://doi.org/10.1007/978-3-662-53015-3_18
8. Chiesa, A., Forbes, M.A., Spooner, N.: A zero knowledge sumcheck and its applications. Cryptology ePrint Archive, Report 2017/305 (2017). http://eprint.iacr.org/2017/305
9. Damgård, I., Fehr, S., Lunemann, C., Salvail, L., Schaffner, C.: Improving the security of quantum protocols via commit-and-open. In: Halevi, S. (ed.) CRYPTO 2009. LNCS, vol. 5677, pp. 408–427. Springer, Heidelberg (2009). https://doi.org/10.1007/978-3-642-03356-8_24
10. Damgård, I., Nielsen, J.B.: Perfect hiding and perfect binding universally composable commitment schemes with constant expansion factor. In: Yung, M. (ed.) CRYPTO 2002. LNCS, vol. 2442, pp. 581–596. Springer, Heidelberg (2002). https://doi.org/10.1007/3-540-45708-9_37
11. Danezis, G., Fournet, C., Groth, J., Kohlweiss, M.: Square span programs with applications to succinct NIZK arguments. In: Sarkar, P., Iwata, T. (eds.) ASIACRYPT 2014. LNCS, vol. 8873, pp. 532–550. Springer, Heidelberg (2014). https://doi.org/10.1007/978-3-662-45611-8_28
12. Daza, V., González, A., Pindado, Z., Ràfols, C., Silva, J.: Shorter quadratic QA-NIZK proofs. In: Lin, D., Sako, K. (eds.) PKC 2019. LNCS, vol. 11442, pp. 314–343. Springer, Cham (2019). https://doi.org/10.1007/978-3-030-17253-4_11
13. Döttling, N., Garg, S., Ishai, Y., Malavolta, G., Mour, T., Ostrovsky, R.: Trapdoor hash functions and their applications. In: Boldyreva, A., Micciancio, D. (eds.) CRYPTO 2019. LNCS, vol. 11694, pp. 3–32. Springer, Cham (2019). https://doi.org/10.1007/978-3-030-26954-8_1
14. Döttling, N., Ghosh, S., Nielsen, J.B., Nilges, T., Trifiletti, R.: TinyOLE: efficient actively secure two-party computation from oblivious linear function evaluation. In: ACM CCS 2017, pp. 2263–2276 (2017)

15. Döttling, N., Kraschewski, D., Müller-Quade, J.: Statistically secure linear-rate dimension extension for oblivious affine function evaluation. In: Smith, A. (ed.) ICITS 2012. LNCS, vol. 7412, pp. 111–128. Springer, Heidelberg (2012). https://doi.org/10.1007/978-3-642-32284-6_7

16. Escala, A., Herold, G., Kiltz, E., Ràfols, C., Villar, J.: An algebraic framework for Diffie-Hellman assumptions. In: Canetti, R., Garay, J.A. (eds.) CRYPTO 2013. LNCS, vol. 8043, pp. 129–147. Springer, Heidelberg (2013). https://doi.org/10.1007/978-3-642-40084-1_8

17. Fauzi, P., Lipmaa, H., Pindado, Z., Siim, J.: Somewhere statistically binding commitment schemes with applications. Cryptology ePrint Archive, Report 2020/652 (2020). https://eprint.iacr.org/2020/652

18. Fauzi, P., Meiklejohn, S., Mercer, R., Orlandi, C.: Quisquis: a new design for anonymous cryptocurrencies. In: Galbraith, S.D., Moriai, S. (eds.) ASIACRYPT 2019. LNCS, vol. 11921, pp. 649–678. Springer, Cham (2019). https://doi.org/10.1007/978-3-030-34578-5_23

19. Fuchsbauer, G., Orrù, M., Seurin, Y.: Aggregate cash systems: a cryptographic investigation of Mimblewimble. In: Ishai, Y., Rijmen, V. (eds.) EUROCRYPT 2019. LNCS, vol. 11476, pp. 657–689. Springer, Cham (2019). https://doi.org/10.1007/978-3-030-17653-2_22

20. Gennaro, R., Gentry, C., Parno, B., Raykova, M.: Quadratic span programs and succinct NIZKs without PCPs. In: Johansson, T., Nguyen, P.Q. (eds.) EUROCRYPT 2013. LNCS, vol. 7881, pp. 626–645. Springer, Heidelberg (2013). https://doi.org/10.1007/978-3-642-38348-9_37

21. Gentry, C., Wichs, D.: Separating succinct non-interactive arguments from all falsifiable assumptions. In: 43rd ACM STOC, pp. 99–108 (2011)

22. Ghosh, S., Nielsen, J.B., Nilges, T.: Maliciously secure oblivious linear function evaluation with constant overhead. In: Takagi, T., Peyrin, T. (eds.) ASIACRYPT 2017. LNCS, vol. 10624, pp. 629–659. Springer, Cham (2017). https://doi.org/10.1007/978-3-319-70694-8_22

23. González, A., Hevia, A., Ràfols, C.: QA-NIZK arguments in asymmetric groups: new tools and new constructions. In: Iwata, T., Cheon, J.H. (eds.) ASIACRYPT 2015. LNCS, vol. 9452, pp. 605–629. Springer, Heidelberg (2015). https://doi.org/10.1007/978-3-662-48797-6_25

24. González, A., Ráfols, C.: New techniques for non-interactive shuffle and range arguments. In: Manulis, M., Sadeghi, A.-R., Schneider, S. (eds.) ACNS 2016. LNCS, vol. 9696, pp. 427–444. Springer, Cham (2016). https://doi.org/10.1007/978-3-319-39555-5_23

25. González, A., Ràfols, C.: Shorter pairing-based arguments under standard assumptions. In: Galbraith, S.D., Moriai, S. (eds.) ASIACRYPT 2019. LNCS, vol. 11923, pp. 728–757. Springer, Cham (2019). https://doi.org/10.1007/978-3-030-34618-8_25

26. Groth, J.: Short pairing-based non-interactive zero-knowledge arguments. In: Abe, M. (ed.) ASIACRYPT 2010. LNCS, vol. 6477, pp. 321–340. Springer, Heidelberg (2010). https://doi.org/10.1007/978-3-642-17373-8_19

27. Groth, J., Maller, M.: Snarky signatures: minimal signatures of knowledge from simulation-extractable SNARKs. In: Katz, J., Shacham, H. (eds.) CRYPTO 2017. LNCS, vol. 10402, pp. 581–612. Springer, Cham (2017). https://doi.org/10.1007/978-3-319-63715-0_20

28. Groth, J., Sahai, A.: Efficient non-interactive proof systems for bilinear groups. In: Smart, N. (ed.) EUROCRYPT 2008. LNCS, vol. 4965, pp. 415–432. Springer, Heidelberg (2008). https://doi.org/10.1007/978-3-540-78967-3_24

29. Hubacek, P., Wichs, D.: On the communication complexity of secure function evaluation with long output. In: ITCS 2015, pp. 163–172 (2015)
30. Jutla, C.S., Roy, A.: Shorter quasi-adaptive NIZK proofs for linear subspaces. In: Sako, K., Sarkar, P. (eds.) ASIACRYPT 2013. LNCS, vol. 8269, pp. 1–20. Springer, Heidelberg (2013). https://doi.org/10.1007/978-3-642-42033-7_1
31. Libert, B., Yung, M.: Concise mercurial vector commitments and independent zero-knowledge sets with short proofs. In: Micciancio, D. (ed.) TCC 2010. LNCS, vol. 5978, pp. 499–517. Springer, Heidelberg (2010). https://doi.org/10.1007/978-3-642-11799-2_30
32. Lipmaa, H.: Progression-free sets and sublinear pairing-based non-interactive zero-knowledge arguments. In: Cramer, R. (ed.) TCC 2012. LNCS, vol. 7194, pp. 169–189. Springer, Heidelberg (2012). https://doi.org/10.1007/978-3-642-28914-9_10
33. Okamoto, T., Pietrzak, K., Waters, B., Wichs, D.: New realizations of somewhere statistically binding hashing and positional accumulators. In: Iwata, T., Cheon, J.H. (eds.) ASIACRYPT 2015. LNCS, vol. 9452, pp. 121–145. Springer, Heidelberg (2015). https://doi.org/10.1007/978-3-662-48797-6_6
34. Pedersen, T.P.: Non-interactive and information-theoretic secure verifiable secret sharing. In: Feigenbaum, J. (ed.) CRYPTO 1991. LNCS, vol. 576, pp. 129–140. Springer, Heidelberg (1992). https://doi.org/10.1007/3-540-46766-1_9
35. Poelstra, A.: Mimblewimble (2016). https://download.wpsoftware.net/bitcoin/wizardry/mimblewimble.pdf
36. Ràfols, C., Silva, J.: QA-NIZK arguments of same opening for bilateral commitments. In: Nitaj, A., Youssef, A. (eds.) AFRICACRYPT 2020. LNCS, vol. 12174, pp. 3–23. Springer, Cham (2020). https://doi.org/10.1007/978-3-030-51938-4_1

Another Look at Extraction
and Randomization of Groth's zk-SNARK

Karim Baghery[1], Markulf Kohlweiss[2,3], Janno Siim[4], and Mikhail Volkhov[3(✉)]

[1] imec-COSIC, KU Leuven, Leuven, Belgium
karim.baghery@kuleuven.be
[2] IOHK, Hong Kong, China
[3] The University of Edinburgh, Edinburgh, UK
{mkohlwei,mikhail.volkhov}@ed.ac.uk
[4] University of Tartu, Tartu, Estonia
janno.siim@ut.ee

Abstract. Due to the simplicity and performance of zk-SNARKs they are widely used in real-world cryptographic protocols, including blockchain and smart contract systems. Simulation Extractability (SE) is a necessary security property for a NIZK argument to achieve Universal Composability (UC), a common requirement for such protocols. Most of the works that investigate SE focus on its strong variant which implies proof non-malleability. In this work we investigate a relaxed weaker notion, that *allows proof randomization*, while guaranteeing statement non-malleability, which we argue to be a more natural security property. First, we show that it is already achievable by Groth16, arguably the most efficient and widely deployed SNARK nowadays. Second, we show that because of this, Groth16 can be *efficiently* transformed into a black-box weakly SE NIZK, which is sufficient for UC protocols.

To support the second claim, we present and compare two practical constructions, both of which strike different performance tradeoffs:

- Int-Groth16 makes use of a known transformation that encrypts the witness inside the SNARK circuit. We instantiate this transformation with an efficient SNARK-friendly encryption scheme.
- Ext-Groth16 is based on the SAVER encryption scheme (Lee et al.) that plugs the encrypted witness directly into the verification equation, externally to the circuit. We prove that Ext-Groth16 is black-box weakly SE and, contrary to Int-Groth16, that its proofs are fully randomizable.

Keywords: zk-SNARKs · Simulation extractability · UC security

1 Introduction

Succinct non-interactive arguments of knowledge (SNARK) have revolutionized the deployment of zero-knowledge proofs, particularly in the blockchain and cryptographic currency space [BCG+14, KMS+16, KKK20, BCG+20, SBG+19].

© International Financial Cryptography Association 2021
N. Borisov and C. Diaz (Eds.): FC 2021, LNCS 12674, pp. 457–475, 2021.
https://doi.org/10.1007/978-3-662-64322-8_22

The ready availability of cryptographic libraries implementing SNARKs has also inspired numerous other applications [NT16, DFKP16][1].

Due to its exceptional performance and simplicity, currently the most widely deployed SNARK is Groth16 [Gro16]. In this work, we consider an important perspective on security analysis of Groth16, namely the limits of its malleability (and non-malleability). The lack of study in this direction is surprising considering the importance of non-malleability in distributed settings such as blockchain and the popularity of Groth16 for practical applications.

Arguably, the strongest extraction and non-malleability property for SNARK systems is *simulation-extractability* (SE) [Sah99, DDO+01], a security notion that extends knowledge-soundness (KS) by giving the adversary access to the simulation oracle. One of the important properties of this notion is that its straight-line extractable, black-box variant is necessary to achieve universally composable (UC) security [Can01] for non-interactive zero-knowledge (NIZK) proof systems, as shown by [CLOS02, GOS06, Gro06]. This is an important practical concern since applications employing SNARKs often use the UC framework due to its flexibility and expressive power [KMS+16, KKKZ19, KKK20]. Moreover, SE is needed in game-hopping style proofs [Sho04] in which one game hop introduces the simulator and a subsequent game hop relies on extraction [KMS+16, CDD17].

Simulation-extractability comes in two flavors: the adversary against the stronger flavor is required to produce a proof that differs from any simulated proof that the adversary obtained from the simulator. In this work, we focus on the weaker flavor [KZM+15], that allows for a limited malleability of proofs but requires the adversary to produce a proof for a statement that differs from any of the statements queried from the simulator. Weak SE and strong SE of *proof systems* are in analogy to chosen message attack (CMA) and strong CMA unforgeability of *signatures*.

Another important parameter of a SE notion is whether it supports white-box (WB) or black-box (BB) extraction. A well-known impossibility result [GW11] states that SNARKs cannot be proven secure under falsifiable assumptions. In practice, the non-falsifiability of the assumptions used for SNARKs comes from their white-box nature; that is, they imply some knowledge of the adversary's internals. This prevents proving black-box extraction (and black-box SE), which requires extracting from the adversary only using its "input/output" interface. Since precisely this notion is required for UC security, in practice compilers lifting zk-SNARKs to black-box SE are used [KZM+15, AB19, Bag19], and, crucially, their efficiency can benefit from a stronger (white-box) property of the input SNARK as we show in this work.

Although black-box strong SE is sometimes a desirable property, (black-box) weak SE is sufficient for many UC applications, for instance in Hawk [KMS+16], as argued in [KZM+15]. Hawk uses SE NIZKs directly as a raw primitive (without employing a functionality), and it suggests to use a non-succinct strong SE NIZK, since no other candidates were known at that time. Kosba

---

[1] See also the application chapter of [ZKP19].

et al. [KZM+15] point out that a weak SE NIZK can be used instead. We also note that weak SE is sufficient for the SNARKs to signatures of knowledge (SoK) compiler of [GM17] that embeds a hash of the message into the statement proven. Thus applications employing SoK, such as [BMRS20], can also benefit from our work. Note that in weak SE it is the statement rather than the proof that cannot be mauled. The resulting SoK satisfies CMA unforgeability.

Our Contributions. Our results are twofold. First, we show that Groth16, as described in the literature and deployed in practical applications, is already white-box weak SE.

Surprisingly, this was not known before. Proof malleability was noted by [GM17] as an obstacle for proving the strong SE property for Groth16, which resulted in them constructing a new non-malleable SNARK. Allowing proof randomization in the definition resolves the issue differently by proving a security property for the original system that lies in strength between knowledge soundness and strong SE. Additionally, we show that only a specific type of proof malleability is possible and that rerandomized proofs have the same distribution as fresh proofs of the same statement. We show in the algebraic group model (that we state as an assumption) that the extractor can either obtain the witness or point to the unique simulated proof that was randomized to obtain the proof produced by the adversary. Thus, even if the adversary queries multiple proofs for the same statement, it cannot combine them into a new proof of the same statement, which is the main technical challenge in proving white-box weak SE.

As our second contribution, we give two optimized constructions for black-box weak SE: Int-Groth16 and Ext-Groth16. Int-Groth16 is based on the (strong) WB-to-BB SE compiler of [Bag19]. It adds a public key of a cryptosystem to the CRS and a ciphertext containing encryption of the witness to the proof. It then employs a SNARK to prove an extended statement to ensure that the witness is correctly encrypted. We show that this compiler can be used for *weak* WB-to-BB conversion, and therefore instantiated with the more efficient Groth16.[2] We optimize the encryption scheme and employ a SNARK-friendly variant of ElGamal with randomness reuse [Kur02]. A noteworthy technical detail is that the witness needs to be mapped to SNARK-friendly elliptic curve points. The downside of this construction is that even state-of-the-art SNARK-friendly public-key operations incur a substantial overhead in the circuit size.

Ext-Groth16 uses a verifiable encryption technique of Lee et al. [LCKO19] to overcome this limitation. We again encrypt the witness, but with a different encryption scheme in which resulting ciphertexts enter Groth16 verification equation directly and thus have almost no effect on the circuit structure. To show Ext-Groth16 secure, we need to directly prove black-box weak simulation-extractability, which we do by a reduction to white-box weak SE of Groth16. The main technical challenge is, again, to show which transformations exactly are available to the adversary. Additionally, we prove that the zero-knowledge

---

[2] In fact, even weak simulation soundness without extractability is sufficient for the compiler.

property of Ext-Groth16 can rely on the standard Decisional Diffie-Hellman assumption rather than the novel assumption stated in [LCKO19].

To compare the efficiency of these two constructions, we estimate CRS and proof size, prover time, and verifier time as a function of the encrypted witness size. Our results show that both constructions have low overhead compared to the commonly used generic transformations. In particular, Ext-Groth16 leads to almost no increase in CRS size and prover time, while resulting in slightly bigger proofs and verification time.

Related Work. Simulation-extractability is relevant for both CRS-based and Random-Oracle (RO) based NIZKs. Faust et al. [FKMV12] show that NIZKs obtained from Σ-protocols using the Fiat-Shamir heuristic satisfy simulation-extractability in the RO model. In this work we focus on simulation-extractability of CRS-based NIZKs, and on the Groth16 SNARK in particular.

White-Box Constructions. White-box SE SNARKs have been discovered only recently. Groth and Maller [GM17] presented the first construction in 2017, targeting the language of Square Arithmetic Programs (SAPs). They also proved a lower bound of three group elements for the proof size and two verification equations for all *non-interactive linear proof* (NILP) based SNARKs, which covers many previously known pairing-based SNARKs. Weak SE allows us to go below this bound with a single verification equation.

Bowe and Gabizon [BG18] give a RO-based variant of Groth16 for Quadratic Arithmetic Programs (QAPs) that is simulation-extractable, and has five group elements and two verification equations. Lipmaa [Lip19] presents a different technique that allows to construct SE SNARKs for QAP and the three other arithmetization techniques from the QAP family (namely, SAP, SSP, and QSP). Kim, Lee, and Oh [KLO19] present a SE SNARK for QAP with three elements but just a single verification equation, avoiding the lower bound of Groth and Maller by using a RO in addition to a knowledge extraction assumptions and a CRS. Recently, Baghery, Pindado, and Ràfols [BPR20] revised Bowe and Gabizon's construction [BG18] and presented a new variation which saves 1 paring in the verification, and gets rid of the RO at the cost of a collision-resistant hash function.

Black-Box Transformations. A generic transformation that makes ordinary NIZKs black-box SE has been known at least since [DDO+01]. Along this direction, Kosba et al. [KZM+15] extend, analyse, and optimize this transformation technique—they present three transformations; two of which build weak SE NIZKs, while the third builds a strong SE NIZKs. Atapoor and Baghery [AB19] adapt Kosba et al.'s work directly to Groth16 and evaluate the efficiency of the resulting strong SE argument. Baghery [Bag19] analyses a transformation from white-box SE to black-box SE, and instantiates it with the strong SE SNARK by Groth and Maller. We show that this technique also works for lifting white-box *weak* SE to black-box *weak* SE. Other generic transformations take into account CRS subversion and updatability [ARS20,BS20].

2   Preliminaries

Notation. We denote the security parameter by $\lambda \in \mathbb{N}$. We say that a function $f : \mathbb{N} \to \mathbb{R}$ is negligible, if for a big enough λ, $f < 1/p(\lambda)$ for all polynomials $p(\lambda)$. We write $g(\lambda) = \mathrm{negl}(\lambda)$ to mean that g is some negligible function. For a distribution X we denote random sampling by $x \xleftarrow{\$} X$, and when this notation is used with a finite set S, $x \xleftarrow{\$} S$ denotes uniform sampling from S. We write vectors in bold, and write $\boldsymbol{a} \cdot \boldsymbol{b}$ for the inner product of two vectors $\boldsymbol{a}$ and $\boldsymbol{b}$.

When working with polynomials, we generally use upper case letters for indeterminates as X, Y, Δ, X_γ, and lower case for concrete values x, y, δ, γ. We use vector notation to denote a list of formal variables, so for $\boldsymbol{X} = X_1, \ldots, X_n$, we write $P(\boldsymbol{X}) \in \mathbb{F}[X_1 \ldots X_n] = \mathbb{F}[\boldsymbol{X}]$ for a polynomial in these variables, and for a $\boldsymbol{x} \in \mathbb{F}^n$, $P(\boldsymbol{x})$ will denote the polynomial evaluation $P(x_1 \ldots x_n)$.

PPT stands for (uniform) probabilistic polynomial-time. An *execution transcript* $\mathrm{trans}_{\mathcal{P}}$ of an algorithm $\mathcal{P}$ contains $\mathcal{P}$'s private coins, inputs and outputs, including interactions with any oracles that it is provided with. Having access to $\mathrm{trans}_{\mathcal{P}}$ implies white-box access to $\mathcal{P}$.

Bilinear Groups. Let $(\mathbb{G}_1, \mathbb{G}_2, \mathbb{G}_T, e(\cdot, \cdot), p)$ be a Type III[3] bilinear group of prime order p with generators G, H, and $e(G, H)$ for the three groups respectively. The pairing $e : \mathbb{G}_1 \times \mathbb{G}_2 \to \mathbb{G}_T$ is a bilinear map. We will write $\mathbb{G}_1$, $\mathbb{G}_2$, and $\mathbb{G}_T$ additively. It will be convenient to use square brackets notation to represent group elements by specifying their exponents: $[a]_\iota \triangleq [a]G_\iota$. We will denote the (exponent-level) pairing for the square brackets notation as $[a]_1 \bullet [b]_2 \triangleq e([a]G, [b]H)$. When $\boldsymbol{a}$ is a vector of values $a_i \in \mathbb{Z}_p$, we will overload the square brackets notation, and denote a vector of $[a_i]_\iota$ by $[\boldsymbol{a}]_\iota$. In the same way we will overload $[\{a, b, c, \ldots\}]_\iota = \{[a]_\iota, [b]_\iota, [c]_\iota, \ldots\}$ for sets. When set or vector A contains elements from several groups, we will denote it by combining all the group indices in the subscript, e.g. $[A]_{1,2,T}$ if A contains elements from all the three groups.

Circuit Form and Quadratic Arithmetic Programs (QAP). Let $\mathcal{R}$ be a relation for an NP language $\mathcal{L}$, such that $(\phi, w) \in \mathcal{R} \Leftrightarrow \phi \in \mathcal{L}$. When $\mathcal{R}$ is implemented as an arithmetic circuit $\mathcal{C}$, we assume it to be of the following form. The input wires are split into: l public input wires corresponding to $\phi_1, \ldots, \phi_l$, and l_w private input wires, corresponding to $w_1, \ldots, w_{l_w}$. We denote the total number of wires by m, and thus the remaining $m - l - l_w$ wires are called intermediate—they can be computed from ϕ and w.

A quadratic arithmetic program (QAP, [GGPR13]) for the circuit $\mathcal{C}$ consists of the quotient polynomial $t(x)$ of degree n, and three sets of polynomials $\{u_i(X)\}_{i=0}^m$, $\{v_i(X)\}_{i=0}^m$ and $\{w_i(X)\}_{i=0}^m$ of degree $n - 1$. A particular QAP

---

[3] Asymmetric, with $\mathbb{G}_1 \neq \mathbb{G}_2$ and without any efficiently computable nontrivial homomorphism in either direction between $\mathbb{G}_1$ and $\mathbb{G}_2$, according to the classification of [GPS06].

assignment $\{a_i\}_{i=0}^{m}$ contains assignments to the circuit wires, and $a_0 = 1$ is a fixed parameter. We will refer to the sets $\{\phi_i\} \cup \{w_i\}$ and $\{a_i\}$ interchangeably when there is no risk of confusion, with ϕ_0 corresponding to a_0. The assignment $\{a_i\}$ satisfies the QAP if and only if $(\sum_{i=0}^{m} a_i u_i(X))(\sum_{i=0}^{m} a_i v_i(X)) - (\sum_{i=0}^{m} a_i w_i(X)) = h(X)t(X)$ for some $h(X)$ of degree $n-2$. That is, $t(x)$ divides the left hand side of the equation.

As QAP relations are defined over a finite field that determines suitable bilinear groups, they need to be compatible with the desired security level λ. Our asymptotic security notions are all quantified over λ-compatible relations $\mathcal{R}_\lambda$. In practice SNARK systems use very specific pre-defined groups for a fixed security level. For these reasons we elide most of these details in our formal modelling and typically write $\mathcal{R}$ instead of $\mathcal{R}_\lambda$.

Algebraic Modelling and Assumptions. Following [FKL18,Lip19], we say that the algorithm $\mathcal{A}$ is *algebraic*, if there is a way to represent any group element it returns using elements it has seen before, specifically as a linear combination of these elements with known (extracted) coefficients. Security against algebraic adversaries can be formalized either as a standard model white-box knowledge-extraction assumption [BV98,PV05,Lip19], or by defining a separate cryptograpic model as done in the algebraic group model (AGM) [FKL18]. We are following the extraction assumption style from [Lip19], without considering the stronger hashed version that additionally allows $\mathcal{A}$ to sample random elements in $\mathbb{G}$ without knowing their exponents.

Definition 1 (Algebraic Algorithm, [Lip19]). *A PPT algorithm $\mathcal{A}$ is algebraic with respect to a cyclic group $\mathbb{G}_\iota$ of prime order p, if there exists a polynomial time extractor $\mathcal{X}_{\mathcal{A}}^{alg}$ returning a coefficients matrix K, such that for all m and all efficiently sampleable distributions $\mathcal{D}$ over $(\mathbb{Z}_p^*)^m$,*

$$\Pr\left[\boldsymbol{\sigma} \xleftarrow{\$} \mathcal{D}_\lambda; e \xleftarrow{\$} \mathcal{A}([\boldsymbol{\sigma}]_\iota); K \leftarrow \mathcal{X}_{\mathcal{A}}^{alg}(\mathsf{trans}_{\mathcal{A}}) : e \neq [K\boldsymbol{\sigma}]_\iota \right] = \mathrm{negl}(\lambda).$$

It is easy to see how this definition extends to the asymmetric bilinear groups ($\mathcal{X}_{\mathcal{A}}^{alg}$ should return K with $m_1 + m_2$ rows, and $(e_1\ e_2)^T = \left[K(\boldsymbol{\sigma}_1\ \boldsymbol{\sigma}_2)^T \right]_{1,2}$), and to the case when $\mathcal{A}$ obtains elements from an oracle ($\mathsf{trans}_{\mathcal{A}}$ captures communication with it). That means that in the soundness and knowledge soundness games, an algebraic adversary $\mathcal{A}$ gets only CRS elements as an input, and in the simulation-based definitions $\mathcal{A}$ additionally sees the simulated proof elements.

In proofs with algebraic adversaries, we use the following variant of the discrete logarithm assumption [FKL18].

Definition 2 ((q_1, q_2)-Discrete Logarithm Assumption). *Let $(\mathbb{G}_1, \mathbb{G}_2, \cdot, \cdot, p)$ be a Type III bilinear group. We say that (q_1, q_2)-**dlog** holds if for all PPT $\mathcal{A}$,*

$$\Pr\left[x \xleftarrow{\$} \mathbb{Z}_p^*; z \xleftarrow{\$} \mathcal{A}([x, \ldots, x^{q_1}]_1, [x, \ldots, x^{q_2}]_2) : x = z \right] = \mathrm{negl}(\lambda).$$

Non-interactive Zero-Knowledge Arguments. We introduce security notions for non-interactive zero-knowledge (NIZK) arguments that we use throughout the paper. In particular, we define proof rerandomization and different flavors of simulation-extractability. In the following, NIZK denotes a tuple of efficient algorithms (Setup, Prove, Verify, Sim) unless specified otherwise.

Weak simulation extractability (SE) is an extension of knowledge soundness where adversary can query simulated proofs (even for false statements) and finally has to come up with a statement and a proof for which an extractor cannot recover a witness. Moreover, the statement cannot be any of the statements queried from the oracle. First, we give a definition for white-box version which allows there to be a different extractor for each adversary.

Definition 3 (White-box Weak Simulation-Extractability, [KZM+15]). *We say that NIZK is white-box weak SE if for any PPT adversary $\mathcal{A}$ there exists a polynomial time extractor $\mathcal{X}_\mathcal{A}$ such that for $\mathcal{R}_\lambda$,*

$$\Pr\left[\begin{matrix}(\boldsymbol{\sigma},\tau) \leftarrow \mathsf{Setup}(\mathcal{R}_\lambda); (\phi,\pi) \leftarrow \mathcal{A}^{\mathcal{S}_{\sigma,\tau}}(\boldsymbol{\sigma}); \\ w \leftarrow \mathcal{X}_\mathcal{A}(\mathsf{trans}_\mathcal{A})\end{matrix} : \begin{matrix}\mathsf{Verify}(\boldsymbol{\sigma},\phi,\pi) = 1 \wedge \\ (\phi,w) \notin \mathcal{R}_\lambda \wedge \phi \notin Q\end{matrix}\right] = \mathrm{negl}(\lambda),$$

where $\mathcal{S}_{\sigma,\tau}(\phi)$ is a simulator oracle that calls $\mathsf{Sim}(\boldsymbol{\sigma},\tau,\phi)$ internally, and also records ϕ into Q.

The important distinction between this notion and *strong* SE lies in the last condition in the security game. Strong SE requires $(\phi,\pi) \notin Q$, where $\mathcal{S}$ records pairs of queried instances and simulated proofs. If NIZK is randomizable, $\mathcal{A}$ can just pass re-randomized simulated proof for an instance it does not know a witness of and win the strong SE game. This is forbidden, thus the strong SE scheme must be non-malleable. Honest proofs are also non-randomizable, otherwise zero-knowledge would not hold. Weak SE relaxes this non-malleability requirement by allowing to produce $\pi' \neq \pi$ for the simulated (and thus also real) proof π.

The black-box variant of weak SE specifies the existence of a single extractor that works for all adversaries.

Definition 4 (Black-box Weak Simulation-Extractability, [KZM+15]). *We say that NIZK = (Setup, Prove, Verify, Sim, Ext) is black-box weak SE if for any PPT adversary $\mathcal{A}$ and $\mathcal{R}_\lambda$,*

$$\Pr\left[\begin{matrix}(\boldsymbol{\sigma},\tau,\tau_{ext}) \leftarrow \mathsf{Setup}(\mathcal{R}_\lambda); \\ (\phi,\pi) \leftarrow \mathcal{A}^{\mathcal{S}_{\sigma,\tau}}(\boldsymbol{\sigma}); w \leftarrow \mathsf{Ext}(\boldsymbol{\sigma},\tau_{ext},\phi,\pi)\end{matrix} : \begin{matrix}\mathsf{Verify}(\boldsymbol{\sigma},\phi,\pi) = 1 \wedge \\ (\phi,w) \notin \mathcal{R}_\lambda \wedge \phi \notin Q\end{matrix}\right] = \mathrm{negl}(\lambda),$$

where $\mathcal{S}_{\sigma,\tau}(\phi)$ is a simulator oracle that calls $\mathsf{Sim}(\boldsymbol{\sigma},\tau,\phi)$ internally, and also records ϕ into Q.

Proof malleability can also be a beneficial security property. We call the proof system for the relation $\mathcal{R}$ *randomizable* or *proof malleable*, if there exists a (non-trivial) PPT procedure Rand such that $\Pr[\mathsf{Verify}(\boldsymbol{\sigma},\phi,\mathsf{Rand}(\pi))] = 1$ for all honestly generated proofs π for $\boldsymbol{\sigma}$ and ϕ. The notion of proof rerandomization we use is similar to [BCC+09] and the ciphertext rerandomization in [LCKO19]:

Definition 5 (Proof Rerandomization). *A proof system is* rerandomizable *with respect to relation* $\mathcal{R}_\lambda$ *and randomization transformation* Rand, *if for all* $(\phi, w) \in \mathcal{R}_\lambda$, *all* σ *output by* Setup$(\mathcal{R}_\lambda)$ *and all* π *such that* Verify$(\sigma, \phi, \pi) = 1$: $\{$Prove$(\sigma, \phi, w)\}_\lambda = \{$Rand$(\sigma, \phi, \pi)\}_\lambda$, *where the randomness is over the random variables used in* Prove *and* Rand.

We elide standard definitions of knowledge soundness (KS), zero-knowledge, and a weaker simulation-soundness notion that is only used by our compiler in Sect. 4.1 (it is obtained by removing the extractor from SE, similarly to the distinction between KS and soundness).

3   White-Box Weak SE and Randomizability of **Groth16**

In this section, we show that Groth16 is white-box weakly simulation extractable, which to our knowledge is the first SNARK construction that is proved to (only) achieve this notion. Additionally, we provide some facts about randomization of Groth16. We start by recalling Groth16 in Fig. 1.

To simplify notation we denote $q_i(\alpha, \beta, x) = \beta u_i(x) + \alpha v_i(x) + w_i(x)$ and $y_i(\alpha, \beta, \gamma, x) = q_i(\alpha, \beta, x)/\gamma$, and use it as $q_i(x)$ and $y_i(x)$ omitting other variables when it is clear from the context. As explained before, $a = \phi \parallel w$.

Setup$(\mathcal{R})$:

$\quad \tau = x, \alpha, \beta, \gamma, \delta \xleftarrow{\$} \mathbb{Z}_p^*$

$\quad \sigma_1 \leftarrow \left[\alpha, \beta, \delta, \{x^i\}_{i=0}^{n-1}, \left\{ \frac{x^i t(x)}{\delta} \right\}_{i=0}^{n-2}, \{y_i(x)\}_{i=0}^{l}, \left\{ \frac{q_i(x)}{\delta} \right\}_{i=l+1}^{m} \right]_1$

$\quad \sigma_2 \leftarrow \left[\beta, \gamma, \delta, \{x^i\}_{i=0}^{n-1} \right]_2$

$\quad$ **return** $(\sigma = \sigma_1 \cup \sigma_2, \tau)$

Prove$(\sigma, \phi = \phi_1 \ldots \phi_l, w = w_1 \ldots w_{m-l})$:

$\quad r_a, r_b \xleftarrow{\$} \mathbb{Z}_p^*$

$\quad [a]_1 \leftarrow \left[\alpha + \sum_{i=0}^{m} a_i u_i(x) + r_a \delta \right]_1; \quad [b]_2 \leftarrow \left[\beta + \sum_{i=0}^{m} a_i v_i(x) + r_b \delta \right]_2$

$\quad [c]_1 \leftarrow \left[\sum_{i=l+1}^{m} a_i \frac{q_i(x)}{\delta} + \frac{h(x)t(x)}{\delta} + a r_b + b r_a - r_a r_b \delta \right]_1$

$\quad$ **return** $([a]_1, [b]_2, [c]_1)$

Verify$(\sigma, \phi = \phi_1 \ldots \phi_l, \pi = (a, b, c))$:

$\quad$ **assert** $e(a, b) = e([\alpha]_1, [\beta]_2) + e(\sum_{i=0}^{l} \phi_i [y_i(x)]_1, [\gamma]_2) + e(c, [\delta]_2)$

Sim$(\tau, \phi = \phi_1 \ldots \phi_l)$:

$\quad \mu, \nu \xleftarrow{\$} \mathbb{Z}_p^*;$ **return** $\left([\mu]_1, [\nu]_2, \left[\frac{\mu\nu - \alpha\beta - \sum_{i=0}^{l} \phi_i q_i(x)}{\delta} \right]_1 \right)$

Rand$(\sigma, \pi = (a, b, c))$:

$\quad r_1, r_2 \xleftarrow{\$} \mathbb{Z}_p^*;$ $a \mapsto (1/r_1)a;$ $b \mapsto r_1 b + r_1 r_2 [\delta]_2;$ $c \mapsto c + r_2 a$

$\quad$ **return** (a, b, c)

Fig. 1. Groth16 zk-SNARK with simulation and randomization procedures.

White-Box Weak SE. Our proof is in the AGM and relies on the same hardness assumptions ((q_1, q_2)-discrete logarithm) as Groth16 knowledge soundness. Additionally we require a form of linear independence from QAP polynomials—a similar requirement was used for square arithmetic programs in [GM17].

Theorem 1. *Assume that $\{u_i(x)\}_{i=0}^{l}$ are linearly independent and* $\mathrm{Span}\{u_i(x)\}_{i=0}^{l} \cap \mathrm{Span}\{u_i(x)\}_{i=l+1}^{m} = \emptyset$. *Then Groth16 achieves weak white-box SE against algebraic adversaries under the $(2n-1, n-1)$-dlog assumption.*

Proof (Sketch). The proof splits in two branches—we show that either $\mathcal{A}$ uses simulated elements, and in this case it can only use them for a single simulation query k, or it does not use them at all. In particular, this implies that $\mathcal{A}$ cannot combine several elements from different queries algebraically for the π it submits. We then argue that the non-simulation case reduces to knowledge soundness, and in the simulation case we show that $\mathcal{A}$ supplies ϕ that is equal to one of the simulated instances, which proves that $\mathcal{A}$ reuses a simulated proof, potentially randomized. An interesting detail not captured in the weak SE definition is that not only can we decide whether the proof π' provided by algebraic $\mathcal{A}$ is a modification of the simulated proof π queried before in the simulation case, but we can pinpoint which exact simulated proof it was derived from. More details are provided in the full version [BKSV20]. □

Transforming the Proof. It is known that Groth16 has malleable proofs. It is not hard to extend this statement to show that Groth16 is rerandomizable, that is its output of Rand is indistinguishable from honest proofs, even if Rand is applied to maliciously generated (but verifiable) proofs.

Theorem 2. *Groth16 zk-SNARK is rerandomizable[4] with respect to the randomization transformation Rand presented in Fig. 1.*

Proof. In a nutshell, the proof elements a and b output by Rand are random and independent of each other; and the verification equation fixes a unique c based on $a, b, \boldsymbol{\sigma}, \boldsymbol{\phi}$. As before, more details are provided in the full version [BKSV20]. □

Together with white-box weak SE forbidding instance malleability, and perfect ZK, Theorem 2 implies that randomization is equivalent to any other way to transform the honest (or simulated) proofs. But this does not give an explicit algebraic characterization of the transformation—that is, we do not know if there is any other way to create an honest proof, or any other way to rerandomize it (that would produce the same distribution). One of the interesting properties of the proof of Theorem 1 is that it can be extended to show that Rand is the only algebraic transformation possible, which we present as an independent result. We also show that the most-general algebraic form of the honest generation procedure has at most three random "axes", any two of which are required for perfect zero-knowledge.

---

[4] This property has been observed before, for example in [LCKO19] in a similar context.

Observation 1. The only form of algebraic transformation on Groth16 proofs that is possible without violating its verification equation is the randomization procedure $\text{Rand}(\sigma, \pi = (a, b, c); r_1, r_2)$, where r_1, r_2 are chosen by the adversary.

4   Black-Box Weak SE

We study two approaches to achieve black-box weak SE by encrypting the witness. The first construction Int-Groth16 integrates ciphertexts directly to the relation, and the second construction Ext-Groth16 proves the correctness of ciphertexts with external techniques.

4.1   Black-Box Weak SE with Internal Encryption

First, we describe a generic transformation for achieving black-box weak SE. We let the prover encrypt the witness w with a IND-CPA secure cryptosystem and then use a weak simulation sound NIZK (e.g., Groth16) to prove the relation

$$\mathcal{R}' \triangleq \{((\phi, \mathsf{pk}, c), (w, r)) : (\phi, w) \in \mathcal{R} \land c = \mathsf{Enc}(\mathsf{pk}, w; r)\},$$

where ϕ is the statement the prover wants to prove and $\mathcal{R}$ is the corresponding relation. Since we make the public key pk a part of the reference string, it will be possible to black-box extract the witness from the ciphertext. Full details of the construction can be seen in Fig. 2.

$\text{Setup}(\mathcal{R}_\lambda)$: $(\mathsf{pk}, \mathsf{sk}) \leftarrow \mathsf{KGen}(1^\lambda)$; $(\sigma', \tau') \leftarrow \text{Setup}'(\mathcal{R}')$;
  return $(\sigma = \sigma' \cup \mathsf{pk}, \tau = \tau', \tau_{ext} = \mathsf{sk})$;

$\text{Prove}(\sigma = \sigma' \cup \mathsf{pk}, \phi, w)$:
  $r \xleftarrow{\$} \mathbb{Z}_p^*$, $c \leftarrow \mathsf{Enc}(\mathsf{pk}, w; r)$; $\pi' = \text{Prove}'(\sigma, (\phi, \mathsf{pk}, c), (w, r))$ **return** (c, π');

$\text{Verify}(\sigma = \sigma' \cup \mathsf{pk}, \phi, \pi = (c, \pi'))$: **assert** $\text{Verify}'(\sigma, (\phi, \mathsf{pk}, c), \pi')$;

$\text{Sim}(\sigma = \sigma' \cup \mathsf{pk}, \tau, \phi)$:
  $c \leftarrow \mathsf{Enc}(\mathsf{pk}, 0; r)$ for $r \xleftarrow{\$} \mathbb{Z}_p^*$; $\pi' \leftarrow \text{Sim}'(\sigma', \tau, (\phi, \mathsf{pk}, c))$; **return** (c, ϕ);

$\text{Ext}(\sigma, \tau_{ext}, \phi, \pi = (c, \pi'))$: **return** $\mathsf{Dec}(\tau_{ext}, c)$;

Fig. 2. The construction for black-box weak SE NIZK where $\mathsf{NIZK}' = (\text{Setup}', \text{Prove}', \text{Verify}', \text{Sim}')$ is a weak simulation sound NIZK and $(\mathsf{KGen}, \mathsf{Enc}, \mathsf{Dec})$ is a IND-CPA secure cryptosystem.

This transformation was first analyzed in [Bag19], where it was shown to lift a white-box *strong* SE NIZK to a black-box *strong* SE. Below we sketch a proof that it also lifts a weak simulation sound NIZK to a black-box weak SE NIZK.

Theorem 3. *Let* NIZK' = (Setup', Prove', Verify', Sim') *be a complete, weak simulation sound, and computational zero-knowledge non-interactive proof system and* (KGen, Enc, Dec) *an IND-CPA secure cryptosystem. Then the* NIZK *construction in Fig. 2 is complete, black-box weak SE, and computational zero-knowledge.*

Proof (sketch). Completeness of NIZK follows from the completeness of NIZK' and correctness of the cryptosystem. Computational zero-knowledge holds since $\mathsf{Enc}(\mathsf{pk}, 0)$ is computationally indistinguishable from $\mathsf{Enc}(\mathsf{pk}, w)$ and since NIZK' already has computational zero-knowledge. Finally, suppose that there exists a PPT adversary $\mathcal{A}$ that can break black-box weak SE of NIZK. We can easily construct a PPT adversary $\mathcal{B}$ that can break weak simulation soundness of NIZK'. $\mathcal{B}$ gets σ' as an input and generates pk itself. Now $\mathcal{B}$ can run $\mathcal{A}(\sigma' \cup \mathsf{pk})$ internally and whenever $\mathcal{A}$ makes a simulation query ϕ, $\mathcal{B}$ makes a simulation query $(\phi, \mathsf{pk}, c = \mathsf{Enc}(\mathsf{pk}, 0))$ and gets back a proof π' which allows him to send (c, π') to $\mathcal{A}$. Finally, $\mathcal{A}$ outputs $(\phi^*, (c^*, \pi^*))$ such that ϕ^* has not been queried and either ϕ^* is an invalid statement or c does not encrypt the correct witness. Now $\mathcal{B}$ can output $((\phi^*, c^*), \pi^*)$ which will break weak simulation soundness.   □

We can obtain good efficiency if we instantiate the above construction by taking Groth16 as NIZK' and by using vector ElGamal as a cryptosystem (see the full version for details). We call this instantiation Int-Groth16. In Sect. 5 we discuss further optimization of this construction.

Corollary 1. *Int-Groth16 is a complete, black-box weak SE, and computational zero-knowledge NIZK argument.*

4.2 Black-Box Weak SE with External Encryption

The disadvantage of the previous construction is that one needs to encode the extended relation as an arithmetic circuit, that is shown, e.g. in Hawk, to result in a considerably larger public parameters and a slower prover. Thus, we propose a second construction Ext-Groth16 which is closely based on the SAVER cryptosystem [LCKO19] which in a sense gives ciphertexts as a public input to Groth16. Having the encryption outside of the circuit allows us to have smaller circuit overhead which results in smaller CRS size and higher prover efficiency. As before, proof size is linear, and is dominated by the size of the encrypted witness (this is inevitable for black-box constructions, as discussed before [GW11]). The formal description is presented on Fig. 3. Roughly speaking, we reinstantiate SAVER, but also prove that the construction is black-box weak simulation extractable. Additionally we re-prove computational zero-knowledge under the weaker and more standard DDH assumption.

Technical Details. As Ext-Groth16 is based on SAVER, we point out the important ways it is different from Groth16. First, we extend the CRS with the pk elements, similarly to how it is done in Int-Groth16 (since pk uses Groth16 trapdoors, it changes the security proof). Second, Groth16 itself is modified: while

$\mathsf{Setup}(\mathcal{R})$:

$\quad \tau_1 = x, \alpha, \beta, \gamma, \delta \xleftarrow{\$} \mathbb{Z}_p^*; \; \tau_2 = \{s_i\}_{i=1}^{l_w}, \{t_i\}_{i=0}^{l_w} \xleftarrow{\$} \mathbb{Z}_p^*;$

$\quad \sigma_1 \leftarrow \left[\alpha, \beta, \delta, \{x^i\}_{i=0}^{n-1}, \left\{ \frac{x^i t(x)}{\delta} \right\}_{i=0}^{n-2}, \{y_i(x)\}_{i=0}^{l+l_w}, \left\{ \frac{q_i(x)}{\delta} \right\}_{i=l+l_w+1}^{m} \right]_1;$

$\quad \sigma_2 \leftarrow \left[\beta, \gamma, \delta, \{x^i\}_{i=0}^{n-1} \right]_2;$

$\quad \mathsf{pk}_1 \leftarrow \left[\{\delta s_i\}_{i=1}^{l_w}, \{y_{l+i}(x)t_i\}_{i=1}^{l_w}, \delta(t_0 + \sum_{i=1}^{l_w} t_i s_i), \gamma(1 + \sum_{i=1}^{l_w} s_i) \right]_1;$

$\quad \mathsf{pk}_2 \leftarrow \left[\{t_i\}_{i=0}^{l_w} \right]_2;$

$\quad$**return** $(\sigma = \sigma_1 \cup \sigma_2 \cup \mathsf{pk}_1 \cup \mathsf{pk}_2, \tau = \tau_1 \cup \tau_2, \tau_{\mathsf{ext}} = \{s_i\}_{i=1}^{l_w});$

$\mathsf{Prove}(\sigma, \phi = \phi_1 \dots \phi_l, w = w_1 \dots w_{l_w} \dots w_{m-l})$:

$\quad r, r_a, r_b \xleftarrow{\$} \mathbb{Z}_p^*;$

$\quad c_0 \leftarrow r[\delta]_1; \; c_i \leftarrow r[\delta s_i]_1 + w_i[y_{l+i}(x)]_1 \text{ for } i \in [1 \dots l_w];$

$\quad \psi \leftarrow r\left[\delta(t_0 + \sum_{j=1}^{l_w} t_j s_j) \right]_1 + \sum_{i=1}^{l_w} w_i[y_{l+i}(x)t_i]_1;$

$\quad [a]_1 \leftarrow \left[\alpha + \sum_{i=0}^{m} a_i u_i(x) + r_a \delta \right]_1; \; [b]_2 \leftarrow \left[\beta + \sum_{i=0}^{m} a_i v_i(x) + r_b \delta \right]_2;$

$\quad [c]_1 \leftarrow \left[\sum_{i=l+l_w+1}^{m} w_{i-l} \frac{q_i(x)}{\delta} + \frac{h(x)t(x)}{\delta} + a r_b + b r_a - r_a r_b \delta \right]_1 - r\left[\gamma(1 + \sum_{i=1}^{l_w} s_i) \right]_1;$

$\quad$**return** $(([a]_1, [b]_2, [c]_1), \mathcal{CT} = (c_0, \dots, c_{l_w}, \psi));$

$\mathsf{Verify}(\sigma, \phi = \phi_1 \dots \phi_l, \pi = ((a, b, c), (c_0, \dots, c_{l_w}, \psi)))$:

$\quad$**assert** $\sum_{i=0}^{l_w} e(c_i, [t_i]_2) = e(\psi, H);$

$\quad$**assert** $e(a, b) = e([\alpha]_1, [\beta]_2) + e(\sum_{i=0}^{l} \phi_i[y_i(x)]_1 + \sum_{i=0}^{l_w} c_i, [\gamma]_2) + e(c, [\delta]_2);$

$\mathsf{Sim}(\tau, \phi = \phi_1 \dots \phi_l)$:

$\quad \mu, \nu, c_0, \dots, c_{l_w} \xleftarrow{\$} \mathbb{Z}_p^*;$

$\quad (a, b, c) \leftarrow \left([\mu]_1, [\nu]_2, \left[\frac{\mu\nu - \alpha\beta - \gamma(\sum_{i=0}^{l} \phi_i y_i(x) + \sum_{i=1}^{l_w} c_i)}{\delta} \right]_1 \right);$

$\quad \psi \leftarrow \left[\sum_{i=0}^{l_w} t_i c_i \right]_1;$

$\quad$**return** $((a, b, c), \mathcal{CT} = ([c_0]_1, \dots, [c_{l_w}]_1, \psi));$

$\mathsf{Ext}(\sigma, \tau_{\mathsf{ext}} = \{s_i\}_{i=1}^{l_w}, \phi, \pi = (\cdot, (c_0, c_1, \dots, c_{l_w}), \cdot))$:

$\quad$**for** $i \in [1 \dots l_w]: [y_i(x)w_i]_1 \leftarrow c_i - s_i c_0; \; w_i \leftarrow \mathsf{dlog}_{[y_i(x)]_1}([y_i(x)w_i]_1);$

$\quad$**return** $w_1, \dots, w_{l_w};$

$\mathsf{Rand}(\sigma, \pi = ((a, b, c), (c_0, c_1, \dots, c_{l_w}, \phi)))$:

$\quad r_1, r_2, r' \xleftarrow{\$} \mathbb{Z}_p^*;$

$\quad c_0 \mapsto c_0 + r'[\delta]_1; \; c_i \mapsto c_i + r'[\delta s_i]; \; \psi \mapsto \psi + r'[\delta t_0 + \sum_{j=1}^{l_w} \delta t_j s_j]_1;$

$\quad a \mapsto (1/r_1)a; \; b \mapsto r_1 b + r_1 r_2 [\delta]_2; \; c \mapsto c + r_2 a - r'[\gamma(1 + \sum_{i=1}^{l_w} s_i)]_1;$

$\quad$**return** $((a, b, c), (c_0, c_1, \dots, c_{l_w}, \phi));$

Fig. 3. Ext-Groth16: the black-box-extractable SAVER-inspired variant of Groth16. The relation $\mathcal{R}$ must assert that inputs on witness input wires $l \dots l + l_w$ are small enough to be efficiently decryptable. $q_i(x)$ and $y_i(x)$ are as for Groth16, e.g. in Fig. 1.

constructing the proof, element c has an additional coefficient, that is needed to balance out ciphertext randomness.

Crucially, Ext-Groth16 cannot achieve black-box strong SE, because it is proof malleable (and rerandomizable). First, the rerandomization of embedded Groth16 still works, because it does not interfere with the "ciphertext randomness cancelling term" of c. Second, ciphertexts are also rerandomizable: we can replace r with $r + r'$ additively in all c_i, in ψ and c (as shown in Fig. 3).

Another important distinction is that in order for the decryption to work efficiently (since it relies on solving discrete logarithm), plaintexts should be small enough. This is critical to guarantee the extraction—to prevent $\mathcal{A}$ from creating un-extractable proofs, we require the circuit itself to make range-checks on plaintext values. We account for the circuit growth in our efficiency evaluation, but in this section we assume the circuit transformation to be an implicit part of the construction, since this suffices for our security analysis.

Finally, we estimate the resulting performance parameters of Ext-Groth16. Construction CRS size (omitting constants) is $(m + 2n + 2l_w)\ \mathbb{G}_1$, and $(n + l_w)\ \mathbb{G}_2$. Proof size is $(l_w + 4)\ \mathbb{G}_1$ and $1\ \mathbb{G}_2$, so $l_w + 2$ times more $\mathbb{G}_1$ than in Groth16. Prover time is (omitting constants) $(m + 3n - l + 2l_w)\ E_1$ and $n\ E_2$. Verifier time is $l\ E_1$ and $(l_w + 5)\ P$, so $l_w + 2$ pairings more than in Groth16.

Security. We give a direct proof for the security of Ext-Groth16, as opposed to relying on the security of a transformation as for Int-Groth16. We prove computational zero-knowledge under the standard DDH assumption, as compared to a decisional polynomial assumption introduced and used in SAVER. The weak SE proof is structurally similar to the proof of Theorem 1: that is, we show that either $\mathcal{A}$ reuses a simulated proof (potentially randomizing it), or it does not use simulated data at all, and in that case we can extract the witness. The crucial difference now is that extractor Ext is black-box and operates by decrypting the ciphertext. The proof of the following theorem is deferred to [BKSV20].

Theorem 4. *The Ext-Groth16 NIZK argument in Fig. 3 achieves perfect completeness; computational zero-knowledge under the DDH assumption; and black-box weak SE against algebraic adversaries under linear independence of $U = \{u_i(X)\}_{i=0}^{l+l_w}$, and span independence between U and rest of $u_i(X)$.*

Lemma 1. *The Ext-Groth16 NIZK is rerandomizable with Rand in Fig. 3.*

Proof. Follows directly from rerandomizability of SAVER in [LCKO19] ☐

5 Performance

In this section, we evaluate the efficiency of Int-Groth16 and Ext-Groth16. First, in Table 1, we give a high-level comparison of Groth16 and (the most efficient) C∅C∅ black-box SE transformation [KZM+15, Section 4]. It shows the asymptotic dependence of the performance metrics on the witness size l_w and the blow-up of the QAP size due to the use of cryptographic primitives for the transformation. Enc_{l_w} denotes an encryption scheme with sufficiently large plaintext size to encrypt the witness. We note that even for Ext-Groth16 a small circuit modification is required, and therefore m grows by $2l_w$ bits, and n grows by

l_w; additionally, l_w wires for Ext-Groth16 have 6 times less capacity than for Int-Groth16 and C0C0. Clearly, in Table 1, an overhead of C0C0 in CRS size and prover time is strictly bigger than in both constructions we suggest, due to the use of PRF and commitment scheme, and Ext-Groth16 encryption overhead (thus proof size and verification time) is bigger than in first two transformations because of the expansion factor.

Table 1. A comparison of Groth16 with the overhead of C0C0 framework and our constructions. Constants are omitted in the case of CRS size and prover's computation. $\mathbb{G}_1$ and $\mathbb{G}_2$: group elements, E: exponentiations and P: pairings. l_w is the number of secret input wires. $e(l_w) = |\mathsf{Enc}_{l_w}|$, $c(l_w) = e(l_w) + |\mathsf{Com}| + |\mathsf{Prf}|$, where $|\mathsf{Op}|$ denotes the number of *constraints* required for the operation $\mathsf{Op} \in \{\mathsf{Enc}_{l_w}, \mathsf{Com}, \mathsf{Prf}\}$. $e_i(l_w), c_i(l_w)$ denote an additional increase in *input wires* (counted in m, but not in n). k_e is Enc expansion factor, can be assumed ≤ 2. The highlighted cells indicate the best efficiency. Top-level parentheses between expressions and units are omitted for better readability.

Construction	Security	CRS	Proof	Prover	Verifier
Groth16, Sect. 3	KS, Weak	$m + 2n$ $\mathbb{G}_1$	2 $\mathbb{G}_1$	$m + 3n - l$ E_1	l E_1
	WB-SE	n $\mathbb{G}_2$	1 $\mathbb{G}_2$	n E_2	3 P
Groth16 + [KZM+15]	Weak	$+3c(l_w) + c_i(l_w)$ $\mathbb{G}_1$	$+k_e l_w$ $\mathbb{G}_1$	$+4c(l_w) + c_i(l_w) - O(l_w)$ E_1	$+k_e l_w$ E_1
	BB-SE	$+c(l_w)$ $\mathbb{G}_2$		$+c(l_w)$ E_2	
Int-Groth16, Sect. 4.1	Weak	$+3e(l_w) + e_i(l_w)$ $\mathbb{G}_1$	$+k_e l_w$ $\mathbb{G}_1$	$+4e(l_w) + e_i(l_w) - O(l_w)$ E_1	$+k_e l_w$ E_1
	BB-SE	$+e(l_w)$ $\mathbb{G}_2$		$+e(l_w)$ E_2	
Ext-Groth16, Sect. 4.2	Weak	$+36 l_w$ $\mathbb{G}_1$	$+6 l_w + 2$ $\mathbb{G}_1$	$+42 l_w$ E_1	$+6 l_w + 2$ P
	BB-SE	$+12 l_w$ $\mathbb{G}_2$		$+12 l_w$ E_2	

We also estimate the *concrete* performance of our two black-box constructions, along the same four performance parameters defined in Table 2, as depending on the bit-size of the encrypted witness. For both NIZKs we will use a 255-bit BLS12-381 curve, defined over a 381 bit prime field. Let us assume that witness size is B_w bits, and it is provided in bit-decomposed form in the original circuit. We aim to optimize proof size, which is important for SNARKs, and thus will only consider encrypting secret inputs at the maximum possible capacity (e.g. we do not encrypt individual bits); the two approaches have different block capacities, so the number of plaintext (and ciphertext) blocks is different in both cases. For Int-Groth16, block size is 248 bits, where the 6 remaining bits are reserved for Koblitz [Kob87] message embedding padding. For Ext-Groth16 we split the plaintext in 43-bit blocks, thus assuming that we can solve 43-bit discrete logarithm for black-box extraction. This explains Ext-Groth16 expansion factor of $6 = \lceil 248/43 \rceil$. We base our circuit design estimates, which are especially relevant to Int-Groth16, on zcash implementation, description of which is provided in [HBHW20] (Section "Circuit Design").

Due to space limits, we cover the concrete performance estimation and analysis in [BKSV20].

Table 2. Overhead comparison of our constructions over plain Groth16. $\mathbb{G}^{\mathbb{J}}$ stands for bit-size of an encoded JubJub point, and $\mathbb{G}_i$ is the size of an encoded BLS12-381 point. Highlighted cells indicate efficiency improvement.

Construction	CRS	Proof	Prover	Verifier
Int-Groth16	$3286 + 16.4B_w$ $\mathbb{G}_1$ $1010 + 5.1B_w$ $\mathbb{G}_2$	$\left(\lceil\frac{B_w}{248}\rceil + 1\right)\mathbb{G}^{\mathbb{J}} + B_w$	$4296 + 21.6B_w$ E_1 $1010 + 5.1B_w$ E_2	$3\lceil\frac{B_w}{248}\rceil$ E_1
Ext-Groth16	$0.14B_w$ $\mathbb{G}_1$ $0.05B_w$ $\mathbb{G}_2$	$\left(\lceil\frac{B_w}{43}\rceil + 2\right)\mathbb{G}_1$	$0.16B_w$ E_1 $0.05B_w$ E_2	$\left(\lceil\frac{B_w}{43}\rceil + 2\right) P$

Performance Comparison. Our estimates, summarized in Table 2, suggest that both constructions are quite efficient practically. Ext-Groth16 achieves better prover time and CRS size at the expense of slightly bigger proofs and verification time. CRS size and prover time of Ext-Groth16 incur a very small overhead, and are asymptotically *much* smaller than the same numbers for Int-Groth16, giving almost a 100–135× performance gain. Hence, we focus our detailed analyses on the proof size and verifier time:

1. *Proof size.* Assuming that encoded BLS12-381 $\mathbb{G}_1$ takes 381 bits, and that JubJub point $\mathbb{G}^{\mathbb{J}}$ takes 256 bits, Int-Groth16 overhead is $\left(\lceil\frac{B_w}{248}\rceil + 1\right)256 + B_w \approx 2.03B_w + 256$ bits, and for Ext-Groth16 it is $\left(\lceil\frac{B_w}{43}\rceil + 2\right)381 \approx 8.86B_w + 762$ bits. Asymptotically, Int-Groth16 proof size is ×4.4 times smaller.

2. *Verifier time.* To compare the increase in exponentiations in Int-Groth16 with the increase in pairings in Ext-Groth16, we use the estimation that micro benchmarks ([AB19, Fig. 2], also consistent with [FLSZ17, Table 3] for BN-254) show pairings to be approximately $N = 35$ times slower than processing one element of a multi-exponentiation. Thus, the verification overhead of Int-Groth16 is small for practical witnesses, e.g. $1600 \cdot 3/248 \approx 20$ wires for encrypting 200 bytes, comparing to tens of thousands circuit constraints. The overhead of Ext-Groth16 therefore is about 70× more than for Int-Groth16, although for real-world witnesses it takes less than just a few tens milliseconds, and becomes immaterial for bigger public input sizes.

6 Conclusion and Future Work

We prove two important theorems about [Gro16] and [LCKO19] enabling the composable analysis of provable secure protocols. We conjecture that both our white-box and black-box results generalize to other SNARKs. In fact, we first showed white-box weak SE in a modification of [GM17] with the second equation removed. We decided to focus on Groth16 as the most important SNARK in this family to give a targeted proof and performance analysis. Besides improving performance, we expect weak SE and proof randomization to also have positive cryptographic applications that would be impossible with strong SE—just as for Groth-Sahai proofs [GS08, BCC+09].

Acknowledgements. We thank Mary Maller for encouraging discussions and technical feedback on the white-box weak-SE theorem. This work has been supported in part by the European Union's Horizon 2020 research and innovation programme under grant agreement No. 780477 (project PRIViLEDGE). Janno Siim was additionally supported by the Estonian Research Council grant PRG49. Most of the work was done while Janno Siim was affiliated with the University of Edinburgh. Karim Baghery has been supported in part by the Defense Advanced Research Projects Agency (DARPA) under Contract No. HR001120C0085, and by Cyber Security Research Flanders with reference number VR20192203.

References

[AB19]   Atapoor, S., Baghery, K.: Simulation extractability in Groth's zk-SNARK. In: Pérez-Solà, C., Navarro-Arribas, G., Biryukov, A., Garcia-Alfaro, J. (eds.) DPM/CBT-2019. LNCS, vol. 11737, pp. 336–354. Springer, Cham (2019). https://doi.org/10.1007/978-3-030-31500-9_22

[ARS20]   Abdolmaleki, B., Ramacher, S., Slamanig, D.: Lift-and-shift: obtaining simulation extractable subversion and updatable SNARKs generically. In: ACM SIGSAC Conference on Computer and Communications Security, CCS 2020 (2020)

[Bag19]   Baghery, K.: On the efficiency of privacy-preserving smart contract systems. In: Buchmann, J., Nitaj, A., Rachidi, T. (eds.) AFRICACRYPT 2019. LNCS, vol. 11627, pp. 118–136. Springer, Cham (2019). https://doi.org/10.1007/978-3-030-23696-0_7

[BCC+09] Belenkiy, M., Camenisch, J., Chase, M., Kohlweiss, M., Lysyanskaya, A., Shacham, H.: Randomizable proofs and delegatable anonymous credentials. In: Halevi, S. (ed.) CRYPTO 2009. LNCS, vol. 5677, pp. 108–125. Springer, Heidelberg (2009). https://doi.org/10.1007/978-3-642-03356-8_7

[BCG+14] Ben-Sasson, E., et al.: Zerocash: decentralized anonymous payments from bitcoin. In: 2014 IEEE Symposium on Security and Privacy, pp. 459–474. IEEE Computer Society Press (May 2014). https://doi.org/10.1109/SP.2014.36

[BCG+20] Bowe, S., Chiesa, A., Green, M., Miers, I., Mishra, P., Wu, H.: ZEXE: enabling decentralized private computation. In 2020 IEEE Symposium on Security and Privacy, pp. 947–964. IEEE Computer Society Press (May 2020). https://doi.org/10.1109/SP40000.2020.00050

[BG18]   Bowe, S., Gabizon, A.: Making Groth's zk-SNARK simulation extractable in the random oracle model. Cryptology ePrint Archive, Report 2018/187 (2018). https://eprint.iacr.org/2018/187

[BKSV20] Baghery, K., Kohlweiss, M., Siim, J., Volkhov, M.: Another look at extraction and randomization of Groth's zk-SNARK. Cryptology ePrint Archive, Report 2020/811 (2020). https://eprint.iacr.org/2020/811

[BMRS20] Bonneau, J., Meckler, I., Rao, V., Shapiro, E.: Coda: decentralized cryptocurrency at scale. IACR Cryptol. ePrint Arch., 2020:352 (2020). https://eprint.iacr.org/2020/352

[BPR20]   Baghery, K., Pindado, Z., Ràfols, C.: Simulation extractable versions of Groth's zk-SNARK revisited. In: Krenn, S., Shulman, H., Vaudenay, S. (eds.) CANS 2020. LNCS, vol. 12579, pp. 453–461. Springer, Cham (2020). https://doi.org/10.1007/978-3-030-65411-5_22

[BS20]   Baghery, K., Sedaghat, M.: Tiramisu: black-box simulation extractable NIZKs in the updatable CRS model. Technical report, Cryptology ePrint Archive, Report 2020/474 (2020)

[BV98]   Boneh, D., Venkatesan, R.: Breaking RSA may not be equivalent to factoring. In: Nyberg, K. (ed.) EUROCRYPT 1998. LNCS, vol. 1403, pp. 59–71. Springer, Heidelberg (1998). https://doi.org/10.1007/BFb0054117

[Can01] Canetti, R.: Universally composable security: a new paradigm for cryptographic protocols. In: 42nd FOCS, pp. 136–145. IEEE Computer Society Press (October 2001). https://doi.org/10.1109/SFCS.2001.959888

[CDD17] Camenisch, J., Drijvers, M., Dubovitskaya, M.: Practical UC-secure delegatable credentials with attributes and their application to blockchain. In: Thuraisingham, B.M., Evans, D., Malkin, T., Xu, D. (eds.) ACM CCS 2017, pp. 683–699. ACM Press (October/November 2017). https://doi.org/10.1145/3133956.3134025

[CLOS02] Canetti, R., Lindell, Y., Ostrovsky, R., Sahai, A.: Universally composable two-party and multi-party secure computation. In: 34th ACM STOC, pp. 494–503. ACM Press (May 2002). https://doi.org/10.1145/509907.509980

[DDO+01] De Santis, A., Di Crescenzo, G., Ostrovsky, R., Persiano, G., Sahai, A.: Robust non-interactive zero knowledge. In: Kilian, J. (ed.) CRYPTO 2001. LNCS, vol. 2139, pp. 566–598. Springer, Heidelberg (2001). https://doi.org/10.1007/3-540-44647-8_33

[DFKP16] Delignat-Lavaud, A., Fournet, C., Kohlweiss, M., Parno, B.: Cinderella: turning shabby X.509 certificates into elegant anonymous credentials with the magic of verifiable computation. In: 2016 IEEE Symposium on Security and Privacy, pp. 235–254. IEEE Computer Society Press (May 2016). https://doi.org/10.1109/SP.2016.22

[FKL18] Fuchsbauer, G., Kiltz, E., Loss, J.: The algebraic group model and its applications. In: Shacham, H., Boldyreva, A. (eds.) CRYPTO 2018. LNCS, vol. 10992, pp. 33–62. Springer, Cham (2018). https://doi.org/10.1007/978-3-319-96881-0_2

[FKMV12] Faust, S., Kohlweiss, M., Marson, G.A., Venturi, D.: On the non-malleability of the Fiat-Shamir transform. In: Galbraith, S., Nandi, M. (eds.) INDOCRYPT 2012. LNCS, vol. 7668, pp. 60–79. Springer, Heidelberg (2012). https://doi.org/10.1007/978-3-642-34931-7_5

[FLSZ17] Fauzi, P., Lipmaa, H., Siim, J., Zajac, M.: An efficient pairing-based shuffle argument. In: Takagi, T., Peyrin, T. (eds.) ASIACRYPT 2017. LNCS, vol. 10625, pp. 97–127. Springer, Cham (2017). https://doi.org/10.1007/978-3-319-70697-9_4

[GGPR13] Gennaro, R., Gentry, C., Parno, B., Raykova, M.: Quadratic span programs and succinct NIZKs without PCPs. In: Johansson, T., Nguyen, P.Q. (eds.) EUROCRYPT 2013. LNCS, vol. 7881, pp. 626–645. Springer, Heidelberg (2013). https://doi.org/10.1007/978-3-642-38348-9_37

[GM17]   Groth, J., Maller, M.: Snarky signatures: minimal signatures of knowledge from simulation-extractable SNARKs. In: Katz, J., Shacham, H. (eds.) CRYPTO 2017. LNCS, vol. 10402, pp. 581–612. Springer, Cham (2017). https://doi.org/10.1007/978-3-319-63715-0_20

[GOS06] Groth, J., Ostrovsky, R., Sahai, A.: Perfect non-interactive zero knowledge for NP. In: Vaudenay, S. (ed.) EUROCRYPT 2006. LNCS, vol. 4004, pp. 339–358. Springer, Heidelberg (2006). https://doi.org/10.1007/11761679_21

[GPS06] Galbraith, S.D., Paterson, K.G., Smart, N.P.: Pairings for cryptographers. Cryptology ePrint Archive, Report 2006/165 (2006). http://eprint.iacr. org/2006/165

[Gro06] Groth, J.: Simulation-sound NIZK proofs for a practical language and constant size group signatures. In: Lai, X., Chen, K. (eds.) ASIACRYPT 2006. LNCS, vol. 4284, pp. 444–459. Springer, Heidelberg (2006). https://doi. org/10.1007/11935230_29

[Gro16] Groth, J.: On the size of pairing-based non-interactive arguments. In: Fischlin, M., Coron, J.-S. (eds.) EUROCRYPT 2016. LNCS, vol. 9666, pp. 305–326. Springer, Heidelberg (2016). https://doi.org/10.1007/978-3-662-49896-5_11

[GS08] Groth, J., Sahai, A.: Efficient non-interactive proof systems for bilinear groups. In: Smart, N. (ed.) EUROCRYPT 2008. LNCS, vol. 4965, pp. 415–432. Springer, Heidelberg (2008). https://doi.org/10.1007/978-3-540-78967-3_24

[GW11] Gentry, C., Wichs, D.: Separating succinct non-interactive arguments from all falsifiable assumptions. In: Fortnow, L., Vadhan, S.P. (eds.) 43rd ACM STOC, pp. 99–108. ACM Press (June 2011). https://doi.org/10.1145/1993636.1993651

[HBHW20] Hopwood, D., Bowe, S., Hornby, T., Wilcox, N.: Zcash protocol specification, version 2020.1.13 (2020). https://github.com/zcash/zips/blob/master/protocol/protocol.pdf. Accessed 19 Aug 2020

[KKK20] Kerber, T., Kiayias, A., Kohlweiss, M.: Kachina - foundations of private smart contracts. IACR Cryptol. ePrint Arch., 2020:543 (2020). https://eprint.iacr.org/2020/543

[KKKZ19] Kerber, T., Kiayias, A., Kohlweiss, M., Zikas, V.: Ouroboros crypsinous: privacy-preserving proof-of-stake. In: 2019 IEEE Symposium on Security and Privacy, pp. 157–174. IEEE Computer Society Press (May 2019). https://doi.org/10.1109/SP.2019.00063

[KLO19] Kim, J., Lee, J., Oh, H:. Qap-based simulation-extractable SNARK with a single verification. Technical report, Cryptology ePrint Archive, Report 2019/586 (2019)

[KMS+16] Kosba, A.E., Miller, A., Shi, E., Wen, Z., Papamanthou, C.: Hawk: the blockchain model of cryptography and privacy-preserving smart contracts. In: 2016 IEEE Symposium on Security and Privacy, pp. 839–858. IEEE Computer Society Press (May 2016). https://doi.org/10.1109/SP.2016.55

[Kob87] Koblitz, N.: Elliptic curve cryptosystems. Math. Comput. **48**(177), 203–209 (1987)

[Kur02] Kurosawa, K.: Multi-recipient public-key encryption with shortened ciphertext. In: Naccache, D., Paillier, P. (eds.) PKC 2002. LNCS, vol. 2274, pp. 48–63. Springer, Heidelberg (2002). https://doi.org/10.1007/3-540-45664-3_4

[KZM+15] Kosba, A., et al.: How to use SNARKs in universally composable protocols. Cryptology ePrint Archive, Report 2015/1093 (2015). http://eprint.iacr.org/2015/1093

[LCKO19] Lee, J., Choi, J., Kim, J., Oh, H.: SAVER: snark-friendly, additively-homomorphic, and verifiable encryption and decryption with rerandomization. Cryptology ePrint Archive, Report 2019/1270 (2019). https://eprint.iacr.org/2019/1270

[Lip19] Lipmaa, H.: Simulation-extractable SNARKs revisited. Cryptology ePrint Archive, Report 2019/612 (2019). https://eprint.iacr.org/2019/612

[NT16] Naveh, A., Tromer, E.: PhotoProof: cryptographic image authentication for any set of permissible transformations. In: 2016 IEEE Symposium on Security and Privacy, pp. 255–271. IEEE Computer Society Press (May 2016). https://doi.org/10.1109/SP.2016.23

[PV05] Paillier, P., Vergnaud, D.: Discrete-log-based signatures may not be equivalent to discrete log. In: Roy, B. (ed.) ASIACRYPT 2005. LNCS, vol. 3788, pp. 1–20. Springer, Heidelberg (2005). https://doi.org/10.1007/11593447_1

[Sah99] Sahai, A.: Non-malleable non-interactive zero knowledge and adaptive chosen-ciphertext security. In: 40th FOCS, pp, 543–553. IEEE Computer Society Press (October 1999). https://doi.org/10.1109/SFFCS.1999.814628

[SBG+19] Steffen, S., Bichsel, B., Gersbach, M., Melchior, N., Tsankov, P., Vechev, M.T.: zkay: specifying and enforcing data privacy in smart contracts. In: Cavallaro, L., Kinder, J., Wang, X., Katz, J. (eds.) ACM CCS 2019, pp, 1759–1776. ACM Press (November 2019). https://doi.org/10.1145/3319535.3363222

[Sho04] Shoup, V.: Sequences of games: a tool for taming complexity in security proofs. Cryptology ePrint Archive, Report 2004/332 (2004). http://eprint.iacr.org/2004/332

[ZKP19] ZKProof. ZKProof community reference, version 0.2 (December 2019). https://docs.zkproof.org/pages/reference/reference.pdf/. Accessed 26 Jun 06. Updated versions at https://zkproof.org

BooLigero: Improved Sublinear Zero Knowledge Proofs for Boolean Circuits

Yaron Gvili[1], Sarah Scheffler[2(✉)], and Mayank Varia[2]

[1] Cryptomnium LLC, New York, USA
yaron.gvili@cs.tau.ac.il
[2] Boston University, Boston, USA
{sscheff,varia}@bu.edu

Abstract. We provide a modified version of the Ligero sublinear zero knowledge proof system for arithmetic circuits provided by Ames et al. (CCS '17). Our modification "BooLigero" tailors Ligero for use in Boolean circuits to achieve a significant improvement in proof size. Although the original Ligero system could be used for Boolean circuits, Ligero generally requires allocating an entire field element to represent a single bit on a wire in a Boolean circuit. In contrast, our system performs operations over words of bits, allowing a proof size savings of between $O((\log|\mathbb{F}|)^{1/4})$ and $O((\log|\mathbb{F}|)^{1/2})$ compared to Ligero, where $\mathbb{F}$ is the field that leads to the optimal proof size in original Ligero. We achieve improvements in proof size of approximately 1.1–1.6x for SHA-2 and 1.7–2.8x for SHA-3. In addition to checking constraints of standard Boolean operations such as AND, XOR, and NOT over words, BooLigero also supports several other constraints such as multiplication in $\mathrm{GF}(2^w)$, bit masking, testing for zero bits, bit rearrangement within and across words, and bitwise outer product. Most of these techniques batch very efficiently, with only a constant overhead regardless of how many constraints of the same type are tested. Like Ligero, our construction requires no trusted setup and no computational assumptions, which is ideal for blockchain applications. It is plausibly post-quantum secure in the standard model. Furthermore, it is public-coin, perfect honest-verifier zero knowledge, and can be made non-interactive in the random oracle model using the Fiat-Shamir transform.

1 Introduction

Zero knowledge proofs and arguments have become the backbone of modern cryptography. In addition to their uses in building other cryptographic primitives such as signatures, multiparty computation (MPC), and identification schemes, they play a pivotal role in the design of anonymous and privacy-preserving cryptocurrencies [4,15,27,32].

Since Kilian's seminal work on probabilistically checkable proofs [28], their interactive version [26], and their generalization into interactive oracle proofs [7], many zero knowledge argument systems have been created from such proofs. In this work, we focus on and improve Ligero [1], a protocol that achieves a balance between proof size and prover runtime.

© International Financial Cryptography Association 2021
N. Borisov and C. Diaz (Eds.): FC 2021, LNCS 12674, pp. 476–496, 2021.
https://doi.org/10.1007/978-3-662-64322-8_23

1.1 Our Contributions

This paper makes three contributions.

BooLigero: Ligero for Boolean Circuits. In this paper, we present BooLigero, an improvement to Ligero tailored for Boolean circuits. Our method allows us to utilize the "full" field element and store $\log |\mathbb{F}|$ bits of the witness per element, rather than storing only a single bit per (larger) field element and enforcing an additional constraint as is required in Ligero. We can utilize the full field for XOR and NOT operations; for AND we can use $\sqrt{\log |\mathbb{F}|}$ bits of the field element. This buys us an improvement in the proof size between $O((\log |\mathbb{F}|)^{1/4})$ and $O((\log |\mathbb{F}|)^{1/2})$ compared to original Ligero, depending on the proportion of ANDs in the circuit. The prover and verifier runtime should not change much compared to original Ligero. We do this while maintaining Ligero's properties of being public coin, perfect honest-verifier zero knowledge, amenability to the Fiat-Shamir heuristic, being plausibly post-quantum secure in the standard model, and requiring no trusted setup.

Efficient Zero-Checking and Bit-Pattern Constraint Tests. In Ligero, the witness is encoded, and constraints are checked by ensuring that the prover's claims are consistent with parts of the encoded witness that were randomly chosen by the verifier. We add the ability to reveal masked elements of the witness directly, in such a way that the verifier may check properties on the masked elements that will enable them to test properties of other hidden witness elements. Tests with a certain kind of linearity are extremely efficient, requiring only a constant overhead in the number of witness elements to test arbitrarily many instances of the property on existing variables. This enables us to test properties that would normally be difficult to test while representing many bits per word, such as testing whether certain bits are zero, or testing bit "patterns" such as masking and shifting. We can also use these to build range tests. These tests may be helpful in frameworks outside BooLigero as well.

Concrete 1.1–2.8x Improvement Over Ligero. We evaluate our performance on the hash functions SHA-3 and SHA-2, which are common benchmarks and have particular appeal to the cryptocurrency community. We achieve a 1.7–2.8x improvement over Ligero for Merkle trees of SHA-3 from 2^1 to 2^{15} leaves. Our circuit for SHA-3 utilizes one of our specialized tests to perform the bit-rotation step of the SHA-3 main loop. For SHA-2, we achieve a 1.1–1.6x improvement over Ligero for Merkle trees from 2^1 to 2^{15} leaves. Note that this is in spite of the fact that SHA-2 uses some addition modulo 2^{32} operations, which Ligero supports directly and BooLigero does not.

1.2 Related Work

In general, zero knowledge proofs are evaluated for performance on three metrics: proof/argument size, prover runtime, and verifier runtime. There is a spectrum of zero-knowledge proof/argument systems.

On one extreme of the spectrum, large, fast proofs construct ZK proofs from various flavors of MPC: the garbled-circuit based approach of ZKGC [25] (with improvements from [29]) or approaches that use the GMW [19] paradigm (e.g. [24], improved in [18] and [11]). All of these are fairly quick to compute, but they incur a linear proof size (except the very recent work of [37], which cannot be made non-interactive, and is therefore not usable in most blockchain scenarios).

On the other extreme, we have "succinct" sublinear-size arguments. The smallest arguments are constant size, but generally suffer from two problems – assumptions and trusted setup. Many of these arguments use unfalsifiable assumptions (e.g., [5,8,13,16,20,30,33]) and this is inherent at a certain level [17]. Others require a trusted setup step performed by a central authority or a trusted committee operating a costly multiparty computation (e.g. [4,5,9,12, 14,16,20,21,31,33,38]), both being undesirable or even unacceptable in many financial use cases.

In the middle, there exist transparent protocols that achieve sublinear (but not constant) size without the need for trusted setup. A number of these protocols use assumptions that render them vulnerable to quantum attacks (e.g. [10,23,34,36]). There are three different approaches to sublinear transparent protocols without trusted setup that are plausibly post-quantum secure: Ligero [1], Stark [3], and Aurora [6].

Compared to Ligero and BooLigero, Stark's proof size is asymptotically smaller ($O(\log^2 s)$ instead of $O(\sqrt{s})$ for circuit size s), but concretely larger for circuits smaller than approximately 10^6 gates, as shown in [36]. Its prover runtime is more expensive than Ligero's both asymptotically by a $\log s$ factor, and is also concretely longer. For circuits with repeated sub-circuits, Stark has significantly improved verifier runtime, but there is no asymptotic difference for circuits without this property.

Aurora [6] also has a significantly smaller proof size than Ligero and BooLigero ($O(\log^2 s)$ instead of $O(\sqrt{s})$) and the same asymptotic prover and verifier runtime. However, its interactive version has a $O(\log s)$ round complexity compared to Ligero and BooLigero's $O(1)$, and its prover runtime is concretely higher than Ligero's. Moreover, without a certain unproven conjecture involving Reed-Solomon codes, it becomes much less efficient (see discussion in [34]).

2   Preliminaries

Notation. We use $\mathbb{F}$ to refer to a finite field, and $GF(2^w)$ to refer to a finite field with order 2^w. We also often use w to refer to the "word size" and refer to elements of $GF(2^w)$ as "w-words" when we use their w-bit representations.

For operations, we use $\oplus$ for bitwise XOR and & for bitwise AND, over bits or w-words depending on context. We use $*$ to denote Galois field multiplication, and $\cdot$ for element-wise multiplication of vectors.

Bit indexing, denoted with square brackets, always begins at 1. Bitstrings are always shown in big endian. Thus, if $x = 0001$, then $x[1] = 1$ is the least significant bit of x.

Zero Knowledge IOPs. A ZKIOP is an interactive oracle proof (IOP) [7] that is additionally zero-knowledge. Let $\mathcal{P}$ and $\mathcal{V}$ be probabilistic polynomial-time interactive Turing machines. An interactive oracle protocol between $\mathcal{P}$ and $\mathcal{V}$ occurs over several rounds. $\mathcal{P}$ reads messages sent by $\mathcal{V}$ fully, but $\mathcal{V}$ queries random parts of $\mathcal{P}$'s message rather than reading them entirely. At the end, $\mathcal{V}$ either accepts or rejects. Let $\langle \mathcal{P}(x, w), \mathcal{V}(x) \rangle$ refer to the output of $\mathcal{V}(x)$ when executing an interactive oracle protocol with $\mathcal{P}(x, w)$. Let R be a relation for language L so that $(x, w) \in R$ if w is a witness for x's membership in L.

Definition 1 (Zero knowledge interactive oracle proof). $\langle \mathcal{P}, \mathcal{V} \rangle$ *is a* zero knowledge interactive oracle proof system *for R with soundness error δ if:*

- Completeness*: For any $(x, w) \in R$, $\langle \mathcal{P}(x, w), \mathcal{V}(x) \rangle = 1$.*
- Soundness*: If $x \notin L$, then for all $\mathcal{P}^*$, $\Pr[\langle \mathcal{P}^*, \mathcal{V}(x) \rangle = 1] \leq \delta$*
- Perfect honest-verifier zero knowledge*: Let $\mathsf{View}_{\mathcal{V}}(\mathcal{P}, \mathcal{V}, x, w)$ be the view of $\mathcal{V}$ upon completion of $\langle \mathcal{P}(x, w), \mathcal{V}(x) \rangle$. The protocol is perfect honest-verifier zero knowledge if there exists a probabilistic poly time simulator $\mathcal{S}$ such that for all (x, w), the distribution of $\mathcal{S}(x)$ equals the distribution of $\mathsf{View}_{\mathcal{V}}(\mathcal{P}, \mathcal{V}, x, w)$.*

The IOPs we deal with in this paper are also *public-coin*, meaning that $\mathcal{V}$'s messages to $\mathcal{P}$ are always chosen randomly from a known distribution, and $\mathcal{V}$'s queries to $\mathcal{P}$ depend only on messages that have already occurred and that $\mathcal{P}$ has seen. Zero knowledge IOPs can be converted to zero knowledge arguments in a standard way using the Fiat-Shamir transform [7].

3 Ligero Background

In this section we provide relevant background from [1].

Proof Size of Ligero. Ligero [1] is a zero-knowledge argument that achieves $O(\sqrt{s})$ proof size, where s is the size of the verification circuit.

Ligero encodes the witness using an Interleaved Reed-Solomon code, which can be considered an m-vector of Reed-Solomon (RS) codewords. Each RS codeword can itself be considered a vector of n elements which encode ℓ unencoded elements, for $n = O(\ell)$. Thus, the overall interleaved Reed-Solomon code can be considered an $m \times n$ matrix encoding $m \times \ell$ variables.

Ligero achieves $O(\sqrt{s})$ proof size by being clever about how the verifier checks constraints on this matrix. Roughly speaking, the communication will consist of some (linear combinations of) rows and some columns of the matrix, with simplified complexity $O(n + m)$. Thus, one can balance m against ℓ and set both[1] to $O(\sqrt{s})$ to achieve a proof size of $O(\sqrt{s})$.

We let $L = \mathsf{RS}_{\mathbb{F}, n, k, \eta}$ be a Reed-Solomon code with minimal distance. L^m refers to the interleaved code, which has codewords that are simply m codewords of L. L^m is best understood as a matrix where the m rows are L-codewords. The details of interleaved Reed-Solomon codes as they relate to Ligero are provided in the full version [22], but they should not be necessary to understand this paper.

---

[1] Actually, m is set to $O(\sqrt{s/\kappa})$ and ℓ is set to $O(\sqrt{s\kappa})$, where κ is a security parameter.

Tests in Ligero. As a zero-knowledge IPCP between the prover $\mathcal{P}$ and verifier $\mathcal{V}$, the prover begins by encoding its witness as a L^m codeword – an $m \times n$ matrix encoding $m \times \ell$ variables in the witness. Ligero creates three tests for constraints over this matrix: **Test-Interleaved** ([1] Sect. 4.1), **Test-Linear-Constraints-IRS** ([1] Sect. 4.2), and **Test-Quadratic-Constraints-IRS** ([1] Sect. 4.3). Each of these tests consists of two phases:

1. **Oracle phase:** $\mathcal{P}$ creates an oracle to the L^m-encoded witness (possibly with some additional info).
2. **Interactive testing phase:** $\mathcal{P}$ and $\mathcal{V}$ interact with each other. $\mathcal{P}$ sends some linear combinations of rows of the matrix. $\mathcal{V}$ makes queries to the oracle to obtain columns of the L^m codeword (without receiving any L codeword "rows" fully). After the interaction, $\mathcal{V}$ checks whether the linear combinations given to it by $\mathcal{P}$ match the columns it queried, and either accepts or rejects.

When used as a zero-knowledge argument (instead of a ZKIPCP), the oracle is replaced with a commitment. Before the interactive testing phase, $\mathcal{P}$ commits to all columns of its encoded witness as the leaves of a Merkle tree that uses a statistically hiding commitment scheme. To make the proof non-interactive, the verifier's messages can be replaced with a random oracle call on the prover's messages up to that point.

Boolean Circuits in Ligero. Ligero is presented for arithmetic circuits over a prime field. It is possible to use Ligero for a Boolean circuit as well, but this has two downsides.

The first downside is that one must use an entire field element to represent a single bit. This causes a blowup of $\log |\mathbb{F}|$ in the number of witness elements, which causes a blowup of $O(\sqrt{\log |\mathbb{F}|})$ in the proof size.

How small of a field can we use? There is a minimum requirement that $|\mathbb{F}| \geq \ell + n$ ([1] §5.3), which is required so that there are sufficient evaluation points for L. Furthermore, if the field gets too small, one must repeat the protocol several times in order to achieve the desired soundness. At very small field sizes, the costs of the commitments ($\log s$ times a constant hash output length) also start growing in comparison to the rest of the proof. Concretely, testing out different field sizes for Boolean circuits on the order of 10^6 to 10^9 gates tends to yield optimal field sizes of about 14–20 bits. This suggests that there is approximately a 3.7–4.4x gain to be had by packing the bits efficiently.

The second downside is that this costs additional constraints. First, each extended witness element e must be proven to be 0 or 1 by adding a quadratic constraint that $e^2 - e = 0$. Second, XOR and AND are also both quadratic constraints: the constraint $e_1 + e_2 = a_0 + 2 \cdot a_1$, along with bit constraints on all variables, enforce that a_0 is the XOR of e_1 and e_2, and that a_1 is the AND of e_1 and e_2. Computing only one or the other necessitates the creation of a dummy variable for the other, and enforcing bit constraints on all. Hence, the number of constraints is twice the maximum number of AND and XOR gates combined.

Unlike linear constraints, which can be evaluated using only an encoding of the witness itself, evaluating quadratic constraints like $x * y = z$ requires providing encodings of x, y, and z, separately from (but related to) the encoding of the witness itself. Although the number of quadratic constraints will asymptotically be $O(s)$, this suggests that there may be concrete room for improvement by reducing the number of quadratic constraints.

4   BooLigero Techniques

We make one minor change and two major changes to Ligero [1], which we described in Sect. 3.

The minor change is that we use $GF(2^w)$ instead of the prime field $GF(p)$. Ligero's methods work for any finite field, where addition and multiplication now use operations in the new field. Since we are still using Interleaved Reed-Solomon codes, we can directly reuse Ligero's **Test-Interleaved, Test-Linear-Constraints-IRS**, and **Test-Quadratic-Constraints-IRS**. The latter two now test bitwise XOR/NOT constraints and $GF(2^w)$ multiplication rather than arithmetic addition and multiplication. We lose the ability to natively check linear arithmetic constraints in mod 2^w, but we gain the ability to cheaply check XORs. We can still check linear arithmetic constraints in power-of-two moduli by building an adder out of the constraint tests we have.

The following two larger changes to Ligero are the focus of our work:

Change 1: Additional constraint tests that reveal variables directly. We add a number of tests for additional constraints. These new tests operate differently than the Ligero tests, and in fact the new tests rely on the Ligero tests in order to check linear and quadratic constraints. In the new tests, the prover modifies and extends the witness with additional variables, some of which are based on a "challenge" sent by the verifier. As part of the proof oracle, the prover sends some (masked) elements of the witness to the verifier directly, and the verifier must check to see whether the revealed elements have a certain property. These tests can be nested inside other tests – e.g., our **Test-And-Constraints** procedure involves invoking **Test-Pattern-Zeros-Constraints**, as described in Sect. 4.3.

Most of our tests use only linear constraints and cost $O(\kappa)$ (a security parameter) in the proof size, independent of the circuit size and the number of constraints. Our **Test-And-Constraints** involves adding approximately $3\sqrt{w}N$ hidden variables, where N is the number of AND gates. This is still an improvement over the approximately wN added elements that are required to represent wN Boolean wires in plain Ligero. We describe our constraint tests in Sect. 4.3.

Change 2: Two oracles/rounds of commitment. Unlike original Ligero, many of the tests we add require verifier input in order to choose which constraints we will check – generally, the verifier will pick a random linear combination of the variables to use in constraints. However, for this to be sound, the original variables must already have been available in an oracle (or been committed to). This necessitates splitting the proof oracle in two: one that presents an encoding of the "original" witness, and one that is parameterized by the verifier's random choices and returns an encoding of the added variables. We call the first oracle the "initial oracle" and the second the "response oracle". Thus, whereas Ligero had two phases of procedures – the oracle phase and the interactive testing phase – we have four: initial phase (creation of initial witness to be provided as oracle or commitment), challenge phase (verifier sends random bits as challenge), response phase (creation of witness extension to be provided as a second oracle or commitment), and the interactive testing phase We describe each of these phases in Sect. 4.1. This process is based on the circuit sampling idea of [2].

4.1   Test Procedures

In original Ligero, each test consists of an oracle and an interactive test procedure which will ensure that the oracle is valid. In our protocol, each test consists of two oracles, separated by a verifier challenge, and followed by an interactive test procedure. The second oracle is the response to the challenge. We describe each of our constraint test procedures in four phases:

1. **Initial phase:** $\mathcal{P}$ adds elements to the witness, encodes it, and provides the encoding as the first proof oracle.
2. **Challenge phase:** $\mathcal{V}$ sends random bits to $\mathcal{P}$, which will be required to generate the second proof oracle.
3. **Response phase:** Based on the bits received in the challenge, $\mathcal{P}$ adds more elements to the witness, and adds additional constraints. $\mathcal{P}$ encodes the extensions to the witness, and provides the encoding (which can be combined with the first oracle's output) as well as the revealed variables.
4. **Interactive testing phase:** $\mathcal{P}$ and $\mathcal{V}$ run an interactive testing protocol. At the end, $\mathcal{V}$ has acceptance criteria for determining whether to accept or reject the proof. Our tests augment the original Ligero acceptance criteria with additional checks on properties of the revealed variables.

In slightly more detail, the variables in the witness consist of:

- v_0 original variables
- v_1 added hidden variables in the initial phase
- v_2 added hidden variables in the response phase
- v_3 added revealed variables in the response phase

$\mathcal{P}$ and $\mathcal{V}$ first set ℓ, m_1, m_2, and m_3 so that $\ell m_1 \geq v_0 + v_1$, $\ell m_2 \geq v_2$, and $\ell m_3 \geq v_3$. $\mathcal{P}$ creates the initial witness encoding $U^{\mathbf{w}_1} \in L^{m_1}$ from the v_0 original variables and v_1 added hidden variables in the initial phase, and sets this as the initial oracle. After receiving $\mathcal{V}$'s challenge, it creates the response witness encoding $U^{\mathbf{w}_2} \in L^{m_2}$ from the v_2 newly added hidden variables. As in original Ligero, it also creates encodings U^x, U^y, and $U^z \in L^{m'}$ needed for testing quadratic constraints (where m' is set so that $m'\ell$ is at least the number of quadratic constraints). $\mathcal{P}$ sets the response oracle as the vertical concatenation of $U^{\mathbf{w}_2}$, U^x, U^y, U^z, along with all revealed variables in the clear.

When doing the interactive testing phase, $\mathcal{P}$ also creates $U^{\mathbf{w}_3} \in L^{m_3}$ which contains the revealed variables added in the response phase. During this phase,

$\mathcal{P}$ treats its witness encoding $U^{\mathbf{w}}$ as the vertical concatenation of $U^{\mathbf{w}_1}$, $U^{\mathbf{w}_2}$, and $U^{\mathbf{w}_3}$. The verifier will do the same with the revealed variables.

Our new BooLigero tests rely on executing the interactive testing phase of Ligero tests on $U^{\mathbf{w}}$. (The encodings of x, y, and z needed for **Test-Quadratic-Constraints-IRS** are also built relative to the full $\mathbf{w}$.) They also add additional linear and quadratic constraints to be tested in this way. These tests may be useful in frameworks outside BooLigero as well.

Adding Linear Constraints. Ligero's **Test-Linear-Constraints-IRS** checks whether an encoding of a secret vector x is a solution to linear equation $Ax = b$, where A is a public matrix and b is a public vector. In the context of testing the protocol in a full circuit, x is the witness vector, b is the all 0s vector, and A is set so that the jth row of Ax equals $in_1 + in_2 - out$, where the jth addition gate in the circuit computes $out = in_1 + in_2$. To add an additional linear constraint, we simply add an additional row to A along with an additional element to b. Doing so does not affect the proof size.

Adding Quadratic Constraints. Ligero's **Test-Quadratic-Constraints-IRS** tests whether encodings of vectors x, y, z meet the condition that $x \cdot y + a \cdot z = b$, where $\cdot$ represents element-wise multiplication in $\mathbb{F}$. When using the protocol for testing a circuit, the x, y, z vectors are built so that their jth entries are in_1, in_2, out, where the jth multiplication gate in the circuit computes $out = in_1 * in_2$. These vectors are constructed in a public way from the witness, i.e. $\mathcal{P}$ and $\mathcal{V}$ both construct P_x such that $x = P_x \mathbf{w}$. Unlike the linear constraint test, separate encodings of x, y, and z must be provided to the verifier; thus, increasing the number of quadratic constraints increases the proof size.

4.2 Testing Linear Operations that Yield Zero Over Bits

We first define a useful class of tests that can be batched very efficiently.

Let ℓ_1 and ℓ_2 be positive integers, and let $t_1 = \ell_1 w$ and $t_2 = \ell_2 w$. Let $T \in \{0,1\}^{t_2 \times t_1}$ be a public $t_2 \times t_1$ binary matrix. Then T defines a test on $x \in \{0,1\}^{t_1}$ which checks whether $Tx = \vec{0}$, where $\vec{0}$ is of length t_2.

To incorporate this into Ligero, we observe that one can represent a vector of Ligero variables $x \in \mathrm{GF}(2^w)^{\ell_1}$ as a vector in $\{0,1\}^{t_1}$ of $t_1 = \ell_1 w$ bits. Adding two variables in one of these representations exactly corresponds to adding the variables in the other representation. So, we abuse notation and treat the vector $x \in \mathrm{GF}(2^w)^{\ell_1}$ as vector in $\mathrm{GF}(2)^{t_1}$.

Observe that, given $a \in \{0,1\}^{t_1}$ (which can also be represented by a vector in $\mathrm{GF}(2^w)^{\ell_1}$) such that $Ta = \vec{0}$, this implies that $T(x+a) = \vec{0}$ if and only if $Tx = \vec{0}$. In the full protocol, rather than guaranteeing that Ta will be 0, we will write a test that will check whether *both* Ta and Tx are 0 simultaneously. To achieve privacy, we blind any Ligero variables we wish to test with T. $\mathcal{P}$ will generate a random a subject to the constraint that $Ta = \vec{0}$ and then open the variable $(x + a)$ directly to the verifier, who can independently check that $T(x + a) = \vec{0}$. Figure 1 shows a construction for a perfect zero-knowledge protocol between $\mathcal{P}$ and $\mathcal{V}$ to test T for a batch of N variables with low soundness error. Observe that the communication complexity for this batched test of N ℓ_1-tuples is only the size of one tuple: ℓ_1 elements of $\mathrm{GF}(2^w)$. Note that it is also independent of t_2; it depends only on t_1 and w.

We will embed this construction into BooLigero to test properties discussed in Sect. 4.3, such as rearranging bits in a "pattern," checking whether certain bits are zero, or both at the same time.

Test-$T(\kappa, \mathbb{F}; x_1 = (x_{11}, \ldots, x_{1t}), \ldots, x_N = (x_{N1}, \ldots, x_{Nt}))$

Auxiliary input: Soundness parameter κ. Field $\mathrm{GF}(2^w)$ Positive integers ℓ_1 and ℓ_2; let $t_1 = w\ell_1$ and $t_2 = w\ell_2$. Binary matrix $T \in \{0, 1\}^{t_2 \times t_1}$.

Inputs: A batch of N secret variables in $\mathrm{GF}(2^w)^{\ell_1}$ held by $\mathcal{P}$, $x_1 = (x_{11}, \ldots, x_{1\ell_1})$, $\ldots$, $x_N = (x_{N1}, \ldots, x_{N\ell_1}) \in \mathrm{GF}(2^w)^{\ell_1}$. where $\mathcal{P}$ claims that (abusing notation and treating each x_i as a binary t_1-vector) $Tx_i = \vec{0}$ for all $i \in [N]$.

Protocol:

1. **Initial phase:** For $j \in [\kappa]$, $\mathcal{P}$ picks and adds hidden variable $a^{(j)} \in \mathrm{GF}(2^w)^{\ell_1}$ such that $Ta^{(j)} = \vec{0}$ to the witness.
2. **Challenge phase:** $\mathcal{V}$ sends $N\kappa$ bits: $r_i^{(j)}$ for $i \in [N]$ for $j \in [\kappa]$.
3. **Response phase:** $\mathcal{P}$ adds

$$u^{(j)} = a^{(j)} \oplus \bigoplus_{\substack{i \in [N] \\ \text{s.t.} \\ r_i^{(j)} = 1}} x_i \tag{1}$$

for $j \in [\kappa]$ (a total of $\ell_1 \kappa$ elements) as revealed elements to the witness. $\mathcal{P}$ and $\mathcal{V}$ add the κ instances of Eqn. 1 to the list of linear constraints to check.
4. **Interactive testing phase:** $\mathcal{P}$ and $\mathcal{V}$ run **Test-Linear-Constraints-IRS** and **Test-Interleaved**. $\mathcal{V}$ accepts if both tests pass and additionally (abusing notation and treating each $u^{(j)}$ as a binary t_1-vector) $Tu^{(j)} = \vec{0}$ for all $j \in [\kappa]$.

Fig. 1. Test construction for any binary matrix T

Note that the test itself is not sound without the additional tests provided by Ligero – the soundness of the main part of the test depends on the revealed variables being well-formed. We ensure that the all variables are well-formed by using **Test-Linear-Constraints-IRS** and **Test-Interleaved**, and ensuring that the initial elements are provided in an oracle (or committed to) before receiving the challenge. Note also that sometimes T itself will reveal certain information about x – for example, that x is 0 at certain bit locations. But the protocol will not reveal anything about x other than the fact that $Tx = \vec{0}$, which is already true if $\mathcal{P}$ is honest.

Lemma 1. (Security of Test-T). *The protocol described in Fig. 1 is complete, perfect zero-knowledge, and has soundness error $1/2^\kappa + \delta_1 + \delta_2$, where δ_1 is the* soundness error of **Test-Linear-Constraints-IRS** and δ_2 is the soundness error of **Test-Interleaved**.

The proof is given in the full version [22].

4.3 New Constraint Tests

In this section, we describe our added tests for BooLigero. Each of these calls one of the original Ligero tests **Test-Linear-Constraints-IRS** or **Test-Quadratic-Constraints-IRS**. The later tests additionally call on the earlier BooLigero tests as well.

Properties Tested by **Test-T**. We proceed to name two useful properties (and their conjunction) that can be tested using the construction from the previous section. As described in the previous section, they can test the property on arbitrarily many input variables for only a constant overhead over the cost of the variables themselves. Since we will reuse them later, we name each of these special cases of **Test-T**.

- **Test-Zeros-Constraints**: This tests whether particular bit locations in the input are 0. Let $Z \subseteq [t_2]$ be a set of indices to be zero-tested. Formally, let T_Z be a square matrix with 1s on the diagonal for indices in Z, and 0 for all other elements. Observe that $T_Z x = \vec{0}$ if and only if x is 0 at the Z indices.
- **Test-Pattern-Constraints**: We informally define a "pattern" as a relationship between between $(t_i = t_1 - t_2)$ "input bits" and t_2 "output bits." The pattern property enforces that each "output bit" is an XOR of some subset of the input bits. In general, pattern matrices T_π are defined as a matrix that is a concatenation between a matrix $\pi \in \{0,1\}^{t_2 \times t_i}$ and a $t_2 \times t_2$ identity matrix. Several useful functions can be defined as patterns:
  - Masking. Suppose we wished to show in Ligero that $x \& \mu = y$ for some public mask μ, for Ligero variables $x, y \in \mathrm{GF}(2^w)^{\ell_2}$ and mask $\mu \in \{0,1\}^{t_2}$. Let M be the t_2-square matrix with μ comprising the diagonal and zeros elsewhere. Then we can test whether $x \& \mu = y$ using the pattern $T_\mu = [\, M \mid I \,]$, because:

$$[\, M \mid I \,] \begin{bmatrix} x \\ y \end{bmatrix} = \vec{0}$$

  which, for diagonal matrix M, implies that $Mx = y$.
  - Even parity. Suppose we wished to show that $y \in \mathrm{GF}(2^w)$ is the parity of $x \in \mathrm{GF}(2^w)^{\ell_1 - 1}$. This can be tested by checking that

$$\begin{bmatrix} \begin{matrix} \ddots & & \cdot \\ \cdots & 0 & \cdots \\ 1 & \cdots & 1 \end{matrix} & I \end{bmatrix} \begin{bmatrix} x \\ y \end{bmatrix} = \vec{0}$$

  which will check that the least significant bit of y equals a sum of all bits of x. Even-parity can be batch-tested by using Zeros, testing the parity of many variables simultaneously.

- **Test-Pattern-Zeros-Constraints**: Notice that a Zeros test can be performed on the same revealed values as a pattern test, if the blinding variables are chosen to meet both constraints. We will often perform these tests on the same revealed variables to save space.

Bitwise AND Test. Next, we describe our test for bitwise AND. Note that AND cannot be tested using the method in the previous section, since it is not a linear operation. Instead, we write a new test that calls **Test-Pattern-Zeros-Constraints**.

As a first step, one way to test AND would be to fully bit-decompose our single w-bit element into w elements each representing a single bit. This would let us use quadratic constraints directly to show AND constraints. However, doing so is expensive. This method would yield roughly the same proof size as original Ligero, since it uses an entire w-bit element to represent a single bit. Instead, we exploit the nature of Galois field arithmetic to compute the AND of $w_0 = \lfloor \sqrt{w} \rfloor$ bits simultaneously in a w-bit element using a GF multiplication. We then use our Pattern test to convert between the original variables and the w_1 decomposed variables, where w_1 is the minimum integer such that $w_0 w_1 \geq w$. Each of these w_1 "split" variables contains w_0 bits of the original element (except the last, which may contain fewer if $w_0 \nmid w$).

Suppose we have elements $x, y \in \mathrm{GF}(2^w)$, and want to find $z = x \& y$. We start by using a Pattern to split x into w_1 variables $\hat{x}_1, \ldots, \hat{x}_{w_1}$, and to split y into w_1 variables $\hat{y}_1, \ldots, \hat{y}_{w_1}$. First, consider the x variables. Each split variable $\hat{x}_h$ will consist of w_0 chunks of w_0 bits each. (Recall that by construction $w_0^2 \leq w$.) The least significant bit of each chunk will be a bit of x, and all other bits will be 0. This is illustrated in Eq. 2. The y variables will be split differently: each $\hat{y}_h$ will consist of a single chunk of w_0 bits from y, starting with the least significant bit. This is shown in Eq. 3.

We then set $\hat{z}_h = \hat{x}_h * \hat{y}_h$. The effect of multiplying $\hat{x}_h$ by $\hat{y}_h$ is that the chunk of w_0 bits in $\hat{y}_h$ is "copied" to each of the w_0 chunks of output for which the corresponding chunk of $\hat{x}_h$ was 1. Thus, in order to figure out which bits were shared between x and y, we go to the kth bit of the kth chunk of $\hat{z}_h$. This will equal the kth bit of $\hat{y}_h$ times the LSB of the kth chunk of $\hat{x}_h$. This is shown in Eq. 4. Recomposing from the $\hat{z}_h$ variables back to z by using Pattern once again, we have exactly computed the bitwise AND of x and y.

Figure 2 shows an example of how to split (x, y, z), where $z = x \& y$. The full **Test-And-Constraints** procedure is shown in Fig. 3. The patterns π_x, π_y, and π_z, described formally in Fig. 3 step 1(d).

Lemma 2. (Security of Test-And-Constraints). *The protocol described in Fig. 3 is complete, perfect zero-knowledge, and has soundness error $3(1/2^\kappa) + \delta_1 + \delta_2 + \delta_3$, where δ_1 is the soundness error of **Test-Quadratic-Constraints-IRS**, δ_2 is the soundness error of **Test-Linear-Constraints-IRS**, and δ_3 is the soundness error of **Test-Interleaved**.*

A full proof of security for the test is shown in §A. Additionally, the $\hat{z}$ variables can be used to compute bitwise outer product if desired.

$$x = 10110 \rightarrow (\hat{x}_{w_1} = 000\,\overset{w_0}{\overset{\frown}{01}}, \hat{x}_2 = 0\,0\overset{w_0}{\overset{\frown}{0}}\overset{w_0}{\overset{\frown}{01}}, \hat{x}_1 = 0\,0\overset{w_0}{\overset{\frown}{01}}\,\overset{w_0}{\overset{\frown}{00}}) \tag{2}$$

$$y = 11101 \rightarrow (\hat{y}_{w_1} = 0000\,\overset{\frown}{1}, \hat{y}_2 = 000\,\overset{\frown}{1}\,\overset{\frown}{1}, \hat{y}_1 = 000\,\overset{\frown}{0}\,\overset{\frown}{1}) \tag{3}$$

$$\updownarrow \qquad\qquad \updownarrow \qquad\qquad \updownarrow \; \hat{z}_h = \hat{x}_h * \hat{y}_h$$

$$z = 10100 \leftarrow (\hat{z}_{w_1} = 000\,\overset{w_0}{\overset{\frown}{01}}, \hat{z}_2 = 0\,\overset{w_0}{\overset{\frown}{00}}\,\overset{w_0}{\overset{\frown}{11}}, \hat{z}_1 = 0\,0\overset{w_0}{\overset{\frown}{01}}\,\overset{w_0}{\overset{\frown}{00}}) \tag{4}$$

Fig. 2. Example variable splits for **Test-And-Constraints** for $w = 5$, $w_0 = 2$, $w_1 = 3$. Pattern constraints enforce the relationship between x and $\hat{x}$, and similar for y and z. The $\hat{z}$ variables are related to $\hat{x}$ and $\hat{y}$ via a quadratic constraint.

In the full version [22] we show how to do cheap range tests for power-of-two ranges, and how to build an adder and use it to perform non-power-of-two range tests. Our full modifications to the protocol from [1] are shown in Fig. 4.

5   Performance

We primarily evaluate our proof on its size compared to original Ligero, since our asymptotic prover and verifier runtime should be the same as Ligero. Recall that a proof for a Boolean circuit in original Ligero requires using an entire field element to represent a single bit value on a wire. Like original Ligero, the parameters for BooLigero can be set so that the proof size is $O(\sqrt{s})$ elements, where s is the circuit size. If the field size in Ligero is $b = \lceil \log \mathbb{F} \rceil$ bits, then we would expect BooLigero to save a factor of $O(\sqrt{b})$ in the proof size. For example, if a Ligero proof used a field with 18 bits, we would expect a $\sqrt{18} \approx 4.2x$ improvement in the BooLigero proof size. For AND gates we require $w_1 \approx \sqrt{w}$ variables to compute the AND of a single w-bit variable. If the Ligero and BooLigero field sizes require the same number of bits to represent, BooLigero will use only $\sqrt{b}$ fewer variables, a proof size improvement of $O(b^{1/4})$ for AND-heavy circuits. We also add a small constant up-front cost for the revealed variables.

Determining the Size of the Extended Witness and Proof. If the verification circuit C consists of only XOR gates, NOT gates, and Galois field multiplications, then the size of the witness $\mathbf{w}$ is simply the number of wires in C, which we call v_0 as described in Sect. 4.1. If C contains ANDs, or uses any other BooLigero test (e.g. using **Test-Pattern-Constraints** to perform a bit shift), then $\mathbf{w}$ is augmented with the ($v_1 + v_2$ hidden and v_3 revealed) variables described in Sect. 4.3. The combined proof oracle becomes an L^m encoding of the $v_0 + v_1 + v_2$ hidden variables in the witness, plus the v_3 revealed variables in the clear. Once the extended witness is created, the process of choosing the parameters proceeds in the same way as original Ligero: the number of rows m is balanced against the number of variables per row ℓ to achieve sublinear proof size. For more details, see [1] Sect. 5. In the non-interactive version of BooLigero, the Merkle path part of the proof is doubled since the initial and response variables were committed

---

Test-And-Constraints($\mathbb{F} = \mathrm{GF}(2^w), \kappa; x_1, \ldots, x_N, y_1, \ldots, y_N, z_1, \ldots, z_N$)

Inputs: Soundness parameter κ. Secret variables $x_1, \ldots, x_N, y_1, \ldots, y_N, z_1, \ldots, z_N \in \mathbb{F}$ where $\mathcal{P}$ claims that $x_i \& y_i = z_i$ for all $i \in [N]$.

Constraint enforced: $x_i \& y_i = z_i$ for all $i \in [N]$.

Procedure:

1. Initial phase:
   (a) Let $w_0 = \lfloor \sqrt{w} \rfloor$. Let w_1 be the minimum integer such that $w_0 w_1 \geq w$. (Note that $w_1 \leq w_0 + 2$.)
   (b) Add $3Nw_1$ new variables to the witness as described below.
       i. For $i \in [N]$, for $h \in [w_1]$, add new variable $\hat{x}_{i,h}$ where $\hat{x}_{i,h}[(k-1)w_0 + 1] = x_i[((h-1)w_0) + k]$ for $k \in [w_0]$ (if the index is defined), and all other bits are 0. An example is shown in Equation 2.
       ii. For $i \in [N]$, for $h \in [w_1]$, add new variable $\hat{y}_{i,h}$ where $\hat{y}_{i,h}[k] = x_i[((h-1)w_0) + k]$ for $k \in [w_0]$ (if the index is defined), and all other bits are 0. An example is shown in Equation 3.
       iii. For $i \in [N]$, for $h \in [w_1]$, add new variable $\hat{z}_{i,h} = \hat{x}_{i,h} * \hat{y}_{i,h}$, where $*$ denotes multiplication in $\mathrm{GF}(2^w)$. Observe that within $\hat{z}_{i,h}$, each of w_0 "chunks" of w_0 bits, the kth bit of the kth chunk is 1 if and only if the corresponding bits in x_i and y_i are 1. An example is shown in Equation 4.
   (c) For all $i \in [N], h \in [w_1]$, add a quadratic constraint that $\hat{x}_{i,h} * \hat{y}_{i,h} = \hat{z}_{i,h}$.
   (d) We define patterns π_x, π_y, π_z which describe the relationship between the variables and their "hatted" versions described in 1(b) and with examples in Equations 2, 3, and 4.
       i. T_{π_x} enforces the following on column-vector $[x_i, \hat{x}_{i,1}, \ldots, \hat{x}_{i,w_1}]$:
          A. For all $h \in [w_1]$, $\hat{x}_{i,h}$ is 0 everywhere except at indices $(1 + kw_0)$ for all valid k. Additionally, $\hat{x}_{i,w_1}$ is also 0 at indices where $k+1 > w \bmod w_0$.
          B. For $k \in [w]$, $x_i[k] = \hat{x}_{i, \lfloor \frac{k+1}{w_0} \rfloor}[1 + w_0((k-1) \bmod w_0)]$
       ii. T_{π_y} enforces the following on column-vector $[y_i, \hat{y}_{i,1}, \ldots, \hat{y}_{i,w_1}]$:
          A. For all $h \in [w_1]$, $\hat{y}_{i,h}$ is 0 everywhere except at indices $1, \ldots, w_0$. Additionally, $\hat{y}_{i,w_1}$ is also 0 at indices greater than $w \bmod w_0$.
          B. For $k \in [w]$, $y_i[k] = \hat{y}_{i, \lfloor \frac{k+1}{w_0} \rfloor}[k \bmod w_0]$
       iii. T_{π_z} enforces the following on column-vector $[z_i, \hat{z}_{i,1}, \ldots, \hat{z}_{i,w_1}]$:
          A. For all $h \in [w_1]$, $\hat{z}_{i,h}$ is 0 at all indices greater than w_0^2. Additionally, $\hat{z}_{i,w_1}$ is also 0 at indices greater than $w_0(w \bmod w_0)$.
          B. For $k \in [w]$, $z_i[k] = \hat{z}_{i, \lfloor \frac{k+1}{w_0} \rfloor}[1 + ((k-1) \bmod w_0) + w_0((k-1) \bmod w_0)]$

       Run the initial phase of 3 **Test-Pattern-Zeros-Constraints** tests, one for each of these predicates, using all of the corresponding variables from 1(b) as input. That is, do a batch test for T_{π_x}, T_{π_y}, and T_{π_z} for all $i \in [N]$. Each test's initial phase adds hidden $(w_1 + 1)\kappa$ elements, for a total of $3(w1 + 1)\kappa$.
2. Challenge phase: Run the challenge phase of each of the three **Test-Pattern-Zeros-Constraints**, which involves picking $N\kappa$ bits for each test.
3. Response phase: Run the response phase of each of the three **Test-Pattern-Zeros-Constraints**, which will add $(w_1 + 1)$ revealed variables and some linear constraints on them.
4. Interactive testing phase: Run **Test-Quadratic-Constraints-IRS** on the constraints described in 1(c), and run the interactive testing phase of **Test-Pattern-Zeros-Constraints**, which involves running **Test-Linear-Constraints-IRS** and ensuring that **Test-Pattern-Zeros-Constraints** passes using the revealed variables.

Fig. 3. Witness modification procedure and costs for **Test-And-Constraints**

Protocol ZKIOP($C, \mathbb{F} = \mathrm{GF}(2^w)$)

- **Input:** The prover $\mathcal{P}$ and the verifier $\mathcal{V}$ share a common input circuit $C : \mathrm{GF}(2^w)^{n_i} \to \mathrm{GF}(2^w)$ and input statement x. $\mathcal{P}$ additionally has input $\overline{\alpha} = (\alpha_1, \ldots, \alpha_{n_i})$ such that $C(\overline{\alpha}) = 1$.
- **Initial oracle:** Let v_1 be the total number of variables added by $\mathcal{P}$ in the initial phase all BooLigero tests. Let v_2 and v_3 be the number of hidden and revealed variables added by $\mathcal{P}$ in the response phase all BooLigero tests. The variables themselves cannot be known until the challenge, but the number is fixed. Let m_1, m_2, m_3, ℓ be integers such that $m_1 \cdot \ell > n_i + s + v_1$, $m_2 \cdot \ell > v_2$, and $m_3 \cdot \ell > v_3$, where s is the number of gates in the circuit. $\mathcal{P}$ generates an extended witness $\mathbf{w}_1 \in \mathbb{F}^{m_1\ell}$ where the first $n_i + s$ entries of $\mathbf{w}$ are $(\alpha_1, \ldots, \alpha_{n_i}, \beta_1, \ldots, \beta_s)$ where β_i is the output of the ith gate when evaluating $C(\overline{\alpha})$. The next v_1 variables are those for the **initial phase** section of all BooLigero tests. Let $L = \mathsf{RS}_{\mathrm{GF}(2^w), n, k, \eta}$, and let $\zeta = (\zeta_1, \ldots, \zeta_\ell)$ be a sequence of distinct elements disjoint from $\eta_1, \ldots, \eta_n$. The prover samples random codeword $U^{\mathbf{w}_1} \in L^{m_1}$ subject to $\mathbf{w}_1 = \mathsf{Dec}_\zeta(U^{\mathbf{w}_1})$.
- **Challenge:** $\mathcal{V}$ chooses and sends random bits as described in the **challenge phase** section of all BooLigero tests.
- **Response oracle:** $\mathcal{P}$ generates witness extension $\mathbf{w}_2 \in \mathbb{F}^{m_2\ell}$ where the first v_1 variables in $\mathbf{w}_2$ are the hidden variables for the **response phase** section of all BooLigero tests. $\mathcal{P}$ also generates witness extension $\mathbf{w}_3 \in \mathbb{F}^{m_3\ell}$, where the first variables in $\mathbf{w}_3$ are the revealed variables for the **response phase** section of all BooLigero tests. Let $m = m_1 + m_2$ and let $m' = m_1 + m_2 + m_3$. Let $\mathbf{w} \in \mathbb{F}^\ell$ be the vertical concatenation of $\mathbf{w}_1$ and $\mathbf{w}_2$. Let $\mathbf{w}' \in \mathbb{F}^{(m_1+m_2+m_3)\ell}$ be the vertical concatenation of $\mathbf{w}$ and all revealed variables. $\mathcal{P}$ deterministically chooses codeword $U^{\mathbf{w}_3} \in L^{m_3}$. $\mathcal{P}$ samples random codeword $U^{\mathbf{w}_2} \in L^{m_2}$ subject to $\mathbf{w}_2 = \mathsf{Dec}_\zeta(U^{\mathbf{w}_2})$ and sets $U^{\mathbf{w}} \in L^m$ to be the vertical concatenation of $U^{\mathbf{w}_1}$ and $U^{\mathbf{w}_2}$. Let m'' be an integer such that $m''\ell$ is greater than the number of multiplication gates plus additional quadratic constraints in BooLigero tests. $\mathcal{P}$ constructs vectors $x, y, z \in \mathbb{F}^{m''\ell}$ where the jth entry of x, y, z contains the values $\beta_a, \beta_b, \beta_c$ corresponding to the jth multiplication gate in $\mathbf{w}$. The following entries of x, y, z contain the values for additional constraints added in BooLigero tests. $\mathcal{P}$ and $\mathcal{V}$ construct matrices $P_x, P_y, P_z \in \mathbb{F}^{m''\ell \times m''\ell}$ such that $x = P_x\mathbf{w}', y = P_x\mathbf{w}', z = P_z\mathbf{w}'$. $\mathcal{P}$ constructs matrix $P_{\mathbf{add}} \in \mathbb{F}^{m''\ell \times m''\ell}$ such that the jth row of $P_{\mathbf{add}}\mathbf{w}$ equals $\beta_a + \beta_b - \beta_c$ where β_a, β_b, and β_c correspond to the jth addition gate of the circuit in $\mathbf{w}$, and the subsequent rows correspond to additional linear constraints added in BooLigero tests. It also samples $U^x, U^y, U^z \in L^{m''}$ subject to $x = \mathsf{Dec}_\zeta(U^x)$, $y = \mathsf{Dec}_\zeta(U^y)$, and $z = \mathsf{Dec}_\zeta(U^z)$. Let $u'_h, u^x_h, u^y_h, u^z_h, u^0_h, u^{\mathbf{add}}_h$ be auxiliary rows sampled randomly from L for every $h \in [\sigma]$ where each of $u^x_h, u^y_h, u^z_h, u^{\mathbf{add}}_h$ encodes an independently sampled random ℓ messages $(\gamma_1, \ldots, \gamma_\ell)$ subject to $\sum_{c \in [\ell]} \gamma_c = 0$ and u^0_h encodes 0^ℓ. $\mathcal{P}$ sets the combined oracle as $(U \in L^{m+3m''}, R)$ where U is set as the vertical juxtaposition of the matrices $U^{\mathbf{w}} \in L^m$, $U^x, U^y, U^z \in L^{m''}$, and R is the set of all v_3 revealed variables. When the combined oracle is queried on $Q \subset [n]$, the response will be the columns of U that are in Q, as well as R sent in the clear.
- **The interactive protocol:**
  1. For every $h \in [\sigma]$, $\mathcal{V}$ sends the first verifier message of the testing process for **Test-Interleaved**, **Test-Linear-Constraints-IRS** applied to $A = P_{\mathbf{add}}, b = \vec{0}$ on $U^{\mathbf{w}}$, and **Test-Quadratic-Constraints-IRS** applied to U^x, U^y, U^z.
  2. For every $h \in [\sigma]$, $\mathcal{P}$ responds with the appropriate next step of the testing process for **Test-Interleaved**, **Test-Linear-Constraints-IRS**, and **Test-Quadratic-Constraints-IRS**.
  3. $\mathcal{V}$ picks a random set $Q \subset [n]$ of size t, and queries $U[j]$ that is the vertical juxtaposition of $U^x_h[j], U^y_h[j], U^z_h[j], U^{\mathbf{w}}_h[j], u^x_h[j], u^y_h[j], u^z_h[j], u^{\mathbf{add}}_h[j], u'_h[j], j \in Q$. It also receives R, the list of revealed variables. It uses the same deterministic process as $\mathcal{P}$ to generate $U^{\mathbf{w}_3}$ and appends this to the bottom of the queried columns for testing. It accepts if all acceptance criteria for **Test-Interleaved**, **Test-Linear-Constraints-IRS**, **Test-Quadratic-Constraints-IRS**, **Test-Pattern-Zeros-Constraints** and **Test-And-Constraints** are met.

Fig. 4. ZKIOP of [1] with our modifications shown in blue. (Color figure online)

to separately. We computed the parameters using our own optimizer written in SciPy and validated them with an optimizer obtained from [35].

5.1   Concrete Results

For both SHA-2 and SHA-3, we evaluate our proof sizes compared to Ligero on proving membership in the list captured by a Merkle tree. For a Merkle tree with M leaves, $(2M - 1)$ hash computations are done. This has become a common benchmark for evaluating the scalability of zero-knowledge proofs to larger predicates.

SHA-3. SHA-3 only uses bit operations, so there is no special benefit from using an arithmetic system. Both BooLigero and Ligero may do the wordwise rotations for free; they can be achieved by re-indexing constraints for the next step. Ligero can do the bitwise rotations for free (since each variable represents only a single bit), but in BooLigero we must write the additional variable and use **Test-Pattern-Constraints** to enforce the constraint. Using SHA-3 as the hash function in a Merkle tree, each invocation of the hash function consists of a single call to the f-function (Fig. 5).

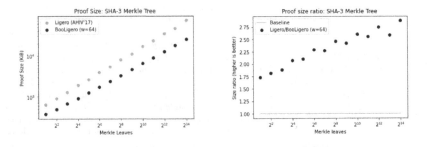

Fig. 5. BooLigero and Ligero absolute and relative proof sizes for SHA-3 Merkle trees

SHA-2. SHA-2 contains a mixture of Boolean operations and mod-2^{32} addition. Although the SHA-2 circuit used in [1] was not provided, we reconstruct a similar circuit using the same techniques. As described in [1], Ligero computes modular addition by using a dummy variable. Our SHA-2 circuit for original Ligero tracks 16 32-bit variables (11 main variables plus 5 dummy variables) throughout 64 iterations of the SHA-2 loop.

BooLigero prefers a different strategy. Although we can compute mod-2^{32} addition in BooLigero by implementing an adder, it turns out that a standard 135840-wire Boolean circuit for SHA-2 leads to a smaller proof size since it uses far fewer ANDs (Fig. 6).

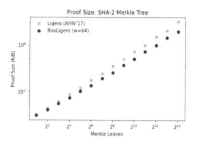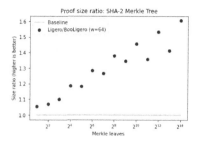

Fig. 6. BooLigero and Ligero absolute and relative proof sizes for SHA-2 Merkle trees

Acknowledgments. The authors graciously thank Muthu Venkitasubramaniam for providing us with a parameter optimizer [35], and the anonymous reviewers for their insightful comments. The second author is supported by a Google PhD Fellowship. The third author is supported by the DARPA SIEVE program under Agreement No. HR00112020021 and the National Science Foundation under Grants No. 1414119, 1718135, 1801564, and 1931714.

A   Proofs of Lemmas

*Proof. (Security of **Test-And-Constraints**).* We must show that **Test-And-Constraints** is complete, zero-knowledge, and sound up to error $3(1/2^\kappa) + \delta_1 + \delta_2 + \delta_3$, where δ_1 is the soundness error of **Test-Quadratic-Constraints-IRS**, δ_2 is the soundness error of **Test-Linear-Constraints-IRS**, and δ_3 is the soundness error of **Test-Interleaved**.

Completeness: If $\mathcal{P}$ is honest, then all variables are well-formed. We must show that following the process described in step 1(b) of Fig. 3 will lead to computing bitwise AND. Elements in $GF(2^w)$ are polynomials over $GF(2)$ of degree at most $(w-1)$, and multiplication in $GF(2^w)$ is polynomial multiplication modulo an irreversible polynomial. As in step 1(a), let $w_0 = \lfloor \sqrt{w} \rfloor$. Fix $i \in [N]$.

By construction, the polynomial representations of all $\hat{y}_{i,h}$ variables (for $h \in [w_1]$) have degree at most $w_0 - 1$. They can be written as $\sum_{k=0}^{w_0-1} c_k v^k$, where v is the polynomial variable and c is the coefficient (either 0 or 1).

The $\hat{x}_{i,h}$ variables are of the form $\sum_{k=0}^{w_0-1} d_k v^{kw_0}$ (using d as the coefficient). Thus, if we multiply $\hat{x}_{i,h} * \hat{y}_{i,h}$, the result can be written as:

$$\hat{z}_{i,h} = \hat{x}_{i,h} * \hat{y}_{i,h} = \left(\sum_{k=0}^{w_0-1} d_k v^{kw_0}\right)\left(\sum_{k=0}^{w_0-1} c_k v^k\right)$$

$$= d_0\left(\sum_{k=0}^{w_0-1} c_k v^k\right) + d_1\left(\sum_{k=0}^{w_0-1} c_k v^{w_0+k}\right) + \ldots + d_{w_0-1}\left(\sum_{k=0}^{w_0-1} c_k v^{(w_0-1)w_0+k}\right)$$

$$= \left(d_0 c_0 v^0 + \ldots + d_0 c_{w_0-1} v^{w_0-1}\right)$$

$$+ \left(d_1 c_0 v^{w_0} + \ldots + d_1 c_{w_0-1} v^{2w_0-1}\right)$$

$$+ \ldots + \left(d_{w_0-1} c_0 v^{(w_0-1)w_0} + \ldots + d_{w_0-1} c_{w_0-1} v^{w_0^2-1}\right)$$

$$= \sum_{k=0}^{w_0^2-1} d_{\lfloor k/w_0 \rfloor} c_{(k \mod w_0)} v^k$$

First, notice that the degree of this polynomial is at most $w_0^2 - 1$, so by construction, this polynomial will not need to be reduced modulo the irreducible polynomial. Next, notice that the coefficient e_k of v^k can be written as $e_k = d_{\lfloor k/w_0 \rfloor} c_{(k \mod w_0)}$. But the c and d coefficients correspond to the bits of $\hat{x}_{i,h}$ and $\hat{y}_{i,h}$, which in turn correspond to the bits of x_i and y_i. So if we wish to know the AND of $c_{k'}$ and $d_{k'}$, we can look at the coefficient of v^k, for the k for which $k' = \lfloor k/w_0 \rfloor = (k \mod w_0)$, This will occur at $k = k'w_0 + k'$. Thus, each $\hat{z}_{i,h}$ can be used to find the AND of w_0 bits. For $k' \in \{0, \ldots, w_0 - 1\}$, bit $\hat{z}_{i,h}[1 + k' + k'w_0]$ is the AND of $\hat{x}_{i,h}[1 + w_0 k']$ and $\hat{y}_{i,h}[1 + k']$.

Zooming back out to z_i, we find that each bit of z_i can be found as $z_i[k] = \hat{z}_{i,\lfloor \frac{k+1}{w_0} \rfloor}[1+((k-1) \mod w_0)+w_0((k-1) \mod w_0)]$. Since the $\hat{z}_{i,h}$ variables were formed correctly from the $\hat{x}_{i,h}$ and $\hat{y}_{i,h}$ variables, which were formed correctly from x_i and y_i, z_i will be the AND of x_i and y_i for all $i \in [N]$, as desired.

Zero-knowledge: Deferred to full version [22].

Soundness: Suppose $\mathcal{P}$ is cheating, that is, there is at least one (x_i, y_i, z_i) triple for which $z_i \neq x_i \& y_i$. Without loss of generality, let $i = 1$ be an index on which the prover cheats.

If the Ligero matrix is not well-formed, **Test-Interleaved** will fail with probability at least $1 - \delta_3$; we assume this is not the case for the rest of the proof.

If $z_1 \neq x_1 \& y_1$, then one of the following must be true:

1. There exists an $h \in [w_1]$ for which $\hat{z}_{1,h} \neq \hat{x}_{1,h} * \hat{y}_{1,h}$.
2. The $\hat{x}_{1,h}$ variables were not properly formed from x_1. That is, $T_{\pi_x}[x_1, \hat{x}_{1,1}, \ldots, \hat{x}_{1,w_1}, x_1]^\perp \neq \vec{0}$. The same may be true for T_{π_y} on the y variables, or T_{π_z} on the z variables.

If the former is true, then **Test-Quadratic-Constraints-IRS** will fail with probability at least $1 - \delta_1$. If the latter is true, then either **Test-Linear-Constraints-IRS** will fail with probability at least $1 - \delta_2$, or the pattern-checking part of **Test-Pattern-Zeros-Constraints** for R_x will fail with probability at most $1/2^\kappa$. Similarly for R_y and R_z. Thus, by a Union bound, the overall protocol has soundness error $3(1/2^\kappa) + \delta_1 + \delta_2 + \delta_3$ over the verifier's coins.

References

1. Ames, S., Hazay, C., Ishai, Y., Venkitasubramaniam, M.: Ligero: lightweight sublinear arguments without a trusted setup. In: Thuraisingham, B.M., Evans, D., Malkin, T., Xu, D. (eds.) ACM CCS 2017, pp. 2087–2104. ACM Press, Dallas, TX, USA, 31 October–2 November 2017. https://doi.org/10.1145/3133956.3134104
2. Baum, C., Nof, A.: Concretely-efficient zero-knowledge arguments for arithmetic circuits and their application to lattice-based cryptography. In: Kiayias, A., Kohlweiss, M., Wallden, P., Zikas, V. (eds.) PKC 2020, Part I. LNCS, vol. 12110, pp. 495–526. Springer, Heidelberg, 4–7 May 2020, Germany, Edinburgh, UK. https://doi.org/10.1007/978-3-030-45374-9_17
3. Ben-Sasson, E., Bentov, I., Horesh, Y., Riabzev, M.: Scalable, transparent, and post-quantum secure computational integrity. Cryptology ePrint Archive, Report 2018/046 (2018). https://eprint.iacr.org/2018/046
4. Ben-Sasson, E., et al.: Zerocash: decentralized anonymous payments from bitcoin. In: 2014 IEEE Symposium on Security and Privacy, pp. 459–474. IEEE Computer Society Press, 18–21 May 2014, Berkeley, CA, USA. https://doi.org/10.1109/SP.2014.36
5. Ben-Sasson, E., Chiesa, A., Genkin, D., Tromer, E., Virza, M.: SNARKs for C: verifying program executions succinctly and in zero knowledge. In: Canetti, R., Garay, J.A. (eds.) CRYPTO 2013, Part II. LNCS, vol. 8043, pp. 90–108. Springer, Heidelberg, 18–22 August 2013, Germany, Santa Barbara, CA, USA. https://doi.org/10.1007/978-3-642-40084-1_6
6. Ben-Sasson, E., Chiesa, A., Riabzev, M., Spooner, N., Virza, M., Ward, N.P.: Aurora: transparent succinct arguments for R1CS. In: Ishai, Y., Rijmen, V. (eds.) EUROCRYPT 2019, Part I. LNCS, vol. 11476, pp. 103–128. Springer, Heidelberg, 19–23 May 2019, Darmstadt, Germany. DOI: https://doi.org/10.1007/978-3-030-17653-2_4
7. Ben-Sasson, E., Chiesa, A., Spooner, N.: Interactive oracle proofs. In: Hirt, M., Smith, A.D. (eds.) TCC 2016-B, Part II. LNCS, vol. 9986, pp. 31–60. Springer, Heidelberg, 31 October–3 November 2016, Germany, Beijing, China. https://doi.org/10.1007/978-3-662-53644-5_2
8. Ben-Sasson, E., Chiesa, A., Tromer, E., Virza, M.: Succinct non-interactive zero knowledge for a von neumann architecture. In: Fu, K., Jung, J. (eds.) USENIX Security 2014, pp. 781–796. USENIX Association, 20–22 August 2014, San Diego, CA, USA (2014)
9. Bitansky, N., Chiesa, A., Ishai, Y., Ostrovsky, R., Paneth, O.: Succinct non-interactive arguments via linear interactive proofs. In: Sahai, A. (ed.) TCC 2013. LNCS, vol. 7785, pp. 315–333. Springer, Heidelberg, Germany, Tokyo, Japan, 3–6 March 2013. https://doi.org/10.1007/978-3-642-36594-2_18
10. Bootle, J., Cerulli, A., Chaidos, P., Groth, J., Petit, C.: Efficient zero-knowledge arguments for arithmetic circuits in the discrete log setting. In: Fischlin, M., Coron, J.S. (eds.) EUROCRYPT 2016, Part II. LNCS, vol. 9666, pp. 327–357. Springer, Heidelberg, 8–12 May 2016, Germany, Vienna, Austria. https://doi.org/10.1007/978-3-662-49896-5_12
11. Chase, M., et al.: Post-quantum zero-knowledge and signatures from symmetric-key primitives. In: Thuraisingham, B.M., Evans, D., Malkin, T., Xu, D. (eds.) ACM CCS 2017, pp. 1825–1842. ACM Press, 31 October–2 November 2017, Dallas, TX, USA (2017). https://doi.org/10.1145/3133956.3133997

12. Chiesa, A., Hu, Y., Maller, M., Mishra, P., Vesely, N., Ward, N.P.: Marlin: pre-processing zkSNARKs with universal and updatable SRS. In: Canteaut, A., Ishai, Y. (eds.) EUROCRYPT 2020, Part I. LNCS, vol. 12105, pp. 738–768. Springer, Heidelberg, 10–14 May 2020, Germany, Zagreb, Croatia (2020). https://doi.org/10.1007/978-3-030-45721-1_26

13. Costello, C., et al.: Geppetto: versatile verifiable computation. In: 2015 IEEE Symposium on Security and Privacy, pp. 253–270. IEEE Computer Society Press, 17–21 May 2015, San Jose, CA, USA. https://doi.org/10.1109/SP.2015.23

14. Gabizon, A., Williamson, Z.J., Ciobotaru, O.: PLONK: permutations over Lagrange-bases for oecumenical noninteractive arguments of knowledge. Cryptology ePrint Archive, Report 2019/953 (2019). https://eprint.iacr.org/2019/953

15. Ganesh, C., Orlandi, C., Tschudi, D.: Proof-of-stake protocols for privacy-aware blockchains. In: Ishai, Y., Rijmen, V. (eds.) EUROCRYPT 2019, Part I. LNCS, vol. 11476, pp. 690–719. Springer, Heidelberg, 19–23 May 2019, Darmstadt, Germany. https://doi.org/10.1007/978-3-030-17653-2_23

16. Gennaro, R., Gentry, C., Parno, B., Raykova, M.: Quadratic span programs and succinct NIZKs without PCPs. In: Johansson, T., Nguyen, P.Q. (eds.) EUROCRYPT 2013. LNCS, vol. 7881, pp. 626–645. Springer, Heidelberg, 26–30 May 2013, Germany, Athens, Greece. https://doi.org/10.1007/978-3-642-38348-9_37

17. Gentry, C., Wichs, D.: Separating succinct non-interactive arguments from all falsifiable assumptions. In: Fortnow, L., Vadhan, S.P. (eds.) 43rd ACM STOC, pp. 99–108. ACM Press, 6–8 June 2011, San Jose, CA, USA. https://doi.org/10.1145/1993636.1993651

18. Giacomelli, I., Madsen, J., Orlandi, C.: ZKBoo: faster zero-knowledge for Boolean circuits. In: Holz, T., Savage, S. (eds.) USENIX Security 2016, pp. 1069–1083. USENIX Association, Austin, TX, USA, 10–12 August 2016

19. Goldreich, O., Micali, S., Wigderson, A.: How to play any mental game or a completeness theorem for protocols with honest majority. In: Aho, A. (ed.) 19th ACM STOC, pp. 218–229. ACM Press, 25–27 May 1987, New York City, NY, USA (1987). https://doi.org/10.1145/28395.28420

20. Groth, J.: On the size of pairing-based non-interactive arguments. In: Fischlin, M., Coron, J.S. (eds.) EUROCRYPT 2016, Part II. LNCS, vol. 9666, pp. 305–326. Springer, Heidelberg, 8–12 May 2016, Germany, Vienna, Austria (2016). https://doi.org/10.1007/978-3-662-49896-5_11

21. Groth, J., Kohlweiss, M., Maller, M., Meiklejohn, S., Miers, I.: Updatable and universal common reference strings with applications to zk-SNARKs. In: Shacham, H., Boldyreva, A. (eds.) CRYPTO 2018, Part III. LNCS, vol. 10993, pp. 698–728. Springer, Heidelberg, 19–23 August 2018, Germany, Santa Barbara, CA, USA (2018). https://doi.org/10.1007/978-3-319-96878-0_24

22. Gvili, Y., Scheffler, S., Varia, M.: BooLigero: improved sublinear zero knowledge proofs for Boolean circuits. Cryptology ePrint Archive, Report 2021/121 (2021). https://eprint.iacr.org/2021/121

23. Hoffmann, M., Klooß, M., Rupp, A.: Efficient zero-knowledge arguments in the discrete log setting, revisited. In: Cavallaro, L., Kinder, J., Wang, X., Katz, J. (eds.) ACM CCS 2019, pp. 2093–2110. ACM Press, 11–15 November 2019 (2019). https://doi.org/10.1145/3319535.3354251

24. Ishai, Y., Kushilevitz, E., Ostrovsky, R., Sahai, A.: Zero-knowledge from secure multiparty computation. In: Johnson, D.S., Feige, U. (eds.) 39th ACM STOC, pp. 21–30. ACM Press, 11–13 June 2007, San Diego, CA, USA (2007). https://doi.org/10.1145/1250790.1250794

25. Jawurek, M., Kerschbaum, F., Orlandi, C.: Zero-knowledge using garbled circuits: how to prove non-algebraic statements efficiently. In: Sadeghi, A.R., Gligor, V.D., Yung, M. (eds.) ACM CCS 2013, pp. 955–966. ACM Press, 4–8 November 2013, Berlin, Germany. https://doi.org/10.1145/2508859.2516662

26. Kalai, Y.T., Raz, R.: Interactive PCP. In: Aceto, L., Damgård, I., Goldberg, L.A., Halldórsson, M.M., Ingólfsdóttir, A., Walukiewicz, I. (eds.) ICALP 2008, Part II. LNCS, vol. 5126, pp. 536–547. Springer, Heidelberg, 7–11 July 2008, Germany, Reykjavik, Iceland (2008). https://doi.org/10.1007/978-3-540-70583-3_44

27. Kerber, T., Kohlweiss, M., Kiayias, A., Zikas, V.: Ouroboros crypsinous: Privacy-preserving proof-of-stake. Cryptology ePrint Archive, Report 2018/1132 (2018). https://eprint.iacr.org/2018/1132

28. Kilian, J.: A note on efficient zero-knowledge proofs and arguments (extended abstract). In: 24th ACM STOC, pp. 723–732. ACM Press, 4–6 May 1992, Victoria, BC, Canada (1992). https://doi.org/10.1145/129712.129782

29. Kondi, Y., Patra, A.: Privacy-free garbled circuits for formulas: size zero and information-theoretic. In: Katz, J., Shacham, H. (eds.) CRYPTO 2017, Part I. LNCS, vol. 10401, pp. 188–222. Springer, Heidelberg, 20–24 August 2017, Germany, Santa Barbara, CA, USA (2017). DOI: https://doi.org/10.1007/978-3-319-63688-7_7

30. Lipmaa, H.: Succinct non-interactive zero knowledge arguments from span programs and linear error-correcting codes. In: Sako, K., Sarkar, P. (eds.) ASIACRYPT 2013, Part I. LNCS, vol. 8269, pp. 41–60. Springer, Heidelberg, 1–5 December 2013, Germany, Bengalore, India (2013). https://doi.org/10.1007/978-3-642-42033-7_3

31. Maller, M., Bowe, S., Kohlweiss, M., Meiklejohn, S.: Sonic: zero-knowledge SNARKs from linear-size universal and updatable structured reference strings. In: Cavallaro, L., Kinder, J., Wang, X., Katz, J. (eds.) ACM CCS 2019, pp. 2111–2128. ACM Press, 11–15 November 2019. https://doi.org/10.1145/3319535.3339817

32. Miers, I., Garman, C., Green, M., Rubin, A.D.: Zerocoin: anonymous distributed E-cash from Bitcoin. In: 2013 IEEE Symposium on Security and Privacy, pp. 397–411. IEEE Computer Society Press, 19–22 May 2013, Berkeley, CA, USA (2013). https://doi.org/10.1109/SP.2013.34

33. Parno, B., Howell, J., Gentry, C., Raykova, M.: Pinocchio: nearly practical verifiable computation. In: 2013 IEEE Symposium on Security and Privacy, pp. 238–252. IEEE Computer Society Press, 19–22 May 2013, Berkeley, CA, USA (2013). https://doi.org/10.1109/SP.2013.47

34. Setty, S.: Spartan: Efficient and general-purpose zkSNARKs without trusted setup. In: Micciancio, D., Ristenpart, T. (eds.) CRYPTO 2020, Part III. LNCS, vol. 12172, pp. 704–737. Springer, Heidelberg, 17–21 August 2020, Germany, Santa Barbara, CA, USA (2020). https://doi.org/10.1007/978-3-030-56877-1_25

35. Venkitasubramaniam, M.: Personal communication, September 2020

36. Wahby, R.S., Tzialla, I., Shelat, A., Thaler, J., Walfish, M.: Doubly-efficient zkSNARKs without trusted setup. In: 2018 IEEE Symposium on Security and Privacy, pp. 926–943. IEEE Computer Society Press, 21–23 May 2018, San Francisco, CA, USA. https://doi.org/10.1109/SP.2018.00060

37. Weng, C., Yang, K., Katz, J., Wang, X.: Wolverine: fast, scalable, and communication-efficient zero-knowledge proofs for Boolean and arithmetic circuits. Cryptology ePrint Archive, Report 2020/925 (2020). https://eprint.iacr.org/2020/925

38. Xie, T., Zhang, J., Zhang, Y., Papamanthou, C., Song, D.: Libra: succinct zero-knowledge proofs with optimal prover computation. In: Boldyreva, A., Micciancio, D. (eds.) CRYPTO 2019, Part III. LNCS, vol. 11694, pp. 733–764. Springer, Heidelberg, 18–22 August 2019, Germany, Santa Barbara, CA, USA (2019). https://doi.org/10.1007/978-3-030-26954-8_24

Mining for Privacy: How to Bootstrap a Snarky Blockchain

Thomas Kerber[✉], Aggelos Kiayias, and Markulf Kohlweiss

The University of Edinburgh and IOHK, Edinburgh, Scotland
papers@tkerber.org, {akiayias,mkohlwei}@ed.ac.uk

Abstract. Non-interactive zero-knowledge proofs, and more specifically succinct non-interactive zero-knowledge arguments (zk-SNARKs), have been proven to be the "Swiss army knife" of the blockchain and distributed ledger space, with a variety of applications in privacy, interoperability and scalability. Many commonly used SNARK systems rely on a *structured reference string*, the secure generation of which turns out to be their Achilles heel: If the randomness used for the generation is known, the soundness of the proof system can be broken with devastating consequences for the underlying blockchain system that utilises them. In this work we describe and analyse, for the first time, a blockchain mechanism that produces a secure SRS with the characteristic that security is shown under comparable conditions to the blockchain protocol itself. Our mechanism makes use of the recent discovery of *updateable* structured reference strings to perform this secure generation in a fully distributed manner. In this way, the SRS emanates from the normal operation of the blockchain protocol itself without the need of additional security assumptions or off-chain computation and/or verification. We provide concrete guidelines for the parameterisation of this setup which allows for the completion of a secure setup in a reasonable period of time. We also provide an incentive scheme that, when paired with the update mechanism, properly incentivises participants into contributing to secure reference string generation.

1 Introduction

In the domain of distributed ledgers, non-interactive zero-knowledge proofs have many interesting applications. In particular, they have been successfully used to introduce privacy into these inherently public peer-to-peer systems. Most notably, Zerocash [2] demonstrates their usefulness in the creation of private currencies. Beyond this, there are numerous suggestions [21,25,29] to apply the same technology to smart contracts for increased privacy. Beyond privacy, other applications of zero knowledge include blockchain interoperability, e.g., [17], and scalability, e.g., [9].

For the practical efficiency of these designs, two things are paramount: The succinctness of proofs, and the speed of verifying these proofs. The distributed

© International Financial Cryptography Association 2021
N. Borisov and C. Diaz (Eds.): FC 2021, LNCS 12674, pp. 497–514, 2021.
https://doi.org/10.1007/978-3-662-64322-8_24

nature of the ledgers mandates that a large number of users store and verify each proof made, rendering many zero-knowledge proof systems not fit for purpose.

Research into so-called zk-SNARKs [18–20, 26, 27] aims at optimising exactly these features, with proof sizes typically under a kilobyte, and verification times in the milliseconds. It is a well-known fact that non-interactive zero-knowledge requires some shared randomness, or a *common reference string*. For many succinct systems [18–20, 26, 27], a stronger property is necessary: Not only is a shared random value needed, but it must adhere to a specific *structure*. Such structured reference strings (or SRS) typically consist of related group elements: g^{x^i} for all $i \in \mathbb{Z}_n$, for instance.

The obvious way of sampling such a reference string from public randomness reveals the exponents used – and knowledge of these values breaks the soundness of the proof system itself. To make matters worse, the security of these systems typically relies (among others) on *knowledge of exponent* assumptions, which state that to create group elements related in such a way *requires* knowing the underlying exponents and hence any SRS sampler will have to "know" the exponents used and be trusted to erase them, becoming effectively a single point of failure for the underlying system. While secure multi-party computation can be, and has been, used to reduce the trust placed on such a setup process [31], the selection of the participants for the secure computation and the verification of the generation of the SRS by the MPC protocol retain an element of centralisation. Using an MPC setup remains a controversial element in the setup of a decentralised system that requires SNARKs.

Recent work has found succinct zero-knowledge proof systems with *updateable* reference strings [19, 26]. In these systems, given a reference string, it is possible to produce an updated reference string, such that knowing the trapdoor of the new string requires both knowing the trapdoor of the old string, *and* knowing the randomness used in the update. [19] conjectured that a blockchain protocol may be used to securely generate such a reference string. Nevertheless, the exact blockchain mechanism that produces the SRS and the description of the security guarantees it can offer has, so far, remained elusive.

1.1   Our Contributions

In this work we describe and analyse, for the first time, a blockchain mechanism that produces a secure SRS with the characteristic that security is shown for similar conditions under which the blockchain protocol is proven to be secure. Notably different, we make implicit use of secure erasure, and require honest majority only during a specific initialisation period. The SRS then emanates from the normal operation of the blockchain protocol itself without the need of additional security assumptions or off-chain computation and/or verification.

We rely primarily on the *chain quality* property of "Nakamoto-style" ledgers [14] – distributed ledgers in which a randomised process selects which user may append a block to an already established chain. Such ledgers rely on an honest majority of hashing power (or some other resource) – and can be shown to guarantee a chain quality property which suggests that any sufficiently long chain segment will have some blocks created by an honest user, cf. [14,15,28].

Our construction, described in Sect. 3 integrates reference string updates into the block creation process, but we face additional difficulties due to update calculation being a computationally heavy operation (albeit, contrary to brute-force hashing, useful). The issues arising from this are two fold. Firstly, an adversarial party can take shortcuts by supplying a low amount of entropy in their updates, and try to utilise this additional mining power to subvert the reference string which potentially has a large benefit for the adversary. Secondly, even non-colluding rational block creators may be incentivised to use bad randomness which would reduce or remove any security benefits of the updates. Our work addresses both of these issues.

We prove formally that our mechanism produces a secure reference string in the full version of this paper [22, Appendix F] by providing an analysis in the universal composition framework [10]. Furthermore, the full version of this paper [22, Section 4] demonstrates via experimental analysis how to concretely parameterise a proof-of-work ledger to ensure that an adversary which takes shortcuts (while honest users do not) will still fail in subverting the reference string. The concrete results provided in our experimental section can be used to inform the selection of parameters in order to run our reference string generation mechanism in live blockchain systems.

We further introduce an incentive scheme in Sect. 4, which ensures that rational participants in the protocol, who intend to maximise their profits, will avoid low-entropy attacks. In short, the incentive mechanism mandates that a random fraction of update contributors in the final chain will be asked to reveal their trapdoor, which will be verified to be the output of a random oracle by the underlying ledger rules. Only if a user can demonstrate that their update is indeed random do they receive a suitably determined reward for their effort. Careful choice of the reward assignment enables us to demonstrate that rational participants will utilise high entropy exponents, thus contributing to the SRS computation.

1.2   Related Work

Beyond the obvious relation to the works introducing updateable reference strings in [19,26] (most notably Sonic [26], which we follow closely in our instantiation in the full version of this paper [22, Appendix A]), there have been attempts of practically answering the question of how to securely generate reference strings. These have been in a setting where the string is *not* updateable.

Notably [5] describes the mechanism used by Sprout, the first version of Zcash, during the initial setup of the cryptocurrency's SRS. It uses multi-party computation to generate a reference string, with a root of trust on the initial group of people participating. Due to performance constraints on the MPC protocol, the set of parties participating is relatively small, although only the honesty of a single participating party is required.

For the Sapling version of Zcash, a different approach was used when their reference string was replaced (due to an upgrade of the zero-knowledge statement, and proof system used). Their second CRS generation mechanism, described in [6] uses a multiple-phase round-robin mechanism to generate a reference string for Groth's zk-SNARK [18]. They utilise a random beacon to ensure the uniform distribution of the result, and a coordinator to perform deterministic auxiliary computations.

A great deal of work has also gone into the design of non-interactive zero-knowledge which does not require structure in it's references, such as DARK [8], STARKs [1], and Bulletproofs [7]. While these pose a promising alternative which does not require the techniques used in this work, leveraging updatability of reference strings may permit greater efficiency without additional security assumptions, and may be useful in instantiating generic constructions, such as the polynomial commitments-based Halo Infinite [3].

2   Updateable Structured Reference Strings

While updateable structured reference strings (uSRSs) are modelled in the works we are building on [26, Section 3.2], we model their security in the setting of universal composability (UC) [10]. Here, a uSRS is a reference string with an underlying trapdoor τ, which has had a structure function S imposed on it. $S(\tau)$ is the reference string itself, while τ is not revealed to the adversary. In the full version of this paper [22, Appendix A], we prove that Sonic [26] (with small modifications for extraction, as described in Subsect. 2.2), satisfies all the properties we require in this section. Our main proof is independent of the Sonic protocol however, and applies to any updateable reference string scheme satisfying the properties laid out in the rest of this section.

2.1   Standard Requirements

A uSRS scheme S consists of a trapdoor domain T, an initial trapdoor τ_0, a set P of permissible (and invertible) permutations over T (i.e. bijective functions whose domain and codomain is T), and a structure function S with the domain T. We require P to include the identity function id, and to be closed under function composition: $\forall p_1, p_2 \in P : p_1 \circ p_2 \in P$. An efficient permutation lifting † should exist, such that for any permutation $p \in P$ and $\tau \in T$, $p^{\dagger}(S(\tau)) = S(p(\tau))$. Finally, there must exist algorithms $\rho \leftarrow \mathrm{ProveUpd}(S(\tau), p)$ and $b \leftarrow \mathrm{VerifyUpd}(S(\tau), \rho, S(p(\tau)))$ for creating and verifying update proofs respectively. The format of these update proofs is not specified, however the following constraints must be met:

1. **Correctness.** Applying an honestly generated update proof will verify: $\forall p \in P, \tau \in T : \mathrm{VerifyUpd}(S(\tau), \mathrm{ProveUpd}(S(\tau), p), S(p(\tau)))$.
2. **Structure preservation.** Applying *any* valid update is equivalent to applying *some* permutation $p \in P$ on the trapdoor: $\forall \rho, \tau, \mathrm{srs}' : \mathrm{VerifyUpd}(S(\tau), \rho, \mathrm{srs}') \implies \exists p \in P : \mathrm{srs}' = S(p(\tau))$.

3. **Update uniformity.** Applying a random permutation is equivalent to selecting a new random trapdoor: Let D be the uniform distribution over T, and for all $\tau \in T$, let D_τ be the uniform distribution over the multiset $\{ p(\tau) \mid p \in P \}$. Then $\forall \tau \in T : D = D_\tau$.

We define a corresponding UC functionality $\mathcal{F}_{\text{uSRS}}$, which provides a reference string $S(p(\tau_{\mathcal{H}}))$, which the adversary can influence by providing the permutation $p \in P$, given only $S(\tau_{\mathcal{H}})$ as input, for a randomly sampled $\tau_{\mathcal{H}} \in T$.

Functionality $\mathcal{F}_{\text{uSRS}}$

The updateable structured reference string functionality $\mathcal{F}_{\text{uSRS}}$ allows the adversary to update a reference string by applying a permutation from a set of permissible permutations P.

  The functionality is parameterised by a trapdoor domain T, a structure function S, and a set of permissible permutations P over T.

State variables and initialisation values.

Variable	Description
$\tau_{\mathcal{H}} := \bot$	The honest part of the trapdoor
$\tau := \bot$	The trapdoor

When receiving a message HONEST-SRS *from $\mathcal{A}$:*

  if $\tau_{\mathcal{H}} = \bot$ **then let** $\tau_{\mathcal{H}} \xleftarrow{R} T$
  return $S(\tau_{\mathcal{H}})$

When receiving a message SRS *from a party ϕ:*

  query $\mathcal{A}$ **with** (PERMUTE, ϕ) **and receive the reply** p
  if $\tau = \bot$ **then**
      assert $p \in P \wedge \tau_{\mathcal{H}} \neq \bot$
      let $\tau \leftarrow p(\tau_{\mathcal{H}})$
  return $S(\tau)$

We believe this functionality to be of independent interest, and it is not explicitly tied to our implementation. Notably, while we use a distributed ledger as a weak form of a broadcast channel, other broadcasts can be considered without modification to this functionality. While, as presented, the functionality does not dictate any specific usage, we conjecture that when parameterised with an appropriate structure function and permutation set it can be used to securely instantiate updateable SRS-based SNARKs, such as Sonic [26], Marlin [11], or Plonk [13]. Due to the UC setting, this would require additional lifting to enable UC knowledge extraction, such as that of C∅C∅ [24].

2.2 Simulation Requirements

In addition to the basic properties of correctness, structure preservation, and update uniformity, any simulator wishing to help realise $\mathcal{F}_{\text{uSRS}}$ via updates will need to have access to two additional properties:

1. **Update proof simulation.** From an initial SRS $S(\tau)$ for which the simulator knows the trapdoor, it can produce a valid update to any (correctly structured) SRS. Formally: $\exists S_\rho \forall \tau_1, \tau_2 \in T$: VerifyUpd$(S(\tau_1),$ $S_\rho(\tau_1, S(\tau_2)), S(\tau_2))$, where S_ρ is a PPT algorithm.
2. **Permutation extraction.** The simulator must be capable of extracting the permutation p underlying any valid adversarial update proof.

The most natural method to achieve permutation extraction would be using white-box extractors, as the updates themselves typically rely on some form of knowledge assumption, such as knowledge-of-exponent. However, white-box extractors cannot be used in UC proofs. Instead, we will assume that the update proof is proven to correspond to a specific trapdoor through a lower-level NIZK. Crucially, this lower-level NIZK should not require a *structured* reference string, and rely only on a common random string, or a random oracle. Fortunately, it is not subject to stringent efficiency requirements as the full version of this paper [22, Section 4] demonstrates.

Specifically, we assume that the basic update proof ρ is a statement in a NIZK relation $\mathcal{R}$ where the witness is an encoding of the corresponding permutation p. We require each update proof to have one and only one corresponding permutation, formally expressed by requiring $\mathcal{R}$ to be a bijection. This results in a straightforward modification to the ProveUpd and VerifyUpd algorithms that permits the extraction of the underlying permutations even in the UC setting: ProveUpd also creates a NIZK proof π of (ρ, p), and returns (ρ, π), While VerifyUpd returns true only if this newly embedded NIZK proof also verifies.

The addition of this NIZK trivially preserves all security properties including correctness, due to the definition of $\mathcal{R}$:

Definition 1. *A uSRS scheme is permutation extractable if the relation*

$$\mathcal{R} := \{(\text{ProveUpd}(S(\tau), p), p) \mid \tau \in T, p \in P\}$$

is a bijection, and in NP.

We show in [22, Appendix A] that the relation required for the case of Sonic [26] can be efficiently constructed, and leave the question of how to achieve extraction without the reliance on a further NIZK to future work.

3   Building uSRS from Chain Quality

This section shows how to securely initialise a uSRS using a distributed ledger by requiring block creators to perform updates on an evolving uSRS during an initial setup period. After waiting for agreement on the final uSRS, it can be safely used. To formally model this approach, we discuss the ideal and real worlds used in our simulation proof. Both worlds have access to a ledger, however the ideal world's ledger is independent of the reference string (which is instead provided by the independent $\mathcal{F}_{\text{uSRS}}$ functionality), while the real world's ledger is programmed to generate it using updates.

3.1   High-Level Overview

This basic premise of this paper relies on Nakamoto-style ledgers' basic means of operation: Different users can extend a chain of blocks if they can satisfy some condition, with this condition being associated with a type of hardness which ensures attackers are limited in the number of extensions they can perform. Given such a structure, we associate a uSRS update with each block prior to a time δ_1. This time is selected such that the security properties of the ledger ensure at least one of the blocks is honest in each competitive chain at this point.

In our modelling, we construct this from a ledger functionality with an additional *leadership state*, which is derived from information miners embed in their blocks. Specifically for our case, these encode uSRS updates. We leave this sufficiently general to allow other uses as well. The basic idea is to show that a ledger which performs uSRS updates in its leadership state is equivalent to one which doesn't, but is accompanied by the $\mathcal{F}_{\mathrm{uSRS}}$ functionality. They make up our real and ideal worlds respectively. After time δ_1, users wait a further time period δ_2 until common prefix ensures that all parties agree on the reference string.

While ledger functionalities are often treated as global, our approach effectively constructs one ledger from another – the ledger is not a dependency of our protocol, but a component. In this context, globality is irrelevant, as the environment already has direct access to the functionality. We expect protocols building on the ledger to use it in a global fashion, however. The same is not true for the uSRS – most usages will likely rely on the simulator being able to extract its trapdoor.

3.2   Our Ledger Abstraction

Our construction of the updateable structured reference string functionality relies heavily on the properties of *common prefix*, *chain quality*, and *chain growth* defined in the "Bitcoin backbone" analysis by Garay et al. [14], for Nakamoto-style consensus algorithms. Despite our use in the section title, we make use of all three properties, not just that of chain quality. We emphasise chain quality, as it is the property central to ensuring an honest update has occurred. We briefly and informally restate the three properties:

- **Common prefix.** Given the current chains Π_1 and Π_2 of two parties, and removing k blocks from the first, it is a prefix of the second: $\Pi_1^{\lceil k} \prec \Pi_2$.
- **Chain quality.** For any party's current chain Π, any consecutive l blocks in this chain will include μ blocks created by an honest party.
- **Chain growth.** If a party's chain is of length c, then s time slots later, it will be at least of length $c + \gamma$.

These parameters determine the length of the two phases of our protocol. In the first phase, we construct the reference string itself from the liveness parameter (assuming $\mu \geq 1$), and in the second phase, we wait until this reference string has propagated to all users. The length of the first phase is at least $\delta_1 \geq \lceil l\gamma^{-1} \rceil s$, and that of the second at least $\delta_2 \geq \lceil k\gamma^{-1} \rceil s$. Combined, they make up the total uSRS generation delay $\delta \geq (\lceil l\gamma^{-1} \rceil + \lceil k\gamma^{-1} \rceil)s$.

We assume a ledger which guarantees the backbone properties. While we do not prove any specific existing proof-of-work ledger (or those based on a different leader-selection mechanism) formally UC-realise this specific formalisation, we argue all ledgers with "Nakamoto-style" (as opposed to BFT-style) consensus do so.. Both ledger and argument are presented in the full version of this paper [22, Appendix B]. Our functionality further depends on a *global clock* $\mathcal{G}_{\text{clock}}$, defined in [22, Appendix E.1]. For the purposes of this paper, it is sufficient that this is a beacon providing monotonically increasing values representing the current time to any party requesting them.

In addition to this, we assume each block created can contain additional information, provided by its creator (the "miner"), which can be aggregated to construct a "leader state". Each created block is associated with an *update a*, and the ledger is parameterised by two procedures, Gen, and Apply, which describe the honest selection of updates, and the semantics of updates respectively. Looking forward, these utilise ProveUpd and VerifyUpd internally, although the formalism is sufficiently general to allow usage of the leader state for other, parallel purposes. The exact parameters differ in our ideal and real world, with the ideal world "hiding" the uSRS updates. Additionally, the real world adds time-sensitivity: It does nothing to the SRS after the setup period. Gen is randomised, takes a leader state σ and the current time t as inputs, and produces an update a. Apply takes a leader state σ, an update a, and an update time t, and returns a successor state σ': $\sigma' = \text{Apply}(\sigma, (a, t))$. For a chain, the leader state may be computed by sequentially applying all updates in the chain, starting from an initial state $\varnothing$.

The adversary controls when and which party creates a new block, as well as the transactions each new block contains (provided it does not violate the backbone properties). For transactions created by a corrupted party, the adversary can further control the block's timestamp (within the reasonable limits of not being in the future, and being after the previous block), and the desired update a itself. For honest parties updates, Gen is used instead.

The UC interfaces our ledger provides are:

- SUBMIT. Submitting new transactions for the ledger.
- READ. Reading the confirmed sequence of transactions.
- PROJECTION. Reading the current chain's sequence of (potentially unconfirmed) transactions.
- LEADER-STATE. Reading the confirmed leader state.
- ADVANCE. The adversary switches a party to a longer chain.
- EXTEND. The adversary instructs a party to create a block.

While this ledger abstraction is not the focus of this paper, we believe it to be of independent interest in cases where finer control over miner's actions, or better access to the competing chains is desired.

3.3 The Ideal World

Our ideal world consists of two functionalities, composed in parallel (by which we mean: the environment may address either, and they do not interact). The first is a variant of $\mathcal{F}_{\text{uSRS}}$, with the modification that it cannot be addressed by honest parties before δ time slots have passed. Formally, this modification is made with a wrapper functionality $\mathcal{W}_{\text{delay}}(\mathcal{F}, \delta)$, described in [22, Appendix E.4].

The second is the Nakamoto-style ledger functionality, parameterised with arbitrary leader-state generation and application procedures which are also partially used in the hybrid world: Gen = GenIdeal and Apply = ApplyIdeal, and the following ledger parameters:

1. A common prefix parameter k.
2. Chain quality parameters μ and l.
3. Chain growth parameters γ and s.

Formally then, our ideal world consists of the pair $(\mathcal{W}_{\text{delay}}(\delta, \mathcal{F}_{\text{uSRS}}), \mathcal{F}_{\text{nakLedger}}^{\text{ideal}})$, as well as the global functionality $\mathcal{G}_{\text{clock}}$.

3.4 The Hybrid World

In our hybrid world, we use a uSRS scheme $\mathcal{S}$, with algorithms ProveUpd, VerifyUpd, the structure function S, permissible permutations P, permutation lifting $\dagger$, initial trapdoor τ_0. The hybrid world consists of a separate Nakamoto-style ledger $\mathcal{F}_{\text{nakLedger}}^{\text{real}}$, a NIZK functionality $\mathcal{F}_{\text{NIZK}}^{\mathcal{R}}$, and the global clock $\mathcal{G}_{\text{clock}}$. The ledger is then parameterised by the same chain parameters as those in the ideal world, and the following leader-state procedures:

> **procedure** Apply$((\text{srs}, \sigma^{\text{ideal}}), ((\text{srs}', \rho, \pi, a^{\text{ideal}}), t))$
>   **if** srs $= \varnothing$ **then let** srs $\leftarrow S(\tau_0)$
>   **if** $t \leq \delta_1 \wedge$ VerifyUpd(srs, ρ, srs$'$) **then**
>   **send** (VERIFY, ρ, π) **to** $\mathcal{F}_{\text{NIZK}}^{\mathcal{R}}$ **and receive the reply** b
>   **if** b **then**
>   **let** srs $\leftarrow$ srs$'$
>   **return** (srs, ApplyIdeal($\sigma^{\text{ideal}}, a^{\text{ideal}}, t$))
> **procedure** Gen$((\text{srs}, \sigma^{\text{ideal}}), t)$
>   **if** $t > \delta_1$ **then**
>   **return** $(\epsilon, \epsilon, \epsilon, \text{GenIdeal}(\sigma^{\text{ideal}}, t))$
>   **else**
>   **let** $p \xleftarrow{R} P; \rho \leftarrow$ ProveUpd(srs, p)
>   **send** (PROVE, ρ, p) **to** $\mathcal{F}_{\text{NIZK}}^{\mathcal{R}}$ **and receive the reply** π
>   **return** $(p^\dagger(\text{srs}), \rho, \pi, \text{GenIdeal}(\sigma^{\text{ideal}}, t))$

Note that these parameterising algorithms use $\mathcal{F}_{\text{NIZK}}^{\mathcal{R}}$, and are therefore the reason the ledger depends on this hybrid functionality.

Key here is that once a block is received after the initial chain quality period, any reference string update it may declare is no longer carried out – at this point the uSRS is not necessarily stable, as the chain may still be reorganised, but should not change for this particular chain. Further, these procedures always mimic the ideal-world behaviour, extending it rather than replacing it. This demonstrates the composability of allowing block leaders to produce updates: One system using updates for security does not impact other parallel uses of the leadership state.

There is little additional work to be done to UC-emulate the ideal-world behaviour, besides ensuring that queries are routed appropriately, especially how the reference string is queried in the hybrid world. We describe this with a small "adaptor" protocol in the full version of this paper [22, Appendix C], LEDGER-ADAPTOR. This forwards most queries, and treats uSRS queries as querying the appropriate part of the leader state after time δ, and by ignoring them before. Formally, our real world consists of the global clock $\mathcal{G}_{\text{clock}}$, and the system LEDGER-ADAPTOR$(\delta, \mathcal{F}^{\text{real}}_{\text{nakLedger}}(\mathcal{F}^{\mathcal{R}}_{\text{NIZK}}))$.

3.5   Alternative Usage of $\mathcal{G}_{\text{clock}}$

In both worlds, $\mathcal{G}_{\text{clock}}$ is used to determine the cutoff point after which the reference string is deemed secure. A simple alternative to this usage of the clock is to instead rely on the length of the chain for this purpose. We did not make this choice as it complicates the ideal world: The delay wrapper would have to communicate with the ideal world ledger, and query it for the length of parties' chains. We do not regard a clock as a significant additional assumption, however little of the remainder of this paper differs if chain lengths are used instead. Even in this case, a clock is present to guarantee liveness, although it is used only to constrain the adversary.

3.6   UC Emulation

Our security is derived through UC-emulation, stated in the following theorem:

Theorem 1. *For any updateable reference string scheme $\mathcal{S}$, satisfying correctness, structure preservation, update uniformity, update simulation with $\mathcal{S}_\rho$, and permutation extraction, LEDGER-ADAPTOR (in the $(\mathcal{F}^{\text{real}}_{\text{nakLedger}}, \mathcal{F}^{\mathcal{R}}_{\text{NIZK}})$-hybrid world, parameterised as in Subsect. 3.4) UC-emulates the pair of functionalities $(\mathcal{F}^{\text{ideal}}_{\text{nakLedger}}, \mathcal{W}_{\text{delay}}(\delta, \mathcal{F}_{\text{uSRS}}))$, parameterised as in Subsect. 3.3, in the presence of the global clock functionality $\mathcal{G}_{\text{clock}}$, with the simulator $\mathcal{S}_{\text{LEDGER-ADAPTOR}}$.*

A full security proof and simulator may be found in the full version of this paper [22, Appendix F & D].

4   Low-Entropy Update Mitigation

While our analysis indicates that in a Byzantine, honest majority setting, our protocol produces a trustworthy reference string, it also asks participants to dedicate computational resources to updates. It follows that in a rational setting, players need to be properly incentivised to follow the protocol. We emphasise that the rational setting is not the focus of this paper, and optimistically, in a setting where the majority of miners are rational and a small fraction honest, the few honest blocks are sufficient to eliminate the issue described in this section.

For Sonic, a protocol deviation exists that breaks the security of the reference string: By choosing the exponent in a specific low-entropy fashion, (e.g., $y = 2^l$) the computation of the update, which primarily relies on repeated squaring, can be done significantly faster. More generally, some permutations in P may be more efficiently computable. In more detail, instead of using a random permutation p, a specific choice is made that eases the computation of srs′ – in the most extreme case, for any uSRS scheme, the update for $p =$ id is trivial.

4.1   Proposed Construction

In order to facilitate a mitigation for this class of attacks, we will need to assume an additional property of the underlying ledger, in particular it must provide a "resettable" randomness beacon: With each ADVANCE operation (where adversary must be restricted in how often it may do such ADVANCE queries), a random beacon value is sampled in a variable bcn and is associated with the corresponding block. Beacons of this kind are often easily available, for instance by hashing the proof-of-work [4], and are inherent in many proof-of-stake designs. Prior work [12] demonstrates that such beacon values allow for the adversary to bias them only by "resetting" it at most a certain number of times, say t, before they are fixed by entering the ledger's confirmed state, with the exact value of t depending on the chain parameters.

We can then amend Gen to derive its random values from the random oracle, by sending the query (bcn, nonce) to $\mathcal{F}_{RO}$, where nonce is a randomly selected nonce, and bcn is the previous block's beacon value. The response is used to index the set of trapdoor permutations P, choosing the result p, and the nonce is stored by miners locally, and kept private. We adapt the Phase 1 period δ_1 so that at least $l' := l(1 - \theta)^{-1} + c$ blocks will be produced, where θ and c are new security parameters (to be discussed below). Next, after Phase 2 ends, we can be sure that the beacon value associated with the end of Phase 1 has been reset at most t times.

We extract from bcn l' biased coins, each with probability θ. For each block, if the corresponding coin is 1, it is required to reveal its randomness within a period of time at least as long as the liveness parameter. Specifically, a party which created one of the selected blocks may reveal its nonce. If its update matches this nonce, the party receives an additional reward of value R times the standard block reward.

While this requires a stricter chain quality property, with the ledger functionality instead enforcing that one of these l non-opened updates are honest, we sketch why this property still holds in the next section.

4.2 Security Intuition

Consider now a rational miner with hashing power α. We know that, at best, using an underlying blockchain like Bitcoin, the relative rewards such a miner may expect are at most $\alpha/(1 - \alpha)$ in expectation; this assumes a selfish mining strategy that wins all network races against the other rational participants. Now consider a miner who uses low entropy exponents to save on computational power on created blocks and, as a result, boosts their hashing power α to an increased relative hashing power of $\alpha' > \alpha$. The attacker can further try to influence the blockchain by forking and selectively disclosing blocks which has the effect of resetting the bcn value to a preferred one. To see that the impact of this is minimal, we prove the following lemma.

Lemma 1. *Consider a mapping $\rho \mapsto \{0,1\}^{l'}$ that generates l' independent biased coin flips, each with probability θ, when ρ is uniformly selected. Consider any fixed $n \leq l'$ positions and suppose an adversary gets to choose any one out of t independent draws of the mapping's random input with the intention to increase the number of successes in the n positions. The probability of obtaining more than $n(1 + \epsilon)\theta$ successes is $\exp(-\Omega(\epsilon^2 \theta n) + \ln t)$.*

Proof. In case $t = 1$, result follows from a Chernoff bound on the event E defined as obtaining more than $n(1+\epsilon)\theta$ successes, and has probability $\exp(-\Omega(\epsilon^2\theta n))$. Given that each reset is an independent draw of the same experiment, by applying a union bound we obtain the lemma's statement. □

The optimal strategy of a miner utilising low-entropy attacks is to minimise the number of blocks of other miners are chosen, to increase its relative reward. Lemma 1 demonstrates that at most a factor of $(1+\epsilon)^{-1}$ damage can be done in this way. Regardless of whether a miner utilises low-entropy attacks or not, their optimal strategy beyond this is selfish mining, in the low-entropy attack mining in expectation $l'\alpha'/(1 - \alpha')$ blocks [14]. A rational miner utilising low-entropy attacks will not gain any additional rewards, while a miner not doing so will gain at least $l'\alpha/(1-\alpha)(1+\epsilon)^{-1}\theta R$ rewards from revealing their randomness, by Lemma 1. It follows that for a rational miner, this strategy can be advantageous to plain selfish mining only in case:

$$\frac{\alpha'}{1 - \alpha'} > (1 + \theta(1 + \epsilon)^{-1}R)\frac{\alpha}{1 - \alpha}$$

If we assume a miner can increase their effective hash rate by a factor of c, using low-entropy exponents, then their advantage in the low entropy case is $\alpha' = \alpha c/(\alpha c + \beta)$, where $\beta = 1 - \alpha$ is the relative mining power of all other miners. If follows that the miner benefits if and only if:

$$\frac{\alpha c}{\alpha c + \beta} \cdot \frac{\alpha c + \beta}{\beta} > (1 + \theta(1 + \epsilon)^{-1}R)\frac{\alpha}{\beta}$$
$$\iff c > 1 + \theta(1 + \epsilon)^{-1}R$$

If we adopt a sufficiently large intended time interval between blocks it is possible to bound the relative savings of a selfish miner using low-entropy exponents;

following the parameterisation of the full version's simulation [22, Section 4.2], if a selfish miner using such exponents can improve their hashing power by at most a multiplicative factor c then we can mitigate such attack by setting R to $(c-1)/(\theta(1+\epsilon)^{-1})$.

5 Discussion

While the clean generation of a new reference string from a ledger protocol is itself useful, real-world situations are likely to be more complex. In this section we discuss practical adjustments that may be made.

5.1 Upgrading Reference Strings

As distributed ledgers are typically long-lived, and may well outlive any reference string used within it – or have been running before a reference string was needed. Indeed, the Zcash protocol has seen upgrades in its reference string. A reference string being replaced with a new one is innocuous without further context, however it is important to consider how they are usually used in zero-knowledge proofs. If the proof they are used in is stateless, upgrading from an insecure to a secure reference string behaves as one may naively expect: It ensures that after the upgrade, security properties hold.

In the example of Zcash, which runs a variant of the Zerocash [2] protocol, the situation is more muddy. Zerocash makes *stateful* zero-knowledge proofs. Suppose a user is sceptical of the security of the initial setup – and there is good reason to be [30] – but is convinced the second reference string is secure. Is such a user able to use Zcash with confidence in its security?

Had Zcash not had safeguards in place, the answer would be no. While the protocol may operate as intended currently, and the user can be convinced of that, due to the stateful nature of the proofs, the user cannot be convinced of the correctness of this state. The Zcash cryptocurrency did employ similar safeguards to those we outline below. We stress the importance of such here, as not every project may have the same foresight.

Specifically, for a Zerocash-based system, an original reference string's backdoor could have been used to create mismatched transactions, and to effectively "mint" large coins illicitly. This process is undetectable at the time, and the minted coins would persist across a reference string upgrade. Our fictitious user may therefore be rightfully suspicious as to the value of any coins he is sold – they may be a part of an almost infinite pool!

Such an attack, once carried out (especially against a currency) is hard to recover from – it is impossible to identify "legitimate" owners of the currency, even if the private transaction history were deanonymised, and the culprit identified. The culprit may have traded whatever he created already. Simply invalidating the transaction would therefore harm those he traded with, not himself. In an extreme case, if he traded one-to-one with legitimate owners of the currency, he would succeed in effectively stealing the honest users funds. If such an attack is identified, the community has two unfortunate options: Annul the funds of potentially legitimate users, or accept a potentially large amount of inflation.

We may assume a less grim scenario however: Suppose we are *reasonably confident* in the security of our old reference string, but we are *more confident* of the new one. Is it possible to convince users that we have genuinely upgraded our security? We suggest the usage of a type of *firewalling* property. Such properties are common in the domain of cross-chain transfers [17], and are designed to prevent a catastrophic failure on one chain damaging another.

For monetary transfers, the firewall would guarantee an upper-bound of funds was not exceeded. Proving the firewall property is preserved is easy if a small loss of privacy is accepted – each private coin being re-minted before it can be used after the upgrade, during which time its value must be declared. Assuming everything operates fine, and the firewall property is not violated, users interacting with the post-firewall state can be confident as to the upper bound of funds available. Further, attacks on the system can be identified: If an attacker mints too many coins, eventually the firewall property will be violated, indicating that too many coins were in circulation – bringing the question of how to handle this situation with it. We believe that a firewall property does however give peace of mind to users of the system, and is a practical means to assuage concerns about the security of a system which once had a questionable reference string.

In Zcash, a soft form of such firewalling is available, in that funds are split across several "pools", each of which uses a different proving mechanism. The total value of each pool can be observed, and values under zero would be considered a cause for alarm, and rejected. Zcash use the terminology "turnstiles" [32], and no attacks have been observed through them.

A further consideration for live systems is that as the full version's simulation [22, Section 4.2] shows, the time required strongly depends on the frequency between blocks. This may conflict with other considerations for selecting the block time – a potential solution for this is to only perform updates on "superblocks": blocks which meet a higher proof-of-work (or other selection mechanism) criteria than usual.

5.2   The Root of Trust

An important question for all protocols in the distributed ledger setting is whether a user entering the system at some point during its runtime can be convinced to trust in its security. Early proof-of-stake protocols, such as [23], did poorly at this, and were subject to "stake-bleeding" attacks [16] for instance – effectively meaning new users could not safely join the network.

For reference strings, if a newly joining user is prepared to accept that the honest majority assumption holds, they may trust the security of the reference string, as per Theorem 1. There is a curious difference to the security of the consensus protocol however: to trust the consensus – at least for proof-of-work based protocols – it is most important to trust a *current* honest majority, as these protocols are assumed to be able to recover from dishonest majorities at some point in their past. The security of the reference string on the other hand only relies on assuming honest majority during the initial δ time units. This may become an issue if a large period of time passes – why should someone trust the intentions of users during a different age?

In practice, it may make sense to "refresh" a reference string regularly to renew faith in it. It is tempting to instead continuously perform updates, however as noted in Subsect. 5.1, this does not necessarily increase faith in a stateful system, although is can remove the "historical" part from the honest majority requirement when used with stateless proofs.

Most subversion attacks are detectable – they require lengthy forks which are unlikely to occur during a legitimate execution. In an optimistic case, where no attack is attempted, this may provide an additional level of confirmation: if there are no widespread claims of large forks during the initial setup, then the reference string is likely secure (barring large-scale out-of-band censorship). A flip side to this is that it may be a lot easier to sow doubt, however, as there is no way to *prove* this: A malicious actor could create a fork long after the initial setup, and claim that it is evidence of an attack to undermine the credibility of the system.

5.3   Applications to Non-updateable SNARKs

Updateable SNARK schemes have two distinct advantages which our protocol makes use of: First, they have an explicit update procedure which allows a party ϕ to replace a reference string whose security depends on some assumption A, with one whose security depends on $A \vee (\phi$ is honest$)$. Second, they can survive with a partially biased reference string, a fact which we don't use directly in this paper, however the functionality $\mathcal{F}_{\mathrm{uSRS}}$ we provide permits rejection sampling, encoding it into the ideal world.

The lack of an update algorithm can be resolved for some zk-SNARKs, such as [18], by the existence of a weaker property: In two phases, the reference string can be constructed with (potentially different) parties performing round-robin updates (also group exponentiations) in each phase. This approach is also detailed in [6], and it implies a natural translation to our protocol, in which the first phase is replaced with two phases of the same length, performing the first and second phase updates respectively.

The security of partially biased references strings has not been sufficiently analysed for non-updateable SNARKs, however this weakness can be mitigated. Following [6], it is possible to use a pure random beacon (as opposed to the resettable one used in Sect. 4) to create a "pure" reference string from the "impure" one presented so far. To sketch the design: The random beacon would be queried after time δ, and the randomness used to select a trapdoor permutation over the reference string. This would then be applied by each party independently, arriving at the same – randomly distributed – reference string.

As this is not required for updateable SRS schemes, we did not perform this analysis in depth. However the approach to the simulation would be to perform the SRS generation identically, and then program the random beacon to invert all permutations applied to the honest reference string. Since this includes the one honest permutation applied on every honest update, this is indistinguishable from a random value to the adversary. It is worth noting that the requirement of a random beacon is on the stronger side of requirements, especially as it should itself not allow adversarial influence to provide the desired advantage. Approaches using block hashes for randomness introduce exactly the limited influence which we are attempting to remove!

Acknowledgements. The second and third author were partially supported by the EU Horizon 2020 project PRIVILEDGE #780477. We thank Eduardo Morais for providing data on the required depth of reference strings for Zcash's Sapling protocol.

References

1. Ben-Sasson, E., Bentov, I., Horesh, Y., Riabzev, M.: Scalable, transparent, and post-quantum secure computational integrity. Cryptology ePrint Archive, Report 2018/046 (2018). https://eprint.iacr.org/2018/046
2. Ben-Sasson, E., et al.: Zerocash: decentralized anonymous payments from bitcoin. In: 2014 IEEE Symposium on Security and Privacy, pp. 459–474. IEEE Computer Society Press, May 2014
3. Boneh, D., Drake, J., Fisch, B., Gabizon, A.: Halo infinite: recursive zk-SNARKS from any additive polynomial commitment scheme. Cryptology ePrint Archive, Report 2020/1536 (2020). https://eprint.iacr.org/2020/1536
4. Bonneau, J., Clark, J., Goldfeder, S.: On bitcoin as a public randomness source. Cryptology ePrint Archive, Report 2015/1015 (2015). http://eprint.iacr.org/2015/1015
5. Bowe, S., Gabizon, A., Green, M.D.: A multi-party protocol for constructing the public parameters of the Pinocchio zk-SNARK. In: FC 2018. LNCS, vol. 10958, pp. 64–77. Springer, Heidelberg (2019). https://doi.org/10.1007/978-3-662-58820-8_5
6. Bowe, S., Gabizon, A., Miers, I.: Scalable multi-party computation for zk-SNARK parameters in the random beacon model. Cryptology ePrint Archive, Report 2017/1050 (2017). http://eprint.iacr.org/2017/1050
7. Bünz, B., Bootle, J., Boneh, D., Poelstra, A., Wuille, P., Maxwell, G.: Bulletproofs: short proofs for confidential transactions and more. In: 2018 IEEE Symposium on Security and Privacy, pp. 315–334. IEEE Computer Society Press, May 2018
8. Bünz, B., Fisch, B., Szepieniec, A.: Transparent SNARKs from DARK compilers. In: Canteaut, A., Ishai, Y. (eds.) EUROCRYPT 2020. LNCS, vol. 12105, pp. 677–706. Springer, Cham (2020). https://doi.org/10.1007/978-3-030-45721-1_24
9. Buterin, V.: On-chain scaling to potentially 500 tx/sec through mass tx validation. https://ethresear.ch/t/on-chain-scaling-to-potentially-500-tx-sec-through-mass-tx-validation/3477
10. Canetti, R.: Universally composable security: a new paradigm for cryptographic protocols. In: 42nd FOCS, pp. 136–145. IEEE Computer Society Press, October 2001
11. Chiesa, A., Hu, Y., Maller, M., Mishra, P., Vesely, N., Ward, N.: Marlin: preprocessing zkSNARKs with universal and updatable SRS. In: Canteaut, A., Ishai, Y. (eds.) EUROCRYPT 2020. LNCS, vol. 12105, pp. 738–768. Springer, Cham (2020). https://doi.org/10.1007/978-3-030-45721-1_26

12. David, B., Gaži, P., Kiayias, A., Russell, A.: Ouroboros Praos: an adaptively-secure, semi-synchronous proof-of-stake blockchain. In: Nielsen, J.B., Rijmen, V. (eds.) EUROCRYPT 2018. LNCS, vol. 10821, pp. 66–98. Springer, Cham (2018). https://doi.org/10.1007/978-3-319-78375-8_3

13. Gabizon, A., Williamson, Z.J., Ciobotaru, O.: PlonK: permutations over Lagrange-bases for oecumenical noninteractive arguments of knowledge. Cryptology ePrint Archive, Report 2019/953 (2019). https://eprint.iacr.org/2019/953

14. Garay, J., Kiayias, A., Leonardos, N.: The bitcoin backbone protocol: analysis and applications. In: Oswald, E., Fischlin, M. (eds.) EUROCRYPT 2015. LNCS, vol. 9057, pp. 281–310. Springer, Heidelberg (2015). https://doi.org/10.1007/978-3-662-46803-6_10

15. Garay, J., Kiayias, A., Leonardos, N.: The bitcoin backbone protocol with chains of variable difficulty. In: Katz, J., Shacham, H. (eds.) CRYPTO 2017. LNCS, vol. 10401, pp. 291–323. Springer, Cham (2017). https://doi.org/10.1007/978-3-319-63688-7_10

16. Gaži, P., Kiayias, A., Russell, A.: Stake-bleeding attacks on proof-of-stake blockchains. Cryptology ePrint Archive, Report 2018/248 (2018). https://eprint.iacr.org/2018/248

17. Gazi, P., Kiayias, A., Zindros, D.: Proof-of-stake sidechains. In: 2019 IEEE Symposium on Security and Privacy, pp. 139–156. IEEE Computer Society Press, May 2019

18. Groth, J.: On the size of pairing-based non-interactive arguments. In: Fischlin, M., Coron, J.-S. (eds.) EUROCRYPT 2016. LNCS, vol. 9666, pp. 305–326. Springer, Heidelberg (2016). https://doi.org/10.1007/978-3-662-49896-5_11

19. Groth, J., Kohlweiss, M., Maller, M., Meiklejohn, S., Miers, I.: Updatable and universal common reference strings with applications to zk-SNARKs. In: Shacham, H., Boldyreva, A. (eds.) CRYPTO 2018. LNCS, vol. 10993, pp. 698–728. Springer, Cham (2018). https://doi.org/10.1007/978-3-319-96878-0_24

20. Groth, J., Maller, M.: Snarky signatures: minimal signatures of knowledge from simulation-extractable SNARKs. In: Katz, J., Shacham, H. (eds.) CRYPTO 2017. LNCS, vol. 10402, pp. 581–612. Springer, Cham (2017). https://doi.org/10.1007/978-3-319-63715-0_20

21. Juels, A., Kosba, A.E., Shi, E.: The ring of gyges: investigating the future of criminal smart contracts. In: Weippl, E.R., Katzenbeisser, S., Kruegel, C., Myers, A.C., Halevi, S. (eds.) ACM CCS 2016, pp. 283–295. ACM Press, October 2016

22. Kerber, T., Kiayias, A., Kohlweiss, M.: Mining for privacy: how to bootstrap a snarky blockchain. Cryptology ePrint Archive, Report 2020/401 (2020). https://eprint.iacr.org/2020/401

23. Kiayias, A., Russell, A., David, B., Oliynykov, R.: Ouroboros: a provably secure proof-of-stake blockchain protocol. In: Katz, J., Shacham, H. (eds.) CRYPTO 2017. LNCS, vol. 10401, pp. 357–388. Springer, Cham (2017). https://doi.org/10.1007/978-3-319-63688-7_12

24. Kosba, A., et al.: C0c0: a framework for building composable zero-knowledge proofs. Cryptology ePrint Archive, Report 2015/1093 (2015). https://eprint.iacr.org/2015/1093

25. Kosba, A.E., Miller, A., Shi, E., Wen, Z., Papamanthou, C.: Hawk: the blockchain model of cryptography and privacy-preserving smart contracts. In: 2016 IEEE Symposium on Security and Privacy, pp. 839–858. IEEE Computer Society Press, May 2016

26. Maller, M., Bowe, S., Kohlweiss, M., Meiklejohn, S.: Sonic: zero-knowledge SNARKs from linear-size universal and updatable structured reference strings. In: Cavallaro, L., Kinder, J., Wang, X., Katz, J. (eds.) ACM CCS 2019, pp. 2111–2128. ACM Press, November 2019

27. Parno, B., Howell, J., Gentry, C., Raykova, M.: Pinocchio: nearly practical verifiable computation. In: 2013 IEEE Symposium on Security and Privacy, pp. 238–252. IEEE Computer Society Press, May 2013

28. Pass, R., Seeman, L., Shelat, A.: Analysis of the blockchain protocol in asynchronous networks. In: Coron, J.-S., Nielsen, J.B. (eds.) EUROCRYPT 2017. LNCS, vol. 10211, pp. 643–673. Springer, Cham (2017). https://doi.org/10.1007/978-3-319-56614-6_22

29. Steffen, S., Bichsel, B., Gersbach, M., Melchior, N., Tsankov, P., Vechev, M.T.: zkay: specifying and enforcing data privacy in smart contracts. In: Cavallaro, L., Kinder, J., Wang, X., Katz, J. (eds.) ACM CCS 2019, pp. 1759–1776. ACM Press, November 2019

30. Swihart, J., Winston, B., Bowe, S.: Zcash counterfeiting vulnerability successfully remediated. ECC Blog, February 2019. https://electriccoin.co/blog/zcash-counterfeiting-vulnerability-successfully-remediated/

31. Zcash. Parameter generation (2018). https://z.cash/technology/paramgen/

32. Zcash. Address and value pools in Zcash (2019). https://zcash.readthedocs.io/en/latest/rtd_pages/addresses.html#turnstiles

Author Index

Printed in the United States
by Baker & Taylor Publisher Services